Politics UK

Third edition

Bill Jones (Editor)
Andrew Gray
Dennis Kavanagh
Michael Moran
Philip Norton
Anthony Seldon

With additional material by Simon Bulmer, Andrew Flynn, Bill Jenkins, Jonathan Tonge, The Rt Hon. Lord Biffen, David Coates, The Rt Hon. Lord Mackay of Clashfern, Peter Riddell, David Vincent and David Walker

PRENTICE HALL

London   New York   Toronto   Sydney   Tokyo   Singapore
Madrid   Mexico City   Munich   Paris

First published 1991 by Philip Allan
Second edition published 1994
This third edition published 1998 by
Prentice Hall Europe
Campus 400, Maylands Avenue
Hemel Hempstead
Hertfordshire, HP2 7EZ
A division of
Simon & Schuster International Group

Typeset in $9\frac{1}{2}$/12pt Sabon
by Mathematical Composition Setters Ltd, Salisbury, Wilts

Printed and bound in Great Britain by
The Bath Press

Library of Congress Cataloging-in-Publication Data

Politics UK / Bill Jones ... [et al.]. – 3rd ed.
    p. cm.
   Includes bibliographical references and index.
   ISBN 0-13-269606-1 (pbk.: alk. paper)
   1. Great Britain–Politics and government–1945–   I. Jones, Bill,
1946–
JN231.P69   1998   97-3711
320.941–dc21   CIP

British Library Cataloguing in Publication Data

A catalogue record for this book is available from
the British Library

ISBN 0-13-269606-1 (pbk)

---

  2 3 4 5   02 01 00 99 98

Contents

Authors

Bill Jones studied International Politics at the University College of Wales, Aberystwyth, before working for two years as an Assistant Principal in the Home Civil Service. In 1973 he joined the Extra-Mural Department at Manchester University as Staff Tutor in Politics and was Director of the Department from 1987–92. His books include *The Russia Complex* (Manchester University Press, 1978), *British Politics Today* (with Dennis Kavanagh, Manchester University Press, 5th edn, 1994) and *Political Issues in Britain Today* (Manchester University Press, 4th edn, 1994). He also undertakes regular consultancy work for publishers, radio and television. He also writes books and articles on political education and continuing education. He was chairman of the Politics Association 1983–85 and became a vice-president in 1993. In 1992 he retired from full-time work but still maintains his writing and consultancy interests and is currently a Research Fellow in the Department of Government, University of Manchester.

Andrew Gray is Professor of Public Sector Management at the University of Durham where he is Director of its Centre for Public Sector Management Research and Convenor of the Public Policy Studies Group. He has also taught at the Universities of Kent, Southern California, California State (Los Angeles), Exeter and Manchester Polytechnic. His interests in public management have taken him on teaching, research and consulting assignments in a dozen countries on four continents and produced a variety of books and articles. His chapters are written with research collaborators Bill Jenkins, University of Kent, with whom he published *Administrative Politics in British Government* (Wheatsheaf Books, 1985), *Budgeting, Auditing and Evaluation* (Transaction Publishers, 1993) and a range of articles, and Andrew Flynn, University of Wales, Cardiff.

Dennis Kavanagh is Professor of Politics at the University of Liverpool. He is the author of numerous books, including *British Politics: Continuities and Change* (Oxford University Press, 3rd edn, 1996), *Thatcherism and British Politics: The End of Consensus* (Oxford University Press, 2nd edn, 1990) *Election Campaigning: The Marketing of Politics* (1995) and *The British General Election of 1997*, with David Butler (1997).

Michael Moran began his academic career at Manchester Polytechnic (now Manchester Metropolitan University) before joining the Department of Government at Manchester University, where he is Professor of Government. He has written widely on British politics and comparative public policy. His current interests lie in the field of health care policy. He lectures on the main introductory undergraduate course at Manchester and is a frequent lecturer to sixth-form conferences. His publications include *The Politics of Banking* (Macmillan, 1986), *Politics and Society in Britain* (Macmillan, 1989) *The Politics of the Financial Services Revolution* (Macmillan, 1990), *States, Regulation and the Medical*

Profession (with Bruce Wood, 1993). Since 1993 he has edited the journal *Political Studies*.

Philip Norton is Professor of Government and Director of the Centre for Legislative Studies at the University of Hull, and founding editor of *The Journal of Legislative Studies*. His publications include more than 20 books, among them *The Conservative Party* (Prentice Hall/Harvester Wheatsheaf, 1996), *National Parliaments and the European Union* (Frank Cass, 1996), *The British Polity* (Longman, 3rd edn, 1994), *Does Parliament Matter?* (Harvester Wheatsheaf, 1993), *Back from Westminster* (with D. Wood, University Press of Kentucky, 1993), *Parliamentary Questions* (ed., Oxford University Press, 1993) and *Legislatures* (Oxford University Press, 1990). He is president of the Politics Association in the UK and a past president of the British Politics Group in the USA. He has been described in *The House Magazine* – the journal of both Houses of Parliament – as 'our greatest living expert on Parliament'.

Anthony Seldon was educated at Oxford and the London School of Economics. His first book was *Churchill's Indian Summer* (Hodder, 1981). In 1987, with Peter Hennessy, he established the Institute of Contemporary British History and became its first director. He has helped initiate four journals: *Contemporary Record, Modern History Review, Twentieth Century British History* and *Contemporary European History*. He edits the Blackwell series *Making Contemporary Britain*. His edited books include (with Peter Hennessy) *Ruling Performance* (Blackwell, 1987); (with Andrew Graham) *Governments and Economics Since 1945* (Routledge, 1990); (with Dennis Kavanagh) *The Major Effect* (Macmillan, 1994); (with David Marquand) *The Ideas that Shaped Post-war Britain* (HarperCollins, 1996), *How Tory Governments Fall* (HarperCollins, 1996); and (with Stuart Ball) *The Conservative Century* (Oxford University Press, 1994). He is currently Headmaster of

Brighton College. His biography of John Major will be published in late 1997.

Additional material has been supplied by the following:

Simon Bulmer, Professor of Government, University of Manchester.

Andrew Flynn, Lecturer in Environmental Planning and Policy at the University of Wales, Cardiff.

Bill Jenkins, Reader in Public Policy and Management at the University of Kent at Canterbury where he teaches public administration, public policy and management and contemporary British politics; associate editor of *Public Administration*.

Jonathan Tonge, Lecturer in Politics at Salford University.

John Biffen, former Chief Secretary to the Treasury and Leader of the House of Commons.

David Coates, Professor of Labour Studies, Department of Government, University of Manchester.

Lord (James) Mackay of Clashfern, a Scottish jurist, became Lord Advocate of Scotland in 1979 and a life peer and then was Lord Chancellor from 1987 to 1997.

Peter Riddell, political columnist and commentator of *The Times* and author of two books on the policies of the Thatcher governments and one on career politicians; he also has a book on parliament appearing in autumn 1997.

David Vincent, Deputy Vice Chancellor and Professor of Modern History, University of Keele.

David Walker, principal leader writer for *The Independent* and co-author of *The Times Guide to the New British State*.

Preface

The three years since the second edition of *Politics UK* have been full of political incident and developments, all of which have been digested and are reflected in this new edition. All chapters have been substantially rewritten, many completely so, and a number of new features have been introduced. Firstly, we have reined in the historical content in favour of increased emphasis on the social context. Secondly, we have reorganised the ideology section and included a chapter on concepts. Thirdly, we have a new chapter on Northern Ireland, by guest author Jonathan Tonge. Fourthly, we have developed the Concluding Comments at the end of each major section by inviting well-known guest writers, such as: Peter Riddell, columnist on *The Times*; former minister Lord Biffen, and Professor David Vincent of Keele University.

Nor have we neglected the presentational side of the book, which from the outset has been so important in making it accessible and fun to read. We retain and supplement our innovative practice of plentiful boxes, tables, photographs and diagrams but have added something new: two colours. Since the first edition appeared in 1991 other publications have adopted some of our style; this flatters us and suggests the book has been influential in publishing terms as well as useful to students. We sincerely hope this major rewrite will prove as useful and popular as the earlier two editions have been.

Bill Jones
January 1997

Acknowledgements

Thanks are due to: all our authors, for assiduously preparing so much material before the 1992 election; our guest contributors; and Ruth Pratten of Prentice Hall for the complex and occasionally thankless task of nursing the project through to completion with so much dedication and skill.

Grateful acknowledgement is made to the following sources for permission to reproduce material in this book previously published elsewhere. Every effort has been made to trace copyright holders, but if any have been inadvertently overlooked the publisher will be pleased to make the necessary arrangement at the first opportunity.

Photographs of Alastair Campbell, Tony Blair, John Major, Lord Bingham, David Trimble, Ian Paisley, John Hume, Gerry Adams, John Maynard Keynes, John Locke, Jean-Jacques Rousseau, David Owen and Leon Trotsky supplied by Popperfoto; Peter Mandelson by Guardian News Services; Mary Wollstonecraft by courtesy of the National Portrait Gallery, London.

Figures

Fig. 3.1 © *The Economist*, London (20 June 1992). Fig. 3.2 *Social Trends*, 1996. Crown Copyright 1996. Reproduced by permission of the Controller of HMSO and of the Office of National Statistics; Fig. 3.3 © *The Economist*, London (11 December 1993). Fig. 3.4 © *The Economist*, London (20 February 1993). Fig. 4.1 © *The Economist*, London (15 June 1996). Fig. 4.2 *The Independent*, 3 March 1996. Fig. 4.3 © *The Economist*, London (18 May 1996). Fig. 5.1 © *The Economist*, London (16 April 1994). Fig. 8.1 Tressell, *The Ragged Trousered Philanthropists*, HarperCollins Publishers Ltd (1965). Fig. 9.1 Martin Rawson. Fig. 13.1 Grant, 'Pressure Groups and the Policy Process', *Social Studies Review* Vol. 3:4 (March 1988); Fig. 13.2 Grant, 'Insider and Outsider Pressure Groups', *Social Studies Review* Vol. 1:1 (September 1985). Fig. 13.3 McCullagh, 'Politics and the Environment', *Talking Politics*, autumn 1988. Fig. 15.2 Norton, 'The Case against a Bill of Rights', *Talking Politics*, Vol. 5:3 (1993). Fig. 20.3 *The Independent*, 10 July 1995. Fig. 22.4 Leach *et al.*, *The Changing Organisation and Management of Local Government*, Macmillan Press Ltd. Fig. 22.7 Audit Commission, 1993. Fig. 22.8 Leach *et al.*, *The Changing Organisation and Management of Local Government*, Macmillan Press Ltd. Fig. 24.1 *The Guardian*, 27 March 1996, Home Office data. Fig. 24.2 Home Office, Crown Copyright. Reproduced with the permission of the controller of Her Majesty's Stationery Office. Fig. 24.3 *The Guardian*, 23 April 1997, British Crime Survey data and Home Office data. Fig. 24.4 *The Guardian*, 11 January 1996, British Crime Survey data. Fig. 24.5 *The Guardian*, 12 October 1993. Fig. 25.1 Burch, 1978 (Manchester University Press). Fig. 25.3 Baggott, 'Pressure Groups', *Talking Politics*, autumn 1988. Fig. 25.4 Jones 1986, Tyne Tees Television 1986. Fig. 26.1 © *The Economist*, London (27 April 1996). Fig. 26.2 *Social Trends*, 1996. Crown Copyright 1996.

Reproduced by permission of the Controller of HMSO and of the Office of National Statistics. Fig. 26.3 © *The Economist*, London (15 June 1996). Fig. 26.4 *Times Higher Education Supplement*, 4 September 1992. Fig. 27.1 *Social Trends*, 1996. Crown Copyright 1996. Reproduced by permission of the Controller of HMSO and of the Office of National Statistics. Fig. 28.1 *British Foreign Policy* – M. Smith, S. Smith and B. White, Routledge (Allen & Unwin). Fig. 30.1 McCullagh and O'Dowd, 'Northern Ireland: The Search for a Solution', *Social Studies Review*, Vol. 1:4 (March 1986). Fig. 30.2 *The Independent*/Peter Macdiarmid. Fig. 31.3 European Communities, *Europe in Figures*.

Tables

Table 3.1 *Regional Trends*, 1995. Crown Copyright 1995. Reproduced by permission of the Controller of HMSO and the Office for National Statistics. Table 3.2 *Social Trends*, 1996. Crown Copyright 1996. Reproduced by permission of the Controller of HMSO and of the Office of National Statistics. Table 5.1 Parry *et al.*, *Political Participation and Democracy in Britain* (Cambridge University Press, 1992). Table 5.3 *Social Trends*, 1996. Crown Copyright 1996. Reproduced by permission of the Controller of HMSO and of the Office of National Statistics. Table 11.5 © Mori/ *Sunday Times*, 1992. Table 12.3 Negrine, *Politics and the Mass Media* (Routledge, 1996). Table 12.5

Reprinted by permission of Sage Publications Ltd from McQuail, *Mass Communications Theory: An Introduction*, 1983. Table 13.1 Baggott, 'Pressure groups', *Talking Politics*, autumn 1988. Table 16.1 Gallup, *Political and Economic Index*, April 1996. Table 16.2 Gallup, *Political and Economic Index*, December 1995. Table 17.4 Somit and Roemmele, *The Victorious Incumbent* (Dartmouth Publishing Company, 1995). Table 17.5 House of Commons Sessional Information Digest 1987–92. Table 17.6 figures calculated from House of Commons Sessional Information Digest 1994–95. Table 18.1 Shell and Beamish (eds), *The House of Lords at Work* (Oxford University Press, 1993). Table 18.2 *Dod's Parliamentary Companion, 1996*. Table 18.3 Shell and Beamish (eds), *The House of Lords at Work* (Oxford University Press, 1993). Table 19.2 Burch and Moran 1985 'The Changing British Parliamentary Elite', *Parliamentary Affairs*, Vol. 38:1. Table 27.1 *Social Trends*, 1996. Crown Copyright 1996. Reproduced by permission of the Controller of HMSO and of the Office of National Statistics. Table 30.1 E. Moxon-Brown; Table 30.2 adapted from the Northern Ireland Census 1991 Religion Report by permission of the Controller of HMSO and the Department of Finance and Personnel. Table 31.2 *Agence Europe*, 23 June 1996. Table 31.3 European Communities, Annual Economic Report from 1995 – European Economy No. 59, 1995.

PART ONE

Context

CHAPTER ONE

Introduction: Explaining politics

BILL JONES AND MICHAEL MORAN

LEARNING OBJECTIVES

- To explain and illustrate the concept of what politics is.

- To discuss why politicians become involved in their profession.

- To explain the essence of decision-making in political situations.

- To discuss the kind of questions political science addresses and the variety of approaches that exist.

- To introduce some of the main political relationships between the state and the individual.

- To look at the rationales for studying politics together with some of the major themes and issues in the study of British politics.

INTRODUCTION

This opening chapter is devoted to a definition of 'politics' and the way in which its study can be approached. In the first section, we discuss decision-making and identify what exactly is involved in the phrase 'political activity'. In the second section we examine the critical political questions. We then go on to describe how the more general activity called 'politics' can be distinguished from the workings of 'the state'. In the fourth section, we describe some of the most important approaches used in the study of politics and examine the chief reasons for its study in schools and colleges. The fifth section explains the purpose of studying politics and the final section sketches some of the themes raised in the study of British politics.

'There has never been a perfect government, because men have passions; and if they did not have passions, there would be no need for government.'

Voltaire, *Politique et legislation*

Definitions and decision making

Is politics necessary?

'A good politician', wrote the American writer H.L. Mencken, 'is quite as unthinkable as an honest burglar.' Cynical views of politics and politicians are legion. Any statement or action by a politician is seldom taken at face value but is scrutinised for ulterior personal motives. Thus, when Bob Hawke, the Australian Prime Minister, broke down in tears on television in March 1989, many journalists dismissed the possibility that he was genuinely moved by the topic under discussion. Instead they concluded that he was currying favour with the Australian electorate – who allegedly warm to such manly shows of emotion – with a possible general election in mind.

Given such attitudes it seems reasonable to ask why people go into politics in the first place. The job is insecure: in Britain elections may be called at any time, and scores of MPs in marginal seats can lose their parliamentary salaries. The apprenticeship for ministerial office can be long, hard, arguably demeaning and, for many, ultimately unsuccessful. Even if successful, a minister has to work cripplingly long days, survive constant criticism – both well and ill informed – and know that a poor debating performance, a chance word or phrase out of place can earn a one-way ticket to the back benches. To gamble your whole life on the chance that the roulette wheel of politics will stop on your number seems to be less than wholly rational behaviour. Why, then, do politicians put themselves into the fray and fight so desperately for such dubious preferment?

In some political cultures, especially the undemocratic ones, it seems clear that politicians are struggling to achieve and exercise power, power for its own sake: to be able to live in the best possible way; to exercise the power of life and death over people, to be in fact the nearest thing to a god it is possible for a human being to be. We see that some early rulers were actually deified: turned into gods either in their lifetimes or soon after their deaths.

The Serbian leader, Slobodan Milošević fought hard to retain control of Serbia during the cruel civil war which racked the country from 1989 onwards. Someone who knows him well explained: 'I do not think he believes in anything, only in his own power. It is even possible he could be a peacemaker

if he thinks that is what he has to do to hold on to power' (*Sunday Times*, 4 July 1993). George Orwell suggested in his famous novel, *Nineteen Eighty-Four*, that the state had potentially similar objectives (see quotations).

George Orwell suggested that for the totalitarian state, power was potentially an end in itself. Towards the end of his famous *Nineteen Eighty-Four*, the dissident Winston Smith is being interrogated under torture by O'Brien, a senior official of 'The Party'. O'Brien asks why the Party seeks power, explaining:

George Orwell and the abuse of power

> Now I will tell you the answer to my question. It is this. The Party seeks power entirely for its own sake. We are not interested in the good of others; we are interested solely in power. Not wealth or luxury, or long life or happiness: only power, pure power. What pure power means you will understand presently. We are different from all oligarchies of the past, in that we know what we are doing. All the others, even those who resembled ourselves, were cowards and hypocrites. The German Nazis and the Russian Communists came very close to us in their methods, but they never had the courage to recognize their own motives. They pretended, perhaps they even believed, that they had seized power unwillingly and for a limited time, and that just round the corner there lay a paradise where human beings would be free and equal. We are not like that. We know that no one ever seizes power with the intention of relinquishing it. Power is not a means, it is an end. One does not establish a dictatorship in order to safeguard revolution; one makes the revolution in order to establish the dictatorship. The object of persecution is persecution. The object of torture is torture. The object of power is power.

Later on he offers a chilling vision of the future under the Party:

> There will be no loyalty, except loyalty towards the Party. There will be no love, except love of Big Brother. There will be no laughter, except the laugh of triumph over a defeated enemy. There will be no art, no literature, no science. When we are omnipotent we shall have no more need of science. There will be no distinction between beauty and ugliness. There will be no curiosity, no enjoyment of the process of life. All competing

pleasures will be destroyed. But always – do not forget this, Winston – there will be the intoxication of power, constantly increasing and constantly growing subtler. Always, at every moment, there will be the thrill of victory, the sensation of trampling on an enemy who is helpless. If you want a picture of the future, imagine a boot stamping on a human face – for ever.

Orwell, 1955, pp. 211–15

In developed democratic countries the answer is more complex, although one, somewhat cynical school of thought insists that naked power is still the chief underlying motivation (see below: ambition and the career politician).These countries have realised the dangers of allowing politicians too much power. Checks and balances, failsafe constitutional devices and an aware public opinion ensure politicians, however much they may yearn for unlimited power, are unable realistically to expect or enjoy it. We have instead to look for more subtle motivations.

Biographies and interviews reveal an admixture of reasons: genuine commitment to a set of beliefs, the desire to be seen and heard a great deal, the trappings of office such as the official cars, important-looking red boxes containing ministerial papers and solicitous armies of civil servants. Senator Eugene McCarthy suggested politicians were like football coaches: 'smart enough to understand the game and dumb enough to think it's important'. A witty remark, but true in the sense that politics is an activity which closely resembles a game and which similarly exercises an addictive or obsessive hold upon those who play it. Tony Benn cheerfully admits to being consumed with politics and I remember once asking an exhausted ex-Labour minister, David Ennals, why he continued to work so hard. 'Ah, politics', he replied 'is just so fascinating you see.' But is the game worth playing? Words like 'betrayal', 'opportunism', 'exploitation', 'distortion' and 'fudge' are just some of the pejorative terms frequently used in describing the process. Would we not be better off without politics at all?

In his classic study *In Defence of Politics* (1982), Bernard Crick disagrees strongly. For him politics is 'essential to genuine freedom … something to be valued as a pearl beyond price in the history of the human condition'. He reminds us of Aristotle's view that politics is 'only one possible solution to the problem of order. It is by no means the most usual. Tyranny is the most obvious alternative, oligarchy the next.' Crick understands 'politics' as the means whereby differing groups of people with different, often conflicting, interests are enabled to live together in relative harmony. For him 'politics' describes the working of a pluralist political system 'in advanced and complex societies' which seeks to maximise the freedom and the power of all social groups. The system may be far from perfect but it is less imperfect than the various authoritarian alternatives.

This line of thinking provides an antidote to overly cynical analyses of politics. The compromises inherent in the process tend to discredit it: few will ever be wholly satisfied and many will feel hard done by. Similarly politicians as the imperfect practitioners of an imperfect system receive much of the blame. But without politicians to represent and articulate demands and to pursue them within an agreed framework we would be much the poorer. Whether Crick is right in reminding us to count our democratic blessings is a question which the reader must decide, and we hope that this book will provide some of the material necessary for the making of such a judgement.

Ambition and the career politician

'Politics is a spectator sport,' writes Julian Critchley (1995, p. 80). An enduring question which exercises us spectators is: 'Why are they doing it?' Dr Johnson, in his typically blunt fashion said politics was 'nothing more nor less than a means of rising in the world'. But we know somehow this is not the whole truth. Peter Riddell of *The Times* in his wonderfully perceptive book, *Honest Opportunism* (1993), looks at this topic in some detail. He quotes Disraeli, who perhaps offers us a more rounded and believable account of his interest in politics to his Shrewsbury constituents: 'There is no doubt, gentlemen, that all men who offer themselves as candidates for public favour have motives of some sort. I candidly acknowledge that I have and I will tell you what they are: I love fame; I love public reputation; I love to live in the eye of the country.'

Riddell also quotes F.E. Smith, who candidly gloried in the 'endless adventure of governing men'. For those who think these statements were merely expressions of nineteenth-century romanticism, Riddell offers the example of Richard Crossman's comment that politics is a 'never ending adventure… with its routs and discomfitures, rushes and sallies', its 'fights for the fearless and goals for the eager'. He also includes Michael Heseltine whom he heard asking irritatedly at one of Jeffrey Archer's parties in 1986: 'Why shouldn't I be Prime Minister then?' The tendency of politicians to explain their taste for politics in terms of concern for 'the people' is seldom sincere. In the view of Henry Fairlie this is nothing more than 'humbug'. William Waldegrave agrees: 'Any politician who tells you he isn't ambitious is only telling you he isn't for some tactical reason; or more bluntly, telling a lie… I certainly wouldn't deny that I wanted ministerial office; yes, I'm ambitious.' As if more proof were needed, David Owen once said on television – and 'he should know', one is tempted to say – that 'Ambition drives politics like money drives the international economy.' Riddell goes on in his book to analyse how the ambitious political animal has slowly transformed British politics. He follows up and develops Anthony King's concept of the 'career politician', observing that a decreasing number of MPs had backgrounds in professions, or 'proper jobs' in the Westminster parlance, compared with those who centred their whole on politics and whose 'jobs' were of secondary importance, merely supporting the Westminster career. In 1951 the figure was 11 per cent; by 1992 it was 31 per cent. By contrast, the proportion of new MPs with 'proper jobs' fell from 80 per cent to 41 per cent. Many of this new breed begin life as researchers for an MP or in a party's research department, then proceed to seek selection as a candidate and from there into parliament and from then on ever onwards and upwards. The kind of MP who enters politics in later life is in steep decline; the new breed of driven young professionals has tended to dominate the field, proving firmer of purpose and more skilled in execution than those for whom politics is a later or learned vocation. The kind of businessman who achieves distinction in his field and then goes into politics is now a rarity rather than the familiar figure of the last century or the earlier years of this one.

Some silly quotations by politicians

"Politicians pride themselves on being fluent and always in control, but however powerful and mighty they might be, they can say some seriously stupid things as the examples below illustrate:

I would have made a good Pope.   *Richard Nixon*

OK we've won. What do we do now?
Brian Mulroney upon being re-elected Prime Minister of Canada

Outside the killings we have one of the lowest crime rates in the country   *Marion Barry, former Mayor of Washington DC*

I have opinions of my own – strong opinions – but I don't always agree with them   *George Bush*

I didn't go down there with any plan for the Americas or anything. I went down to find out from them and learn their views. You'd be surprised. They're all individual countries.
Ronald Reagan on how his Latin American trip had changed his views

An obscene period in our nation's history
Dan Quayle in 1988 on the Nazi Holocaust

The real question for 1988 is whether we're going forward to tomorrow or past to the – back!   *Dan Quayle*

Hawaii has always been a very pivotal role in the Pacific. It is part of the United States that is an island that is right here.   *Dan Quayle (again)*

What a waste to lose one's mind – or not to have a mind. How true that is.   *Dan Quayle*

And finally (though there are many more): I stand by all the mis-statements.   *Dan Quayle*

Oliver, 1992 "

Defining politics

Politics is difficult to define yet easy to recognise. To some extent with the word 'politics' we can consider current usage and decide our own meaning, making our own definition wide or narrow according to our taste or purposes. From the discussion so far politics is obviously a universal activity; it is concerned with the governance of states, and (Crick's special concern) involves a conciliation or harmonisation process. Yet we talk of politics on a micro- as well as a macro-scale: small groups like families or parent/teacher associations also have a political dimension. What is it that unites these two levels? The answer is: the conflict of different interests. People or groups of people who want different things – be it power, money, liberty, etc. – face the potential or reality of conflict when such things are in short supply. Politics begins when their interests clash. At the micro-level we use a variety of techniques to get our own way: persuasion, rational argument, irrational strategies, threats, entreaties, bribes, manipulation – anything we think will work. At the macro-level, democratic states establish complex procedures for the management of such conflicts, often – though famously not in Britain's case – codified in the form of written constitutions. Representatives of the adult population are elected to a legislature or parliament tasked with the job of discussing and agreeing changes in the law as well as exercising control over the executive: those given responsibility for day-to-day decisions in the running of the country.

Is the political process essentially peaceful? Usually, but not exclusively. If violence is involved on a widespread scale, e.g. war between states, it would be fair to say that politics has been abandoned for other means. But it must be recognised that:

1. Political order within a state is ensured through the implicit threat of force which a state's control of the police and army provides. As John Adams (nineteenth-century US President) pointed out, 'Fear is the foundation of most governments.' Occasionally passions run high and the state's power is explicitly exercised – as in the 1984–5 miners' strike.
2. There are many situations in the world, for example in Northern Ireland or the Lebanon, where violence is regularly used to provide both a context for and an alternative to peaceful political processes.

So, while political activity is peaceful for most of the time in most countries, the threat of violence or its reality are both integral parts of the political process.

We should now be able to move towards a definition:

Politics is essentially a process which seeks to manage or resolve conflicts of interest between people, usually in a peaceful fashion. In its general sense it can describe the interactions of any group of individuals but in its specific sense it refers to the many and complex relationships which exist between state institutions and the rest of society.

Peaceful political processes, then, are the alternative, the antidote to brute force. As the practitioners of this invaluable art politicians deserve our gratitude. It was interesting to note that in July 1989 when Ali Akbar Rafsanjani emerged as the successor to the Iranian extremist religious leader, Ayatollah Khomeini, several Iranians were quoted in the press approving him as 'a political man': someone who would be likely to steer the country away from the internal violence which religious conflicts threatened at the time.

Does this mean that cynical attitudes towards politicians should be discouraged? Not exactly, in our view. It is wrong that they should be widely undervalued and often unfairly blamed, but experience suggests that it is better to doubt politicians rather than trust them unquestioningly. After all, politicians are like salesmen and in their enthusiasm to sell their messages they often exaggerate or otherwise distort the truth. They also seek power and authority over us and this is not a privilege we should relinquish lightly. Lord Acton noted that 'all power tends to corrupt' and history can summon any number of tyrants in support of this proposition. We are right to doubt politicians, but, as John Donne advised, we should 'doubt wisely'.

Decision-making

Much political activity culminates in the taking of decisions and all decisions involve choice. Politicians are presented with alternative courses of action – or inaction – and once a choice has been made they have to try to make sure their decisions are accepted. Two examples follow which illustrate the micro- and macro-senses of politics and which also introduce some important related terminology.

Decision-making I: micro-politics

When the outgoing school captain of chess goes to university a struggle ensues between three candidates for his position: John is a little short of things to cite as 'other activities' on his application forms to university, especially as he is not very good at more traditional sports; David is something of a 'chess prodigy' and wants to convince his father he can go on to become a Grand Master and earn his living from the game; Graham is already captain of soccer but enjoys the status of being in charge and thinks the addition of this more cerebral title might clinch the position of Head Boy for himself.

On the face of it, this commonplace situation has little to do with politics – yet it is an example of politics with a small 'p' or 'micro-politics', and political science terms can fruitfully be used to analyse the situation.

Interests in politics are defined as those things which people want or care about: usually financial resources but other things too like status, power, justice, liberty or the avoidance of unwanted outcomes. In this example one boy (Graham) is interested mainly in the prestige and status of the office and the possible knock-on effect it may provide for an even more sought-after goal, whilst the other two are interested for future educational and career reasons.

Political actors in this instance include the three boys, the headmaster and Mr Stonehouse, the master with responsibility for chess in the school. Other actors, however, might easily be drawn into the political process as it develops.

Power in politics is the ability to get others to act in a particular way. Typically this is achieved through the exercise of threats and rewards but also through the exercise of *authority*: the acceptance of someone's right to be obeyed.

The power relationship in this case might be seen in the following terms. The boys are bereft of any real power: all the cards are held by the master in charge who has been given authority by the head to choose the boy for the job. Conceivably the two disappointed candidates might exercise a threat of disruptive behaviour if their claims are overlooked, but this threat, if it existed, would lack any real credibility and would be unlikely to affect the outcome. All three boys, moreover, accept the authority of Mr Stonehouse to make the decision and are likely to accept his verdict. The outcome of this conflict of interests will depend upon a number of factors:

1. *Political will*: How prepared are any of the boys to advance their cause? John, for example, arranges to play a public simultaneous game against a visiting Nigel Short to give his candidature some extra weight – but such a strategy could backfire, if he loses badly, for example.

2. *Influence*: How open are either actors to rational argument, appeals to loyalty and so forth? Mr Stonehouse, for example, was once employed by David's father to give him extra chess lessons. Will this former contact create a sense of loyalty which will tip the balance in David's favour?

3. *Manipulation*: How effectively can the candidates involve the other actors? Graham's mother is a close friend of Mr Stonehouse and his father is a school governor. Could ambitious parents be mobilised to pull these possible levers of influence?

The political process would take place largely through face-to-face contacts, nods and winks in the case of Graham's father, for example (lobbying for his son could scarcely be done openly: such influence is not after all thought to be 'proper')'. John, however, could advance his claim through a good performance against a Grand Master. The whole political process could therefore take place virtually unseen by anyone except the actors themselves as they make their moves. Open discussion of their claims is unlikely to occur between candidates and Mr Stonehouse (not thought to be good form either). How did it pan out? (This is only a hypothetical situation but the reader may have got interested by now so I'll conclude the mini-drama.)

Well, John did well against Nigel Short and was the last to be beaten after an ingenious defensive strategy which actually put Short in difficulty after he lost a rook. David's ambitious father made an excuse to ring up Mr Stonehouse and at the end of the conversation just 'happened' to raise the subject of his son's chess prowess and his great commitment to the school team. Despite his efforts however the approach was a little unsubtle and Mr Stonehouse was unimpressed. Graham's father (the school governor remember), however, had heavier guns to fire. He met Mr Stonehouse at a parents' evening and contrived to meet him afterwards in the pub for a quiet drink. There he was able to suggest in oblique but unmistakable terms that he would support Mr Stonehouse's interest in becoming head of his subject in exchange for Graham becoming head of chess. I would like to say that Mr Stonehouse was above such petty manoeuvring but he too was ambitious and was being urged by his wife to be more so. After some wrestling with his conscience, he ignored David and (arguably the most deserving) John, and appointed Graham. Moral: justice is seldom meted out by the political process and human frailties often intervene to ensure this is so.

Decision-making II: macro-politics

A major national newspaper breaks a story that Kevin Broadstairs, a Cabinet minister, has been having an affair with an actress. The PM issues a statement in support of his colleague and old friend from university days. However, more embarrassing details hit the front pages of the tabloids, including the fact that the same actress has been also carrying on with a senior member of the Opposition. The 1922 Committee meet and influential voices call for a resignation.

This somewhat familiar situation is quintessentially political.

Interests: The PM needs to appear above suspicion of 'favouritism' but also needs to show he is loyal and not a hostage to either groups of backbenchers or the press. Broadstairs obviously has an interest in keeping his job, retaining respect within his party and saving his rocky marriage. The governing party needs to sustain its reputation as the defender of family values. The press wishes to sell more newspapers.

Actors in this situation are potentially numerous: the PM, Broadstairs, the actress, her former lovers, back-bench MPs, editors, television producers, the Opposition, Mrs Broadstairs and (unfortunately) her children, the church, feminists and anyone else willing to enter the fray.

Power: The power relationship in these circumstances is naturally influenced by the ability of each side to enforce threats. The PM has the power of political life or death over the minister but would like to show his strength by resisting resignation calls, Broadstairs effectively has no power in this situation and is largely dependent on the PM's goodwill and possible press revelations.

Authority: No one questions the PM's right to sack Broadstairs. The press's right to force resignations, however, is very much resisted by politicians. The ultimate authority of the governing party to call for the minister's head is also not questioned.

Political process: Will Broadstairs survive? Sir Bernard Ingham used to say that if no new

developments in a story occurred after nine days it was effectively dead. Our minister in this situation is a hostage to the discretion of his mistress and other people either involved or perceiving an interest in the affair. The outcome will depend on the following:

1. *Political will*: How prepared are the PM and Broadstairs to stand firm against resignation calls? How long could he hold out once the 1922 Committee has given the thumbs down? How long would this Committee stay silent as it saw the issue eroding voter support? How effective also would Broadstairs' enemies in his own party be in hastening his downfall?
2. *Influence*: How much influence does the PM have in Fleet Street? The evidence suggests political sympathies of a paper count for nothing when a really juicy scandal is involved. Does Broadstairs have a body of support on the back benches or is he a 'loner'?
3. *Manipulation*: How good is the minister at coping with the situation? Can he make a clean breast of it like Paddy Ashdown in January 1992 and get away with it? Can he handle hostile press conferences and media interviews (as David Mellor did with aplomb)? Can the minister call up old favours on the back benches?

Let's suppose things quieten down for a few days, the PM defends his friend at Question Time and the wife says she'll stand by her man. If this was all there was to it, Broadstairs would survive and live to fight again, albeit with his reputation and prospects damaged. We saw that in the somewhat similar David Mellor case the revelations kept on rolling (much to everyone's amusement and his embarrassment) but the crucial revelations concerned acceptance of undeclared favours by the minister. After this, back-bench calls for a resignation and an excited press ensured Mellor had to go.

The political process in this case is a little haphazard and depends to some extent upon each day's tabloid headlines. It will also depend on the PM's judgement as to when the problem has ceased to be an individual one and has escalated to the point when his own judgement and the political standing of his party are in question. Once that point has been reached it is only a matter of time before the minister's career is over. There was much in ex-Prime Minister Harold Wilson's tongue-in-cheek comment that 'much of politics is presentation, and what isn't is timing'.

The critical political questions

Because politics studies the making and carrying out of decisions, the student of politics learns to ask a number of important immediate questions about the political life of any institution:

1. Who is included and who is excluded from the process of decision-making? It is rare indeed for all the members of a community or organization to be allowed a part in the decision-making process. Mapping the divide between those taking part and those not taking part is an important initial task of political inquiry.
2. What matters are actually dealt with by the political process? This is sometimes called 'identifying the political agenda'. Every community or body has such an agenda – a list of issues which are accepted as matters over which choices can be made. In a school the agenda may include the budget and the curriculum; in a church, the religious doctrine of the institution; within the government of a country such as Britain the balance of spending between defence and education. But the range of subjects 'on the political agenda' will vary greatly at different times and in different places. In modern Britain, for instance, the terms on which education is provided by the state is a major item of political argument. But before 1870, when compulsory education was first introduced, this was a matter which did not concern decision makers.
3. What do the various individuals or groups involved in the political process achieve? What are their interests and how clearly can they be identified?
4. What means and resources do decision-makers have at their disposal to assist them in getting their way? When a decision is made, one set of preferences is chosen over another. In practice this means that one person or group compels or persuades others to give way. Compulsion or persuasion is only possible through the use of

some resources. These are highly varied. We may get our way in a decision through the use of force, or money, or charm, or the intellectual weight of our argument. Studying politics involves examining the range of political resources and how they are employed.

Politics, government and the state

Every human being has some experience of politics, either as the maker of decisions or as the subject of decisions, because politics is part and parcel of social organisation. An institution which did not have some means of making decisions would simply cease to be an institution. But this book is not long enough to deal with the totality of political life in Britain; it concentrates upon politics inside government and the organisations which are close to government.

The best way of understanding the special nature of politics with a capital 'P' is to begin by appreciating the difference between the state and other institutions in society. In a community like Britain there are thousands of organisations in which political activity takes place. By far the most significant of these is that body called 'the state', which can be defined as follows (for another analysis of the term 'the state' see Chapter 7):

That institution in a society which exercises supreme power over a defined territory.

Three features of the state should be noted:

1. *The 'state' is more than the 'government'*: The state should not be equated with 'government', let alone with a particular government. When we speak of 'a Conservative government' we are referring to the occupancy of the leading positions in government – such as the office of Prime Minister – by elected politicians drawn from a particular party. This in turn should be distinguished from 'government' in a more general sense, by which is meant a set of institutions, notably departments of state such as the Treasury and the Home Office, concerned with the conduct of policies, and everyday administration. The state certainly encompasses these departments of state, but it also embraces a wider range of institutions. Most important, it

includes the agencies whose role it is to ensure that in the last instance the will of the state is actually enforced: these include the police, the courts and the armed forces.

2. *Territory is a key feature of the state*: What distinguishes the state from other kinds of institutions in which politics takes place is that it is the supreme decision-maker in a defined territory. Other institutions in Britain take decisions which their members obey; but power in a family, a school or a firm is ultimately regulated by the will of the state. In Britain, this idea is expressed in the notion of sovereignty. The sovereign power of the state consists in the ability to prescribe the extent and limits of the powers which can be exercised by any other organisation in British society.

It follows that this sovereignty is limited territorially. The British state lives in a world of other states, and the extent of its rule is defined by its physical boundaries – which inevitably abut onto the boundaries of other states.

Disputes about the physical boundaries of state sovereignty are among the most serious in political life. It might be thought that an 'island state', which is how Britain is conventionally pictured, would have no difficulty in establishing its boundaries. In practice, identification is complicated and often leads to fierce disputes with other states over claims to territory. In 1982 a rival sovereign state, Argentina, had to be expelled by force when it occupied territory (which Britain claims for its own) in the Falkland Islands of the South Atlantic. Another source of dispute arises from the fact that the boundaries of a state are not identical with its land mass: states like Britain also claim jurisdiction over the air space above that land mass and over territorial waters surrounding the land. In recent decades, for instance, Britain has extended its 'territorial limits' – the area of sea over which it claims sovereignty – from three miles to two hundred miles beyond the shoreline, in order to possess the fishing and mineral exploration rights of those waters. This extension has often caused disputes between rival claimants.

The fact that there exists on earth only a finite amount of land, sea and air space means

that the sovereignty of a particular state over territory is always subject to potential challenge from outside. Occasionally the ferocity of this challenge may actually lead to the destruction of a state: in 1945, for instance, the defeat of Germany at the end of the Second World War led to the destruction of the German state and the occupation of all German territory by its victorious opponents.

A state's sovereignty is, however, not only subject to external challenge; it can also be disputed internally. In 1916, for instance, the boundaries of the British state encompassed the whole island of Ireland. Between 1916 and 1921 there occurred a military uprising against British rule which ended in agreement to redraw territorial boundaries, creating an independent Irish state covering most of what had hitherto been British sovereign territory.

3. *State power depends on legitimacy*: As the example of the Falklands, the destruction of the German state after 1945 and the creation of an independent state in Ireland all show, control of the means of coercion is an important guarantor of sovereignty. But the sovereign power of a state depends not only on its capacity to coerce; it also rests on the recognition by citizens that the state has the authority or right to exercise power over those who live in its territory. This is commonly called legitimacy. It would be extremely difficult for a state to survive if it did not command this legitimacy. Britain, like most other large communities with sophisticated and advanced economies, is far too complex a society to be governed chiefly by force. This is why the state in Britain, as in other advanced industrial nations, claims not only to be the supreme power in a territory, but also to be the supreme legitimate power.

This right to obedience is asserted on different grounds by different states at different times. The German social theorist Max Weber offered a famous distinction between three types of legitimacy: *traditional*, *charismatic* and *rational–legal*. The first of these rests on custom and appeals to continuity with the past. It is the principal ground, for instance, by which rule through a hereditary monarchy is justified. The second appeals to the divine-like, 'anointed' quality of leadership: in our century many of the greatest dictators, like Adolf Hitler, have commanded obedience through their charismatic qualities. Rational–legal legitimacy rests on the ground that in making decisions agreed rules and agreed purposes are observed.

Although in any state elements of all three sorts of legitimacy can be identified, they will be emphasised in different ways. In Britain, charisma is relatively unimportant. Although some politicians are occasionally described as 'charismatic' personalities, this is no more than a journalistic way of saying 'exciting' or 'appealing'. Political leadership in Britain does not rest on a claim that governors are 'anointed' with divine-like qualities. Tradition in Britain, by contrast, does have some importance. The crown is the symbol of political authority and the Queen's right to that crown of course rests on inheritance – she was born to the succession, like the monarch who preceded her and the one who will follow her. However, the legitimacy of the state in Britain rests only in part on tradition; for the main part it is rational–legal in character: its actions are taken in accordance with agreed procedures, in particular, laws passed by Parliament. It is an absolute principle of the exercise of state authority that the state cannot legitimately command the obedience of citizens if its demands do not carry the backing of legislation, or the force of law (see also Chapter 7 on concepts).

Also central to the study of politics as well as the concept of 'the state' are the concepts of 'power' and 'authority'.

Power is one of the founding organising concepts in political science. We talk of a government being in 'power', of Thatcher being a 'powerful' Prime Minister. We talk of people with the 'power to make decisions'. In essence the concept means a quality, the ability of someone or some group to get others to do what they otherwise would not have done. In crude terms this can be achieved by coercion: a man with a gun can induce compliance through the fear which people naturally have of the consequences.

In real-life politics this rarely happens outside brutal tyrannies like Iraq, but the notion of compul-

sion in the face of threats lies somewhere close to the heart of political power; after all, when the chips are down, states go to war to either impose their will on other states or to prevent this happening to them. Normally, though, power is exercised by recognised politicians acting within an established system making important decisions on behalf of communities or nations.

Bachrach and Baratz (1981) argued that decisions not made by politicians were just as important as those actually made. If a matter can be marginalised or ignored completely through the ability of someone to exclude it, that person can be said to exercise power. For example, it could be argued that cars have been choking our cities for decades, that this problem has been recognised but that remedial action has been postponed for so long because the motor industry is so important to the economy and voters themselves have a potent love/hate relationship with their cars.

It can also be argued that power can be exercised through the ability of some groups to induce people to accept certain decisions without complaint. Marx believed the ruling class was able to permeate the institutions of the state with its values so that the exploitation of capitalism was fully accepted and approved and consequently perceived as simultaneously natural unavoidable and 'common sense' (see Box 5.3, p. 63). With the advent of the modern media other theorists like Antonio Gramsci argued the exploited masses had been induced through a ruling class permeated culture to 'love their servitude'.

Authority is closely associated with power but is crucially different from the crude version of, say, a man with a gun. When our politicians announce new laws we accept them and obey them even if, say, we disagree with them, because we accept the right of politicians to discuss and pass legislation through a popularly elected chamber. In other words MPs have 'authority' to pass laws on our behalf. Something similar occurs when a traffic warden gives us a ticket: we may be furious but we pay up as we respect his/her authority, backed up as it is by statute law.

I think the critial difference between a dictatorship and a democracy is that in a dictatorship there are only two people out of every hundred who take a personal interest in politics; in a democracy there are three. (*Healey*, 1990, p. 156)

Approaching the study of politics

We now have some idea of the nature of politics as an activity and some familiarity with the central ideas of state, power and authority. Politics, then, is the process by which conflicting interests are managed and authoritative choices made in social institutions as different as the family, the school and the firm. The most important set of political institutions are conventionally called 'the state', and it is the state which is the focus of the discipline called 'political science'.

Political science is now a large and well-established academic discipline in both Europe and North America. For instance, the American Political Science Association has 12,000 members and in Britain the Political Studies Association and the Politics Association have over 1,000 members each. However, this is a relatively recent development. The emergence of political science as a separate discipline organised on a large scale in universities and colleges first developed in the United States in the early decades of this century. Even now, the overwhelming majority of people called 'political scientists' are American. Before the emergence of political science the subject was divided between specialists in different disciplines (see Figure 1.1). Constitutional lawyers studied the legal forms taken by states. Historians studied the relations between, and the organisation of, states in the past. Philosophers discussed the moral foundations, if any, of state authority. In large part, the modern discipline is the heir to these earlier approaches. It is

important to be aware of the main approaches, because the approach employed in any particular study influences the kind of questions it asks, the evidence it considers relevant and the conclusions it draws.

Three important approaches are sketched here: the *institutional*, the *policy cycle* and the *sociopolitical* (see Table 1.1 for summary). These, it should be emphasised, are not mutually exclusive. They are indeed complementary approaches; and just as we usually gain an appreciation of a physical object like a work of art if we look at it from a variety of angles, so we understand a system of government better if we examine it in a similarly varied way.

The *institutional or constitutional approach* to the study of politics was until recently dominant in the study of government in Britain. It has three distinctive features: its focus, its assumptions and its choice of evidence. The focus of the institutional approach is upon the formal institutions of government. In Britain this means a concentration on the bodies at the heart of what is sometimes called 'central government' in London: the two Houses of Parliament, the Cabinet, the individual ministries and ministers and the permanent civil servants in those ministries. The working assumption of this approach is that the legal structure of government and the formal organisations in which government activities happen have an importance in their own right. In other words, they are not just the reflections of other social influences; on the contrary, they are assumed to exercise an independent influence over the life of the community. In practical terms this means that the approach is dominated by an examination of the legal rules and the working conventions which govern the operation of these formal institutions.

It is sometimes objected that this approach is static, that it has a tendency to stress the character of government at one fixed moment, and to neglect the fact that political life is characterised by constant cycles of activity.

The *policy cycle approach* tries to capture this cyclical quality. Government is examined as a series of 'policy cycles'. It is pictured as a system of inputs and outputs, as shown in Figure 1.2. Political activity is pictured as a series of stages in the making and execution of decisions about policy. At the stage of

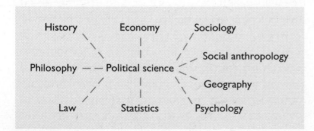

Figure 1.1 Some of the disciplines contributing to political science

Table 1.1   Summary of important approaches to the study of politics

Approaches	Focus	Main assumptions	Examples of characteristic evidence examined
Institutional	Formal machinery of government	Formal structures and legal rules are supreme	Structure of parliaments cabinets, civil services
Policy cycle	Choices made by government	Government action shaped by mix of demands and resources; policy affects wider society	Kinds of resources (money, etc). Patterns of policy-making and implementation
Socio-political	Social context, links between government and society	Structure and production of government shaped by wider society	Economic and class structure; organisation of interest groups

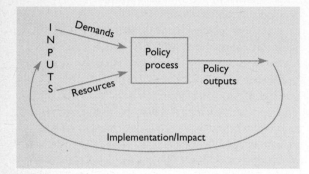

Figure 1.2   The policy cycle

policy initiation there exist both demands and resources. At any one moment in a community there will be a wide range of views about what government should do, which will manifest themselves as demands of various kinds: that, for instance, government should provide particular services, such as free education for all under a certain age; that it should decide the appropriate balance of resources allocated to different services; or that it should decide the exact range of social activity which is appropriate for government, rather than for other social institutions, to regulate. Making and implementing policy choices in response to these demands requires resources. These are the second major input into government and include: people, like the administrators and experts necessary to make policy choices and to implement them; and money, which is needed to pay government personnel. These resources can be raised in a wide variety of ways: for example, revenue can be raised by taxation, by

borrowing or by charging for the services that governments provide.

After examining the initial stages of resource raising and allocation, the policy cycle approach describes the processing of inputs; in other words, how the balance of different demands and the balance between demands and resources is allocated to produce policy choices. Finally, the process of what is sometimes called policy implementation and policy impact (see Figure 1.2) studies how government policies are put into effect and what consequences they may have for the subsequent balance of demands and resources. It is this emphasis on the linked nature of all stages in the policy process which leads us to speak of the policy cycle approach (see also Chapter 25). This approach is also distinguished by its particular focus, assumptions and choice of evidence. Although it resembles the institutional approach in concentrating attention on the institutions of government its focus is primarily on what these institutions do, rather than on how they are organised, because the most important assumption here is that what is interesting about government is that it makes choices – in response to demands and in the light of the scarce resources at its command. In turn this affects the sort of evidence on which the 'policy cycle' approach concentrates. Although much of this evidence concerns practical functioning and organisation of government, it also involves the wider environment of government institutions. This is necessarily so because the demands made on government and the resources which it can raise all come from that wider society. In this concern with the wider social context of government institutions the policy approach shares some of the concerns of the socio-political approach.

The *socio-political approach* has two particularly important concerns: the social foundations of the government order; and the links connecting government to the wider organisation of society. Close attention is paid to the wider social structure and to the kinds of political behaviour which spring from it. It is a working assumption of this approach that government is indeed part of a wider social fabric, and that its workings can only be understood through an appreciation of the texture of that wider fabric. Some versions make even stronger assumptions. For instance, most Marxist scholars believe that the workings of government in a community are at the most fundamental level determined by the kind of economic organisation prevailing in that community. The focus and assumptions of the socio-political approach in turn shape the kind of evidence on which it focuses. This includes information not only about the social structure, but also about the social influences which shape important political acts, such as voting and the kinds of economic and social interests (like business and workers) who influence the decisions taken in government.

Why we study politics

It is not difficult to understand why many individuals wish to take part in political activity. Some people have a desire to control the lives of their fellow human beings; most people wish to control their own lives. Political activity offers the chance to exercise such control. But the study of politics is an altogether different matter. It offers the chance of gaining understanding rather than power. What is the purpose of attempting to acquire this understanding? In a country like Britain, the reasons are threefold.

1. *Training in citizenship*: Even when not studied as part of an examinable course, knowledge of how the system of politics works is an important part of training in citizenship. Citizenship conveys the right to make choices: between different parties at elections; between different forms of political activity, or no

activity at all; between opposition to, or support for, the policies designed to meet the pressing problems of the day. Making these choices sensibly and intelligently obviously demands some thought about, and knowledge of, the substance of the issues involved. It is not sensible, for instance, to form definite views about how the National Health Service should be organised without knowing at least a little about the problem of providing health care for the community.

But another kind of knowledge is necessary to make a sensible choice as a citizen: knowledge not just about the substance of the issue in question, but about the means by which decisions can be made and the processes by which they can be put into effect. This latter sort of knowledge comes from an examination of the political process in a community like Britain. Wishing a particular result is, in politics, a very long way from achieving it. The effective citizen who wishes to have some say over how the community is governed needs to be in a position to make some appreciation of political and administrative possibilities. This is particularly important in Britain because, as we will discover, one of the characteristic features of the British political system is that citizens are offered choices by fiercely competitive teams (political parties) who wish to be selected as governors of the country. Assessing the realism of the competing promises made by these teams demands a knowledgeable and educated citizenry – educated not only in the substantive nature of particular policies, but also in the realities of political power and in the administrative capacities of the state. The study of politics is, then, about the way a person can become educated so as more effectively to play the part of a democratic citizen. But there is also a second use to which political knowledge can be put.

2. *Improving the effectiveness of government*: Political institutions are in part the product of conscious human design. They are created by people in particular circumstances to achieve certain purposes. The civil service in Britain, for instance, was reformed in the later decades of the nineteenth century in an attempt

to produce an efficient and corruption-free administrative machine capable of putting into effect the laws passed by Parliament. Because political and administrative institutions can be designed, they can also be changed and reformed in order to ensure that they achieve their goals more effectively. One purpose of the study of politics is to examine institutions with a view to assessing that effectiveness and discovering how it can be increased. Judgements of this order are far from simple. Different institutions have different objects, so the assessment of effectiveness will vary greatly: what constitutes effectiveness in a political party will be very different from what constitutes effectiveness in a civil service department. Nor is producing increased effectiveness a straightforward matter. The kind of knowledge we acquire from the study of politics does not allow us to engage in social engineering. A malfunctioning engine or a defective bridge can be dismantled and rebuilt to cure defects; the problems of an institution such as the House of Commons cannot be solved by simply abolishing that body and starting again.

Nevertheless, the study of politics can make a practical contribution to the workings of institutions. It encourages discussion about the goals to which they should aim; it examines cases of successful achievement and of failure and offers the possibility of making recommendations for reforms and improvements.

Part of the purpose of the study and teaching of politics is, then, to encourage citizens to become more knowledgeable and sophisticated and to produce a better appreciation of the purposes and functioning of institutions in order to improve their working effectiveness. But the study of politics is not simply an activity whose existence has immediate practical justifications. Understanding political life also illuminates the wider nature of a society.

3. *Understanding British society*:   The political life of a community is part and parcel of its total social life. Nobody could claim to understand Britain who knew nothing of its history or its literature. In other words, political life is an integral part of the culture of a community, and understanding the culture of Britain demands a knowledge of British political institutions. Therefore, we study British politics in part for exactly the same reasons that we study English literature or the history of the country: it is quite simply a necessary part of any person's knowledge of the experience of being British.

Themes and issues in British politics

Britain's system of government is one of the most intensively examined in the world; not surprisingly, therefore, there is no shortage of issues and themes. We conclude this introductory chapter by selecting four which are of special importance and which recur in different ways in the chapters following. These themes are: democracy and responsibility; efficiency and effectiveness; the size and scope of government; and the impact of government on the wider society.

Democracy and responsibility

British government is intended to be democratic and responsible: it is meant to be guided by the choices of citizens, to act within the law and to give an account of its actions to society's elected representatives. The issue of how far democracy and responsibility do indeed characterise the political system is central to the debates about the nature of British government. Defenders of the system point to a variety of features. Democratic practices include the provision for election – at least once every five years – of the membership of the House of Commons by an electorate comprising 43 million from Britain's 57 million inhabitants. The membership of the Commons in turn effectively decides which party will control government during the duration of a Parliament's life, while all legislation requires a majority vote in the Commons. In addition to these formal practices, a number of other provisions support democratic political life. Freedom of speech, assembly and publication allow the presentation of a wide variety of opinions, thus offering the electorate a choice when they express a democratic preference. The existence of competing political parties similarly means that there are clear and realistic choices facing voters when they go to the polls in elections.

Democracy means that the people can decide the government and exercise influence over the decisions, governments take. *Responsibility* means that government is subject to the rule of law and can be held to account for its actions. Those who think British government is responsible in this way point to a variety of institutions and practices, some of which are formal in nature. They include the right to challenge the activities of government in the courts and to have the actions of ministers and civil servants overturned if it transpires that they are done without lawful sanction. They also include the possibility of questioning and scrutinising – for instance in the House of Commons – government ministers over their actions and omissions. In addition to these formal provisions responsibility rests on wider social restraints which are intended to hold government in check. The mass media report on and scrutinise the activities of politicians and civil servants while a wide range of associations and institutions, such as trade unions and professional bodies, act as counterweights in cases where government threatens to act in an unrestrained way.

Against these views a variety of grounds have been produced for scepticism about the reality of responsible democratic government in Britain. Some observers are sceptical of the adequacy of democratic institutions and practices. Is it possible, for instance, to practise democracy when the main opportunity offered to the population to make a choice only occurs in a general election held once every four or five years? It is also commonly observed that the links between the choices made in general elections and the selection of a government are far from identical. The workings of the British electoral system (see Chapter 11) mean that it is almost unheard of for the 'winning' party in a general election to attract the support of a majority of those voting.

Even greater scepticism has been expressed about the notion that government in Britain is 'responsible'. Many observers argue that the formal mechanisms for restraining ministers and civil servants are weak. Widespread doubt, for instance, has been expressed of the notion that the House of Commons can effectively call ministers and civil servants to account. Indeed, some experienced observers and participants have spoken of the existence of an 'elective dictatorship' in Britain: in other words, of a system where government, though it requires the support of voters every four or five years, is able in the intervening period to act in an unrestrained way. There have also been sceptical examinations of the wider mechanisms intended to ensure restraint and accountability. Some insist that the mass media, for instance, are far from being independent observers of the doings of government; that, on the contrary, they are systematically biased in favour of the powerful and against the weak in Britain. Similar claims have been made by observers of the judiciary – a key group since, according to the theory of responsible government, judges are vital in deciding when government has acted in a way which is not sanctioned by law. Finally, some radical observers go further and argue not merely that 'democratic responsibility' is defective, but that there is a 'secret state' in Britain; in other words, a system of unchecked power which operates outside the scrutiny of public institutions and which is able to act systematically outside the law.

Efficiency and effectiveness

Arguments about democracy and responsibility touch on the moral worth of the system of government in Britain, but government is not only to be evaluated by its moral credentials. It also is commonly judged by its working effectiveness – and justifiably so, for the worth of a system of government is obviously in part a function of its capacity to carry out in an effective way the tasks which the community decides are its responsibility.

Until comparatively recently it was widely believed that British government was indeed efficient and effective in this sense. Britain was one of the first countries in the world, for instance, to develop a civil service selected and promoted according to ability rather than to political and social connections. In the last quarter century, however, the efficiency and effectiveness of British government have been widely questioned. Critics focus on three issues: the skills of public servants, the evidence of the general capabilities of successive British governments and the evidence of particular policy failures.

The most important and powerful public servants in Britain are acknowledged to be 'senior civil servants' – a small group of senior administrators, mostly based in London, who give advice about policy options to ministers. This senior civil service is largely staffed by what are usually called 'generalists' – individuals chosen and promoted for their general intelligence and capabilities rather than because they possess a particular managerial or technical skill. However, critics of the efficiency of British government have argued that the nature of large-scale modern government demands administrators who are more than generally intellectually capable; it demands individuals trained in a wide range of specialised skills (see Chapter 20).

The absence of such a group, drawn from disciplines like engineering and accountancy, at the top of British government is often held to explain the second facet of poor effectiveness – the general inability of British government to manage its most important tasks effectively. In recent decades the chief task of government in Britain has been to manage the economy. That task has, measured by the standards of Britain's major competitors, been done with conspicuous lack of success. In the 1950s Britain was one of the richest nations in Western Europe; by the 1980s she was one of the poorest.

The debate about the general competence of British government has been heightened by a series of more particular instances of policy failure in recent decades. One observer, surveying the history of British policy initiatives, concluded that there existed only one instance of a major policy success (the introduction of 'clean air' legislation in the 1950s). On the other hand, every observer can produce numerous instances of policy disasters: the Concorde aeroplane, which should have assured the country a first place in modern aircraft manufacture, and which turned out to be an expensive commercial failure; a series of financial and technical disasters in the field of weapons development; and a comprehensive disaster in the building, during the 1950s and 1960s, of uninhabitable high-rise tower blocks in the effort to solve the country's housing problems.

The belief that the efficiency and effectiveness of British government have been defective has dominated debates about the organisation of the system in the last thirty years and has produced numerous proposals for reform in the machinery. A few of these have even been implemented. Local government, for instance, was reorganised in the early 1970s into larger units which, it was believed, would deliver services more efficiently. Within the last decade, however, a new argument has entered the debate. The belief that the problems of efficiency and effectiveness were due to a lack of particular skills, or lack of an appropriate organisational structure, has been increasingly displaced by a more radical notion: that the failings of the system were intrinsic to government, and that more efficient and effective institutions could only come when government itself was reduced to a more manageable size and scope. In other words, there is a link between the debates about efficiency and effectiveness and our third theme – the size and scope of government.

Size and scope of government

British government is big government. Major public services – the provision of transport, health care, education – are performed wholly or largely by public institutions. Many of the institutions are, by any standards, very large indeed, for example the National Health Service. As we will see in Chapter 4, Britain has a 'mixed' economy. In other words, goods and services are produced by a combination of private enterprise and public institutions. Nevertheless, an astonishing variety of goods and services are provided by what is commonly called 'the public sector'. What is more, until very recently this sector was steadily growing at the expense of the private sector.

The growth of government to gigantic proportions has prompted two main debates, about its efficiency as a deliverer of goods and services; and about the impact of a growing public sector on the wider economy. The efficiency debate we have already in part encountered. In the last decade, however, many free market economists have argued that government failures are due to more than the failings of particular people and structures. They are, it is argued, built into the very nature of government. According to this view, the public sector lacks many of the most important disciplines and spurs to effectiveness under which private firms have to work. In particular, say its critics, the public sector rarely has to provide services in competition with others. Because the taxpayer always stands behind a public enterprise the discipline exercised by the possibility of losses and bankruptcy, which guides private firms, is absent in the case of government. Thus government has an inherent tendency towards wastefulness and inefficiency. Defenders of the public sector, on the other hand, while not denying the possibility of waste and inefficiency, argue that failures also happen in the private sector; and that, indeed, one of the most important reasons for the growth of government is the failure of private enterprise to provide vital goods and services on terms acceptable to consumers.

A more general argument about the problems of having a large-scale public sector concerns the resources which are needed to maintain this sector. In the 1970s perhaps the most influential explanation of the failings of the British economy rested on the claim that Britain had 'too few producers'. It was argued that non-productive services had grown excessively at the expense of the sector of the economy producing manufactured goods for the home market and for export. A large proportion of the excessive expansion of the 'service' sector consisted in the growth of public services such as welfare, health and education. These were in effect 'crowding out' more productive activities. Against this view, it has been argued that the growth of 'services' is more a consequence than a cause of the contraction of manufacturing in Britain, and that in any case 'non-productive' services, such as education, are actually vital to sustaining a productive manufacturing sector.

Whatever the rights and wrongs of these arguments we will see in succeeding chapters that critics of 'big government' have, in the 1980s and 1990s, enjoyed much influence over policy. Many activities once thought 'natural' to the public sector – such as the provision of services like a clean water supply and energy for the home – have been, or are being, transferred to private ownership. Arguments about 'privatisation', as these transfers are usually called, have also cropped up in the final major theme we sketch here – the impact of government.

The impact of government

We already know from our description of the 'policy cycle' approach that government has powerful effects on the wider society. Modern government takes in society's resources – money, people, raw materials – and 'converts' them into policies. In turn, these policies plainly have a great effect on the lives of us all. On this there is general agreement, but there is great disagreement about the precise impact of government. This disagreement has crystallised into a long-standing argument about the extent to which the effects of government activity are socially progressive or regressive – in simpler terms, whether the rich or poor get most out of the policy process.

The most important way government raises resources in a country like Britain is through taxation. The taxation system in Britain is guided by the principle of 'progression': in other words, the wealthier the individual or institution, the greater the liability to pay tax. On the other hand, the services provided by government are either consumed collectively (e.g. national defence), consumed individually but are freely available to all (e.g. free art galleries) or are designed for the poor (e.g. supplementary welfare payments). By contrast, it is difficult to think of a public service which is designed to be consumed only by the rich. These considerations should ensure that the impact of government is redistributive between rich and poor. At the extremes of poverty, for instance, the poor should contribute nothing to taxation but nevertheless be eligible for a wide range of benefits paid for from the general taxes paid by everyone else in the community.

Critics of the view that the impact of government is redistributive in this way rest their case on several arguments. Firstly, some services of government, while not designed for the benefit of the better-off, may nevertheless be worth more to the rich than to the poor. An efficient police service, for instance, which deters theft, is correspondingly desirable according to the amount of property one stands to lose to thieves. Secondly, some services, while again designed to be universally enjoyed, may in practice be almost totally consumed by the better-off. In the arts, for example, opera attracts large public subsidies but is rarely patronised by the poor and is highly fashionable among the rich. Thirdly, some services, while designed actually to ensure equality of treatment for all, or even preferential treatment for the deprived, may nevertheless in practice be more widely used by the better-off than by the poor.

It is widely alleged, for instance, that the National Health Service in Britain actually disproportionately devotes its resources to caring for the better-off. This is partly because the poorest in the community are least knowledgeable about the services available and least willing to make demands for these services; and partly because the actual distribution of resources inside the Health Service is alleged to be biased towards the more vocal and better-off groups in society.

Most of the argument about the redistributive effects of government focus on where the services provided by the public sector actually end up, but some observers also question how far the formally 'progressive' character of the taxation system is realised in practice. It is commonly argued that the very richest are also the most sophisticated at minimising their taxation obligations by the use of skilled advisers like accountants and tax lawyers, whose speciality is to arrange the financial affairs of a company or an individual so as to minimise the amount of tax which must legally be paid.

This opening chapter has discussed the meaning of politics, the characteristics of the state, approaches to the study of politics, reasons for studying the subject and some important themes and issues in British politics. The rest of the book, organised in eight parts, follows directly from the definition we adopted on page 7.

Politics is about conflicting interests: Part I provides the historical, social and economic contexts from which such conflicts emerge in Britain. Part II, on ideology, examines the intellectual basis of such conflicts.

Politics is also centrally concerned with how state institutions manage or resolve conflicts within society: Parts III, IV, V and VI deal respectively with the representative, legislative, executive and judicial processes whereby such management takes place or is attempted. Finally, Part VII examines how these institutions handle the major policy areas.

Chapter summary

This introductory chapter has explained that politics is about the management and resolution of conflicts by what people want to do and achieve. The study of the subject focuses on how this process is

performed, especially the way individuals relate to the state. Three approaches – institutional, policy cycle and socio-political – are outlined and it is suggested we study politics for understanding and improved citizenship. Major themes include the control citizens have over their government, the efficiency of the system and the extent of its intervention in everyday lives.

Discussion points

■ Why do you think people go into politics and make it their life's work?

■ Think of a typically political scenario and analyse it in the way demonstrated in the chapter.

■ Which approach to politics, from the ones outlined, seem to be the most interesting and helpful to you in explaining political phenomena?

Further reading

Crick's classic work (1982) is essential reading as is Duverger (1966). Leftwich (1984) is worth reading as an easy-to-understand initiation and Laver (1983) repays study too. Renwick and Swinburn (1987) is useful on concepts though Heywood (1994) is by any standards a brilliant textbook. Riddell (1993) is both highly perceptive and very entertaining – a must for anyone wondering if the subject is for them. O'Rourke (1992) is a humorous but insightful book. Oliver (1992) is a hilarious collection of silly quotations by politicians. A shorter introduction to British politics is Jones and Kavanagh (1994).

References

Bachrach, P. and Baratz, M. (1981) 'The Two Faces of Power', in F.G. Castles, D.J. Murray and D.C. Potter (eds), *Decision, Organisations and Society* (Penguin).

Crick, B. (1982) *In Defence of Politics*, 2nd edn (Penguin).

Critchley, J. (1995) *A Bag of Boiled Sweets* (Faber and Faber).

Duverger, M. (1966) *The Idea of Politics* (Methuen).

Healey, D. (1990) *The Time of My Life* (Penguin).

Heywood, A. (1994) *Political Ideas and Concepts* (Macmillan).

Jones, B. and Kavanagh, D. (1994) *British Politics Today*, 5th edn (Manchester University Press) (6th edn forthcoming in 1998).

Laver, M. (1983) *Invitation to Politics* (Martin Robertson).

Leftwich, A. (1984) *What is Politics? The Activity and its Study* (Blackwell).

Oliver, D. (1992) *Political Babble* (John Wiley).

O'Rourke, P.J. (1992) *Parliament of Whores* (Picador).

Orwell, G. (1955) *Nineteen Eighty-Four* (Penguin).

Renwick, A. and Swinburn, I. (1989) *Basic Political Categories*, 2nd edn (Hutchinson).

Riddell, P. (1993) *Honest Opportunism* (Hamish Hamilton).

CHAPTER TWO

The historical context

ANTHONY SELDON

LEARNING OBJECTIVES

- To examine the areas of continuity of policy.

- To explain the only two significant turning points in policy since 1945, towards collective policies after 1945 and back towards the private sector after 1979.

- To investigate why continuity has been the norm in British history since 1945.

INTRODUCTION

Over fifty years have now passed since the ending of the Second World War. Fifteen general elections have seen a slow but steady alternation of Labour and Conservative governments, with the Liberals remaining throughout only a minor force at Westminster. Yet despite all the changes of government, and of prime ministers, what is remarkable is not the fluctuations in policy, but the continuities in the policy pursued by both parties in office.

The world in 1945

In 1945 the biggest war in the history of humankind ended. Unlike the First World War of 1914–18, which was largely a European affair, the Second World War was truly international, spreading from the Far East through the Indian subcontinent, the Middle East and North Africa down to the South Atlantic. By 1945 the world was exhausted.

Germany was decisively beaten, and the Third Reich, which Hitler had said would endure for a thousand years, had lasted just twelve. The British contribution to the war effort was eclipsed by that of the USSR and USA, but up to their entry into the war it had fought almost alone against the menace of the German and Italian dictators.

Long before the surrender of Germany in May and of Japan in August 1945, it had become clear that Britain would not be able to compete on equal military or political terms after the war with the Soviet and American superpowers. Both these countries had vastly greater military might than Britain, the former by virtue of its concentration of economic resources on defence, the latter backed up by its almost limitless economic wealth. The war had shown how dependent Britain had become on other countries for economic resources, and even for physical protection. Like the First World War, the war would not have been won without the intervention of the USA, which after 1945 came to dominate the international economy.

While the former European great powers before 1914 had constantly jockeyed for power, no major doctrinal difference had separated them. Yet the USA and USSR after 1945 were indomitably opposed, respectively championing the opposing ideologies of capitalism and communism. Within months of the ending of war in 1945 it became clear that these two nations, allies during the war from 1941 to 1945, would now become implacable enemies. The world was quickly dividing itself into two hostile camps, with a numerically large but politically weak 'non-aligned' group of nations in the middle. The high ideals which launched the United Nations (UN), the international body which superseded the ill-fated League of Nations of the interwar years, quickly foundered on the rocks of the Cold War – the war of words, propaganda and worse fought between the East and West.

Where stood Britain in the face of this rearrangement of the balance of power in the world? It is necessary to appreciate how devastating a blow the war was to Britain. A quarter of a million dead, with many more wounded, often for life, provides a clue to the extent of the trauma. Britain's homes and factories were severely damaged, especially in London, south-eastern towns and towns with ports. The whole economy was severely dislocated, with debts and loans much increased and exports devastated, never fully to recover. The USA also suffered a similar number of dead, but the ability of the US economy to recover from the expense and shock of the war drain was far greater than Britain's, which, in truth, was already in relative economic decline by 1939: the war merely provided another decisive downward push.

The country yearned for peace and security, where the electorate would be free of the fears of unemployment and poverty of the world before 1939, and of fear of invasion. The mood was ready for a government to offer a new agenda for British politics.

Origins of the Keynesian social democratic consensus of 1945–79

'Consensus' is a key concept in understanding the recent past. The word 'consensus' is Latin for agreement, and its use implies a set of common assumptions and a continuity between the policies pursued by both the main parties when they were in power. It does not mean that there were not disagreements: there were many. But it does suggest that the differences in the policies practised when the parties were *in office* were relatively small rather than fundamental.

The term permits the existence of major differences between the radical elements within each of the main parties, but it recognises that when the parties were in power they were dominated by pragmatists for whom continuity and slow change were more important than major policy departures. There were two different periods of consensus in the post-war world: from 1945 to 1979, when a Keynesian social democratic consensus prevailed, and after 1979, when it was replaced by a qualified free enterprise consensus.

The first consensus was largely consolidated by the post-war Labour government (1945–51), presided over by Clement Attlee, but its genesis is found in the war years, 1939–45.

1. *Six years of war united the country* against a common enemy while the privations of war instilled a widespread desire for a new and better beginning. The comradeship of war had also helped blunt some of the sharper edges of British class differences.
2. *Coalition government (1940–5)* had fostered social and intellectual links between Labour and Conservatives. The common everyday effort to defeat Hitler had taken much of the bite out of ideological differences between the two parties.
3. *Acceptance of Keynesianism* had been evident both in Chancellor Kingsley Wood's 1941 Budget and in the 1944 White Paper, which commanded full support from all three main political parties for its aim of 'full employment'.
4. *Planned economy*: Conservatives had always maintained that central planning of the economy would not work, but the spectacular success of the government's tightly controlled war economy supported the case for planning.
5. *Trade unions*: In 1940 Ernest Bevin, General Secretary of the Transport and General Workers' Union (TGWU), was appointed Minister of Labour in recognition of the unions' importance to the war effort. Their enthusiastic cooperation was vital to success and established a strong claim for regular post-war consultation.

BOX 2.1   IDEAS AND PERSPECTIVES

Was there a post-war consensus?

The 'post-war consensus', little heard of before the 1980s, became in that decade a buzzword among political scientists and contemporary historians. Controversy surrounding it focused on three areas, Did it, in fact, ever exist? If so, when did it reach its high point? Was it a net benefit, or a cause of the nation's decline?

Prime among the sceptics about consensus is Ben Pimlott (see Pimlott 1989), who argues that 'the consensus is a mirage, an illusion that rapidly fades the closer one gets to it'. He argues that it was only from the perspective of the 1980s that there appears to have been harmony before; during the period from 1945 to 1979 the divisions were bitter and almost continuous, and politicians from both main parties never regarded themselves as belonging to a 'consensus'. Keynes and Beveridge, the intellectual fathers of the alleged consensus, Pimlott argues, were by no means accepted uncritically by the Labour and Conservative parties, particularly by their

radical wings. The notion of a consensus, he argues, is a rose-tinted view of what the electorate felt. Ordinary voters were, he says, more divided during the period of the so-called consensus than since its conclusion after 1979. Pimlott sums up his views in a memorable expression: 'Sandbagged in their electoral trenches, the early post-war voters can be seen as the anonymous infantry of two implacably opposed armies in an era of adversarial policies, with the middle-way Liberals floundering in no-man's land' (Pimlott 1989).

More recently, the existence of consensus has come under fire from a group of historians, notably in Jones and Kandiah (1996). These qualifications are valuable, but do not undermine the fundamental notion of two periods of consensus since 1945, a Keynesian social democratic one lasting until 1979, and a qualified free market one which will endure probably long into the twenty-first century.

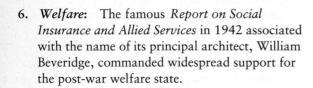

6. *Welfare*: The famous *Report on Social Insurance and Allied Services* in 1942 associated with the name of its principal architect, William Beveridge, commanded widespread support for the post-war welfare state.

By 1945 all the ingredients for a new widely supported consensus were present in the political culture. All three parties went to the polls in 1945 committed to a broad range of economic and social policies of a qualitatively different kind to anything envisaged in the interwar years. The stage had been set.

The Attlee government, 1945–51

A major problem with history is that one can never know with any certainty what might have happened had circumstances been different. It is possible that,

had the Conservatives won the general election of 1945, they would have implemented as radical a set of policies as those enacted by Labour. But it seems most unlikely that the Conservatives would have gone as far as Labour did, or executed policies in quite the same way. The Attlee government has been chiefly credited with creating the post-war consensus. As the historical examination above has made clear, it did not create the consensus, but it did consolidate it and gave it its particular form. The post-war consensus can be said to have six main aspects or 'planks':

1. *Full employment*: The Attlee government pledged itself to abide by the 1944 White Paper on Employment to achieve full employment. This meant in practice a mix of interventionist economic and fiscal policies to ensure that

unemployment never rose above a minimum level of 2–3 per cent. This contrasted markedly with the high levels of the interwar period.

2. ***Mixed economy and Keynesian policies***:   This entailed a mixture of private and state ('public') ownership of industry and services. The 1945 Labour manifesto advocated nationalisation of public utilities and an extension of state ownership over other aspects of the private sector. Once in office, it proceeded to nationalise hitherto private companies, for example coal (1946), electricity (1947), railways (1947) and gas (1948). Major manufacturing industries, however, remained in the private sector. Keynesian principles of economic management were now accepted as orthodoxies.

3. ***Welfare state***:   The government's social policies from 1945 to 1951, which included setting up the National Health Service (NHS) in July 1948, and expansion of free education, public housing, sickness benefit and family allowances, far exceeded the tentative groping towards welfarism before 1939. The core principles of this aspect of the consensus included universal and free welfare benefits for all in need.

4. ***Trade unions***:   The Attlee government, for the first time in peacetime, brought unions into both formal and informal contact with government in a continuing relationship. They gave the unions the feeling that they had a virtual 'right' to be consulted.

5. ***Equality***:   The Attlee government pursued active economic and social policies to try to *reduce* (if not eliminate) inequalities of income, wealth and region. Heavily progressive taxes were thus pursued to flatten out inequalities in salaries and wages and an active regional policy was followed to bolster employment and income in areas of higher than average unemployment, such as the north-east of England.

6. ***Foreign policy***:   It is tempting, but wrong, to see the consensus wholly in terms of the continuity in economic and social policies pursued by Labour and Conservative government. There also existed a marked overlap in the foreign and defence spheres. Thus it was Labour which decided in 1946 that Britain must be a nuclear nation, which forged NATO in 1949 with full Conservative support, and again it was Labour which decided in 1950 that it could not submerge Britain in the European Coal and Steel Community (ECSC).

The first consensus endures, 1951–5

In October 1951, the Conservatives won the general election. It was a narrow victory of just seventeen seats, and in fact they won 200,000 fewer votes overall than Labour. But for the vagaries of the British electoral system, therefore, the Conservatives would have lost the election. What type of Conservative government would there now be? Labour had warned during the election campaign, as it had done during the earlier campaigns of 1945 and February 1950, that if elected the Conservatives would return to their interwar policies.

They did not do so, although there were some minor modifications to the consensus. A variety of factors explain why they chose to accept rather than reject so much of the Attlee settlement. The narrowness of the majority had much to do with it. For 1952 and much of 1953, the Conservatives were not performing strongly in either the opinion polls or by-elections: unpopular moves were ruled out and to have cut back on, for example, the welfare state or to have been confrontational towards the trade unions were moves deemed likely to lose support. (The popularity of privatisation was only discovered after 1979, when the climate of opinion had changed considerably.)

As important was the fact that the Conservative right wing lacked cohesion, leaders and even supporters. Potential leaders of a right-wing reaction were either not given jobs by Churchill (Prime Minister 1951–5), for example Waterhouse, or were to an extent marginalised, as in the case of Lord Salisbury.

Churchill's own continued presence was of considerable importance in explaining the continuation of moderate policies after 1951. Churchill, who as a younger man had often been identified with radical policies, now saw himself as a conciliator. His policy preferences, his appointments and his very presence were central to the consolidation of the consensus.

The Conservative Party, too, had changed its spots since 1945. Reforms to parliamentary candidate requirements meant that it was no longer necessary to have private capital to stand as a Conservative. In consequence the 1950 election saw a vast influx of a new type of middle-class Conservative MP, typified by the grammar school-educated Ted Heath. On policy, R.A. Butler, the wartime Education Minister, had been reforming and modernising party policy at the Conservative Research Department. Aided by some bright young assistants who went on to play major parts in the subsequent history of the party (Reginald Maudling, Iain Macleod and Enoch Powell), Butler was responsible for a stream of policy documents and statements, notably the *Industrial Charter* (1947) and *The Right Road for Britain* (1949). These documents played a part, albeit a small one, in assisting the transfer of the Conservatives from an arguably *laissez-faire* party before the war to an interventionist one after it.

A final factor that accounted for the Conservative acceptance of the consensus after 1951 was the collapse of the centre vote. The year 1951 was the worst result ever for the Liberal Party: 2.5 per cent of the votes cast, and six MPs. Many middle-class voters abandoned not just the Liberals but also the Conservatives, either not voting at all or voting Labour. The Conservatives knew they had to woo back these left-inclined voters if they were to consolidate their hold on power.

In consequence, all areas of the consensus were held up largely intact. *At the Treasury* the moderate Butler was appointed Chancellor rather than the right-wing Oliver Lyttelton, who had been tipped for the job. Butler's economic policies, aimed at full employment, were so similar to those of the Labour Chancellor Hugh Gaitskell that *The Economist* coined a new term 'Butskellism' to honour the continuity.

The mixed economy was retained virtually intact. Only two industries were privatised (or 'denationalised' as it was then called), both in 1953. But one of these, iron and steel, had barely had time to be nationalised and even after 1953 retained a large measure of state supervision; the other, road haulage, was scarcely of first-rate significance.

The welfare state was accepted, and in some areas extended. Initial plans for instituting cuts and other economies were dropped. There was no doctrinal attack on welfare, nor was there any

social policy offered by the Conservatives that could be said to have been distinctly Conservative.

At the Ministry of Labour (currently called the Department of Education and Employment) Walter Monckton was preferred to David Maxwell Fyfe, a more hard-line politician who had shadowed the ministry in opposition. Monckton was given precise instructions from Churchill to avoid industrial confrontation. Trade union leaders quickly realised that Monckton was a soft touch: no wonder he was regarded as their favourite post-war Minister of Labour – of any party. As employers were encouraged not to resist wage demands, Monckton earned himself the title of 'the oil can'. Union leaders meanwhile were frequent visitors at 10 Downing Street and in the corridors of Whitehall. There was to be no return to their second-rank stature of the interwar years and before.

The concept of equality, albeit of opportunity, was also subscribed to by the Conservatives. An excess profit tax was introduced to howls of protest from businessmen. Progressive income taxes were retained, as were regional policies.

On the foreign and defence fronts, there were no right-wing hawkish policies. Defence spending, following the close of the Korean War, was cut back. Following the death of Stalin in March 1953, a policy of trying to bring about closer relations with the Soviet Union was actively pursued by Churchill, to the intense annoyance of the USA. Progress towards decolonisation was continued, especially in West Africa. True, the government did decide to build the hydrogen bomb in 1953, but this decision was a logical follow-on from Attlee's decision to build the atomic bomb (tested in 1952).

High noon of the first consensus, 1955–70

The Churchill government of 1951–5 set the tone for the entire period of Conservative rule to the Labour victory in the general election of October 1964. The policies that Labour inherited were strikingly similar to those it had bequeathed the Conservatives in 1951. No further denationalisations occurred after 1953; the welfare state was little changed; trade unions became an even more permanent fixture, with the formation of the National Economic Development Council in 1962, of which they were partners; full employment policies were still being pursued; and Britain's defence and foreign policy stances were maintained. Indeed, the period after 1955 witnessed a great acceleration in the granting of independence to Britain's former colonies. The Conservative Party, once the party of empire, was now the party of decolonisation and self-government.

Labour won a narrow victory in 1964 but consolidated it with a ninety-six majority in the general election of March 1966. The party held office until June 1970. In opposition before 1964, Labour had made radical policy proclamations, as parties tend to do when relieved of the shackles of office, and when the (usually) moderate leadership is less able to marginalise the fervour of its back-bench followers. In 1960, for example, the Labour Party conference voted against nuclear weapons, which would have meant sweeping changes to Britain's defence and foreign policy commitments. The party leadership managed to persuade conference to reject the proposal the following year. But radical zeal was not quenched, and when the apparently left-wing Harold Wilson beat the right-wing candidate, George Brown, for the party leadership in 1963, the stage looked set for a future Labour government which would advance radical socialism, thereby breaking the consensus. But Labour in power from 1964 was not a radical force: moderation, continuity and pragmatism continued to be the order of the day.

Britain's poor economic health was the reason given for the conspicuous lack of radicalism. 'Socialism costs money' was the answer given to an increasingly restless left wing; 'but when the economy recovers …'. The economy, however, never did recover. True, there were some left-wing policies – comprehensive schooling (in place of grammar and secondary moderns) was given a decisive push and the steel industry was renationalised in 1967. The government also presided over a wide range of permissive reforms in divorce, race relations and abortion.

None of these policies, however, could be regarded as a serious challenge to the consensus. The Conservatives from 1951 to 1964 had themselves done little to discourage the drift towards comprehensivisation. The renationalisation of steel was denounced, but no serious plans were made to reprivatise it. And the reforms in the personal sphere owed more to the traditions, and occasionally even the instigation, of the Liberal Party.

Hence, there are two related problems in understanding why the consensus continued until 1970: why the Conservatives adhered to it after Churchill's departure in 1955; and why Labour did not abandon it after 1964. The first is probably the easier to explain. Churchill was succeeded as Prime Minister by the moderate Anthony Eden, and when he resigned prematurely, in January 1957, the even more middle-of-the-road Harold Macmillan took over. With a leadership determined to stick by consensual policies and their proven popularity at the polls (the election victory in May 1955 was followed by an even bigger one in October 1959) there was neither will nor incentive to introduce new-style policies. Why bother when the present mix appeared to be working? Alternative policies, moreover, were not on offer: no one in the parliamentary party was seriously suggesting abandoning the principles of the welfare state, pursuing wholesale privatisation, suppressing trade union power or arresting the pace of decolonisation. Those voices raised on the far right of the party were few and far away from the mainstream.

Radical anti-consensus policies were, in contrast, being widely advocated by Labour. Why, then, did the consensus hold after 1964? In practical terms, a left-wing Labour programme would have entailed a massive nationalisation programme, which would have tipped the scales away from a mixed economy; abolition of private education and health care; and unilateral nuclear disarmament and a withdrawal from NATO. Economic difficulties provide part but by no means all of the explanation why such policies were not pursued. The small size of the majority (five) after the October 1964 election, and the desire not to repel potential voters, helps explain why radical policies were not followed before the March 1966 election, but not after it. One could make a case for saying that Labour lacked the time, in the four years between 1966 and 1970, to introduce anti-consensus policies. But the evidence does not suggest that Labour would have produced more radical policies if it had remained in office after 1970. The overwhelming reason why Labour did not abandon consensual policies wholesale between 1964 and 1970 was the lack of desire by senior figures in the party to implement left-wing socialism. Had they really wanted to introduce radical anti-consensual policies, they could have done and would have done.

The moderating influence of the civil service also played a part, if an unquantifiable one, in explaining why the consensus continued throughout the period. Civil servants tend to like continuity and moderation and to resist sudden change. The general unpopularity of, even unfamiliarity with, non-consensual economic and social philosophies, is also important. Both Labour and Conservative parties until the 1970s broadly accepted the ideas of Keynes and Beveridge. Those who seriously challenged their prevailing orthodoxy were regarded as mavericks and outsiders.

Keynesian social democratic consensus under stress, 1970–9

The election of the Conservative government under Thatcher in May 1979 can correctly be identified as the principal catalyst in the breaking of the consensus. It had, however, come under severe stress between 1970 and 1979, first from Conservatives, then from Labour. Not all commentators, however, would agree that the period saw the consensus under stress: in particular Holmes and Horsewood (1988) argue that the post-war consensus reached its high point only in the years 1972–6. This period, they argue, saw trade union involvement in government, welfare spending, state control in industry and Keynesian economic policies all reaching new heights.

There is much in what Holmes and Horsewood say. But one should not overlook the fact that the pre-1972 Conservative government under Edward Heath offered the most serious challenge the post-war consensus had faced up to that point. It also provided the first taste of the right-wing economic and anti-union policies which after 1979 became known as 'Thatcherism'. Heath's government was elected in June 1970 determined to free industry from wide measures of state control, to legislate on trade union power and to promote the free market and self-reliance in place of welfarism. In the event, as unemployment rose above half a million, Heath lost his nerve when the unpopularity of his policies was felt, and in consequence he brought about the so-called 'U-turn' in 1972. From that point until the

election; as Holmes describes, the government embraced consensual policies. Nationalisation was even extended, unique for a Conservative post-war government, and the 1972 Industry Act greatly increased state controls, in direct contrast to the direction of policy between 1970 and 1972. Trade union leaders were consulted as never before and it was ironical, and personally very painful for Heath, that it was the failure to bring to a conclusion the strike with the miners that precipitated his decision to call an election for February 1974. He lost.

Labour returned to power with a minority government led by Harold Wilson. A second election followed in October when he was able to achieve an outright, though wafer-thin, majority of three. Several senior Labour figures, notably Tony Benn and Michael Foot, whose views were well supported on both front and back benches, now pressed hard for the introduction of radical policies, in particular: withdrawal from the European Community, which Britain had joined in 1973; unilateral nuclear disarmament; and an extension of state ownership and control.

Not one of these policies was adopted. Wilson, and then Callaghan, who succeeded him as Prime Minister in 1976, were both able to outflank the left, to its growing dismay and anger. Labour's small majority, which disappeared altogether following by-election defeats in 1977, was offered as one reason. The 'Lib.–Lab. pact' of 1977–8, when the tiny Liberal Party maintained Labour in power, provided another reason for the government to reject doctrinaire policies. Recurrent economic difficulties, which resulted in the International Monetary Fund (IMF) being called in to help out the government in 1976, also help explain Labour's moderation in office, especially as the IMF made the setting of monetary targets and cuts in spending a condition of the provision of stand-by facilities.

Other policies, normally associated with right of centre governments, followed the IMF loan, including the imposition of cash limits on many departmental programmes and the sale of some government shares in British Petroleum to the private sector. At the same time Labour was gradually abandoning its commitment to Keynesian belief in spending one's way out of recession, and hence to full employment. Without the twin constraints of no parliamentary majority and a weak economy, Labour might conceivably have adopted more genuinely socialist policies after 1974. As it was, the consensus was still virtually intact when Thatcher entered Downing Street in May 1979. It had largely survived the twin attacks on it in the 1970s, from the right in 1970–2 and (ironically) from Labour, 1976–9.

Why the Keynesian social democratic consensus broke down

Why was there a fundamental change in the policies pursued by British governments after 1979? Kavanagh and Pimlott (1989) list three main reasons, which together explain the breakdown.

1. *Ideas*: No challenge to the prevailing Keynesian–Beveridge orthodoxy had captured the imagination of a critical mass of policy makers since before the war until the 1970s. The challenge came from the right (what had become known as the 'radical right'), which exalted free enterprise in place of state control and provisions. The new ideology rested heavily on the work of two men: F.A. Hayek, in his influential book *The Road to Serfdom* (1944), who subsequently argued that state power was a potential menace to individual liberty and should be everywhere curtailed if individuals were to enjoy maximum benefit; and Milton Friedman, who spearheaded an economist's challenge to the principles of Keynesianism, and in attempting to overturn Keynes's teaching substituted a new theory, popularly known as monetarism, which laid great stress on the control of the money supply and the reduction of inflation, even at the expense of maintaining full employment (see also Chapter 8).

    The ideas of Hayek, Friedman and others were initially articulated in a little-known international annual conference, the Mont Pelerin Society, formed soon after the war. Like-minded academics, mainly economists, met at this forum and advocated many of the ideas which were later adopted by Margaret Thatcher. The Mont Pelerin Society provided the spur for the establishment in London in 1957 of the Institute of Economic Affairs, which, together with the later Centre for Policy Studies (1974),

gradually persuaded academics and politicians of the benefits of 'free enterprise' policies over Keynesian state involvement.

2. *People*: Ideas need people with political weight to articulate them and give them force if they are to have any significance. The earliest influential convert in the Conservative Party to the radical right was Enoch Powell, and after his dismissal from the Shadow Cabinet in 1968 the banner was kept flying by John Biffen and most importantly Keith Joseph. Joseph in turn had been influenced principally by Peter Bauer, a London School of Economics (LSE) economist, and by Alfred Sherman, a journalist and propagandist; he did more than anyone to persuade Thatcher of the virtues of free enterprise policies. And it was Thatcher who possessed the single-mindedness and personal conviction to see that the policies were carried through without deflection after 1979.

3. *Circumstance*: Ideas and people alone would not have been sufficient to bring about the major policy shift; circumstance provided the opportunity. Without the collapse and discrediting of Keynesian social democrat policies in the 1960s and especially the 1970s, as described by Marquand (1988) and Skidelsky (1988), 'Thatcherism' would never have had its chance. The policies with which Keynesianism was associated – demand management and income policies – were shown to have failed as unemployment and inflation both rose and governments seemed incapable of running the government effectively, or indeed of containing the trade unions. Thatcher seized her opportunity with both hands.

The qualified free market consensus after 1979

Although John Vincent (1987) has argued that what was remarkable about Thatcher was how little, not how much, she changed, such a stance distorts her historical importance. He is right to stress the difficulties she faced overturning policies and assumptions which had endured for over twenty years. Nevertheless, most of the six planks of the consensus were overturned, or at least seriously modified, by Thatcher after 1979. Four aspects of the consensus listed below went through major transformation:

1. *Employment:* She never pursued full employment policies. Heath had panicked when unemployment threatened to reach one million in 1972. Thatcher kept her nerve and watched unemployment rise to more than two and then three million, levels that had existed in the dreaded interwar years. No one had believed before 1979 that unemployment would ever be allowed to rise that high, nor that a government would survive if it were allowed to happen. This was proved wrong on both counts. The reduction of inflation, in line with the teachings of Friedman rather than Keynes, was placed above the reduction of unemployment. Under her chancellors Geoffrey Howe (1979–83) and Nigel Lawson (1983–90) she refused to expand the economy in the hope of reducing unemployment. She argued that her task was to create real not artificially stimulated jobs.

2. *Trade union industrial and political power* diminished greatly in the 1980s. Consultations, which amounted almost to a veto, over government policies had risen to an all-time high in the 1970s. Unions were indirectly associated in toppling three governments (1970, February 1974 and 1979). Thatcher decided that she was not going to continue the close relationship and in consequence formal and informal contacts between union leaders and government ministers and officials all but ceased. Trade unions were effectively pushed to one side in policy formulation, and a series of acts (1980, 1982, 1984, 1988 and 1989) greatly reduced their industrial and political power.

3. *The mixed economy* was also changed beyond recognition. The steady programme of privatisation – gas, steel (again!), electricity: the list is long and well known – decisively pushed the balance in the economy in the direction of private rather than public ownership. The rise in private share ownership was mirrored by the increase in home ownership through the government's policy of encouraging tenant purchase of council properties. The country still had a mixed economy, but it had become fairly lop-sided.

4. *A duty to further equality:* In place of equality, Thatcher appeared to prefer a 'stimulating inequality', believing that differential pay acts as an incentive to effort and enterprise, and that intervention by the state distorts the operation of the free market. Regional aid to reduce inequalities between different parts of Britain was consistently cut back after 1979, with the result that differentials between north and south have increased markedly. The steady reduction in income tax rates has benefited the better off, and helped widen inequalities in income. Although many sections of the working class became more prosperous after 1979, the number in the 'underclass', comprising the long-term unemployed, many single-parent families and those dependent on state benefits, grew considerably. Britain became a more polarised country as a direct consequence of Thatcherite policies.

Two planks, however, were not removed. *The welfare state* remained largely intact during Thatcher's first two terms of office (1979–87). Its survival was in some ways paradoxical. Bodies such as the Institute of Economic Affairs had for many years been campaigning for a move away from the universal to selective provision of welfare benefits, and at the same time advocated the extension of market forces throughout the various parts of the welfare empire. But partly for fear of risking unpopularity over such a sensitive issue, and partly because the government's hands were full with other matters, the welfare state was left intact. In Thatcher's third term (1987–90) the NHS in particular was subjected to new market pressures, but it would be wrong to exaggerate the extent to which Thatcher disturbed the welfare state. Its key principles, which include universal and free provision, and flat rate benefits, remained. Private provision increased but the welfare state continued to provide support for those who either could or would not pay. Thatcher realised it would be electoral suicide for her to do anything else (see also Chapter 26).

The foreign and defence consensus has also continued very much intact. Policy since 1979 has been based upon Britain's continued maintenance and upgrading of its nuclear deterrent (Polaris to

Trident); granting of independence to some remaining colonies (notably Zimbabwe in 1980); close cooperation with NATO and the USA; and qualified support for the European Community. If we include a determination to contain terrorism in Northern Ireland and to remain there providing military and economic support, then the continuity of consensus policy in this area is complete.

The emergence of the second consensus in the 1980s

Did Thatcher manage, in largely breaking the old, to forge a new consensus? Returning to the definition of consensus given at the opening of this chapter, it matters not what parties say in opposition (when they tend to make pronouncements more extreme than they carry out in office): it is their policies *in power* that matter. We do not know what a Labour government might have done if elected in 1983 or 1987. Only if their policies had been manifest could a definitive answer have been given to this question.

The decade saw the Labour party becoming steadily more moderate. Its high point of non-moderation came in the period 1980–3 after Michael Foot succeeded James Callaghan as party leader. Its 1983 manifesto was as socialist as any since 1945, promising the unilateral abandonment of Britain's nuclear weapons, extensions of nationalisation, as well as opposition to the (capitalist) EEC.

After 1983, however, with Neil Kinnock replacing Michael Foot as party leader, the party progressively moved away from left-wing policies. Labour's 1987 election programme was moderate. Defeat that year further stiffened Kinnock's resolve to fight off his left wing and remove from the party doctrinaire policies which no longer commanded widespread support of the electorate. Old-style left-wing figures such as Tony Benn and Eric Heffer were gradually marginalised, a task made easier by their defeat in their challenge for the party leadership in October 1988. Kinnock was assisted in his task by his deputy Roy Hattersley and by the promotion into senior frontbench positions of able pragmatic figures like John Smith, Bryan Gould and Gordon Brown.

The endorsement given by the party conference in October 1989 to the party's moderate policy review was a major endorsement of Kinnock's policy of 'modernising' Labour policies. In practice it meant that the party had come to realise that if it clung to its traditional socialist politics, it would never again be elected. The class composition and preferences of the electorate have been changing throughout the post-war period in favour of the Conservative Party. With the exception of its strong showing in the March 1966 election, Labour had undergone a steady loss of support at every election between 1951 (48.6 per cent) and 1983 (27.6 per cent). The 1987 result was a slight improvement at 30.8 per cent of the popular vote, which could have been interpreted as an endorsement for Labour's more popular policies, but the party was still 10 percentage points behind the Conservatives. The period since 1979 saw the pace of social change increase. From 1979 to 1987, according to the opinion-polling organisation MORI, union membership fell from 30 to 23 per cent, home owner-occupation rose from 52 to 62 per cent, share ownership increased from 7 to 19 per cent and households defined as middle class rose from 35 to 42 per cent. Much of the increase in Conservative support in the 1983 and 1987 elections came from those affected by these changes. The Conservatives gained 36 per cent of the working-class vote in 1987, the highest percentage in any post-war election, and did especially well among those living in the south who worked in the private sector (see Chapter 11).

Two responses were possible for Labour. Either it could have adapted its policies to appeal to the new electorate or it could have argued, as the left did, that the reason for the defeats was that the party was insufficiently socialist. In the 1980s the party gradually but decisively adopted the former course. Thatcher, and the Social Democratic Party, founded in 1981, played a significant role in moderating Labour's policies by 1990. It would have taken an election and a Labour victory to have shown if Labour in power would have accepted much of the Thatcher agenda, and whether a new, more right-wing consensus had emerged. In the event, no Labour victory transpired. But Tories might have wished they had lost in 1992 after the drubbing they eventually took in 1997. On this occasion the swing away from them occurred in all classes and massively so. The alliance of middle classes with the skilled working classes which had sustained Thatcher throughout the 1980s was shattered by New Labour.

The swing amongst C1 and C2 voters was 16 and 15 per cent respectively according to the BBC/NOP exit poll. Voters aged between 18 and 29 swung an incredible 19 per cent and the gender gap closed with an 11 per cent swing to Labour amongst women. Even mortgage payers and home owners swung by 15 and 12 per cent respectively. A major realignment had occurred in May 1997 to see in the new millenium.

The qualified free market consensus solidifies in the 1990s?

The new consensus solidified in the 1990s, when it became clear that under Major the Conservatives reined back on going for a full-blooded free market agenda, and Labour, under John Smith (1992–4) and Tony Blair (1994–) accepted much of the reforms of the 1980s without promising to take the country back in a statist direction if elected to office. There are three reasons for the parties drawing closer since 1990.

1. *Leaders*:   John Major has defined his distinctive brand of Conservatism as 'Thatcherism with a human face'. It is clear that on many issues he is to the left of Thatcher, and hence is often closer to New Labour's policies. Tony Blair, Labour leader since 1994, is also to the right of Kinnock and Smith. Labour and Conservative leaders are closer philosophically now than at any time since 1975. Both Blair and Major have less confrontational personalities than many of their predecessors.
2. *Ideas*:   The 1980s was the decade of the radical right think-tanks. Hardly a week went by without some pronouncement from the Institute of Economic Affairs, the Centre for Policy Studies or the Adam Smith Institute. Intellectuals, often exiles from the left like Alfred Sherman or Paul Johnson, queued up to write articles or books about an aspect of 'Thatcherism', usually in approving style. In the 1990s the guns of think-tanks and the pens of intellectuals have lost much of their force. The radical right found its champion in John Redwood, but after his defeat in the party leadership contest in July 1995, the cause of those who wanted unbridled free market policies was in the descendant. Following the May 1997 election defeat, ideological groups within the Conservative Party were evenly balanced, with the centre of power being commanded by the centre. In Labour, Blair has further marginalised the far left, who want to reintroduce socialism. New Labour has effectively extinguished socialist policies – for the foreseeable future especially after Blair's 'presidential' landslide victory in May 1997.
3. *Circumstance*:   The 1997 general election taught both main parties different lessons. Labour realised it would have to go further to purge itself of its remaining socialist ideas and ties if it was to avoid a fifth election defeat in a row. Conservatives realised how narrow was their margin of victory, and subsequent by-election disasters raised further the clamour for moving away from doctrinaire free enterprise to capture the centre vote. Widespread acceptance that market economics alone will not cure unemployment, and the imperatives of the global economy and money markets, are further circumstances pushing the two parties closer.

We need to examine the six planks of the consensus to see how they stand in the eyes of Conservatives and Labour in the mid-1990s:

1. *Full employment*:   By mid-1997, unemployment still stood at under 2 million. When Britain left the exchange rate mechanism, the possibility of a more active government economic policy presented itself. Labour and many Conservatives called for reflation of the economy, but Major resisted. To that extent the parties differed. But even Labour agreed that to hope to return to full employment (with 2–3 per cent unemployed) would be a pipe dream.
2. *Mixed economy*:   Since 1979, two-thirds of state-owned industries and services have been returned to private enterprise. Labour initially said it would renationalise. But by 1989 under the Kinnock review the party declared it accepted the market economy, albeit better regulated, and would not try to reintroduce wholesale socialism. Nor will the party alter the policy on sale of council houses. Blair confirmed the intention to extend privatisation. The main difference remaining between the parties is Labour's liking for greater regulation and more emphasis on directed investment.

3. *Welfare state*:   This was the last domestic area of the post-war consensus to be attacked by Thatcher. Her government had long been pressed by the Institute of Economic Affairs and other groups to abandon *universal* provision of benefits in favour of *selective* benefits, and to extend charging for services (if necessary on a loan basis), private provision of welfare benefits and greater freedom of choice. Thatcher resisted this pressure in the main, but after 1987 progressively adopted 'contracting out' to private suppliers of services and the introduction of 'internal markets'. John Major continued this trend, e.g. by hospitals being allowed in 1991 to become self-governing trusts (i.e. local authorities' oversight over hospitals weakened). But these plans fall a long way short of abandoning or even privatising the welfare state *en masse*. Labour by 1997 was forced to accept much of the logic of the Conservatives' policy; relative economic decline and the unpopularity of high taxes have led Labour to search for more cost-effective ways to target social policy. In other words, Labour realises that universal free benefits may need to yield a greater use of the market.

4. *Trade unions*:   Under Michael Foot (Labour leader 1980–3) Labour was committed to restoring trade union 'rights' taken away in the Acts of 1980 and 1982. By the end of the decade Labour accepted that some aspects of Conservative policy, e.g. ending the 'closed shop', and the formal election by members of union officials, should be retained. Some differences remained between the parties; above all, Labour supported the European Union's Social Charter. But the differences were not major and became even less when Blair acceded to pressure within the party (and from outside) to distance it from the trade unions. Such a move, it was argued, would be welcomed by the electorate.

5. *Equality*:   This area remains one of some difference. In the 1980s and early 1990s, the gulf between rich and poor individuals and the north and south of Britain grew. All four chancellors, Howe (1979–83), Lawson (1983–9), Lamont (1990–93) and Clarke (1993–7) lowered tax burdens on the better-off, and refused to use government expenditure significantly to reduce regional unemployment (influenced by the banker's maxim 'don't throw good money after bad'). Until Blair, Labour was committed to raising taxes on the better-off and to pursuing a more effective regional policy. By the 1990s Labour had abandoned its doctrinaire commitment to socialist equality, but it had not fully given up a belief in the need to reduce inequality.

6. *Foreign and defence policy*:   Labour in the early 1980s was opposed to Britain's place in NATO, its nuclear deterrent and even membership of the European Community. By 1989 Labour had abandoned its attachment to unilateral nuclear disarmament, and from 1993 often appeared closer to the Clinton administration in Washington than the Conservatives. On Europe, Labour is more enthusiastic than the Conservatives, who remain split on the issue.

It seems likely, from the perspective of the late 1990s, that the Thatcher governments of 1979–90 succeeded in shifting the policy agenda to the right, much as the Attlee government of 1945–50 shifted it to the left. But the position stabilised in the 1990s. Had Thatcher remained in office, it is quite possible that she would have taken Britain irrevocably in a free market direction. But under Major, the forces of moderation prevailed. His concern was not to abolish the public sector, but via the Citizen's Charter to make it work better, just as under Blair, the aim of a future Labour government is not to abolish capitalism, but to make it work more efficiently. It is conceivable that Labour will introduce socialism in power and tilt the agenda firmly back leftwards. But such a scenario seems at best unlikely and we will in all probability see a qualified free market consensus continue well into the twenty-first century.

Chapter summary

British politics since 1945 have seen two dominant periods. A Keynesian social democratic consensus lasted from 1945 to 1979, and was based on the economic ideas of J.M. Keynes and the social philosophy of Beveridge. In this period, the state had a major role to play as a provider of services and a redistributor of income and wealth. A second consensus was inaugurated with the Thatcher government coming to power in 1979. This pushed the agenda in a right-wing or free market direction, in favour of greater private rather than state provision. But it was a *qualified* free market consensus because many aspects of policy, such as the welfare state, which did not exist before 1945, were retained in whole or in part. There was no wholesale return to private sector provision.

Discussion points

■ Do consensus policies enhance or detract from the quality of democracy in Britain?

■ Is it a distortion of the facts to assert that consensus politics have been the norm in postwar Britain?

■ Is 'qualified free market' an adequate description of the politics of the 1980s and 1990s?

■ Why might the policies of Labour and the Conservatives be so similar when the parties are in office?

Further reading

For critical accounts on the existence of consensus, see Pimlott (1989), Jones and Kandiah (1996) and Jones (1996). For sympathetic accounts, see Kavanagh and Morris (1994), Seldon (1994) and Marquand (1996).

References

Holmes, M. and Horsewood, N. (1988) 'The consensus debate', *Contemporary Record*, Summer.

Jones, H. (1996) 'The postwar consensus in Britain: thesis, antithesis and synthesis?', in B. Brivati, J. Buxton and A. Seldon (eds), *Contemporary History Handbook* (Manchester University Press).

Jones, H. and Kandiah, M. (eds) (1996) *The Myth of Consensus* (Frank Cass).

Kavanagh, D. and Morris, P. (1994) *Consensus Politics*, 2nd edn (Blackwell).

Marquand, D. (1988) 'Postwar consensus and its decline', *Contemporary Record*, Autumn.

Marquand, D. (1996) 'Moralists and Hedonists', in D. Marquand and A. Seldon (eds), *The Ideas That Shaped Postwar Britain* (HarperCollins).

Pimlott, P. (1989) 'Is the postwar consensus a myth?', *Contemporary Record*, Summer.

Seldon, A. (1994) 'Consensus: a debate too long?', *Parliamentary Affairs*, October.

Skidelsky, R.S. (ed.) (1988) *Thatcherism* (Chatto and Windus).

Vincent, J. (1987) 'The Thatcher governments, 1979–87', in P. Hennessy and A. Seldon (eds) *Ruling Performance: British Governments from Attlee to Thatcher* (Basil Blackwell).

CHAPTER THREE

The social context

MICHAEL MORAN

LEARNING OBJECTIVES

- To sketch some of the most important sources of social hierarchy in Britain.

- To outline how those hierarchies have changed, and continue to change, over time.

- To show the sorts of political tensions to which those hierarchies give rise.

INTRODUCTION

The social context refers to a wide range of factors. It covers social institutions which we would immediately recognise as such because they are part of our daily experience, such as the school or college. But it also refers to social groupings which have a less immediately recognisable form. For instance, every society has social groupings which arrange members into hierarchies, whether the hierarchies are those of wealth, esteem or power. This social environment provides the context within which politics takes place, and its understanding is vital to making sense of the politics of a country.

The parts of Britain

The simplest way to start is with the basic geography of the United Kingdom. Viewed in this way several features of the UK become clear:

1. *It is small*: Only 244.1 thousand square kilometres.
2. *It is densely populated*: The number of persons per square kilometre in 1993 was just over 240, against an average for the fifteen members of the European Union of 115.
3. *It is industrial*: Only 2 per cent of those employed work on the land.
4. *It is rich*: We live in one of a small number of rich countries in a largely poor world. Viewed internationally, the arguments about the allocation of resources in Britain are arguments *between* comparatively well off groups of people. Figure 3.1 illustrates Britain's long-term position in the 'league table' of world wealth. Despite long-term decline we remain in the 'premier league' of wealth. That is reflected in the life chances of the British people compared with those of other inhabitants of the globe: life expectancy in the United Kingdom is 76 years, in Africa 53.

5. *It is capitalist*: 'capitalism' here is a neutral description: it describes a system where property is privately owned, and where goods and services are traded for a price by free exchange in markets.

Viewed from the 'outside', therefore, British society can look uniform. But when we examine it more closely, variety appears.

One of the most striking sources of variation is *geography*. Britain is a 'multinational state': that is, it is a political unit ruled by a single sovereign authority but composed of territories which historically were different nations, and whose populations still retain distinct national identities.

There are at least five different national groupings in the United Kingdom: the English, Welsh, Scottish, Irish and those (mostly Protestants in Northern Ireland) who identify with 'Ulster'. Identity has been further complicated by immigration. The United Kingdom has periodically received waves of immigrants from abroad and in the 1950s and 1960s received particularly large numbers from what is conventionally called the 'new Commonwealth' – notably from our former colonial possessions in the West Indies and the Indian subcontinent. These immigrants and their children are

for the most part permanently settled in Britain and are citizens of the community. They are conventionally called 'black Britons' but this oversimplifies the question of identity. Groups from the Indian subcontinent, in particular, often retain close connections with their place of origin and in Britain retain their own distinctive cultures, language and religious practices.

The question of national identity in Britain is therefore more complicated than the simple existence of a political unity called the United Kingdom would suggest. But there is a further aspect to territorial differences. Even the most casual traveller in Britain soon realises that within national areas there exist striking variations – differences ranging from the most profound cultural and economic matters to the most mundane aspects of everyday life. Even inside the biggest nation in the United Kingdom, England, there exist striking regional differences.

Although the actual figures change with time, for several decades real income in the south-east of England, and accompanying measures of well-being like employment, have been more favourable than in any other part of the United Kingdom. While in the 1990s the impact of economic recession and a slump in the housing market narrowed this gap, the south-east still

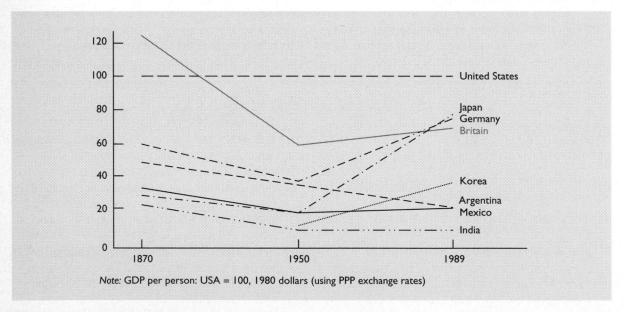

Note: GDP per person: USA = 100, 1980 dollars (using PPP exchange rates)

Figure 3.1 The wealth of Britain, compared over time with other countries
Source: The Economist, 20 June 1992, p. 155

remains the powerhouse of the kingdom. Conversely, areas like Northern Ireland and the north-west of England have for decades been among the poorest. The scale of this is illustrated in Table 3.1.

The regional differences identified here have been widely noticed in recent years and have given rise to the argument that in Britain there exists a 'north–south' divide between the prosperous and the poor parts of the United Kingdom. But despite the undoubted gaps in the wealth of different regions, such characterisations are, at best, only a part of the truth. There exist numerous prosperous communities in the north of Britain. In the heart of the prosperous south in parts of London and Bristol, by contrast, there are communities so impoverished that they have in recent years been the source of serious social unrest. Part of the reason for this is that overlaying any divisions between regions are important differences between various parts of urban areas in Britain.

Urban problems and the city

It is common to speak of the 'urban problem' in Britain or, in the same breath, of 'the problems of the inner city'. But there is actually a wide array of social features summed up in a single phrase like 'the urban problem'. Similarly, although the 'inner city' has become a byword for poverty and misery, many areas of inner cities (witness parts of London) are the homes of the rich and fashionable, while in outer suburbs and even in rural areas there are, especially on public housing estates, areas of deep poverty. Nevertheless, a number of long-term social changes have combined to change the character of the giant cities which were the characteristic creation of Britain's industrial revolution. Two should be noted.

Firstly, long-term shifts in population have changed both the numbers living in many inner city areas and the social balance of the population. The figures of movement tell the story. Between 1981 and 1994, for instance, the population of Cheshire rose by 4.6 per cent, while that of Greater Manchester fell by 1.6 per cent. In the 'booming' south-east the population of Greenwich fell by 1.0 per cent, while the population of Buckinghamshire rose by 15.4 per cent.

This shift of population out of established areas of cities to suburbs and small towns reflects a

Table 3.1 Regional inequality in Britain, 1995

	South-east	West Midlands	East Anglia	South-west	East Midlands	Wales	North-west	Yorks and Humberside	North	Scotland	Northern Ireland
% of working age with a degree	17.1	10.6	12.1	11.6	10.6	11.5	12.1	11.4	9.9	12.7	11.0
Gross average weekly earnings per head (£)	437.5	346.3	341.2	349.6	338.2	331.4	354.2	337.1	331.7	350.7	330.9
Unemployed rate (%)	7.9	8.4	6.2	7.0	7.7	8.5	8.8	8.8	10.6	8.2	11.4
Perinatal mortality rate 1984–6[a]	5.5	5.3	5.2	5.3	6.9	6.2	6.2	7.7	6.3	6.2	6.1
% of households with one car or more (1994)	71	69	69	65	69	67	69	67	59	62	65

Source: Regional Trends, 1995
[a] Births and deaths under one week of age per 1,000 live and still births.

second change: population decline is commonly a reflection of economic decline and social crisis. The cities of the industrial revolution have seen their economic foundations decay as the traditional industries have decayed, with important consequences for prosperity and financial stability. In the biggest cities, especially London, 'averages' conceal huge inequalities in wealth, health and life chances.

Work and unemployment

Work is a central part of each individual's life – whether the worker is the unrewarded housewife or company chief executive earning £500,000 a year. But the nature of work is also important for wider social reasons. *Occupation* is the single most important influence on the social structure. The kind of work done is a key determinant of the material rewards and the status an individual enjoys. Indeed the class structure in Britain closely corresponds to the occupational structure. Definitions of class commonly mean *occupational class*: 'working class', for instance, usually refers to those people – and their families – who earn a living from 'manual' jobs. The central place of occupation in the political life of the country is well illustrated by the case of voting and elections, where occupational class has been, and remains, a key influence on the way people vote. Work is central to the life of the individual, but it is also central to the economic structure. Five aspects of this centrality are notable.

Most people in Britain live by selling their labour

Britain is a market economy in which the only significant tradable resource controlled by the majority of the population is labour. There are indeed exceptions: a small minority of the wealthy control sufficient productive property to be able to live on the returns of that property; a larger group – like pensioners, unemployed, some students – live off state-provided benefits. But most individuals either live by selling their labour to others, or – as in the case of children – are dependent on 'breadwinners'. Figure 3.2, which compares the rates of 'self-employment' for different ethnic groups in the population, reinforces this point.

Most people sell their labour to private firms

Because Britain is a capitalist society only a minority of the workforce is employed in the public sector. Until the beginning of the 1980s a long-term increase had occurred in the size of this minority – so marked that some observers argued that excessive growth of public sector employment was a main cause of Britain's economic difficulties. This trend has been reversed. A combination of cuts in numbers employed in public services and the privatisation of many important industries means that the dominance of private firms as employers has been reinforced in recent years.

Changes in the balance between private and public sector employment are connected to a third notable feature of the workforce – the changing balance between sectors.

Service employment is displacing manufacturing employment

Great economic changes always produce changes in the kind of work done in an economy. The industrial revolution meant, in the long run, that agriculture ceased to be the main source of jobs in Britain. For several decades now a further development has been taking place – a new stage in the industrial revolution has shifted jobs into the 'service' or 'tertiary' sector. There are both proportionately and absolutely fewer workers in industries like steel and coal and more in banking, insurance and health care.

These changes are sometimes described as involving a shift away from manual, working-class occupations to non-manual, middle-class ones. It is certainly true that there has been a long-term increase in the number of 'professional', highly qualified workers in Britain. It is also true that most of the new 'service' jobs involve little of the strenuous physical effort or extreme working conditions associated with a job such as mining. But it is not the case that the service sector necessarily demands skilled work. On the contrary: in recent years some of the fastest growth has been in areas like cleaning and catering, which provide unskilled and usually casual or part-time jobs.

The expansion of the service sector as an employer is also sometimes equated with the growth of public sector employment. This is an exaggeration. It is

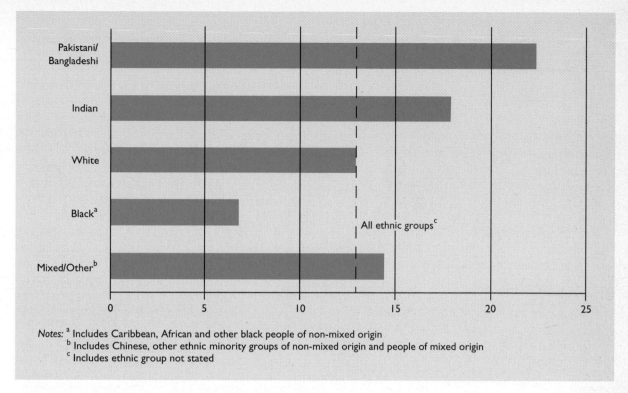

Notes: [a] Includes Caribbean, African and other black people of non-mixed origin
       [b] Includes Chinese, other ethnic minority groups of non-mixed origin and people of mixed origin
       [c] Includes ethnic group not stated

Figure 3.2   Self-employed as a percentage of all in employment: by ethnic group, spring 1994
Source: Social Trends, 1996

indeed the case that some services – like education and health care – which have seen large increases in numbers employed in recent decades are delivered by the public sector. But some of the industries where numbers have declined most rapidly – like coal and steel – were also publicly owned. By contrast one of the fastest growing industries in the last decade, financial services, is largely privately owned.

Women are becoming important in the workforce

Women have always worked but they have not always been paid for working. For example, until the beginning of this century 'domestic service' was a major source of paid employment for women. Social change has since almost eliminated domestic servants and their jobs are now done for nothing by mothers, wives and daughters. In recent decades women – especially married women – have taken paid employment in large numbers. The trends are illustrated in Figure 3.3.

Three features of women's work should be noticed. Firstly, it is disproportionately concentrated in the 'service' sector and in what is sometimes called 'light manufacturing' – work involving, for instance, assembling and packing components. Secondly, while just over half the population are women, far more than half of working women are in jobs with low pay and status and far less than

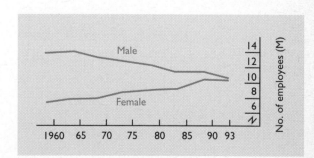

Figure 3.3   Trends in male and female employment in Britain
Source: The Economist, 11 December 1993

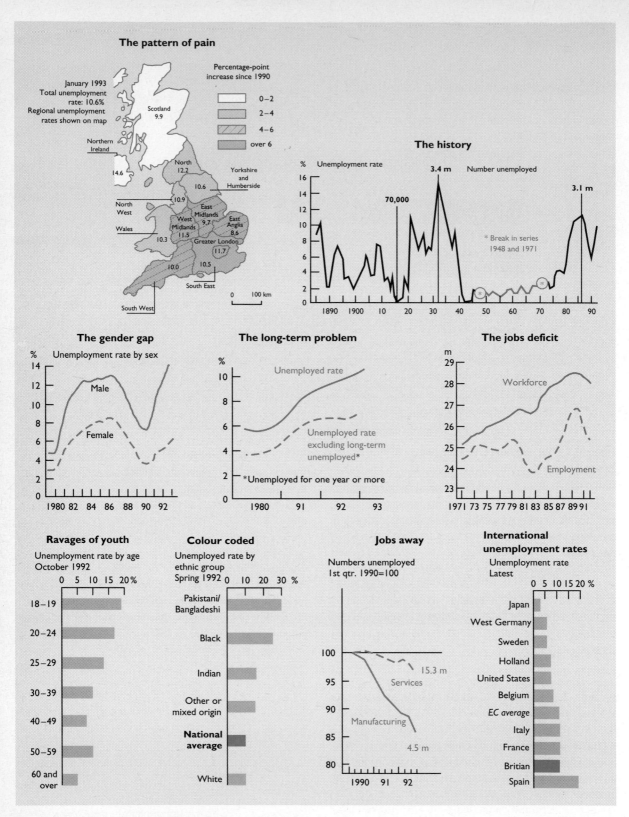

Figure 3.4 Anatomy of unemployment

Source: The Economist, 20 February 1993

half are in high-status jobs: a disproportionately high proportion of women are cleaners in universities, and a disproportionately low number are teachers in them. Thirdly, women occupy a disproportionate number of casual and part-time jobs in the workforce. This observation links to the final feature of work and employment on which we focus.

Unemployment and part-time work have become more common

There has always been unemployment in Britain. For over three decades after 1940, however, it was conventional to speak of the existence of 'full employment'. Only a small proportion of the workforce was out of a job: as recently as 1975, for instance, there were only 838,000 registered unemployed. Unemployment, moreover, was largely accounted for by individuals who were unemployable (for instance, through ill health) and by relatively high levels of joblessness in a few depressed parts of the country (for example, communities over-reliant on a single declining industry).

This era of full employment has gone. For over a decade now, large-scale unemployment has been the norm: the figure for registered unemployed topped one million by 1976, two million by 1981, three million by 1984. Even more significantly, unemployment has ceased to be a transient experience because the numbers of long-term unemployed have grown greatly. The unemployed are disproportionately concentrated among predictable groups: those with few or no formal educational qualifications; those who live in areas where the local economy is depressed; and those who come from some ethnic minorities (see Figure 3.4).

It is often pointed out that even in an era of mass unemployment the overwhelming majority of adults are nevertheless in work and that while jobs are lost in some industries they are being created in others. This is correct, but simple measures of job numbers fail to reveal important changes which are occurring in the structure of the workforce. Full-time jobs in manufacturing have been lost and have been disproportionately replaced by temporary or part-time jobs in the service sector. This hints at a division in the population which may in time become as significant as the divide between the employed and the unem-

---

BOX 3.1

Labour as an economic resource

The vast majority of employees in Britain are united by one single important feature: their labour power is their only significant economic resource.

But otherwise employees in Britain are fragmented into numerous groups:

1. public sector and private sector workers;
2. manual and non-manual workers;
3. workers in service and manufacturing sectors;
4. part-timers and full-timers.

---

ployed. To an increasing degree large employers are dividing their workforce into a 'core' and a 'periphery'. The 'core' consists of workers in secure, long-term employment. There is also a tendency for these to be the better qualified and to enjoy the best pay and fringe benefits. The 'periphery' consists of a shifting group of temporary employees who can be taken on, and laid off, according to demand. There is a corresponding tendency for these workers to be disproportionately women, to be doing less skilled jobs and to be comparatively poorly rewarded. The 'dual' labour market, as it is sometimes called, offers considerable advantages to employers. Temporary and casual labour is comparatively cheap, most workers are poorly organised in unions and legal protection against such eventualities as dismissal is more limited than in the case of the permanent workforce. Thus employers can use their 'peripheral' workforce in a highly flexible way to respond to changing market conditions.

Wealth, property and the social structure

Only one thing can be said with certainty about the distribution of wealth in Britain: it has long been, in statistical terms, highly unequal. But the meaning and even the accuracy of the bald statistics are perhaps more uncertain here than in any other area of British society. Beyond the general proposition that a statistically small group owns an arithmetically large amount of the nation's wealth, there exists little agreement.

Debate starts with the very significance of inequality. For some, the existence of a minority of very wealthy people in Britain is a good thing and any diminution of the wealth of the few a bad thing. According to this argument, great wealth is desirable because it shows the ability of the market system to reward the enterprising with great incentives, thus encouraging innovation and risk-taking in the economy. In addition, the wealthy are a socially important group because although a minority they are still, in absolute terms, large in number. This means that they support social diversity by, for example, sponsoring a variety of political causes, charities and artistic activities. Without the wealthy, according to this view, society would be dull, uniform and dominated by the state. On the other hand, critics of the social order in Britain maintain that control of great wealth by a minority is illegitimate. It appropriates what is properly the wealth of the community for a few and contradicts the aim of democracy by lodging wealth – and thus power – in the hands of a minority.

These arguments are, in the long run, inconclusive because they involve competing notions of what a just social order should look like. But they have also proved inconclusive for a more mundane reason: nobody can agree on how definitively to measure wealth and its distribution. Most of us think we could recognise the existence of great wealth – but we would soon disagree about what exactly to include as a measure of wealth, and how to value what is actually included. We could probably agree, for instance, that the great landed estates still owned by some aristocrats are a form of wealth and should be counted as such. But should this also be said of even the most humble property, such as the family semi-detached house? In an age where domestic houses often fetch high prices, and where over 60 per cent of dwellings are owner-occupied, this decision can make a big difference to estimates of the distribution of wealth. Similarly, there would probably be general agreement that

ownership of a body of shares in a large business corporation is a form of wealth. But should this also be said of more indirect stakes in ownership? In many of the largest corporations in Britain a substantial proportion of shares are owned by 'institutions' – organisations like insurance companies and pension funds, which invest the proceeds of the contributions of individual policy-holders or those paying into pension schemes. Since an individual making such contributions is entitled to a return on the investments, just as certainly as the direct shareholder is entitled to a dividend, it may be thought that participants in insurance schemes and pension funds should be counted as owning some of the wealth of the economy. If this is indeed so, it suggests that not only is wealth quite widely distributed but that it has become more equally distributed in recent decades, because the beneficiaries of life insurance and pension schemes have grown greatly in number. (For instance, in 1953 only 28 per cent of workers were in a pension scheme; thirty years later the figure was 52 per cent.) Table 3.2 shows how sensitive the figures can be to the definition of wealth, by comparing the results when we include or exclude the value of dwellings.

An additional complication is introduced by the difficulty of actually valuing wealth, even when we agree on what is to be included in a definition. The

Table 3.2 Distribution of marketable wealth in Britain, Inland Revenue estimates

Marketable wealth – percentage of wealth owned by:	1976	1992
Most wealthy 1%	21	18
Most wealthy 5%	38	37
Most wealthy 10%	50	49
Most wealthy 25%	71	72
Most wealthy 50%	92	92
Marketable wealth less value of dwellings: percentage owned by:		
Most wealthy 1%	29	29
Most wealthy 5%	47	53
Most wealthy 10%	57	65
Most wealthy 25%	73	82
Most wealthy 50%	88	94

Source: Social Trends, 1996, p. 96.

values of shares in companies, for instance, are decided on the open market. Falls in share prices can thus drastically reduce estimates of the riches of the (mostly wealthy) groups of large shareholders.

It is important to bear these cautionary remarks in mind when discussing arguments about wealth distribution and in interpreting the figures presented in Table 3.2. Nevertheless, three observations seem beyond reasonable doubt. Firstly, there is indeed a minority which owns a statistically disproportionate amount of the community's total wealth. Secondly, there is a very large group at the other end of the social scale which is virtually propertyless. Thirdly, over time there is some redistribution of wealth away from the very richest, but the trickle of resources down the social scale is slow and uneven.

The social environmental: continuity and change

In a famous introduction to the social fabric of British politics, published over thirty years ago, Jean Blondel (1963) summarised Britain as a homogeneous society. By this he did not mean that social divisions were absent, but that Britain, when compared with the USA or with other important European nations, was marked by comparatively few important lines of divisions. Whereas religion, race, territory, were important lines of division elsewhere, the social context of British politics could be pretty fully understood by reference to class divisions alone: the most important 'blocs' in British society were classes, identified by their occupation. The key division was between manual and 'white-collar' workers.

That line of division remains important, and more generally the divisions between the rich and poor remain significant in British society. But two developments have combined to make this line of division less crucial.

Firstly the unity of the two big class 'blocs' has declined. This is most obvious in the case of the manual working class: the numbers of manual workers have declined; they have been internally divided between those in permanent, full-time jobs and those in temporary and/or part-time work; and there has been a growth in unemployment among those who would formerly have done manual work. Conversely, there has been a big increase in the

numbers of white-collar workers, but this increase has also brought more internal variety: a wider span of jobs, and important divisions between those in fairly secure permanent work, and those on short-term and temporary contracts.

Secondly, there has been a rise in new kinds of social identification, and a strengthening of old ones. Of the first of these, perhaps the most important has been the rise of different *ethnic* identities. The most important cause of this development is the large-scale migration, especially from the West Indies and the Indian subcontinent, which took place into Britain, especially in the 1950s and 1960s. These groups had very distinctive racial identities; many also brought a very strong sense of religious identity to a society where religion had been, for most of the population, a comparatively unimportant matter. The diversity and the complexity of the ethnic 'mix' in different parts of the UK are illustrated by Table 3.3.

At the same time, there has been a revival of traditional identities, notably those based on the different nations that make up the 'United Kingdom'. This is especially noticeable in the case of Scotland.

A second very important source of identity beyond ethnicity is that based on *gender*. There is a close connection between changes in the job market and

Table 3.3 The ethnic composition of Great Britain at the last (1991) census (per cent)

Ethnic group	Great Britain	England	Wales	Scotland
White	94.5	93.8	98.5	98.7
Ethnic minorities	5.5	6.3	1.4	1.4
Black	1.6	1.9	0.3	0.1
Caribbean	0.9	1.1	0.1	0.0
African	0.4	0.4	0.1	0.0
Other	0.3	0.4	0.1	0.0
South Asian	2.7	3.0	0.6	0.6
Indian	1.5	1.8	0.2	0.2
Pakistani	0.9	1.0	0.2	0.4
Bangladeshi	0.3	0.3	0.1	0.0
Chinese and other	1.2	1.3	0.6	0.5
Chinese	0.3	0.3	0.2	0.2
Other Asian	0.4	0.4	0.1	0.1
Other other	0.5	0.6	0.3	0.2
Total population (000s)	54,860	47,026	2,835	4,998

Source: Layton-Henry, 1996

change in both perceptions *of* women and perceptions *by* women. The rise of the (paid) working woman has had important consequences even beyond the labour market itself. It undoubtedly lies at the root of a new sense of self-confidence and self-consciousness among many women, reflected in, for instance, a heightened sense of dissatisfaction with long-established inequalities within and outside the workplace between men and women. It has greatly affected the culture and the structure of family life. In many groups – notably in traditional working-class communities – the spread of paid employment among women has accompanied a decline in the very occupations where manual workers were traditionally employed. The result is that the historical role of 'breadwinner' now lies with women rather than men in many instances, inevitably enforcing changes in power and authority within the family.

Chapter summary

In this chapter we have: seen how Britain as a society compares with the societies of other nations around the globe; seen how the different nations and regions of Britain differ; seen how the changing nature of work is reshaping British society; seen how the social structure and the distribution of wealth are intertwined; and seen how lines of division beyond those of work and property, like gender and race, are becoming important.

Discussion points

- What are the most important political consequences of the fact that Britain is both a rich and a capitalist society?

- What are the most likely political results of recent changes in the nature of work in Britain?

- What is the most important line of division in British society: nationality, class, race or gender?

Further reading

Esping-Andersen (1990), while rather advanced for the beginning student, is excellent in 'setting' Britain in an international context. Halsey (1986) remains one of the best introductions to the social structure. Perkin (1989), not easy-going, is invaluable in describing historical evolution. Atkinson (1974) is still invaluable in describing the problems of estimating the distribution of wealth. Halsey (1988) brings together long-term surveys of change in structure. Blondel (1963), while now dated, nevertheless remains the most successful attempt to summarise the social fabric of British politics. The two most invaluable sources of up-to-date information on society and economy are published annually by Her Majesty's Stationery Office: *Regional Trends* and *Social Trends*. Rose (1971 and 1982) are classics on the nature of national identity in the United Kingdom.

References

Atkinson, A.B. (1974) *Unequal Shares* (Penguin).

Blondel, J. (1963) *Voters, Parties and Leaders* (Penguin).

Esping-Andersen, G. (1990) *The Three Worlds of Welfare Capitalism* (Polity Press).

Halsey, A.H. (1986) *Change in British Society* (Macmillan).

Halsey, A.H. (1987) 'Social trends since World War II', in Central Statistical Office, *Social Trends*.

Halsey, A.H. (ed.) (1988) *British Social Trends since 1900* (Macmillan).

Layton-Henry, Z. (1996) 'Immigration and contemporary British politics', *Politics Review*, February.

Perkin, H. (1990) *The Rise of Professional Society: England since 1880* (Routledge).

Rose, R. (1971) *Governing without Consensus: An Irish Perspective* (Faber).

Rose, R. (1982) *Understanding the United Kingdom* (Longman).

CHAPTER FOUR

The economic context

MICHAEL MORAN

LEARNING OBJECTIVES

- To sketch the nature of the division between the public sector and the private sector in the British economy.

- To describe how the structure of production has changed over time.

- To show how changes have taken place in the way enterprises are owned and controlled, and to show why these changes are politically relevant.

INTRODUCTION

The economic structure is vital to the political system in Britain for many reasons, of which three are especially important. Firstly, the way property is distributed is a major influence over political organisations. As we examine elections, political parties and pressure groups later in this book we will see that the voting behaviour of citizens, the divisions between parties and the structure of pressure groups are all closely tied to the wider economic context. Secondly, in the economy lies, obviously, the wealth of the country – and, therefore, the resources on which government can draw to support its operations. Finally, in Britain today the management of the economic structure and the cure of economic problems is the most visible task of government. The economic structure influences political organisation, provides the resources of government and involves major responsibilities of government.

The economic structure: the public and the private

The United Kingdom, as we saw in the last chapter, is a capitalist country: private ownership of property dominates; most people rely on the sale of their labour to make a living. But this capitalist country, like most others, also has a large *public sector*: the state is important in economic life. State involvement in economics is often thought of as meaning 'public ownership'; in fact that is only one way among many by which the state shapes economic structures.

The government as owner

Public ownership is the most visible form of state participation in the economic structure. Government has long been a major owner of productive property:

for instance, the crown was already a great property holder when land was the main source of wealth in the community. In the nineteenth century government established a public monopoly in a major new industry of the time, posts and telecommunications. In modern Britain government is still a major owner of society's natural resources, like coal, oil and gas. (The right to exploit these is only given by licence to private firms.) However, the best-known instances of public ownership are the result of what is usually called *nationalisation*. The nationalised industries are the product of conscious political choices. For most of the century until the start of the 1980s the nationalised sector grew, with successive governments of different political outlooks adding to the range. In the years between the two world wars, for instance, industries as different as broadcasting and electricity supply were nationalised (by the creation of, respectively, the British Broadcasting Corporation and the Central Electricity Generating Board). The years immediately after the Second World War saw a substantial increase in public ownership: coal, steel and railways were all taken into the state sector. The main reason for the post-war growth of public ownership was the belief that the enterprises, if left in private hands, would be run inefficiently or would even fail. This motivation also explains many of the important pieces of nationalisation accomplished in the 1960s and 1970s. These included shipbuilding and important sections of the aircraft and motor vehicle production industries.

Until the mid-1970s it seemed that the continued expansion of public ownership was an irreversible trend in Britain. However, Margaret Thatcher's Conservative administrations of the 1980s destroyed this assumption. Through a programme of 'privatisation' they sold into private hands about 40 per cent of what was in public ownership at the start of the decade. The 'privatised' concerns include many once thought 'natural' to the public sector, such as the gas supply and telecommunications industries. Privatisation marks a radical shift in the balance between the state and the market in Britain. However, the retreat of state ownership does not necessarily mean that total public participation in the economy is in decline. On the contrary, in most of the other five cases which we will consider the importance of government is apparently growing.

The government as partner

The state can act as a partner of private enterprise in numerous ways. Publicly controlled institutions in the financial sector commonly provide investment capital to allow private enterprises to set up or to expand. The major area of growth in partnership in recent years, however, has been at the local level. Faced with the need to redevelop declining and derelict areas of the cities, local authorities and local development corporations have embarked on numerous joint developments with private firms. Some of the best known examples of policy initiatives at the local level – such as the redevelopment of London's docklands – are the result of precisely such partnerships.

The government as regulator

Although most debate about public intervention in the economy concerns ownership, it is arguably the case that the structure of the market economy in Britain is less influenced by ownership than by public regulation – in other words by sets of rules either contained in law or otherwise prescribed by government.

Public regulation is of three kinds. Firstly, the state sets a general framework for the conduct of life, including economic life. Criminal and civil law defines and enforces commercial contracts, identifies what constitutes honesty and dishonesty and provides a means for detecting and preventing fraud. Without this general framework of enforced rules the market economy could not operate.

A second category of regulation is directed at particular industries or sectors of the economy, governing the conduct of affairs inside individual enterprises. For instance, there now exists a large body of law governing relations in the workplace. Industrial relations law places obligations on both employers and trade unions in industrial bargaining. Health and safety legislation prescribes rules safeguarding the life and health of employees.

Finally, there is regulation governing the relations between firms in the private sector and the rest of society. The importance of this kind of regulation has grown greatly in recent years. Two of the most important instances concern pollution control and consumer protection. Pollution regulations govern the nature of industrial processes and restrict the emissions which firms can allow into the atmosphere. Consumer protection regulates the content of many products (in the interests of safety), how they can be advertised (in the interests of honesty and accuracy) and the terms of competition between firms (in the interests of ensuring fair prices).

One important form of regulation is sometimes called 'self-regulation'. Under this system an industry or occupation determines its own regulations and establishes its own institutions for policing and enforcement. Some important professions (like the law) and major industries (like advertising) are organised in this way. But most self-regulation should more accurately be called regulation under public licence, because what happens is that the state licenses a group to regulate itself – thereby saving the difficulty and expense of doing the job directly. This links to our next instance of public participation in the market economy.

The government as licensee

When government does not wish to engage directly in a particular economic activity, but nevertheless wants to retain control over that activity, it has the option of licensing a private firm to provide goods and services under prescribed conditions. This method is historically ancient: in the seventeenth and eighteenth centuries, for instance, government often granted monopolies to private corporations to trade in particular products or in particular areas. In the modern economy licensing is used extensively. The exploitation of oil reserves in the North Sea has largely been accomplished by selling licences to explore for oil to privately owned companies. The service of providing commercial radio and commercial television is handled in a similar way: thus the licence or 'franchise' to provide a commercial television service for the north-west of England has been held by a private firm, Granada TV, since the foundation of commercial television.

One of the most common ways of allocating licences is through a system of competitive bidding; the government, of course, can also use the competitive system by going to the private sector as a customer for goods and services.

The government as customer

We saw in the opening chapter that government can use a variety of means, including coercion, to raise goods and services. But government in Britain in fact normally uses the market. In other words, it employs the state's revenues (from such sources as taxation) to buy the goods and services it needs. A glance around any classroom or lecture theatre will show the importance of the public sector as a customer. The room itself will almost certainly have been built as the result of a contract with private firms of builders and architects. The teacher at the front of the room is a private citizen hired on the labour market. Virtually every piece of equipment in the room will also have been bought from private firms. This simple example is illustrated on a wider scale throughout government. Take the example of national defence. Although we usually think of government as providing the defence of the country, it actually buys most of the means of defence in the marketplace: soldiers, sailors and airforce personnel have to be recruited from the labour market in competition with other recruiters of labour, like private firms; most defence equipment is bought under contract from the private sector; and the everyday necessities of the forces – from the food eaten in the regimental mess to the fuel used by a regimental staff car – is bought in the marketplace.

The government is a customer in the market economy, but it is a very special kind of customer. Because government is the biggest institution in British society it is also the biggest customer. In some important areas it is to all intents and purposes the only customer. To take the example given above, in the supply of most important defence equipment – rockets, military aircraft, warships – the public sector is the sole purchaser. Here the 'producer–customer' relationship is obviously a very special one. Firms producing defence equipment, while nominally in private ownership, operate in such close contact with government agencies that they are in practical terms often indistinguishable from public bodies.

That the state is a customer of the private sector is well recognised; but in understanding the country's economic structure it is as important to emphasise the role of the public sector as a supplier of goods and services.

The government as supplier

Until recently government had a major role as a direct supplier of goods and services in Britain. Housing (council dwellings), transport (bus and rail services), energy (coal, gas, electricity), health care (NHS hospitals), education (schools and universities): these were just some of the important goods and services that were provided directly by central or local government, or by nationalised corporations. Perhaps the biggest change in the role of government produced by Conservative governments after 1979 was to shrink its importance as the direct supplier of goods and services. Even where the state has retained some responsibility in this area it has become a 'contract state', contracting out the delivery of services to private agencies. Nevertheless, the state retains a residual importance in this area, notably in the fields of education and health care.

The various ways in which the state is a pervasive presence in the economic structure are illustrated in Table 4.1 The list is significant both because it shows how important the state is and because it shows how far the issues that are argued about in British politics concern the balance between its various roles. Take the single example of ownership. In the 1980s government 'privatised' many enterprises like gas supply and the telephone service. At the same time it set up public bodies to regulate the newly privatised concerns: to fix prices and other conditions under which services are supplied to customers. Arguments between supporters and opponents of privatisation are not, therefore,

Table 4.1 Varying roles of government in the economic structure

Forms	Examples
Ownership	Minerals, land
Partnership	Development schemes in inner cities
Licensing	Oil exploration, commercial radio and television
Regulation	Health and safety at work
Purchase	Defence contracting
Supply	Health care, education

arguments about whether or not government should be present in the economic structure; they turn on differences about whether, in particular cases, it is better for the state to be an owner or a regulator.

Economic structure: the balance of sectors

The role of public institutions is obviously a key aspect of a country's economic structure, but just as important is the balance between what are sometimes called 'sectors'. We often speak of Britain as an 'industrial' economy, but the industries dominant in the economy have changed greatly in the recent past and continue to change. These alterations have momentous wider consequences: they affect the social structure, noticeably the class structure, and thus feed through to politics. For instance, the declining proportion of manual workers in the economy was until recently a cause of declining votes for the Labour Party, once the party of most manual workers.

It is conventional to make a distinction between 'primary', 'secondary' and 'tertiary' (or 'service') sectors. The 'primary' sector extracts the basic raw material of production from nature: obvious examples include mining, forestry and agriculture. The 'secondary' sector is most closely identified with manufacturing – in other words, with turning raw materials into finished goods, be they cars, refrigerators or aeroplanes. The 'tertiary' (or service) sector refers to activities designed neither to extract and process materials, nor to manufacture goods, but to deliver services; hence the alternative, commonly used name. We saw in the last chapter that many important services – like health and education – are provided by public institutions; but others, ranging from catering and tourism to financial services, are provided by privately owned firms operating in the market.

The three categories of sector are extremely broad, but their changing importance illuminates aspects of the developing economic structure. The decisive historical event in the evolution of the British economy was the industrial revolution. It began in the latter half of the eighteenth century and within a hundred years transformed the country. This revolution involved a shift in the balance between sectors. The key change was the decline in agriculture as a source of wealth and as a source of jobs. At the same time the economy began to depend increasingly on the production and sale of finished goods – at first cotton, then a wide range of manufactures based on the iron and steel industries. Thus the industrial revolution coincided with the rise of the 'secondary' or manufacturing industries. But in recent decades there has occurred a second stage in structural change: the decline of manufacturing and the rise of service industries in the 'tertiary' sector. In part this change is not specific to Britain. It reflects the characteristic development of most industrial economies. The reasons for the expansion of service industries are various. Technical advance has made the activities of extraction and manufacture much more efficient than in the past: in agriculture, for instance, a workforce which is the tiniest in Britain's history produces more food than ever before because of the use of advanced technology on the farm. At the same time, growing prosperity has created an increased demand for services of all kinds, ranging from education to catering and tourism. Britain, because it is a classic example of an advanced industrial economy, has shared in this common experience of economic change.

In Britain 'sectoral' change has been especially marked. The great industries on which Britain's nineteenth-century industrial might were built have almost universally declined – both in world markets and as components of the British economy. Coal, shipbuilding, steel and iron – all once major centres of economic power and employment – have become much less significant. This decline can be traced back over a century in the case of many industries, but in recent decades it has accelerated. The changing balance between sectors and the rapid rise of the 'service' sector, are illustrated in Figures 4.1 and 4.2

The important changes in the balance between the sectors are also reflected in another important feature of the economy – the structure of ownership.

The structure of ownership

We have already examined one aspect of ownership in Britain's economy – the balance between enterprises owned and controlled in the public and private sectors. But the simple phrase 'private ownership' is complex, and deserves close scrutiny. The legal vesting of the ownership of productive property – factories, equipment, and so on – in private hands is an outstanding important feature of the British economy. The changing structure of that ownership has implications for the functioning of the whole social system and for the kinds of policies which governments can pursue.

In the early stages of the industrial revolution, Britain, like many other capitalist economies, was

---

BOX 4.1

Phases of economic development

Before the industrial revolution most economic activity involved agriculture.

After the industrial revolution manufacturing was supreme.

In recent decades service industries have become increasingly important.

This is changing the class structure from one dominated by manual to one dominated by non-manual workers.

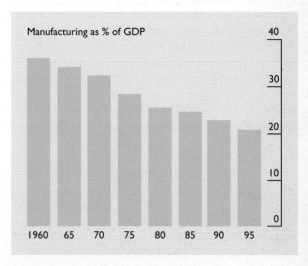

Figure 4.1   The decline of manufacturing
Source: *The Economist,* 15 June 1996

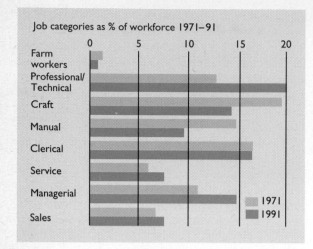

Job categories as % of workforce 1971–91

Figure 4.2 Changing patterns of employment, 1971–91
Source: *The Independent*, 3 March 1996

marked by what is sometimes called *the unity of ownership and control*: firms were for the most part small by modern standards; they were controlled by families or by partnerships; and the legal owners were usually those who took the main part in daily management. Like much else in Britain, this pattern has changed in modern times. Three developments are important: the separation of the managerial function from the role of ownership; the changing structure of legal ownership in the most important enterprises; and the changing size and scope of firms' activities.

The development of a *division of functions between those responsible for the daily control of firms and those vested with legal ownership* actually began in the nineteenth century; it is now predominant among larger firms in the economy. It has been prompted by the growing complexity of the task of running a large business enterprise, which has resulted in the emergence of a wide range of specialised managerial jobs covering finance, production, personnel, sales, and so on. No one seriously disputes that there now exists in most large corporations a separation between, on one hand, individuals responsible for the daily running of the enterprise and, on the other, groups vested with legal ownership. There is, however, a serious argument about the implications – including the political implications – of this shift. Some commentators argue that Britain is only one of a range of advanced capitalist nations where a 'separation of ownership

from control' has occurred. In other words real power in firms is no longer exercised by owners, but by salaried managers. The consequence is that one of the traditional characteristics of the capitalist system – the concentration of economic resources in the hands of private individuals motivated largely by the desire for profit – has been modified. Salaried managers, it is argued, have a wider set of motivations than pure profit and are responsive to the needs and wishes of the community. Other commentators argue that, by contrast, the rise of the manager has only allocated traditional tasks in a new way. Managers, it is claimed, run firms in the traditional interests of owners – with profits in mind above all. They do this because many managers are also in part owners; because owners who are not managers still retain the power to dismiss managers who ignore the pursuit of profits; and because in any case most managers accept the philosophy that the point of a firm is to make profit.

The original notion that owners were no longer powerful in big firms arose because of changes in the legal nature of firms. Most big enterprises in Britain are no longer family-owned firms or partnerships. They are 'joint stock' companies – which means that ownership is vested jointly in a multiplicity of individuals who own the stock, or shares, in the firm. Where the owners are many and scattered, and managers are few and concentrated, it is natural that the latter should more effectively control decisions inside the company.

This connects to the second main development identified at the beginning of this section – *the changing form of legal ownership*. The largest and most important firms in the economy are typically owned jointly by many people scattered around the country – and in some cases around the world. Since important decisions – like contests for membership of the board of directors – are decided by majority votes, with shareholders allotted votes in proportion to the number of shares owned, it is virtually impossible for numerous small shareholders to combine together in sufficient number to control decisions.

In recent years, however, changes in the nature of share ownership have altered this state of affairs. Although the number of individuals owning shares in Britain grew in the 1980s – principally because of widespread buying of the stock of newly privatised concerns like British Telecom and British Gas – the proportion of total shares owned by private individuals has shown a long-term fall over recent decades. The facts are illustrated in Figure 4.3. In place of the private shareholder, ownership is increasingly in the hands of what are conventionally called 'institutions', notably insurance companies and pension funds. This change has an important implication for the debate about the separation of ownership from control. The institutions' shareholdings are concentrated in the biggest and most important firms. Hence, the argument that managers have the power to wield influence over a dispersed mass of owners no longer holds. Indeed, there have been striking cases in recent years where the institutions have wielded their numerical resources to control and discipline managements of individual firms.

The rise of the giant firm is the third important feature of the structure of ownership in the private sector. Most firms in Britain are tiny, but a small number of giant enterprises nevertheless dominate the economy. This is the result of a long-term trend: the domination of big firms has grown greatly in the twentieth century, a change mirrored in other advanced industrial economies. The giant firms dominant in the economy are also usually multi-

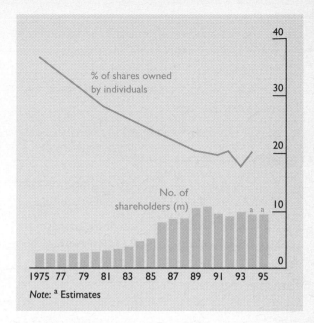

Note: [a] Estimates

Figure 4.3 Patterns of share ownership
Source: The Economist, 18 May 1996

national in character. A multinational firm is a concern which produces its goods in different nations, and sells them in many different national markets. The most sophisticated firms operate an international 'division of labour': it is common, for instance, for different components of a motor car to be produced in a variety of factories in different countries, and then to be assembled in yet another country. In the years since the Second World War the significance of multinational companies in Britain has grown greatly. Many of the biggest British concerns have taken on a multinational character. British markets have also themselves been deeply penetrated by foreign multinationals. Britain is one of the most popular locations for American firms expanding abroad, and even when firms are not located in Britain there are whole markets – for instance in motor cycles, electrical goods and automobiles – where the products of foreign multinationals either dominate or are a substantial part of the supply.

Chapter summary

In this chapter we have: identified the different ways in which government is present in the economic structure in Britain, emphasising the variety of roles performed by government; described the long-term decline of manufacturing industry in Britain; and summarised the debates about the changing nature of ownership and control in the economy.

Discussion points

- Why has the balance between the different roles of government in the economy changed in the last two decades?

- What have been the main political problems caused by the decline of manufacturing industry in Britain?

- Does the rise of the giant firm in the economy have any important political consequences?

Further reading

Introductions to the history and changing structure of the economy include Cairncross (1992), Curwen (1990) and Pollard (1992). The impact of the Thatcher 'revolution' is discussed in Edgell and Duke (1991) and in Marsh (1992). The best overall introduction to the 'ownership and control' debate remains Nichols (1970).

References

Cairncross, A. (1992) *The British Economy Since 1945* (Blackwell).

Curwen, P. (ed.) (1990) *Understanding the UK Economy* (Macmillan).

Edgell, S. and Duke, V. (1991) *A Measure of Thatcherism: A Sociology of Britain* (HarperCollins).

Marsh, D. (ed.) (1992) *Implementing Thatcherite policies: Audit of an Era* (Open University Press).

Nichols, T. (1970) *Ownership, Control and Ideology* (Allen and Unwin).

Pollard, S. (1992) *The Development of the British Economy* (Edward Arnold).

CHAPTER FIVE

Political culture and political participation

MICHAEL MORAN

LEARNING OBJECTIVES

- To define the meaning of 'political culture' and to explain its importance in the study of British politics.

- To identify the main elements of the dominant political culture in the United Kingdom.

- To show that this dominant political culture exists alongside dissenting cultures.

INTRODUCTION

Politics can be visualised as a sort of game, albeit a deadly serious game, played according to particular rules between groups of contestants. This chapter is about the 'rules of the game' in British politics, and how those rules affect the way the mass of the population take part in politics. Britain is a 'democracy', so we examine what this word means, and what it means when applied to Britain. We note the gap that appears to exist between theoretical ideas of democracy, and the reality of democratic participation. We then use the idea of 'political culture' to explore what this gap tells us about the nature of the British political system.

Democracy and equality

'Government of the people, by the people, and for the people.' These words of the great American President, Abraham Lincoln, are usually taken as the most succinct account of the nature of democracy. Viewed from this perspective democracy in the United Kingdom has a number of puzzling features.

Government *by* the people is rare, if by that we mean the large-scale participation of the population at large in the government process. Table 5.1 is taken from the main study of political participation in Britain; it shows that, beyond voting in general elections, which occurs only once every four or five years, and signing petitions, participation is rare.

Lincoln's phrase 'for the people' echoes a tradition in democracy which goes back to its first great theorist, the Greek political thinker Aristotle (384–22 BC). In Aristotle's view democracy literally meant 'rule by the people', in the sense that in democratic political systems the poor and property-less would rule at the expense of those with

Table 5.1 Percentage of population who have engaged in different forms of participation

	% 'yes'/ at least once
Voting	
1. Vote local	68.8
2. Vote general	82.5
3. Vote European	47.3
Party campaigning	
4 Fund-raising	5.2
5 Canvassed	3.5
6 Clerical work	3.5
7 Attended rally	8.6
Group activity	
8 Informal group	13.8
9 Organised group	11.2
10 Issue in group	4.7
Contacting	
11 Member of Parliament	9.7
12 Civil servant	7.3
13 Councillor	20.7
14 Town hall	7.4
15 Media	3.8
Protesting	
16 Attended protest meeting	14.6
17 Organised petition	8.0
18 Signed petition	63.3
19 Blocked traffic	1.1
20 Protest march	5.2
21 Political strike	6.5
22 Political boycott	4.3
23 Physical force	0.2

Source: Parry *et al.*, 1992, p. 44

property. This fear of the propertyless was one of the main reasons historically for opposing democratic measures like extending voting rights to all adults. The UK has had democratic political procedures (like free elections involving almost all adults) for over seventy years, yet nothing like Aristotle's fears have been realised. We saw in Chapter 3 that there is considerable economic inequality in Britain. This inequality extends to politics. A recent study shows how select is the group which still reaches the top of the most important institutions in Britain. Of this hundred top people identified in the early 1990s, only four

were women; 66 per cent were educated at public (fee-paying) schools; and 54 per cent were graduates of the elite universities of Oxford and Cambridge.

British democracy, therefore, presents some puzzling features. On the one hand, the rules of government are undoubtedly democratic. There are elections by secret ballot in which contesting parties compete for the votes of most of the adult population. On the other hand, the fears of the historical opponents of democracy have not been realised: inequality of class, region, gender still remain.

The study of *political culture* tries to understand these puzzles. How does a system of government which is formally based on principles of equality coexist with highly unequal outcomes? Box 5.3 at the end of this chapter offers a brief discussion on this, but the body of this chapter is concerned to explain the meaning and usefulness of 'political culture' as applied to the United Kingdom.

The meaning of political culture

Political culture refers to the patterns of beliefs and practices which govern social life in a community. It thus covers an immense range: the character of religion and morality, the conventions and customs governing everyday social life – and the beliefs and practices concerning the conduct of politics. It is usual to refer to the last of these as the *political culture* of a community. The political culture governs the 'rules of the political game' in a society. These rules are not written down but comprise attitudes which can be discerned by social scientists through questionnaires and other methods of research. Political culture encompasses beliefs about the nature of political leadership and authority, about the proper and improper way to settle political differences and about the proper and improper functions of government. Thus, when we try to decide whether the British have a special respect for the monarchy, we are examining an aspect of the political culture. Similarly, when we examine the attitudes of the people in Britain to the role of violence in settling political differences we are also looking at a part of the British culture. And when we try to decide how far there exists in Britain general agreement about how much the state should control our lives we are looking yet again at the political culture. These features explain why 'political culture' is so important in understanding the nature and limits of British democracy. Having said this it should also be emphasised that political culture is not an 'independent variable': the operation of British democracy itself serves to shape and change it.

Two further things should be noticed about this notion of political culture. Firstly, it is obviously both part of a wider communal culture and is affected by that wider culture. In a society where violence is a generally accepted way of settling social differences, for instance, it will also be a generally accepted way of settling political differences. Secondly, although we speak in a shorthand way about the patterns of beliefs and practices in a community, this does not mean that there always exists an agreed set of cultural values held by everyone. On the contrary, in all communities there are some disagreements on the fundamental rules of the political game. In most communities there is a 'dominant' political culture adhered to by those who exercise most power, and a set of 'subcultures' which mark off various minorities (see again Box 5.3). In some important communities – for instance, Northern Ireland – there actually exists a deeply divided political culture in which there are fundamental disagreements between groups about the rules of the political game.

The political culture concerns the rules by which politics is conducted in a community. In analysing those rules we should distinguish between those relating to how decisions are taken, and those relating to the substance of the policies which government can pursue. In other words, we should separate *procedural* and *substantive* aspects of the political culture.

Procedure covers much more than formal rules in a body like Parliament. It also encompasses more general views about how decisions should be taken and how those decisions should be put into effect. How far, for instance, is government a matter for the public at large to decide, and how far is it an activity left to a specially qualified minority? Under what circumstances, if any, is force used in political conflict? When, if ever, do citizens resist the decisions of a government to the point of breaking the law? These are all questions about the political culture of a community. They illuminate a particularly important point: political culture consists not just of what people believe, and say they believe, about the rules of politics; it also consists in what they actually do. If citizens say – for instance in opinion polls – that the law should always be obeyed, however bad it may be, this tells us something important about an aspect of the political culture. But to get a full picture we are also obliged to look at whether in reality laws are indeed obeyed. It is perfectly common in politics, as in most other areas of life, for us to say and believe one thing and to act in a quite different way.

A moment's thought will now show that the political culture involves something much wider than attitudes to the formal machinery of government. As the example of opinions about law-breaking suggests, it spills over into social life generally. We can infer important evidence about attitudes to authority from such apparently 'non-political' matters as the extent to which people obey regulations like those governing traffic speeds or the declaration of income to the tax authorities.

The procedural element is certainly the most important part of a political culture, because it goes to the very heart of politics – how decisions are to be taken and how they are to be put into effect. But this should not lead us to neglect the importance of the *substantive* part of the political culture. What people think government should do is no less important than their views about how politics should be conducted. How far, for instance, is there agreement about the substance of what government should do, and to what extent is political debate dominated by fierce divisions between conflicting political philosophies? Of course, there always exist in any group some differences between members about the content of the decisions which the group should make – whether the group is a family, a school, a firm or a government. But in a nation as large and diverse as Britain these differences will inevitably be more numerous, and more clearly organised.

Any examination of a political culture therefore involves (see Table 5.2) four different aspects of the 'rules of the political game' in a community:

1. What people say about the procedures by which government should be conducted.
2. What we can infer from behaviour about how those procedures actually work.

Table 5.2 Examining the political culture

	Procedure	Substance
Action	*Example*: how laws are actually obeyed	*Example*: how far political parties implement radically different policies in government
Opinion	*Example*: popular views about when laws should be disobeyed	*Example*: how far political parties express radically different political philosophies

3. What is said about the fundamental purpose of governments.
4. What we can infer about this from practice.

It can hardly be stressed too strongly that it is important to look at both what is said and what is done. If a nation has a large political party whose programme demands the fundamental overthrow of existing social institutions, this constitutes an important piece of evidence about the nature of the political culture. But we should also look at how far that programme is reflected in the actual behaviour of the party. For instance, many Western European countries in the years after the Second World War had communist parties with a large following, formally committed to the overthrow of capitalist society. Britain had no such well-supported communist movement. This is often taken as a sign that left-wing radicalism is weaker in Britain than in Europe. Yet the actions – as distinct from the slogans – of communist parties in France and Italy often suggested movements which were more cautious and conservative than many parts of the labour movement in Britain.

It should now be obvious that identifying the nature of the British political culture demands a wide range of evidence. There is one other subtlety which should also be borne in mind. We find it a useful form of shorthand to speak of *a* British political culture, because it is indeed the case that it is possible to identify a pattern of beliefs and practices which is dominant in the country. But we should always bear in mind that we are indeed talking about precisely that – the **dominant** political culture. Britain, like any large and sophisticated society, is highly diverse. There are many significant groups whose way of life – including political way of life – does not conform to, and in some cases seriously challenges, that dominant culture. We

begin therefore with the dominant pattern and then describe the most important kinds of dissent.

The dominant political culture

Four features of the dominant political culture in Britain are noteworthy: deference, secrecy, civility and consensus. We will explain the meaning of each in turn and sketch its significance.

Deference

The first great essay on the nature of English attitudes to politics was Walter Bagehot's *The English Constitution*, which appeared in 1867 (Bagehot, 1964). Bagehot's work also popularised the single most influential idea in the study of the country's political culture: that we are a particularly *deferential* people. When we speak of the 'deferential' part of the culture, we are usually referring to a number of different things. Perhaps the most common modern meaning refers to a tendency to defer to the commands or wishes of public authority. Until recently in Britain this sort of deference was widespread. Law-breaking on any large scale was rare. This meant not only the comparative absence of any riotous behaviour but, perhaps even more significantly, the readiness to obey the law and the officers of the law in everyday matters. This readiness was reflected in numerous ways: for instance, in the willingness of the population to obey without close supervision regulations like those governing traffic: and in the fact that for the most part the police could enforce the law without being armed and with only occasional use of significant force.

This kind of deference is probably in decline. A second kind, of great importance in the past, is also certainly less common nowadays. When Bagehot spoke of deference he was thinking not of the tendency to defer to authority in general, but of preference for government by rulers born into a separate governing class. In other words deference was not to *any* authority, but to the 'well-born' as the natural wielders of authority.

The respect and affection in which the monarchy used to be held in Britain are a shorthand expression of this sort of deference. A sizeable group in the population believed that government should be the prerogative of those born to rule. Although sections of the working class received the vote as long ago as 1867, and the whole adult population has had the vote for over sixty years, those selected by the population to govern were disproportionately drawn from groups connected to the traditional aristocracy. A significant proportion of manual workers habitually supported a party, the Conservatives, precisely because the Conservatives were associated with, and were often led by, people with aristocratic connections.

Deference is an attribute of the population at large, but it has had an important effect on the culture of the governing groups in Britain. In particular it helps explain a second key feature of the political culture: a strong attachment to secrecy in the theory and practice of British government.

Secrecy

The secretive character of the British political culture is built into the very structure of the law. Most countries have legislation prohibiting the publication of 'official secrets' – on grounds, for instance, of national security. But Britain's official secrecy laws are recognised to be especially comprehensive. In recent years, for instance, prosecutions have included those of Clive Ponting, a civil servant who leaked documents to a Member of Parliament (see Box 5.1). But the significance of secrecy legislation lies in more than its substance. It is a reflection of a widespread predisposition favouring the conduct of government out of the public gaze. British government was historically ruled by the monarch and a small number of aristocratic advisers. The democratic politics which we now associate with Britain operated alongside a traditional assumption, that government was the proper business of a specialised class. This is reflected in a variety of characteristic British institutions. The 'lobby' system, for instance, is an arrangement under which an accredited group of journalists is given confidential, anonymous briefings about government on condition that they observe prescribed limits on what they report. The doctrine (as it is usually called) of *collective Cabinet responsibility* similarly tries to ensure that Cabinet discussions and arguments remain secret, by binding each member of Cabinet not to dissent in public from decisions collectively arrived at. The doctrine of *individual ministerial responsibility* also serves the function of preserving secrecy in important parts of government. The formal meaning of the doctrine is that ministers are answerable for actions taken by their department. This shields from public scrutiny the many civil servants who in reality take numerous decisions in the minister's name.

| BOX 5.1 | | EXAMPLE |

The Ponting affair and secrecy

The Ponting affair tested the limits of the Official Secrets law in Britain. After the Falklands War in 1982 there were allegations that an Argentinian ship, the *General Belgrano*, had been sunk with loss of many lives for unnecessary political reasons, not on military grounds. Clive Ponting, a senior official in the Ministry of Defence, anonymously leaked ministry papers to a critical Labour MP. When Ponting's identity was discovered he was prosecuted under the Official Secrets law. Ponting argued that he owed a duty above the level of the law to inform an MP about a major constitutional impropriety. The jury, despite strong guidance from the judge to bring in a guilty verdict, acquitted Ponting.

Source: Peele, 1988

These practices and constitutional doctrines are themselves a product of an important foundation of the traditionally secretive aspect of British government. Until comparatively recently there existed in Britain an identifiable governing class – an 'establishment', as it was sometimes called. This group was quite small in number and tended not only to work together but to share a common social round in London and in upper-class society. A great deal of the business of government was therefore carried out in a private and informal way, often in gentlemen's clubs like the famous Athenaeum. The 'secrecy' of British government was therefore not a conspiratorial secrecy; it was the reflection of the sort of closed social world inhabited by the rulers of the country. As we will see shortly, the decline of this socially united governing group has placed the institutions of secrecy under great strain.

Civility

The term 'civic culture' was coined over thirty years ago by two American scholars, Gabriel Almond and Sidney Verba (1963; see also 1981), to describe a kind of political culture of which Britain was held to be a prime example. 'Civility' in this connection means not the everyday usage which suggests politeness, but a certain attitude to authority and to the settling of political disputes. It signifies a willingness to respect the views of lawful authority, and is therefore related to the phenomenon of deference. But it also conveys something wider: a tolerance of opposing political views and a readiness to settle political differences by peaceful means rather than by resort either to violence or to aggressive public demonstrations. Political civility is also part of a wider social civility – in other words, part of a readiness in everyday life to tolerate others of different views and to respect the differing sensibilities of others in social life.

The judgement that Britain's was a 'civic' political culture was heavily influenced by foreign comparisons. By the standards of most countries Britain's modern political history has been remarkably peaceful. The last great armed struggle over the nature of political authority on the mainland of Britain was in the seventeenth century. Violent street clashes between political rivals or between political factions and the authorities were largely unknown in modern times, the case of Northern Ireland excepted (see below). Trade unions have only once (in 1926) used a general strike of all members to try to impose their views on an elected government, and then only in a half-hearted way. Popular support for those using or advocating violence, or some more limited means of direct action designed to secure concessions from government, has been low: such groups have in modern times never gained the support of more than a minority of the population in, for instance, election contests.

This political civility seems to be part of a more general social civility. Though comparisons between countries in this respect have to be treated with caution, it really does seem to be the case that social relations generally are in Britain less abrasive and more peaceable than is common elsewhere. Support for this view comes in part from the admittedly unsystematic reflections of foreign observers but also from more systematically gathered material. Violent crime is, for instance, low by international standards, while the most violent of crimes – murder – is at a minuscule level compared with the USA, as Figure 5.1 illustrates (see also Chapter 24).

Thus far we have identified aspects of the political culture which bear most closely on the procedural

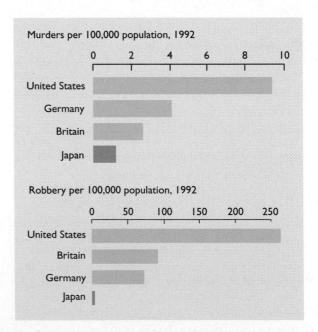

Figure 5.1 Crime in an international context
Source: The Economist, 16 April 1994

rules of the political game. The final element – consensus – links more closely the theory and practice of the substance of politics.

Consensus

The everyday meaning of consensus is agreement in opinion, but when we speak of consensus as an aspect of the British political culture we mean something more limited. The consensual character of British politics refers to a high level of agreement, both among the population at large and among the politically active, about the economic and social system which should prevail in Britain and about the proper function of government in that system. Of course, in a society such as Britain, with a diverse and sophisticated culture and complex economy, there exist many disagreements about the particular policies which governments should pursue. Underneath these important differences, however, there also exists almost universal support for two sets of institutions: for constitutional democracy under a constitutional monarchy; and for a market economy supported by a substantial state sector. This consensus can be summed up as support for *liberal democracy* and the *mixed economy*.

All the major political parties in Britain in this century have overwhelmingly supported the political principles on which the country is governed. 'Liberal democracy' indicates the joining together of two sets of principles: the practice of 'liberal' freedoms (like freedom of speech, worship and association) with a democratic method for changing or confirming the party which controls government. This democratic method involves periodic competitive elections in which almost all adults are entitled to vote. These two principles also have important consequences for the daily practice of politics. For instance, freedom of association and freedom to voice opinion mean that in British politics there are numerous groups (conventionally called pressure groups) who demand, and receive, the right to be heard in the process of policy-making.

The consensus about the liberal democratic nature of the British political system remains relatively unshaken. As we shall see, this is not so true of the consensus about the mixed economy. Nevertheless, for over half a century disagreements in this area concerned only the exact 'mix' of the mixed economy,

not the principle of its existence. The Labour Party, the most important radical force in the country, never challenged the continuation of the market order. In the party there exists a group of socialists who would like to replace capitalism, but they have always been a minority in a varied alliance of reformers and radicals who wish only to regulate capitalist institutions more closely. Similarly, there were until recently few in the Conservative Party who wished to develop an economy in which the state did nothing more than cater for a few traditional functions like public order and external defence. In both parties leaders sometimes found it expedient to use language suggesting that they did not support the mixed economy. It was common for Conservative leaders to make strongly 'free market' speeches and for Labour leaders to attack capitalism, when addressing audiences made up of party activists. But the gap between what was said on these occasions and what was actually privately believed, and actually done in government, was very wide. This illustrates to perfection the point made earlier: in assessing the nature of a political culture we must attend to what is done as well as to what is said. This is especially true in a country like Britain, where the demands of democratic politics force politicians who wish to win elections to adjust their speeches to the particular audience they are addressing.

This sketch of a 'dominant' political culture has in parts deliberately been phrased in the past tense, because in recent years the extent to which it is open to challenge have become clearly marked. We now examine these challenges.

Challenges to the dominant political culture

The account of the British political culture which we have just outlined undoubtedly describes a historically important aspect of British life – and an aspect which still powerfully endures. But it would be wrong to imply that this is the whole picture. There exist powerful challenges to the prevailing orthodoxy. Two sources of minority dissent are particularly important. The first is *nationalism*. Britain's constitution and boundaries have been the subject of controversy and even of armed conflict. In recent years substantial minorities in Wales and

Scotland have supported parties advocating separation from the United Kingdom – and have also supported the demands for independence of those parties. But the most important source of nationalist dissent has come from the Irish. Until 1921 the 'United Kingdom' encompassed the whole island of Ireland, and Irish constituencies sent Members to Parliament in Westminster. In that year, after five years of a war of secession, the Irish Free State gained independence. The episode displays many of the features – fundamental disagreement about the nature of the state, the use of violence to challenge authority – conspicuously absent from the dominant political culture. This source of challenge has been renewed since the revival of the Ulster troubles in 1969. Since then British troops have been required in Northern Ireland to combat a violent campaign for secession organised from within a part of the Catholic community which believes in Irish nationalism as an alternative to British rule.

A second source of challenge can be found in *class organisation*. Although the British labour movement has undoubtedly been marked by a special respect for the authority of elected governments, this respect is far from universal. At periodic moments in the country's history – in the years immediately before and after the First World War, in the so called 'General Strike' of 1926 and in a wide range of individual strikes in the 1970s and 1980s – trade union militancy mounted a significant challenge to existing political and economic hierarchies. In many individual working-class communities – especially those formed around heavy manual occupations like coal mining – there have long existed powerful and deep-rooted radical traditions which reject many aspects of the dominant culture, especially the consensus favouring a market economy. To some degree this dissenting culture based on class coincides with the dissenting culture based on national differences, because many of the most important centres of class dissent have been in such places as the South Wales coalfields. This observation alerts us to an important point. The features usually described as characteristic of the *British* political culture are not so much British as English, and, at that, are particularly characteristic of the southern half of England.

The dissenting challenges of nationality and class are not new in British politics, but cultural change

in recent years has made us more sensitive to them. The political culture of a country is neither fixed in content nor independent of the wider society. On the contrary, it is intimately affected by the wider pattern of social institutions and it will be subjected to change and stress as the wider social surroundings change. British society has, in recent decades, changed greatly. The structure of the economy has altered, with important traditional sectors in decline. The ethnic composition of the population in selected areas has changed as a result of large-scale immigration in the 1950s and 1960s. The traditional organisation of family life has altered greatly, notably in the expanded numbers of people living either alone or in single-parent families.

Partly as a result of social changes a number of important challenges to the dominant political culture can be observed. They can be summarised under two headings: the *challenge to deference* and the *challenge to consensus*.

Although considerable argument exists about how widespread 'deference' ever was in Britain, there is no doubt that, however defined, its level has fallen in recent years. The evidence for this comes from systematic surveys, from observation of political practice and from more general changes in social behaviour. We saw earlier that one important form of deference consisted in a preference for rule by individuals with aristocratic connections. These preferences are disproportionately held by older people and are thus literally dying out. The everyday conduct of political life also indicates a growing unwillingness simply to take authority on trust. For instance, the reporting of politics by journalists has displayed a growing readiness to question politicians sceptically. The signs of this include the rise of more investigative styles of journalism and the challenges now being mounted to the 'lobby' system of political reporting. Indeed, the decline of 'deference' has had important general effects on the 'secrecy' with which British government is conducted. Secrecy became a major issue in the 1980s. The traditionally secretive character of the system was sustained by a deference among political journalists and political activists towards the governing class. The strenuous attempts made by governments in recent years to preserve the secret nature of the government system reflect the declining hold of these traditional attitudes. It is much more common than was formerly the case for official documents to be 'leaked' to newspapers, increasingly common for civil servants to be discussed by name in debates about government decisions, and perfectly common for divisions expressed in the supposedly 'confidential' Cabinet room to be widely reported in the newspapers. The problem of leaks and of the inadequacy of their present means of control was dramatised by the Ponting case (see Box 5.1 above).

The declining hold of deference is also plain at the level of popular participation. There has been a growing willingness, especially on the part of the young, to participate in politics outside the conventional channels represented by elections and by membership of old-established political parties. Membership of the dominant parties, Labour and Conservative, shows a long-term decline. Labour used to boast over a million members in the early 1950s, but during the next decade dissatisfaction at slow or non-existent progress towards socialist goals led to a substantial exodus of members opening the door for 'entryist' groups like Militant with a

---

BOX 5.2 **EXAMPLE**

Political activists

Political activists are often represented as rather unusual, perhaps even a little odd. The reality is often reassuringly mundane. In August 1986, Tyne Tees television screened a series, *Is Democracy Working?* One of the programmes featured three party workers in the north east of England.

Mrs Karen Johnson, chairperson of her constituency Conservative women's committee, helped her husband run his business: they were comfortably well off and sent their children to private school. She subscribed to the Conservative values of 'freedom, good housekeeping and the individual. ... Capitalism is a better way than the state being in charge of everything in that under capitalism the individuals have a chance to prove themselves.'

Mr Wal Hobson was born into a working-class family but became a careers officer. He was an active ward member of the Labour Party and believed 'Socialism is the only political theory that is really concerned about the ordinary people ... social justice is the key word for me – and equality.'

Mrs Jane Young was chairperson of the Liberal Party in Newcastle North and a schoolteacher. She saw Liberals as standing for 'tolerance, rights of the individual – as long as those rights don't infringe on anyone else's liberty ... consensus and cooperation.'

While these values obviously differ and clash all three saw politics as a practical and effective way of realising them. As Mr Hobson put it: 'I think politics does determine how your life runs. ... If you do not work at grassroots politics you cannot improve things for ordinary people. ... It's everything I've ever believed turned into something real, instead of just abstract ideas inside my head.'

All three were united in their concern for the democratic process. 'I am defending democracy by being active in a political party,' said Karen Johnson. 'I do think it's important that some people are prepared to do it. I only wish that more people would be prepared to give a little of their time.'

The Liberal's view was similar. 'I bother because I think it is important to be a participating member of a democracy. If you are not willing to participate then I feel you have no ground for complaining about anything that is done. If you want things changed and you want to improve conditions for yourself and for the country as a whole then to be involved is very important.'

These activists did not come over in any way as power hungry ideologues. Rather, they seemed hard-working, intelligent, sincere and public-spirited. But are they typical? Of political activists, probably yes – but not of society as a whole. Of the 4 per cent of the population who are party members, less than 1 per cent can be described as genuinely active. It would seem that the democratic links between government and society are becoming increasingly tenuous. And this is worrying if, as the American economist Henry George once said, 'We cannot safely leave politics to politicians. The people themselves must think.'

different agenda. This loss of support – membership slumped to about 200,000 – damaged the party and must have been instrumental in its failed electoral efforts in the 1980s. There was, however, a strong revival of Labour Party membership after Tony Blair became leader: nearly doubling to nearly half a million.

On the other hand, participation in a wide range of loosely organised movements has grown. The 1980s were a booming decade for the Campaign for Nuclear Disarmament (CND) and a wider 'peace movement' in Britain. At one time, CND claimed over 100,000 members. Peace movements are now in decline, but they are only part of a wider shift to new kinds of political activity – in the women's movement, in groups formed to protect the environment and in numerous particular groups formed to campaign on local issues.

The scale of this shift into participation in new sorts of social organisations concerned with the protection and care of the physical environment is shown in Table 5.3. Not all members of these organisations are 'political' by any means – but the organisations themselves are often significant pressure groups. If we set alongside this growth the declining membership of more conventional groups, like trade unions and political parties, we get a striking sense of a changing culture and a changing balance of group participation.

If the 'procedural' part of the political culture is changing, the same is true of the consensus over substance. The consensual nature of British politics was until recently one of its characteristic features. For most of the period since the end of the Second World War there was agreement across the political

Table 5.3 The rise of the environmental movement: membership of selected groups (United Kingdom, thousands)

	1971	1993
National Trust	278	2,189
Royal Society for the Protection of Birds	98	850
Greenpeace	–	410
Friends of the Earth	1	120
Ramblers' Association	22	94

Source: Social Trends, 1996, Table 11.4

spectrum about the broad content of public policy: in particular, on the desirability of full employment, state provision of extensive welfare and the existence of a large number of publicly owned industries providing goods and services. In the 1970s and 1980s this agreement came under great pressure. The most important reason was the increasingly severe crisis of the British economy.

In the 1950s – the period when consensus was especially strong – the nation's prosperity grew rapidly. While Britain was not as successful as many of its international competitors, there nevertheless existed full employment and sustained economic growth. From the early 1960s increasingly severe problems appeared and by the middle of the 1970s a full crisis was apparent: inflation was at a historically high level, unemployment was rising and international confidence in the economy was declining. Governments began to abandon key parts of the post-war consensus, beginning with the commitment to full employment. But the most radical departures came in 1979 with the election of Margaret Thatcher's first government. Since 1979 the country has been governed by administrations consciously intent on rejecting the post-war consensus. In the view of Thatcherites the state sector of the economy is inefficient, public spending is a burden destroying the ability of the people to create wealth, and many welfare services sap the capacity of the people to act in an enterprising and independent way. Since 1979 governments have pursued radical alternatives to the post-war consensus. These have included the large-scale disposal of public industries to private shareholders; the sale of council houses to their tenants; the closure of industries held to be too inefficient to compete in world markets; and the subjection of welfare, health and education provision to increasingly strong market forces. When Thatcher was succeeded by John Major as Prime Minister and Conservative Party leader in November 1990 there was a change to a less challenging and adversarial style, but the thrust of the Thatcherite revolution was maintained.

The election of the Blair Government in the landslide of May 1997 might be thought to have disrupted this new consensus. In the field of constitutional reform the Blair programme does represent a radical departure. However, the Labour Party, in opposition and in office, has been careful not to try to reverse any of the significant economic reforms of the Thatcher years.

A new consensus?

It may be that we are now witnessing the creation of a new consensus in British politics. The Thatcher revolution, like all revolutions, was accompanied by great political division. But the Labour Party, after nearly two decades of electoral failure, has now refashioned itself as 'New Labour', and this involves accepting many of the radical policies of the Thatcher years. We have seen in this chapter that the cultural context of British politics is a mixture of

---

BOX 5.3 **IDEAS AND PERSPECTIVES**

Dominant values

'Nothing appears more surprising' wrote David Hume, 'than the easiness with which the many are governed by the few.' The aspect of this question which has most intrigued political theorisers is why the poor accept their blatantly unequal position in relation to the rich; where, for example, in the USA, 5 per cent of the population can own over 50 per cent of the wealth.

Marx's explanation was that 'In every epoch the ideas of the ruling class are the ruling ideas.' In other words those with the power and wealth are able to convince the rest of society that their wealth and power is legitimate; just as slave owners were able to convince slaves that their servitude was somehow perfectly proper. Marx believed this was done through the creation of a 'false consciousness', whereby the working classes were induced to believe the capitalist economic system was natural, fair, unavoidable and more efficient than any alternative. Antonio Gramsci developed this approach, arguing that this trick was managed through manipulation of 'civil society' – the church, schools and the media. The result was an irresistible wave of messages – a subtle brainwashing whereby the proletariat came to wear their chains willingly – which delivered to the ruling capitalist class a 'hegemony' over society.

Sociologists have also offered their explanations. David Lockwood discerned three working-class perspectives which together suggested opposition to dominant values was likely to decline: 'proletarian traditionalists' in the older, fading industries, living in closely knit cultures, provided the bedrock of trade union and socialist support; 'deferential traditionalists' in agriculture and small businesses were isolated from the organised masses and unlikely to share their perspective; finally the 'new working class', working in new industries, living on new estates and earning well, tended to reject traditional working-class perspectives in favour of money, home and family.

Another sociologist, Mann, perceived a pragmatic acceptance by workers of the status quo: they are not fooled by the ruling class messages but, in the absence of anything better, they simply adapted to its requirements. Dominant values are so powerfully ubiquitous that workers cannot avoid absorbing them, but their social and work subcultures foster 'deviant' values in an unsystematic, unideological way. This explanation makes sense: working people may not swallow dominant values uncritically but it is unlikely their circumstances would afford a consistently radical critique of capitalist society. Working people have to be pragmatic; while they earn a fraction of their bosses' wages, they receive enough for their families to survive and even better the lot of their parents. Radical strategies, on the other hand, carry the risk of economic hardship, widespread social dislocation or violence with no proven alternative economic model available. In other words the poor cannot afford a revolution: the rich, who can, don't need one.

Sources: Femia, 1987; Mann, 1973

stability and change. In some ways it is astonishing how little Britain has altered in this century. The British have experienced two world wars, decades of economic decline, the loss of an empire, a revolution in welfare provision and forms of housing tenure, astonishing changes in technology and a transformation of material standards of life. Yet the country remains recognisably what it was in 1900: a rich capitalist society formally governed by parliamentary institutions. The impact of democracy on inequality has been nothing like as great as the fears of its opponents or the hopes of its supporters. Politics and government are closely connected to the social structure, but plainly they are not just moulded by that structure. The relationship between the political system and its social, economic and cultural surroundings consists of a subtle and varied interaction. Precisely what kind of political practices and institutions have resulted from that interaction we will discover in the following chapters.

Summary

In this chapter we have: described the meaning of political culture and its relevance to understanding democracy in Britain; outlined the main parts of the dominant political culture; and described the dissenting political cultures to be found in the United Kingdom.

Discussion points

- Why is deference apparently in decline in Britain?

- Does 'political culture' refer to anything more than the ideology of the ruling class in Britain?

- Why are new forms of political participation becoming popular in Britain?

Further reading

Parry *et al.* (1992) is the authoritative study of participation. Macpherson (1973) examines the meaning of a democratic political culture. Bagehot (1964) is the first great essay in British political culture. Almond and Verba (1963) gave a more orthodox political science view, and Kavanagh (1972, 1981) revisited their arguments. Byrne and Lovenduski (1983) introduced the idea of participation in new social movements. Gamble (1988) is the outstanding interpretation of the meaning of the Thatcherite refashioning of political culture in the 1980s.

References

Almond, G. and Verba, S. (1963) *The Civic Culture* (Princeton University Press).

Almond, G. and Verba, S. (eds) (1981) *The Civic Culture Revisited* (Little Brown).

Bagehot, W. (1964) *The English Constitution* (Watt; first published 1867).

Byrne, P. and Lovenduski, J. (1983) 'Two new protest groups: the peace and women's movement' in H. Drucker *et al.* (eds), *Developments in British Politics* (Macmillan).

Femia, J. (1987) *Gramsci's Political Philosophy* (Oxford University Press).

Gamble, A (1988) *The Free Economy and the Strong State* (Macmillan).

Kavanagh, D. (1972) *Political Culture* (Macmillan).

Kavanagh, D. (1981) 'Political culture in Great Britain: the decline of the civic culture', in G. Almond and S. Verba (eds), *The Civic Culture Revisited* (Little Brown).

Macpherson, C.B. (1973) *Democratic Theory: Essays in Retrieval* (Oxford University Press).

Mann, M. (1973) *Consciousness and Action among the Western Working Class* (Macmillan).

Parry, G., Moyser, G. and Day, N. (1992) *Political Participation and Democracy in Britain* (Cambridge University Press).

Peele, G. (1983) 'The state and civil liberties', in H. Drucker *et al.* (eds), *Developments in British Politics* (Macmillan).

Poverty and exclusion

DAVID VINCENT

In 1991 I sent off to a publisher the manuscript of a textbook on the history of relations between the poor and the state entitled *Poor Citizens*. The editor pointed out that as I had adopted a thematic rather than a strictly chronological approach, the intended student audience might find difficulty in navigating its way around the book, and asked if a glossary could be attached. This I set about compiling more out of duty than interest, and by the end of the alphabet, my patience was wearing thin. Against the last entry, 'Work-Shy', I simply wrote, '*See also* fiddlers, layabouts, parasites, residuum, scroungers, underclass, undergraduates, undeserving (Categories of abuse rather than analysis).' The penultimate noun was included to see if the readers were paying attention, but there was a genuine coherence to the remainder of the list. Since the modern notion of poverty began to emerge in the mid-nineteenth century, alongside and partly in response to the growth of mass democracy, there has been a constant manufacture of pejorative terms designed to separate those who do not deserve support from those who do. From Henry Mayhew's isolation in 1850 of the 'dishonest poor', 'distinguished from the civilised man by his repugnance to regular and continuous labour', to the importation from America at the end of the 1980s of the notion of the 'underclass', there has been a rich tradition of excluding by language all or some section of the poor from the benevolent consideration of the more fortunate.

Those who use these terms would want to resist my intemperate distinction between abuse and analysis. They would point out that such categories are not just the invention of privileged outsiders, but are often deployed within the communities in which the poor live. To assume that the dispossessed do not exercise moral judgement in their own lives and over those of their neighbours is to exclude them from the realm of civilised society in a more profound fashion than the harshest form of material discrimination. Criticism of misbehaviour, it is argued, is in reality an inclusive act, and, if founded on detailed knowledge, is as susceptible to systematic study as any other aspect of the lives of the poor. Charles Murray, who in the closing months of Margaret Thatcher's regime sought to apply to the British case the concept of the 'underclass' which he had developed during his of work on poverty programmes in the United States, mounted a robust defence of his enterprise. There could be no resolution of the growing crisis of the welfare society, he asserts, unless commentators ceased to be embarrassed about condemning forms of behaviour which were simply wrong. In three areas in particular – unemployment, illegitimacy and crime – it was not only possible but necessary to distinguish those who made the effort to act in a responsible fashion from whose who did not, and to apply the conclusions to a new estimation of the proper role of the state in achieving a good society.

The line that runs from the undeserving to the underclass overlaps in a confusing fashion with the history of distinctions based on material well-being. When Frank Field, the Labour MP and former Director of the Child Poverty Action Group, endorses the notion of underclass, he refers to those who have been denied the fruits of economic growth since 1979, particularly the frail elderly, the long-term unemployed and single-parent families. The decision in 1980 to up-rate benefits levels by price rather than income inflation ensured that those dependent on the welfare system fell further and further behind the standard of living of the majority of society. The tripling of unemployment, the continued rise in the numbers of both pensioners and single parents dependent on the state, together with the growth of low-paid work, ensured that the proportion existing on or below the Income Support level rose from one in seven to almost one in four of the population. This growth of relative, and in many cases absolute, poverty reversed the trends set in motion by the creation of the post-war welfare state, and threatened to bequeath to the next millennium a society more divided than at any time since the industrial revolution began.

What both the behavioural and the structural notions of the underclass have in common is a critical linkage between politics and society. They raise the related questions of what the excluded might do to the political system, and what government should be doing for them. For readers of *Politics UK*, the most interesting aspect of the first of these questions is how unimportant it is. As mass unemployment grew in the 1930s, observers were much occupied with the notion of 'demoralisation', which implied not just a lack of optimism, but rather, in Murray's sense, a systemic collapse of self-respect and self-discipline which would lead to the overthrow of all established forms of authority. In the event, the political culture survived more or less unaltered, to the relief of the right and the deep disappointment of the left. As the jobless total rose once more above three million in the early 1980s, similar fears were expressed, but apart from some scattered though destructive urban disturbances, the basic structures of the state were not seriously threatened. If the poll tax rioters played a significant role in the ultimate demise of Margaret Thatcher, the drama as a whole demonstrated the time-honoured capacity of the establishment to maintain its position through tactical retreat.

The more diffuse issues of apathy and disillusion which have concerned political scientists are confined neither to the poor nor to the 1980s. Indeed it may be argued that rather than the losers abandoning the system, it is the winners in the contemporary economy who are departing most radically from established patterns of participation. The real victims of progress, the dependent elderly, the unsupported mothers, the long-term unemployed, have always found the utmost difficulty in taking an active part even in those political organisations which claim to represent their interests. The casualties of the Great Depression had the National Unemployment Workers' Movement through which to give some expression to their exclusion from the institutions of organised labour, but its attempted successor of the modern era, the Claimants' Union, enjoyed nothing like the same membership or impact. Since the creation of the Child Poverty Action Group in 1965, the characteristic vehicle of protest has been the pressure group, which has furthered the fragmentation of the political process without transforming the opportunities of the dispossessed for direct participation in the search for a solution to their problems.

It is the second of the questions which contains the greater possibility of debate. Those concerned with deprivation rather than depravity put forward policies ranging from a simple reversal of all that the Conservatives have done since 1979 to a search for new forms of citizenship rights which empower individuals and their families to exercise control over their own lives and the larger institutional forces which influence them. Commentators seeking to revive Victorian categories of moral censure have in view nothing less than the wholesale retreat of the state from the lands it has progressively colonised since the welfare reforms of the Edwardian Liberals. There is bitter dispute between those claiming to be new left or new right, with the former accused of disguising in the name of revision a profound political conservatism, and the latter of dressing up in the guise of civilisation a fundamental retreat from civilised compassion.

To understand this debate, it is necessary to think carefully about concepts which often appear interchangeable. If the issue of exclusion represents, as Ralf Dahrendorf (1978) claims, the biggest challenge facing the contemporary polity, the notion of the underclass may well be the largest obstacle to grasping its implications. The Marxist notion of class which the term echoes is a category of both experience and action. At the lower end of society, common suffering generates collective strength; the dispossessed represent both the casualties and gravediggers of bourgeois power. To import such a term to an analysis of material inequality in the modern world obscures the key difference between the present and the past. If the various categories of poverty can be added up to a grand total, they remain a far less homogeneous group than their predecessors in the 1930s or the Victorian period, and for that reason are even less able to exert influence in the political arena. Equally, those seeking to come to terms with fundamental issues of occupational, criminal or sexual morality merely compromise their arguments by insisting on a single composite mass of delinquency. Their critics can bring to bear the powerful arguments which have by now qualified the use of class in many more traditional contexts, that those who display one characteristic do not necessarily display another, that individuals move in and out of positions and attitudes with great and still unmeasured frequency, and that linguistic categories bear no necessary relation to objective behaviour.

Instead of deploying a neologism to echo an older vocabulary, Murray and his sympathisers would have done better simply to use the original terminology which they profess to admire. The Victorian phrase 'undeserving poor' still perfectly well conveys what is meant, and highlights not only the differences between the two responses to exclusion, but also important areas of overlap. It is, for instance, an error for the New Right to characterise their opponents as indifferent to personal failing. Whilst it is true that Beveridge's welfare state sought to diminish the sphere of moral judgement, it could never allow itself to do so entirely. The original structure embodied a concept of the nuclear family identical to Murray's, and contained reserve powers of discrimination against those who would not work or support their dependants. If, by the 1960s, a more liberal attitude was being adopted to alternative domestic arrangements, the reappearance of large-scale unemployment was exposing powerful continuities of suspicion and censure. The apprehension felt by the employed working class and their leaders about the able-bodied poor has never departed. Well before the era of Thatcher and Blair, the old left as

much as the old right were doing battle against the work-shy and the scroungers.

There is a further, and for students of modern politics, still more interesting area of common concern. Imaginative thinkers on the left are at one with their radical opponents in asserting that the centripetal tendencies of the twentieth-century state have to be attacked. Individual empowerment, again a shared if variable goal, requires a reversal of trends which Liberals and socialists set in motion at the beginning of the twentieth century and Conservatives completed at the end. By some means, resources and the authority to control their allocation have to be redistributed from the centre to the periphery. Implicit in such a transformation, regardless of perspective, would be a larger and more effective role for the values and standards of the poor and their neighbours. It is at the point where the precise nature of such local power and its connection to whatever is left in the centre have to be considered, that the differences between New Left and New Right become at once more stark and more uncertain. In one sense it is simple enough. Murray wants nothing less than a return to Jeffersonian democracy, with the state playing a residual role in maintaining the fabric of the nation. His critics attack the scale of his pessimism about the constructive potential of large-scale democratic institutions, and seek instead to rearticulate the relationship between the different layers of collective resource allocation. As elsewhere, the advocates of the moral underclass ease the road of their opponents by the extremity of their position. Merely denying the likelihood or practicality of so total an abandonment of twentieth-century British history does not resolve the problems which remain.

Some insight into the difficulties is given by Murray's celebration of his childhood locality at the end of the attempt to apply his underclass theory to the British context:

When I think of autonomous communities, I think of the midwestern town where I grew up. I remember school rooms where the children of corporate executives were best buddies with the children of assembly line workers, church congregations in which every social class was mixed, children growing up thinking that being a garbage collector or a cleaning lady or a janitor was respectable, because the first lesson we were taught was that the only degrading kind of work was no work. (Murray, 1990)

Whether this world ever in fact existed must be left to students of US politics. On this side of the Atlantic it crucially did not. In the early post-war era about which Murray is writing, class in its full, corrosive sense created a fissure through schooling and most other local institutions. The tight, supportive, decent, neighbourhoods of the pre-war towns and cities, which the right as well as the left now invoke with nostalgia, were created by exclusion not inclusion. It is precisely the absence of Murray's memory, whether mythical or not, which makes the projection of a new democratic community so difficult for English political scientists. We have never been there, even in our dreams. Nineteenth-century critics from Thomas Carlyle to William Morris tried to locate it in the Middle Ages, but the tedious scholarship of modern historians has closed off that avenue of escape and progress.

It is indicative of the contemporary debate that the Conservative government's most creative response in late 1996 was to set up a hotline to facilitate the reporting of suspected benefit abuse by neighbours and workmates. In doing so, it was at least conforming to a real tradition. The classic slums were rife with slanderous gossip about precisely the topics that concern Murray – who was in bed when they were supposed to be working, who was in someone else's bed when they were supposed to be in their own, who had found a suspiciously rapid means of paying off debts From the early means-test inspectors onwards, the state and local welfare systems have always made extensive if covert use of anonymous reports about alleged fraud. At least in the past, the censorious tale-telling was accompanied by various structures of moral and physical support. The material context for such informal services has in most instances gone beyond recall as the public life of the streets has dissolved into the private home and the distant place of work and entertainment. In its emaciated form, the historic British neighbourhood can bear neither the expectations of government seeking to transfer its responsibilities, nor the hopes of reformers searching for new vehicles of progress. Deprivation has always provoked suspicion and intolerance. The community as an inclusive, moralising entity must be the consequence as much as the condition of an attack on poverty.

Reference

Dahrendorf, Ralf (1987) 'The erosion of citizenship and the consequences for us all', *New Statesman*, 12 June.

Murray, C. (1990) *The Emerging British Underclass* (IEA).

PART TWO

Defining the political world

CHAPTER SIX

Ideology and the liberal tradition

BILL JONES

LEARNING OBJECTIVES

- To elucidate the concept of ideology.

- To trace the transition of new ideas from revolutionary stage to point when they were accepted.

- To show how Classical Liberalism developed into New Liberalism, a creed which set the agenda for the next century.

INTRODUCTION

This chapter begins by discussing what we mean by the term 'ideology'. It goes on to explain how liberal ideas entered the political culture as heresies in the seventeenth and eighteenth centuries but went on to become the orthodoxies of the present age. Classical Liberalism in the mid-nineteenth century is examined together with the birth of modern liberalism in the early twentieth century.

What is ideology?

For up to two decades after 1945 it seemed as if ideology as a factor in British politics was on the wane. The coalition comradeship of the war had drawn some of the sting from the sharp doctrinal conflicts between the two major political parties and in its wake the Conservatives had conceded – without too much ill grace – that Labour would expand welfare services and nationalise a significant sector of the economy. Once in power after 1951 the Conservatives presided over their socialist inheritance of a mixed economy and a welfare state. Both parties seemed to have converged towards a general consensus on political values and institu-

tions: there was more to unite than to divide them. By the end of the 1950s some commentators – notably the American political scientist Daniel Bell – were pronouncing 'the end of ideology' (see Bell, 1963) in Western societies.

The faltering of the British economy in the 1960s, however, exacerbated in the early 1970s by the rise in oil prices, industrial unrest and raging inflation, reopened the ideological debate with a vengeance. A revived Labour left hurled contumely at their right-wing Cabinet colleagues for allegedly betraying socialist principles. Margaret Thatcher, meanwhile, leader of the opposition after 1975, began to elaborate a position far to the right of her predecessor Edward Heath (Prime Minister 1970–4). The industrial paralysis of the 1978–9 'winter of discontent' provided a shabby end for Jim Callaghan's Labour government and a perfect backcloth against which Thatcher's confident assertions could be projected. From 1979 to 1990 ideology in the form of Thatcherism or the New Right triumphed over what has subsequently been labelled the 'post-war consensus'.

Ideology as a concept is not easy to define. It is to some extent analogous to philosophy but is not as open-ended or as disinterested. It shares some of the moral commitment of religion but is essentially secular and rooted in this world rather than the next. On the other hand, it is more fundamental and less specific than mere policy. Perhaps it is helpful to regard ideology as applied philosophy. It links philosophical ideas to the contemporary world; it provides a comprehensive and systematic perspective whereby human society can be understood; and it provides a framework of principles from which policies can be developed.

Individuals support ideologies for a variety of reasons: moral commitment – often genuine, whatever cynics might say – as well as self-interest. Clearly, ideology will mean more to political theorists active within political parties, elected representatives or the relative minority who are seriously interested in political ideas. It has to be recognised that most people are ill informed on political matters and not especially interested in them. It is quite possible for large numbers of people to subscribe to contradictory propositions – for example that welfare services should be improved while taxes should be cut – or to vote for a party out of sentiment while disagreeing with its major policies. But the broad mass of the population is not completely inert. During election campaigns they receive a crash course in political education, and leaving aside the more crass appeals to emotion and unreason, most voters are influenced to some extent by the ideological debate. The party with the clearest message which seems most relevant to the times can win elections, as Labour discovered in 1945 and the Conservatives in 1979.

Classifying ideologies

This is a difficult and imperfect science but the following two approaches should help clarify it.

The horizontal left–right continuum

Left	Centre	Right

This is the most familiar classification used and abused in the press and in everyday conversations. It arose from the seating arrangements adopted in the French Estates General in 1789 where the aristocracy sat to the right of the King and the popular movements to his left. Subsequently the terms have come to represent adherence to particular groups of principles. Right-wingers stress freedom or the right of individuals to do as they please and develop their own personalities without interference, especially from governments, which history teaches are potentially tyrannical. Left-wingers believe this kind of freedom is only won by the strong at the expense of the weak. They see equality as the more important value and stress the collective interest of the community above that of the individual. Those occupying the centre ground usually represent various kinds of compromise between these two positions.

The implications of these principles for economic policy are obviously of key importance. Right-wingers champion free enterprise, or capitalism: the rights of individuals to set up their own businesses, to provide goods and services and reap what reward they can. Left-wingers disagree. Capitalism, they argue, creates poverty amidst plenty – much better to move towards collective ownership so that workers can receive the full benefit of their labour. Politicians in the centre dismiss both these positions as extreme and damaging to the harmony of national life. They tend to argue for various combinations of left and right principles or compromises between them: in practice a mixed economy plus efficient welfare services. The left–right continuum therefore relates in practice principally to economic and social policy.

Left	Centre	Right
Equality	Less inequality	Freedom
Collectivism	Some collectivism	Individualism
Collective ownership	Mixed economy	Free enterprise

The vertical axis or continuum

The inadequacies of the left–right continuum are obvious. It is both crude and inaccurate in that many people can subscribe to ideas drawn from its whole width and consequently defy classification. H. J. Eysenck suggested in the early 1950s that if a 'tough' and 'tender' axis could bisect the left–right continuum, ideas could be more accurately plotted on two dimensions. In this way ideological objectives could be separated from political methodology – so tough left-wingers, e.g. communists, would occupy the top left-hand quarter, tough right-wingers, e.g. fascists, the top right-hand quarter, and so on. The diagram below illustrates the point.

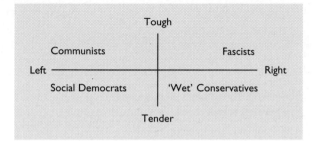

The vertical axis can also be used to plot other features:

1. An authoritarian–democratic axis is perhaps a more precise variation on the tough and tender theme.
2. A status quo–revolutionary axis is also useful. The Conservative party has traditionally been characterised as defending the established order. Margaret Thatcher, however, was a committed radical who wanted to engineer major and irreversible changes. It was Labour and the Conservative 'wets' who defended the status quo in the 1980s. This approach produces some interesting placements on our two-dimensional diagram.

```
                    Status quo
                        |
            Labour      |  Conservative
            right       |  'wets'
   Left ─────────────────────────────── Right
            Bennite     |  Thatcherite
            left        |  right
   Socialist        Revolutionary    National
   Workers'                          Front
   Party
```

Political parties and the left–right continuum

Despite its inadequacies the left–right continuum is useful because it is commonly understood. It will be used as a guide to the following sections, but first a word on the way in which political parties relate to the political spectrum.

For most of the post-war period the major ideological divisions have not occurred between the two big parties, but within them. The Labour Party has covered a very wide spectrum from the revolutionary left to cautious social democrat right. Similarly, two major Conservative schools of thought developed in the late 1970s: traditional ('wet') Conservatism and the New Right or Thatcherite Conservatism. The centre ground for many years was dominated by the Liberal Party, but during the 1980s it was first augmented by the Social Democratic Party (which split off from the Labour Party in 1981) and then was fragmented when the merger initiative following the 1987 election resulted in the awkward progeny of the Social and Liberal Democrats plus the rump Social Democratic Party led defiantly by David Owen until May 1990 when the party formally folded.

Ideas and values in politics

In politics, ideas and values cannot exist in isolation. They need a vehicle by which they can be transformed from abstract ideology into practical legislative effect. The vehicle is the political party. ...

It is more than nostalgia that justifies the party system. It is essentially the belief that some of the 'ideas and values' of politicians have a permanent importance. The policies by which those ideas and values are implemented may change with time and circumstance but the ideology abides.

Roy Hattersley, The Guardian, 30 September 1989

The liberal tradition

The word 'liberalism' was originally a pejorative term used to describe radical or progressive ideas. Since then, like so many other political labels coined as forms of abuse ('tory' was once a name given to Irish outlaws), the word has lost its derogatory connotations and fully traversed the ground between vice and virtue. Now liberalism denotes opinions and qualities which are generally applauded. Most people would like to think they are liberal in the sense of being open-minded, tolerant, generous or rational. This is partly because the ideas of the English liberal philosophers from the mid-seventeenth to mid-nineteenth centuries became accepted as the dominant elements in our political culture. These were the ideas which helped create our liberal democratic political system in the late nineteenth century and since then have provided its philosophical underpinning.

Interestingly in the USA the term came to assume a pejorative meaning in the early 1980s when the Republicans successfully linked it to being 'soft on communism' and therefore anti-American.

An important distinction clearly has to be made between liberal with a small 'l' and the Liberalism associated with the party of the same name until the 1987 merger. The Liberal Party always claimed a particular continuity with liberal philosophical ideas; but so deeply ingrained have these views become that most political parties also owe them substantial unacknowledged philosophical debts. For their part Liberals have made contributions to political, social and economic thinking which have been hugely influential and have been plundered shamelessly by other parties. It makes sense, therefore, to begin with some consideration of the liberal tradition of both the 'l' and 'L' variety.

Philosophical liberalism

Bertrand Russell attributes the birth of English liberal thought in part to the French philosopher, René Descartes (1596–1650). His famous proposition 'I think, therefore I am' made 'the basis of knowledge different for each person since for each the starting point was his own existence not that of other individuals or the community' (Russell, 1965, p. 579). To us such propositions seem unexceptional; but in the mid-seventeenth century they were potentially revolutionary because they questioned the very basis of feudal society. This relied upon unquestioning acceptance of the monarch's divine right to rule, the aristocracy's hereditary privileges and the church's explanation of the world together with its moral leadership. Feudal society was in any case reeling from the impact of the Civil War (1642–9), the repercussions of which produced a

limited constitutional monarchy and the embryo of modern parliamentary government. Descartes had inaugurated a new style of thinking.

Rationality

John Locke (1632–1704) did much to set the style of liberal thinking as rational and undogmatic. He accepted some certainties like his own existence, God and mathematical logic, but he respected an area of doubt in relation to most propositions. He was inclined to accept differences of opinion as the natural consequences of free individual development. Liberal philosophers tended to give greater credence to facts established by scientific enquiry – the systematic testing of theories against reality – rather than to assertions accepted as fact purely on the basis of tradition.

Toleration

This lack of dogmatism was closely connected with a liberal prejudice in favour of toleration and compromise. Conflicts between crown and Parliament, Catholicism and Protestantism had divided the country for too long, they felt: it was time to recognise that religious belief was a matter of personal conscience, not a concern of government.

Natural rights and the consent of the governed

This idea emerged out of the 'contract' theorists of the seventeenth and eighteenth centuries. These thinkers believed that each individual had made a kind of agreement to obey the government in exchange for the services of the state, principally protection from wrong-doing. The logical extension of this mode of thought was that if a contract of this sort had been somehow agreed, then the citizen had a right to reject a government which did not provide services up to the requisite standard. It was not suggested that anything had actually been signed; the idea was more of an application of the legal concept of rights to the philosophical realm. It was all a far cry from Sir Robert Filmer's doctrine that the divine authority of monarchs to receive absolute obedience could be traced back to Adam and Eve from whom all monarchs were originally descended (see also Chapter 7 on the concept of rights).

Individual liberty

The idea of natural rights was closely allied to the concept of individual liberty which had already been established by the eighteenth century:

These liberties included the freedom from arbitrary arrest, arbitrary search and arbitrary taxation; equality before the law, the right to trial by jury; a degree of freedom of thought, speech and religious belief; and freedom to buy and sell. (Gamble, 1981, p. 67; see also Chapter 7 on the concept of freedom)

Such liberties in practice were protected by constitutional checks and balances, limited government and representation.

Constitutional checks and balances

Locke argued that to ensure that executive power was not exercised arbitrarily by the King, the law-making or legislative arm of government should be separate, independent and removable by the community. This doctrine of the 'separation of powers' informed liberal enthusiasm for written constitutions (though ironically Britain has never had a written constitution nor, indeed, an effective separation of powers).

Limited government

Instead of the absolute power which Filmer argued the monarch was free to exercise, liberal philosophers, mindful of past abuses, sought to restrict the legitimacy of government to a protection of civil liberties. It was held to be especially important that government did not interfere with the right to property or the exercise of economic activity.

Representation

It followed that if the legislature was to be removable then it needed to be representative. Many liberal Whigs in the eighteenth century believed that Parliament was generally representative of the nation even though the franchise was small and usually based upon a highly restrictive property qualification. Such positions were destined to be eroded, however, by the inherent logic of natural rights: if everyone had equal rights then surely they should have an equal say in removing a government not of their liking?

The influence of the liberal philosophers perhaps seems greater in retrospect than it was because they were often seeking to justify and accelerate political trends which were already well under way. Nevertheless, they were of key importance and provide ideas still used as touchstones in the present day.

Some commentators, like Eccleshall and Gamble, see liberalism as providing the philosophical rationale for modern capitalist society. Certainly the idea of individual freedom, property rights and limited government suited the emergent entrepreneurial middle classes destined to come of political age in the next century. Liberal views on government, however, have enjoyed a general acceptance not just in Britain but in the USA, Western Europe and elsewhere. They have provided the commonly accepted ground rules of democratic behaviour, the 'procedural values' of toleration, fair play and free speech which Bernard Crick argues should be positively reinforced in our classrooms (see Chapter 1). They have provided in one sense an 'enabling' ideology which all major parties have accepted. Indeed, it is in some ways surprising that a creed originating in an agrarian, largely non-industrialised country should have provided a political framework which has survived so tenaciously and indeed triumphantly into the present day.

Classical Liberalism

The American and French Revolutions applied liberal principles in a way which shocked many of their more moderate adherents. The Napoleonic interlude caused a period of reaction but during the mid- to late nineteenth century Classical Liberalism took shape. Claiming continuity with the early liberals, this new school was based upon the economic ideas of Adam Smith and the radical philosophers Jeremy Bentham, James Mill and his son John Stuart Mill. Liberalism with a capital 'L' then took the stage in the form of the Liberal Party, a grouping based upon the Whigs, disaffected Tories and the Manchester Radicals led by Richard Cobden and John Bright. Classical Liberalism was characterised by:

An acceptance of the liberal conception of the independent, rational and selfgoverning citizen as the basic unit of society.

An embrace of the concept would be a better word in that it now represented a goal or vision to be worked for. Liberals hoped that through the erosion of aristocratic privilege and the moral transformation of the working class, social differences would give way to a new society of equals.

Human nature

The liberal view of human nature was fairly optimistic. John Stuart Mill, for example, doubted whether working for the common good would induce citizens to produce goods as efficiently as when self-interest was involved. He warned against too rapid a rate of social progress. At the heart of Liberal philosophy, however, was Locke's civilised reasonable human being, capable of being educated into responsible citizenship. Many Liberals felt such an education would take a great many years but that it was possible, especially through direct involvement of citizens in the economy and the political system.

Freedom

Classical Liberalism retained the emphasis on freedom. In his essay *On Liberty*, for example, Mill felt: 'It was imperative that human beings should be free to form opinions and to express their opinions without reserve.' The only constraint should be that in the exercise of his freedom, an individual should not impinge upon the freedom of others (again see Chapter 7).

Utilitarianism

Jeremy Bentham (1748–1832) took the rationality of liberal philosophy to new levels with his science of utilitarianism. His approach was based upon what now seems an extraordinarily simplistic view of human psychology. He argued that human beings were disposed to seek pleasure and avoid pain. While they sought what was best for themselves they frequently made mistakes. The role of government therefore was to assist individuals in making the correct choices, thus achieving the greatest happiness for the greatest number. While Bentham embraced the *laissez-faire* economic system as highly utilitarian, he believed that most laws and administrative arrangements reflected aristocratic privilege and therefore were in need of reform.

Minimal government

Bentham's influence paradoxically led to far-reaching legal and administrative reforms; for example, the regulatory framework for mines and factories. Other liberals, however, were strongly opposed to such regulation both as a violation of *laissez-faire* principles and as an interference in the moral education of the poor. Liberals like Herbert Spencer (1820–1903) argued that welfare provision was wrong in that it sheltered the poor from the consequences of their behaviour. 'Is it not manifest', he argued, 'that there must exist in our midst an immense amount of misery which is a normal result of misconduct and ought not to be dissociated from it?' State support for the poor was therefore a dangerous narcotic likely to prevent the right lessons being learnt. The stern lesson Classical Liberals wished to teach was that the poorer classes would face the penalties of poverty unless they adopted the values and lifestyles of their economic superiors: thrift, hard work, moderate indulgence and self-improving pastimes.

Representative government

Bentham and James Mill (1773–1836) introduced an alternative argument in favour of representative government. Bentham dismissed the natural rights argument as 'nonsense on stilts'. His own utilitarian reasoning was that such a form of government was the most effective safeguard for citizens against possibly rapacious rulers or powerful 'sinister interests'. As both men believed the individual to be the best judge of where his own interests lay they favoured universal franchise (though Mill sought to restrict it to men over 40). His son, J. S. Mill (1806–73), is probably the best known advocate of representative government. He urged adult male and female suffrage but to guard against a 'capricious and impulsive' House of Commons he advised a literacy qualification for voting and a system of plural voting whereby educated professional people would be able to cast more votes than ill-educated workers. Mill also believed that a participatory democracy and the sense of responsibility it would imbue would contribute towards the moral education of society: 'Democracy creates a morally better person because it forces people to develop their potentialities.'

Laissez-faire economics

Laissez-faire economics was predicated upon the tenet of individual freedom: it asserted that the ability to act freely within the marketplace – to buy and sell property, employ workers and take profit – was central to any free society. Adam Smith's (1723–90) broadsides against the trade protection of the eighteenth-century mercantilist system provided the clearest possible statement of the case for economic activity free from political restrictions. According to Smith, producers should be allowed to supply products at the price consumers are willing to pay. Provided that competition was fair the 'hidden hand' of the market would ensure that goods were produced at the lowest possible price commensurate with the quality consumers required. Producers would be motivated by selfish pursuit of profit but would also provide social 'goods', through providing employment, creating wealth and distributing it in accordance with the energy and ability of people active in the economic system. Smith believed government intervention and regulation would impede this potentially perfect self-adjusting system. Liberals were not especially worried by the inequalities thrown up by *laissez-faire* economics, nor did they waste any sleep over the socialists' claim that the wage labour system enabled the middle-class property owners to exploit their workers. Classical Liberals were opposed to inherited financial advantages but not so concerned with the differences created by different performances in relation to the market. They favoured the meritocracy of the market: they were the high priests of capitalism.

Peace through trade

Liberals, especially the so-called Manchester Radicals, also applied their free trade principles to foreign affairs. Richard Cobden, for example, regarded diplomacy and war as the dangerous pastimes of the aristocracy. His answer to these perennial problems was: 'to make diplomacy open and subject to parliamentary control'; eliminate trade barriers; and encourage free trade worldwide. Commerce, he argued, was peaceful, beneficial and encouraged cooperation and contact between nations. If the world were a completely open market, national economies would become more integrated and interdependent and governments would be less likely to engage in conflicts or war.

The New Liberalism

The emphasis of Classical Liberalism was upon *laissez faire*, wealth production, toleration of inequality, minimal welfare, individual responsibility and moral education. Towards the end of the nineteenth century, however, Liberals themselves began to move away from their own ascetic economic doctrines. John Stuart Mill had argued that government was only justified in intervening in society in order to prevent injury to the life, property or freedom of others. To some Liberals it appeared that capitalist society had become so complex and repressive that the freedom of poor people to develop their potential was being restricted: even if they were inclined to emulate their middle-class betters their capacity to do so was held back by poverty, poor health and education, squalid living and working conditions. Liberal thinkers began to shift their emphasis away from 'negative' freedom – freedom from oppression – towards providing 'positive' freedom – the capacity of people to make real choices regarding education, employment, leisure, and so on.

State responsibility for welfare

T.H. Green (1836–82) helped initiate this movement for positive action to assist the poor by calling for a tax upon inherited wealth. Alfred Marshall (1842–1924) believed capitalism now provided such material plenty that it had the capacity to redistribute some of its largesse to the disadvantaged so that they would be able genuinely to help themselves to become self-reliant. But it was L. T. Hobhouse (1864–1929) who perhaps marked the key shift of Liberals towards paternalism:

The state as over-parent is quite as truly liberal as socialistic. It is the basis of the rights of the child, of his protection against parental neglect, of the equality of opportunity which he may claim as a 'future citizen'.

Hobhouse insisted that his version of paternalism should not be oppressively imposed; he favoured a basic minimum standard of living which would provide 'equal opportunities of self development'. He followed Green in proposing taxation to finance such welfare innovations as health insurance and pensions. The great Liberal victory of 1906 enabled the government to implement many of these new measures. Thereafter Liberals became firm advocates of welfarism; in 1942 the Liberal William Beveridge produced his famous blueprint for the post-war welfare state.

The mixed economy: Hobsonian and Keynesian economics

Government intervention of a different kind was proposed by J.A. Hobson (1858–1940). He was the first major Liberal economist (he later became a socialist) to argue that capitalism was fatally flawed. Its tendency to produce a rich minority who accumulated unspent profits and luxury goods meant that the full value of goods produced was not consumed by society. This created slumps and, indirectly, the phenomenon of economic imperialism. Capitalists were forced by such underconsumption to export their savings abroad, thus creating overseas interests with political and colonial consequences. Hobson argued that the state could solve this crisis with one Olympian move: redirect wealth from the minority to the poor via progressive taxation. The section of society most in need would then be able to unblock the mechanism which caused overproduction and unemployment, thus making moral as well as economic sense.

J.M. Keynes (1883–1946) completed this revolution in Liberal economic thought by arguing that demand could be stimulated not by redistribution of wealth to the poor but by government-directed investment into new economic activity. Confronted by a world recession and massive unemployment, he concentrated upon a different part of the economic cycle. He agreed that the retention of wealth by capitalists under a *laissez-faire* economic system lay at the heart of the problem, but believed the key to be increased investment, not increased consumption. Instead of saving in a crisis governments should encourage businessmen to invest in new economic activity. Through the creation of new economic enterprises wealth would be generated, consumption increased, other economic activities stimulated and unemployment reduced. He envisaged

a mixed economy in which the state would intervene with a whole range of economic controls to achieve full employment and planned economic growth. Keynes was not just concerned with the cold science of economics: his view of the mixed economy would serve social ends in the form of alleviated hardship and the extension of opportunity. But while Keynes was unhappy with capitalism in the 1930s he did not propose to replace it – merely to modify it. He was no egalitarian, unlike socialist economists, and disagreed with Hobsonian calls for wealth redistribution which he felt would adversely affect the incentives to achieve which human nature required: 'for my own part I believe there is social and psychological justification for significant inequalities of income and wealth' (Keynes, 1973, p. 374).

Internationalism

Radical Liberals like J.A. Hobson, Norman Angel, E.D. Moorel, C.R. Buxton, H.N. Brailsford, Lowes Dickenson and Charles Trevelyan produced an influential critique of the international system, arguing that the practice of secret diplomacy, imperialist competition for markets, haphazard balance of power policies and the sinister role of arms manufacturers made war between nations tragically inevitable. The First World War appeared to vindicate their analysis and encouraged them to develop the idea of an overarching international authority: the League of Nations. The idea was picked up by political parties and world leaders including the US President, Woodrow Wilson, and through the catalyst of war was translated into the League of Nations by the Versailles Treaty. Most of the Radical Liberals joined the Labour Party during and after the war but the Liberal Party subsequently remained staunchly internationalist and in favour of disarmament proposals throughout the interwar period.

Further development of democratic government

The New Liberals were no less interested than their predecessors in the development of representative democracy through extension of the franchise and the strengthening of the House of Commons. Lloyd George's device of including welfare proposals in his

BOX 6.1   JOHN MAYNARD KEYNES (1883–1946)   BIOGRAPHY

By courtesy of Popperfoto

Born in Cambridge, Keynes was the son of an academic. He was educated at Eton and King's College, Cambridge, where he mixed in avant-garde intellectual circles, such as the 'Bloomsbury group', and taught sporadically. He served in the India Office (1906–8) and later wrote his first book on this subject. In the First World War he advised the Treasury and represented it at the Versailles Treaty negotiations but resigned at the terms proposed. His essay *The Economic Consequences of the Peace* (1919) brought his powerful radical intellect to the notice of the country's ruling elite. He attacked Churchill's restoration of the gold standard in 1925 and the unemployment caused by the Depression inspired his most famous work, *General Theory of Employment, Interest and Money* (1936). His views won support on the left and in the centre as well as helping to inspire the New Deal policies of Roosevelt in the USA.

Keynes married a Soviet ballerina and with her father founded the Vic-Wells ballet. In 1943 he established the Arts Theatre in Cambridge. In the same year he played a leading role in the Bretton Woods agreement, which set up a new international economic order, the establishment of the International Monetary Fund and negotiations following the ending of lend-lease (a financial agreement whereby aid was channelled to the UK during the war) after the war to secure a major loan to help Britain survive the rigours of the immediate post-war world. Most people achieve only a fraction in their lifetimes of what Keynes managed to do. He was one of the truly great figures of the century and his influence lives on today.

1909 Budget – a measure which the House of Lords had traditionally passed 'on the nod' – precipitated a conflict between the two chambers which resulted in the House of Lords' power being reduced from one of absolute veto over legislation to one of delay only. In the early 1920s Liberals gave way to Labour as the chief opposition party, returning 159 MPs in 1923, 59 in 1929 and only 21 in 1935. The dramatic decline in the party's fortunes coincided with its support for a change in the electoral system from the 'first-past-the-post' system, which fav-oured big parties, to alternatives which would provide fairer representation to smaller parties, like the Liberals, with thinly spread national support.

This chapter has sought to emphasise the centrality of the liberal (note small l) tradition in the evolution of modern British political thought. In the eighteenth century it helped establish reason, toleration, liberty, natural rights and the consent of the governed in place of religious dogma, feudal allegiance and the divine right of monarchs to rule. In the nineteenth century it added representative, demo-cratic government with power shared between various elements. Having provided key guidelines for our modern system of government, Classical Liberalism argued for minimal government interven-tion in social policy and an economy run essentially in harmony with market forces.

The New Liberals, however, engineered a new intellectual revolution. They argued for government intervention to control an increasingly complex economy which distributed great rewards and terrible penalties with near-random unfairness. They also saw commerce not as the healing balm for international conflicts but as the source of the conflicts themselves. The irony is that the Liberals Keynes and Beveridge proved to be the chief architects of the post-war consensus between Labour and Conservatives while, as we shall see, Margaret Thatcher wrought her revolution not through application of traditional Conservatism but through a rediscovery of Classical Liberalism.

Postscript: Fukuyama and the end of history

No account of the development of the liberal tradi-tion in politics can end without some reference to Francis Fukuyama, the obscure official in the US State Department who argued in articles and a book that the liberal tradition had developed to the extent that it, allied to free enterprise economics, had eclipsed all its rivals on the left and right – commu-nism, fascism, socialism – thus producing the 'universalisation of Western Liberal democracy as the final form of human government'.

He founded his reasoning on the Hegelian notion that civilisations successively develop, resolve internal conflicts and change for the better. The 'end of history' is when a point is reached whereby conflict is eradicated and the form of society best suited to human nature has evolved.

The importance of the article lay partly in its timing. The British Empire took a couple of decades to expire but Stalin's went up in a few years at the end of the 1980s. The intellectual world was deafened by the crashing of rotten regimes and astonished by the apparent vibrancy of their demo-cratic successors. Moreover after decades of defending liberal values against a grey and predatory

communist bloc, the Western intelligentsia responded warmly to a thesis which appeared to say 'We've won'. Fukuyama's bold thesis fitted the facts and suited the mood of the times. Even in Britain the triumph of Thatcher in three successive elections between 1979 and 1987 seemed to reflect the thrust of the argument and her stated resolve to destroy socialism in her country. However, Fukuyama's thesis seems to ignore the exponential forces for change which are changing society at breakneck speed: computer technology and the information revolution; the huge pressure on finite world resources; the spread of nuclear weapons; the increasing concentra-tion of wealth in a few hands; the huge and growing gap between rich and poor. Who is to say these forces will not undermine the liberal consensus and possibly usher in a new authoritarianism?

To assume the liberal underpinnings of many world political systems will survive can be seen as at best naive and at worst complacent.

Chapter summary

Ideology is a kind of applied philosophy. It can be classified on the right–left continuum, a flawed but still much used form. The liberal tradition, based on rights, freedom and representation, developed from the seventeenth century and set the ground rules for political activity during the nineteenth and twentieth. Classical Liberalism elevated the market economy but the New Liberalism, which was concerned to protect society from its excesses, still provides the rationales for the welfare state and the mixed economy.

Discussion points

- Are there better ways of classifying ideology than the left–right continuum?

- What are the grounds for thinking all human beings have rights?

- Should government resist interfering in the economy?

- Have the Liberals been exploited/robbed in ideological terms by the other two big parties?

- Defend the Fukuyama thesis that the evolution of political systems has reached its end point in liberal democratic free enterprise.

Further reading

Two excellent books have recently become available which introduce politics students to ideology. Adams (1993) is well written and subtly argued. Heywood (1992) is also essential reading. Useful in general terms are Eccleshall (1984) and Gamble (1981). Plant (1991) is more difficult but no less rewarding. On Liberalism, the texts by J. S. Mill in the References (1975, 1985a, 1985b) are as good a starting point for understanding liberalism as any. Eccleshall (1986) lays some claim to be the definitive text but Arblaster (1984) and Manning (1976) address wider readerships. Fukuyama (1991) elaborates the 'end of history' theory.

References

Adams, I. (1993) *Political Ideology Today* (Manchester University Press).

Arblaster, A. (1984) *The Rise and Fall of Western Liberalism* (Blackwell).

Bell, D. (1960) *The End of Ideology* (Free Press).

Eccleshall, R. (1984) *Political Ideologies* (Hutchinson).

Eccleshall, R. (1986) *British Liberalism* (Longman).

Fukuyama, F. (1982) *The End of History and the Last Man* (Hamish Hamilton).

Gamble, A. (1981) *An Introduction to Modern Social and Political Thought* (Macmillan).

Heywood, A. (1992) *Political Ideologies: An Introduction* (Macmillan).

Keynes, J.M. (1985) *A General Theory of Employment, Interest and Money*, Vol. VII of his *Collected Works* (Macmillan; first published 1936).

Manning, D.J. (1976) *Liberalism* (St Martin's Press).

Mill, J.S. (1975) *Representative Government* (Oxford University Press; first published 1861).

Mill, J.S. (1985a) *On Liberty* (Penguin; first published 1859).

Mill, J.S. (1985b) *Principles of Political Economy* (Penguin; first published 1848).

Plant, R. (1991) *Modern Political Thought* (Blackwell).

Russell, B. (1965) *The History of Western Philosophy* (Unwin)

CHAPTER SEVEN

Political ideas: key concepts

BILL JONES

LEARNING OBJECTIVES

- To introduce the conceptual approach to understanding political ideas as an alternative to the ideology-centred perspective traditionally employed.

- To explain the essence of some key concepts in the study of political science.

- To explain how these concepts are employed in the real world of politics.

INTRODUCTION

Chapter 6 touched on some key concepts; this one takes the examination further. It examines the field of political ideas through the perspective of concepts and it goes on to discuss some of the most familiar and most used ones, relating them to broader questions concerning political ideas. The most obvious starting point is with the notion of a concept itself.

What is a concept?

A concept is usually expressed by a single word or occasionally by a phrase. Concepts are frequently general in nature, representing a specific function or category of objects. For example the word 'table' usually refers to an individual human artefact, but it also embodies the whole idea of a table, which we might understand as a flat platform usually supported by legs designed to have objects rested upon them. Without this definition a table would be a meaningless object; it is the concept which gives it purpose and function. As Andrew Heywood (1994, p. 4) explains:

a concept is more than a proper noun or the name of a thing. There is a difference between talking about a chair, a particular and unique chair, and holding the concept of a 'chair', the idea of a chair. The concept of a chair is an abstract notion, composed of the various features which give a chair its distinctive character – in this case, for instance, the capacity to be sat upon.

It follows, therefore, that the concept of a 'parliament' refers not to a specific parliament in a given country but to the generality of them; the abstract *idea* underlying them. By the same token, as we grow up, we come to attribute meaning and function to everyday objects through learning the appropriate concepts – plates, cups, windows, doors, and so forth. Without these concepts we would be totally confused, surrounded by a mass of meaningless phenomena. In one sense concepts are the meaning we place upon the world, impose upon it, to enable us to deal with it. Similarly we come to understand the political world through concepts which we learn from our reading, the media and our teachers. Over the years we come to extend them and refine them in order to achieve a sophisticated understanding, to become 'politically literate'. To use a slightly different analogy, concepts are like the different lenses opticians place in front of us when attempting to find the one which enables us to see more effectively; without them we cannot bring a blurred world into focus – with them we achieve clarity and sharpness.

Some political concepts are merely descriptive, for example 'elections', but others embody a 'normative' quality – they contain an *ought*. 'Representation' is both descriptive, in that it describes why MPs sit in legislatures, and normative, in that it carries the message that states ought to base their political system on some kind of electoral principle.

Ideologies are composites of complex concepts and we can understand them by focusing on these constituent elements. This chapter will proceed to examine briefly six key concepts in political science: human nature, freedom, democracy, equality, social justice and rights.

Human nature

It is appropriate to refer again to the quotation by Voltaire which opens Chapter 1: 'There has never been a perfect government, because men have passions; and if they did not have passions, there would be no need for government.' Voltaire sums up the concern of the political scientist and philosopher with the vexed subject of human nature. Many other thinkers have been concerned with our relationships, individually and collectively, with political institutions and it is understandable they should focus on the nature of what is being organised and governed: ourselves. Many seek to identify something which explains what 'mankind is all about', a central core to our natures. Martin Hollis (cited in Plant, 1991, p. 28) writes:

All political and social theorists ... depend on some model of man in explaining what moves people and accounts for institutions. Such models are sometimes hidden but never absent. There is no more central or persuasive topic in the study of politics.

Often these models will be the template of the related philosophy. Thomas Hobbes, for example, believed man outside society, in a 'natural' state, was disposed towards pleasure and against pain but in each case would be impelled to make individual choices. This would mean that agreement on what was desirable or undesirable would be lacking, resulting in a kind of perpetual state of war; life; in his famous description would consequently be 'solitary, poor, nasty, brutish and short'. There would be no security of property 'no thine and mine distinct; but only that to be everyman's, that he can get; and for so long as he can keep it.'

He points out, to those who may doubt his pessimistic analysis, that a man already arms himself when taking a journey, locking doors and chests at night, even when he knows there are officers whose job it is to protect him. 'Does he not ... as much accuse all mankind by his actions?' Hobbes goes on to argue the need for a sovereign power, a Leviathan, to impose order on society, to quell the inherent civil war of 'all against all'. Rousseau similarly predicated a state of nature in his philosophy based on man's nature in which the 'savage' was uncivilised though basically kindly. It was only the effects of organised modern society which made him bad. Already in this discussion it is possible to discern a pessimistic view of human nature, like that of Hobbes, and a more optimistic one, as in Rousseau and Locke (see Boxes 7.1 and 7.2).

In the nineteenth century the same tendencies can be seen. Marx was an optimist, believing mankind was much better than it appeared because of the corrupting effects of the harsh economic system of privately owned capital. Marx believed that human nature was a rogue product of a sick society: 'Environment determines consciousness.' It followed that to change the social environment for the better would be to improve human nature too. However, experience has tended to disappoint Marxist expectations. The Soviet Union was established after the 1917 revolution as a new experiment in political organisation. Progressive intellectuals and the working class the world over rallied to its cause, confidently expecting it to transform human nature, as, according to Marxist reasoning, the underlying capitalist economic system had been abolished. Right-wing politicians opposed it and sought to expose it as a harsh police-supported tyranny disguised by stirring rhetoric and naive leftwing support.

The debate continues but it is hard to deny the pessimists were proved right. Through skilful manoeuvring and ruthless opportunism Joseph Stalin moved himself into a position of total power and exercised a bloody hegemony over a huge state for over two decades. Far from transforming human nature, the Soviet Union merely demonstrated that in Herzen's phrase 'we are not the doctors, we are the disease'.

In the late nineteenth century, Charles Darwin formulated his theory of evolution, which argued that all species did not replicate themselves perfectly on all occasions; they sometimes developed exceptions or mutations in their bodily form. Those mutations which suited the environment survived and thrived and went on to establish a new strain which carried the banner for the species whilst the remaining strains faded away into extinction. This notion of the 'survival of the fittest' was used by a number of classical liberal thinkers – like Herbert Spencer – to justify capitalism as the way in which the species was developing itself and to argue against government interference with the 'natural order' of things.

Despite their differences, these philosophies were united in assuming the basic rationality of man, that humans make rational decisions about their lives and act in accordance with reason for most of the time. The later part of the century, however, saw the emergence of a revolutionary new approach which had widespread repercussions for many kinds of thinking: the ideas of Sigmund Freud:

Men and women in Freud's view are radically amphibious. They live in two dimensions: the realm of instinctual drives dominated by the pleasure principle; and the social existence controlled and directed in the individual case by the reality principle. (Plant, 1991, p. 55)

BOX 7.1   JOHN LOCKE (1632–1704)   BIOGRAPHY

By courtesy of Popperfoto/Reuter

Locke was one of the founding fathers of the English empirical approach and of liberal democracy. Born in Somerset and educated in Oxford, he was fascinated by medicine and science and became the personal physician of Lord Shaftesbury. After a spell in government service he retired to France (1675–9) where he made contact with the country's leading intellectual figures. When his patron fell from power he fled to Holland, where he supported, presciently enough, William of Orange, who was invited to take the English crown in 1688. Locke's *Two Treatises of Government*, (1690, see Locke, 1956) were intended as a riposte to the divine right ideas of Robert Filmer and the 'total sovereignty' of Hobbes. Locke's works are characterised by tolerance and moderation and a less pessimistic view of human nature; sentiments often perceived as typically English.

To live any kind of ordered life excludes the continuance of the pleasure principle, so drives are repressed and sublimated into socially useful activities like work and achievement:

Sublimation of instinct is an essentially conspicuous feature of cultural development: it is what makes it possible for the higher psychical activities, in [the] scientific, artistic or ideological, to play such an important part in civilised life. (Freud, 1963, p. 34)

But whereas Freud applauds the constructive consequences of repression, others, like Fromm and Marcuse, believed it to be harmful. Fromm argued that it created an alienated person who was in one sense mentally ill. To achieve 'mental health' he called for a number of reforms, many of them socialist in form. Critics like Thomas Szasz pointed out shrewdly that 'mental health and illness are new ways of describing moral values'.

Marcuse agreed with Freud that some degree of repression – he called it 'basic repression' – is necessary for a society to function acceptably, but he believed that in Western society the degree of what he called 'surplus repression' based on class domination was unjustifiable and a revolution was necessary to correct the imbalance. Another variety of idea is based upon a biological approach. Racialists, for example, posit different characteristics for different races. Nazis believed the Aryans to be the 'master race' and others to be inferior; others argue that some races are genetically inferior in terms of intelligence. Radical feminists also perceive huge irreconcilable 'essential' differences between the sexes, based on the male sex's disposition to dominate through rape or the fear of rape and violence (Brownmiller, 1975).

Freedom

The sense of liberty is a message read between the lines of constraint. Real liberty is as transparent, as odourless and tasteless as water.

(Michael Frayn, *Constructions*, 1974)

Freedom, as the above quote suggests, is not easy to define or describe, partly because it is so emotive: most politicians declare commitment to it or its synonym, 'liberty' and it is generally held to be a 'good thing'. To explore some of the intricacies and difficulties of this concept, consider the five cases listed below:

1. A man is locked in a cell for twenty-four hours a day; his fellow prisoners are beaten when they break the rules of the prison.
2. A man is left on a desert island where he can walk around but not escape.
3. A man lives in Toxteth on social security, unable to support his children or fulfil his ambition of becoming a professional musician.
4. A man is held up by a mugger and told to hand over his money or be attacked with a knife.
5. A man lives in a comfortable house in East Grinstead and fulfils his dream of becoming a successful novelist.

If the question is put 'are these men free?' then what can we conclude? Clearly the first man is not free in any sense; his movements are wholly restricted and he is prevented from leaving his cell by the locked door – he is the archetype of the person denied freedom. The second man is free to walk around but not beyond this to leave the restricted space of the island; he is effectively exiled or imprisoned. The third is free to walk wherever he wishes and in theory to do anything he pleases, but in practice he is prevented by lack of money/resources and is unable to fulfil his desire or life goal. The fourth man faces a dilemma: he can refuse to hand over his money but if he does he will face the prospect of being badly wounded, even killed, raising the question of whether he has any kind of choice. The final man is the archetypal successful man: he has the ability to move freely according to his choice; he can holiday abroad and has the resources to do so; he has fulfilled his ambitions regarding his career. It seems fair to conclude there are degrees of freedom with the first example the least free, the last, most so.

The cases discussed above reveal the range of debate about this elusive concept. The first and fourth men face physical coercion: if they refuse to obey what they are told, force will be used against them. They are classic victims of loss of freedom. Marginally close behind them is the occupant of the desert island: he is free from physical fear but he is not free to leave his restricted space. The argument gets difficult with the third man who lives in poverty. He is free from coercion but the problem is this: can he be said to be free if he has no resources to leave his less than salubrious living area, is uneducated and unable to become the person he wants to be?

These cases demonstrate the difference between 'freedom from' and 'freedom to': 'negative' and 'positive' freedom. Philosophers might say that men in cases one, two and possibly four were unfree in the negative sense: they are the victims of coercion, they are oppressed in one way or the other. The third man is free, though in the negative sense, free to improve himself, 'get on his bike' and look for a job. This sort of freedom is seen by certain thinkers, including nineteenth-century Classical Liberals, and politicians as the real core or 'essential' definition. Poverty, they argue, is not necessarily restrictive; it might even be the spur to prosperity and hence the route to more viable choices. Such thinkers defended the *laissez-faire* economic system and opposing regulatory government intervention as unjustifiable incursions

into the freedoms of factory owners and other employers, not to mention the best interests of the individuals concerned.

It was the liberal philosopher T.H. Green (1988[1911]) who first argued, in modern times for 'positive freedom'. He believed that anyone prevented from realising his/her full potential was in a real sense unfree. He defined freedom as the ability of people to 'make the best and most of themselves'. If they were not able to do this then they were not free. This definition, so attractive to socialists, opened up in theory the whole field of government intervention, especially via welfare services. Such a formulation of the concept also carries with it the clear implication that wealth should be redistributed to give more chances to more people.

Opponents of this approach, echoing Classical Liberals, claim that it is self-defeating: the government takes away the individual's freedom to improve

BOX 7.2   JEAN-JACQUES ROUSSEAU (1712–78)   BIOGRAPHY

By courtesy of Popperfoto/Reuter

Rousseau's mother died giving birth in Geneva and he had little family life nor any formal education. In 1728 he ran away to Italy and became the lover of a baroness before moving to Paris in 1741, where he made a living from secretarial work and copying music. He established a lifelong relationship with an illiterate servant girl, Thérèse le Vasseur. He had four children by her and despite his expressed concern for children delivered them all to orphanages. He was a friend of famous intellectuals like Voltaire and Diderot, writing music and contributing articles to the latter's *Encyclopédie*, but his first famous work was his prize-winning essay on arts and sciences which argued that civilisation was corrupting man's natural goodness. He developed these ideas in a further essay on inequality in which he attacked private property. In 1762 he published his classic *Du Contrat social* (see Rousseau, 1913), which begins with the famous line: 'Man is born free but everywhere he is in chains.' This work, plus his slogan 'Liberty, Equality, Fraternity', became the founding text of the French Revolution.

his/her lot; it takes away the freedom of employers to employ workers at rates the market requires; it is part, in fact, of a subtle, incremental tyranny. In the twentieth century Friedrich Hayek and the economist Milton Friedman argued this case passionately, insisting that such a position was the 'road to servitude'. Sir Keith Joseph, a disciple of both thinkers, stated flatly 'Poverty is not unfreedom'.

Defenders insist that unless the individuals are empowered to realise their personal potential, then they are not truly free. They also argue that the kind of freedom right-wingers and classical liberals want is the freedom of the strong to dominate the weak, or, as R.H. Tawney (1969) vividly put it, 'the freedom of the pike is death to the minnows'.

Some dictatorial regimes claim to be 'free' when they are not. Fascist regimes, for example, claimed that the only 'true' freedom occurred when people were obeying the will of the national leader, i.e. total subjugation, not freedom as we in Western European countries would understand it. We in these countries tend to believe we are not free from government oppression unless it can be removed via unfettered elections.

Anarchists argue for a much wider kind of freedom; in fact they believe there is no need for any kind of authority and advocate complete freedom. This is generally not thought to be desirable, for it would give licence to murderers, child molesters, robbers and the like. J.S. Mill tried to solve this problem by advocating that people should be allowed all freedoms except those which were harmful to others; the 'harm principle'. According to this approach, personal harm – like suicide or addictive drugs – would be acceptable as others would not be involved. Modern libertarians use similar arguments to urge the legalisation of harmful drugs like heroin and cocaine.

Democracy

'There are no wise few. Every aristocracy that has ever existed has behaved, in all essential points, exactly like a small mob.'

G.K. Chesterton, *Heretics*, 1905

As with freedom/liberty, democracy is a universally regarded 'good thing' with many oppressive regimes claiming the title for propaganda purposes.

Rousseau's conception of democracy was based on his unusual idea of what constituted freedom; for him it had to be small-scale and 'direct'. Citizens had to contribute personally to the formation of a 'general will' of the community by participating constantly in its governance. They could only be truly 'free' when they obeyed the imperatives which they themselves had helped create. It followed that those who failed to obey this general will were not obeying their 'true' natures and should be impelled to conform or be 'forced to be free'. Bertrand Russell believed this doctrine to be pernicious and the thin end of what eventually became the totalitarian wedge. Rousseau's idea of direct democracy hearkened back to the Greeks, but it must be clear to most enthusiasts for democracy that such a form of governance is not possible in the context of large nation-states. Even small groups find it hard to agree on simple things so it is stretching credence to the limits to believe large groups can agree on big issues.

To maximise direct democracy, one of the aims of the left, some advocate the introduction of more and more referendums, but such devices would surely introduce unacceptable delays into government when decisions often have to be made quickly and emphatically. Some point out that today computer technology enables government to be carried out in theory on an 'interactive' basis, and some experiments along these lines have been tried in the USA and elsewhere. From one point of view our existing system is superior to any direct method, whether using ballot boxes or new technology, as many popular attitudes are authoritarian and illiberal. For example on penal policy (see Chapter 24) the public tend to favour harsh sentences for criminals and the death penalty for murderers. They can also be nationalistic and xenophobic. At least our existing system allows these extremes to be filtered out in favour of views which are the result of rational debate and intensive research. Still others accept the difficulties of scale and number and advocate instead the devolution of decision-making down to the lowest level compatible with efficiency.

As a result of the inadequacies of direct democracy, an indirect form of it has been developed, called 'representative democracy', whereby people are elected to serve the community for a space of years; they become more or less full-time professional politicians, experienced in understanding the complexities both of public affairs and of interpreting the public mood. Most importantly they are also accountable to the public at election times and hence removable if they are deemed ineffective or unsuitable. This has also been called liberal democracy, the triumph of which some have discerned with the demise of communism in the late 1980s (see section on Fukuyama in Chapter 6, p. 80). Churchill famously said that this was the worst kind of government except for all the rest; but this should not blind us to its manifest imperfections.

On democracy

" No one pretends that democracy is perfect or all wise. Indeed, it has been said that democracy is the worst form of government, except for all the others that have been tried from time to time.   *Winston Churchill*

The task of parliament is not to run the country but to hold to account those who do.

William Ewart Gladstone "

1. Most people are bored by politics and functionally politically illiterate. This makes them a prey to unscrupulous politicians who can use the freedom of the system to abuse its fundamentals – Hitler subverted the Weimar Republic to seize power in the early 1930s.
2. Politicians, as already suggested, cannot be trusted to be wholly disinterested servants of the community. Dr Johnson once declared that politics was 'nothing more nor less than a means of rising in the world'; and the Nolan Committee's investigations have revealed that the cupidity of politicians remains a danger to the independence and honesty of our elected representatives.
3. Voting is an occasional ritual whereby the citizen briefly has the chance to change the government; as Rousseau dismissively pointed out, the electorate in Britain have power only on election days; once they have voted their power is vested in a body which is essentially able to do what it likes. He was right to the extent that majority voting is a fine principle but majorities can be as tyrannical as minorities; for example, the Protestant voters in Northern Ireland who used their position to disadvantage the

Catholic minority over a number of decades. Lord Hailsham in the mid-1970s declared the British system of government had become an 'elective dictatorship' for the five years parties were allowed to govern before the next election (though, ever the politician, he seemed to lose his indignation when his party came to power in 1979).

4. As the German sociologist Robert Michels (1949) argued, there is a tendency for any democracy to be subverted by small elite groups: his so-called 'iron law of oligarchy'. Interestingly, Sir Anthony Eden supported this theory in the British case when he told the House of Commons in 1928 that 'We do not have democratic government today ... What we have done in all the progress of reform and evolution is to broaden the basis of oligarchy.' Marxists tend to agree with Michels and argue further that the liberal democratic system is merely a decoration; behind the façade of elections and democratic process, the richest groups in society take all the major decisions in their own interests and against those of the masses.
5. In the modern era issues are increasingly complex, for example the arguments over the desirability of a unified European currency. This has meant that the natural reluctance of voters to involve themselves in politics has been accentuated through their inability to absorb the complexity.
6. The political process is now dominated by the media – elections are essentially media events – and the politicians have been able to use their skills in manipulating the media, via the infamous 'spin doctors' and others, to disguise and obfuscate the real issues. Often issues are abandoned altogether in favour of 'negative campaigning'; a good example is the ploy of character assassination, as in the case of Neil Kinnock in the 1992 election who was the object of a highly personal campaign by the Murdoch-owned *Sun* newspaper.

Equality

What makes equality such a difficult business is that we only want it with our superiors.

Henri Becque, *Querelles Littéraires*, 1890

Equality is yet another hotly disputed concept. There is 'equality of opportunity' and 'equality of outcome'. The left prefer the latter, the right the former. Equality of opportunity is agreed now by all shades of opinion as a desirable thing; the liberal view has prevailed. Even South African supporters of the National Party now claim to have renounced their old apartheid attitudes which caused so much suffering and injustice. (Whether they have or not, of course, is hard to tell, but at least they no longer claim their racist views are correct, fair and God-given.)

The problems arise when the equality of outcome argument is considered. For many on the left any inequality is deemed to be bad and remediable through government action. If the analogy of a race is employed, then everyone stands on the same starting line when embarking on their lives. The right-winger tends to say that how far and fast individuals progress in the race of life is a function of their ability, their energy and their will to succeed: 'winners' will strive and achieve and be admired; 'losers' will fall behind, be looked down on and make excuses. Whilst the consensus after the war in Britain was that inequality was something to be deplored and reduced, Margaret Thatcher asserted the right of people to be 'unequal', to excel, to be better. In March 1995 John Major was asked in the House of Commons if he believed inequality should be reduced; perhaps surprisingly, he replied 'Yes'. Nevertheless Major would not accept the left-wing argument regarding the requirement to help those who fall behind in life's race. He would be likely to argue that some differences in outcome were the consequence of 'natural inequalities', which are likely to affect anyone: some can run faster, others have exceptional memories, musical gifts, and so on. To interfere with 'nature' in this way is harmful, say right-wing theorists, likely to distort the internal dynamics of society.

The left-winger tends to interpret the 'equal start in life' argument as an illusion: most people carry handicaps; for some it might be a broken home, resulting in emotional turmoil and underachievment in school; for others it might be lack of resources, poverty, lack of adequate role models, and so forth. To maintain everyone has an equal chance in present society is to say, according to the left, that

the fleet of foot have a clear opportunity to excel without any impediment over others less gifted or blessed by birth.

So the left tend to argue for a system which helps the slower to catch up, for their poverty to be alleviated, their special needs met; in some cases for special 'affirmative action', whereby those groups regularly excluded from success, like racial minorities and women, are given some preference, perhaps in the form of 'quota' allocations for university entrance, as in the USA.

The right claim that, to work effectively, people need to be given an incentive. If wages are equalised, for example, then the lazy will have no incentive to work and will be idle whilst the industrious are exploited and denied proper reward for their effort. They claim this is fundamental for the effective functioning of the economy which is fuelled by incentives: when a role needs performing in society the market puts a price on filling it; when it is a freely available skill, like sweeping the streets, the rate is low but when the skills are rare and dependent on years of study plus high intellectual ability – as in the case running a major company – the rates are high and rightly so. This argument was also employed by the Conservatives in the 1980s when they cut taxes for high earners. A corollary of this argument is that a hierarchy of reward stimulates effort: if someone desires advancement in the form of riches or status they are prepared to work for it and strain every effort. In the USA this is part of the so-called 'American Dream' whereby immigrants often arrived with nothing except their clothes yet within a generation or two had accumulated large fortunes or won senior places in society. Similarly Sir Keith Joseph was making the same point when he stated the apparent paradox that for 'the poor to become richer, we have to make society more unequal'.

Finally, right-wing polemicists claim that remedial intervention by the state is implicitly tyrannical as it involves taking away from the able – sometimes through the law, backed up by force – some of their just rewards. They also point to the former communist regimes where 'equality' was imposed on society through the agency of an oppressive regime complete with police powers, work camps and punitive prison sentences.

Social justice

Justice is the right of the weakest
                    Joseph Joubert, Pensées, 1842

Who should get what in society? The left tend to favour an approach based on 'needs' and the right one based on 'rights' or 'desert'. In his book, *Modern Political Thought* (1991), Raymond Plant investigates this by positing the problem of the just distribution of one hundred oranges in a society of one hundred people. The obviously fair approach, especially if all members have been involved in the production process, is to give one orange to each person. However, if some people have a particular physical need for vitamin C, then the question arises whether their needs justify an unequal distribution. Maybe these special needs people need two each? Or three or even more? This is the kind of debate social justice discussions stimulate and it obviously has wider implications for the way in which income and wealth are distributed together with other material goods like welfare benefits, taxation, housing, and so forth.

Karl Marx declared that in a communist society the principle of material distribution would be: 'From each according to his ability, to each according his needs!' A charming fictional version of what life might be like in a truly socialist society is found in William Morris's novel *News from Nowhere* (1891; see Morris, 1993), in which the main character finds himself in a future socialist England in which money has been abolished, people work happily for the community and take what they need for basic consumption and leisure purposes. In reality this utopian vision would probably remain a mere vision, but some vestige of its moral force still informs current thinking on the left.

At the heart of this notion of social justice is that large accumulations of wealth, juxtaposed by poverty and ill health, are not justifiable. It follows, according to this approach, that wealth should be redistributed in society and, indeed, between nations. On the other hand, even left-wing theorists agree that some economic inequality is necessary to make the economic system work, so the real debate is how much redistribution is needed to achieve justice?

One influential thinker on the left has been John Rawls, whose book *A Theory of Justice* (1971) has occasioned much debate. He asked us to consider what distribution of goods we would endorse if we were rational people planning a society but, crucially, were unaware of our own capacities. In this way it would be possible to prevent people from favouring their own talents and strengths, for example preventing a clever person from advocating a meritocracy or a physically strong person a free-for-all society. This ensures that any decisions reached would be neutral. Rawls argues that all would agree on the greatest possible degree of liberty in which people would be able to develop their talents and life plans. In addition, however, Rawls posits the 'difference principle' whereby he maintains that social and economic inequalities – differences in wealth, income and status – are only just if they work to the advantage of most disadvantaged members of society and only if they can be competed for fairly by all. Rawls argues that in such a situation rational people would choose, through a sense of insecurity, a society in which the position of the worst-off is best protected; this would be a market economy in which wealth is redistributed through tax and welfare systems up to the point when it becomes a disincentive to the economic activity.

Right-wing theorists tend to ignore this notion of needs, indeed the very notion of social justice is denied by some (e.g. Friedrich Hayek). The right tend to favour 'rights'-based approaches, for example the fact that someone has made an artefact endows a property right upon the craftsman/woman. Similarly if a person has bought something, the same right is presumed to be in place as money can be seen as an symbolic exchange for labour. Work, or the exercise of talent, is held to establish a right to material reward; 'Well, he's earned it' is often said about wealthy hard-working people. Alternatively if someone is rich through unusual talent, as a writer maybe or an exceptional entertainer, the usual response is that 'he's worth it'. Robert Nozick (1974) has been an influential theorist on the right, arguing that wealth is justifiable if it is justly acquired in the first place – for example has not been stolen – and has been justly transferred from one person to another. He goes on to argue that if these conditions have not been met the injustice should be rectified. Nozick rejects the notion of 'social justice' or the idea that inequality is somehow morally wrong. If transfers of wealth take place between one group in society and another, it should be on the basis of private charity, made on the basis of personal choice. But Nozick's views do not necessarily bolster right-wing views on property as the rectification principle could imply the redistribution of much wealth, especially when it is considered that so much of the wealth of the West has been won at the expense of plunder and slavery in Third World countries.

Right-wing thinkers are also attracted by Social Darwinism. Herbert Spencer (see Spencer 1982) argued that material circumstances were merely the reflection of differing innate abilities and talents: people are rich because they are more able than others and therefore deserving of reward. In his view this reflected the 'natural' order of things and as such should not be disturbed. He also believed it was wrong to intervene to assist people who had fallen on hard times: 'If we protect people from the consequences of their own folly we will people the world with fools.'

Rights

Rights that do not not flow from duties well performed are not worth having.

    Mohandas K. Ghandi, *Non-Violence in Peace and War*,
1948

Human 'rights' embodies the idea that every human has certain basic entitlements, and gives rise to a number of questions:

1. What is the basis of these rights? Are they legal?

Some are embodied in the law but others are not.

2. Are they related to religious ideas?

To some extent but not necessarily.

3. What are the sources of human rights?

Their origins lie more in moral than political philosophy. They were implicit in the notion of the social contract, popular in the seventeenth century and revived in a singular form by Rawls in the 1970s, as mentioned above. Before the seventeenth century political ideas were dominated by God and feudalism. All authority was vested in the monarch, sanctioned by God via the 'divine right of kings' theory. There were no thoughts of individuals having any rights

beyond those invested by the law. Hobbes' theory was so unorthodox as it rested on the notion of a contract between individuals and the state whereby allegiance was given in exchange for protection from the anarchic disorder of an ungoverned society. However, if the state failed in its duty of providing protection then the obligation of citizens would 'last as long, and no longer, than the power by which he is able to protect them'. In other words, according to Hobbes, citizens retain a right of independence even under an all-powerful ruler. This notion of a social contract and fundamental rights was revolutionary in his time; it gathered strength during the century and in the thought of John Locke became a means whereby 'equal and independent people' in a state of nature could decide whether or not 'by their own consent to make themselves part of some political society'. It followed that: everyone had rights independent of the state; and the authority of the government depended on the consent of the governed. Nearly a century later – 1776 – these ideas were neatly and wonderfully summarised in the American Declaration of Independence:

We hold these truths to be self-evident, that all men are created equal, that they are endowed by their creator with certain unalienable rights, that among these are Life, Liberty and the pursuit of Happiness. That to secure these rights, Governments are instituted among men, deriving their just powers from the consent of the governed.

There is a clear distinction to be made between moral and legal rights. Legal or 'positive' rights are included in the law and can be enforced in the courts. Such rights can be a right to do something should one choose – like walk on the highway; or a right not to be treated in a certain way – like not be the victim of violence; or they can be the empowering right to vote in an election. In Britain basic rights like freedom of speech and worship are not enshrined in law; but instead they are not excluded – so are therefore allowed. In contrast, in the USA such rights are included in the constitution and are more easily defended (though similar legal safeguards in despotic regimes, like the former USSR, have not protected human rights). Internationally human rights are held to exist as the basic conditions for a tolerable human existence. The United Nations issued its Universal Declaration of Human Rights, which 'set a common standard of achievement for all peoples and all nations'. Similar declarations exist in relation to economic, social and cultural rights. The European Union has its own set of declarations along very similar lines. Interestingly the European Convention has been the source of rulings made by virtue of British membership of the EU, which have over-ruled domestic law, as in the case of corporal punishment in schools. These international organisations have been very important in advancing the cause of human rights as they have brought them to the attention of transgressing and law-abiding nations alike.

As in the case of freedom and justice, there is a familiar left–right dichotomy over rights which relate to the operation of the economy. The right tend to stress 'negative' rights: the right to be left alone, not to be imprisoned or attacked by the state. The left stress 'positive rights', like the UN's 'right to work' (Article 23), and 'right to education' (Article 26). Such rights are denied by the right; this conflict can also be seen in the Labour Party's adherence to the Social Chapter of the Maastricht Treaty and the Conservatives' opposition to it.

Some thinkers champion animal rights. Logically, if humans have rights by virtue of being alive, then other forms of life must have rights too. This makes vegetarianism a difficult philosophy to refute. True, animals cannot think and express themselves, but their very helplessness offers a reason why humans should protect and not exploit them through killing and eating them. The Animal Liberation Front feels especially strongly about experiments inflicted upon animals for medical, or, much worse, cosmetic research.

Chapter summary

A concept is like a lens placed in front of one's

perception of the world and can be descriptive and normative. Many key concepts are interpreted differently according to the political perspective (see Figure 7.1 for summary of left and right versions of key concepts). Power is a crucial organising concept used in analysing why people do the bidding of politicians, and authority is essentially power plus legitimacy.

Discussion points

- In what ways does the study of concepts tell us more about political ideas than approaches based on looking at different ideologies?
- Of the seven concepts studied in this chapter, which three are the most central to the study of politics?
- Is the left-wing interpretation of concepts more defensible than that of the right?

Further reading

The best book on political concepts is Andrew Heywood's simply excellent *Political Ideas and Concepts* (1994). Also very useful is Plant (1991), Russell (1965) and Plamenatz (1963).

References

Brownmiller, S. (1975) *Against Our Will: Men, Women and Rape* (Simon and Schuster).

Freud, S. (1963) *Civilisation and its Discontents* (Hogarth Press; first published 1930).

Green, T. H. (1988) *Works*, ed. R. Nettleship (Oxford University Press; first published 1911).

Heywood, A. (1994) *Political Ideas and Concepts* (Macmillan).

Locke, J. (1956) *The Second Treatise on Government*, ed. J. Gough (Blackwell; first published 1690).

Michels, R. (1949) *Political Parties* (Free Press).

Morris, W. (1993) *News from Nowhere* (Penguin; first published 1891).

Nozick, R. (1974) *Anarchy, State and Utopia* (Blackwell).

Plant, R. (1991) *Modern Political Thought* (Blackwell).

Rawls, J. (1971) *A Theory of Justice* (Harvard University Press).

Rousseau, J.-J. (1913) *The Social Contract and Discourses* (Dutton; first published 1762).

Spencer, H. (1982) *The Principles of Ethics*, ed. T. Machan (Liberty Classics; first published 1887).

Tawney, R. H. (1969) *Equality* (Allen and Unwin).

Left		Right
Optimistic	Human nature	Pessimistic
Positive	Freedom	Negative
Direct	Democracy	Indirect
Equality of outcome	Equality	Equality of opportunity
Needs	Social justice	Deserts
Positive	Rights	Negative
Interventionist	State	Minimal

Figure 7.1 Concepts and ideology

CHAPTER EIGHT

Political ideas: the major parties

BILL JONES

LEARNING OBJECTIVES

- To explain the provenance of Conservatism and the ideology of capitalist free enterprise; explain the difference between 'one nation' and neo-liberal Conservatism; assess the impact of Margaret Thatcher on her party's ideas.

- To trace the origins of Labour thinking to the rejection of nineteenth-century capitalism; its maturing into corporate socialism and revisionism plus the left-wing dissenters in the 1970s and 1980s; to analyse the impact of Labour's rapid move into the centre and the apparent embrace of neo-Thatcherite ideas by Tony Blair.

- To sum up the message of the Liberal Party over the years including its alliance with the SDP and its evolution into the Liberal Democrats.

INTRODUCTION

In the aftermath of the Second World War some commentators felt that the two major political parties in Britain were 'converging' ideologically. Daniel Bell, the American sociologist, wrote of 'the end of ideology' and in the 1970s a post-war 'consensus' was discerned between the two parties on the desirability of a welfare state and a mixed economy. Britain's relative economic decline inclined both parties to adopt more radical remedies which drew upon their ideological roots. Margaret Thatcher swung the Conservatives violently to the right whilst Labour swung radically to the left in the early 1980s. Once Thatcher had gone, Major adopted a less overtly ideological stance, whilst Labour, following the failed experiment of Foot as leader, successively under Kinnock, Smith and Blair has moved rapidly into the centre. This chapter analyses the evolution of the ideas of the major parties and traces the most recent changes.

"The language of politics is now a Conservative language…. It is we who have changed the whole thrust of politics and moved it in our direction.

John Major, Conservative

We live in a world of dramatic change and the old ideologies that have dominated the last century do not provide the answers.   *Tony Blair, Labour*

We are beginning to see the break-up of the two great monoliths that dominate British politics.

Paddy Ashdown, Liberal Democrat

Whether you are from the left, right or centre, it is your country, your future and it should be your choice.

Sir James Goldsmith, Referendum Party"

The Conservative Party

Key elements

Conservatism has a long history stretching back before its formal emergence in the 1830s. Critics have doubted whether the party has ever possessed a coherent philosophy, and indeed Lord Hailsham (1959) has described it as a not so much a philosophy as an attitude. However, it is possible to discern a number of key tenets upon which this attitude and Conservative policies have been based:

1. *The purpose of politics is social and political harmony*: Conservatives have traditionally believed that politics is about enabling people to become what they are or what they wish to be. They believe in a balance, a harmony in society. They have avoided too much ideological baggage in favour of measured pragmatism which has always kept options open. Like Edmund Burke, they have tended to believe that 'all government … is founded on compromise'.

2. *Human nature is imperfect and corruptible*: This notion of 'original sin' lies at the heart of Conservatism, leading its supporters to: doubt the altruism of humankind beyond close family; perceive most people as more interested in taking rather than giving; and see them as fairly easy to corrupt without the external disciplining force of strong government.

3. *The rule of law is the basis of all freedom*: Law restricts freedom yet without it there would be no freedom at all, but – given humanity's selfish, aggressive nature – anarchic chaos. Accepting the authority of the law is therefore the precondition of liberty.

4. *Social institutions create a sense of society and nation*: Social and political institutions help to bind together imperfect human beings in a thing called society. Living together constructively and happily is an art and this can be learnt. At the heart of the learning process lies the family, and the institution of marriage. The royal family provides an idealised and unifying 'model' at a kind of micro-level. At the macro-level is the idea of the nation, ultimately a cause worth dying for.

5. *Foreign relations is the pursuit of state interests in an anarchic world*: States exhibit all the dangerous characteristics of individuals plus a few more even more unpleasant ones of their own. A judicious defence of national interests is the best guide for any country in the jungle of international relations.

6. *Liberty is the highest political end*: Individuals need freedom to develop their own personalities and pursue their destinies. Conservatives agree with Mill that it should entail freedom from oppression and extend until it encroaches upon the freedom of others. It should not embrace the 'levelling' of wealth, as advocated by socialists, as this redistribution would be imposed upon a reluctant population by the state (see also Chapter 6).

7. *Government through checks and balances*: 'Political liberty', says Lord Hailsham, 'is nothing else than the diffusion of power.' This means in practice institutions which divide power between them and all have a measure of independence and thus prevent any single arm of government from being over-mighty. Hailsham also argues that political factions should balance each other, each taking a turn at government rather than allowing it to be the preserve of one party alone.

8. *Property*: Conservatives, like David Hume, believe that the right to property is the 'first principle of justice' on which the 'peace and security of human society entirely depend'. Norton and Aughey (1981) take this further,

arguing that it is an 'education. It enlightens the citizens in the value of stability and shows that the security of small property depends upon the security of all property' (p. 34). The Conservative policy of selling council houses was in line with this belief in that it was assumed, probably rightly in this case, that people would cherish their houses more once they enjoyed personal ownership.

9. *Equality of opportunity but not of result*: Conservatives believe everyone should have the same opportunity to better themselves. Some will be more able or more motivated and will achieve more and accumulate more property. Thus an unequal distribution of wealth reflects a naturally unequal distribution of ability. Norton and Aughey maintain the party is fundamentally concerned with justifying inequality in a way which 'conserves a hierarchy of wealth and power and make[s] it intelligible to democracy' (p. 47). To do this, Conservatives argue that inequality is necessary to maintain incentives and make the economy work; equality of reward would reward the lazy as much as the industrious (see also Chapter 7).

10. *One nation*: Benjamin Disraeli, the famous nineteenth-century Conservative prime minister, added a new element to his party's philosophy by criticising the 'two nations' in Britain, the rich and the poor. He advocated an alliance between the aristocracy and the lower orders to create one nation. His advice was controversial and remains so.

11. *Rule by elite*: Conservatives believe the art of government is not given to all; it is distributed unevenly, like all abilities, and is carefully developed in families and outside it most commonly in good schools, universities and the armed forces.

12. *Political change*: Conservatives are suspicious of political change as society develops organically as an infinitely complex and subtle entity; precipitate change could damage irreparably things of great value. Therefore they distrust the system-builders like Marx, the root and branch reformers like Tony Benn. But they do not deny the need for all change; rather they tend to agree with the Duke of Cambridge that the best time for it is 'when it can be no longer resisted', or

with Enoch Powell that the 'supreme function of a politician is to judge the correct moment for reform'.

Impact of Thatcherism

This collection of pragmatic guides to belief and action was able to accommodate the post-war Labour landslide which brought nationalisation, the managed Keynesian economy, close cooperation with the trade unions and the welfare state. The role of Harold Macmillan was crucial here. In the 1930s he wrote *The Middle Way*, a plea for a regulated *laissez-faire* economy which would minimise unemployment and introduce forward planning into the economy. He was able to accept many of the reforms introduced by Labour and reinterpret them for his own party.

The post-war consensus continued with little difference over domestic policy between Macmillan and Gaitskell, Wilson and Heath. But when the economy began to fail in relation to competitors in the late 1960s and early 1970s a hurricane of dissent began to blow up on the right of the Conservative Party – and the name of the hurricane was Margaret Thatcher. She had no quarrel with traditional positions on law, property and liberty, but she was passionately convinced of a limited role for government (though not necessarily a weak one); she wanted to 'roll back' the socialist frontiers of the state. She was uninterested in checks and balances but wanted to maximise her power to achieve the things she wanted. She was opposed to equality and favoured the inequalities caused by a dynamic economy. She had scant respect for the aristocracy as she admired only ability and energy, qualities she owned in abundance. She was not in favour of gradual change but wanted radical alterations now, in her lifetime. She was a revolutionary within her own party and it has still not stopped reverberating from her impact.

Thatcherite economics

1. Margaret Thatcher was strongly influenced by Keith Joseph who was in turn influenced by the American economist Milton Friedman. He urged that to control inflation it was merely necessary to control the supply of money and credit circulating in the economy.

2. Joseph was also a disciple of Friedrich Hayek, who believed that freedom to buy, sell and employ, i.e. economic freedom, was the foundation of all freedom. Like Hayek, he saw the drift to collectivism as a bad thing: socialists promised the 'road to freedom' but delivered instead the 'high road to servitude'.

3. Hayek and Friedman agreed with Adam Smith that if left to themselves, market forces – businessmen using their energy and ingenuity to meet the needs of customers – would create prosperity. To call this 'exploitation' of the working man, as socialists did, was nonsense as businessmen were the philanthropists of society, creating employment, paying wages, endowing charities. When markets were allowed to work properly they benefited all classes and everyone.

4. Thatcher believed strongly that state intervention destroys freedom and efficiency through: taking power from the consumer – the communist 'command' economies were inefficient and corrupt; protecting employment through temporary and harmful palliatives; controlling so much of the economy that the wealth-producing sector becomes unacceptably squeezed.

5. Trade unions were one of Thatcher's *bêtes noires*. She saw them as undemocratic, reactionary vested interests which regularly held the country to ransom in the seventies. She was determined to confront and defeat them.

6. She believed state welfare to be: expensive; morally weakening in that it eroded the self-reliance she so prized; and monopolistic, choice-denying and less efficient than private provision.

7. Her defence of national interests was founded in a passionate patriotism which sustained her support for the armed forces and the alliance with the USA. During the Falklands War she showed great composure and courage in taking risks and ultimately triumphing. The reverse side of this was her preference for the US link over the European Union, which she suspected of being a Trojan horse for German plans to dominate the whole continent.

Margaret Thatcher therefore drove a battering ram through traditional Conservatism but it was in effect a return to the Classical Liberalism of the early/mid-nineteenth century (see Chapter 6). Andrew Heywood (see Further Reading) discerns another thread in Thatcherism, that of Neo-Conservatism, a pre-Disraelian emphasis on duty, responsibility, discipline and authority; a reaction to the permissiveness of the 1960s, the defining decade of post-war socialistic culture. Many claimed to have been converted to her ideas but the 1980s witnessed a tough internal battle, which the prime minister finally won, between her and the so-called 'wet' wing of the party, which still hearkened back to the 'one nation' variety of the party's creed.

When John Major succeeded her following the virtual 'coup' in November 1990, many thought he would be the best hope of stern and unbending Thatcherism, but he seemed much more conciliatory, more concerned with achieving unity even at the cost of compromise, a very un-Thatcherite course of action. As the years passed by, however, it became apparent that this initial analysis is far away from what happened. Major's government was almost wholly circumscribed by the ideas of his predecessor. As Andrew Heywood has pointed out, the Major government accepted her ideas; there was no conflict with 'wets' and even Heseltine, Clarke and Patten accepted the supremacy of markets by the mid-1990s. But he took her ideas further even than she dared in her day, privatising British Rail and introducing the market principle into many hitherto forbidden areas of the welfare state.

Heywood points out that the changes have been in style rather than substance. In the 1980s Thatcherism adopted a 'heroic' mode, smashing socialism and the power of the trade unions; it was like a continuous war or revolution as the Prime Minister tried to change 'the hearts and minds of the nation'.

Major replaced that style with a 'managerial' version. However, he also added another element: a return to Neo-Conservatism with a renewed emphasis on morality ('the back to basics' campaign), obligation and citizenship. Conservatives have long been worried by the downside of market forces: growing inequality, the emergence of an underclass, insecurity at work and the loss of the 'feelgood factor'. There was a feeling in the mid-1990s that the nation's social fabric was in dire need of repair. Added to this market individualism plus Neo-Conservatism has been a shift towards a 'Little Englandism'. Most commentators do not believe

Major is this kind of politician by instinct but he was forced to adjust his position on Europe quite drastically by the determined Euro-sceptic minority, elevated in the early 1990s, through the disappearance of the Conservatives' overall majority, into a position of great influence and potential power.

Major was criticised for being too weak on ideology and a poor leader. The *Sun* editorials attacked him as showing 'poor judgement and weak leadership'. Lord Rees-Mogg, a pillar of the right-wing establishment, has written: 'He is not a natural leader, he cannot speak, he has no sense of strategy or direction.' Kenneth Clarke frankly stated that when he was first mooted as leader he thought him 'a nice bloke but not up to the job'. Norman Lamont applied the cruellest cut when he said the government gave the 'impression of being in office but not in power'. Major's predecessor wrote in her memoirs that he was prone to compromise and to be 'drifting with the intellectual tide'.

Losing Conservative themes

> The truth is that the European debate will not subside. It is at the heart of our economic and constitutional traditions. It will proceed into the next parliament with a vitality that challenges loyalties.
>
> *John Biffen, The Guardian, 17 February 1996*

We are unpopular, above all, because the middle classes – and all those who aspire to join the middle classes – feel that they no longer have the incentives and opportunities they expect from a Conservative government.

Margaret Thatcher's attack on 'one nation' Conservatism, 11 January 1996

The Labour Party and socialism

Socialism

Socialism developed as a critique and alternative to capitalism and its political expression, Conservatism. It focused on economics as the key activity, but the full sweep of its message provided guidance on virtually all aspects of living. Perhaps the clearest statement of the idea is still provided in Robert Tressell's *Ragged Trousered Philanthropists* (1965), when the hero, Owen, addresses his scornful workmates on the subject by drawing an oblong in the dust with a charred stick to represent the adult population of the

country: 'all those who help consume the things produced by labour'. He then divides the oblong up into five to represent five classes of people:

1. *All those who do nothing*, e.g. tramps, beggars and the aristocracy.
2. *All those engaged in mental work* which benefits themselves and harms others, e.g. employers, thieves, bishops, capitalists.
3. *All those engaged in unnecessary work* 'producing or doing things which cannot be described as the necessaries of of life or the benefits of civilisation'. This is the biggest section of all, e.g. shop assistants, advertising people, commercial travellers.
4. *All those engaged in necessary work* producing the 'necessaries, refinements and comforts of life.'
5. *The unemployed.* (Figure 8.1)

Underneath the oblong he then draws a small square which, he explains, is to represent all the goods produced by the producing class: group four. The crucial part comes next: how are all these goods shared out under the 'present imbecile system'?

As the people in divisions one and two are universally considered to be the most worthy and deserving we give them – two-thirds of the whole. The remainder we give to be 'Shared out' amongst the people represented by divisions three and four.

(Tressell, 1965[1914], p. 272).

Owen then proceeds to point out that it is groups three and four which battle most ferociously for their third while 'most of the people who do nothing get the best of everything. More than three quarters of the time of the working class is spent making things used by the wealthy.'

Despite his eloquence, Owen's workmates are reluctant to listen, so, as playwright Alan Sillitoe observes in his introduction to the 1965 edition, he calls them:

philanthropists, benefactors in ragged trousers who willingly hand over the results of their labour to the employers and the rich. They think it the natural order of things that the rich should exploit them, that 'gentlemen' are the only people with the right to govern. (p. ii)

Towards the end of the book another character, Barrington, orates his vision of a socialist society: nationalisation of land, railways and most forms of production and distribution; the establishment of

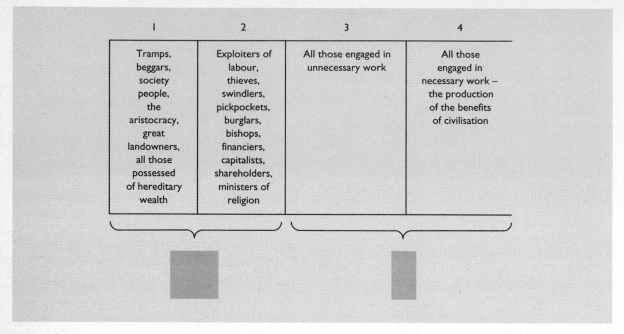

Figure 8.1   How the things produced by people in division 4 are 'shared out' among the different classes of the population
Source: Tressell, 1965[1914]

community culture and leisure facilities; the ending of unemployment; the abolition of the now redundant police force; equal pay; good homes for all; automation of industry and consequent reduction of the working day to four or five hours; free education to 21 and retirement at full pay at 45; and the ending of military conflict worldwide.

This classic account of socialism issues from a fundamental set of assumptions; provides a critique of capitalism and its related ideology; and offers a superior form of society as an achievable objective.

Critique of capitalism

Socialism asserted that capitalism 'exploited' the working masses by selling the fruits of their labour, taking the lion's share of the revenue and paying only subsistence wages. This produced huge disparities in income and disparities between the suburban living rich and the urban-based poor. Because the ruling capitalists dominate all the institutions of the state they subtly intrude their values into all walks of life and a complex web of mystifications produce a 'false consciousness' (see Box 5.3, p. 63) in which the

working class believe wrongly their best interests are served by supporting capitalist values. Capitalist championing of 'individualism' and 'freedom' are mere cloaks for the exploitation of the weak by the strong. The ruthlessness of the system induces a similar quality in society. Wage labour merely relieved employers of their obligations to their workers. By living in large urban settlements working men were alienated from each other whilst the automating of industry denied workers their creative satisfaction. A final criticism is that capitalism with its booms and slumps is inevitably inefficient and inferior to a planned economy. Two large antagonistic classes of populace emerge in capitalist societies: a small wealthy ruling class and a large impoverished proletariat living in the city.

Underlying principles of socialism

Socialism developed out of this critique of nineteenth century capitalism. The principles underlying the new creed included the following:

1. ***Human nature is basically good***: only capitalism distorts it.

2. *Environment creates consciousness*: A superior environment will create a superior kind of person.
3. *Workers create the wealth*: They should receive the full fruits of their effort.
4. *Equality*: The strong should not impose themselves on the weak.
5. *Freedom*: The poor need more resources to be truly free.
6. *Collectivism*: Social solidarity should take the place of selfish individualism.

The Labour Party

Labour in power

Labour held power briefly in the 1920s and began to formulate a more pragmatic and less incoherent version of socialism. During the 1930s and the war years socialist thinkers like Hugh Dalton (1887–1962) and Herbert Morrison (1888–1965) developed what has since been called 'corporate socialism' comprising:

1. *Keynesian economics*: Management of the economy, using investment to cure slumps and squeeze out unemployment.
2. *Centralised planning of the economy*: this was the corollary of the Keynesian approach; it had worked brilliantly during the war and would do the same for the peace, promised Labour.
3. *Nationalisation*: Morrison devised this approach based on bringing an industry out of private and into public control via a board accountable to Parliament. Once in power Labour nationalised 20 per cent of the economy, including the major utilities; established the National Health Service and expanded universal social services into a virtual 'welfare state'.
4. *Mixed economy*: The extent of nationalisation was not defined but, unlike the Soviet command economies, it was intended to maintain a private sector, albeit one subordinate to the public.
5. *Social services*: An expansion of existing support services for the needy – the young (education), the poor (benefits), the old (pensions) and the sick (health service) – was envisaged.
6. *Socialist foreign policy*: The trauma of two world wars convinced Labour a new approach was needed based on disarmament and international collective security. The USSR proved resistant to fraternal overtures from a fellow left-wing government and ultimately Labour's combative Foreign Secretary, Ernest Bevin (1881–1952), was forced to attract the USA into the NATO alliance.

Revisionism

Some Labour intellectuals – such as Hugh Gaitskell (1906–63), Hugh Dalton (1887–1962), Roy Jenkins (1920–), Denis Healey (1917–) and, most importantly, Anthony Crosland (1918–77) – were not content, like Morrison, to declare that 'socialism is what the Labour government does'; they looked for a new direction after the huge achievements of Clement Attlee (1883–1967) and his government. Crosland's book, *The Future of Socialism* (1956) asserted that: Marx's predictions of capitalist societies polarising before revolutions established left-wing governments had been proved wrong; the working class had been strengthened by full employment and the business class tamed by the achievments of socialism. Crosland argued that the ownership of the economy was no longer relevant as salaried managers were now the key players. He attacked another sacred cow by maintaining that nationalisation was not necessarily the most effective road to socialism and that other forms of collective ownership were more effective. He concluded that Labour should now concentrate its efforts on reducing inequality through progressive taxation and redistributive benefits and class differences through ending selection in education.

In practice revisionism was Labour's policy for the next thirty years, but when in government in the 1970s its fatal flaw was exposed: it was dependent on an expanding economy, and when this fell into decline cuts in public expenditure became inevitable.

The left wing of the party never accepted revisionism and first Aneurin (Nye) Bevan, then Michael Foot opposed the new drift towards a diluted ideology. In the 1960s Wilson defied the left in the parliamentary party, but when it teamed up with the trade unions trouble was in store for the 1970s administrations under both Wilson and Callaghan. Led by Tony Benn, the left now offered an alternative economic strategy based on: workers' control;

BOX 8.1	*e.g.*	EXAMPLE

The brief, eventful life of the Social Democratic Party

On 1 August 1980, Shirley Williams, David Owen and William Rodgers published an open letter to the Labour Party in *The Guardian*: the famous 'Gang of Three' statement. It followed in the wake of Roy Jenkins' Dimbleby Lecture, in which he had suggested a new party might 'break the mould' of British politics. Members of the 'gang' had opposed previous proposals on the grounds that a centre party would 'lack roots and a coherent philosophy'; they warned, however, that if Labour's drift to the left continued, they would have to reconsider their position.

After the Wembley Conference in January 1981, which pushed through measures strenghtening the control of left-wing party activists over the election of the leadership and the reselection of MPs, the three ex-Cabinet ministers joined Jenkins in creating the Social Democratic Party (SDP). Over the ensuing months some twenty to thirty centre-right Labour MPs made the journey over to the new party, plus a fair number of peers and other figures, not forgetting the solitary Conservative MP.

The Guardian article had called for a 'radical alternative to Tory policies ... rejecting class war, accepting the mixed economy and the need to manage it efficiently'. The SDP fought the 1983 election in tandem with the Liberals, gaining 26 per cent of the vote, but their high hopes were dashed in 1987 when they only mustered 22 per cent. The resultant merger negotiations split the SDP into 'Owenite' and 'mergerite' camps and appeared to disperse finally the heady optimism which had attended its birth.

During its brief life, did the SDP truly offer a 'radical alternative'? Certainly SDP members elaborated on *The Guardian* manifesto in a spate of articles and books. Shirley Williams in *Politics is for People* drew heavily upon the ideas of Robert Owen and Tawney, whilst Owen's *Face the Future* drew upon Mill, William Morris and G.D.H. Cole. Both authors acknowledged their debts to the Fabians and Anthony Crosland.

The SDP was formed in a blaze of publicity and 'breaking the mould' rhetoric, but a genuine alternative was probably not on offer. In one sense its message represented an amalgam of policies picked up across the political spectrum. Decentralisation was close to the Liberal, Bennite and Green position; SDP views on the market economy and trade unions were close to Margaret Thatcher's position – she actually praised Owen for being 'sound' on both; and on social policy and defence the SDP was close to the position of the Callaghan government to which the SDP leaders had once belonged. This is not to say the SDP lacked a carefully worked out and detailed programme; merely that it lacked a distinctive alternative or even radical quality. History will judge the SDP as a party of protest with a limited appeal outside the middle classes.

When its twelve-point plan was announced in March 1981, *The Times* concluded that this 'new beginning' was no more than a modern version of 'Butskellism' which was 'seeking essentially to bring that consensus up to date'. In other words, the SDP was merely developing Labour revisionist policies free of the political and rhetorical restrictions caused through working within the Labour Party. In Samuel Beer's (1982) view: 'What had happened was quite simple: the Labour Party had been a socialist party ... [and] many of its adherents ceased to believe in socialism.'

In August 1980 the Gang of Three had written that a 'Centre Party ... would lack roots and a coherent philosophy'. The final irony of the SDP is that its leaders succeeded in writing its obituary before its birth had even taken place.

extended state control of the economy; participatory democracy at all levels of national life; fresh injections of funds into the welfare state; encouragement of extra-parliamentary activity; and unilateral abandonment of nuclear weapons. The revisionist leadership tried to ignore the left but when the 1979 election was lost to a new and militantly ideological leader, Margaret Thatcher, the left insisted that a similar return to the roots of socialist ideology was necessary. With the revisionist leadership defeated and discredited, the left made its move, managing to impose its candidate, Michael Foot, as leader in 1980, plus a radically left-wing set of policies on the party which resulted in the 1983 manifesto being dubbed by Gerald Kaufman 'the longest suicide note in history'. More significantly the left's ascendancy led to the defection of an important wing of the party to form the Social Democratic Party which split the anti-Tory vote and helped keep Thatcher in power for a decade.

Neil Kinnock, elected as Foot's successor, was a child of the left but soon recanted, dismissing its prescriptions as 'Disneyland thinking'. He assiduously began to nudge his party towards the centre ground via a series of policy reviews which essentially accepted the 'efficiency and realism' of the market as the best model of economic organisation. It was implicit in this new analysis – though hotly denied – that socialism was no longer relevant, and even the word disappeared from policy documents and manifestos. When he lost the crucial 1992 election, he resigned and John Smith continued this 'desocialising' work. When Smith died tragically of a heart attack in May 1994, Tony Blair was elected leader and soon placed his stamp on a party denied power for nearly fifteen years.

BOX 8.2   DAVID OWEN (1938–)   **BIOGRAPHY**

By courtesy of Popperfoto/Reuter

Dr David Owen trained as a doctor, becoming Labour MP for Plymouth in 1966. After a spell as junior minister he became Minister of State at Health and Social Security (1976–8) moving on to the Foreign Office the following year. In 1977 he became the youngest Foreign Secretary for over forty years. Always to the right of the parliamentary party, he became infuriated at the control exerted by the left after the Thatcherite victory in 1979. He joined with Shirley Williams and Bill Rodgers in proposing a pro-European moderate socialism but soon joined up with Roy Jenkins to form the Social Democratic Party in 1981. He took over as leader from Jenkins in 1983 but won few friends with his insensitive, arrogant style. When David Steel suggested a merger of the two centre parties in 1987, Owen refused and took a small section of the party into a reconstituted SDP, but this vehicle for a single politician's ambition folded ignominiously in 1990. During the war occasioned by the break-up of Yugoslavia (now) Lord Owen was given the task of negotiating peace for the European Union but his efforts were ultimately no more successful than any others.

Views by Labour leaders past and present

"As for Tony Blair, I still think, as I thought when I first met him, we're lucky to have him – both the Labour Party and the nation. He might have gone off and joined the Social Democrats and no-one would have heard of him again.   *Michael Foot, The Observer, 6 September 1996*

My view of Christian values has led me to oppose what I perceived to be a narrow view of self-interest that Conservatism – particularly in its modern, more right-wing form – represents.

Tony Blair, September, 1995"

Having already abandoned its former policies of opposition to the European Community/Union, unilateral nuclear disarmament and nationalisation, Blair shifted the party even further to the right by attacking the power of trade unions in the party. He waged a spectacularly successful war against the 'collective ownership' Clause Four in the party's constitution. Not content with this he nudged the party away from the social democratic heartland of full employment and welfare spending. This was because it was deemed the requisite taxation would never be endorsed by voters and recognised that the world's economy had changed. With modern technology the economy has become globalised so that flows of capital can break companies and even currencies in minutes. To maintain policies of high taxation risks massive withdrawals of capital from any economy contemplating such socialistic measures.

'New Labour' has effectively embraced the economic side of Thatcherism: tax cuts, low inflation, a market economy plus encouragement of entrepreneurial activity. Tony Blair has even felt able to praise aspects of Thatcher's legacy and to endorse some of them as worth keeping. He has tried to strike out, however, and devise some distinctive policies for his party. He has eschewed a major 'big' idea but has come up with a middling sized one instead, a 'stakeholder society'. This is the idea associated with the economist John Kay and Will Hutton, a columnist of *The Guardian* who has been aiming his thoughts at the Labour leadership for a number of years. The basic thinking here is that everyone, individuals and groups, should have some investment in society, everyone should feel part of their community at all levels, economic,

cultural and social. To the same end Blair wishes to encourage parental responsibility and social solidarity. The other biggish idea alighted on by Blair has been constitutional reform; Labour has embraced devolved assemblies for both Scotland and Wales plus reform of the House of Lords and a referendum on the electoral system. However, plans are vague and pitted with flaws, none more so than the unresolved so-called 'Mid-Lothian Question', whereby Scottish MPs would have the ability to vote on English issues but English MPs would not have the ability to reciprocate as the internally elected assembly would assume this role.

It is often said that Blair has moved Labour so far to the centre he is now even to the right of the 'one nation' Tories. Certainly his approach bears comparison with this strain of Conservatism and it must be significant that he has in the past used the phrase 'one nation' socialism.

The massive endorsement of New Labour in the election of 1 May 1997 was fulfilment of the strategy conceived and implemented by Tony Blair and his close collaborator Peter Mandelson to move the Labour Party into a position where it embraced the market economy and removed the fear of old style socialism felt by the middle class occupants of 'Middle England'. 'Blairism' is vaguely expressed and lends itself to wide interpretation but sceptical commentators wonder if he has a framework of belief strong enough to survive the vicissitudes of several years in office and to resist the atavistic influences of the union-based old Labour ideology.

The Liberal Democrats

After the war the Liberal Party continued to decline politically but still offered an alternative to voters in the centre of political ideas. At heart the party still adhered to the ideas of 'New Liberalism' covered in Chapter 6, with emphases upon: individual liberty, equality, a mixed economy, a developed welfare state and a reformed democratised system of government. Under the skilful leadership of Jo Grimond, Jeremy Thorpe and David Steel, the party survived the post-war decades but hardly prospered. And then in 1981 it joined forces with the breakaway SDP to form the Alliance. It was not difficult to unite on policies, which were very close, rather it was personalities who caused the foundering of this short-lived alliance. In 1987 the two elements of the alliance formally merged and fought the 1992 election as the Liberal Democrats. Its manifesto, *Changing Britain for Good*, called for a shift of power to the consumer and ordinary citizen, the development of worker shareholding, and a market economy in which the market is the 'servant and not the master'. In addition the party repeated the traditional call for reform of the voting system and devolution of power to the regions. Following the 1992 election its new leader, Paddy Ashdown (elected 1988), made steady progress, and the Liberal Democrats' policy of 'equidistance' between the two big parties was replaced by one of open cooperation. Iain McWhirter, writing in *The Observer* (17 April 1995), suggested, interestingly, that if indeed the Lib. Dems come to support a Labour government, they can find a role to the left of Labour, acting as its conscience on constitutional reform and the welfare state.

In 1996 a joint Labour/Lib. Dem. committee was set up to liaise on constitutional reform, a notoriously time-consuming set of proposals over which

---

BOX 8.3 THE BATTLEGROUND   **DEBATE**

Tory	**Labour**
Economy	
■ Maintain British opt-out on single currency.	■ Support single currency in principle, but no entry until real economies converge.
■ Bring spending below 40 per cent of GDP.	■ Introduce a growth and possibly a jobs creation target.
■ Move towards a 20p standard rate income tax band.	■ No tax rises, except possibly for the super rich.
■ Step by step privatisation of welfare state.	■ Bring £80bn welfare state programme down by welfare to work package.
Constitution	
■ Maintain constitution largely unchanged.	■ Scottish parliament within 3 years of election with tax raising powers. Set up Welsh Assembly.
■ Fend off greater powers for Brussels.	■ Remove voting rights of hereditary peers.
■ Introduce an elected assembly in Northern Ireland.	■ Introduce Freedom of Information Act.
■ Attack Labour for break-up of Britain.	■ Hold referendum on electoral system for Commons.
Values	
■ Individualism.	■ Community.
■ Freedom.	■ Rights balanced by duties.
■ Responsibility.	■ Meritocracy.
■ One Nation.	■ One Nation.
■ Attack labour hypocrisy.	■ Attack Tories as organised hypocrisy.

Source: The Guardian, 29 January 1996

Labour felt it wise to maximise agreement in case votes from the smaller party were needed.

The strong showing by the Liberal Democrats in the 1997 general election buttressed the claim of that party to be the *de facto* left-of-centre conscience of the new Blair order regarding constitutional reform and the nurturing of the welfare state, especially the educational system.

Chapter summary

Conservatism is more than mere pragmatism in the ruling interest but includes a concern for unity, harmony and balance in a society based on property, equal opportunity, elite rule and gradual change. Margaret Thatcher gave major prominence to the neo-liberal strand in Conservatism which stressed the primacy of markets in economics. Major returned to the rhetoric of 'one nation' Conservatism but contained the practice of Thatcherism. Labour began as a socialist party dedicated to the replacement of capitalism by a collectively owned economy, but in government translated this into nationalisation, a policy of doubtful success. In opposition during the 1980s it gradually shed its socialist clothes and donned those of the free market and restricted public spending: in effect a compromise with Thatcherism. Liberal Democrats inherited the New Liberal ideas to which they have added a disposition to work with the Labour Party in office.

Discussion points

- To what extent was Margaret Thatcher a Conservative?

- Did John Major contribute anything distinctive to Conservative thinking?

- Did Labour sell out its principles during the 1980s?

- Is there room for a distinctive third set of political ideas in Britain, and do the Lib. Dems offer them?

Further reading

I am grateful to Andrew Heywood for his lecture to the Politics Association Revision Week (April 1996) for some of the points included in this chapter. His book on *Political Ideologies* (1992) was also a valuable source, as was the similar book by Ian Adams (1993). Michael Foley's *Ideas that Shape Politics* (1994) is a useful collection of essays.

References

Crosland, C.A.R. (1956) *The Future of Socialism* (Cape).

Foley, M. (1994) *Ideas that Shape Politics* (Manchester University Press).

Norton, P. and Aughey, A. (1981) *Conservatives and Conservatism* (Temple Smith).

Tressell, R. (1965) *The Ragged Trousered Philanthropists* (Panther; first published 1914).

CHAPTER NINE

Political ideas: themes and fringes

BILL JONES

LEARNING OBJECTIVES

- To explain and put into context the themes of:
  - feminism;
  - nationalism;
  - environmentalism.

- To chart and elucidate the political fringe on the far left and far right.

INTRODUCTION

The first three chapters in this section looked at ideology, political concepts, and party political ideas. This fourth chapter addresses three major themes – feminism, nationalism and environmentalism – followed by the rarefied world of the political fringe.

Feminism

In 1980 a United Nations report stated:

While women represent 50 per cent of the world's population, they perform nearly two-thirds of all working hours, receive one-tenth of world income and own less than 1 per cent of world property.

Despite the existence of a worldwide feminist movement, the position of women has improved very slightly, if at all, since the dawn of feminism in the late eighteenth century. The rights of women were implicit in the recognition of the rights of 'men', but thinkers like Locke did not include women in their scheme of things. Rousseau did, however, and in 1792 Mary Wollstonecraft's *Vindi-cation of the Rights of Women* (see Wollstonecraft 1967) articulated their rights explicitly (see Box 9.1) just as the French Revolution was asserting the rights of oppressed people everywhere. Whether women were 'oppressed' or not was a moot point. Most men assumed that women existed to perform domestic roles: producing and rearing children and caring for their husbands as well as all the household chores. Probably most women would have agreed had they ever been thought important enough to be consulted. They had no possibility of pursuing careers, voting or participating in public life. Their consolation was the power they exercised through this domestic role, influencing their men-folk and maybe even dominating them behind the scenes. But the legal position of women at this time

BOX 9.1   MARY WOLLSTONECRAFT (1757–97)   BIOGRAPHY

By courtesy of the National Portrait Gallery, London

Mary Wollstonecraft was an Anglo-Irish writer and is often cited as the first modern feminist. At the age of 28 she wrote a semi-autobiographical novel, *Maria*. She moved to London to become the 'first of a new genus' of women, a full-time professional writer and editor specialising in women and children. She was closely associated with the group of radical reforming writers called the English Jacobins, where she met her future husband, the philosopher William Godwin. In her *Vindication of the Rights of Women* (1792) she argued for equal rights for women in society, especially regarding educational opportunities. Her daughter with Godwin was Mary Shelley, the author of *Frankenstein*.

was dire: they had no right to divorce (unlike their husbands); no right to marital property, and their husbands could beat them quite legally – even rape them should they wish. Moreover, men regularly used prostitutes whilst preaching fidelity for their wives and divorcing them when this failed to be upheld. In 'exchange' women were praised for their femininity, sensitivity and were idealised by the notion of romantic love. An unequal relationship indeed.

Emergent socialist ideas supported the position of women. Engels argued in his *Origin of the Family, Private Property and the State* (1884) that the prehistorical position of women had been usurped by men so that property now was passed on through the male line instead of the female because men wished to pass on property to their sons. The exploitative relationship between the propertied

class and the proletariat was mirrored within the family by the relationship between men and women. A socialist revolution would sweep away private property and remove the economic basis of the monogamous marriage.

During the nineteenth century the women's movement, such as it was, concentrated on gaining the vote, the belief being that once this citadel had fallen the other injustices regarding the imbalance of political and legal rights compared with men, would soon be remedied.

To an extent these early feminists were operating with the grain of history as the franchise for men was being progressively extended at this time. Nevertheless it took a bitter and militant struggle for the 'suffragettes', led by Emmeline and Christabel Pankhurst, to win through: in 1918 women received the vote but only if they fulfilled certain educational and property qualifications and were, bizarrely, over the age of 30! In 1928 they finally achieved equal political rights, but this did not automatically transform their position. The women's movement subsided for a number of decades but the impact of two world wars, where women played leading roles on the home front, advanced their claims for better treatment. Their purpose was to put an end to the discrimination in a male-dominated world resulting from the widespread male belief that women should look after the home and leave the important jobs to the men. Simone de Beauvoir's *The Second Sex* (1952) attacked the asymmetry whereby men were defined as free independent beings and women merely in terms of their relationships with men.

But the so-called 'second wave' of feminism began with Betty Friedan's *The Feminine Mystique* (1963). This major work rejected the myth that women were different and were happy being domestic adjuncts to men. Having nominally equal rights did not deliver real equality in a world controlled by men and discriminating against women. In the late 1960s and 1970s, the work of Germaine Greer (*The Female Eunuch*, 1971) and Kate Millett (*Sexual Politics*, 1969) moved the focus of debate from the wider world of career and public life to the micro-worlds which we all inhabit. Greer developed some of the ideas of Herbert Marcuse (1964, 1969a, 1969b), who argued that western society was sexually repressed. She suggested that women had absorbed the male idea of their sexuality as soft and yielding – a kind of sex image stereotype – whilst their true and possibly quite different nature was not allowed to be fulfilled. Concomitant with this went an assertion of lesbianism as a socially demonised activity. Instead of living out expected roles, Greer was insisting that people could be true to themselves, being 'male' or 'female' according to their own natures. Millett's emphasis was on how women are brainwashed into accepting a given image of themselves regarding their role and even their appearance. This image, according to her, was a reflection of 'patriarchy'; constructed by men with their interests in mind. What was attributed to gender roles was in fact no more than a socially constructed role which women were induced to accept from birth via a battery of socialising agencies, including family, tradition,

law, the media, and popular culture. Women were forced to accept a role of being gentle caring mother figures, whose job was to tend their men. Alternatively they were seen as whores and temptresses, equally subservient but this time more dangerous. Millett also directed attention at the family and home, pointing out that here was the most important arena in which the male controlled the key sexual relationship, dominating the female; it followed from this, in that key feminist phrase, that 'the personal is the political'.

In the 1970s it was observed that liberal feminists, who believed reform and a high degree of equality was possible in society as it is, coexisted with socialist feminists, who believed the main inequality was still between classes and not the sexes. They believed in major changes to the economy and society before women could be truly free. A third group soon emerged, the radical feminists. For them the problem lies not in society or the economy but in human nature, more precisely, male human nature. The problem with women, in other words, is men. In *The Dialectic of Sex* (1980, originally published 1971), Shulamith Firestone perceives a fundamental oppression of women by men in consequence of their biological role. Sex domination precedes and exceeds economic exploitation. What she advocates is a 'sexual revolution much larger than – inclusive of – a socialist one' to 'eradicate the tapeworm of exploitation'. She argues for a restructuring of society through science, whereby children would be produced artificially and looked after communally so that women's physical and psychological burdens would be removed and they would be free for the first time in history.

Susan Brownmiller – *Against our Will* (1975) – shifts the focus to the violence which men use to threaten women; the fear of rape is used to maintain male dominance and rapists act for all men in demonstrating the consequences of non-compliance. Other feminist writers, like Andrea Dworkin and Dale Spender – often called 'supremacists' – assert female moral superiority and argue that the world would be better if women were in control. Often this type of feminist will be separatist in relation to men; their lesbianism consequently has a political quality to it. For them men are not necessary for women and women who live with men are 'man identified' instead of being 'woman identified'.

BOX 9.2   **IDEAS AND PERSPECTIVES**

Sexual inequality at work

- The total number of women on the boards of major companies is 3.72 per cent.
- Women make up just 2.8 per cent of senior managers and 9.8 per cent of managers.
- The average female worker earns nearly 40 per cent less than the average male earner.

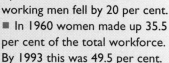

- Women managers earn 16 per cent less than their male counterparts.
- Between 1960 and 1990 the number of women working rose 34 per cent while the number of working men fell by 20 per cent.
- In 1960 women made up 35.5 per cent of the total workforce. By 1993 this was 49.5 per cent.

Source: The Guardian, 6 March 1995

It is often said that since the 1970s the women's movement has lost momentum. Certainly the tone has become milder; Greer (1985), and Friedan (1982) have both disappointed radicals by writing approvingly of domesticity and child-rearing. The New Right in the USA and UK, moreover, have reinforced 'traditional values' of women's roles and the desirability of marriage (and by implication the subversive effects of one-parent families) to hold society together. In their book *Contemporary Feminist Politics* (1993), Lovenduski and Randall applaud the progress made by the women's movement in permeating institutions and professions and in disseminating feminist values so effectively that they have become widely accepted as orthodoxies. However, they lament the failure to replace activists when they bow out of activity, and the internecine squabbling and fragmentation which has weakened the movement. The strong showing of women candidates in the 1997 election – they virtually doubled from 62 to 120, most of them Labour – cheered campaigners for more female representation and those who defended the special Labour measures to favour women candidates in winnable seats.

Nationalism

Nationalism derives from the view that the world is divided naturally into national communities, all of which have the right to independence and the right to govern themselves. Nations often, though not necessarily, coincide with state frontiers; the notion of 'national territory' is potent, often stimulating countries to resort to war in its defence or reacquisition. Argentina's military rulers attempted to win popularity by invading the 'Malvinas Islands', as they called the Falklands, in 1982, but were resisted and defeated by Britain, which defended the islands not essentially because they were part of the British state, but more for a mixture of pride, principle and political expedience.

States usually contain a dominant racial type, but most have minorities living within their borders too, either indigenous or immigrant. Well-established countries usually have a sense of 'community', a combination of shared history, language and culture. In these circumstances it is normal for citizens to share a patriotic love of their country, to feel a sense of duty towards it and, ultimately, a willingness to die for it.

This was not always the case. It was not unusual for people to feel strong attachments to their country, as far back as the Ancient Greeks and Romans. In Shakespeare's time patriotism was acknowledged in, for example, Henry V's stirring address at Harfleur ('Cry God for Harry, England and Saint George!'). But it was quite possible for royal houses to be 'borrowed' from other countries or imported by invitation, as in the case of William and Mary from Holland to Britain in 1689.

Modern nationalism, the notion that nations have the right to be in charge of their own destiny, was a product of the French Revolution. Here the liberal idea of natural rights, with its concomitant right of citizens to reject governments, was allied with Rousseau's idea of the General Will, that nations had a sense of what they wanted which could be interpreted and which endowed both freedom and 'sovereign' power: the first appearance of the idea that the will of the people was superior to any other, including the head of state and ruling class.

So the French, always patriotic and intensely proud of their country, acquired an additional mission: to carry the idea of national self-determination into the wider world. A further element was added through the Romantic movement in the late eighteenth century, which idealised national myths and heroes. In Germany Gottfried von Herder (1744–1803) attacked the tendency of the German ruling class to ape French customs and culture in an attempt to appear sophisticated. He believed a nation's language was the repository of its spirit, that it should be nurtured and artists working within it revered.

During the nineteenth century nationalism grew in two ways. Firstly, through nations developing the will to unite, as in the cases of Germany and Italy, and, secondly, within the large multinational empires of Austria-Hungary and Turkey. In 1848 a number of revolutions erupted based on emergent nationalism.

Towards the end of the century the major European powers embarked on a kind of 'super'-nationalism – imperialism – whereby they colonised huge tracts of Africa and Asia, extracting wealth and brutally denying the native populations the rights to self-determination they insisted upon for European peoples. Nationalism in Europe took on an ugly complexion, combining authoritarianism with ideas of racial superiority.

The emergent doctrine of socialism appeared initially to be the antithesis of nationalism when the Second International at Stuttgart in 1906 passed a resolution committing the working classes in the event of war to intervene to 'bring it promptly to an end'. And yet in the summer of 1914 the military machines of Europe proved firmer of purpose, more swift in motion than the ponderous political armies of socialism. One by one the major socialist parties accepted the *fait accompli* of the war and rallied to their respective national causes. On Saturday, 2 August over 100,000 British socialists demonstrated against the war, but on 15 October a Labour Party manifesto duplicated the Liberal view of the war as a struggle between democracy and military despotism. Shortly afterwards, Labour took its place in the wartime coalition government. Socialism had briefly stood up to nationalism but the result had been a pushover.

At Versailles in 1918 a number of states were invented (Czechoslovakia) or reinvented (Poland) as the notion of self-determination reached its high-water mark. But by this time the colonial possessions of the imperial powers had begun to imbibe some of the ideas of their masters and apply them to their own cases. In India and Africa independence movements began to emerge and gained much impetus when Europe was weakened by the Second World War, itself initiated by the murderously aggressive nationalism of Nazi Germany, supported by that of Italy as well as Japan. In its wake India gained its freedom (1947) and during the 1950s and 1960s the map of the British Empire was effectively rolled up as the anti-colonial 'wind of change' gathered force.

The establishment of the United Nations in 1945, followed by many other international organisations like the North Atlantic Treaty Organisation (NATO) and the Organisation of Petroleum Exporting Countries (OPEC) marked the advance of internationalism at the expense of nationalism. This was especially true of the European Economic Community, set up in the 1950s and rapidly perceived as spectacularly successful. However, nationalism is still very much a motivating force in world politics, and in places like the former Yugoslavia, Russia and the Middle East is capable of a virulent expression.

British people like to portray themselves as not especially nationalistic – theirs is a longstanding and confident union – but occasions like the Euro '96 soccer championships and other sporting events reveal the British to be as fervently supportive of their country as any other. Within British politics nationalism also has an important role to play.

Ireland

Ireland was joined to the United Kingdom by the Act of Union in 1800 but the marriage was far from happy given the background of exploitation and savage suppression of revolts by the British.

In 1922 Ireland won its independence, but the six counties in the north-east of the island remained part of the UK, dominated by the Protestant majority, which discriminated against the Catholic minority, many of whom supported a united Ireland and are often referred to as the 'Nationalists'. Negative feelings were reciprocated; the BBC correspondent Fergal Keene described in a radio broadcast (Radio 4, November 1996) how, as a Catholic child, he regarded Protestants as being as weird as any 'Martian'.

After decades of misrule the province exploded into violence in the late 1960s and has been a tragic source of conflict ever since. The 'peace process' (1994–6) promised to provide a negotiated solution between the nationalists under Gerry Adams and the Unionist representatives of the Protestants but violence broke out again in the summer of 1996. With the IRA still insisting on its policy of violence, its political wing, Sinn Fein, performed surprisingly well in the 1997 election, winning two seats.

Scotland

In 1707 Scotland merged with England and Wales, but before then was an independent nation-state and even when part of Britain retained its own legal and educational systems plus a proud sense of national identity. In 1934 John McCormick founded the Scottish National Party (SNP) as a response to alleged English indifference to Scottish economic needs. It has always sought independence from Westminster with continued membership of the Commonwealth. To maximise support it has tended to be no more than mildly left of centre and has concentrated on economic issues like demanding the alleged 'share' of North Sea oil to which Scotland was entitled.

Throughout the 1970s the SNP increased its electoral support and in 1992 it had three MPs (down from the seven it achieved in 1974, when it gained its highest share of the vote). In 1978 the referendum on devolution returned a majority in favour but not by the 40 per cent majority upon which its parliamentary opponents had insisted. The SNP vote benefited from the widspread collapse of the Conservative vote in Scotland in May 1997, harvesting three new seats, making six in all.

Labour's promise of a separate assembly for Scotland may well steal the thunder of the SNP as the Blair administration continues.

Wales

Welsh nationalism is more of the romantic cultural variety, concentrating on the health of the language as a major theme. Plaid Cymru draws it greatest support, unsurprisingly, from the Welsh-speaking parts of Wales: the rural areas of the north and the centre. Politically the movement is anti-Conservative and mildly to the left; less so now than when the party was overtly socialist but probably more so than Labour in 1997. The chief objective of the party is a national assembly for Wales, but it is interesting that when a referendum was held on this issue in 1978 the proposal was soundly defeated. At the 1997 election, Plaid Cymru's vote held up well and it retained its four MPs.

England

Whilst Welshmen and Scots and those from Northern Ireland have their own distinctive identity, most of them also feel themselves to be 'British', though – with the exception of Ulster Unionists – this is seldom an important issue. The key issue in the 1990s regarding English nationalism has been that of the European Union. When Margaret Thatcher was deposed in 1990, the issue which sparked off her fall from power was the EU and its alleged aim of increasing integration to the point where national identities would be threatened. A band of loyal followers kept alive her passionate opposition within the governing party and indeed forced Major to trim his position in their favour between 1994 and 1997. The Conservative Party has always sought to present itself as the 'patriotic', party and to outflank his Euro-sceptical critics Major adeptly shrouded himself in the Union Jack throughout 1996.

The split in the Conservative Cabinet in the run up to the 1997 election ran deep with Portillo, Lilley and Howard highly sceptical and others like Dorrell and Rifkind positioning themselves towards the Eurosceptics for possible post election leadership reasons. During the election campaign over 200 Conservative candidates declared publicly that they were opposed to the single currency, in violation of the official 'wait and see' policy. The wipe-out result for the Conservatives in the May election removed Portillo and other leading sceptics but left the parliamentary party still deeply split between supporters and opponents of closer European integration. Some wish the UK to withdraw completely; others wish it to pursue a more independent line, advancing national interests more aggressively; whilst still others fear the possible domination of Europe by its most powerful economy, Germany.

Labour also has dissenters to its basically pro-EU stance, but they are quieter and less numerous than the Conservatives. In November 1996, Labour, partly for tactical political reasons, announced it would hold a referendum before taking the country into a single currency. This policy shift brought the party into line with Sir James Goldsmith's generously funded single-issue Referendum Party, which ran against every candidate unwilling to support such a measure. Despite the sound and fury of an expensive campaign the Referendum Party polled only 800,000 votes, yet this did not stop it claiming to have assisted the demise of a number of leading Europhiles including its arch enemy David Mellor in Putney.

In a chapter of the *13th British Social Attitudes Survey*, Dowds and Young (1996) distinguish four sub-sets of attitudes on nationalism:

1. *Supranationalists* (20 per cent of respondents): This group wishes to include foreign influences ('inclusive') and is not high on 'national' sentiment like pride in national culture and heritage; likely to be educated, female, *Guardian* reading, Labour supporter.
2. *Patriots* (20 per cent): High on national sentiment but not so as to wish to exclude foreign influences ('exclusive'); likely to be well educated, attached to locality, likely to be *Daily Telegraph* readers and Conservative voters.
3. *John Bulls* (24 per cent): High on exclusion and national sentiment; attached to locality; *Mail* reading and Conservative voting.
4. *Belligerents* (17 per cent): High on exclusion; low on national sentiment; more likely to be male, authoritarian, not well educated, *Sun* reading.

According to the study, all four groups are more or less equally sized. The first two believe membership of the EU is beneficial but only the supranationalists favour full integration, and of them only 28 per cent supported a single currency. The authors conclude that, taken overall, the 'moderate line' on the EU, favoured by both major parties, of a 'pragmatic pursuit of national interests within the sturdy framework of national sovereignty, is the position of a beleaguered minority' (*The Guardian*, 21 November 1996).

So nationalism in Britain is still a powerful force, though it operates in very different ways. In Ireland it threatens the peace; in Wales it takes a cultural/language-based form; in Scotland it is more economic and concerned with identity. In England, forgetting Mebyon Kernow, which wants independence for Cornwall, and similar rumblings from Yorkshire, nationalism is more inward-looking, defending the status quo and consisting of hostility to Germany, fear of federalism, bureaucracy and old-fashioned suspicion of foreigners. Yet this English form of nationalism is no less powerful than that of the Celtic fringe; it reaches to the very heart of government, for years was responsible for a gaping chasm in the governing party and still defines deep fault lines in Labour and Conservatives.

Green thinking

The ecological perspective rejects philosophies of the right, left and centre as more similar than dissimilar. Jonathan Porritt characterises them collectively as 'industrialism'. This 'super-ideology', which is 'conditioned to thrive on the ruthless exploitation of both people and planet, is itself the greatest threat we face.' Conservatives, socialists and centre politicians argue about rival economic approaches – individualism versus collectivism and how the cake of national income should be sliced up and distributed – but they all agree that the size of the cake should be increased through vigorous economic growth. This is the central proposition which the Greens most emphatically reject. Industrialism, they say, is predicated on the continuous expansion of the goods and services and on the promotion of even more consumption through advertising and the discovery of an increasing range of 'needs'. It creates great inequalities whereby a rich and envied minority set the pace in lavish and unnecessary consumption while a substantial number – in many countries a majority – are either unemployed or live in relative poverty. The Conservatives have presided over an increase in income differentials but have offered economic growth as a panacea: more for the rich and more for the poor. Porritt observes:

If the system works, i.e. we achieve full employment, we basically destroy the planet; if it doesn't, i.e. we end up with mass unemployment, we destroy the lives of millions of people. … From an industrial point of view it is rational to … promote wasteful consumption, to discount social costs, to destroy the environment. From the Green point of view it is totally irrational, simply because we hold true to the most important political reality of all: that all wealth ultimately derives from the finite resources of our planet. (Porritt, 1984, pp. 46–7.)

The Green view goes on to adduce a number of basic principles:

1. *A world approach*: All human activity should reflect appreciation of the world's finite resources and easily damaged ecology.
2. *Respect the rights of our descendants*: Our children have the right to inherit a beautiful and bountiful planet rather than an exhausted and polluted one.
3. *Sufficiency*: We should be satisfied with 'enough' rather than constantly seeking 'more'.
4. *A conserver economy*: We must conserve what we have rather then squander it through pursuit of high growth strategies.
5. *Care and share*: Given that resources are limited, we must shift our energies to sharing

Table 9.1   Two worlds: industrialism versus ecology

Industrialism	Ecology
The environment	
Domination over nature	Harmony with nature
Environment managed as a resource	Resources regarded as strictly finite
High energy, high consumption	Low energy, low consumption
Nuclear power	Renewable sources of energy
Values	
An ethos of aggressive individualism	Cooperatively based communitarian society with emphasis on personal autonomy
Pursuit of material goods	Move towards spiritual non-material values
Rationality and packaged knowledge	Intuition and understanding
Patriarchal values, hierarchical structure	Post-patriarchal feminist values, non-hierarchical structure
Unquestioning acceptance of technology	Discriminating use and development of science and technology
The economy	
Economic growth and demand stimulation	Sustainability, quality of life and simplicity
Production for exchange and profit	Production for use
High income differentials	Low income differentials
A free market economy	Local production for local need
Ever-expanding world trade	Self-reliance
Employment as a means to an end	Work as an end in itself
Capital-intensive production	Labour-intensive production
Political organisation	
Centralisation, economies of scale	Decentralisation, human scale
Representative democracy	Direct democracy, participative involvement
Sovereignty of nation-state	Internationalism and global solidarity
Institutionalised violence	Non-violence

Source: Adapted from Porritt, 1984, pp. 216–17

what we have and looking after all sections of society properly.

6. *Self-reliance*: We should learn to provide for ourselves rather than surrendering responsibility to specialised agencies.

7. *Decentralise and democratise*: We must form smaller units of production, encourage cooperative enterprises and give people local power over their own affairs. At the same time international integration must move forward rapidly.

Porritt maintains this amounts to a wholly alternative view of rationality and mankind's existence. He contrasts the two world views of industrialism and ecology in Table 9.1 below.

Inevitably the other major parties have done all they can to climb aboard the green bandwagon, cloaking their policies in light green clothes and shamelessly stealing the rhetoric of the environmentalists.

As it currently stands the Greens' political programme is unlikely to fall within the 'art of the possible'. But as Malcolm Muggeridge once pointed out 'utopias flourish in chaos', and if environmental chaos does arrive, it may well be the Greens who inherit what is left of the earth, if it is not already too late by then.

The political fringe

The political fringe is the name given to those small factions and groups which often do their political work outside the conference halls of the main parties rather than within them. Those who belong are often determined ideologues, given to regular argument in groups prone to splits and factions. They do have some intrinsic interest, however, as microcosms of

---

BOX 9.3 LEON TROTSKY (1879–1940)　　　**BIOGRAPHY**

By courtesy of Popperfoto

Leon Trotsky was a Russian Jewish revolutionary politician born in the Ukraine. He was arrested for being a Marxist at the age of 19 but escaped from Siberia in 1902. After teaming up with Lenin, he became President of the first Soviet in St Petersburg after the abortive 1905 revolution. He escaped to the West but returned to Russia in March 1917 to assist Lenin in organising the Bolshevik Revolution in November of the same year. He conducted peace negotiations with Germans and led the Red Army of five million men in the ensuing civil war. An inspiring and charismatic leader as well as brilliant intellectually, Trotsky should have succeeded Lenin in 1924, but his theories of permanent world revolution were less well suited to the times than Stalin's pragmatic 'socialism in one country'. Moreover, Stalin was too devious and ruthless for him and he was eventually exiled in 1929, being assassinated in Mexico with an ice pick in 1940 by Ramon del Rio, an agent of Moscow. His ideas live on, but mostly on the radical intellectual fringe in developed countries.

political ideas and conflicts. It must also be remembered that in the early part of this century the Labour Party was just such a small faction, snapping around the heels of the Liberal Party – yet within a couple of decades it was actually in power.

Left and right extremes

We recognise only two classes in society. ... Our problems are the result of a rotten capitalist system.
Arthur Scargill, Socialist Labour Party

But what I am saying is that the prospect of the collapse of everything that is opposed to us is greater than at any time in 20th century Britain.
John Tyndall, British National Party

Far left

Marx, Lenin and Stalin

Most far left groups owe their intellectual debts to Karl Marx. He argued that under a capitalist economy rich property owners would so drive down wages in pursuit of profits and a competitive edge that a vast army of impoverished workers would eventually rise up and sweep away the whole corrupt system. Once private property had been abolished, working people would begin to live new and better lives in an economy in which people would work willingly for each other and not reluctantly for an employer. It did not quite work out that way.

After the Marxist takeover of power in Russia in 1917, a period of great hardship and economic instability followed. Lenin established a political system based upon centralised control supported by a network of secret police. He believed in the need for a 'vanguard party' of professional revolutionaries to lead the masses when the time came. There had to be rigid discipline and acceptance of the vanguard party's 'dictatorship of the proletariat' while it implemented socialism. Communists claimed this was the transitional stage the USSR was in by the early 1920s when Lenin died.

Trotsky – advocate of 'worldwide revolution' – was the heir apparent but the dogged and unintellectual Joseph Stalin, Secretary of the Party, was cleverer than his brilliant colleague. He urged 'socialism in one country' rather than an inter-

national conflagration; he outmanoeuvred his rivals and plotted ruthlessly, succeeding in presenting Trotsky as a traitor to the revolution. He eventually drove him into exile in Mexico, where his agents succeeded in assassinating him in 1940.

Stalin, by then, was a brutal dictator, both paranoid and obsessed with power, claiming to be implementing communism but in reality imposing industrialisation and collective farming on a reluctant and starving peasantry. Anyone less than obsequiously worshipful of their leader was imprisoned, exiled or shot. Overseas communist parties were employed essentially to assist the development of the 'home of socialism' and any deviation from the party line was punished by expulsion or worse.

This is the legacy inherited by extreme left-wing parties in Britain. The Communist Party of Great Britain (CPGB) was founded in 1920 and became the willing tool of Moscow's message in this country, interpreting all the shifts in the official line and condemning anyone perceived as an enemy of the USSR. Members managed to survive the astonishing *volte-face* when Stalin ceased to oppose Hitler as first priority and signed a deal with him in 1939 to partition Poland. Once Hitler invaded Soviet Russia in 1941, British communists breathed a sigh of relief; they were at last able to luxuriate in a vast amphitheatre of approving views as the whole country applauded the heroic Soviet effort. After the war, Stalin's expansion into Eastern Europe, his blockade of Berlin in 1948 and the crushing, by his machine, of the Hungarian rising in 1956 quickly disillusioned communists and Moscow 'fellow travellers' alike. The Cold War effectively ruined the chances of communist parties of achieving power anywhere in Europe and they began to wither and atrophy.

In the 1970s and 1980s opposition to communism in Eastern Europe intensified and the accession to power of the liberal Gorbachev in Moscow was the signal for the bloodless revolutions throughout the former communist bloc, with only Cuba and China being spared. The CPGB split into a hardline pro-Moscow rump and a liberal 'Eurocommunist' wing, with the latter seizing control. It tried to transform itself into 'an open, democratic party of the new pluralistic and radical left'. In 1991 it ceased to be the CPGB and renamed itself the Democratic Left.

Trotskyism

A number of Trotskyite bodies sprung up during and after his lifetime calling for worldwide revolution. Ted Grant, a South African, was involved with some of them like the Militant Labour League in the 1930s. With Peter Taafe, Grant set up the *Militant* newspaper and adopted the tactic of 'entryism', the idea being to infiltrate members of a 'Militant Tendency' (notice only a 'tendency', and not a separate party, which would have breached Labour rules) into the decaying structure of the 1960s Labour Party and seize leadership at the grassroots level of that party and, in theory, the country once the time for revolution arrived. The Tendency virtually controlled Liverpool City Council in the 1980s and two members, Dave Nellist and Terry Fields, were elected MPs. They advocated a number of radical measures, including: nationalisation of the top two hundred companies; extension of state control over the whole economy; workers' control in state-owned industries; nationalisation of the media; a slashing of defence spending; withdrawal from the EC; and abolition of the House of Lords. In 1992 the Tendency gave way to Militant Labour, still attempting to 'enter' the Labour Party, but most of the prominent members had faded away and the MPs lost their seats.

The Socialist Labour Party

This was formed in 1996 by miners' leader Arthur Scargill, following his failure to prevent the rewriting of Clause Four at Labour's conference in 1995 (Figure 9.1). 'We recognise only two classes in society, both of which are recognised by their relationship to the means of production,' he explained. 'Our problems are the result of a rotten capitalist system.' Accordingly, his party favours common ownership of the economy, full employ-

Figure 9.1 The ghost of old Labour
Source: *The Guardian*, 29 January 1996

ment, a four-day week, a ban on non-essential overtime, retirement at 56, restoration of union rights, abolition of the monarchy, House of Lords and public schools, and withdrawal from the EU. Only 500 attended the launch in May 1996.

The Workers' Revolutionary Party

Gerry Healy, expelled from Labour for his Trotskyite views, put his energies into a new party to express and promote the views of his hero. The idea of the party is to build up battle-hardened cadres to seize power when capitalism collapses, as it must, in its view. Membership was never high but celebrity members like Vanessa Redgrave and her brother Corin gave the party a high media profile.

The Socialist Workers' Party

Tony Cliff, who founded this organisation, was also expelled from Labour for being a Trotskyite. His party has concentrated on international revolution and international links are stressed. Paul Foot, nephew of Michael and a national columnist, is a high-profile member.

The Socialist League

Ken Coates was the guru of this party, once known as the International Marxist Group; Tariq Ali was also a 1960s luminary and helped to win headlines when the International Marxist Group were seeking to emulate in Britain the exploits of 'Danny the Red' (Daniel Cohn-Bendit) and others in Paris, the home of left-wing activism in that decade. The SL wished to 'transform consciousness' and achieve liberation through ending 'alienation'.

Far right

Fascism

This set of ideas developed by Benito Mussolini in the 1920s and supplemented by Adolf Hitler in the 1930s was founded on xenophobic nationalism and total submission to the state. Democracy was scorned as the language of weakness and mediocrity; a one-party totalitarian state led by a charismatic leader was the preferred alternative. The leader and his team were seen as the result of an evolving process whereby the best people and ideas won through. It followed that

the same thing happened when nations fought; war was the means whereby nations grew and developed. Hitler added a racial twist: the Aryans were the founding race of Europe, a race of conquerors and the Germans were their finest exemplars; all other races were inferior, and the Jews in particular were lower than vermin and should therefore be destroyed. In the stressful interwar years, racked by economic depression and unemployment, these unwholesome ideas seemed attractive and full of hope to many who faced despair as their only alternative. It is emotionally satisfying perhaps to blame one's troubles on a single group in society, especially one which is quite easily recognisable physically and very successful economically and culturally.

In Britain Sir Oswald Mosley founded a party which evolved into the British Union of Fascists, offering himself as the strong charismatic national leader who would end the party bickering and lead the country into new successes. Mosley proposed that: employers and workers should combine in the national interest and work in harmony; strikes and lock-outs should be banned; all major elements in the productive process should work together to plan the economy (corporatism). Moreover, he argued that the Empire would provide all the things the country needed and imports which could be made in Britain would be banned. Parliament and the old parties would be reformed and MPs would be elected according to occupational groups. Once elected, Parliament would pass on power to the leader to introduce the 'corporate state'. Parties and parliament would be ended; everyone and everything would be 'subordinated to the national purpose'. Mosley's anti-semitism was disguised in Britain but his coded references to 'alien influences' were clear enough to most Britons; he favoured sending all the Jews in the world to a barren reservation. When it was revealed that Hitler's remedy to his self-invented 'Jewish problem' had been genocide of the most horrifying kind, a revulsion set in against fascist ideas. But they have proved unnervingly resilient and still appear in the present time in a different form.

In 1967 the National Front (NF) was formed. Its central message is a racist one, warning against dilution of the British race via intermarriage with 'backward and primitive races', producing an 'inferior mongrel breed and a regressive and degenerate culture of tropical squalor'. Repatriation of black Britons is the answer offered. At the level of theory, however, the Jews are offered as the main threats, being characterised as an international conspiracy to subvert the Western economies and introduce communism before setting up a world government based in Israel. This side of the NF and its utter contempt for democracy is disguised in public expressions, but it exercised considerable appeal to young men with a taste for violence and racial hatred. In 1983 the 'New' NF – later the British National Party – was born; this is dedicated to infiltration and is more secretive, having many contacts with neo-Nazi groups abroad and many terrorist groups too. Football supporters are often infiltrated by NF members and in 1994 a friendly football match between Ireland and England was ended by thuggish violence instigated by the NF. A related body called Combat 18 (the number in the name relates to the order in the alphabet of Hitler's initials: AH) openly supports Nazi ideas and embraces violence as a political method.

1997 election

As previously the general election of May 1997 saw the usual multicoloured rainbow of fringe joke candidates, but for the far left and far right as well as the pranksters the result was widespread loss of deposits; voters may flirt with the fringe from time to time but when the election arrives they revert to 'sensible voting'.

Chapter summary

Feminism is concerned with the unequal position of women in society and falls into liberal, socialist and radical categories. Nationalism emerged in the nineteenth century, and, whilst it is now contested by internationalism, still retains much of its destructive force. Green thinking applies environmentalism to politics, calling for a revolutionary change in the way developed societies live. Far left fringe groups tend to draw on the ideas of Marx and Trotsky; their relevance has declined since the anti-communist revolutions but many followers still keep up the struggle. Far right groups tend to be neo-fascist and racialist; their support is small but their influence subversive.

Discussion points

- Has feminism achieved any major victories and if so what are they?

- Is nationalism more dangerous than terrorism?
- What chance is there of the Greens ever winning power in the UK?
- Why do you think people join fringe political groups?

Further reading

Lovenduski and Randal (1993) is a thorough review of feminism in Britain; the political ideas books by Adams (1993) and Heywood (1992) have good sections on nationalism; and Dobson (1990) and Porritt (1984) are good on ecology. An excellent study of totalitarianism is Arendt (1951). On fascism, also recommended is Wolf (1981) and Cheles *et al.* (1991); Thurlow (1986) is a history of British fascism to the present day.

References

Adams, I. (1993) *Political Ideology Today* (Manchester University Press).

Arendt, H. (1951) *The Origins of Totalitarianism* (Allen and Unwin).

Brownmiller, S. (1975) *Against our Will: Men, Women and Rape* (Simon and Schuster).

Cheles, L., Ferguson, M. and Wright, P. (1991) *Neo-Fascism in Europe* (Longman).

de Beauvoir, S. (1968) *The Second Sex* (Bantam; first published 1952).

Dobson, A. (1990) *Green Political Thought* (Unwin Hyman).

Dowds, M. and Young, J. (1996) *13th British Social Attitudes Survey* (SPCR).

Firestone, S. (1980) *The Dialectic of Sex* (Women's Press).

Friedan, B. (1963) *The Feminine Mystique* (Norton).

Friedan, B. (1982) *The Second Stage* (Norton).

Greer, G. (1971) *The Female Eunuch* (Granada).

Greer, G. (1985) *Sex and Destiny* (Harper and Row).

Heywood, A. (1992) *Political Ideologies* (Macmillan).

Lovenduski, J. and Randall, V. (1993) *Contemporary Feminist Politics* (Oxford University Press).

Marcuse, H. (1964) *One Dimensional Man* (Beacon).

Marcuse, H. (1969a) *An Essay on Liberation* (Penguin).

Marcuse, H. (1969b) *Eros and Civilisation* (Sphere).

Millett, K. (1969) *Sexual Politics* (Granada).

Porritt, J. (1984) *Seeing Green* (Blackwell).

Thurlow, R. (1987) *Fascism in Britain* (Blackwell).

Wollstonecraft, M.A. (1967) *A Vindication of the Rights of Women* (Norton; originally published 1792).

Dominant ideas and moments of choice

DAVID COATES

Democratic politics is all about the representation of interests, but, as we have already seen, the formulation of those interests is itself a very complex process, in which the sets of ideas dominant in the society as a whole play a critical part. Each of us needs ideas in order to build a mental picture of the world that surrounds us, and in order to formulate our own concerns within that world, and those ideas are not things that we individually create afresh. Rather, in formulating our picture of the world and of our interests within it, we draw on the stock of ideas that have come down to us over time, and that collectively constitute our own particular political culture. Political options are therefore critically shaped by the nature of that political culture, and as that culture changes democratic electorates find themselves with real moments of choice.

The stock of ideas available to us in the UK for the understanding of our own politics and interests is a particularly rich one. Each of us, to varying degrees, carry within our heads concepts and understandings whose origins can be traced back to a range of coherent intellectual traditions and associated political ideologies. As we have just seen, some of those intellectual roots are of long standing: conservatism, liberalism and a sense of nationhood. Others are more recent: social democracy (new liberalism), feminism, even ecology. Not all of us will draw on all of those intellectual packages, but none of us can entirely escape the impact of at least some of them: and therefore there is much to be gained from an understanding of the distribution of

ideologies over time, and from an assessment of their relative strengths in the contemporary world. Figure 1 constitutes, in the broadest sense, a first stab at such a mapping of ideologies in time. It suggests, in the UK case, that the rise and fall of ideologies coincides roughly with the fifty-year cycles of economic expansion and decline that have been such a feature of UK economic life since the nineteenth century. It also indicates the strength of classical *liberal* ideas as the dominant common sense of the nineteenth century. Electoral cycles also arguably follow a half-century rhythm too, witness 1906, 1945 and 1997. It shows conservatism, socialism and ideas of imperial glory as its main challengers then; and it suggests that the second half of the twentieth century is best understood as an ideological battleground between liberalism and a milder form of socialism that draws heavily on Keynesian economics.

Two things follow from Figure 1 for an understanding of contemporary UK politics. One is the persisting strength of liberal ideas. The other is the regularity and tenacity of the challenges to their dominance. Both are vital ingredients of contemporary UK life.

UK political culture is deeply liberal: in the sense that categories of thought and sets of social understandings that derive from the liberal tradition are deep in all of us, whether we like it or not. It is axiomatic in UK political life to think in terms of individuals rather than of groups, to think of individuals as essentially equal in value and in rights, and to subscribe to aspirations for individual

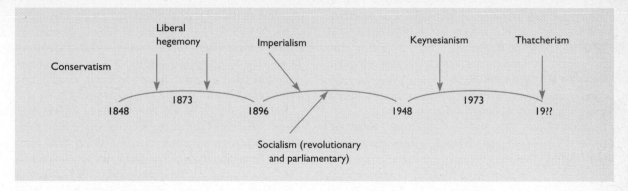

Figure 1   Mapping ideologies in time

freedom and well-being. It is normal to think that property should be privately owned, that the state should be limited in the scale of its activity, and that markets are the prime instrument through which to organise a successful economy. Those ideas were deeply embedded in UK political culture in the nineteenth century; and were given a new lease of life, a new dominance, by the rise of Thatcherism after 1979. We have lived since 1979 under a set of governments imbued with a particular mix of liberal and conservative ideas: governments which have now spent nearly twenty years arguing that our interests are best served by extending private ownership and market processes, by rolling back state involvement in the economy, and by restraining welfare provision. The Thatcher and Major governments have always offered liberalism tempered by conservatism – they have never sought to end the welfare state or to withdraw the state entirely from economic intervention; but they have shifted the whole political landscape in the UK back towards a reliance on the quintessentially liberal institutions of *private property* and *the market.*

The capacity of recent Conservative governments to retain power for so long has not been the product of any inevitable superiority of the liberal ideas to which they subscribe. On the contrary, liberal ideas lost their dominance once before (after 1896) and could do so again. Thatcherite liberal-conservatism established its initial popularity in the late 1970s only because of the emerging weakness of its main ideological opponent: namely post-war social democracy. As an intellectual/political tradition, social democracy had attempted to *manage the market* and to *mix private and public ownership*,

in the belief that market forces and private property, if left unregulated, would produce unacceptable levels of unemployment and social inequality. Both main political parties had subscribed to versions of this social democratic alternative to unbridled liberalism throughout the 1950s and 1960s; but the Labour Party in particular had adopted such views as its own. So when Labour governments in the 1970s found that they could no longer use state ownership and activity to produce full employment and growth – when they found that Keynesianism had stopped working – they eventually lost more than government power. In a real sense, they also lost their way. They lost confidence in their underlying ideological package. In fact, ever since 1979 the Labour Party has been on a quest (one that in truth it shares with the entire centre-left in the UK), a quest for a *new way* of running a modern economy and society, one that is both more socially equal and more economically successful than that offered by liberal conservatism. The Bennites thought they possessed such an alternative in the early 1980s, and gave the Labour Party its most socialist programme since the 1930s; but that was resoundingly rejected by the electorate in 1983, to leave Labour seeking a more moderate alternative that was still to the left of the Conservatives. The claim now, by the Blairite leadership of the Labour Party, is that at last it has found that more moderate alternative.

The big claim now on offer is that Labour in power will deliver a *stakeholder* society. The idea of stakeholding offers – to those who find it credible – both a critique of the dominant liberalism and a set of proposals for a new dominant order. Its criticism of liberalism is that unregulated markets create too selfish and too unstable a universe. The resulting universe is too selfish, in that social policies inspired by liberal ideas encourage each of us to pursue only short-term and private interests, without adequate regard for the long-term needs of us all. It is also too unstable, in that economic policies inspired by liberal ideas then entrench that short-termism, because no one can be sure they will be employed tomorrow. Stakeholding, on the other hand, it is claimed, gives all of us long-term rights: to education and training, to job security, and to basic welfare. It also imposes upon us responsibilities to work collectively to create an internationally competitive economy, and to spend and save wisely to minimise the welfare burden we might otherwise impose upon others. A stakeholder economy, we are now being told, will be successful, as stakeholder-based economies elsewhere (in Germany and in Asia) already are, because economic relationships will be built on *a balance of competition and trust*; and a stakeholder society will be more ordered, more secure, less divided than the society created by the years of liberal conservatism, because it will be built on high levels of *mutual reciprocity*. That at least is the claim.

So as in 1945 and 1979, the UK electorate in 1997 faced a moment of choice: not just between political parties broadly imbued with the same ideas, but between different ideas themselves. Liberal capitalism versus stakeholder capitalism seems now to be on the agenda. Indeed the contemporary debate on the UK centre-left is much more about whether an incoming Labour government will actually deliver a stakeholder society, rather than about whether such a society is desirable. That debate has focused intellectually around Will Hutton's best-selling book, *The State We're In* (1995); and it has focused politically around the degree of radicalism to be expected from Tony Blair's New Labour. The gap between Hutton and Blair may yet mean that a future Labour government will not in the end create a qualitatively new form of capitalism based on mutuality and trust; but be that as it may, the *idea* of such an alternative to market-based liberal capitalism is definitely gathering a wider and wider audience. As it does so, it is adding a new and fascinating element to the rich tapestry of UK political culture, and so is widening political options again.

Reference

Hutton, W. (1995) *The State We're In* (Jonathan Cape).

PART THREE

The representative process

CHAPTER TEN

Elections

DENNIS KAVANAGH

LEARNING OBJECTIVES

- To understand the purpose of elections.

- To evaluate the electoral system and its strengths and shortcomings.

- To study changes in campaigns.

INTRODUCTION

This chapter begins by discussing the framework in which elections are held. It then considers who is entitled to vote, the rules of the electoral system, the nomination of candidates, expenditure and the role of election campaigns.

Competitive elections to choose governments lie at the heart of the democratic process; a crucial difference between democratic and non-democratic states is to be found in whether or not they hold com-petitive elections. The best indicator of such competition is the existence of a number of political parties at elections. In addition to choice there must also be widespread electoral participation. In Britain the entire adult population has the right to vote at least once every five years for candidates of different parties in the House of Commons.

Elections in Britain matter for other reasons. They are the most general form of political participation; at general elections since 1945 an average of 75 per cent of adults on the electoral register turns out to vote (Table 10.1). Secondly, these votes are import-ant, for they determine the composition of the House of Commons and therefore which party forms the government. Thirdly, elections are a peaceful way of resolving questions which in some other countries are settled by force; above all the question 'who is to rule?' They are also important in giving legitimacy to government and therefore oblige the public to obey the laws passed by Parlia-ment. Voting in general elections is how we decide who is to govern us.

What are elections?

Elections are a mechanism of social choice, a device by which people choose representatives to hold office and carry out particular functions. In a direct democracy, usually in small societies, people may of course do the tasks themselves or take turns

Table 10.1   Election turnouts 1945–87

Date	%
1945	73.3
1950	84.0
1951	82.5
1955	76.8
1959	78.7
1964	77.1
1966	75.8
1970	72.0
Feb. 1974	78.1
Oct. 1974	72.8
1979	76.0
1983	72.7
1987	75.4
1992	77.8
1997	71.3

Table 10.2   Extension of the suffrage

Date	Adult population with the vote (%)
1832	5
1867	13
1884	25
1919	75
1928	99
1969	99

the cessation of hostilities in 1918 and 1945, respectively. The USA has calendar elections prescribed by the constitution; even in wartime elections for the Congress and Presidency went ahead.

Purpose of elections

> What are elections for? As a first answer, most people would probably reply along the lines of: 'To express the democratic will of the electorate.' That answer, however, simply raises more questions. Are national elections about choosing effective executives or selecting competent legislatures? Should they provide each voter with a local MP, or each party with its fair share of MPs? In an ideal society one might like an election system which achieved all six objectives. However, except in very rare circumstances, that is impossible. We have to decide priorities and strike compromises.
>
> Peter Kellner, *The Observer*, 24 March 1996

(rotation) to carry them out. In large-scale societies, however, the election of representatives is necessary.

Election is not the only method by which rulers are chosen. Leaders may emerge, for example, through heredity (e.g. monarchy) or force (e.g. the military). Indeed, appointments in many walks of life are made without elections: in the civil service and in many professions appointment is on merit (demonstrated, for example, by passing competitive examinations, serving an apprenticeship or gaining diplomas or other marks of competence). But today competitive elections are widely regarded as the symbol of legitimate and representative democracy.

In Britain competitive elections were well established in the eighteenth and nineteenth centuries, even though only small numbers of males had the vote. The suffrage, or right to vote, was steadily broadened during the nineteenth century. Britain effectively had mass suffrage by 1928, when the vote was extended to virtually all men and women over the age of 21 (see Table 10.2).

General elections for the House of Commons are called under either of two circumstances: when the Parliament has run its full five years (until 1911 the permissible life span of a Parliament was seven years) or when it is dissolved by the monarch on the advice of the Prime Minister of the day. In the exceptional conditions of war the elections due to be held by 1916 and by 1940 were delayed until

Some commentators have argued that the advent of opinion polls and the power to time economic booms for the run-up to an election gave the incumbent too great an advantage (Hailsham, 1979). While the Thatcher victories of 1983 and 1987 may support this thesis, Wilson's defeat in 1970, Heath's in 1974, Callaghan's in 1979 and Major's in 1997 do not. Indeed, the 1992 election turns some of the conventional wisdom on its head. John Major had delayed calling an election until late in the Parliament – hoping that signs of economic recovery would be more visible and that the opinion polls would move decisively in his favour. Neither had occurred when he called the election for April 1992. It is likely that the polls underestimated the Conservative share of the vote – and that the party was leading before and during the campaign – but

BOX 10.1   **IDEAS AND PERSPECTIVES**

Opinion polls

Opinion polls are increasingly used to report on the state of public opinion. These are surveys of the views of a sample of between one and two thousand voters drawn randomly from the electorate. Sampling is done either by *quota* or *probability* methods. A *quota* sample is obtained by allowing the interviewer to find respondents who together match the known age, sex, class and other characteristics of the population. A *probability* sample is drawn by choosing every *n*th name on the electoral register. Today most polls reply on *quotas*. At elections the polls attract an enormous amount of attention for their prediction of which party will win. They claim to be able to predict parties' share of the votes to within 3 per cent in 95 per cent of cases.

The 1992 general election was the most exhaustively polled ever and the newspapers and television broadcasts often led with the latest results of the opinion poll. The polls do have a good record of predicting winners, though they came unstuck in the 'upset' elections of 1970, February 1974 and 1992. In the 1992 election the eve of poll predictions by the main polling organisations overestimated the Labour final share of the vote by 4 per cent, underestimated the Conservatives' by 4 per cent and overestimated the Alliance by 1 per cent. The average forecast of the four major polls published on polling day was for a Labour lead of 0.9 per cent. In the event the Conservatives won by 7.6 per cent – an 8.5 per cent error, the largest ever.

Subsequent analysis suggests that a number of factors contributed to the error (Kavanagh, 1992). They include:

- **A late swing** amongst undecided voters which the pollsters were unable to pick up. Usually 80 per cent of voters have made up their minds before the campaign;

this time the figure was much lower at 63 per cent.

- **The don't knows:** At 5 per cent, these represented an unusually large percentage of respondents just before polling day, and are thought to have voted disproportionately for the Conservatives.

- **Secret Tories:** ICM's re-interviewing of its eve-of-poll respondents who refused to divulge their voting intentions revealed that a number eventually voted Conservative, a view supported by MORI's inquest.

- **Respondents may have lied** through a sense of guilt at voting for the low-taxation, low-spending Conservatives.

- **Protest votes:** Some voters may have used the polls to vent their anger against the government – as in a by-election – but returned to the fold on election day.

- **Sampling error:** Most respondents were interviewed on the street on the same day – a practice which some experts say favours Labour. Weekend polls by Harris tended to produce Conservative leads.

- **Differential turnout:** MORI claims that Conservatives displayed a greater willingness to turn out and vote than Labour supporters.

- **Non-registration:** A significant number of people polled, maybe 1 per cent, had not registered to vote in order to avoid poll tax payment and were more than likely to be Labour voters; this could explain some of the distortion.

Opinion polls also have a demonstrated influence at by-elections. Voters are able to use the knowledge provided by the polls to vote tactically against the incumbent. By-election polls were extremely important in helping the Alliance and Liberals gain some spectacular by-election victories in the 1980s.

Major was not to know that. The poor performance of the opinion polls may increase the politicians' scepticism about their forecasting ability (see Box 10.1).

The government is expected to resign and recommend a dissolution if it is defeated on a major issue, or it loses a vote of censure in the Commons. To date the only post-war case of a forced dissolution was in 1979, when the Labour government lost a vote of confidence following the failure of its Scottish and Welsh devolution plans to be carried by the necessary majorities in referendum in those two countries. This was unusual because the government was in a minority in the Commons.

The other opportunity which British voters have for a nation-wide election of representatives is for members of the European Assembly every five years. To date elections have been held in 1979, 1984, 1989 and 1994 for eighty-seven Euro-MPs (see Chapter 31). Voters cast their ballots largely on what they think of the government of the day. In 1994, Labour gained 44 per cent of the vote (an increase of 9 per cent on the 1992 general election), the Conservatives 27.8 per cent (a drop of 15 per cent). The Conservative share was the lowest gained by either major party in a national election this century.

A significant feature is that the turnout, usually around a third of the electorate, has regularly been the lowest or second lowest, in any EU member state.

One might also note the introduction of referendums on constitutional issues – over British membership of the European Community in 1975, and in Scotland and Wales over devolution in 1979. Supporters of a referendum claim that when there is a single issue, particularly one which raises constitutional questions, and on which the parties are broadly agreed (so reducing the role of a general election is providing a choice for voters) a referendum is appropriate. In 1996, the Labour Party announced that the creation of planned assemblies for Scotland and Wales would be subject to prior approval in referendums in the two nations. Labour also favours a referendum on electoral reform. All parties have agreed to hold a referendum before Britain enters a single European currency.

Who votes?

To be entitled to vote a person must have his or her name on the electoral register of the constituency in which he or she resides. The register is a list compiled each year by the local Registration Officer. For inclusion on the register the person must be resident in the constituency on the given date, be over 18 years of age and be a British subject. Persons lacking a fixed address cannot be registered. One apparent anomaly is that citizens of the Irish Republic are also entitled to vote if they have had three months' continuous residence in the United Kingdom before the qualifying dates. Peers, aliens, people judged insane in mental homes and people disqualified upon conviction of corrupt electoral practices and certain types of prison offenders are not eligible to vote.

Referendums provide an opportunity for the electorate to vote on issues, and may be binding on Parliament or advisory. They have been held in Britain as a whole once (on whether Britain should remain in the European Community in 1975), in Northern Ireland once (on the Border in 1973) and in Scotland and Wales once (in 1979 on the proposals for assemblies in Scotland and Wales). Interestingly, each of these was held on a constitutional matter. The Scotland Act 1978 provided for a devolved assembly in Edinburgh but subject to approval by 40 per cent of the electorate in an advisory referendum. The Scottish voters approved by 33 per cent to 31 per cent; the proposal therefore failed. Only 12 per cent of Welsh voters supported a proposal for a Welsh assembly, compared to 47 per cent who voted against.

In 1993 there were growing demands for a referendum to be held on the Maastricht Treaty. This was resisted by the leadership of the two main parties on the grounds that it is for Parliament to decide such issues; they also may have feared the display of divisions in their parties.

Sir James Goldsmith has founded a Referendum Party, which seeks a referendum on future integration of Britain in the EU. In the 1997 general election he ran candidates against Conservatives who did not support the idea. In June 1996, the anti-EU Tory MP, Bill Cash introduced a bill, under the ten-minute rule, providing for a referendum on Britain's future relations with the EU. It gained over

90 votes (including seventy-four Conservatives). John Major had argued that in the event of his government deciding to enter a single European currency he would hold a referendum and the government would campaign for entry.

Inaccuracies in the state of the register when it is compiled, combined with the greater mobility of people, mean that the register is often out of date when it is published. It becomes less accurate after publication, as voters die or change residence. The register for the April 1992 election was based on voters' residence on 10 October 1991 and contained 43,252,865 names. But there have been increasing complaints about the register's accuracy. The actual number of registered voters in 1992 was up by 0.2 per cent on 1987 but the Registrar General's estimate of the population was that it had grown by 1.2 per cent. Some of the non-registration in 1992 may have been because of the unwillingness of some voters to pay the poll tax. A turnout of 78 per cent (as in 1992) may actually mean that over 80 per cent of eligible voters have cast a vote in the election. Not surprisingly, many of the non-voters are drawn from the unemployed, very old, young and poor. These people also tend to participate less in other social activities; many are poorly informed about politics and see little point in participating.

Constituency boundaries

The division of the country into constituencies is in the hands of permanent electoral **Boundary Commissions**. There is a separate Commission for each of the four nations of the United Kingdom and each has the task of establishing an approximately equal size of constituency electorate. The Commissions periodically (between ten and fifteen years) review and make recommendations about the size of the constituency electorates. They arrive at a notional quota for each nation by dividing the total electorate by the available number of seats.

Notwithstanding the Commission's efforts, once allowances are made for such features as respecting the existing boundaries of counties and London boroughs, sparsely populated constituencies and the sense of 'community' in an existing seat, there are many inequalities in the size of the constituency electorates. In 1983, for example, the average electorate per constituency was around 65,000, yet a third of seats varied from this figure by some 15,000. Recent boundary reviews have had to take account of the more rapid growth of electorates in the south of Britain and the suburbs compared to the north and cities, and award relatively more seats to the former. Over time the recommendations have been helping the Conservative Party at the expense of Labour. It was largely for this reason that the Labour government avoided implementing the recommendations of the 1969 Boundary Review, which was calculated to be worth between five and twenty seats to the Conservative Party. Scotland and Wales have long been given more seats in the House of Commons than the size of their populations strictly justifies, in part because both were guaranteed a minimum number of seats by the 1944 Redistribution of Seats Act. At present their 'bonus' is nineteen seats; this helps Labour, which in the 1992 election won twenty-seven of the thirty-six Welsh seats and forty-nine of the seventy-two Scottish seats. New boundaries operated for the 1997 election. Once again Labour lost out, perhaps to the extent of about 8 seats, as the major metropolitan conurbations lose, and the south-east and suburbs gain.

The electoral system

An electoral system is a set of rules governing the conduct of elections. Electoral systems aim to produce a legislature that is broadly representative of the political wishes of the voters, to produce a government that is representative of the majority of voters and to produce strong and stable government. These aims are not necessarily compatible with one another. A key feature prescribes how popular votes are translated into seats in the legislature. There are, broadly speaking, two types of electoral systems (Urwin, 1982). In *proportional* systems there is an attempt to establish a close relationship between the distributions of votes between parties and the allocation of seats in the legislature. How close depends on the type of system used. Proportional systems may be subdivided into party list and transferable vote systems (see Box 10.2). Setting a high threshold (e.g. 5 per cent of votes in Germany) for a party to gain a seat can limit the number of parties represented. A low one (e.g. 0.67 per cent in the Netherlands) encourages fragmentation. In *first-past-the-post majoritarian systems* the candidate who achieves a plurality of votes wins the seat. These may be subdivided into *plurality* and *absolute majority* systems. At the risk of oversimplifying, one may say that proportional systems are found largely in Western European states and majoritarian systems are found in Anglo-American societies (the UK, Canada, Australia, and the USA).

The two systems also broadly correlate with multi-party versus two-party systems, respectively. But this list of countries may be about to change. In a referendum in 1993 Italians voted by a large majority to abandon PR and adopt a largely first-past-the-post system, tempered by proportionality, and New Zealanders by a large majority voted for the German additional member system. Desire for a change to the electoral rules is often a symptom of broader dissatisfaction with the political system. The 1995 New Zealand election failed to produce a party with a majority and increased the power of small parties.

The different types of electoral systems do seem to reflect national outlooks about government and politics. Proportional systems are often adopted in divided societies – to provide a form of reassurance to minorities and emphasise the importance of the legislature being broadly representative of society. Plurality systems are defended on the grounds that they help to provide a more stable government and, where there is one party in government, allow the voters to hold the government responsible for its record at the next election. Their disproportionality also means that a party often has a majority of seats for a minority of the vote. In October 1974 Labour

---

BOX 10.2   **IDEAS AND PERSPECTIVES**

How proportional systems work

The *alternative vote system* is employed in Australia. Each elector lists the candidates in order of preference. Any candidate who has over 50 per cent of first preferences is elected. If no one has over 50 per cent, the candidate finishing bottom on first preferences is eliminated and his or her second preference is transferred to other candidates. This process continues until one of the remaining candidates gains over 50 per cent, or until only two candidates remain (and the leading candidate is elected). One member is elected for each seat. This system passed the Commons in 1918 and 1931, with Liberal and Labour support, but was defeated in the Lords. It preserves the link between the member and constituency.

The *additional member system* (AMS) as used in Germany elects two types of MPs. A proportion are elected in single-member constituencies on a plurality basis, as in Britain. Others are elected by a second vote from party lists which are produced regionally. This allocation is used to achieve some proportionality between the totals of votes and MPs, although the degree depends on the balance struck between the two types of MP.

The *single transferable vote* (STV) is used in Ireland for large constituencies with several members. It is favoured by the Liberal Democrats. Each elector has the same number of votes as there are seats and ranks the candidates in order of preference 1, 2, 3, etc. A quota is calculated from the formula: number of votes divided by number of seats plus one. Surplus votes for a candidate who has achieved the quota are transferred to other candidates according to the voters' second and lower preferences. Votes for candidates at the bottom are also redistributed as they are eliminated. This process continues until all the requisite number of candidates with votes above the quota are elected.

The list systems are also applied to large constituencies. The order of candidates is decided by the party machine and there is no direct link between member and constituency.

won a majority of seats with only 39.2 per cent of the vote and in 1983 the Conservatives amassed 61 per cent of seats for 42 per cent of the vote.

Until recently the British public and much of the elite assumed that the electoral system was satisfactory. Undoubtedly it enjoyed the virtues of familiarity and clarity; in the post-war period, only in February 1974 has one party failed to gain an overall majority of seats. This assumption also accompanied the belief that the British system of government was superior to that of many Western European states. For much of the twentieth century Britain was an economic and industrial power of the first rank. Its record in resisting Hitler's military aggression, avoiding political extremism (of both the left- and right-wing varieties) and maintaining political stability was superior to that of many West European states which had various forms of proportional representation.

Britain is also unique in not having any form of proportional representation (PR) for direct elections to the European Parliament. Because these elections are not about choosing a government, the familiar objection that PR would lead to unstable government does not apply. But the leaders of the two main parties have not wished to set a precedent for the introduction of PR for Westminster elections. After all, the Parliamentary strengths of the two main parties would be substantially reduced under PR. In 1973 the Royal Commission on the Constitution proposed PR for elections for the recommended Scottish and Welsh assemblies, and Labour has proposed it for a future Scottish Assembly.

In recent years, however, that complacency has been challenged. In part this has reflected the more general dissatisfaction with Britain's economic performance and international standing. The electoral system, like so much else, has come in for criticism. It is not clear, however, how much responsibility for the country's poor economic performance rests with the political system in general, with the electoral and party systems in particular, or with other factors. A study of the economic performance of 21 advanced industrial countries shows that in the past three decades the rates of economic growth and unemployment were virtually identical in countries electing MPs by PR or on first-past-the-post. But on both economic indicators Britain has performed worse than the great majority of countries in either type of system (Rose, 1992).

One has only to look at Northern Ireland to see the shortcomings of the British electoral system when it operates in a bitterly divided society. The use of the first-past-the-post system meant that, as long as religion dictated voting, the Catholics were in a permanent minority and this is hardly calculated to build consent. Northern Ireland politics is different from Great Britain in that the elections for local elections and for its three seats to the European Parliament now use PR.

Among the criticisms of Britain's first-past-the-post are the following:

1. The system does not invariably produce secure majorities for one party. In three of the last nine general elections (1964, February 1974 and October 1974) the winning party did not have a majority sufficient to last for a full Parliament. Many commentators felt that in the era of three-party politics in the 1980s the chances of an indecisive outcome were greatly increased (Butler, 1983).

2. Because some three-quarters of seats are safe for the incumbent party many voters are denied an effective choice in most seats. It produces a House of Commons and government which do not fairly represent the party support across the nation.

3. As the Liberal and Social Democratic Alliance parties gained significant support (over 20 per cent) in the 1980s, so the disproportional effects of the electoral system became more glaring (Table 10.3). It can be argued that when the Liberals were gaining less than 10 per cent of the vote this disproportionality was not too objectionable; but when a party gains over 25 or 23 per cent of the vote and gets only 3.5 per cent of the seats (as in 1983 and 1987) the distortion is less acceptable. It is worth noting that the British system does not discriminate against all minor political parties. Where a party can consolidate its votes in a region, e.g. the Nationalists in Wales or the Unionists in Northern Ireland, then it can collect a representative number of seats. However, the system does penalise those parties which spread their votes widely, like the Liberals.

Table 10.3   Third party seats in House of Commons

Date	No. of seats
1945	34
1950	11
1951	9
1955	8
1959	7
1964	9
1966	14
1970	12
Feb. 1974	37
Oct. 1974	39
1979	27
1983	44
1987	44
1992	44
1997	75
Average	29

4. Critics of the adversarial party system (in which the opposition routinely attacks what the government does and promises to do) complain that the all-or-nothing nature of the British system encourages abrupt discontinuity in policy when one party replaces the other in government. Frequent reversals in policy in such fields as education, regional policy, housing, finance, incomes restraints and the economy may be highly damaging. Coalitions (a probable consequence of PR elections) would, it is claimed, provide for more consistency.

5. As the two main parties have become more regionally based between the north and south and between urban and suburban/rural areas, so they may become less national in their outlooks. It is certainly true that until 1992 the south of Britain and the Midlands have cumulatively become more Conservative, while the north and Scotland have become more solidly Labour.

The year 1992 saw a reversal of the north–south division which had operated in all elections since 1959, and particularly during the 1980s. Labour actually gained ground in the south and Midlands, while the Conservatives increased their share of the vote in Scotland and held their own or increased slightly in the north. Some part of the explanation for the reversal of the north–south variation in swing was that most of the south experienced an economic recession and a sharp fall in house prices after 1989. Unemployment in much of the south was actually higher in 1992 than in 1987, in contrast to the north.

But over the long run the 'two nations' thesis holds. Compared to 1979 when the Lab.–Con. shares of seats and votes were pretty similar to 1992, Labour has managed to increase its share of the vote only in Wales, the north and north-west, and seen it fall sharply in the south. Over the same period the Conservative share of the vote has fallen by over 5 per cent in the north, north-west and Scotland, and remained pretty stable in the south.

In 1987 there was much opposition criticism of the Conservatives gaining 57 per cent of the seats for only 43 per cent of the votes. But in Scotland Labour gained 70 per cent of the seats for 42 per cent of the votes and in Wales, 63 per cent of seats for 45 per cent of the votes. There is now a sharp disparity between shares of votes and of seats in Britain as a whole and in different regions; the effect is to 'overrepresent' Labour in north Britain and the Conservatives in south Britain. Only in 1977 did a good number of Labour MPs sit for the affluent and growing population in the south-east of Britain; Conservatives are hardly represented in the major cities and have no representation at all in Liverpool, Manchester, Glasgow, Bradford, Stoke, Newcastle upon Tyne or Leicester.

One may point to shortcomings in most schemes of proportional representation and the coalitions that usually ensue. For example, it is difficult for the voters to assign responsibility to any one party for a government's record if there are coalition or minority governments. If a coalition government is formed then its programme will very likely be a result of post-election bargaining between the party leaders. Under the present British system disillusioned voters can turn a government out, but under PR some members of the ousted coalition would be members of the new one. Critics also argue that, apart from wartime – when the overriding goal is national survival – coalitions are likely to be unstable and lack coherence. There is some irony in the fact that the Italians have become so disillusioned with their political system – its weak coalitions, the lack of effective choice at elections, which means that the same parties and personalities are usually always in government, the lack of political responsibility and the corruption – and regard the PR electoral system as a major cause of the weaknesses. They wish to adopt the Westminster system.

It is also likely that if a *party list* system is used (as in many West European states) and the party headquarters draws up the list of candidates in multi-member seats, then the direct link between an MP and his or her constituents will be weakened. Another form of PR – the *additional member system* in West Germany – also retains the link between constituency and MP. Finally, if a party is short of a working majority by a few seats in the House of Commons the bargaining power of a small party will be greatly increased. In West Germany the 'Free Liberals' have been 'perpetual' partners in coalition governments with Christian Democrats or Social Democrats. The crucial party may not necessarily be a centrist one. It could be the Ulster Unionists or a nationalist party.

Prospects for electoral reform

The public does not regard proportional representation as an important issue, certainly in comparison to the attention given by political scientists, commentators and politicians. Before the 1992 elections, surveys showed that there was a positive response to questions asking whether Britain should move to a fairer or a more proportional electoral system. But by polling day the surveys indicated that there was preference for the present system and for one-party government over coalition government. Slight alterations in question wording account for some of the differences, but the differences were more a consequence of few people having well-formed views on the subject. An attempt to ask a series of questions on the issue and so establish the degree of consistency of views found that many voters supported their party's views: 71 per cent of Liberal Democrats and 58 per cent of Labour voters were consistently for PR, and 54 per cent of Conservative supporters were consistently against (Dunleavy *et al.*, 1992, p. 642).

Since 1987 there has been growing interest in electoral reform. In the past, supporters complained about the way in which the present system discriminated against the large Liberal vote and in the late

1970s it was argued that coalitions would provide more continuity and consensus on policy. The significant new factor is that many Labour politicians have come to support reform. Having by 1987 lost three successive elections to the Conservatives, who were able to gain landslide victories with only 42 per cent of the vote, and aware that a large number of Labour voters were virtually unrepresented in the south of England, some Labour leaders had second thoughts. The odd spell of Labour government seemed to be a poor return from the first-past-the-post system. Charter '88, a cross-party group, but drawn mainly from the Liberal and Labour parties, advocated constitutional reform, including proportional representation.

A decisive step for Labour was when Neil Kinnock agreed to set up a working party under Professor Plant to look at the electoral systems for a reformed second chamber and regional assemblies. Neil Kinnock agreed to the appointment of a committee as a way of promoting discussion, educating the public and party, appealing to the Liberal Democrats and also avoiding a split on the issue before the 1992 election. At the 1991 party conference delegates successfully pressed for the committee also to review electoral arrangements for the House of Commons. The issue is divisive for Labour. Both Roy Hattersley, deputy leader until 1992, and his successor until 1994, Margaret Beckett opposed reform. In 1993 the Plant Committee made a majority recommendation for a switch to the supplementary vote, only a minimal change from the present system. But John Smith rejected it, agreeing that a referendum could be held on the issue in the next Parliament, and Tony Blair has endorsed the position. In 1997, a joint Lab.–Lib. commission agreed to support a referendum on retaining the present system or switching to PR. Tony Blair says that he is not persuaded of the need for change.

In the last week of the 1992 election electoral reform came to the forefront. Neil Kinnock promised to enhance the authority of the Plant Committee and extend its membership. But with the opinion polls pointing to deadlock, the initiative was seen as an opening to the Liberals. Conservative ministers warned against a Lib.–Lab. government and the destabilising results of proportional representation. In retrospect, some Labour campaigners felt that they may have lost votes by raising the issue and that it prevented them from concentrating public attention on their favoured social issues.

Paradoxically, in 1992 the electoral system did not quite work along traditional lines. Firstly it produced a more proportional relationship between seats and votes. Although the bias to the winner meant that the Conservatives were 'overrepresented' by sixty-two extra seats, Labour also profited by forty-six and the Liberals were 'underrepresented' by ninety-seven, the overall distortion was much greater in the 1983 and 1987 elections. Parties like the SDLP in Northern Ireland and nationalists in Wales which concentrated their votes, had a 'fair' return.

Secondly, the multiplier affect, by which small shifts in votes are converted to a larger turnover of seats, was less evident in 1992. Labour was helped by tactical voting by Liberal Democratic voters in marginal seats and by the overrepresentation of Scotland and Wales. Both factors resulted in Labour ending up with a more efficient distribution of its seats across the country (Crewe, 1992, p. 117). Each of these factors was at work in 1997, but Labour gained most of all from the effect of the electoral system. It gained nearly two-thirds of seats for 44 per cent of the vote.

According to one study (Dunleavy *et al.*, 1992) different PR electoral systems will have different outcomes. For example, the alternative vote system (in which voters number the candidates in order of preference) would have made little difference to the final outcome in 1992. But a form of the additional member system (in which half MPs are elected in constituencies under the first-past-the-post system and half are chosen from a regional list to bring each party's share of seats into line with the share of votes in the region) would have produced a much more proportional outcome. It would have produced a minority government. The single transferable vote system would have had similar effects.

Unless the Labour Party comes out for proportional representation, electoral reform is unlikely to be a major political issue. But if there were a series of deadlocked Parliaments and it seemed that minority governments were here to stay, then a coalition – which involved at least two parties – might seem the only way of ensuring stable government. In that case PR would be a logical development. The introduction of coalitions and/or a proportional representation system would be likely to alter radically the conduct of British government and politics.

The electoral process

Nomination

For election to the House of Commons it is virtually necessary to be nominated as a candidate by a *major* political party. Each constituency party nominates a candidate and, if approved by the party headquarters, he or she becomes the constituency's prospective parliamentary candidate. Each major party maintains a list of approved candidates from which local parties may select. If a candidate is not already on the party list, then he or she has to be approved by party headquarters.

This power has been important in the Labour Party. In the 1950s the party's National Executive Committee (NEC) turned down a number of left-wing nominations by constituencies. In the early 1980s the NEC came under left-wing control and this power was not exercised. Indeed reforms at this time (see below) gave more power to constituency activists, who were usually more left-wing than MPs. But under Neil Kinnock the NEC, as part of its drive against Militant, became more interventionist in candidate selection at by-elections and this has continued since. In the 1992 Parliament it insisted, against some constituency opposition, on a number of all-women short-lists in safe Labour seats as part of the campaign to boost the number of women MPs. These were subsequently ruled illegal and abandoned, although not before a large number of women had been adopted.

To be nominated, a parliamentary candidate must him- or herself be eligible to vote, be nominated by ten local voters and pay a deposit of £500 to the returning officer, which is forfeited if he or she fails to gain 5 per cent of the vote. Traditionally few people participate in the selection process; the numbers ranged from a few dozen in some Labour general management committees to a few hundred in some Conservative associations. The introduction of a system of allowing all members to vote in the selection of candidates has made the process more open.

For many years nomination was assured for virtually all MPs. In the late 1970s, however, Labour left-wingers, as part of their campaign to extend democracy in the party, changed the party rules so that all Labour MPs were subject to mandatory reselection in the lifetime of Parliament. This was widely regarded as a device to make MPs more beholden to left-wing activists in the constituencies than to the party whips in Westminster. Some (ten) Labour MPs were de-selected for the 1983 election, and some of the MPs who departed for the Social Democratic Party would probably not have been reselected by their local parties. For the 1987 election six were de-selected. The rule change did not prove to be the major force once expected for the advance of the left in the party. On the contrary, left-wingers have sometimes been threatended with de-selection and a number of constituency parties confine themselves to renominating the sitting MP. By 1990, mandatory resolution was effectively overturned when Conference agreed that contests would take place only if a ballot of local members demanded one.

Conservative activists have usually been a force for loyalty. Sir Anthony Meyer, who challenged Margaret Thatcher for the party leadership in 1989, was shortly afterwards de-selected by his Clwyd North West association, and supporters of Michael Heseltine's challenge to her in 1990 also came under pressure. In 1996 the anti-Major MP Sir George Gardiner encountered strong opposition in his local Reigate party and was eventually de-selected in January 1997.

Expenditure

Elections cost money. In 1992 the cost to the government – more accurately, its Consolidated Fund – was over £42 million. In addition, the annual cost of maintaining the electoral register is £40 million.

British constituency elections are cheap in comparison to those in many other Western states, largely because expenditure by local candidates is strictly limited by law. Each candidate is required to appoint an election agent who is responsible for seeing that the limits on expenses are not broken. The legal limits are usually raised before each election in line with inflation. The maximum per-

mitted in constituencies ranged between £6,000 and £7,000 in 1992. On average candidates for the main three parties spend under £5,000 each, with Conservatives usually spending the most. In 1992 Conservative candidates spent an average of £5,840, Labour £5,090 and Liberals, £3,169. For all parties the victors were more likely to spend near to the maximum permitted. The bulk of this spending goes on printing a candidate's election leaflets and addresses. Local candidates also have free postage for their election leaflets and free hire of school halls for meetings. The limit on spending means that local candidates can legally do little or no opinion polling, telephone canvassing or media advertising.

In sharp contrast, there is no legal limit on the spending by national party organisations and no legal obligation for them to publish their election budgets. Most national spending goes on advertising, opinion polling, financing the leaders' tours and meetings and providing grants to constituency parties. Centrally, the parties in 1987 spent £15 million compared to just over £7 million in 1983. In 1992 the Conservatives estimated that they spent £10 million (in real terms a decline on 1987) and cut back on press advertising. Labour spent some £7 million and the Liberals some £2 million. If the Labour Party is credited with the huge press advertising campaigns run by public sector unions in favour of more spending on public services, the Conservative–Labour differences are reduced.

One important difference between election campaigns in Britain and the USA is that British parties are precluded from purchasing time on the broadcasting media, although they can buy advertising in the press. In the USA there is little doubt that the opportunities for advertising have made elections very expensive and heightened the importance of personalities and the wealth of candidates. Some $100 million was spent by candidates in the 1988 US presidential campaign on television commercials alone. The time made available by television companies for election broadcasts is a considerable subsidy to the parties.

Campaigns

There is a ritual element to British election campaigns. This is particularly so at the constituency level, with candidates and helpers pursuing their time-worn techniques of canvassing, addressing meetings and delivering election addresses to electors' homes. At the national level the party leaders address public meetings in the major cities, attend morning press conferences and prepare for national election broadcasts. Elections today are effectively fought on a national scale through the mass media, particularly television. The activities of the party leaders – visiting party committee rooms, factories, and old people's homes, speaking at evening rallies and making statements at morning press conferences – are conducted with an eye to gaining such coverage. If activities are not covered by peak-time television they are largely wasted as a means of communicating with the public. One of the most famous images of the 1979 election was Margaret Thatcher on a Norfolk farm, cuddling a new-born calf. This had little to do with discussion of political issues but the bonus for the Conservatives was that photographs of the event were carried in almost every national newspaper and on the television screens. There is some Americanisation of campaigning in Britain; local face-to-face meetings have declined in importance, while the national parties employ their own opinion pollsters and advertising agencies and make use of computers, direct mail and other modern devices to 'market' themselves and appeal to target voters in key seats (Kavanagh 1995).

It is difficult to prove that election campaigns make much difference to the final result. One party's good campaign in a constituency may fail to show a marked improvement because the opposition parties have also made strenuous efforts in the seat. There is some evidence that an active new MP, perhaps using local radio and television over the lifetime of a Parliament, can gain up to 700 'personal' votes at the following general election. For many voters, however, the choice of whom to support on polling day is a product of a lifetime of influences, rather than the four weeks of an election campaign. Most observers agreed that in 1983 the Conservative campaign was vastly superior to Labour's, which was something of a disaster. Yet, according to the average score of the opinion polls, the fall in support for both Labour and Conservatives between the first week of the campaign and polling day was identical (4 per cent). In 1987 many observers were critical of the Conservatives' campaign but on polling day they had preserved the eleven-point lead over Labour enjoyed at the outset of the campaign. Compared to the disaster of 1983, Labour's campaign was admired for its smooth organisation and professionalism. But for all this, and Neil Kinnock's campaigning superiority to Michael Foot, Labour added just 3 per cent to its 1983 record low vote. In 1992 once more, communicators and, according to the polls, voters, judged that Labour and Neil Kinnock has campaigned better than the Conservatives and John Major. Even Conservative supporters were critical of their party's campaign. Yet Labour added only 3.6 per cent to its 1987 vote and the Conservative margin of victory in votes was greater than that achieved by any party in elections between 1950 and 1979. Packaging and presentation can only do so much.

Referendums

According to *The Economist* (23 November 1996), referendums in British politics are set to multiply. It quotes the Constitution Unit's Report on this democratic device, which judges 'Across the world, politicians tend to dislike referendums. They take the decisions out of established hands and elected leaders can never take control.' By the autumn of 1996 both main parties had pledged themselves to a referendum before taking the country into a single European currency. In addition Labour pledged, if elected, to hold referendums on Welsh and Scottish assemblies and on electoral reform. Why the popularity? After all, as Stalin's Foreign Minister, Molotov, said: 'The disadvantage with free elections is you can never be sure who is going to win them.' The reasons are complicated.

Firstly, politicians will not have missed the fact that a large majority of voters say in polls they like referendums if the issue is sufficiently important. Secondly, the authority of elected politicians has declined along with their reputations, and this device invokes the authority of the people in a very direct way. Both sides of a big argument can favour a referendum – as over the single currency issue – when both feel they could win the resultant debate. Thirdly, they can be useful when there is a difficult problem on which delay is thought advisable, like devolution for example; and technically referendums are only advisory not binding (though it is hard to believe a government would totally ignore an emphatic result). Fourthly, they can be a useful uniting factor when a party cannot agree, as over membership of the EEC for Labour in 1975; in effect the party says to the country: 'We cannot decide so why don't you?'. Similarly Labour is divided over electoral reform – one group favours no change and another favours proportional representation; the referendum, it is fondly hoped, will square the circle, though it may merely make matters more complex as most voters are baffled by the respective arguments for and against. This also raises the question of whether referendums are a cop-out for politicians, a way of evading their responsibilities. How can voters decide on the arcane arguments over the single currency? Isn't it likely that the debate will be dominated by those who simplify and employ emotive slogans? Don't politicians get elected to make such decisions and use their judgement on behalf of the country? This question can be added to the discussion points below.

Summary

The British electoral system has for a long time been admired for its simplicity and its effects in producing stable government. It is a quality much less admired today and reform is on the agenda. The reforms come from changes in the party system and the European Union. Less is decided on elections than politicians claim, because of the limits on the autonomy of the British government.

Discussion points

There are a number of questions to ask about the working of the electoral system under the role of elections in Britain today:

- *Campaign funding*. How might party funding be improved?

- *Electoral reform*. What considerations lead the Labour and Liberal Democrat Parties to be more sympathetic to electoral reform than the Conservative Party?

- *Scottish devolution*. What consequences might the creation of a Scottish parliament have on the electoral system and style of campaigning?

- *The importance of elections*. Elections have their limitations in deciding public policy. Discuss.

Further reading

On the traditional and contemporary working of the British electoral system see Butler (1963 and 1983, respectively). On the consequences of different systems see Rose (1992) and Urwin (1987).

References

Butler, D. (1963) *The British Electoral System Since 1918*, 2nd edn (Oxford University Press).

Butler, D. (1983) *Governing without a Majority* (Collins).

Crewe, I. (1992) 'Why Did Labour Lose (Yet Again)', *Politics Review* (September).

Dunleavy, P., Margetts, H. and Weir, S. (1992) 'Replaying the election', *Parliamentary Affairs*, Vol. 45, No. 4, October.

Hailsham, Lord (1979) *Dilemma of Democracy* (Collins, 1977).

Kavanagh, D. (1992) 'Polls: predictions and politics', *Politics Review*, November.

Kavanagh, D. (1995) *Election Campaigning: The New Marketing of Politics* (Blackwell)

Rose, R. (1992) *What Are the Economic Consequences of PR?* (Electoral Reform Society).

Urwin, D, (1982) 'The mechanics and effects of various political systems', *Social Studies Review*, March.

CHAPTER ELEVEN

Voting behaviour

DENNIS KAVANAGH

LEARNING OBJECTIVES

- To study how voters are influenced.

- To understand changes and the impact of society and class.

- To analyse and explain the outcome of the 1997 general election.

INTRODUCTION

To discuss the factors which shape voting behaviour, particularly those which have produced changes in party support in recent years. It also tries to assess the likely impact of these changes on the working of the political system.

Explanations of voting behaviour

For the first half of the post-war period (1945–70) it has been comparatively easy to provide broad explanations of voting behaviour in Britain. Three guidelines simplified analysis. The first was that people were regarded as being either middle or working class on the basis of their occupations. Although there were divisions within these groupings, notably between the skilled and unskilled working class, there was a strong correlation between class and vote: the majority of the working class voted Labour and most of the middle class voted Tory. Secondly, an average of about 90 per cent of voters supported either Labour or Conservative in general elections. Finally, most (over 80 per cent) of voters were partisans or identifiers with one

or other of the above parties. Surveys indicated that for most people party allegiance hardened over time so that they were unlikely to turn to a new party. Identifiers were and are also more likely than other voters to agree with their party's policies and leaders.

During the 1960s it was generally believed by psephologists that British people tended to vote according to traditional associations of class and party. By the 1980s, however, such loyalties had waned, allowing issues to become more important. In an era of 'partisan dealignment' (Sarlvik and Crewe, 1983) citizens no longer vote blindly for the party of their parents or workmates but, in the true spirit of pluralist democracy, listen to what the parties have to say on issues and react accordingly – sometimes in a volatile fashion. Sarlvik and Crewe distinguish between 'salience', the extent to which people are aware of an issue, and 'party preferred' in terms of policies on that issue. They believe the Conservative emphasis on taxes, law and order and trade union reform won the 1979 election for them.

In 1987 and 1992, however, Labour led the Conservatives on three of the most salient issues – unemployment, health and education – yet easily lost both elections. Surveys showed that voters expected a Labour government to increase taxes and that most people were prepared to pay higher taxes to fund extra spending on public services.

Perhaps they were. But, crucially, a post-election Gallup poll found that 30 per cent said they would be better off, and 48 per cent worse off under Labour's tax and budget proposals. Despite their identification of key issues and their preferences for Labour prescriptions, voters reacted to a personal consideration when it came to the crunch. They chose to vote for the party which they thought would deliver the highest degree of personal prosperity. This behaviour calls into question: (a) the value of survey responses on issue questions; and/or (b) the significance of issue voting.

A problem with research on issue voting is that one can never prove whether it is the party loyalty or vote which influences the issue preference, or vice versa (which is necessary for issue voting). And such questions are tied up with the broader image of the perceived 'competence' of the party and the party leader (where Conservatives have for long outscored Labour). At present political scientists are more impressed with the 'competence' factor as an influence on the voter.

For most of the post-war period, therefore, social class and partisanship (and, as noted earlier, the electoral system) interacted to buttress the Labour/Conservative party system. There were only small margins of change in the parties' share of the vote from one general election to another. Between 1950 and 1970, for example, the Conservative share of the vote ranged from 49.7 per cent (1959) to 41.9 per cent (1945) and Labour's from 48.8 per cent (1951) to 43.8 per cent (1959). Stability was the order of the day and it was difficult to envisage a change in the party system.

The above description always needed some qualification. The most important is that between a quarter and a third of the working class have usually voted Conservative. Without this 'deviant' vote there would

not have been a competitive two-party system and the Conservatives would hardly have been the 'normal' party of government in the twentieth century. Another is that class distribution was gradually changing as the proportion of the workforce engaged in manufacturing fell and the proportion employed in service and white-collar occupations grew. This trend has accelerated in the past two decades.

Yet in recent years that old two-party, two-class model explains a diminishing part of British election behaviour. Firstly, consider *partisanship*: between 1964 and 1987 the proportion of the electorate identifying with the Labour and Conservative parties fell from 81 per cent to 70 per cent and *strong identifiers* from 38 per cent to 25 per cent over the same period. Since an increasing number of voters have become less tied to parties, more votes are 'up for grabs' at elections.

Secondly, consider *social class*. The relationship between class and voting was fairly strong until the mid-1970s. Yet even in the 1960s surveys suggested that class loyalty was weakening in its intensity for many voters (Butler and Stokes, 1970, 1974). In general elections between 1970 and 1992, Labour's normal two-thirds share of the working-class vote fell to less than a half (and as low as 38 per cent in 1983). Over the same period the Conservatives' normal four-fifths share of the middle-class vote fell to three-fifths. Within the middle class, Labour and Liberal support is much stronger among the public sector, particularly the creative and welfare professions. Quite separate from these trends has been the shift in the balance between the classes in the electorate. From a rough 40–60 split between the middle class and working class, the distribution today is the reverse. In other words, Labour was gaining a diminishing share of a smaller working-class constituency.

Moreover, social changes, promoted in some degree by Thatcher reforms, have weakened the old class bases of the party system. Over 66 per cent of homes are now privately owned; since 1979 the proportion of council-rented properties fell from 45 per cent to 25 per cent of the housing stock. Jobs in services and white-collar professional and managerial occupations have increased, those in manufacturing have fallen. As a proportion of the work-force trade unionists fell from 53 per cent in 1979 to 38 per cent in 1992. Although many people are now in 'mixed' social class groups, e.g. working-class home-owners, Britain is increasingly becoming a middle-class society.

Finally, consider the *level of support* for the two main parties. The Labour and Conservative parties' combined share of 90 per cent of the vote in general elections between 1945 and 1970 has fallen to around 75 per cent in the elections since then. Electoral stability has been replaced by fluidity and the two-party, two-class model by three-party, less-class-based voting since 1983. As the moorings of class and partisanship have declined, so the election campaigns and the build-up to them (and the personalities, issues and events associated with them) may have more influence.

In October 1978, for example, the opinion polls showed Labour ahead of the Conservatives. Yet by February 1979 Labour trailed by 20 per cent. What had intervened of course was the infamous winter of discontent when many public sector workers took industrial action to break the government's incomes policies. Labour's claims to have an 'understanding' with the trade unions and to be uniquely placed to gain their consent were shattered. In the early months of 1982, Labour, Conservatives and the new Alliance parties were pretty level according to opinion polls and some Conservatives were even talking of the need to replace Margaret Thatcher as party leader. Yet after the Falklands victory in April the government shot into an overwhelming lead and gained a landslide victory in the general election a year later. In September 1986 Labour had a clear lead in the opinion polls but by March 1987 it was twelve points adrift of the Conservatives who again won a clear election victory. For the six months following the Conservative general election victory in April 1992, Conservative and Labour were level pegging in the opinion polls. The humiliating exit of Britain from the exchange rate mechanism (ERM) on 'Black Wednesday' in September 1992 produced a sharp and enduring shift in attitudes to the parties. Tory support plummeted and Labour moved into a 20 per cent lead, a margin which it actually increased over the next four years, and in the 1997 general election had a lead of 13 per cent.

British voting behaviour has become less predictable for the following reasons:

1. *Partisanship:* Strong identifiers with parties have reduced in number.
2. *Social class:* Class loyalties have weakened and the working class is diminishing in size.
3. *Social changes:* Housing and occupational patterns have changed.
4. *Level of support for the two parties:* This reduced from 90 per cent in 1945 to 1970 to 75 per cent since.

Social class

There are several different approaches to defining social class and different definitions and measurements have excited debates (Crewe, 1986; Heath *et al.*, 1985). Most researchers have long relied on the six-category scheme of the British Market Research Society (BMRS): A, B, C1, C2, D and E. The first three (professional, managerial and clerical) are conventionally termed 'middle class', and the final three (skilled and unskilled manual workers, and a residual group of old age pensioners, widows and their families) are 'working class'. This scheme relies on occupation combined with lifestyle and incomes as the basis for differentiating classes and splits the population 40–60 per cent between the middle and working class.

Another approach to social class has been developed by researchers at Oxford University in their study into social mobility. This focuses more on the conditions in which incomes are earned and a person's degree of autonomy and authority at work. *How Britain Votes* (Heath *et al.*, 1985) uses this approach. Its middle class broadly corresponds to the ABC1 groups of the BMRS and the proportions are pretty similar. The most dramatic change in this scheme is the reduction in the size of the *working class* of rank and file manual workers to one third of the workforce. The study also creates other non-manual groups, including the *intermediate* class of clerical and sales workers and foremen (24 per cent) and the *salariat* of managers, executives and professionals (27 per cent). In addition they have a *petite bourgeoisie* of employers and *self-employed* which the BMRS allocate to the skilled working class.

Other researchers, writing from a neo-Marxist perspective, are more concerned with dividing classes according to whether individuals do or do not own the means of production, i.e. control of labour. The study of electoral behaviour by Patrick Dunleavy and Chris Husbands, *British Democracy at the Crossroads* (1985), also takes account of what it calls 'consumption' or 'production' classes. This is based on a person's location on a system of production and exchange and the level of power people can exert over their own tasks. For example, people in manual work may differ according to whether they are primarily dependent on private or public provision of services (i.e. by central or local government). Do they own or rent their houses privately or from the local council? Do they have children in private or state schools? Do they use private health care or the National Health Service? One may also make a similar division among manual and non-manual workers according to whether people are employed in the public or private sector. Studies have found some 'sectoral' effects; workers in the public sector, for example, are more likely to vote Labour compared with similar groups in the private sector. The effects, however are rather modest.

There has been controversy over the changing relationships between social class and voting .

According to Crewe (1986), the working class has not only shrunk in size, but Labour's share of its electoral support also fell in the 1980s. For the first half of the post-war period, Labour and Conservative used to gain two-thirds of the class vote, i.e. Labour working class and Conservative middle class, but in the 1970s and 1980s the figure fell to less than half. In other words, there has been a class dealignment. According to another measure of class (Heath *et al.*, 1985), however, class voting has not declined, once we omit – and this is a large assumption – the large centre party vote from the calculation.

Party support

Conservative

The Conservatives have clearly been the dominant party in Britain in the twentieth century. Indeed some would argue that Britain has had a dominant-party system rather than a two-party one (King, 1993). Before the 1997 general election they were in office, alone or in coalition, for over two-thirds of the century and two-thirds of the period since 1945. Indeed, in this century the only four occasions in which the non-Conservative parties have had clear parliamentary majorities have been: the 1906–10 Liberal government; the 1945–50 Labour government; and the 1966–70 Labour government; and the 1997 Labour government. In recent years a significant part of the Conservative dominance in Parliament has been due to the effects of the first-

past-the-post electoral system and the divided opposition. In 1979, 1983 and 1987, for example, 42 per cent of the vote was enough to produce Conservative majorities, including landslides in the House of Commons in 1983 and 1987 as the Alliance or Liberal and the Labour and other parties divided the non-Conservative vote between them. The Conservatives have also been the beneficiary of Labour's internal divisions, and until 1997 enjoyed strong support from the press and such powerful groups as the City, business and the farming sector. Labour supporters feel particularly sensitive about the partisanship of the tabloids in 1992, and Neil Kinnock blamed Labour's defeat on their 'bias'. In 1992 most Labour and working-class voters, because they read a tabloid, were exposed to pro-Conservative papers.

Yet in the 1980s (as in the 1950s) the Conservative Party also identified itself firmly with economic prosperity. In spite of presiding over a return to mass unemployment and increasing levels of homelessness and inequality, Margaret Thatcher's party managed to fashion a constituency which had an interest in the continuation of Conservative rule. Among those who did well in the 1980s were many who lived in the affluent south and suburbs, home-owners, share-owners (who expanded from 7 per cent in 1979 to over 20 per cent) and most of those in work. In spite of the return of high levels of unemployment, the longest economic recession for over fifty years, the collapse of business confidence and a sharp decline in house prices, particularly in the Tory heartland of the south-east, the Conservatives still managed to outscore Labour when voters were asked to rate the parties' competence on economic management. This appears to have been a crucial influence on the vote in 1992 (see Tables 11.1 and 11.2). In view of the modest Conservative economic record, however, it was more of an emphatic thumbs down to Labour. Either in prosperity or in recession, most voters were not willing to trust it. As Ivor Crewe states, given the Conservative disadvantages, the key question about 1992 is 'why did Labour lose yet again?' (1992). In the 1992 Parliament, however, the Conservatives lost their reputation for economic competence and much press support.

Labour

As partisanship and class weakened in the 1970s and 1980s, so Labour's long-term future as a party of

Table 11.1   How the nation voted

	1997	Apr. 1992	June 1987	June 1983
Conservative	31.3	41.9	42.2	42.3
Labour	44.4	34.4	30.8	27.6
Alliance/Lib. Dems	17.0	17.8	22.6	25.4
Others	7.2	5.8	3.4	4.7

Table 11.2   Government parliamentary majorities, 1945–97

	Overall majority
1945	Lab. 147
1950	Lab. 6
1951	Con. 16
1955	Con. 59
1959	Con. 99
1964	Lab, 5
1966	Lab. 97
1970	Con. 31
1974 (Feb.)	None
1974 (Oct.)	Lab. 4
1979	Con. 44
1983	Con. 144
1987	Con. 102
1992	Con. 21
1997	Lab. 179

government became less secure. Its share of the vote fell below 40 per cent in all general elections between 1970 and 1992. Its 1983 share of 27.6 per cent was its lowest since 1918 (when Labour was still a new party and fighting its first nation-wide election). In 1987 and 1992, the party made a modest recovery, but only to 34.4 per cent, over 7 per cent behind the Conservative vote. This was close to the party's 'core' or expected vote (Table 11.3). Increasingly, it seemed that Labour would require a remarkable combination of favourable circumstances to win outright victory at a general election (Table 11.4)

Optimists could claim that Labour lost general elections because of the special circumstances associated with each election. It did badly in 1979 largely because of the public's hostile reaction to the trade unions and Labour government after the 'winter of discontent'. Before the 1983 election, there were bitter internal party rows over militants,

changes in the party's constitution (see p. 193), the breakaway of the Social Democrats, the weakness of Michael Foot as leader and the bitter battle between Healey and Benn for the deputy leadership. The 1987 election was held against a background of rising living standards; the platform of low inflation and falling unemployment would have made any government unbeatable.

It was difficult, however, to find a convincing alibi for 1992. Given the mismanagement of the economy, a Tory campaign that was widely regarded as lacklustre and a government that had been in office for thirteen years, the odds were against the Conservatives. If Labour could not capture 40 per cent of the vote in 1992, let alone win, then when could it? Clearly, fundamental changes have been at work, making the party into an electoral minority. Some political scientists asked if 1992 was, or the following election would be, 'Labour's last chance'? (Heath *et al.*, 1994). The changes are worthy of note. They are:

1. *Demographic*: The faster growth of population in the south compared to the north, spread of home-ownership and decline of council tenancy, contraction of the public sector (through privatisation) and heavy manufacturing jobs and growth of employment in service industries, and fall in membership of unions have all weakened the traditional social sources of support for Labour. The working class today is increasingly divided between home-owners and council tenants, the skilled and unskilled and the affluent and poor. The old working class – members of trade unions, engaged in heavy industrial work, renting property from a council and employed in the public sector – is a steadily diminishing electoral minority. The 'new working class', as Crewe (1987) describes it, is increasingly home-owning, living in south Britain, car-owning, not

Table 11.3 Calculation of the normal vote since 1974 (per cent)

	Con.	Lab.	Lib.	Other
Mean, 1945–70	45.2	46.1	7.1	1.6
Mean, Feb. 1974–92	40.7	34.4	19.5	5.5
Range, Feb. 1974–92	39.8 ± 4.1	33.4 ± 5.8	19.6 ± 5.8	5.5 ± ?.?
Actual result 1992	41.9	34.4	17.8	5.9

Source: Rose, 1992, p. 453

Table 11.4 Social class and vote, 1979–92 (per cent)

	1979		1983		1987		1992	
	Non-manual	Manual	Non-manual	Manual	Non-manual	Manual	Non-manual	Manual
Conservative	55	36	51	35	49	37	49	35
Liberal/other	19	17	31	28	31	23	25	20
Labour	26	46	18	37	20	40	26	45
Non-manual Con + manual Lab as % of total vote	51		45		44		47	

Source: Harris/ITN exit polls, 3 May 1979, 9 June 1983, 11 June 1987, 9 April 1992; Crewe 1993, p. 33

in a union and employed in the private sector – and until 1997 were deserting Labour. Since he became Labour leader in 1994 Tony Blair has determined to win these people over to the party. The party had no future as a party of the working class but had to appeal to the middle class also. The 1997 election reflected his success.

2. *Attitudinal*: Post-election research conducted for the party among wavering Conservatives showed the lack of enthusiasm for voting Labour. These target voters wanted to 'get on' or to consolidate the material gains which they had made under the Thatcher years. Although they liked Labour's social policies, they regarded the party as a threat to their hopes of material advancement; the party was associated with 'equalising down' and 'holding back'.

Third party voting

The growth of 'other' parties – or decline of aggregate support for the two main parties – may have different meanings. In four elections (1983–92) less

than 75 per cent of votes were for Labour and Conservative. In the House of Commons, however, nearly 95 per cent of seats have been Labour and Conservative. The disproportional effects of the first-past-the-post electoral system 'wasted' much Alliance and Liberal Democratic electoral support.

In the House of Commons the third force is particularly heterogeneous. Apart from the Liberal Democrats it also includes Welsh and Scottish nationalists and the various Northern Ireland parties. Much of the popular support to date for 'other' parties outside Northern Ireland has not been translated into a sufficient number of seats to threaten the two main parties. In the 1974 elections the growth in Liberal support (to 19 per cent of the vote in the February election) and the rise of the nationalists in Scotland (to 30 per cent of the Scottish vote in October 1974) represented a potential threat. But these advances were not consolidated and both parties lost seats and votes in 1979. The referendum in March 1979 showed weak support for national devolution (let alone independence) in Scotland and Wales (only 11.9 per cent of Welsh votes supported it). By 1997 nationalist support had climbed to 22 per cent in Scotland and 10 per cent in Wales.

Elections in Britain were pretty *competitive* from 1945 to 1979. Over the period the Labour and Conservative parties were evenly matched in total votes and time in office. Between 1979 and 1992, as in the interwar years, we may say that electoral competition has been *imbalanced*, with the Conservatives clearly the dominant party.

Table 11.3 provides a computation of each main party's *normal* vote, or the share it should gain in normal circumstances. It is derived from each party's average vote share over the 1974–1992 elections. Special factors – e.g. a dynamic leader, the Falklands War or the winter of discontent, or an outstanding or disastrous record – can produce a variation in the figure. It is seen that the Conservatives had a substantial advantage over Labour. Yet speculation about Conservative hegemony was rudely disrupted in the 1992 Parliament. Since the exit from the ERM, no government has fallen so low in public esteem since opinion polling began over fifty years ago (Crewe, 1994). The exit, tax increases and party divisions have provided the circumstances which reduced the normal vote for the Conservatives. The 1997 election confirmed the collapse of Conservative support.

But occasionally, there is also a *realigning* election, or series of elections, when a new party breaks through or there is durable shift in party strength. The most formidable threat yet to the dominance of the Labour–Conservative party system developed in 1981. Following the breakaway of a number of leading right-wingers from Labour to form the Social Democratic Party, its alliance with the Liberals enabled the new force to gain greatly from the unpopularity and the divisions within the two major parties. Between March 1981 and March 1982 the Alliance was regularly first or second in the opinion polls and had a remarkable string of by-election successes. It failed to maintain its support and was disappointed in the 1983 election with its 25 per cent share of the vote and twenty-one seats. Only in 1997 did the Liberal Democrats manage to build on their by-election successes. Because Liberal support is evenly distributed across the country means the electoral system works against it. In 1997, however, it managed to concentrate its support and doubled its seat total with the same share of the vote as in 1992.

The 1997 general election

It is important to emphasise that the significance of an election is only properly evaluated when the trends are confirmed over a number of elections. The Conservative victory in 1992 meant that Britain was experiencing its longest period of one-party rule in the twentieth century and the two-party system clearly remained uncompetitive. Although Labour had narrowed the deficit (for the second successive election) to 7.6 per cent behind the Conservative share of the vote, this lead was greater than any winning party achieved between 1950 and 1979.

The main voting study of the election warned that social trends would continue on balance to erode Labour's traditional social base and that the party would need a post-war record swing of over 4 per cent to win an overall majority at the next election. Labour had not achieved such a swing in 1992, and the next election was likely to be fought in more adverse circumstances. The study concluded that the party's best hope was a hung Parliament. In turn, that would require cooperation with the Liberal Democrats and, probably, some measure of electoral reform, a step that would almost certainly end any party's chances of winning an overall majority. The authors warned: 'So while Labour may indeed be able to stop the Conservatives from winning office for the fifth time in succession, this will not necessarily herald the restoration of Britain's two-party system. Rather it could be its death knell' (Heath *et al.*, 1994, p. 295). But for the period 1993–1997, Labour enjoyed record leads in the opinion polls and the Conservatives sunk to a record low level of support. The 1997 election produced a devastating outcome for the Conservative party. In the House of Commons its number of MPs is at its lowest since 1906. The 13 per cent gap by which it trailed Labour was comparable to its 15 per cent lead over Labour in 1983. One presumes that Conservative support is now down to its base line. Its long-term decline in the Celtic regions continued. Scotland and Wales became Conservative-free nations, suffering less because of the nationalists than the rise in Labour support. Scotland and Wales hold a total of 110 seats.

Although the scale of the disaster came as a surprise to many, it was in line with the by-election and local election results and opinion polls for much of the parliament. Indeed it was also in line with general election polls. Hitherto Conservative strongholds like Hove and Wimbledon were lost. The party has virtually disappeared from the major cities and is more than ever a party of the English shires and suburbs.

The setback was remarkable for a party which has been the normal party of government and long admired for its tactical flexibility and the prowess of its election machine. In fact neither of these qualities has been much in evidence since 1992. The party's bitter divisions over Europe and the loss of membership and declining level of activity at grass roots level proved fatal. Electually and organisationally the Conservative party is in a state of crisis at the end of the twentieth century.

The scale of change in 1997 actually exceeds the previous landslides. Labour's majority of 179 dwarfs the Liberal one of 130 in 1906, Labour's 146 in 1945 and the Conservative's 142 in 1983. Labour's highest ever number of MPs (419) is greater than in 1945 (393). The 10 per cent swing from Conservative to Labour is the largest in any election since 1945.

Most parties, except for the Conservatives, could find some consolation in the 1997 election. Indeed, they all fed on Conservative misfortune. Apart from Labour, the nationalists doubled their share of seats in Scotland and the Liberals gained their largest number of seats (46) in over 60 years.

The election campaign will be much analysed but it is difficult to believe that it made much difference to the outcome. The standing of the parties on election day was almost identical to that in the opinion polls when Britain was ejected from the ERM in September 1992. The 1997 election outcome was a verdict on the five years of the Major government or perhaps the eighteen years of Conservative government. Since 1992 the exit from the ERM, tax increases, sleaze, mishandling of the BSE crisis, divisions over Europe and the defection of three Conservative MPs all sapped the authority of the government. The above factors contributed to a powerful mood for change and the Conservatives had been in office for a very long time. Party divisions diminished the authority of John Major as a national and even as a party leader. There was an economic recovery, with record low levels of inflation, interest rates and mortgage rates, and falling unemployment but voters were not in the mood to give the government any credit.

On the other hand, Labour had changed greatly since 1992. Under Tony Blair it made a hard-headed analysis of what had gone wrong in 1992 and what was required to win the next election. It was determined to abandon its tax and spend issue. It accepted much of the Thatcherite agenda – privatisation, existing income tax rates for the next parliament, and aggregate public spending figures for the next two years, trade union reforms and a 'wait and see' attitude to British membership of the single currency. It also had a leader who made a point of being seen to lead his party.

During the campaign, John Major was forced to deal with the issue that was tearing his party apart. The government line on the single currency was to wait and see, or as Major expressed it to 'negotiate and decide' whether it would be in Britain's interest to join in the first wave planned 1999. He warned that a premature yes or no decision would weaken his hand in negotiations over the currency arrangements. However, nearly half of Conservative candidates broke ranks and declared in their election addresses that they were opposed to membership in principle. The focus on Europe distracted Conservatives from running on their economic record and advertised their disunity. Instead, Major warned that Labour would lead Britain into a federal Europe and that its plans for devolution in Scotland would lead to the break up of the Union.

Labour made pledges to lower class sizes, not increase standard and top rates of income tax, cut hospital waiting lists and impose a windfall tax on the excess profits of utilities to help to get 250,000 young unemployed into work. Two features which had hampered Labour since 1979 were overturned. Thatcher and Major had always led Labour leaders, when voters were asked to rate party leaders as potential prime ministers. In 1997, however, Blair decisively outscored Major as the best prime minister; according to MORI, 40 per cent of voters thought that Blair would be the most capable prime minister compared with 23 per cent for John Major. In 1992 John Major led Neil Kinnock by 38–27 per cent. And on taxation, although most voters expected taxes to go up in the new parliament, Labour led the Conservatives when voters were asked which party they trusted most on handling taxation. Above all, Labour candidates showed an iron discipline during the campaign. No disagreements broke through, compared to the spectacular disagreements among Conservatives.

Liberal Democrats made great play of their proposal to increase income tax by 1p to improve education. Rather than present themselves as the 'tax and spend party' they said they were the only honest party because taxes would have to go up, even to fund existing programmes. They exploited the convergence in policy between Labour and Conservative parties to claim that a vote for Liberal Democrats was the only way to vote for making a difference. They were rewarded with their largest number of seats for over 70 years.

During the 1980s, and particularly during the 1992 election campaign, the Conservative-supporting tabloid newspapers had been relentlessly hostile to Labour. The tabloids helped to convey negative messages, some of them distorted, about Labour's tax plans in 1992. The Conservative party was assured of getting its message across. The reiterated propaganda message that 'You can't trust Labour' struck home. Newspapers like the *Express*, *Mail*, *Sun* and *Telegraph* faithfully echoed Conservative Central Office anti-Labour claims in campaigns. Labour could only rely on the *Mirror* and *Guardian* for support. The tabloids, particularly the *Sun* also had a large Labour-supporting working class readership. That paper's virulent anti-Labour and anti-Kinnock campaign may have had some effect in producing a late swing to the Conservative party among its readers.

By 1997 the position was much changed. Many Conservative papers had been hostile to John Major personally and to his line on Europe throughout the 1992 Parliament. The failure of British participation in the ERM gave them a chance to break free and all but one of the Tory-supporting newspapers backed John Redwood when he challenged John Major for the party leadership in 1995. They had much material for negative coverage throughout the parliament, including tax rises, sleaze, internal divisions, and sex scandals. Although some of the papers returned to the fold by 1997 they did so without the old enthusiasm. *The Times* bolted the Conservative stable door and, crucially, the largest circulation daily, the *Sun*, and the Sunday *News of the World* endorsed the New Labour Party of Tony Blair. Before one assumes that the endorsement of these newspapers won the election for Labour, one should realise that they were only following their readers.

Their editors could read the opinion polls as well as anybody else; the Conservatives were massively unpopular.

Significance of the 1997 election

1. The convergence in policy between Labour and Conservative means that in large part the battles of the 1980s have been settled. Tony Blair has moved Labour to the new centre – largely Conservative defined – ground. There were some differences between the parties, notably over devolution in Scotland and constitutional reforms and entry to the European Social Chapter. But Labour had significantly accepted the principles of a market economy, low levels of direct taxation and flexible labour markets. These are historic breaches with the party's traditions.

2. The election was as presidential as any preceding one, as all leaders dominated their party's coverage. Tony Blair ran ahead of the party in the opinion polls and his appeal for trust was largely for himself. John Major also detached himself from his divided and unpopular party.

3. Third party support was as strong as ever. If we add the 46 Liberal Democrat MPs to the 29 'other' MPs then the total of 75 is the highest in any post-war parliament.

4. The opinion polls had a good election. All were pretty close to the final outcome, in spite of a widespread belief that the outcome would be much closer than the polls had foretold.

5. The economy seems to have been less important than in other elections. Economic prosperity did not work for the Conservatives.

6. The voting returns show that Labour made impressive gains across the country and among all groups (Table 11.5). Among the C1s, or lower-middle class, there was a massive swing to Labour. All regions moved to Labour but the swing was more modest in the north, where Labour was already strong. Labour has long trailed the Conservatives among women but in 1997 women were as likely as men to vote Labour. It also made large gains among the first-time voters (leading the Conservatives by a 3–1 margin), but still trailed among the over 65s, among whom there was only a 2.5 per cent swing to Labour.

Table 11.5 New Labour's conquest of middle Britain

	1997 Vote, % (change on 1992 in brackets)		
	Conservative	Labour	LibDem
All Great Britain voters	31 (−12)	44 (+9)	17 (−1)
Men	31 (−8)	44 (+6)	17 (−1)
Women	32 (−11)	44 (+10)	17 (−1)
AB voters	41 (−11)	31 (+9)	21 (0)
C1	26 (−22)	47 (+19)	19 (−1)
C2	25 (−15)	54 (+15)	14 (−4)
DE	21 (−8)	61 (+9)	13 (0)
1st time voters	19 (−16)	57 (+17)	18 (−3)
All 18–29	22 (−18)	57 (+19)	17 (0)
30–44	26 (−11)	49 (+12)	17 (−3)
45–64	33 (−9)	43 (+9)	18 (−2)
65+	44 (−3)	34 (−2)	16 (+2)
Home owners	35 (−12)	41 (+11)	17 (−3)
Council tenants	13 (−6)	65 (+1)	15 (+5)
Trades union members	18 (−9)	57 (+7)	20 (+2)

Source: 1992 data ITN/Harris exit poll; 1997 data BBC/NOP exit poll

7. For at least the past three decades two political nations have been emerging – a Labour north and a Conservative south. The Conservatives are still largely a party of the south-east as well as the shires and the suburbs in England. However, Labour now has a more national presence. It also profited greatly from the electoral system. It gained two-thirds of the seats (64 per cent) for only 44 per cent of the vote. The Conservative party gained only a quarter of the seats for 31 per cent of the vote and in Scotland for 17.5 per cent of the vote no seats. By contrast, the Liberals with only 12.5 per cent of the vote got 10 seats. Under a PR system the Conservatives would have gained an extra 40 seats.

8. It is too early to talk of the long-term collapse of the Conservative party or the hegemony of Labour. Only time will allow the 1997 election to be placed in a broader context, and to assess if it is a turning point. In the short term, it clearly breaks

with the Conservative dominance of post-1970. Labour's share of the vote is below the level which it reached in the 1960s and only slightly more than the Conservative share in 1992, although it was its highest vote share for over 30 years. If the vote was for change, it is difficult to argue that it was a mandate for radically different policies. After all, Labour had come to accept much of the Thatcher–Major agenda. It needs restating that the landslide in seats is largely a product of the electoral system and Lib–Lab tactical voting. Clearly, if proportional representation were brought about and Labour and Liberal Democrats worked together, it would be difficult for the Conservatives to get back into office.

Elections are largely decided by the performance of parties in government. But opposition parties still have to be electable. Labour was not electable in 1992, it was in 1997. The Conservatives have to resolve their position on the single European currency and European integration. At present the party in parliament and in a constituency seems Euro-sceptical. Although the party ends the twentieth century in disarray, the twentieth century has still been a Conservative century.

Realignment

Until the 1987 election there was talk of *realignment (or change) in the British party system*, largely based on the rise of the Alliance. It then seemed possible that the Alliance might overtake Labour as the second largest party, perhaps replacing that party, or establishing itself as one of three major national parties. Three different forms of realignment have been discussed:

1. The Liberals could replace Labour as the main alternative to the Conservative Party. This was certainly in the minds of those who were behind the original SDP breakaway from the Labour Party in 1981. Since 1987 this is no longer taken seriously. The New Labour Party of Blair has indeed taken on board virtually all the demands.

2. Greater cooperation between the Liberals and Labour parties could be the most effective way of blocking the Conservatives. Election pacts (in which the weaker of the two parties stands down in seats in a bid to oust the Conservative Party) have been ruled out; more promising might be

cooperation between the parties in Parliament to promote the many areas of agreement (e.g. on Europe or devolution) or tactical voting to oust a Conservative MP. In a number of 'hung' local councils Labour and Liberal groups already cooperate, without a formal endorsement from the top. Labour has moved significantly on constitutional reform and some of its leaders are prepared to contemplate PR, with the almost inevitable consequence of coalition government.

3. The Liberal Democrats could become a significant third party (in terms of seats). This would probably be a consequence of PR.

Any of the above developments could have profound consequences for electoral choice. There is, however, a paradox. Liberals have traditionally done better under Conservative governments, not least by attracting disillusioned Tory voters. Yet of the hundred seats which were most likely to fall to the Liberal Democrats in 1992 and 1997 the great majority were Conservative held. In 1997 a Liberal Democrat breakthrough came at the expense of Conservatives. In 1997 Liberals adopted some positions to the left of Labour, e.g. on taxation and redistribution. As a party of the metaphorical 'centre' the Liberals can gain from other parties but they may also get 'squeezed' in a close contest or lose support if they become too closely identified with one of the big two parties.

If there were to be a series of deadlocked Parliaments and coalition or minority governments ensued, *and* there was continued large support for a third party, pressure would almost certainly increase for a new set of rules of the electoral game. There is little historical evidence about how voters might react to such political and constitutional uncertainties. Multi-party politics provides voters with the opportunity to vote tactically – against the party they most dislike. Might they prefer a clear choice of a government with a majority of seats for one party? At present surveys suggest that potential deadlocked Parliaments are not popular.

Chapter summary

For much of the post-war period voting was fairly predictable. The dominance of the Conservatives in the 1980s produced new interpretations. There seemed to be a move to one-party government and

Labour to long-term decline but this was reversed by Labour's landslide in 1997. The shift in voting behaviour has coincided with changes in party system and perhaps in the political system.

Discussion points

■ Compare the impact of party issues in the 1992 and 1997 general elections.
■ What is the effect of opinion polls on election campaigning?
■ Are society and class still important in shaping voting behaviour?

Further reading

On recent electoral behaviour Crewe (1993) and Heath *et al.* (1994) provide different perspectives. A useful collection of articles on voting is in Denver and Hands (1992). On the 1997 election campaign Butler and Kavanagh (1997) is useful.

References

Butler, D. and Kavanagh, D. (1997) *The British General Election of 1997* (Macmillan).

Butler, D. and Stokes, D. (1970, 1974) *Political Change in Britain* (Macmillan).

Crewe, I. (1986) 'On death and resurrection of class voting', *Political Studies*.

Crewe, I. (1987) 'Why Mrs Thatcher was returned with a landslide', *Social Studies Review*, September.

Crewe, I. (1992) 'Why did Labour lose (yet again)?', *Politics Review*, September.

Crewe, I. (1993) 'The changing basis of party choice, 1979–1992', *Politics Review*.

Crewe, I. (1994) 'Electoral behaviour' in D. Kavanagh and A. Seldon (eds), *The Major Effect* (Macmillan).

Denver, D. and Hands, G. (eds) (1992) *Issues and Controversies in British Electoral Behaviour* (Harvester Wheatsheaf).

Dunleavy, P. and Husbands, C. (1985) *British Democracy at the Crossroads* (Longman).

Heath, A., Jowell, R. and Curtice, J. (1985) *How Britain Votes* (Pergamon Press).

Heath, A., Jowell, R. and Curtice, J. (1994) *Labour's Last Chance* (Dartmouth).

King, A. (1993) *Britain at the Polls* (Stratham House).

Rose, R. (1992) 'What are the Economic Consequences of PR?' (Electoral Reform Society).

Sarlvik, B. and Crewe, I, (1983) *Decade of Dealignment* (Cambridge University Press).

CHAPTER TWELVE

The mass media and politics

BILL JONES

LEARNING OBJECTIVES

- To explain the workings of the media: press and broadcasting.

- To encourage an understanding of how the media interact and influence voting, elections and the rest of the political system.

- To assess how ownership of the media affects its operations.

- To discuss different theories of how the media influence society.

INTRODUCTION

Without newspapers, radio and pre-eminently television, the present political system could not work. The media are so omnipresent and all-pervasive that we are often unaware of the addictive hold they exert over our attentions and the messages they implant in our consciousness on a whole range of matters ... including politics. This chapter assesses the impact of the mass media upon the working of our political system and different theories about how they work.

During the wedding of Prince Andrew and Sarah Ferguson in 1986, ITN newscaster Martyn Lewis was moving about among the crowds with a camera crew. 'What for you has been the highlight of the day?' he asked a young man. 'Oh, being interviewed by you, definitely Martyn', was his instant reply. This episode helps illustrate the point made by Canadian writer Marshall McLuhan that the principal means of communication in modern society, television, has become more important than the messages it carries; to some extent 'the medium' has become 'the message'. The impact of the mass media upon society has

been so recent and so profound that it is difficult as yet for us to gauge its impact with any precision.

The term 'mass media' embraces books, pamphlets and film but is usually understood to refer to newspapers, radio and television; since the 1950s television has eclipsed newspapers and radio as the key medium. Surveys indicate that in 1993 69 per cent of people identify television as the most important single source of information about politics (up from 52 per cent in 1980). On average British people now watch over twenty hours of television per week and given that 20 per cent of television output covers news and current affairs, a fair political content is being imbibed. Indeed, the audience for *News at Ten* (ITN) and the *Nine O'Clock News* (BBC) regularly exceeds 20 million. Surveys also show that over 70 per cent of viewers trust television news as fair and accurate.

Television is now such a dominant medium it is easy to forget its provenance has been so recent. During the seventeenth and early eighteenth centuries political communication was mainly verbal: between members of the relatively small political elite, within a broader public at election times, within political groups like the seventeenth-century Diggers and Levellers, and occasionally from the pulpit. Given their expense and scarcity, books and broadsheets had a limited, though important, role to play.

The agricultural and industrial revolutions in the eighteenth century revolutionised work and settlement patterns. Agricultural village workers gave way to vast conglomerations of urban industrial workers who proved responsive to the libertarian and democratic values propagated by the American and French political revolutions. Orator Henry Hunt was able to address meetings of up to 100,000 people (the famous Peterloo meeting has been estimated at 150,000) which he did purely (and in retrospect, astonishingly) through the power of his own lungs. Later in the nineteenth century the Chartists and the Anti-Corn Law League employed teams of speakers supplementing their efforts with pamphlets – which could now be disseminated via the postal system.

The press

By the end of the nineteenth century newspaper editorials and articles had become increasingly important: *The Times* and weekly journals for the political elite and the popular press – the *Mail*, *Mirror* and *Express* – for the newly enfranchised masses. Press barons like Northcliffe, Rothermere and Beaverbrook became major national political figures, wooed and feared by politicians for the power which the press had delivered to them within a democratic political system. Britain currently has eleven daily newspapers and some three-quarters of the adult population read one. The tabloids – the *Daily Mirror* and the *Sun* – have circulations of three million and nearly four million respectively. There is a smaller but growing aggregate circulation for the 'qualities' like *The Guardian*, *The Times*, *The Independent* and the *Daily Telegraph*. The two tabloids have a predominantly working-class circulation, the 'qualities' a more middle-class and well-educated readership. The *Daily Express* and the *Daily Mail* are more up-market tabloids and have a socially more representative readership.

By tradition the British press has been pro-Conservative (see Tables 12.1 and 12.2). In the 1987 and 1992 elections the Labour-supporting press numbered virtually *The Guardian* and the *Daily Mirror*, with the vast majority of dailies and Sundays supporting the government party. However, Major's administration witnessed an astonishing shift of allegiance. It began

Table 12.1 Social class and political leanings of readership, 1992

Paper	Party backed	% of readers in social class				Party backed by readers		
		AB	C1	C2	DE	Con.	Lab.	Lib./Dems
Daily Mirror	Lab.	6	18	36	40	20	64	14
Daily Star	pro.-Con.	4	14	38	44	31	54	12
Sun	Con.	5	17	35	43	45	36	14
Daily Mail	Con.	24	32	25	19	65	15	18
Daily Express	Con.	20	34	26	20	67	15	14
Today	Con.	12	26	37	25	43	32	23
Financial Times	No. Con. maj.	57	30	8	5	65	17	6
Daily Telegraph	Con.	49	32	11	7	72	11	16
The Guardian	Lab./LD	52	27	11	11	15	55	24
The Independent	None	52	29	11	7	25	37	34
The Times	Con.	61	26	8	6	64	16	19

Source: Watts, 1997

Table 12.2   Political affiliation of newspaper readers, 1993

	Sun	Mirror	Star	Mail	Express	Today	Telegraph	Guardian	The Times	Independent	Financial Times
					Daily readership (%)						
Con.	45	20	31	65	67	43	72	15	64	25	65
Lab.	36	64	54	15	15	32	11	55	16	37	17
Lib. Dem.	14	14	12	18	14	23	16	24	19	34	16
Con. lead	9	−44	−23	51	52	11	61	−40	48	−12	48

	News of the World	Sunday Mirror	The People	Mail on Sunday	Sunday Express	The Sunday Times	The Sunday Telegraph	Observer	Independent on Sunday
					Sunday readership (%)				
Con.	40	22	30	60	66	57	71	19	25
Lab.	41	59	52	19	15	18	11	51	40
Lib. Dem.	15	16	15	19	15	22	16	26	31
Con. lead	−1	−37	−22	41	51	39	60	−32	−15

Source: Sevaldson and Vadmand, 1993

with the criticism Major received for being allegedly weak as a leader and insufficiently robust in relation to European issues; stalwart Tory supporters like the *Mail*, *Times* and *Telegraph* aimed their critical shafts at the government. As the election was announced the *Sun* caused a sensation by emphatically backing Blair. Its Murdoch-owned stablemate, the Sunday *News of the World*, followed suit later on in the campaign. As in 1992, the *Financial Times* backed Labour also and the *Express*, now owned by Labour peer Lord Hollick, wobbled temporarily a bit leftwards from its usual true blue course. No such doubts for the *Mail* though, nor the *Telegraph*, despite its determined scepticism over Europe. *The Times* refused to back any party in 1997 but urged its readers to vote for the Eurosceptic cause. Hugo Young in *The Guardian* on 24 April 1997 was amused by the *Sun*'s contortions. Forced by its owner, Murdoch, to support the man he thought would be Prime Minister, the paper found it difficult to avoid snarling over Blair's commitments to 'getting closer to the EU and giving more recognition

to trade unions'. Moreover the *Sun* ran more stories in favour of the Conservatives than Labour during the campaign, according to researchers at Loughborough University.

In recent elections a close correlation was noted between issues run by the Conservatives and lead stories in the tabloids; it was known certain tabloid editors had close links with Conservative Central Office. It remains to be seen how long the pro-Labour stance of the Murdoch press survives the sensational Labour victory in May 1997. In the 1987 general election the *Sun*, *Star* and the *News of the World* chose to publish lurid front-page stories about the private (i.e. sex) lives of Labour and Liberal leaders (David Steel successfully sued the *Sun* and the *Star* over their stories).

A French survey in February 1997 revealed that Britons buy more newspapers than any other Europeans, but are least trustful of what they read in them, preferring to trust the news given out on radio and television.

Tabloids and Tony's spin doctor

" I'm just saying that the weight of newspapers in setting a political agenda is significant. If at the time of an election, the Tory instinct is driving news agendas, then it will affect the way the broadcasters cover it. That's why we focus on the tabloids. They don't like us to acknowledge that the papers that really matter are the tabloids. I think one of the reasons Tony wanted me to work for him, and why I wanted to work for Tony, was that we both acknowledge the significance to the political debate of the tabloids.

Alastair Campbell, Tony Blair's press secretary,
The Guardian, 17 February 1997 "

Broadcasting

Adolf Hitler was the first politician fully to exploit the potential of radio for overtly propaganda purposes; Theodore Roosevelt with his fireside chats and Stanley Baldwin with his similar, relaxed, confidential style introduced the medium more gently to US and British political cultures. Some politicians like Neville Chamberlain were quite skilled at addressing cinema audiences via Pathé News films, but others like (surprisingly) the fascist leader Oswald Mosley – a fiery platform speaker – proved to be wooden and ineffective. During the war radio became the major and much-used medium for political opinion – Churchill's broadcasts were crucial – and news, while film drama was used extensively to reinforce values such as patriotism and resistance.

It was in 1952, however, that the television revolution began in earnest with Richard Nixon's embattled 'Checkers' broadcast, made to clear his name of financial wrongdoing. Offering himself as a hard-working honest person of humble origins, he finished his talk by telling viewers how his daughter had received a puppy as a present: he did not care what anyone said, he was not going to give Checkers back (see quotation). This blatant appeal to sentiment proved spectacularly successful and confirmed Nixon's vice-presidential place on the Eisenhower ticket. Later on, television ironically contributed to Nixon's undoing through the famous televised debates with Kennedy during the 1960 presidential election contest. Despite an assured verbal performance – those listening on the radio thought he had bested Kennedy – Nixon, the favourite, looked shifty with his five o'clock shadow and crumpled appearance. Kennedy's good looks

and strong profile gave him the edge. Politicians the world over looked, listened and learned that how you appear on television counts for as much as what you say.

Richard Nixon – the 'Checkers' speech

" I should say this: Pat doesn't have a mink coat, but she does have a respectable Republican cloth coat. One other thing I should probably tell you, because if I don't they'll be saying this about me too. We did get something, a gift, after the election…a little cocker spaniel in a crate all the way from Texas. … And our little girl, Trisha, the six-year-old, named it Checkers. And you know, the kids love that dog, and I just want to say this right now, that regardless of what they say about it, we're gonna keep it!

Richard Nixon, US Vice-President, in the 'Checkers speech',
after he had been accused of using campaign funds for
his personal gain, 1952 (cited in Green, 1982) "

What they say about the papers

" Four hostile newspapers are more to be feared than a thousand bayonets.   *Napoleon Bonaparte*

The gallery where the reporters sit has become the fourth estate of the realm.   *Lord Macaulay, 1828*

In America the president rules for four years and journalism rules for ever and ever.   *Oscar Wilde*

The business of the New York journalist is to destroy the truth, to lie outright, to pervert, to vilify, to fawn at the feet of Mammon, and to sell his race and his country for his daily bread. … We are the tools and vassals of rich men behind the scenes. … We are intellectual prostitutes.
    John Swinton, US journalist, 1880

As a journalist who became a politician. … I formed rather a different view about the relations between government and the press. What shocked me when I was in government was the easy way in which information was leaked.   *Norman Fowler, Memoirs, 1991*

I am absolved of responsibility. We journalists don't have to step on roaches. All we have to do is turn on the light and watch the critters scuttle.
    P. J. O'Rourke on the duties of journalists in relation to politics
    (Parliament of Whores, 1992, p. xix) "

The British Broadcasting Corporation (BBC) was established as a public corporation in 1926, a monopoly that was defended on the grounds that it provided a public service. At first, under the influence of John (later Lord) Reith it struck a high moral and 'socially responsible' note. The BBC set an example and a standard which influenced emergent broadcasting systems all over the world. Commercial television (ITV) broke the BBC monopoly and began broadcasting in 1955; commercial radio in 1973. The BBC was granted a second television channel (BBC2) in 1964; a second ITV channel (Channel 4) began broadcasting in 1982 and Channel 5 in 1997. In February 1989 Rupert Murdoch's Sky Television began broadcasting using satellite technology. After a quiet start the new technology took hold and was operating at a profit by 1993. Many of the channels offer old films and popular programme repeats from the USA, but Sky News has established itself as a respectable and competent twenty-four-hour news channel.

Although the Prime Minister appoints the chairman of the BBC and its board of governors and the government of the day reviews and renews the BBC's charter, its governors are supposed to act in an independent fashion. The creation of the independent television network under the IBA in 1954 ended the BBC's monopoly in television broadcasting. Independent Television's chairman, like the BBC's, is appointed by the government. However, since ITV is financed out of advertising revenues it enjoys more financial independence from the government.

Broadcasting – especially television – has had a transforming impact on political processes.

Media organisations and the political process

Two minutes of exposure at peak-time television enables politicians to reach more people than they could meet in a lifetime of canvassing, hand-wringing or addressing public meetings. Alternatively, speaking on BBC Radio 4's early morning *Today* programme gains access to an 'up-market' audience of over one million opinion formers and decision-makers (Margaret Thatcher always listened to it and once rang in unsolicited to comment). In consequence, broadcasting organisations have become potent players in the political game: the regularity and nature of access to television and radio has become a key political issue; interviewers like John Humphries, David Dimbleby and Jeremy Paxman have become important national figures; and

investigative current affairs programmes like *World in Action* and *Panorama* have occasionally become the source of bitter political controversy.

Veteran US broadcaster's views on television news

"For all those who either cannot or will not read, television lifts the floor of knowledge and understanding of the world around them. But for the others, through its limited exploration of the difficult issues, it lowers the ceiling of knowledge.

The sheer volume of television news is ridiculously small. The number of words spoken in a half-hour broadcast barely equals the number of words on two-thirds of a standard newspaper page. That is not enough to cover the whole day's major events. Compression of facts, foreshortened arguments, the elimination of extenuating explanation – all are dictated by TV's restrictive time frame and all distort, to some degree, the news on television. The TV correspondent as well as his or her subjects is a victim of this compression. With inadequate time to present a coherent report, the correspondent seeks to craft a final summary sentence that might make some sense of the preceding gibberish. This is hard to do without coming to a single point of view – and a one line editorial is born. The greatest victim in all this is our political process and in my view this is one of the greatest blots on the recent record of television news. Soundbite journalism simply isn't good enough to serve the people in our national elections. Studies have shown that in 1988 the average block of uninterrupted speech by a presidential candidate on the news networks was 9.8 seconds. The networks faithfully promised to do better in 1992. The average soundbite that year was 8.2 seconds. The networks promised to do better in 1996. Further, figures compiled by Harvard researcher Dr Kiku Adatto showed that in 1988 there was not a single instance in which a candidate was given as much as one minute of uninterrupted time on an evening's broadcast.

Compare these figures with those of the newscasts in 1968. Then the average soundbite was 42.3 seconds ... and 21 percent of soundbites by presidential candidates ran at least a minute.

Walter Kronkite, a Reporter's Life, Knopf, 1997, extracted for The Guardian, 27 January 1997"

Television has influenced the form of political communication

In the nineteenth century it was commonplace for political meetings to entail formal addresses from great orators, like Gladstone or Lloyd George lasting an hour or more. Television has transformed this process. To command attention in our living-rooms politicians have to be relaxed, friendly, confidential – they have to talk to us as individuals rather than as members of a crowd. Long speeches are out and orators are obsolete: political messages have to be compressed into spaces of two to three minutes – often less. Slogans and key phrases have become so important that speech writers are employed to think them up. The playwright Ronald Millar was thus employed and helped produce Margaret Thatcher's memorable 'The lady's not for turning' speech at the 1981 Conservative Party conference.

Television and the image

Since the arrival of television appearances have been crucial. Bruce (1992) quotes a study which suggested 'the impact we make on others depends on … how we look and behave – 55%; how we speak – 38% and what we say only 7%. Content and form must therefore synchronise for, if they don't, form will usually dominate or undermine content' (p. 41). So we saw Harold Wilson smoking a pipe to pre-empt what his adviser Marcia Williams felt was an overly aggressive habit of shaking his fist to emphasise a point. Margaret Thatcher was the first leading politician to take image building totally professionally under the tutelage of her media guru, Gordon Reece. Peter Mandelson, Labour's premier spin doctor of the 1980s and 1990s, commented that by the mid-1980s: 'every part of her had been transformed: her hair, her teeth, her nose I suspect, her eyebrows. Not a part of Mrs Thatcher was left unaltered.' Every politician now has a career reason to be vain; Granada television's *World in Action* in 1989 wickedly caught David Owen personally adding the final touch to his coiffure from a hair-spray can just before going on air.

Some politicians are arguably barred from the highest office on account of their looks. Some say Kinnock's red hair (such as it was) and abundant freckles turned people off. Labour's Robin Cook's red hair and gnome-like appearance are said by some experts to disqualify him from the party's leadership despite his brilliant forensic skills and his position as the foremost parliamentarian of his day. American political scientists also conjecture that were he living today, Lincoln would never have been president with his jutting jaw and sunken eyes; similarly Herbert Hoover's obesity would have meant failure at the nomination stage. The perfect candidate was held by some to be Gary Hart, candidate for the presidency in 1988: very good-looking, charismatic, a good speaker, overloaded with charm and extremely intelligent. It was his excessive liking for pretty young women, and being found out, which proved his undoing with an American public which can insist on unreasonably high moral standards in its presidential hopefuls – though the success of the far from perfect Clinton in 1992 and 1996 suggests the nation has become more realistic.

Broadcasters have usurped the role of certain political institutions

Local party organisation is less important now that television can gain access to people's homes so easily and effectively. The message, however, is a more centralised national one, concentrating upon the party leadership rather than local issues and local people. The phenomenon of the SDP, moreover, has shown that a national party can now be created through media coverage without any substantial branch network. It also reveals how quickly such parties can decline once media interest wanes. However, this effect must not be exaggerated. The work of Seyd and Whiteley (1992) has proved that high local party membership and activity rates still have a positive effect on voting behaviour and correlate positively with higher poll results.

The House of Commons has lost some of its informing and educative function to the media. Ministers often prefer to give statements to the media rather than to Parliament and interviewers gain much more exclusive access to politicians than the House of Commons can ever hope for. Even public discussion and debate is now purveyed via radio and television programmes like the BBC's *Today*, *Newsnight* and *Question Time*. Some hoped that televising the House of Commons would win back some of these lost functions but others worried that the 'cure' would have damaging side-effects on the seriousness and efficacy of parliamentary procedures.

The appointment of party leaders

In 1951 Attlee was asked by a Pathé News reporter how the general election campaign was going. 'Very well', he replied. When it became obvious that the Prime Minister was not prepared to elaborate the interviewer asked him if he wished to say anything else. 'No' was the reply. Such behaviour did not survive the 1960s. Sir Alec Douglas-Home's lack of televisual skills was believed to have helped Labour win the 1964 election: he was smartly replaced by Edward Heath – himself not much better as it turned out. The success of Wilson and to a lesser extent Callaghan as television communicators made media skills an essential element of any aspiring premier's curriculum vitae. This is what made the choice of Michael Foot as Labour's leader in 1981 such a risky venture. A powerful and brilliant public speaker, Foot was ill at ease on television, tending to address the camera like a public meeting and to give long rambling replies. Worse, he tended to appear with ill-chosen clothes and on one occasion with spectacles held together with sticking plaster. These shortcomings may seem trivial; but they are important on television. Research shows that viewers make up their minds about people on television within seconds; and, as we saw above, manner and appearance are crucial in determining whether the reaction is positive or negative. It could be argued that Neil Kinnock was elected substantially as the televisual antidote to Foot; he was much better but still tended to give over-elaborate answers.

Personnel

Unsurprisingly, the media and politics have become more closely interrelated with media professionals like David Steel, Tony Benn, Bryan Gould and Austin Mitchell going into politics, and Robert Kilroy-Silk, Brian Walden and Mathew Parris moving out of politics and into the media. The apotheosis of this tendency was represented by former US president, Ronald Reagan, who used his actor's ability to speak lines to the camera to compensate for other political inadequacies. His astonishing political success is testimony to the prime importance of media skills in the current age. Professional help has become commonplace, with many ambitious politicians attending television training courses.

Spin doctors

These fearsome-sounding new actors on the political stage focus their energies on ensuring that the media give the desired interpretation to events or statements. Their provenance is usually thought to have

been the Dole–Mondale 1972 presidential debate when Republican advisers wanted to jump in first with their favourable verdicts on Dole's performance. Since then the popular idea is of somewhat shadowy figures moving around conference floors explaining what the party leader 'really' meant in his speech or on the phone to television executives cajoling and bullying to get their way. Kenneth Baker, when Chairman of the Conservative Party and therefore a *de facto* senior 'spinner', pulled off one of the great coups of the art in 1991 over the local government elections when Labour won 500 seats and the Conservatives lost 900. However, Baker had assiduously targeted the two 'flagship' boroughs of Wandsworth and Westminster – both setting very low poll tax – and when their majorities actually increased a wholly false impression of victory was conveyed to the press and reflected therein (though having a sympathetic press must have helped). The doyen of spin doctors however, and the one most commonly associated with the title in recent years, is the Labour MP Peter Mandelson. His ability to persuade and charm and to exert telling pressure was legendary but he was also highly instrumental in using his concern for presentation to

Peter Mandelson, MP, 'spinner' *extraordinaire*
By courtesy of Popperfoto

influence Labour's swift move to the right after the débâcle of 1987. He fully acknowledges his affinity with his grandfather, Herbert Morrison who 'rebuilt the Labour Party from the ashes of the thirties'.

In an interview in *The Guardian*, on 21 December 1995 he explained that he had given up his old trade: 'Those in my own party who fear my legendary powers with the press can relax. Conservatives, on the other hand, shouldn't relax, because my election experience is still going to be brought to bear' (he was chair of Labour's election planning group). The role of spin doctor in chief has in theory passed on to Alastair Campbell, Blair's press secretary, but few doubt Mandelson was very close to Blair's inner councils in the run up to the election.

The government uses the media more extensively to convey its messages

On 31 January 1989 Kenneth Clarke and other sundry ministers participated in a £1.25 million nationwide television link-up to sell the government's White Paper *Working for Patients*. The Conservative government in the 1980s embraced the media as the key vehicle for favourable presentations of its policies and programmes to the public. In the autumn of 1989 it was revealed that spending on government advertis-

Alastair Campbell, Blair's press secereetary
By courtesy of Popperfoto/Reuter

ing had risen from £35 million to £200 million between 1979 and 1989. This made the government one of the country's ten biggest advertisers. Critics pointed out that a government which had passed legislation to prevent Labour local authorities using ratepayers' money to advance partisan policies seemed to be doing precisely the same at a national level – but on a vastly increased scale.

Public relations hype had been used extensively to sell early privatisations but, allegedly at the instigation of Lord Young (former Trade Secretary), had subsequently been used for party political purposes. This is clearly a grey area in that any government has to spend money to explain new laws and regulations to the public at large, and it is inevitable that such publicity will often reflect party political values. But clear Cabinet rules do exist on this topic: in using advertising governments should exercise restraint, should not disseminate party policy and, most importantly, should not advertise programmes which have not yet been enacted into law. On 4 September 1989 BBC's *Panorama* revealed that over £20 million had already been spent by the water boards to advertise their imminent privatisation. Michael Howard claimed this campaign was not advertising but 'part of an awareness raising campaign'. The same programme looked at the Action for Jobs campaign run just before the 1987 election, which seemed to be aiming reassuring messages at people in work in marginal constituencies in the south-east. However, the Public Accounts Committee investigation concluded no rules had been broken.

The televising of Parliament

The proposal that the proceedings of Parliament be televised was first formally proposed in 1966: it was heavily defeated. While other legislative chambers, including the House of Lords, introduced the cameras with no discernible ill effects, the House of Commons resolutely refused, chiefly on the grounds that such an intrusion would rob the House of its distinctive intimate atmosphere. By the late 1970s, however, the majorities in favour of exclusion were wafer thin and the case would have been lost in the 1980s but for the stance of Margaret Thatcher. In November 1985 it had been rumoured she had changed her mind but at the last minute she decided to vote true to form and a number of Conservative MPs – known for their loyalty, or obsequiousness, depending on your viewpoint – about to vote for the televising of the House instead rushed to join their leader in the 'No' lobby.

Even after the vote in favour of a limited experiment the introduction of the cameras was substantially delayed, and the Select Committee on Procedure introduced severe restrictions on what the cameras could show: for example, only the head and shoulders of speakers could be featured, reaction shots of previous speakers were not allowed and in the event of a disturbance the cameras were to focus immediately on the dignified person of the Speaker. Finally, however, on 21 November 1989 the House appeared on television, debating the Queen's Speech. Margaret Thatcher reflected on the experience as follows:

I was really glad when it was over because it is ordeal enough when you are speaking in the Commons or for Question Time without television, but when you have got television there, if you are not careful, you freeze – you just do. ... It is going to be a different House of Commons, but that is that. (The Times, 24 November 1989)

In January 1990 some of the broadcasting restrictions were relaxed: reaction shots of an MP clearly being referred to were allowed together with 'medium-range' shots of the chamber some four rows behind the MP speaking or from the benches opposite. By the summer of 1990 it was obvious even to critical MPs that civilisation as we know it had not come to an end. On 19 July the Commons voted 131–32 to make televising of the chamber permanent. David Amess MP opined that the cameras had managed to 'trivialise our proceedings and we have spoilt that very special atmosphere we had here'. His was a lone voice, but in December 1993 Michael Portillo joined him, regretting his own vote in favour.

Television has transformed the electoral process

Since the 1950s television has become the most important media element in general elections. Unlike the USA, political advertising is not allowed on British television but party political broadcasts are allocated on the basis of party voting strength. These have become important during elections, have become increasingly sophisticated and some – like the famous Hugh Hudson-produced party political broadcast on Neil Kinnock in 1987 – can have a substantial impact on voter perceptions. More important, however, is the extensive news and current affairs coverage, and here US practice is increasingly being followed:

1. *Professional media managers* – like the Labour Party's Peter Mandelson (now MP for Hartlepool) – have become increasingly important. Brendan Bruce, Conservative Director of Communications 1989–91, discerns four types of media specialist in politics: those who manage the media briefing process (press secretaries, 'spin doctors'); image 'minders' who seek to control and stage-manage media events; 'wordsmiths' who provide speeches, one-liners, and so forth; and the various lobbyists who try to shape media coverage by influencing media and government decision-makers. 'The survival of entire governments and companies now depends on the effectiveness of these advisers yet few outside the inner circles of power even know these mercenaries exist or what their true functions are' (Bruce, 1992, p.128). The Conservatives employ professional public relations agencies, the most famous of which is Saatchi and Saatchi. Political management of media-dominated elections can cause major internal rows – like that between Norman Tebbit and Lord Young during the 1987 election.

2. *Political meetings* have declined. Political leaders now follow their US counterparts in planning their activities in the light of likely media coverage. The hustings – open meetings in which debates and heckling occurs – have given way to stage-managed rallies to which only party members have access. Entries, exits and ecstatic applause are all carefully planned with the audience as willing accomplices. Critics argue that this development has helped to reduce the amount of free public debate during elections and has shifted the emphasis from key issues to marketing hype. Defenders of the media answer that its discussion programmes provide plenty of debate; from 1974 Granada TV ran a television version of the hustings – *The Granada 500* – whereby a representative five hundred people from the north-west regularly questioned panels of politicians and experts on the important issues.

3. Given *television's requirements* for short, easily packaged messages, political leaders insert pithy, memorable passages into their daily election

utterances – the so-called *soundbite* – in the knowledge that this is what television wants and will show in their news broadcasts and summaries throughout the day.

Media and pressure groups

Just as individual politicians influence the media and seek their platforms to convey their messages, so do pressure groups as part of their function of influencing government policy. Pressure group campaigners like Des Wilson are expert in knowing and manipulating the form in which press and television like to receive stories. Because they have been so successful, much pressure group activity now concerns using the media. Anti-blood sports campaigners use yellow smoke when trying to disrupt hunting events as they know television responds well to it. Greenpeace campaigners occupied the ship carrying the French in the Pacific during the nuclear tests in 1995 and kept in touch with the world's press right up to the moment they were forcibly ejected and able to adopt martyrs' clothes on behalf of their organisation. A similar approach was used by Friends of the Earth during the 1995 campaign to prevent Shell's oil platform, Brent Spar, from being disposed of by sinking it in the ocean. On a more mundane but no less effective level, the Snowdrop campaign to achieve a total ban on handguns following the Dunblane massacre of schoolchildren by a crazed gunman in 1996 was able to win the nation's attention through a huge petition and high-profile appearances by its leaders at the 1996 Labour Party conference and on countless news bulletins both on television and radio. To a large extent in modern, developed societies, politics is conducted via the media.

The mass media and voting behaviour

Jay Blumler *et al.* wrote in 1978 that 'modern election campaigns have to a considerable extent become fully and truly television campaigns'. But what impact do the mass media have on the way in which citizens cast their votes? Does the form which different media give to political messages make any major difference? Substantial research on this topic has been undertaken, though with little definite outcome. One school of thought favours the view that the media do very little to influence voting directly but merely reinforce existing preferences.

Blumler and McQuail (1967) argued that people do not blandly receive and react to political media messages but apply a filter effect. Denver (1992, p. 99) summarises this effect under the headings of selective exposure, selective perception and selective retention.

1. *Selective exposure:* Many people avoid politics altogether when on television or in the press, while those who are interested favour those newspapers or television programmes which support rather than challenge their views.
2. *Selective perception:* The views and values which people have serve to 'edit' incoming information so that they tend to accept what they want to believe and ignore what they do not.
3. *Selective retention:* The same editing process is applied to what people choose to remember of what they have read or viewed.

This mechanism is most likely to be at work when people read newspapers. Most people read a newspaper which coincides with their own political allegiances. Harrop's studies produce the verdict that newspapers exert 'at most a small direct influence on changes in voting behaviour among their readers' (quoted in Negrine, 1995, p. 208). Election results in 1983 and 1987 have given support to the reinforcement-via-filter-effect argument. In a thorough empirical study of these elections Newton (1992) found a result which was 'statistically and substantively significant'. The impact seemed to vary from election to election and to be greatest when the result was closest. It would also seem that the Labour press was more important for the Labour vote than the Conservative press for the Conservative vote (Newton, 1992, p. 68). Both these media-dominated election campaigns, moreover, had little apparent impact upon the result. Over 80 per cent questioned in one poll claimed they had voted in accordance with preferences established before the campaign began and the parties' eventual share of the vote accorded quite closely with pre-campaign poll ratings. In 1983 the Conservatives kicked off with a 15.8 per cent lead over Labour and finished with a 15.2 per cent advantage. Some weeks before the election in 1987 the average of five major polls gave Conservatives 42 per cent, Labour 30.5 per cent and the Alliance 25.5 per cent; the final figures were 43, 32 and 23 per cent respectively – and this despite a Labour television campaign which was widely described as brilliant and admired even by their opponents. Perhaps people had 'turned off' in the face of excessive media coverage? Certainly, viewing figures declined and polls reflected a big majority who felt coverage had been either 'too much' or 'far too much'.

The filter-reinforcement thesis, however, seems to accord too minor a role to such an all-pervasive element. It does not seem to make 'common' sense. In an age when party preferences have weakened and people are voting much more instrumentally, according to issues (as we saw in Chapter 11), then surely the more objective television coverage has a role to play in switching votes? Is it reasonable to suppose the filter effect negates all information which challenges or conflicts with established positions? If so, then why do parties persist in spending large sums on party political broadcasts? Some empirical data support a direct-influence thesis, especially in respect of television:

1. Ivor Crewe maintains that during election campaigns up to 30 per cent of voters switch their votes, so despite the surface calm in 1983 and 1987 there was considerable 'churning' beneath the surface. These two elections may have been unusual in any case: the before and after campaign variations were much larger in 1979, 1974 and 1970 though not in the landslide 1997 election.

2. Many studies reveal that the four weeks of an election campaign provide too short a time over which to judge the impact of the media. Major shifts in voting preference take place between elections and it is quite possible that media coverage plays a significant role.

3. Crewe's research also suggests that the Alliance's television broadcasts did have a significant impact in 1983 and to a lesser extent in 1987 in influencing late deciders.

4. Following the Hugh Hudson-produced party political broadcast in 1987 Neil Kinnock's personal rating leapt sixteen points in polls taken shortly afterwards. It could also be that without their professional television campaign Labour might have fared much worse.

5. Other research suggests that the impact of television messages will vary according to the group which is receiving them. This may help explain the pro-Alliance switchers and the responses recorded in Table 12.3. Here the question posed in 1983 was: 'Has television coverage helped you in deciding about who to vote for in the election?' The table shows that people who voted for the same party as in 1979 were less likely to answer 'yes' than those who voted for a different party. It also shows that young people, voting for the first time, were much more likely to attribute a decisive influence to television.

6. In the wake of their 1992 victory the former Conservative Party treasurer, Lord MacAlpine, congratulated the tabloid press for effectively winning the election. The *Sun* responded with the headline (12 April) 'It's the Sun wot won it'. Neil Kinnock agreed. In November 1995 Martin Linton of *The Guardian* reported on a twelve-month study which supported the view that the *Sun* and other tabloids had made a crucial difference to the election result. Labour's post-mortem inquiry calculated that 400,000 votes were swung by the tabloids in the crucial last week of the campaign; MORI's research, based on 22,000 voters, reinforced this claim and the proposition that the tabloids could have made the difference between who won and lost.

Judging the effect of the media on voting behaviour is very difficult, because it is so hard to disentangle it from myriad factors like family, work, region, class, and so forth, which play a determining role. It seems fair to say, however, that:

1. *The media do reinforce political attitudes:* This is important when the degree of commitment to a party can prove crucial when events between elections, as they always do, put loyalties to the test.

2. *The media help to set the agenda of debate:* During election campaigns party press conferences attempt to achieve this but the media do not always conform and between elections the media play a much more important agenda-setting role.

3. *It is clear that media reportage has some direct impact upon persuading voters to change sides*, but research has not yet made clear whether this effect is major or marginal.

1997 election campaign

This campaign was dominated as usual by television and soundbites. However, there is some evidence that the long six-week campaign turned the public off.

Table 12.3 Impact of television on voters: response to question 'Has television coverage helped you in deciding who to vote for in the election?' (per cent)

| | Stability of vote | | |
	Same as 1979	Different from 1979	'New' voters
Yes	13	25	31
No	85	73	63
Don't know	1	2	6

Source: Negrine, 1996, p. 192

Table 12.4 The press, television and political influence

Television	Press
Balanced	Partisan
Trusted	Not trusted
Mass audience	Segmented audience
'Passive' audience politically	'Active' audience
Most important source of information	Secondary source

Source: Lecture by David Denver, September 1996

Ratings for the BBC Nine o'clock News fell from an average of 5.5 million viewers to 3.3 during the election for the specially extended bulletins. Considerable heat was generated by Major's challenge to debate Blair on television. Incumbent candidates usually refuse to give opponents the dignity of such an opportunity and Major's challenge was widely interpreted as a sign of weakness from the 'losing' candidate. In the event negotiations broke down with both sides blaming the other. If the Deputy Prime Ministerial debate involving Prescott, Heseltine and Beith is any indication of how the 'big match' would have played, then the level would not have risen above that of a crude slanging match. The Tory belief that a long campaign would precipitate Blair's collapse into inexperienced gaffes proved well wide of the mark. With remarkable resilience the Labour leader maintained his punishing schedule to the very last day and seemed nerveless in all televised situations, despite an early attempt to shake him by Michael Heseltine, who accused him of being unable to cope, sweating before speeches and on the verge of a breakdown (ironically it was Heseltine's health which broke down shortly after the election). An unusual involvement by television journalism in the election was via the contest for Tatton, where the MP accused of taking cash for asking parliamentary questions, Neil Hamilton, was opposed by the BBC's Martin Bell, standing as an anti-corruption candidate unopposed by Labour or the Lib. Dems. Throughout the bitterly fought campaign Hamilton accused Bell of libel as well as, astonishingly, corruption but on the vital day the voters chose to believe Bell who romped home with an unbelievable 11,000 majority.

Labour's disciplined election machine reacted sharply to neutralise any attempt to link the party with nationalisation, high taxation or a subservient union link. The documentary maker Molly Dineen made an interesting film for a party political broadcast (PPB) about Blair filmed mainly in his own Islington kitchen. The British National Party's PPB, featuring overtly racist comments, was shown on television but only in the face of substantial criticism. Finally, the results service on television was much watched and admired for its superb coverage, the often parodied Peter Snow in particular driving his excellent graphics presentations throughout a fascinating watershed night in British politics.

The political impact of the media: the process

Given the ubiquity of media influence, Seymour-Ure is more than justified in judging that 'the mass media are so deeply embedded in the [political] system that without them political activity in its contemporary form could hardly carry on at all' (Seymour-Ure, 1974, p. 62; see also Table 12.4). He directs attention to the factors which determine the political effects of media messages and which will naturally have a bearing upon the way in which politicians attempt to manipulate them.

The *timing* of a news item 'can make all the difference to its significance' (p. 28). For example, Sir Alan Walters, Margaret Thatcher's part-time economic adviser, wrote an article in 1988 in which he described the European monetary system which Chancellor Nigel Lawson wanted Britain to join as 'half-baked'. Had it appeared immediately it might have caused some temporary embarrassment, but coming out as it did eighteen months later, in the middle of a highly publicised row over this very issue between Margaret Thatcher and her Chancellor, it contributed importantly to Nigel Lawson's eventual resignation on 26 October 1989.

The *frequency* with which items are featured in the mass media will influence their impact. The unfolding nature of the Westland revelations (when Michael Heseltine resigned over a dispute involving Westland Engineering), for example, kept Margaret Thatcher's political style on top of the political agenda for several damaging weeks in January and February 1986. By comparison the resignation of Chancellor Nigel Lawson, although a major cataclysm and one which touched on much more important policy issues, was relatively straightforward and after little more than a week the fuss had subsided.

The *intensity* with which media messages are communicated is also a key element. The Westland crisis and the resignation of Chancellor Nigel Lawson were so damaging to Margaret Thatcher because every daily and Sunday newspaper – serious and tabloid – and every radio and television news editor found these crises irresistible. The Lawson resignation story made the front page for over a week while two successive Brian Walden interviews with Margaret Thatcher and Lawson (29 October and 5 November 1990, respectively) were themselves widely reported news events.

The mass media and the theory of pluralist democracy

If the mass media have such a transforming impact upon politics then how have they affected the fabric of British democracy? It all depends upon what we mean by democracy. The popular and indeed 'official' view is that our elected legislature exerts watchdog control over the executive and allows a large degree of citizen participation in the process of government. This pluralist system provides a free market of ideas and a shifting, open competition for power between political parties, pressure groups and various other groups in society. Supporters of the present system claim that is not only how the system ought to work (a normative theory of government) but is, to a large extent, also descriptive: this is how it works in practice. According to this view the media play a vital political role:

1. They report and represent popular views to those invested with decision-making powers.
2. They inform society about the actions of government, educating voters in the issues of the

day. The range of newspapers available provides a variety of interpretations and advice.
3. They act as a watchdog of the public interest, defending the ordinary person against a possibly overmighty government through their powers of exposure, investigation and interrogation. To fulfil this neutral, disinterested role it follows that the media need to be given extensive freedom to question and publish.

This pluralist view of the media's role, once again both normative and descriptive, has been criticised along the following lines.

Ownership and control influences media messages

Excluding the BBC, the media organisations are substantially part of the business world and embrace profit-making as a central objective. This argument has more force since, following Murdoch's smashing of the union stranglehold over the press through his 'Wapping' revolution, newspapers now make substantial profits. This fact alone severely prejudices media claims to objectivity in reporting the news and reflecting popular feeling. In recent years ownership has concentrated markedly. About 80 per cent of newspaper circulation is in the hands of three conglomerates, Mirror Newspaper Group, United Newspapers and News International. The late Robert Maxwell owned the *Daily Mirror*, *Sunday Mirror* and *Sunday People*; Rupert Murdoch's News International owns the *Sun*, *News of the World*, *The Times*, and *The Sunday Times*. Both of these latter-day press barons also had strong television interests: Murdoch owns Sky Television and Maxwell had an interest in Central TV.

Bilton *et al.* (1996, pp. 66–8) demonstrate how newspaper and television ownership is closely interlinked and have become part of vast conglomerates with worldwide interests. Does it seem likely that such organisations will fairly represent and give a fair hearing to political viewpoints hostile to the capitalist system of which they are such an important part?

True, Maxwell's newspapers supported the Labour Party, but they did not exhibit anything which could be called a coherent socialist ideology. Maxwell was certainly interested, however, in dictating editorial policy, using his papers as a personal memo pad for projecting messages to world leaders (there is little or no evidence that they ever listened). Murdoch's newspapers used to support the Tories loudly, though disenchantment with Major's leadership led a cooling off from about 1994 onwards until the election in 1997 precipitated a 'conversion' to Blair's campaign. In the case of *The Observer* and *The Guardian* it can be argued that ownership is separate from control; but this was not true of Maxwell and is not true of Murdoch, who exerts strong personal editorial control.

Nor is the press especially accountable: the Press Council used to be a powerful and respected watchdog on newspaper editors but in recent years it has meekly acquiesced in the concentration of ownership on the grounds that the danger of monopoly control is less unacceptable than the bankruptcy of familiar national titles. Moreover, since the *Sun* has regularly flouted its rulings, the Council has lost even more respect and has been unable, for example, to prevent the private lives of public figures being invaded by tabloid journalists to an alarming degree.

Television evinces a much clearer distinction between ownership and control and fits more easily into the pluralist model. The BBC, of course, is government-owned and in theory at least its board of governors exercises independent control. Independent television is privately owned and this ownership is becoming more concentrated – five of the companies serve three-quarters of the national audience – but the Independent Broadcasting Authority (IBA) used its considerable legal powers under the 1981 Broadcasting Act to ensure 'balance' and 'due accuracy and impartiality' on sensitive political issues. This is not to say that television can be acquitted of the charge of bias – as we shall see below – but merely that television controllers are forbidden by law to display open partisanship and that those people who own their companies cannot insist upon particular editorial lines.

News values are at odds with the requirements of a pluralist system

In order to create profits media organisations compete for their audiences with the consequent pursuit of the lowest common denominator in public taste. In the case of the tabloids this means the relegation of hard news to inside pages and the promotion to the front page of trivial stories such as sex scandals, royal family gossip and the comings and goings of soap opera stars. On television the same tendency has been apparent with the reduction of current affairs programmes, their demotion from peak viewing times and the dilution of news programmes with more 'human interest' stories. As a result of this tendency it can be argued that the media's educative role in a pluralist democracy is being diminished. Some would go further, however, and maintain that the dominant news values adopted by the media are in any case inappropriate for this role. The experience of successful newspapers has helped to create a set of criteria for judging newsworthiness which news editors in all branches of the media automatically accept and apply more or less intuitively. The themes to which the public are believed to respond include:

1. *Personalities:* People quickly become bored with statistics and carefully marshalled arguments and relate to stories which involve disagreement, personality conflicts or interesting personal details. Westland and the Lawson resignation demonstrated this tendency in action when the clashes between Thatcher and her Cabinet colleagues were given prominence over the important European questions which underlay them.
2. *Revelations:* Journalist Nicholas Tomalin once defined news as the making public of something someone wished to keep secret. Leaked documents, financial malpractice and sexual peccadilloes are assiduously reported and eagerly read.
3. *Disasters:* The public has both a natural and a somewhat morbid interest in such matters.
4. *Visual back-up:* Stories which can be supported by good photographs or film footage will often take precedence over those which cannot be so supported.

It is commonly believed that newspapers which ignore these ground rules will fail commercially and that current affairs television which tries too hard to be serious will be largely ignored and described, fatally, as 'boring'. There is much evidence to suggest these news values are based on fact: these are the themes to which we most readily respond. It does mean, however, that the vast media industry is engaged in providing a distorted view of the world via its concentration upon limited and relatively unimportant aspects of social reality.

The lobby system favours the government of the day

The pluralist model requires that the media report news in a truthful and neutral way. We have already seen that ownership heavily influences the partisanship of the press, but other critics argue that the lobby system of political reporting introduces a distortion of a different kind. Some 150 political journalists at Westminster are known collectively as 'the lobby'. In effect they belong to a club with strict rules whereby they receive special briefings from government spokesmen in exchange for keeping quiet about their sources. Supporters claim this is an important means of obtaining information which the public would not otherwise receive, but critics disagree. Anthony Howard of *The Observer* has written that lobby correspondents, rather like prostitutes, become 'clients' or otherwise 'instruments for a politician's gratification' (Hennessy, 1985, p. 9). The charge is that journalists become lazy, uncritical and incurious, preferring to derive their copy from bland government briefings – often delivered at dictation speed. Peter Hennessy believes that this system 'comes nowhere near to providing the daily intelligence system a mature democracy has the right to expect ... as it enables Downing Street to dominate the agenda of mainstream political discussion week by week' (1985, pp. 10–11). The *Sun*, *The Guardian* and *The Independent* are so opposed to the system that for a while they withdrew from it.

Television companies are vulnerable to political pressure

Ever since the broadcasting media became an integral part of the political process during the 1950s governments of all complexions have had uneasy relationships with the BBC, an organisation with a worldwide reputation for excellence and for accurate, objective current affairs coverage. Margaret Thatcher, however, took government hostility to new lengths, indeed 'abhorrence of the BBC appeared for a while to be a litmus test for the Conservativeness of MPs' (Negrine, 1995, p. 125). Governments seek to influence the BBC in three major ways. Firstly, they have the power of appointment to the corporation's board of governors. The post of chairman is especially important; Marmaduke Hussey's appointment in 1986 was believed to be a response to perceived left-wing tendencies (according to one report he was ordered by Norman Tebbit's

office to 'get in there and sort it out – in days and not months'). Secondly, governments can threaten to alter the licence system (although former Home Secretary, Willie Whitelaw, knew of no occasion when this threat had been used): Margaret Thatcher was known to favour the introduction of advertising to finance the BBC but the Peacock Commission on the financing of television refused to endorse this approach. Thirdly, governments attempt to exert pressure in relation to particular programmes – often citing security reasons. The range of disputes between the Thatcher governments and the BBC is unparalleled in recent history. In part this was a consequence of a dominant, long-established and relatively unchallenged Prime Minister as well as Thatcher's determination to challenge the old consensus – she long suspected that it resided tenaciously within the top echelons of the BBC. During the Falklands War, some Conservative MPs actually accused BBC reports of being 'treasonable' because they questioned government accounts of the progress of the war. On such occasions, they claimed, the media should support the national effort. In 1986 a monitoring unit was set up in Conservative Central Office and in the summer a highly critical report on the BBC's coverage of the US bombing of Libya was submitted together with a fusillade of accusations from Party Chairman, Norman Tebbit. The BBC rejected the accusations and complained of 'political intimidation' in the run-up to a general election. The pressure almost certainly had some effect upon the BBC's subsequent news and current affairs presentation – supporting those who claim that the pluralist analysis of the media's role is inappropriate.

Television news coverage tends to reinforce the status quo

The argument here is that television news cannot accurately reflect events in the real world because it is, to use Richard Hoggart's phrase, 'artificially shaped' (Glasgow University Media Group, 1976, p. ix). ITN's editor, David Nicholas, says that '90 per cent of the time we are trying to tell people what we think they will want to know' (Tyne Tees TV, April 1986). It is what he and his colleagues think people want to know which attracts the fire of media critics. Faced with an infinitely multi-faceted social reality television news editors apply the selectivity of news values, serving up reports under severe time constraints in a particular abbreviated

---

BOX 12.1   **IDEAS AND PERSPECTIVES**

Bias, broadcasting and the political parties

Harold Wilson was notoriously paranoid about the media and believed that not only the press but also the BBC was 'ineradicably' biased against him, full of 'card carrying Tories', in the words of Michael Cockerell. Perhaps it is being in government which explains it as in the 1980s it was Margaret Thatcher and her 'enforcer' Norman Tebbit who seemed paranoid. He launched ferocious attacks on the corporation calling it 'the insufferable, smug, sanctimonious, naive, guilt-ridden, wet, pink, orthodoxy of that sunset home of that third rate decade, the sixties'.

Answering questions in the House can be stressful amidst all the noise but ultimately the barbs can be ignored and the questions avoided easily. But on radio or television well briefed interviewers can put politicians on the spot. This is why ministers have complained so vehemently. Jonathon Aitken (then Chief Secretary to the Treasury) in March 1995 won ecstatic applause from Conservatives when he delivered a No. 10-cleared speech attacking the 'Blair Broadcasting Corporation'. In the firing line on this occasion were *Today* presenter John Humphries (who had given him a bad time on the *Today* programme) and *Newsnight*'s Jeremy Paxman (the *bête noir* of all ministers), accused of 'ego trip

interviewing'. Unfortunately for them the Director-General of the BBC, John Birt, had earlier made a speech in Dublin criticising 'sneering and overbearing' interviewers, though he took the trouble to write to both men denying he was attacking them (though it's hard to think to whom else he could have been referring). Cockerell explains that Humphries is not a 'politically motivated questioner; his aim is to strip away the public relations gloss and to use his own sharp teeth to counter pre-rehearsed soundbites'. He continues, 'Aitken was really objecting to the BBC doing its job: it is one that the politicians of both parties have wanted to do since the earliest days' (*The Guardian*, 28 May 1996).

This probably gets to the heart of the perennial conflict between politicians and the media. Politicians in power ideally would like to control the media – Mrs Thatcher once said she did not like short interviews but would like instead to have four hours of airtime on her own – and resent the criticism which they receive from journalists and interviewers. In a pluralist democracy it is indeed the job of the media to make government more accountable to the public and perhaps it is when politicians do not like it that the media are doing their jobs most effectively.

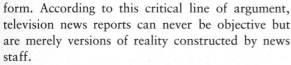

---

form. According to this critical line of argument, television news reports can never be objective but are merely versions of reality constructed by news staff.

Reports will be formulated, furthermore, within the context of thousands of assumptions regarding how news personnel think the public already perceive the world. Inevitably they will refer to widely shared consensus values and perceptions and will reflect these in their reports, thus reinforcing them and marginalising minority or radical alternatives. So television, for example, tends to present the parliamentary system as the only legitimate means of reaching decisions and

tends to present society as basically unified without fundamental class conflicts and cleavages. Because alternative analyses are squeezed out and made to seem odd or alien, television – so it is argued – tends to reinforce status quo values and institutions and hence protect the interests of those groups in society which are powerful or dominant. The Greens offer an interesting case study in that for many years they fell outside the consensus. Towards the end of the 1980s, however, it suddenly became apparent even to the main party leaders that the Green arguments had earned a place for themselves within rather than outside the mainstream of political culture.

The Glasgow University Media Group take this argument further. On the basis of their extensive programme analyses they suggest that television coverage of economic news tends to place the 'blame for society's industrial and economic problems at the door of the workforce. This is done in the face of contradictory evidence, which then it appears is either ignored [or] smothered' (1976, pp. 267–8). Reports on industrial relations were 'clearly skewed against the interests of the working class and organised labour ... in favour of the managers of industry'. The Glasgow research provoked a storm of criticism. David Nicholas dismissed it as a set of conclusions supported by selective evidence (Tyne Tees TV, April 1986). In 1985 an academic counterblast was provided by Martin Harrison, which criticised the slender basis of the Glasgow research and adduced new evidence which contradicted its conclusions.

Marxist theories of class dominance

The Glasgow research is often cited in support of more general theories on how the media reinforce, protect and advance dominant class interests in society. Variations on the theme were produced by Gramsci, in the 1930s by the Frankfurt School of social theorists and in the 1970s by the social-cultural approach of Professor Stuart Hall (for detailed analysis see McQuail, 1983, pp. 57–70; Watts,

1997), but the essence of their case is summed up in Marx's proposition that 'the ideas of the ruling class are in every epoch the ruling ideas'. He argued that those people who own and control the economic means of production – the ruling class – will seek to persuade everyone else that preserving status quo values and institutions is in the interests of society as a whole.

The means employed are infinitely subtle and indirect, via religious ideas, support for the institution of the family, the monarchy and much else. Inevitably the role of the mass media, according to this analysis, is crucial. Marxists totally reject the pluralist model of the media as independent and neutral, as the servant rather than the master of society. They see it merely as the instrument of class domination, owned by the ruling class and carrying their messages into every home in the land. It is in moments of crisis, Marxists would claim, that the fundamental bias of state institutions is made clear. In 1926, during the general strike, Lord Reith, the first Director-General of the BBC, provided some evidence for this view when he confided to his diary, 'they want us to be able to say they did not commandeer us, but they know they can trust us not to be really impartial'. Marxists believe the media obscures the fact of economic exploitation by ignoring radical critiques and disseminating entertainments and new interpretations which subtly reinforce the status quo and help

Table 12.5 Dominance and pluralism models compared

	Dominance	Pluralism
Societal source	Ruling class or dominant elite	Competing political social, cultural interests and groups
Media	Under concentrated ownership and of uniform type	Many and independent of each other
Production	Standardised, routinised, controlled	Creative, free, original
Content and world view	Selective and coherent: decided from 'above'	Diverse and competing views responsive to audience demand
Audience	Dependent, passive, organised on large scale	Fragmented, selective, reactive and active
Effects	Strong and confirmative of established social order	Numerous, without consistency or predictability of direction, but often 'no effect'

Source: McQuail, 1983, p. 68

to sustain a 'false consciousness' of the world based on ruling-class values. For Marxists, therefore, the media provide a crucial role in persuading the working classes to accept their servitude and to support the system which causes it. Table 12.5 usefully contrasts the pluralist with the class dominance model.

Which of the two models best describes the role of the media in British society? From the discussion so far the pluralist model would appear inadequate in a number of respects. Its ability to act as a fair and accurate channel of communication between government and society is distorted by the political bias of the press, the lobby system, news values and the tendency of television to reflect consensual values. The media, moreover, are far from being truly independent: the press is largely owned by capitalist enterprises and television is vulnerable to government pressures of various kinds. Does this mean that the dominance model is closer to the truth? Not really.

While the dominance model quite accurately describes a number of media systems operating under oppressive regimes, it greatly exaggerates government control of the media in Britain.

1. As David Nicholas observes (Tyne Tees TV, April 1986), 'trying to manipulate the news is as natural an instinct to a politician as breathing oxygen', but because politicians try does not mean that they always succeed. People who work in the media jealously guard their freedom and vigorously resist government interference. The *This Week* 'Death on the Rock' programme on the SAS killings in Gibraltar was after all shown in 1988 despite Sir Geoffrey Howe's attempts to pressure the IBA. And Lord Windlesham's subsequent inquiry further embarrassed the government by completely exonerating the Thames TV programme.
2. The media may tend to reflect consensual views but this does not prevent radical messages regularly breaking into the news – sometimes because they accord with news values themselves. Television also features drama productions which challenge and criticise the status quo: for example, at the humorous level in the form of *Spitting Image*; and at the serious level in the form of BBC's 1988 legal series *Blind Justice*. Even soap operas like *EastEnders* often challenge and criticise the status quo.

3. Programmes like *Rough Justice* and *First Tuesday* have shown that persistent and highly professional research can shame a reluctant establishment into action to reverse injustices – as in the case of the Guildford Four, released in 1989 after fifteen years of wrongful imprisonment. Consumer programmes like the radio series *Face the Facts* do champion the individual, as do regular newspaper campaigns.
4. News values do not invariably serve ruling-class interests, otherwise governments would not try so hard to manipulate them. Margaret Thatcher, for example, cannot have welcomed the explosion of critical publicity which surrounded Westland, her July 1989 reshuffle or the Lawson resignation. And it was Rupert Murdoch's *Times* which took the lead in breaking the story about Cecil Parkinson's affair with his secretary, Sarah Keays, in 1983.

Each model, then, contains elements of the truth but neither comes near the whole truth. Which is the nearest? The reader must decide; but despite all its inadequacies and distortions the pluralist model probably offers the better framework for understanding how the mass media affects the British political system.

Language and politics

All this modern emphasis on technology can obscure the fact that in politics language is still of crucial importance. Taking the example of Northern Ireland, we have seen that how the precise meaning of words has provided a passionate bone of contention. When the IRA announced its ceasefire in 1994, its opponents insisted it should be a 'permanent' one. The paramilitary organisation, however, did not wish to abandon its ability to use the threat of violence as a negotiating counter and refused to comply, insisting that its term 'complete' ceasefire was as good as the British government needed or would in any case get. Gerry Adams, President of the political wing of the IRA, Sinn Fein, had a similar problem over his attitude towards bombings. His close contact with the bombers made it impossible for him to condemn the bombing of Manchester in June 1996 so he used other less committing words like 'regret' or 'unfortunate'. Another aspect is tone of voice, which can bestow whole varieties of meaning to a statement or a speech. Sir Patrick Mayhew, for example, John Major's Northern Ireland Secretary, specialises in being 'calm'. After the reopening of violence in the summer of 1996 he had much need for this, enunciating his words slowly and with great care, as if attempting to soothe the wounded feelings of the antagonists and reassure the rest of the country that, contrary to appearances, everything was all right. A more absurd example is Margaret Thatcher's opposition to the wording on a proposed anti-AIDS poster; according to *The Guardian* (18 July 1996), she felt the clearly worded warnings about anal sex were too shocking to be used.

Another example of language being of crucial importance occurred in November 1996 when whip David Willetts was accused of interfering with the deliberations of the Commons Standards and Privileges Committee regarding the investigation of Neil Hamilton's alleged receiving of cash for parliamentary activities on behalf of Mohamed Al Fayed. According to Willetts' own notes of his meeting with the chairman of the committee, Sir Geoffrey Johnson-Smith, he 'wants' advice. On the face of it this seemed as if the government was interfering with the quasi-judicial procedures of the House. In explanation to the committee the whip said he meant the word in the biblical sense of 'needs'. Most commentators were unimpressed.

The media and politics: future developments

The structure of television underwent an upheaval in the early 1990s at the hands of the 'deregulators' led by Thatcher. She had dearly wished to end the licence fee which funds the BBC but the lukewarm response of the Peacock Commission set up to look at this problem headed off this possibility for the time being at least (until 2007). In October 1991 franchises were sold off for independent television regions. Critics complain that these new developments will dilute still further the standards in broadcasting established by the BBC's famous former head, the high-minded Lord Reith. The inception of satellite broadcasting in 1982 via the Murdoch-owned Sky Television has opened up the possibility of an infinite number of channels, all aimed at the same markets and all tending to move the locus of their messages down market. Sky News, a twenty-four-hour news service has allayed some fears by developing, after a

shaky start, into a competent and well-respected service. With over 130 satellite channels in Europe and cable companies making a huge investment in access for their service, the expansion of choice is set to be exponential over the next decade or more. The inception of digital television, which entails the conversion of the broadcast signal into a computerised message, will revolutionise a sector virtually in permanent revolution anyway. This system requires the use of a set-top decoder and can receive signals from satellite or terrestrial stations. The latter fear that Rupert Murdoch will be able to control access to this new technology by being the first in the field to provide the decoders – the argument being that consumers will happily buy one but not any more so that the company in first will effectively be the gatekeeper. Media companies hope that Murdoch will be forced by government regulation to make his technology available to other broadcasters, but the Australian multimillionaire is as much interested in power as in money and is unlikely to relinquish his option for more of both easily, if at all.

Some critics claim the new profusion of television channels will mark the end of quality. They point to the USA, where there is an infinite diversity yet an unremitting mediocrity, and predict that the UK will go the same way.

For politics the technology with the most potential might well prove to be the Internet, for which one needs a telephone line, a modem, some software and a computer. Currently 50 million are logged on worldwide but the service is expanding and has all kinds of implications:

1. *Information*: It is now possible to download immense amounts of up to date information about political issues via the Net.
2. *Email*: It is possible to communicate with politicians and the politically active all over the world, extending enormously the scope of political action.
3. *Interactive democracy*: By being hooked up to the Net it might be possible for politicians or government in democracies to seek endorsement for policies directly from the people. This would have all kinds of drawbacks, e.g. it could slow down the political process even more than at present in developed countries; it could give a platform to unsavoury messages like racism and power-seeking ideologues; it might enthrone the

majority with a power it chooses to abuse. But these opportunities exist and it is virtually certain they will be experimented with if not adopted in the near future.

Chapter summary

The spoken voice was the main form of political communication until the spread of newspapers in the nineteenth century. Broadcasting introduced a revolution into the way politics is conducted as its spread is instant and its influence so great. New political actors have emerged specialising in the media and politicians have learnt to master its techniques. Press news values tend to influence television also, but the latter is more vulnerable to political pressure than the already politicised press. Class dominance theories suggest the media is no more than an instrument of the ruling class but there is reason to believe it exercises considerable independence and is not incompatible with democracy.

Discussion points

- Should British political parties be allowed to buy political advertising on television?

- Has televising Parliament enhanced or detracted from the efficacy of Parliament?

- Does television substantially affect voting behaviour?

- Do the media reinforce the political status quo or challenge it?

- Should interviewers risk appearing rude when confronting politicians?

Further reading

The best available study of the media and British politics is Watts (1997). Also useful is Negrine (1995). The two most readable studies of leadership, the media and politics are both by Michael Cockerell (Cockerell, 1988; Cockerell *et al.*, 1984). Bruce (1992) is excellent on the behaviour of politicians in relation to the media. Blumler and Gurevitch (1995) is an essay on the crisis of communication for citizenship and as such is an interesting source of ideas. See Jones (1993) on the television interview. The most

brilliant and funny book about the press is Chippendale and Orrie's history of the *Sun* (1992).

References

Bilton, A. *et al.* (1996) *Introductory Sociology*, 3rd edn (Macmillan).

Blumler, J.G. and Gurevich, M. (1995) *The Crisis of Public Communication* (Routledge).

Blumler, J.G. and McQuail, D. (1967) *Television in Politics* (Faber and Faber).

Blumler, J.G., Gurevitch, M. and Ives, J. (1978) *The Challenge of Election Broadcasting* (Leeds University Press).

Bruce, B. (1992) *Images of Power* (Kogan Page).

Chippendale, P. and Orrie, C. (1992) *Stick it Up Your Punter* (Mandarin).

Cockerell, M. (1988) *Live from Number Ten* (Faber and Faber).

Cockerell, M., Walker, D. and Hennessy, P. (1984) *Sources Close to the Prime Minister* (Macmillan).

Denver, D. (1992) *Elections and Voting Behaviour*, 2nd edn (Harvester Wheatsheaf).

Glasgow University Media Group (1976) *Bad News* (Routledge and Kegan Paul).

Green, J. (1982) *Book of Political Quotes* (Angus and Robertson).

Harrison, M. (1985) *TV News: Whose Bias* (Hermitage, Policy Journals).

Hennessy, P. (1985) *What the Papers Never Said* (Political Education Press).

Jones, B. (1993) ' "The pitiless probing eye": politicians and the broadcast political interview', *Parliamentary Affairs*, January.

McQuail, D. (1983) *Mass Communication Theory: An Introduction* (Sage).

Negrine, R. (1995) *Politics and the Mass Media*, 2nd edn (Routledge).

Newton, K. (1992) 'Do voters believe everything they read in the papers?', in I. Crewe, P. Norris, D. Denver and D. Broughton (eds), *British Elections and Parties Yearbook* (Harvester Wheatsheaf).

O'Rourke, P.J. (1992) *Parliament of Whores* (Picador).

Sevaldsen, J. and Vardmand, O. (1993) *Contemporary British Society*, 4th edn (Academic Press).

Seyd, P. and Whiteley, P. (1992) *Labour's Grass Roots* (Clarendon Press).

Seymore-Ure, C. (1974) *The Political Impact of the Mass Media* (Constable).

Watts, D. (1997) *Political Communication Today* (Manchester University Press).

Whale, J. (1977) *The Politics of the Media* (Fontana).

CHAPTER THIRTEEN

Pressure groups

BILL JONES

LEARNING OBJECTIVES

- To explain that formal democratic government structures conceal the myriad hidden contacts between government and organised interests.

- To introduce some familiarity with theories regarding this area of government–public interaction.

- To provide some specific examples of pressure group activity.

INTRODUCTION

The Norwegian political scientist Sven Rokkan, writing about his country's system said 'the crucial decisions on economic policy are rarely taken in the parties or in Parliament'. He judged 'the central area' to be 'the bargaining table' where the government authorities meet directly with the trade union leaders and other group leaders. 'These yearly rounds of negotiations mean more in the lives of rank and file citizens than formal elections.'

British politics are not as consensually well organised or cooperative as the Norwegian model, but there is a central core of similarity in respect of pressure group influence. Accordingly this chapter examines the way in which organised groups play their part in the government of the country. Democratic government is supposed to be government of the people, and politicians often claim to be speaking on behalf of public opinion. But how do rulers learn about what people want? Elections provide a significant but infrequent opportunity for people to participate in politics. These are held every four years or so, but pressure groups provide continuous opportunities for such involvement.

Interest or pressure groups are formed by people to protect or advance a shared interest. Like political parties, groups may be mass campaigning bodies, but whereas parties have policies for many issues and, usually, wish to form a government, groups are sectional and wish to influence government only.

The term 'pressure group' is relatively recent; but organised groups have tried to influence government long before the age of representative democracy. The Society for Effecting the Abolition of the Slave Trade was founded in 1787 and under the leadership of William Wilberforce and Thomas Clarkson succeeded in abolishing the slave trade in 1807. In 1839 the Anti-Corn Law League was established, providing a model for how a pressure group can influence government. It successfully mobilised popular and elite opinion against legislation which benefited landowners at the expense of the rest of society and in 1846 achieved its objective after converting the Prime Minister of the day, Sir Robert Peel, to its cause. It proved wrong the cynical dictum that the rich and powerful will always triumph over the poor and weak.   In the twentieth century the scope of government has grown immensely and impinges upon the lives of many different groups. After 1945 the development of the mixed economy and the welfare state drew even more people into the orbit of governmental activity. Groups developed to defend and promote interests likely to be affected by particular government policies. For its own part government came to see pressure groups as valuable sources of information and potential support. The variety of modern pressure groups therefore reflects the infinite diversity of interests in society. A distinction is usually drawn between the following:

1. *Sectional or interest groups*, most of which are motivated by the particular economic interests of their members. Classic examples of these are trade unions, professional bodies (e.g. the British Medical Association) and employers' organisations – the Anti-Corn Law League would also have fallen under this heading.

2. *Cause groups*, which exist to promote an idea not directly related to the personal interests of its members. The Society for Effecting the Abolition of the Slave Trade was such a group and in modern times the Campaign for Nuclear Disarmament (CND), Child Poverty Action Group (CPAG) or the Society for the Protection of the Unborn Child (SPUC) can be identified. Of the environmental groups, the Ramblers Association, Greenpeace and Friends of the Earth are perhaps the best known.

Membership of the former category is limited to those who are part of the specific interest group, for example coal miners or doctors. In contrast, support for a cause like nuclear disarmament or anti-smoking can potentially embrace all adults. The two types of groups are not, however, mutually exclusive. Some trade unions take a stand on many political causes, for example on apartheid in South Africa or sexual equality, and some members of cause groups may have a material interest in promoting the cause, for example teachers in the Campaign for the Advancement for State Education. It should be noted that pressure groups regularly seek to influence each other to maximise impact and often find themselves in direct conflict over certain issues. Baggott (1988) has shown how pressure groups lined up over the issue of longer drinking hours (see Table 13.1).

Table 13.1   Pressure groups and the licensing laws

The lobby in favour of longer drinking hours	Opposed to such changes
Brewers Society (brewery companies)	Action on Alcohol Abuse (a campaigning body set up by the Royal Colleges of Medicine)
Campaign for Real Ale (beer drinkers)	Alcohol Concern (a semi-official body responsible for coordinating services for alcoholics)
British Hotels, Restaurants and Caterers Association	UK Temperance (a moral pressure group concerned about alcohol abuse)
British Tourist authority (a semi-official body which promotes tourism)	The Campaign Against Drink Driving
NULV and NALHM (the pub landlords' associations)	The Royal Colleges of Medicine (e.g. Royal College of Physicians)
	The British Medical Association

Source: Baggott, 1988

Pressure groups and government

The relationship between interest groups and government is not always or even usually adversarial. Groups may be useful to government. Ministers and civil servants often lack the information or expertise necessary to make wise policies, or indeed the authority to ensure that they are implemented effectively. They frequently turn to the relevant representative organisations to find out defects in an existing line of policy and seek suggestions as to how things might be improved. They sound out groups' leaders about probable resistance to a new line of policy. Moreover, an interest group's support. or at least acceptance, for a policy can help to 'legitimise' it and thus maximise its chances of successful implementation. The accession to power of Labour in May 1997 raised the spectre of union influence once again dominating policy, as in the seventies. Blair has been emphatic that unions, like any other group seeking influence, will receive 'fairness but no favours'. Indeed, Blair seems more concerned to woo business groups than the electorally unpopular unions.

In the several stages of the policy process groups have opportunities to play an important role (see Chapter 25). At the initial stage they may put an issue on the policy agenda (e.g. environmental groups have promoted awareness of the dangers to the ozone layer caused by many products and forced government to act). When governments issue Green Papers (setting out policy options for discussion) and White Papers (proposals for legislation), groups may lobby back-benchers or civil servants. In Parliament groups may influence the final form of legislation. As we can see from Figure 13.1 groups are involved at virtually every stage of the policy process.

Insider–outsider groups

Groups are usually most concerned to gain access to ministers and civil servants – the key policy-makers. Pressure group techniques are usually a means to

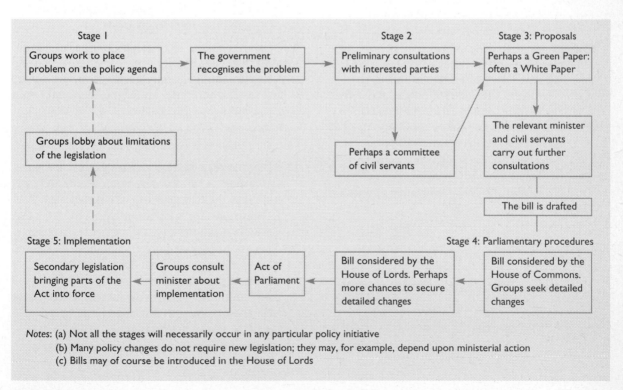

Notes: (a) Not all the stages will necessarily occur in any particular policy initiative

(b) Many policy changes do not require new legislation; they may, for example, depend upon ministerial action

(c) Bills may of course be introduced in the House of Lords

Figure 13.1 Pressure groups and the policy process
Source: Grant, 1988

that end. When government departments are formulating policies there are certain groups which they consult. The Ministry of Agriculture, Fisheries and Food is in continuous and close contact with the Farmers' Union. Indeed in 1989, in the wake of the salmonella food poisoning scandal, it was alleged by some that the ministry neglected the interests of consumers compared to that of the producers. Wyn Grant (1985) has described groups which are regularly consulted as insider groups.

On the other hand, the Campaign for Nuclear Disarmament, for example, mounts public campaigns largely because it has no access to Whitehall; in Grant's language it is an outsider. Not only does it lack specialist knowledge on foreign policy or defence systems, but the policies it advocates are flatly opposed to those followed by every post-war British government. Grant's classification of groups is summarised in Figure 13.2.

To gain access groups usually have to demonstrate that they possess at least some of the following features:

1. *Authority*, which may be demonstrated in the group's ability to organise virtually all its potential members; the National Union of Mineworkers spoke for nearly 100 per cent of miners for a number of years, but its authority was weakened not just by the fall-off in membership after the 1983/4 miners' strike but also by the formation in 1985 of the breakaway Union of Democratic Miners. Similarly, the authority of the teachers' unions has been weakened because of the divisions between so many different groups. Overwhelming support by members for the group leadership's policies is another indicator of authority.

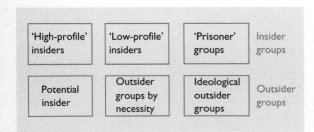

Figure 13.2 Grant's typology of pressure groups
Source: Grant, 1985

2. *Information:* Groups like the British Medical Association or the Howard League for Penal Reform command an audience among decision makers because of their expertise and information.
3. *The compatibility of a group's objectives with those of the government:* For example, trade unions traditionally received a more friendly hearing when pressing for favourable trade union legislation or state intervention in industry from a Labour than a Conservative government. The TUC always received short shrift from Margaret Thatcher who made no effort to disguise her hostility or even contempt. It follows that even when likely to receive a friendly hearing, groups seeking access to the policy process should not put forward demands which the government regards as unreasonable.
4. *Possession of powerful sanctions:* Some groups of workers are able to disrupt society through the withdrawal of their services. The bargaining power of coal miners, for example, was very strong in the mid-1970s when Middle East oil was in short supply and expensive but much weaker a decade later, when cheaper oil was more available as a source of energy.

But becoming and remaining an insider group requires the acceptance of constraints. Group leaders, for example, should respect confidences, be willing to compromise, back up demands with evidence and avoid threats (Grant, 1989, 1990).

Among the favoured activities of groups in the political process are the following:

1. They may try to influence the policies of a party in the areas which concern them, e.g. trade unions in the Labour Party. On the whole, however, groups concentrate their efforts on the government of the day.
2. They try to educate public opinion to their point of view through such activities as rallies, advertising and petitions.
3. They continually lobby government, particularly Whitehall, about the working of legislation or details of impending legislation. Many government ministries grant representation to groups on their departmental inquiries and advisory committees. In recent years the House of Lords has become a popular focus for pressure groups as the unreliable Conservative

majority improved opposition chances of influence.

4. Some try to seek pledges from candidates at elections. This strategy is used by both the pro- and anti-abortion groups.

5. Some may pay MPs a retainer to represent the views of the group in Parliament. Many Tory MPs have such an interest (which they are expected to declare before speaking on the issue). More than a third of Labour MPs are sponsored by trade unions and the majority of Tory MPs are paid retainers by business groups. Sir Giles Shaw MP is employed by Hill and Knowlton, an example of the new breed of professional lobbying organisations which offer their contacts and knowledge of the corridors of power to organisations wishing to influence specific policies. This whole area was transformed by the 'Cash for Questions' row in 1995 leading to the Nolan Committee and its recommendations. (See Box 13.1.)

Pressure group methods include the following:

1. violence, unconstitutional action, illegality (e.g. violent demonstrations, bombings, sit-ins and illegal occupation, as in the campaign to halt the progress of the Newbury bypass in 1996);
2. denial of function (e.g. strikes);
3. publicity-seeking techniques (e.g. petitions, advertisements, leaflets, marches, use of media);
4. expansion of membership, mobilisation and training.

Target groups include all elements in the political system:

1. the public at large;
2. other pressure group members;
3. political parties;
4. Parliament – especially the House of Commons, but in recent years increasingly the House of Lords;
5. ministers;
6. civil servants;
7. the media – as an additional means of reaching all the above groups.

Factors affecting effectiveness

Baggott (1988) points out that the effectiveness of pressure groups is also a function of organisational factors: they need a coherent organisational structure; high-quality and efficient staff; adequate financial resources: good leadership: and a clear strategy. Economic interest groups are usually well financed but cause groups can often compensate for shoestring resources by attracting high-quality committed leadership; for example Jonathon Porritt (Friends of the Earth), Frank Field (CPAG), Mike Daube (ASH) and perhaps the most effective popular campaigner of them all, Des Wilson of Shelter and many other causes.

The American political scientist Robert Downs has suggested that the media and the public's receptivity to pressure-group messages is another potent factor influencing effectiveness. He pointed out that the new cause groups must run the gauntlet of the 'issue-attention' cycle (see Figure 13.3). The pre-problem stage is followed by alarmed discovery coupled with the feeling that something could and should be done. When it becomes clear, as it usually does, that progress will not be easy, interest declines and this is when the pressure group faces its toughest tests. This has certainly been true of environmental, nuclear disarmament and AIDS campaigns, but all three of these reveal that with new discoveries and fresh events the issue-attention cycle can be rerun – possibly frequently over time.

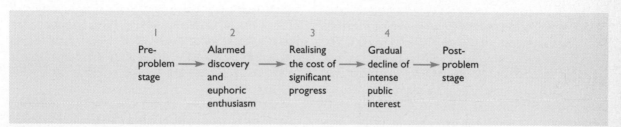

Figure 13.3 The issue-attention cycle
Source: McCulloch, 1988

Economic interest groups

The policies of the government in such areas as interest rates, trading policy and industrial relations are important in providing the context for the economy. Two of the most powerful interest groups which try to influence these policies are business and trade unions.

Business

Business is naturally deeply affected by government economic policies and it is understandable that its representatives will seek to exert influence. Many firms depend on government hand-outs, subsidies and orders and will seek to influence the awarding of contracts. This is particularly true of shipbuilding, highway construction, housebuilding and defence. But others will certainly be interested in policy matters like interest rates, taxation levels and so forth.

In one sense any sizable business organisation acts like a pressure group. Multinational companies – many with turnovers larger than those of small countries – make their own regular and usually confidential representations to government. Particular industries often form federations like the Society of Motor Manufacturers or the Engineering Employers Federation and seek strength in unity. The Confederation of British Industry (CBI) was formed in 1965 and since that date has provided an overall 'peak' organization to provide a forum for discussion – it holds an annual conference – and to represent the views of members to government. It has a membership of 15,000, employs several hundred staff and has an annual budget approaching £5 million. The CBI is dominated by big companies and this helps to explain the 1971 breakaway Small Business Association. For much of Margaret Thatcher's first term of office her policies of high interest and exchange rates damaged manufacturing industry and the CBI criticised the government. It blamed the government for not spending enough on infrastructure, it complained that the high exchange rate made exporting difficult and that high interest rates were discouraging investment. On one famous occasion the then Director-General of the CBI, Sir Terence Beckett, called for a 'bare-knuckle' fight to make Margaret

Thatcher change her deflationary policies – but his violent rhetoric abated after a stormy confrontation with that formidable Prime Minister. In recent years the CBI has been more supportive of the Conservative government line: John Banham, one of Sir Terence's successors, lined up against the European Social Charter in November 1989, for example, but disagreed over the European Monetary System, which the CBI believed Britain could and should join.

The Institute of Directors is a more right-wing and political campaigning body. It opposed prices and incomes restraints, which the CBI was prepared to support in the 1970s, and vigorously supported the Conservative government's policies of privatisation, cutting public spending and encouraging free market economics. The Institute also welcomed Conservative measures to lower direct taxation, reform the trade unions and limit minimum wage regulations, and ideally would like such policies to go further. Other organisations, such as Aims of Industry, are used as means of raising support and indirectly revenue for the Conservative Party. Although no business group has a formal association with the Conservative Party, a number of major firms do make financial contributions (for more details see Chapter 14).

Trade unions

Trade unions perform two distinct roles. The first is political. Since they helped to form the Labour Party in 1900 they have played, and still play, a decisive role in the internal politics of that party (see Chapter 14). Trade unions are involved in party politics more deeply than any other interest group.

The second role of individual trade unions is industrial bargaining, to represent the interests of their members on pay and working conditions in negotiations with employers. Some three-quarters of all unions are affiliated to the Trades Union Congress (TUC), which speaks for the trade union movement as a whole. In the past this function has involved unions directly in the political life of the country.

Various attempts were made by Labour and Conservative governments to win the agreement of unions to pay policies which would keep inflation in check and the cost of British exports competitive in

BOX 13.1   **IDEAS AND PERSPECTIVES**

Trade unions, the Labour party and public opinion

Ever since February 1900, when the Labour Representation Committee, the embryo of the party, was formed, trade unions have played a key role and are the body of pressure groups most closely involved in party politics. In recent years Tony Blair has sought to weaken a link which is not popular with the voters but nevertheless the connections still amount to a virtual umbilical cord.

- **Affiliation:** About half of all trade unionists are affiliated to the party, providing seven-eighths of its membership.

- **Money link:** In 1995 54 per cent of Labour's total income of £12.5 million was provided by the unions. However, in 1985 the percentage was 77 per cent. The practice of 'sponsoring' MPs by unions proved embarrassing politically and was formally abolished; unions now give money direct to local parties, with the result that these contributions are not counted as income centrally.

- **Membership:** Union subs are calculated on the basis of £1.15 per affiliated and 75p per member for the political fund. However, each union decides how many members it wishes to say pay the political levy and some underestimate to save money. In 1995 there were 4.1 million political levy payers and 365,000 individual members. Following Blair's accession to the leadership, membership doubled within two years. Unionists who pay the political levy (it is possible to opt out of this) can pay a reduced membership fee to join the party.

- **Representation:** Unions used to dominate the annual conference through 'block voting' (leaders casting votes on behalf of affiliated members) which accounted for 90 per cent of total votes cast. However, under pressure to remove an undemocratic anomaly this percentage reduced to 50 per cent in 1996. It is the aim of the leadership to move to one member one vote (OMOV) in all conference decisions as in the selection of parliamentary candidates. Trade unions also after 1981 controlled 40 per cent of the votes in the selection of party leader and deputy leader compared to 30 per cent for constituencies and the same for Labour MPs. This division was later changed to $33\frac{1}{2}$ per cent for each sector. They still elect twelve of the twenty-nine seats on Labour's ruling body, the National Executive Council.

- **Volunteers:** Trade unionists supply a fair percentage of the active membership, including local councillors, of the Labour Party and without them the party would be hard pressed to function on the ground. In 1964 73 per cent of trade unionists voted Labour but in 1983 this had fallen to 39 per cent rising to 46 per cent in 1992 (the Conservative voting figures were 31 per cent in both the latter elections).

- **Unions and public opinion:** In the 1970s a record 12.9 million days were lost annually in strikes. In the 1980s that figure dropped to 7.2 million and continued to fall in the 1990s. In 1994 the figure was 0.278 million, though in 95 it rose to 1.24 million. These lower figures were certainly connected to the improving public perception of unions in polls. In September 1979 80 per cent of respondents told MORI researchers (Gallup's figures were similar) unions had 'too much power in Britain today' whilst only 16 per cent disagreed. By 1992 the figures had changed to 27 per cent and 64 per cent respectively.

overseas markets. By the late 1960s Harold Wilson had become exasperated with striking trade unions and proposed measures to curb their tendency to strike and cripple the economy. His White Paper *In Place of Strife,* however, was attacked by the unions and James Callaghan led a successful revolt against it in the Cabinet, destroying the authority of Wilson's government. Ted Heath's administration after 1970 worked hard to solve the problem of union disruption and eventually tried a statutory approach, but this foundered hopelessly and resulted in an election in 1974 which he lost. Labour back in power tried to stem the rocketing inflation by engineering a 'Social Contract' with the unions whereby they agreed to restrain wages demands in exchange for favourable policies on pensions, low pay and industrial legislation. This succeeded to an extent and for a while the UK had a pay regime which was almost Scandinavian but in 1978 Callaghan's call for a 5 per cent limit was rejected and his government descended into the ignominy of the 'winter of discontent' (January–February 1979). Subsequently Margaret Thatcher introduced a series of laws which emasculated union power; five Employment Acts and the 1984 Trade Union Act. These have made unions liable for the actions of their members and made union funds liable to seizure by the courts, as the miners found to their disadvantage in 1984 when their lack of a strike ballot rendered them liable to sequestration of assets. Their bitter strike slowly ran out of steam and they had to suffer a humiliating defeat which set the tone for the rest of the decade. Days lost through strikes fell to an all-time low and a kind of industrial peace held sway although at the cost of much bitterness. Margaret Thatcher refused to consult with the unions and their occasional meetings proved to be cold and wholly unproductive. Unemployment helped to reduce the size of union membership by three million (a quarter) from 1979–1989. The growth of part-time work, mostly by women, did not help either as these workers are notoriously difficult to organise. To minimise the impact of recession and shrinkage some unions decided to merge, like Unison the 1.5 million public service organisation.

The unions' case was not especially aided by Norman Willis, the General Secretary of the TUC in this decade. In contrast to his successor, John Monks, who is an impressive operator and shrewd politician, he was relatively ineffectual. Margaret Thatcher, then, destroyed the power of the unions and John Major has been the beneficiary, though in 1996 some signs of industrial militancy reasserted themselves.

In the run up to the 1997 election the TUC sought to fashion an appropriate new role in relation to the government, which it expected to be a Labour one. Denying there had been any deal with Labour, John Monks said on 26 February 1997: 'We know there will be no special tickets to influence based on history or sentiment.'

Calling for a new 'social partnership', the TUC welcomed Labour's policies on employment rights and proposed greater use of arbitration in public sector disputes. 'Inherent in the social partnership model', said the TUC, 'is the need to minimise industrial disputes.'

'Under the leadership of Mr Monks', responded Tony Blair, 'the TUC has undergone a real process of modernisation ... the unions have changed and must continue to change.'

Yet it is not only trade unions which have been shaken up by the government. Local government, traditionally a strong pressure group on Whitehall. has been much weakened since 1979 and its policy-making role in housing and education reduced. Some of the professions have lost a number of their privileges and been exposed to market forces. Solicitors have lost the monopoly on conveyancing, opticians on the sale of spectacles and university lecturers no longer have guaranteed tenure.

Tripartism

Like political parties, pressure groups want to influence the policies of government. In 1961 the government created the National Economic Development Council (NEDC), a forum in which the government, employers and trade unions could meet regularly to consider ways of promoting economic growth. The activities of NEDC, together with periods of prices and incomes policies and the 1974 Labour government's Social Contract with the unions, were seen at the time as evidence that Britain was moving to a form of corporatism or tripartism in economic policy. Governments would negotiate economic policy with the major producer interest.

Ministers were increasingly aware of the power of producer groups and of how they could frustrate a government's economic policies. They therefore sought the cooperation of leaders of business, employers' and trade union organisations. In spite of objections that such negotiations – notably on prices and incomes policies – bypassed Parliament, this was the path pursued by government in the 1970s.

In 1972 Heath offered the unions a voice in policy making in return for wage moderation. That offer was not accepted, but there were closer relations between the 1974 Labour government and the unions.

Tripartite forms of policy-making and the Social Contract have not been successful. Neither the TUC nor the CBI have sufficient control over their members to make their deals stick. Incomes policies broke down after two or three years. Moreover, after 1979 Margaret Thatcher set her face against such tripartism and relied more on market forces. Before 1979 governments usually tried to pursue consensus policies and their policies (e.g. on regional aid, incomes and price controls) required consultation with the producer groups. After 1979 Margaret Thatcher's determination to break with the consensus and her pursuit of different economic policies shut the groups (particularly the unions) out of the decision-making process. From 1990, John Major showed more of a willingness to meet union leaders, but there were no signs of any return to the pre-Thatcher consensual approach and in April 1993 Major abolished the NEDC.

The growth of professional lobbying

One of the striking features of recent years has been the rapid growth of professional lobbying companies. These offer to influence policy and effect high-level contracts in exchange for large amounts of money. Often, the lobbyists are selling the excellent contacts they have made during a previous career in Parliament or the civil service. In this respect, Britain has once again moved towards the American model, where this kind of activity has been an accepted part of political life on Capitol Hill for decades.

In Britain, over sixty lobbying organisations have been set up, ranging from the small Political Plan-

ning Services to the large (now defunct) Ian Greer Associates. Most major public relations companies have lobbying operations, either in house, or via an established lobbying company. Over thirty Conservative MPs worked for lobbyists before the Nolan Report; consultancies could pay anything up to and beyond £10,000 per year.

There has been pressure for the regulation of such agencies (in Washington, they have to be registered), and one brave voice has dared to suggest that the lobbyist emperors have no clothes. Charles Clarke, former right-hand man to Neil Kinnock, has set up his own company, Quality Public Affairs, offering an alternative and much cheaper service. In *The Guardian* on 30 September 1993, he claimed that lobbying government is a gigantic con trick trading on the mystique of Parliament.

I am telling them that, if they spend £5,000 with me, they can save double the money within a year, once they get to know what to do. …Thousands of pounds are spent by firms getting information that they could easily get for themselves.

Westminster lobbyists can charge clients around £30,000 a year for a full service, including lobbying ministers, civil servants and MPs to push their case.

The Premier Club

Another connection with the Prime Minister was revealed by *The Observer* (21 July 1996), which led with the headline: 'Prime Minister Hired Out'. The story related to the so called 'Premier Club', of which Major is the patron. For £10,000 per year 'ordinary members' were invited to suppers with Cabinet ministers (Heseltine was one such cited) and for £100,000 members could enjoy two dinners per year with the Prime Minister himself. The aim was to contribute funds to the cash-strapped party. However, all companies are obliged by law to declare both direct and indirect political contributions in their annual accounts and the club's advice to potential members that they could file the donation under pre-profit entertainment expenses cut little ice with the eminent QC consulted by the paper. Moreover, it transpired that the chairman of the club, John Beckwith, was also a member of the consortium bidding for the controversial sell-off of

58,000 Ministry of Defence homes, suggesting that the lobbying of at least one businessman extended up to the highest levels, the nexus being funding of the government party itself.

Lord Nolan and the removal of sleaze

On 15 January 1990 the Granada TV programme *World in Action* broadcast its report on MPs and outside interests. It quoted Richard Alexander MP, who had placed an advertisement in the House of Commons magazine as follow: 'Hard working backbench Tory MP of ten years standing seeks consultancy in order to widen his range of activities.' The programme was only one of several investigations at that time and later of how MPs use 'consultancy' often for commercial interests; in effect they are paid to apply pressure through their network of contacts in parliament and Whitehall. In 1994 *The Sunday Times* approached two MPs, under the guise of being a commercial interest, and asked them to place questions on its behalf in exchange for money. In the ensuing media row the newspaper was criticised by many Conservative MPs for its underhand tactics, but the two MPs concerned, Graham Riddick and David Tredinnick, were the object of much more widespread and impassioned obloquy. A commission on 'standards in public life' – 'sleaze' in the popular media interpretation – was set up by John Major under the judge Lord Nolan. This reported in the autumn of 1995 and debated in November. Nolan suggested curbs on the economic activity of MPs and urged they be obliged to reveal the extent of

---

| BOX 13.2 | | EXAMPLE |

Lobbyists and all-party committees

An *Observer* investigation (17 September 1995) revealed an unrecognised aspect of lobbying: commercial infiltration of all-party committees. There are some 130 of these, thirty-eight of which are financed by commercial interests of one kind or another, mostly through the provision of staffing support. The newspaper had acquired a copy of the secret register of this little known Westminster species, showing that in addition to the thirty-eight financed by commercial interests, a further three had connections with lobbying companies. Richard Ottaway MP (Con.) discovered that the charity-sponsored group he supported had been challenged by an identical group financed by drug companies. He complained that these companies:

Decided they should set up an all-party group. They wrote to all members of my group saying they were starting a new one and invited them along. People do not know these groups are paid for by commercial interests. It needs an investigation – and the Register needs to be a public document. All-party groups are one of the most influential set-ups because they are all-party. But that reputation has become sullied.

Danny Barlow, company secretary to the Glass Manufacturers Confederation, explained how the All-Party Glass Group was set up:

In 1988, I personally set up the first meeting that had been held for many many years. We trawled through and contacted our member companies and asked for details of the MPs with glass factories in their constituencies. Now we speak to them ourselves and discuss whatever we feel is of use to us. We were successful in getting some legislation changed.

Nicholas Winterton MP is chair of the All-Party Media Group and is a paid director of the organisation Government Relations, which is given money by its clients, Emap Media and Sony Broadcast and Professional, to fund a researcher for the group who also works for Winterton.

Diana Warwick, a member of the Nolan Committee, was unimpressed:

This lobbyist connection is unhealthy. Their role has become important and substantial, and it has to be made a lot more transparent.

their earnings. This proposal, together with the establishment of an official watchdog, provoked great hostility from Conservative MPs, especially Edward Heath, who refused to divulge his earnings. In the debate Major ignored the opportunity of appearing to cleanse the 'Augean stables' and supported his dissenters. This made him look foolish indeed when the vote went against him on 6 November and introduced a new system whereby MPs are:

- obliged to disclose earnings, according to income bands;
- forbidden from tabling questions and amendments on behalf of outside interests;
- restricted in what they can say in the chamber on behalf of such interests;
- obliged to register all details of contracts with a new and powerful Parliamentary Commissioner (since March 1996).

Edward Heath and David Mellor, both enriched by considerable outside work, declared only that work which was directly attributable to their position as MPs and controversially excluded large amounts of income earned through other activities.

The subject of sleaze, however, was not excluded from the news after Nolan, much as Major would have loved this. *The Guardian* newspaper ran a story accusing a junior trade minister, Neil Hamilton, of accepting money when a back-bench MP in exchange for asking questions and being in the employ of the well-known lobbying company Ian Greer Associates, the then agent of the owner of Harrods, Mr Mohamed Al Fayed, in his campaign to prevent the tycoon Tiny Rowlands from regaining control of the store. Hamilton declared he would sue (as he had successfully and sensationally against the BBC when *Panorama* had accused him of fascist tendencies).

However, in October 1996, in a major climb-down, he announced the withdrawal of his action on grounds of finance. *The Guardian* responded by calling him a 'liar and a cheat' on its front page. The story continued when the subject was referred to the Standards and Privileges Committee. As noted in Chapter 12, Hamilton was trounced in the election by the anti-corruption independent candidate, Martin Bell.

Pressure groups and democracy

Do pressure groups contribute towards a more healthy democracy? As in the debate over the media in Chapter 12, it depends upon what is meant by 'democracy'. The commonly accepted version of British representative or pluralist democracy accords the media a respected if not vital role. According to this view:

1. Pressure groups provide an essential freedom for citizens, especially minorities, to organize with like-minded individuals so that their views can be heard by others and taken into account by government.
2. They help to disperse power downwards from the central institutions and provide important checks against possibly overpowerful legislatures and executives.
3. They provide functional representation according to occupation and belief.
4. They allow for continuity of representation between elections, thus enhancing the degree of participation in the democratic system.
5. They provide a 'safety valve', an outlet for the pent-up energies of those who carry grievances or feel hard done by.
6. Apply scrutiny to government activity, publicising poor practice and maladministration.

Some claim, however, that groups operate in a way which harms democracy. They claim the following:

1. The freedom to organise and influence is exploited by the rich and powerful groups in society; the poor and weak have to rely often on poorly financed cause groups and charitable bodies.
2. Much influence is applied informally and secretly behind the closed doors of ministerial meetings, joint civil service advisory committees or informal meetings in London clubs. This mode of operating suits the powerful insider groups while the weaker groups are left outside and have to resort to ineffective means like influencing public opinion.
3. By enmeshing pressure groups into government policy-making processes a kind of 'corporatism' (see below) has been established which 'fixes'

decisions with ministers and civil servants before Parliament has had a chance to make an input on behalf of the electorate as a whole.

4. Pressure groups are often not representative of their members and in many cases do not have democratic appointment procedures for senior staff.

5. Pressure groups are essentially sectional – they apply influence from a partial point of view rather than in the interests of the country as a whole. This tendency led some political scientists to claim that in the 1970s Britain had become harder to govern (King, 1975), exacerbating conflict and slowing down important decision making processes.

Theoretical perspectives

Pluralism

This approach is both descriptive in that it claims to tell us how things are and normative in that it believes this is generally a good way to be. The importance of pressure group activity was first recognised by commentators in this country in the 1950s, as so often before and since, taking their lead from an American scholar, on this occasion Robert Dahl, who believed major decisions were taken in an American democracy, where power was widely dispersed and shared, through negotiation between competing groups. In 1957 journalist Paul Johnson said pretty much the same thing about his own country adding 'Cabinet ministers are little more than the chairmen of arbitration committees.' Samuel Beer, with his concept of 'new group politics', supported this view: believing the wartime controls in which groups voluntarily aided the government in getting things done, to have survived the peace with the 'main substance' of political activity taking place between the 'public bureaucrats' of the government and the 'private bureaucrats … of the great pressure groups'.

The pluralist approach was much criticised for claiming power was equally dispersed and that access to government was open. Critics maintained that rich business interests would always exercise disproportionate influence and win better access. Writing two decades later, pluralists such as Robert

Dahl and Charles Lindblom adjusted their earlier theories to create a 'neo-pluralism'. This embodied: a stronger role for government in relation to groups and a more explicit recognition of the disproportionate power of some groups.

Corporatism

Corporatism – sometimes prefixed by 'neo-' or 'meso-' (Smith, 1993, Chap. 2) – was in some ways a development of pluralism in that it perceived a contract of sorts taking place between the most powerful groups in the country, rather as Beer saw happening in the war, whereby the government exchanged influence with the groups for their agreement to lead their members along government approved policy lines; for example, the attempts by governments to achieve agreement on a prices and incomes policy in the late 1960s and early 1970s.

Pahl and Winkler (1974) argued that the government was exercising corporatism in that it aimed to: 'direct and control predominantly private-owned business according to four principles: unity, order, nationalism and success'. Corporatism, in one sense, was a means of bridging the gap between a capitalist economy and the socialist notions of planning and democratic consultation. To some extent this altered analysis matched the transition in Britain from a governing Conservative Party whose ethos was against intervention to a Labour one whose ethos was in favour. The drift towards something called corporatism was perceived at the time and criticised by left-wingers like Tony Benn and centrists like David Owen.

The Marxist analysis of pressure groups

Marxists would argue that the greater role accorded the state in corporatism is only an approximation of the real control exercised by business through the state; as Marx said, 'the state is nothing but an executive committee for the bourgeoisie'. The whole idea of pluralist democracy, therefore, is merely part of the democratic window dressing which the ruling economic group uses to disguise its hegemonic control. Naturally, according to this view, the most potent pressure groups will be the ones representing business, while trade unions, for the most part, will be given a marginal role and will in any case act as agents of the capitalist system to a substantial extent. Marxists would also argue that most members of elite decision-making groups implicitly accept the dominant values whereby inequality and exploitation are perpetuated. In consequence most pressure group activity will be concerned with the detailed management of inequality rather than the processes of genuine democracy.

BOX 13.3   IDEAS AND PERSPECTIVES

The importance of citizen campaigning

Des Wilson is probably the best known popular campaigner in the country. On a Tyne Tees TV programme in 1986 he explained his own philosophy on citizen campaigning and suggested ten guidelines for people wishing to become involved in such campaigns.

It is very important to remember that the very existence of campaigners, the fact that people are standing up and saying 'No, we don't want this, this is what we want instead', is terribly important because it makes it impossible for the political system to claim that there is no alternative to what they are suggesting.

Citizen organisations are about imposing citizen priorities on a system which we have set up which doesn't always act as well for us as it should. The more we can impose human values by maintaining surveillance, getting involved in organizations, being prepared to stand up and be counted, the better. Even if we are beaten the important thing is that the case has been made, the voice has been heard, a different set of priorities has been set on the table.

Our movement is, if you like, the real opposition to the political system because I believe all the political parties are actually one political system which runs this country. If we are not satisfied, it's no use just switching our vote around and it's no use complaining 'They're all the same, those politicians'. We can create our own effective opposition through our own lives by standing up and making demands on our own behalf.

Guidelines for campaigners

1. **Identify objectives** – always be absolutely clear on what you are seeking to do. It is fatal to become side-tracked and waste energy on peripheral issues.

2. **Learn the decision-making process** – find out how decisions are made and who makes them.

3. **Formulate a strategy** – try to identify those tactics which will best advance your cause and draw up a plan of campaign.

4. **Research** – always be well briefed and work out alternative proposals to the last detail.

5. **Mobilize support** – widespread support means more political clout and more activists to whom tasks can be delegated.

6. **Use the media** – the media are run by ordinary people who have papers or news bulletins to fill. They need good copy. It helps to develop an awareness of what makes a good story and how it can be presented attractively.

7. **Attitude** – try to be positive, but also maintain a sense of perspective. Decision-makers will be less likely to respond to an excessively strident or narrow approach.

8. **Be professional** – even amateurs can acquire professional research media and presentational skills.

9. **Confidence** – there is no need to be apologetic about exercising a democratic right.

10. **Perseverance** – campaigning on local issues is hard work: this should not be underestimated. Few campaigns achieve their objectives immediately. Rebuffs and reverses must be expected and the necessary resilience developed for what might prove to be a long campaign.

Source: Jones, 1986

New Right

According to the New Right analysis, pressure groups do not enhance democracy as they are primarily interested in their own concerns and not those of wider society. They represent only a section of society, usually the producers, and leave large groups, like the consumers, unrepresented. Also according to this view, pressure groups 'short-circuit' the proper working of the system by promiscuously influencing the legislature and the executive so that the former cannot properly represent the interests of all and the latter cannot implement what has been decided (see Baggott, 1955, pp. 47–53).

Are pressure groups becoming less effective?

The decline of tripartism has led some commentators to answer the question in the affirmative. Certainly trade unions have been virtually excluded from important policy-making processes and almost certainly other pressure groups will have been cold-shouldered by ministers and Whitehall. Margaret Thatcher asserted a powerful self-confident message: she did not need advice. After many years in office this message and *modus operandi* spread downwards to ministers and outwards through the civil service network. Baggott (1995, pp. 46–53) shows how both the authoritarian conservative and free market liberal elements in New Right or Thatcherite thinking (see Chapter 6) were hostile to pressure-group activity, tending to see it as the operation of self-interested sectional interests at odds with the national interest and largely excluding the interests of taxpayers and consumers. According to this view even quite small groups were able to hoodwink or blackmail Labour into acceding to their demands. In consequence, Thatcher and her ministers broke with the tradition of seeking consent for new policies and preferred to impose their views in defiance of outraged group opinion. They did this, as appropriate, through vigorous industrial conflict (miners' strike), providing very short consultation periods – on average only thirty-nine days (Baggott, 1995, p. 126), or, more generally just ignoring certain groups altogether such as the TUC and more or less dismantling the network of consultations constructed during the corporatist seventies. Baggott's survey of pressure groups in 1992 revealed that 38 per cent felt the atmosphere had improved for them but 58 per cent believed it had not changed. As Baggott recognises, this pre-election period was slightly untypical as the government was reaching out to all sections to maximise support in a tight contest.

After the election, Baggott notes a considerable increase in consultation documents but only a slight increase in consultation periods (one twenty-page document in 1994 required comment within twenty-four hours). Major's small majority in the 1992–97 parliament made him vulnerable to interests with the ear of Conservative MPs, but on balance he has pursued similar policies to his predecessor regarding trade unions, even tightening the screw by introducing a public sector pay freeze and ignoring the miners' opposition to the pit closures programme in 1992/3. Doctors angry at the imposition of the internal market in the health service were also ignored.

But what of the pressure groups which are in sympathy: intellectual think-tanks like the Institute for Economic Affairs, business groups like the Institute of Directors or media barons? There is much evidence that their advice is well received, at least it was during the Thatcher years, and it follows that their 'pull' in the highest quarters has been enhanced rather than diminished in recent years. It also needs to be remembered that pressure group activity at the popular level grew apace during the 1970s and 1980s. In Chapter 5, this feature was noted as a major new element in the pattern of participation in British politics. Inglehart (1977) has sought to explain this as a feature of affluent societies, where people are less concerned with economic questions but more with quality of life. Other explanations can be found in the decline of class as the basis of party political activity in Britain. As support for the two big class-based parties has diminished, so cause-based pressure group activity has won popular support. As Moran (1985) notes,

Once established class and party identification weakens, citizens are free to enter politics in an almost infinite variety of social roles. If we are no longer 'working class' we can define our social identity and political demands in numerous ways: so groups emerge catering for nuclear pacifists, radical feminists, homosexuals, real ale drinkers, single parents and any combination of these.

Some of the upsurge in pressure-group activity has been in direct response to the policies of Thatcherism and its style of exclusion – CND provides the best example here – but much of it has been in support of cross-party issues, particularly those relating to the environment. A letter to Greenpeace members in November 1989 reports on activities during the year and comments on the organization's increased effectiveness.

This has been the fastest growing year in Greenpeace history. With 300,000 fellow supporters in the UK and millions more worldwide, you can now count yourself part of one of the most successful campaigning organisations in British history.

And we have campaigned accordingly. Barely a week has gone by without Greenpeace pressing its arguments in the papers, on radio and television and on the streets. The continuing seal crisis, nuclear reactors, pollution of all kinds, sewage sludge, toxic waste shipments, the Greenhouse Effect ... on issue after issue we have taken the initiative, reported the half-concealed facts, presented the alternative case.

The results are obvious. The environment is now a fixed item on the social agenda – not just a fashion item but a core anxiety of millions of people who see the world getting worse and are looking for ways that can prevent us sliding into global catastrophe. The politicians and the industrialists are having to listen and to react. Five years ago this would have been unthinkable.

Greenpeace hasn't done this single-handed. But we have emerged as a respected, radical voice, authoritative as well as provocative. We have, after all, been proved right on issue after issue. It is a long time since we could be dismissed as a bunch of fanciful troublemakers.

Pressure group activity is therefore more widespread and more intense. Much of this is 'outsider' activity, attempting to raise public consciousness, but environmental groups have shown that, with the occasional help of events like the Chernobyl explosion, decision-makers can be influenced and in the case of the protests against the Newbury bypass and the export of veal calves, activists have brought their subjects into the forefront of national consciousness.

While the power of some of the most important groups like trade unions has fallen in recent years, pressure groups remain one of the most important means by which citizens can take part in politics. In this chapter we have given special attention to

unions and business because they have been at the centre of policy processes in Britain in recent decades. But it is important to realise that the range of groups is much wider than the two sides of industry. There has also been a renaissance in grassroots popular movements, especially those concerned with the environment. Important groups can be found in the professions (medicine, law), among the churches and in the wide spectrum of organisations – sporting, charity, artistic – in the community. Virtually everybody is a member of a group that tries to exercise influence on policy because virtually everybody is a member of some organization or other; and sooner or later every organization, even the most unworldly, tries to influence an item of public policy.

Chapter summary

Pressure groups seek to influence policy and not control it. 'Insider' groups which win acceptance by government have a privileged position compared to 'outsider' groups on the periphery, which tend to use high-profile techniques which serve to disguise their lack of real influence. Business groups seek to influence through the CBI and other channels whilst trade unions have lost much power since 1979. Theoretical approaches include pluralism, corporatism and Marxism. On balance pressure-group influence has probably waned since 1979 but some groups concerned with environmental and animal issues have increased their influence and membership.

Discussion points

- Why do pressure groups emerge?
- Why does government seek out groups and try to gain their cooperation?
- Describe an example of pressure group activity from the recent past and consider what it tells you about the way groups operate.
- Why do New Right thinkers dislike the influence of pressure groups?

Further reading

For the student the books and articles by Grant (1985, 1988, 1989, 1990) are the clearest and most useful, but Baggott (1995) is probably the most comprehensive current account and the most accessible. Smith (1993) is an interesting study of some of the more theoretical aspects of the topic. On trade unions, see McIlroy (1985), Taylor (1993) and, on the impact of the Thatcher years, Marsh (1993).

References

Baggott, R. (1988) 'Pressure groups', *Talking Politics*, Autumn.

Baggott, R. (1995) *Pressure Groups Today* (Manchester University Press).

Grant, W. (1985, 1990) 'Insider and outsider pressure groups', *Social Studies Review*, September 1985 and January 1990.

Grant, W. (1988) 'Pressure groups and their policy process', *Social Studies Review*.

Grant, W. (1989) *Pressure Groups, Politics and Democracy in Britain* (Phillip Allan).

Inglehart, R. (1977) *The Silent Revolution: Changing Values and Political Styles among Western Publics* (Princeton University Press).

Jones, B. (1986) *Is Democracy Working?* (Tyne Tees Television).

King, A. (1975) 'Overload: problems of governing in the 1970s', *Political Studies*, June.

Marsh, D. (1993) *The New Politics of British Trade Unionism* (Macmillan).

McCulloch, A. (1988) 'Politics and the environment', *Talking Politics*, Autumn.

McIlroy, J. (1995) *Trade Unions in Britain Today*, 2nd edn (Manchester University Press).

Moran, M. (1985) 'The changing world of British pressure groups', *Teaching Politics*, September.

Pahl, R. and Winkler, J. (1974) 'The coming corporatism', *New Society*, 10 October.

Smith, M. (1993) *Pressure Power and Policy* (Harvester Wheatsheaf).

Taylor, R. (1993) *The Trade Union Question in British Politics* (Blackwell).

CHAPTER FOURTEEN

Political parties

DENNIS KAVANAGH AND BILL JONES

LEARNING OBJECTIVES

■ To examine the functions and major characteristics of the party system together with leadership and organisation features. Inevitably the major focus is on the Conservative and Labour parties, but some attention is also paid to other parties.

INTRODUCTION

In the British political system parties are of central importance. They involve and educate their members who also provide the key personnel for democratic control of central and local government. The majority party in the Commons, providing it can maintain cohesion and discipline, has virtually unrestricted access to the legislative system and command of the executive machine. The second largest party forms the official opposition and, through criticism of the party in power and the shadowing of major policy areas, offers itself as the alternative government.

The role of political parties

While pressure groups are concerned to influence specific policies, political parties set themselves more ambitious objectives. They aim to originate rather than merely influence policy, address the whole range of government policies, and seek to win control of the representative institutions. They do not wish to *influence* the government so much as *become* the government. According to the dominant pluralist theory of democracy, however, political parties perform vital functions.

1. *Reconciling conflicting interests:* Political parties represent coalitions of different groups in society. They provide a means whereby the conflicting elements of similar interests are reconciled, harmonised and then fed into the political system. At general elections it is the party which people vote for rather than the candidate.

2. *Participation:* As permanent bodies parties provide opportunities for citizens to participate in politics, e.g. in choosing candidates for local and parliamentary elections, campaigning during elections and influencing policy at party conferences.

3. *Recruitment:* Parties are the principal means whereby democratic leaders are recruited and trained for service in local councils, Parliament, ministerial and Cabinet office and the premiership itself.

4. *Democratic control:* It is the democratically elected members of political parties who as ministers are placed in charge of the day-to-day running of the vast government apparatus – employing millions of people and spending in total over £350 billion per annum.

5. *Choice:* By presenting programmes and taking stands on issues parties allow voters to choose between rival policy packages.

6. *Representation:* According to the strictly constitutional interpretation, elected candidates represent geographical regions of the country – constituencies – but they also serve to represent in the national legislature a range of socio-economic groups.

7. *Communication:* Parties provide sounding boards for governments and channels of communication between them and society, e.g. when MPs return to their constituencies at weekends to hold surgeries and attend functions.

8. *Accountability:* At election times the party (or parties) forming the government is held accountable for what it has done during its period of office.

Parties, or groups of like-minded MPs, have existed in the House of Commons for centuries. But they emerged in their recognisably modern form of being disciplined, policy oriented, possessing a formal organisation in the country and appealing to a large electorate after the second Reform Act (1867). Indeed, the growth of a large electorate required the parties to develop constituency associations in the country. At that time the two main parties were the Conservatives and Liberals. But with the presence of about eighty Irish nationalists between 1880 and 1918 and then some thirty Labour MPs between 1906 and 1918, Britain had a multi-party system in the early years of this century. After 1918 the Irish nationalists withdrew from the British Parliament and the Liberals declined. The new post-1918 party system pitted the rising Labour Party against the established power of the Conservatives and Liberals, though the latter still gained substantial support until 1929. The interwar years were a period of Conservative dominance of government. Since 1945 the Labour and Conservative parties have together always gained over 90 per cent of the seats in elections to the House of Commons

(Table 14.1), but the Conservatives have been the dominant party.

To a large extent this two-party dominance of Parliament is a consequence of the first-past-the-post electoral system. As noted in Chapter 12, the decline in support for the two main parties in the 1970s and 1980s was largely at the expense of Labour. Yet the three-quarters of the total votes which the Conservative and Labour parties usually now receive still translates into 95 per cent of the seats in the House of Commons. In 1981 the Social Democratic Party broke away from the Labour Party and entered into an alliance with the Liberal Party. For a few heady months, with Alliance poll ratings close to 50 per cent, it seemed as if the mould of two-party policies was about to be broken. The fact that the Alliance parties could gain around a quarter of the vote in 1983 and 1987 created if not a three party system, then at least a 'two and a half' party system. The botched negotiations in 1987 which resulted in a new merged party, the Liberal Democrats, and the defiant rump of the SDP postponed indefinitely the break-up of the dominant post-war two-party system (see section on centre parties below). The Liberal Democrats recovered to gain over 18 per cent of the vote in 1992. The dramatic entry of the Green Party into British politics, when it won 15 per cent of the votes cast in the European elections in June 1989, provided another false dawn for those who hoped for the demise of two-party politics; its rise coincided with the collapse of the Alliance parties and by the end of that year poll support for the Greens had evaporated.

Although the two-party system is based on a selective reading of British party history in the twentieth century, it has been central to perceptions of the British political system. The expectation of one-party majority government lies at the heart of ideas that British government is strong and that the majority party in the House of Commons can virtually guarantee the passage of its legislation through Parliament. The two-party system similarly is alleged to provide a coherent choice at election time, structure debate, and determine the conduct of business in the House of Commons. Finally the two-party system is central to the idea that Britain has responsible government. Because the parties are programmatic, offering

Table 14.1 Election results, 1945–92

Elections	Conservative		Labour		Liberals		Others		Total number of MPs
	Seats	%	Seats	%	Seats	%	Seats	%	
1945	213	39.8	393	47.8	12	9.0	22	3.4	640
1950	298	43.5	315	46.1	9	9.1	3	0.7	625
1951	321	48.0	295	48.8	6	2.5	3	0.7	625
1955	344	49.7	277	46.4	6	2.7	3	1.2	630
1959	365	49.4	258	43.8	6	5.9	1	0.9	630
1964	304	43.4	317	44.1	9	11.2	0	1.3	630
1966	253	41.9	363	47.9	12	8.5	2	1.7	630
1970	330	46.4	287	43.0	6	7.5	7	3.1	630
1974 (Feb.)	297	37.9	301	37.1	14	19.3	23[a]	5.7	635
1974 (Oct.)	277	35.8	319	39.2	13	18.3	26	6.7	635
1979	339	43.9	269	36.9	11	13.8	16	5.4	635
1983	397	42.4	209	27.6	23[b]	25.4	21	4.6	650
1987	375	42.3	229	30.8	22	22.6	24	4.3	650
1992	336	41.9	271	34.4	20	17.8	24	5.8	651
1997	165	31	418	43	46	17	30	9	659

Notes: [a] Northern Irish MPs are counted as 'others' from 1974
[b] In 1983 and 1987 Liberal figures cover the results for the SDP/Liberal Alliance

manifestos at election time, voters are able to deliver a mandate for the winning party. In turn, the electorate is able to hold the government accountable at the subsequent election.

The Conservative Party

The Conservative party is noted for its pragmatism and opportunism, qualities which have helped the party to survive and thrive (see Chapter 8). The party has been in office alone or in coalition for some two-thirds of the twentieth century. Not surprisingly, a recent important study is entitled *Conservative Century* (Seldon and Ball, 1994).

The party suffered a shattering defeat in the 1945 election, the year of a Labour landslide. The electorate was clearly in favour of full employment and the welfare measures Labour promised, as well as greater conciliation of trade unions, and it probably supported an extension of public ownership in the basic industries. The Conservative Party promised to go some way in accepting these, except for public ownership. But the electorate voted for the Labour Party that believed in them more fully and was not associated with the mass unemployment of the 1930s.

Thus, after 1945, the Conservative party faced a problem similar to that which faced the Labour party in the 1980s. Should it carry on clinging to the policies that the electorate had repudiated or should it try to come to terms with what that government had done? On the whole it favoured the latter course. R.A. Butler and Harold Macmillan played an important role in redefining Conservative policies, accepting many of the main planks of the Labour government's programme. Between 1951 and 1964 the Conservative governments largely accepted the greater role of the trade unions and the mixed economy (though in 1953 the government reversed the nationalisation of iron and steel), acquiesced in and continued the passage of many countries from colonial status to independence, protected the welfare state, and maintained a high level of public spending. Finally, the party had also adopted economic planning by the early 1960s. Much of the above was a social democratic consensus and it prevailed regardless of whether Labour or the Conservatives were in office.

Conservative leaders until Margaret Thatcher were careful to position themselves on the party's centre-left. They did this for two reasons. They believed, first, that maintaining the post-war consensus was the only way to run the country. In other words one had to maintain full employment, consult with the main economic interests and intervene in the economy (in the interests of boosting employment, helping exports and assisting the more depressed regions). Secondly, they accepted that such policies were necessary to win that crucial portion of working-class support upon which Conservative electoral success depended.

Yet there have been tensions in the Conservative Party. Historians often distinguish two strands: Tory or '*one nation*' Conservatism, which accepted the above policies, and the *neo-liberal* strand, which upholds the role of the free market and sees much government activity as unnecessary, and even a hindrance.

The authority of the Conservative Party leader has already been mentioned. However, this does not mean that the party leader has a completely free hand. He or she has to keep the leadership team reasonably united and also maintain the morale of the party. When choosing the Cabinet or Shadow Cabinet, a leader has to make sure that people are drawn from different wings of the party. Margaret Thatcher, for example, gave office to many leading 'wets', people who, particularly in her first government, had doubts about her economic policies. In addition, the party leader may have to compromise over policy. Margaret Thatcher was unable to get the public spending cuts that she wished in her first Cabinet and was not able to move as far as she wished in matters such as the introduction of more market-oriented welfare reforms, in part because many Conservatives had doubts about such measures. She was forced, reluctantly on her part, to take Britain into the exchange rate mechanism (ERM) in October 1990 under pressure from her Chancellor (John Major) and Foreign Secretary (Douglas Hurd). She had already lost two previous holders of these posts (Nigel Lawson and Sir Geoffrey Howe) in part over her resistance to this step and was not strong enough to sustain her veto. John Major was particularly constrained in the 1992 Parliament. His room for manoeuvre was limited by his tiny parliamentary majority and party divisions over Europe. On 1 May 1997 Major's battered administration finally came to an end when the forces of New Labour overwhelmed him by a

majority of 179. He immediately announced his resignation and the fight for his succession was enjoined.

Until 1965 the leader 'emerged' when the party was in office (which was usually the case), and the monarch invited a prominent Conservative minister to form a government after consulting senior party figures. (In 1957 the Queen sent for Macmillan rather than Butler to succeed Eden, and in 1963 she sent for Lord Home over the luckless Butler. Both choices angered some Conservative MPs and so involved the monarchy in controversy.) In 1965 the party adopted a system by which MPs elected the leader; Edward Heath was the first leader to be so elected.

The contest has a maximum of three ballots. To win on the first a candidate needs 50 per cent of the votes of the parliamentary party and, in addition, according to the rules, '15 per cent more of the votes … than any other candidates'. If these conditions are not met more candidates can join a second ballot, and if an overall majority still proves elusive, a third ballot can be held involving the top two candidates in a straight fight. In 1975 a new provision was introduced, the annual re-election of the leader, principally to ensure that election losers like Heath could be disposed of efficiently. On 8 May 1997, Lord Jeffrey Archer, former MP, Deputy Chairman of the Conservative Party and well-known friend of Thatcher and Major, criticised the leadership election method pointing out that, unlike in the other two major parties, the Tory leader was selected only by a small electorate of MPs and did not involve the wider party membership to any great extent.

In 1975 Margaret Thatcher was brave enough to challenge the 'loyalty culture' of the Conservatives by standing against Heath and was rewarded – wholly unexpectedly at the time – by a narrow majority in the first ballot. By the time the heavyweights like Willie Whitelaw joined in the second ballot it was too late and she had increased her momentum to romp home. For fifteen years the mechanism lay unused until Sir Anthony Meyer chose to challenge Thatcher in December 1989 – and was easily defeated. The outcome was to be very different when Margaret Thatcher was challenged again in November 1990. On this occasion she had angered her Deputy, Geoffrey Howe and he resigned on 1 November, making a devastating speech on the 13th which encouraged Michael Heseltine to make his leadership move. Thatcher's campaign was badly handled and she fell just four votes short of the required number to be 15 per cent in front of her nearest challenger. After consulting with Cabinet she resigned, and in the subsequent ballot Major, seen as Thatcher's choice, romped home.

John Major has had a troubled tenure as party leader. The personal benefits of the party's unexpected general election victory in 1992 soon disappeared. The turning point in his and his government's future was Britain's humiliating withdrawal from the ERM in September 1992. This was followed by a striking slump in the standing in the polls of himself and his party and by-election and local government election disasters. The party's growing divisions over Europe, already apparent under Thatcher, proved more intractable. His authority was regularly flouted by party rebels, concentrated mainly on the Euro-sceptic and right wing of the party, and the government only just managed to carry the Maastricht bill through the Commons. The whip was withdrawn in November 1994 from eight right-wing back-bench Conservative rebels and the government lacked a majority until the whip was restored in April 1995. The rebels looked to Margaret Thatcher for implicit support and there was talk of the right putting up a leadership challenger to John Major. Finally, in an unprecedented move in June 1995 Major challenged his critics to 'put up or shut up' and

resigned the party leadership. It was rumoured that the discredited ex-Chancellor Norman Lamont would be a candidate, but he withdrew when the Secretary of State for Wales, John Redwood, also on the party's right wing, resigned from the Cabinet and entered the leadership race.

The main difference between the two men concerned Europe. Major adhered to his line of not taking a decision on whether Britain should join a European currency until the political and economic circumstances were known at the time. Redwood wanted to rule out British membership and called for a repatriation of some policies from Brussels to national parliaments. Major won a clear victory by 218 to 89 votes. The 89 Redwood votes probably represent the size of the Euro-sceptic faction in the party. Major followed the election by a Cabinet reshuffle which gave an enhanced position to Michael Heseltine (Deputy Prime Minister) and no concessions to his critics. This was assumed to be the last possible challenge to his leadership before a general election and the opportunity for yet another relaunch.

The election, however, did little to secure Major's authority or reunite the party. Euro-sceptics, aided by traditionally pro-Conservative newspapers, continued to undermine Major. They called, variously, for Britain to declare unilaterally that it would not enter a single European currency, a referendum on continued British membership or on further steps to integration, and reacted angrily to the EU ban on British beef following the BSE crisis in 1996. Two back-bench bills were introduced

---

BOX 14.1   **IDEAS AND PERSPECTIVES**

Conservative groupings

Philip Norton has discerned seven groups in the parliamentary party, according to Philip Cowley.

Neoliberals believe in the rigorous application of market forces; the Tory Right stress moral issues, especially law and order; pure Thatcherites combine a belief in market forces with a desire for law and order;

Wets believe in a role for government intervention in social and economic affairs; Damps believe in the same as wets but not so intensely; Populists reflect popular attitudes, being left on social issues but right on law and order; and the Party Faithful support the party rather than ideological strands of thought.

British Politics Newsletter, No. 86, 1996

under the 10-minute rule, in April and June 1996, by Euro-sceptic Conservative MPs and further embarrassed ministers. The first was to curb the powers of the European Court of Justice, the second a proposal to hold a referendum on Britain's future relations with the EU. These motions showed that a third of the back-bench MPs were hostile to Britain's integration with the EU. Yet Major also had to be careful not to alienate European supporters like Heseltine and Clarke.

Major did not have a distinctive political agenda, unlike his predecessor. There was no Majorism. The 'back to basics' campaign was launched at the 1993 party conference but collapsed, as ministers were forced to resign following various misdemeanours. The Citizen's Charter was designed to improve the quality and responsiveness of public services to citizens (see p. 359), but it did not capture the public imagination. The big deficit in public finances limited scope for tax cuts. But it is worth noting that Major pressed on with privatisations – of coal, nuclear power and the railways.

The work of Philip Norton (1990) showed that Thatcherites were no more than a fifth of Tory MPs at the time of her fall. Dissent had been growing in the party for two decades at least. Some MPs, with little prospect of promotion, are willing to defy the leadership if they calculate their longer term career or constituency popularity will be enhanced. Democratisation (in the form of annual elections for the party leadership) in a divided party only adds to problems of party management. The Conservative Party remains a coalition and the best guarantee of unity is leadership which is strong, consistent and looks like delivering election victory.

Party organisation

The 1922 Committee

The Conservative leader is at the apex of party organisation, in charge of front-bench appointments (whether in or out of office) and of the party bureaucracy. But the leader's writ does not extend to the 1922 Committee, the name given to the Conservative MPs' own organisation. The Committee jealously guards its influence, electing its own officers and executive committee and only giving audiences to the leader by invitation. Usually the Committee provides solid support for the leadership, but behind the scenes discreet influence is often applied and its officers supplement the information flow on party feeling and morale provided by the Chief Whip and his cohorts – a nominated whip, incidentally, always attends Committee meetings. Conservative leaders, if they are wise, take care never to ignore the advice of the 1922 Committee: ultimately, it decides upon their political life or death.

Party committees

The parliamentary party has also established a network of twenty-four specialist committees on policy matters and seven regional groupings. In opposition shadow ministers chair the relevant policy groups but in government the minister does not attend except by invitation. When in government these committees can have considerable influence, often on the detail of policy; individual MPs, for example, might well use them to promote or defend constituency interests. Conservative MPs are also represented on the considerable number of **all-party committees** which exist on a wide range of policy issues.

The National Union of Conservative Associations

This body was set up in 1867 to coordinate local constituency associations in England and Wales: there are separate bodies for Scotland and Northern Ireland. The central council of the National Union, comprising Conservative peers, MEPs, prospective MPs and representatives of regional bodies and advisory committees, meets once a year to elect officers; a smaller executive committee itself appoints a General Purposes Committee. Perhaps the most important function of the National Union is to organise the party conferences each year. Constituency associations are informally consulted during leadership elections but votes are confined to MPs. The National Union is pressing for party members to have a formal voice in the elections.

Conference

The role of conference is formally advisory but in practice it has become important as an annual rallying of the faithful and a public relations exercise in which the leader receives a standing ovation (a regulation ten minutes for Margaret Thatcher in the 1980s) and an impression of euphoric unity is assiduously cultivated for public consumption. As a policy-making body the conference has traditionally been dismissed – Balfour said he would rather take advice from his valet. Richard Kelly (1989), however, argues otherwise. He claims that the consensual conference culture masks an important form of communication: that of 'mood'. Party leaders, he maintains, listen to (or decode?) the messages which underlie the polite contributions from grassroots members and act, or even legislate, accordingly. He also points out that there is a 'conference system' of regional and national conferences involving related sections like Conservative Women, Conservative Trade Unionists and the Federation of Young Conservatives. It was pressure from the conference floor in 1987 which persuaded Margaret Thatcher and Nicholas Ridley to introduce the poll tax in one step, rather than phasing it in – with politically disastrous consequences. Margaret Thatcher confused the enthusiasm of the activists with that of voters. The fact is that the leadership now has to pay attention to the mood of such gatherings – though how important an input they provide into the policy process is difficult to gauge precisely. One may now make a serious case – contrary to caricature and formal party statements – that the Labour conference is now more successfully 'managed' by the leaders than is the Conservative gathering.

Constituency associations

One of the main aims of conference is to send party workers home buoyed up with new enthusiasms for their constituency tasks: recruiting members, attending committees, organising social and fund-raising events, leafleting, exploiting issues at the local level and, most important of all, seeking victory in local and national elections. About half of the local Conservative associations employ full-time agents who provide professional assistance. Despite a nominal membership of about 750,000 the active membership of the Conservative party, the study by Seyd and Whiteley (1995) suggests, is around one-fifth of that number. Conservative Party membership is in bad shape. It is predominantly elderly (an

average age of 61), 'de-energised' and inactive. In terms of their attitudes, Conservative members, according to the study, are pretty typical of party voters (Seyd and Whiteley, 1995). Party workers may well have been discouraged by the steady reduction in the role of local government which means they have fewer opportunities to hold positions of local political responsibility, participate in politics or enjoy patronage. The disastrous local election results since 1992 have greatly reduced the number of Conservative councillors; in many of the great cities – Manchester, Liverpool, Birmingham, Glasgow, Sheffield and Leeds – the party had only a token presence in local government.

Local associations retain the important power of selecting candidates for general elections. They have steadily resisted Central Office measures to secure more women and ethnic minority candidates.

Central Office

Central Office is the organisational core of the Conservative Party. In common with the hierarchical nature of the party, it comes under the direct control of the party leader, who appoints the Party Chairman and other senior officers. Central Office represents an important nexus between party activists in the country and MPs at Westminster, providing advice on small businesses, community groups, trade unions and political education, as well as training for professional constituency agents. Critics in the Charter Movement regularly criticise Central Office for its lack of accountability to the Tory membership. After the 1992 election John Major appointed Sir Norman Fowler to the chairmanship, with a remit to streamline the organisation and reduce its costs. He presided over a major reduction in staffing in the regions and Central Office. In 1993 a new Board of Management was established; this includes senior figures from the National Union, Central Office and the parliamentary party. It assists with fund raising and oversees Central Office budgets. The Party Chairman has a high media profile, particularly during the general election, and is a key organiser of election campaigns. He is usually close to the party leader, e.g. Chris Patten, Party Chairman in the 1992 election, and Brian Mawhinney, who was made Chairman in 1995.

The Research Department was set up in 1925,

becoming a power base for R.A. Butler – who was its head for two decades after the war – and a springboard to the Commons for able young politicians like Iain Macleod, Enoch Powell and Chris Patten. The Department lays on secretarial support for the Shadow Cabinet when the party is in opposition, supports policy groups, briefs the parliamentary party (with officers providing secretarial back-up for subject committees) and produces a range of publications, notably the journal *Politics Today* and the pre-election *Campaign Guide*.

The Department does not originate policy but supports and liaises with the other bodies that do have a policy-making role. Policy work is done in party groups (see below) as well as the 1922 Committee and back-bench committees. Within the voluntary party the National Union Executive Committee also has a role. The Advisory Committee on Policy ceased to meet in the mid-1980s. In government, the main policy initiatives lie with the Prime Minister, Cabinet ministers and the No. 10 Policy Unit, and the Prime Minister and senior colleagues decide the contents of the election manifesto. Some of the think-tanks have also been important in developing ideas of deregulation, competition and the Citizen's Charter. Since 1995 the Director of the party's Research Department has been Danny Finkelstein, a recruit from the think-tank the Social Market Foundation.

Party groupings

Perhaps the oldest group is the **Primrose League**, set up in 1883 by Lord Randolph Churchill to advance the liberal Conservatism of Disraeli and encourage social contact among the grassroots membership. By 1951 the latter function was in the ascendant and it fell to the **Bow Group**, founded in that year, to urge the party's acceptance of the post-war consensus. The Group has a national membership including thirty or so MPs, a number of policy groups and publishes a journal, *Crossbow*.

The **Monday Club** was set up in 1961 in the wake of Macmillan's 'wind of change' African policy and has always concerned itself with defence, external and immigration policies, on which it has invariably taken a strong right-wing and nationalist line – so much so that it has sometimes been accused of being an entry point for National Front influence.

The **Selsdon Group**, formed in 1973, was more concerned to champion the neo-liberal economic policies which Heath's 1972 policy U-turns had appeared to abandon. The **Salisbury Group** is another right-wing intellectual ginger group which exerts influence through its journal *The Salisbury Review*.

The **Tory Reform Group** was set up in 1975 to defend the beleaguered Disraelian tradition; it has some thirty MP members, the most prominent of whom is Peter Walker.

The **No Turning Back Group** is the vehicle for the Thatcherites. Originally formed in 1988 to defend Margaret Thatcher against the 'wets', it believes strongly in cuts in taxes and public expenditure, and a reduction in universal welfare benefits. It has included a number of right-wing figures, such as Michael Portillo, John Redwood and Peter Lilley.

In addition to the above, from time to time the parliamentary party establishes policy groupings, some of which prove ephemeral, like the **Blue Chip Group**, to which Chris Patten belonged in the early 1980s, and **Centre Forward**, the group of twenty-plus MPs formed by Francis Pym in 1983. The anti-European **Bruges Group**, set up in the wake of Thatcher's speech in Bruges in 1988, has proved to be more lasting and more influential. There is also the **92 Group**, whose chairman for several years was the anti-European MP, George Gardiner, de-selected by his constituency association in January 1997. In 1995 he was granted a much publicised meeting with John Major at which he announced he would advocate the promotion of a number of right-wingers to government jobs. He was sent packing. In 1996 the former Cabinet minister David Hunt announced the formation of the **Mainstream Group** to support John Major and Britain's 'constructive' role in the EU.

What the emergence of these general groupings shows is the extent to which the Conservative Party is becoming more factionalised.

Funding

The central organisation of the party receives about one-tenth of its funding via a quota system levied on local constituency organisations. The balance is provided by individual and company donations which flow in directly and often indirectly through what could be called 'front organisations' like British United Industrialists, the Aims of Industry and a number of companies especially set up for the purpose and named after rivers in the United Kingdom. In its evidence to the Houghton Committee in 1974 the party opposed the idea of state aid to political parties. The party has experienced severe financial pressures since 1987 – a consequence of the unwillingness of firms and companies to contribute in the recession, and heavy expenditure. By March 1992 the cumulative deficit was £17 million. The party has reduced expenditure, laid off staff, and in 1993 appointed a Director General in Central Office and a Board of Management to control central finance. By 1996 it announced that the deficit had been wiped out. Perhaps this was just as well since the Conservative's 1997 election campaign was rumoured in *The Guardian* 8 May 1997 to have cost £40 million; in the same edition Labour was predicted to plan stringent restrictions on donations to political parties, especially from foreign donors; Lord Nolan (Chair of the Committee on Standards in Public Life) was to be invited to examine the issue – the funding of political parties – which Major explicitly excluded from his remit.

Conservative difficulties

Some of the difficulties of the Conservative Party have been due to its long period in office. Many groups of voters have become disaffected over time and there is an inevitable desire for change, although there is much less clarity about what should change. The party has also been damaged by several ministerial resignations, in the wake of scandals and sleaze allegations (e.g. paying MPs to ask questions in the Commons), the findings of the Scott Report and divisions in the party. Some of the divisions are long-standing, notably between those who wish to consolidate the Thatcher reforms and those who wish to carry on with radical changes. Since the 1992 election the party has lost its reputation for possessing a clear and consistent sense of direction and for economic competence. These were major advantages enjoyed over Labour in the 1980s. The exit from the ERM (after ministers boasted that it was the cornerstone of their economic policy) and the tax increases forfeited the latter. Some Thatcher-

ites complained that the former is down to weak leadership; John Major is no Margaret Thatcher. The explanation is certainly more complex than that. Thatcher, after all, had lost the support of 40 per cent of the party at the time of her fall and her Cabinet was divided over her attitudes to Europe. Party divisions became more sharply defined as the EU began to take the integrationist philosophy of the 1986 Single European Act seriously and a significant sector of the party became 'sceptical' about the advantages of integration and the erosion of sovereignty.

The Labour Party

The organisation of the Labour Party is different from that of the Conservative Party. The major contrasts are as follows:

1. Unlike the Conservative Party, which developed from within Parliament, Labour developed as a grassroots popular movement *outside* the legislature. In 1900 the trade unions, cooperative and socialist societies formed the Labour Representation Committee (LRC) to represent interests of trade unions and assist the entry of working men into Parliament. In 1906 the LRC changed its name to the Labour Party.
2. The Conservatives have been in power – either alone or as the dominant coalition partner – for two-thirds of the years since 1918, Labour for less than a third.
3. Conservatives have traditionally been the party of the status quo, Labour the party dedicated to reform. Conservatives attracted sober members of the ruling elite who, with some justification, were expecting to preside over an unquestioned existing order. Labour, on the other hand, attracted people whose political style had developed through years of opposition to such an order, who spoke in fiery rhetorical terms and were skilled in manipulating democratic procedures – skills used both against the Conservative enemy and against party comrades with whom they disagreed. In practice the key differences were reduced to those between the gradual and the root and branch reformers: Ramsay MacDonald and John Wheatley in the 1920s; Clement Attlee and Stafford Cripps in

the 1930s; Hugh Gaitskell and Aneurin (Nye) Bevan in the 1950s; Michael Foot and Harold Wilson in the 1960s; James Callaghan and Tony Benn in the 1970s; and Neil Kinnock and Tony Benn in the 1980s. (Williams, 1982).

4. Labour was originally a federation rather than a unified party like the Conservatives, comprising trade unions and intellectual socialist societies, each with their own self-governing mechanisms. Despite the formation of a single party in 1918, a similar coalition still underlies Labour Party politics.

5. The party's written constitution (1918) committed it to certain ideological objectives and laid down democratic procedures for elections, appointments and decision-making. While more democratic than the autocratic Conservative party organisation, the constitution precludes some of the flexible adaptation to changing circumstances which the latter enjoys and when in government offers an alternative source of authority which has on occasions caused Labour embarrassment.

Labour's constitution and the power of the unions

The contrasting 'top-down' and 'bottom-up' provenance of the two big parties explains why the Conservative Party in the country is organisationally separate and subservient to the parliamentary party, while for Labour the situation is – at least in theory – reversed. This proviso is important because the relationship between the parliamentary Labour Party (PLP) and the other party organs is complex and has changed over time. The 1918 constitution aimed to provide a happy marriage between the different elements of Labour's coalition: the trade unions, socialist societies, local constituency parties, party officials and Labour MPs. Institutionally the marriage – which has not been an easy one – expressed itself in the form of the leadership and the parliamentary Labour Party (PLP), the National Executive Committee (NEC), constituency parties and the Conference. The absence of trade unions from this list is misleading because in practice they play a leading role, although one that is being reduced (for more on this see Chapter 13).

Power and leadership in the Labour Party

Unlike the Conservatives, who stress loyalty, hierarchy and strong leadership, Labour's ethos was founded in democracy, egalitarianism and collective decision-making (Minkin, 1980). An 'iron law of oligarchy' theory was propounded before 1914 by the German sociologist Robert Michels (1959): he argued that mass organisations can never be run democratically. This was reinforced by Robert McKenzie (1963) in a classic study of Britain's political parties in which he claimed that, appearances notwithstanding, both major parties reflected similar concentrations of power and authority in the party leadership with the external party organisations playing a merely supportive role. McKenzie argued that: 'By the time the Labour Party had taken office in 1924, its transformation was almost complete. By accepting all the conventions with respect to the office of the Prime Minister and of Cabinet government it ensured that effective power within the party would be concentrated in the hands of the leadership of the PLP' (McKenzie, 1963, p. 639). This made nonsense of Labour's official constitution and the widespread notion that conference constitutes the 'parliament' of the Labour movement.

There is much in this argument. Once elected to Westminster Labour MPs become subject to a different set of forces: they become responsible for all their constituents and not just Labour supporters; they often need to consider their re-election in terms of what non-Labour voters want or will accept; and they become influenced by the dominant Burkean notion that within the House of Commons MPs are not delegates of some outside organisation but individuals elected to use their judgement on behalf of the nation as a whole. Labour's constitution, therefore, particularly when the party is in government, becomes challenged by the constitution of the country. In 1960 party leader Hugh Gaitskell refused to accept a conference resolution embracing unilateralism and succeeded in reversing it in the following year. Harold Wilson as Prime Minister, moreover, ignored a series of conference decisions in the late 1960s and survived while James Callaghan did much the same when Prime Minister in the 1970s. To dismiss Labour's intra-party democracy as unimportant, however, would be foolish.

Minkin (1980) points out that while Harold Wilson was defying conference resolutions and pursuing foreign, economic and industrial policies deeply offensive to the party's left wing, he was also losing the loyalty and hence control of crucial elements in the party. Little by little the constituency parties, the NEC and the trade unions turned against him.

Indeed, the 1970s witnessed the splintering of Labour Party unity. Disillusioned with the revisionism of the Wilson government, the next generation of important trade union leaders found common cause with the left wing of the parliamentary party. In opposition after 1970 conference shifted sharply to the left and by 1974 most constituency parties and the NEC were also firmly in the left wing camp. The result was that Labour governments of Wilson and Callaghan (1974–9) were 'obviously at odds with the party machine … it was if there were two Labour parties, one with the voice of the NEC and the conference and the other with that of the parliamentary leadership' (Butler and Kavanagh, 1980). Disillusion with government policies caused an exodus of party supporters, leaving 'shell' constituency parties vulnerable to takeovers by far left activists, especially members of the Militant Tendency. During the 1970s constituency management committees (GMCs) in many parts of the country were taken over by the left; as these controlled the selection of candidates it was not surprising that the trend gave rise to an increasing number of left-wing candidates.

The limits of the 'iron law' became apparent when Labour again became the opposition party in 1979. The parliamentary leadership was much weaker and in no position to resist the pressures from a more left-wing conference and NEC. The new party policies represented a sharp break with those of the Callaghan government. Labour was now pledged to come out of the European Community (this time without holding a referendum), and adopted a unilateralist defence policy, sweeping measures of public ownership and redistribution, and the repeal of many Tory measures, notably those affecting the trade unions.

The 1981 constitutional changes

Internal party divisions reached a new degree of bitterness in 1979 in the wake of the so-called 'winter of discontent' when the collapse of Labour's incomes policy produced industrial paralysis. On 28 March Callaghan's minority government lost a vote of confidence and a general election was called. The party manifesto is decided jointly by the parliamentary leaders and the NEC but by this time the gulf between the two was immense. When Callaghan vetoed measures which the left wished to include in the manifesto – including the abolition of the House of Lords – he alienated the left still further and set the battle-lines for a fratricidal fight over the reform of the party's constitution.

The party's left wing pressed for radical changes in the rules of the party and in particular they wished to introduce greater 'democracy' into the party. The left insisted that the party leader be elected by an electoral college and not by MPs alone. In 1981 the Wembley conference agreed to set up an electoral college in which the trade unions would have 40 per cent of the vote, constituency parties 30 per cent and MPs 30 per cent. A second aim was for mandatory reselection of MPs within the lifetime of a Parliament. They succeeded in this. But they failed in their third goal, which was to give control of the party's manifesto to the National Executive Committee. The central thrust of all these reforms was to increase the power of the extra-parliamentary elements of the party over MPs. Mandatory reselection was a factor which persuaded some threatened MPs to 'jump' into the SDP in 1981 and 1982, for the reselections favoured the left.

The new machinery for electing the deputy leader was first tried in 1981 when Tony Benn challenged Denis Healey and came within a whisker of toppling him. But the election was time-consuming, bitterly divisive and left many scars. Neil Kinnock and Roy Hattersley contested the leadership in October 1983; Kinnock won easily, while Hattersley decisively won the deputy's post. Yet, if the left managed to overturn the constitution, help drive some disillusioned right-wing MPs to the SDP and force the party to adopt a series of left-wing policies in the 1983 election, its victories were short-lived. The disastrous 1983 general election result, when the party scored its lowest share of the vote in over fifty years and was nearly overtaken by the Alliance parties, forced a rethink. Neil Kinnock gradually

BOX 14.2   TONY BLAIR (1953–)   **BIOGRAPHY**

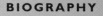

By courtesy of Popperfoto

Tony Blair was born in Edinburgh. He attended an Edinburgh public school, Fettes, then read law at Oxford and qualified as a barrister. He is the first Labour leader to have been educated at a leading public school since Hugh Gaitskell (leader 1955–63).

Blair entered Parliament in 1983, winning the safe seat of Sedgefield. Labour lost the election on its most left-wing manifesto for over fifty years. Conservative critics sometimes attack him for standing on that manifesto – which promised British withdrawal from the European Community, a great extension of public ownership and a unilateralist defence policy. In the House of Commons he proved to be an outstanding debater and was elected to the Shadow Cabinet in 1988. As Shadow Spokesman for employment he presented the trade unions with a *fait accompli*, in announcing that a Labour government would not reintroduce the 'closed shop' which the Conservatives had abolished.

When Neil Kinnock resigned the party

leadership after the 1992 general election, Blair briefly thought about standing. But it was generally felt that it was John Smith's 'turn'. Some Labour modernisers regretted the opportunity to skip a generation and elect a younger leader like Blair or Gordon Brown. Under Smith Tony Blair became Shadow Spokesman on Home Office matters. He was determined to stamp out the widespread perception that Labour was 'soft' on crime and sympathetic to criminals. A popular Blair soundbite was that Labour would be 'tough on crime and tough on the causes of crime'.

When Smith died in 1994 Blair was a candidate and his close friend and rival Gordon Brown, the Shadow Chancellor who for some time had been regarded as the more likely figure, decided not to enter the contest; now he was overtaken by the more junior Blair. It was no surprise that Blair won the election easily in July 1994.

In his first conference speech, Blair called for a review of Clause Four of the party constitution, the clause which committed the party to widespread public ownership. When he learnt that powerful trade unions were opposed, he decided to carry his campaign directly to the membership. At a special conference his redrafted clause was carried by a two-thirds majority. He has continued Neil Kinnock's reforms of the party but further repositioned Labour in an effort to try to steal strong Conservative issues of law and order, low taxes, and standards and traditional forms of education. He has also been accused of authoritarianism, and senior figures have been censured for speaking out of line. Clare Short was reprimanded for expressing 'old' Labour sentiments on taxes (apparently suggesting that people earning over £30,000 per annum should pay more taxes) and public ownership, and David Blunkett for hostility to private schooling. Blair believes in leading from the front, and is determined to create a new Labour Party. Blair survived all criticisms to deliver the promised prize on 1 May 1997: a huge majority of 179 over a shattered and still divided Conservative Party.

managed to impose his authority on the party machine, particularly the NEC: the Militant leaders were expelled from the party; left-wing MPs were marginalised or moved to the centre; more central control was exercised over constituency parties and over the selection of candidates at by-elections; the party's aims and principles were restated in a less left-wing form; and socialism was all but abandoned. In the 1992 election, campaign decisions effectively were taken by Neil Kinnock and his office. When he resigned the leadership in 1992 he left a more centrally controlled party machine to John Smith.

When Smith died tragically in 1994, Tony Blair took over after Gordon Brown agreed to step down as a candidate in favour of his friend. With the help of the formidable Peter Mandelson, policy was not only shifted to the centre right but party discipline was tightened to the point where one backbencher compared Blair to Kim il Sung of North Korea. One of the strengths of the modernisers is their tactic of appealing to the increased, mostly Blairite, membership to endorse new centrist policies and thereby bypass old Labour tendencies. Throughout the long election campaign of 1997 the party's discipline held remarkably and it was the Conservatives who appeared to be the feuding squabbling rabble Labour had traditionally been in the 1970s and 1980s.

The 'modernisation' of Labour

Labour's clear election defeat in 1987 gave reformers the chance to reverse the effects of the party's surge to the left between 1979 and 1983. In spite of high levels of unemployment and its much praised campaign Labour still finished 11 per cent behind the Conservative share of the vote. The Kinnock 'project' of the modernisation of the party was designed to make Labour electable again. The leader was convinced that the party, due to the damage caused by left-wing activists, had lost touch with the concerns of many ordinary Labour voters. The 1981 changes had been a party revolution; now there would be a counter-revolution.

After the election defeat the party launched an ambitious policy review. The consequence was a shift to the political centre and the acceptance of a number of Thatcherite policies (see Chapter 8).

Neil Kinnock was also concerned to strengthen the authority of the leader over the party organisation. The system of one member one vote was extended to the election of parliamentary candidates and members of the NEC; the leader's office became more influential and a shadow communications agency drawn from experts in media and communications played an important role in preparing the party's election strategy.

The project may have resulted in a more leader-dominated and policy centrist Labour Party by 1992. But it did not deliver victory in the general election, its crucial objective. Labour slumped to a fourth successive and unexpected defeat. After the election, party leaders were convinced that it was their spending and taxation proposals, as well as Kinnock's leadership, which had held them back from victory. Survey evidence suggested that the electorate still did not trust Labour, particularly when it came to managing the economy. John Smith succeeded Neil Kinnock as leader in 1992, although it had been his shadow budget during the election campaign which was blamed by many for allowing Conservatives to attack Labour as the party of high taxes. Under Smith the party backed off many of its taxing and spending proposals; it had been scarred by the strong Conservative attack on it as the party of high taxes. John Smith had not been a prominent supporter of Neil Kinnock's party reforms, but in spite of opposition from prominent trade unions, he staked his authority on OMOV (one member one vote) which was carried narrowly at the party conference in 1993. Trade unions' influence in the electoral college for electing the party leader was diluted, as all the three elements – TUs, PLP and constituency parties – had equal shares of $33\frac{1}{3}$ per cent of the vote. Although the union block (winner takes all) vote was abolished and replaced by individual voting, the party has not, strictly speaking, moved to OMOV. Some party members can vote in two or all three sections.

Following John Smith's sudden death from a heart attack in May 1994, Tony Blair, a figure from the party's centre-right, was easily elected leader (see Box 14.2). Blair resumed the Kinnock project with a vengeance. The most important indicator of his determination to reform the party was his decision to rewrite Clause Four of the party's constitution. This was the ideological statement that

BOX 14.3 'OLD' LABOUR VERSUS 'NEW' LABOUR   DEBATE

Old Labour	New Labour
■ Appeal to working class.	■ Appeal to all voters.
■ Importance of public ownership of 'commanding heights' of economy (Clause Four).	■ Rely on markets for economic growth as much as possible.
■ Sweeping redistribution from middle to working class via taxation and public spending.	■ Redistribution via economic growth.
■ Key role of trade unions in party and economy.	■ No privileges for unions.
■ Limits on leadership.	■ Trust the leadership.
■ Campaign through party activists.	■ Campaign through modern communications.
■ Slight interest in constitutional reforms.	■ Constitutional reform to provide more open government and decentralisation.

Labour was a socialist party. In office, however, the party had rarely taken the clause seriously. When it had taken services and industries into public ownership it had done so largely for pragmatic rather than ideological reasons. Yet Clause Four was a gift to political opponents who wished to portray Labour as anti-capitalist and anti-market. At a time when state ownership was becoming widely discredited in the West and even abandoned in Eastern Europe, Blair calculated that it was a liability. Labour should mean what it said and say what it meant. He took his campaign to the membership and it was carried by a two-thirds majority at a special conference in April 1995. Modernisers noted the 9-to-1 majority among local parties, which, significantly, balloted their members. The new clause claims that Labour works for a dynamic economy, a just society, an open democracy and a healthy environment.

The party continued to accept many of the Thatcher and Major government's policies and Blair even spoke favourably about some of them. Labour also redefined its electoral market, realising that it had to reach beyond the working class and trade unions, both now a diminishing minority. Blair wished to appeal to 'all the people', not least middle class voters. Not surprisingly, these policies and theories were leading to further marginalisation of the left and there were complaints that the Blair

leadership was authoritarian. Labour has become a catch-all political party seeking votes across the social spectrum and ditching ideology (Kavanagh, 1996 and see Chapter 6). Traditional divisions between the left and right have been transmuted into divisions between old and new Labour with Roy Hattersley of the old right and Tony Benn of the old left associated with the former (see Box 14.3).

It is interesting to note how democracy in the party had been redefined. The policy role of conference has been modified, as the new more easily managed Policy Forum and its commissions make a more important contribution. Conference is 'managed' to be more supportive of the leadership, so reinforcing the image of Labour as a responsible party of government and with strong leaders. The last three party leaders improved their public standing by challenging conference, e.g. Kinnock's attack on Militant in 1986, Smith's stand on OMOV in 1993, and Blair on Clause Four in 1995. Blair has increasingly relied on ballots of ordinary members to outflank the delegates and activists who could be unrepresentative of Labour voters. The use of ballots among many party members for the Clause Four vote, annual elections for the NEC and parliamentary candidates has on balance helped the leadership. Another example of the *plebiscitarian* style was Blair's decision that Labour's draft election manifesto would be voted on by party members in late 1996. In many respects what has happened in the new Labour Party amounts to a reversal of the traditional analysis of Labour democracy. Persistent electoral defeats, and hunger for office has led to a weakening of the 'old' mechanisms of intra-party democracy, and a rallying behind the leader.

Many factors have contributed to the transformation to what Blair frequently calls New Labour. The four successive crushing election defeats showed the extent to which Britain had changed, socially and culturally. Labour had to take account of these changes if it was to be a credible party of government. The party also had to come to terms with the fact that many of the Conservative policies it had opposed were popular or now too firmly entrenched to be repealed. This included the privatisation measures, changes in industrial relations law, Britain's membership of the European Community and cuts in marginal rates of direct taxation. Academic studies and doorstep feedback showed that the party also had to remove the many 'negatives' in its image, which proved an easy target for Conservative propaganda and hostile tabloids. Above all, a growing awareness of the interdependence of national economies and the need for economic policies to take account of the likely constraints of financial markets showed that socialism in one nation was no longer practical politics (Shaw, 1996).

New Labour in the Commons

The new party which marched onto the benches of the Commons after its historic victory on 1 May 1997 was made up of many new elements. Out of the 419 new entrants, 239 went to university and 68 to Oxbridge, though there are some working class MPs, including a docker, a firefighter, two electricians and Clive Efford, the first ever London cabbie to be an MP. Many were from public sector professions: 55 lecturers; 49 teachers and 12 social workers, plus 16 company directors. Traditional Labour was represented via 28 trade unionists. Most are middle aged – 173 being 41–50; only 3 over 70 and 10 in their twenties. But the really startling thing about New Labour was the 101 women who have already helped to achieve a cultural change in this, 'the best men's club in London'.

Many of the intake were the result of the women-only shortlists rule introduced by Labour and not abandoned before it had engineered an effect. Finally, Labour was able to boast four Asian members, including the first ever Muslim MP, and four black members. Two openly homosexual MPs were returned: Steven Twigg, conqueror of Michael Portillo and Ben Bradshaw, who survived a homophobic campaign by his opponent in Exeter.

Groups in the Labour Party

Given its ideological breadth, it is not surprising that Labour has been even more prone to internal groupings than the Conservatives. The best-known group is the *Fabian Society*, established in 1884 and a founder partner of the Labour Representation Committee in 1900. It has declined in relative terms since the days of its founders, Sidney and Beatrice Webb, but it still boasts a national membership of several thousand and over one half of the PLP (which also provides a fair proportion of the Fabian executive). The Society still performs its traditional roles of initiating debate, gathering information and issuing tracts, many of which contain important policy proposals. As the Fabians favour a gradual reformist path to socialism they are usually perceived as centre-right in the party.

Organised right-wing factions, however, did not appear in the Labour Party until the *Campaign for Democratic Socialism* in 1960, inspired by a group of Gaitskellite MPs and with a degree of nationwide support. This faded away in 1964, but *Manifesto*, a PLP grouping, was set up in 1974 to resist the policies of the left and to press for 'one member one vote' in the selection and reselection of parliamentary candidates. The right was further strengthened in 1981 by the 150 MPs who joined Roy Hattersley and Peter Shore in forming *Solidarity* in response to the sweeping left-wing constitutional changes of that year; this group has also faded.

Unsurprisingly, left-wing groups have also been active. During the 1930s a number thrived, some of them related to the Communist Party as part of the agitation for a Popular Front against fascism. After 1945 the *Keep Left Group* led by Michael Foot, Richard Crossman and Ian Mikardo was established, involving some twenty MPs, urging a more independent and less pro-US foreign policy. During the 1950s elements of this defunct group joined the fifty or so MPs who supported Aneurin Bevan's bid for leadership. *Victory for Socialism*, though founded in 1944, did not become prominent until after 1958 as a Bevanite faction with a national organisation. In 1966 the *Tribune Group* was born, named after the left-wing journal founded in 1937. This group attracted considerable support in the 1970s when the left was vehemently urging alternative policies on Europe with regard to banning nuclear weapons and increased state intervention. During the 1980s *Tribune*'s role as a left-wing ginger discussion group began to alter when one of its leading members, Michael Foot (also an ex-editor of *Tribune*) became leader. A proportion of the group's membership began to shift towards the centre in support of Foot's efforts to formulate an agreed consensus within the party. During the 1982 deputy leadership election a crucial twenty Tribunite MPs either voted for Healey or abstained, thus denying Tony Benn victory. When another left-wing Tribunite, Neil Kinnock, succeeded Foot, Tribune became even 'softer' left; it proceeded to support Kinnock's policy drive towards the centre and has now become, arguably, a leadership support group rather than a critical faction (Seyd, 1987).

The *Campaign Group* was set up in 1982 by twenty-three MPs; it soon attracted a membership of over forty. While Tribune moved to the centre, Campaign has insisted on a more muscular version of familiar left-wing themes, but has added two more important elements: sweeping constitutional changes like the abolition of the House of Lords and the 'proxy' royal prerogatives exercised by the Prime Minister; and the strengthening of links with extra-parliamentary organisations and constituency activists.

The position of *Militant Tendency* has also been exposed by Labour's shift towards the centre with its MPs losing their seats and the Tendency losing its momentum as Labour moved decisively against it (Crick 1984).

Other extra-parliamentary groups, like the *Labour Coordinating Committee* (LCC) and the *Campaign for Labour Party Democracy* (CLPD), which helped the left to win such an ascendancy in the early 1980s, either became isolated or joined the Kinnock-led move into the centre.

Within the PLP the influence of party groups has

also declined and lost sharpness of definition; *Labour Briefing* is a somewhat scurrilous publication but lacks real clout. The 1996 *Labour Reform Group* boasts over a hundred MPs and is seen as a counter to Blair's centralising tendencies. Other groups within the parliamentary party such as regional meetings, the women's caucus, the black caucus (until its demise), as well as closely knit working groups like the shadow policy teams, also contribute to policy and can provide power bases for ambitious MPs.

What needs to be emphasised in the 1990s, however, is the decline of the leftist groups in particular and the decline of factionalism in general in the Labour party. The bitter disputes were important in speeding the party's electoral decline and the party is now often criticised for being too boring and safe. Left-wingers like Benn and Livingstone are now marginal figures and have been voted off the constituency section of the NEC.

Other parties

We all 'know' that the main party battle is between Conservative and Labour. But since 1970 there has been a steady growth of support for 'other' parties. Only the disproportional effects of the electoral system have prevented the 'other' parties' votes being reflected in a large number of seats. In the last four general elections (1983–1997) those parties have gained some 25 per cent of the vote and around 40 seats (as opposed to the 160–170 they would have got under a pure proportional system). But this third force of parties is diverse, including Liberals, Greens, Welsh and Scottish nationalists and five different parties in Northern Ireland.

The centre parties

The main third party after 1918 was the *Liberal Party*. It was one of the two parties of government between 1867 and 1918. However, it steadily declined during the interwar years and attracted only minuscule support for much of the post-war period. In the 1970s it improved its share of the vote, in February 1974 garnering 19 per cent of the poll. However, the first-past-the-post electoral system has been a barrier and prevented it from receiving a proportional share of seats in the House of Commons. Its most distinctive policies in recent years have been political decentralisation and constitutional reform (more open government, proportional representation and a Bill of Rights; see also Chapter 8).

An opportunity for a realignment of the party system came in 1981 when Labour right-wingers broke away to form the Social Democratic Party. In 1983 its twenty-nine MPs (all but one of whom came from Labour) formed a partnership with the Liberals. The two parties had a common programme, a joint leader (the SDP leader Roy Jenkins was Prime Minister designate of an Alliance government), an electoral pact and fought under the label of the Alliance. As noted earlier in the chapter, the Alliance gained 25.4 per cent of the vote in 1983, but only 3.5 per cent of seats. In 1987 the two parties again formed an electoral alliance and gained 22.6 per cent of the vote but few seats. In 1988 the Liberals and a majority of the SDP merged in a Social Liberal Democratic Party, known initially as the 'Democrats' and then after 1989 as the 'Liberal Democrats'.

In June 1990 the SDP gave up the unequal struggle and formally wound itself up. SDP members could comfort themselves with the notion that their party had forced Labour to abandon its left-wing adventures and adopt a programme more in keeping with the expectations of the ordinary voter – a programme in fact very close in essentials to that offered by the SDP throughout its nine-year history.

But electoral support for the Lib. Dems has faded since Tony Blair has taken over the Labour leadership. As Labour has moved to the central ground it has cut into Liberal territory. Paddy Ashdown has repositioned his party from being even-handed between the Conservative and Labour parties, and now takes a pro-Labour stance. The two parties take a similar stance on Europe, devolution and constitutional reform and education and training. The Blair leadership may welcome Liberal support if Labour has only a narrow majority or no majority at all. Liberal support could be used to free the leadership from dependence on Labour left-wing MPs. There is much talk of Lib.–Lab. cooperation and there are certainly very few policy differences between the parties. Ashdown has made clear that the price of Liberal participation in support for a minority Labour government would be proportional representation. For Liberals the danger is that the party may lose any distinctive identity, as Conserva-

tive claims that 'a vote for Ashdown is a vote for Labour' are vindicated.

The Greens

The British Green Party began life in 1973 as an environmental pressure group. In 1985 the party changed its name to the Green Party and thus came into line with environmental parties internationally. During the 1980s Green support in Western Europe grew apace: candidates were elected to eleven national parliaments around the world. In Britain, however, in 1983, 108 candidates mustered barely 1 per cent of the votes (55,000). But after the decline of the Alliance the Greens captured the 'protest' vote. In June 1989 the Greens took an astonishing 15 per cent of the vote in the elections to the European Parliament, overtaking the Liberals. The party's amateurish organisational approach, however, has caused problems, and its electoral support has collapsed. In 1992, it gained an average of 1.3 per cent where a Green candidate stood, worse than in 1987.

Nationalist parties

Party politics in **Northern Ireland** is different from that on the mainland (see Chapter 30). In part this is because of the dominance of issues regarding the border, religious rivalries between Protestants and Catholics and because no mainland party contests any Ulster seat. The two main Protestant parties are the Official Unionists and Democratic Unionists (led by Dr Ian Paisley). They oppose power-sharing with the Catholic community in any Northern Ireland legislature and also oppose the Anglo-Irish agreement (1985) which gives the Irish government a voice in Northern Ireland's affairs. The main Catholic party is the Social Democratic and Labour Party (SDLP) which favours power-sharing. Sinn Fein, the parliamentary wing of the IRA, won one seat in 1983 and 1987 but the MP refused to take his place in Westminster. After losing a single seat to the SDLP in 1992, they gained 15 per cent of the vote in the Assembly elections connected with the peace process. In the general election of 1997 they won two seats, though once again neither was taken up.

In **Scotland** and **Wales nationalist** parties want independence (see Chapter 9) for their countries. They had seven MPs in the 1992 parliament but this increased in 1997 to 6 for the SNP and 4 for Plaid

Cymru. Scotland faces a referendum on a proposed new assembly and it seems a majority favour this, with some tax-raising powers to boot. The non-Conservative parties in 1988 established a constitutional convention to formulate plans for a Scottish parliament which was soon boycotted by the nationalists. Because of the weakness of Conservatives in Scotland many Scots complained they were ruled by an 'alien' English parliament. A large Labour vote had little effect when the party was in a minority south of the border. It will be interesting to see how the SNP regards a Scottish assembly: as a legitimate devolved assembly or as an irrelevant 'half-way house'.

For all the talk of nationalism, it is also worth noting that the majority of MPs in both countries were drawn from pro-union 'national' parties. Since the 1997 election, however, the Conservatives have been wiped out in both countries and Labour has emerged supreme. The referendums in March 1979 showed weak support for national devolution (let alone independence in Scotland and Wales where only 11.9 per cent of Welsh voters supported it). Support since then has grown, fostered by the cross-party Scottish Convention.

The effect of parties

For all the formal strength of British governments in the House of Commons their performance has been much criticised. The failures of most post-war governments, notably in the economic sphere, weaknesses in the face of trade unions in 1974 and 1979 and the frequent reversals of policies both during and between governments, have been seen by many as signs of weak government. According to Professor Richard Rose, in *Do Parties Make a Difference?* (1984), British parties are ill equipped to direct government. Rose argues that they are poorly prepared in opposition and that counter-pressures from other groups like the civil service, the City, business and trade unions are strong. Rose points in particular to the failure of pre-1979 governments to improve macro-economic conditions (like inflation, unemployment, economic growth and balance of payments) to show that parties do not make much difference in reversing the trend. The secular decline is regarded by Rose as proof of the relative weakness of the parties.

Against this, some argue that the parties in government may have too much power. The relative ease

with which they get their legislation through Parliament, for example, in the absence of formal checks and balances or the extension of non-elected quangos (Jenkins 1996) has prompted concern. Adversarial party politics has produced frequent and damaging reversals of policy (Finer, 1975). Critics advocate the introduction of a proportional electoral system, partly on the grounds of fairness (since to have a majority of seats in the Commons, governments would also need the support of a majority of the electorate), and partly on the grounds that coalitions would slow down the damaging reversals of policy resulting from competing party ideologies.

On the whole, the experience since 1979 supports one line of the adversary politics analysis. There have been significant discontinuities in the fields of industrial relations, abandonment of formal incomes policy and tripartite style of decision-making, privatisation of state industries and services. Moreover, the Thatcher record shows that parties can make a difference, particularly when they have a determined leader who has a political strategy and are in office for a lengthy period (Kavanagh, 1990). In particular, recent governments have proved effective in resisting the pressures of interest groups. In the 1970s it was fashionable to argue that groups had excessive influence and that governments were often weak. Powerful groups were able to defy or veto government policies and government usually went out of its way to consult them. But the Thatcher and Major governments have massively reduced the role of the trade unions and local government and have imposed far-reaching changes on the teaching, health and legal professions. Parties also seem to be striving more than ever to show their independence from interests. Labour has distanced itself from the unions, though it still depends heavily on union finances, and Conservative governments, prior to the withdrawal from the ERM in September 1992, were not sympathetic to business complaints about the effects of economic policy. Powerful lobbies still campaign for more public spending in their favoured areas, but the size of the public sector has been reduced (thanks to privatisation) and both major parties are less sympathetic to spending demands.

During the period of Conservative hegemony, some political commentators thought Britain might be developing into a one-party state rather like Japan. Fears were expressed that interest groups would accustom themselves to working with one party alone. Other fears expressed were that the Conservatives would politicise the civil service and make it into an instrument of ideology instead of a neutral vehicle for the public good. There is little evidence for this last suspicion. Rather, Thatcher was concerned to encourage civil servants who were change-oriented, interested in cutting costs and promoting value for money. But Labour may be concerned that for nearly two decades civil servants have been working with governments that have spurned public sector solutions to problems. Conservatives have also had the opportunity to make their policy changes in the early 1980s well nigh irreversible. Many of the controversial policies were soon accepted by Labour, e.g. council house sales, membership of the European Community/Union, some of the privatisations and lower rates of marginal income tax. By the mid-1990s it is reasonable to assume that the education and health changes and some of the trade union reforms will be so well entrenched that they will be difficult to unscramble.

Having read the political runes of the 1980s, Labour policy converged so closely to the Conservatives' it was difficult for voters to distinguish between them. In the end they decided that the Conservatives were too tired and incompetent as well as arguably dishonest, and Labour was returned with the kind of majority it took them 14 years, to overturn after 1983. Labour approached the 1997 election with some of its supporters looking somewhat desperately to constitutional reform to correct the 'one-party-state' tendency. However, once in power with a huge majority it will be interesting to see how much enthusiasm for this perennially difficult subject Labour will be able to sustain.

Problems for parties

Britain is widely regarded as the home of strong parties. They have a reputation for being disciplined, programmatic, providing clear choice for voters at elections and providing stable one-party government. Yet there are signs that parties are in trouble. Symptoms include the following:

1. *Declining popular attachment:* Surveys over the years show that about 15 per cent of the electorate consistently claim to be very interested in politics. Yet the proportion of voters who identify very strongly with the Labour and Conservative parties has fallen, from over two-fifths in 1964 to a quarter today, with the big decline occurring in the mid-1970s. A MORI poll conducted in January 1993 found that only 2 per cent were willing to canvas by telephone for the party they support or stop strangers in the street and discuss their party's strengths.

2. *Declining membership:* Party membership has declined in Britain, as it has in a number of other Western states. The Labour Party had a million individual members in the 1950s and this fell to just over 250,000 in 1992. From the 1950s to the 1990s Conservative membership fell from a claimed 2.8 million to some 500,000. It has risen by an extra 100,000 over the past two years but its membership is relatively old – on average in its sixties – and the dearth of Conservative election posters in the 1997 election campaign revealed that in all but a few constituencies activism was virtually dead. About only 2 per cent of voters are actually party members.

3. *People have other, non-political interests:* Competition for the time and interest of voters has developed from television, various leisure activities and interest groups. If voters are becoming more instrumental in their outlooks, they may find it more profitable to advance their specific concerns through participation in local protest bodies. The decline in party membership has coincided with an increase in membership of many cause groups.

4. *Interest groups are reluctant to associate closely with a political party:* The trade union connection with Labour has not inspired others to follow, and group spokespersons are increasingly likely to seek direct access to ministers rather than to operate through a political party. Parties lack effective control over the mass media. The last national newspaper to be connected to a political party was the *Daily Herald*, and this ceased publication long ago. There is no popular market for a party political newspaper.

5. *Parties are turning elsewhere for relevant skills:* They court think-tanks for ideas rather than their own research departments (e.g. Labour consulted the Institute of Public Policy Research for a Social Justice Commission on the role of the welfare state and the Conservatives turned to the Centre for Policy Studies) and turn to

opinion pollsters, advertising agencies and communication specialists for help with election campaigning (Kavanagh, 1995).

Chapter summary

The strength of the party system suffered because of the weakness of Labour after 1979. It has made changes in policy and it is fair to say that the party has effectively abandoned socialism and in many ways is more leader-driven and disciplined than the Conservative Party. It remains to be seen whether Labour's landslide victory in 1997 will usher in a period during which, especially if the voting system is reformed, it becomes the 'one-party' ruler.

Discussion points

- Compare the nature and effects of the Conservative with Labour's annual conference; does either have any real impact on policy formulation?

- How is Labour's provenance as a party of protest against nineteenth-century capitalism and lack of democracy reflected in its organisation and structure?

- To what extent does the party leader dominate party organisation in the Conservative Party.

- Consider the arguments for and against state funding of political parties.

Further reading

On party structure and internal politics, McKenzie (1963) is still a classic, though dated. Minkin (1992) and Kelly (1989) are good on more recent development in the two main parties. On policy effects of parties see Finer (1975) and Rose (1984).

References

Benyon, J. (1991) 'The Fall of a Prime Minister', *Social Studies Review*, Vol. 6, No. 3.

Butler, D. and Kavanagh, D. (1980) *The British General Election of 1979* (Macmillan).

Callaghan, J. (1987) *The Far Left in English Politics* (Blackwell).

Crick, M. (1984) *Militant* (Faber and Faber).

Finer, S. (1975) *Adversary Politics of Government* (Wigram).

Kavanagh, D. (1987) 'The rise of Thatcherism', *Social Studies Review*, Vol. 3, No. 2.

Kavanagh, D (1990) *Thatcherism and British Politics*, 2nd edn (Oxford University Press).

Kavanagh, D. (1994) 'Changes in electoral behaviour and the party system', *Parliamentary Affairs*, Vol. 47.

Kavanagh, D. (1995) *Election Campaigning: The New Marketing of Politics* (Blackwell).

Kavanagh, D. (1996) *British Politics: Continuities and Change*, 3rd edn (Oxford University Press).

Kelly, R.N. (1989) *Conservative Party Conferences* (Manchester University Press).

Kelly, R.N. (1995) 'Labour's leadership contest and internal organisation', *Politics Review*, February.

McCulloch, A. (1988) 'Shades of Green ideas in the British Green movement', *Teaching Politics* (May).

McKenzie, R.T. (1963) *British Political Parties* (Heinemann).

Michels, R. (1959) *Political Parties* (Dover Publications).

Minkin, L. (1980) *The Labour Party Conference* (Manchester University Press).

Minkin, L. (1992) *The Contentious Alliance* (Edinburgh University Press).

Norton, P. (1990) 'The lady's not for turning: but what about the rest?', *Parliamentary Affairs*.

Norton, P. and Aughey, A. (1981) *Conservatives and Conservatism* (Temple Smith).

Parkin, S. (1989). *Green Parties* (Heretic Books).

Pattie, C., Johnston, R. and Russell, A. (1995) 'The stalled greening of British politics', *Politics Review*, February.

Pelling, H. (1995) *A History of the British Communist Party* (Adam and Charles Black).

Rose, R. (1984) *Do Parties Make a Difference?* 2nd edn (Macmillan).

Seldon, A. and Ball, C. (eds) (1994) *Conservative Century: The Conservative Party since 1900* (Oxford University Press).

Seyd, P. (1987) *The Rise and Fall of the Labour Left* (Macmillan).

Seyd, P. and Whiteley, P. (1995) 'Labour and Conservative Party members compared', *Politics Review* February.

Shaw, E. (1996) *The Labour Party since 1945* (Blackwell).

Taylor, S. (1982) *The National Front in English Politics* (Macmillan).

Williams, P. (1982) 'Changing styles of Labour leadership', in D. Kavanagh (ed.), *The Politics of the Labour Party* (Allen and Unwin).

State of the parties

PETER RIDDELL

Parties and elections are the fixed points of the political world. Journalists write about what goverments and oppositions do and say almost entirely from the viewpoints of the main parties and in terms of their impact on the timing and result of the next general election. Most politicians think and behave in exactly the same way. Parties are still the main vehicles for expressing the preferences of voters and, since 1868, elections have determined which party forms the government of the day. Sir Lewis Namier, the historian of eighteenth-century politics, described elections as locks on the river of British history, controlling the flow of events. David Butler (1995), the founding father of the post-war study of elections in Britain, has argued that elections have replaced the dates of monarchs as the historian's landmarks. The years 1906, 1945, 1964 and 1979 mean more to historians of the twentieth century than 1935 when George V died or 1952 when Queen Elizabeth II succeeded to the throne. Yet Butler adds the caveat, 'elections may decide less than they appear to. Certainly they decide less than is suggested by the rhetoric of campaign speeches.'

A party- and election-focused view of politics can both exaggerate differences and underestimate continuities. The decisive events in post-war British politics are only loosely related to the result of the previous general elections and might have occurred whichever party was in power. For instance, Britain's financial and military resources had been so depleted by the Second World War that even a Conservative government led by Sir Winston Churchill could not have long delayed independence for India and Pakistan. In the 1950s, Britain would almost certainly have remained aloof from the negotiations which led to the creation of the original European Common Market in the Treaty of Rome in 1957 if Labour rather than the Conservatives had been in office. The firm personal commitment of Sir Edward Heath broke the lengthy stalemate over Britain's entry in 1971–2, but that might have occurred a few years later under a Labour government. In the 1970s, the shifts in economic policy towards what became known as monetarism and in the growth in the public sector occurred in the mid- to late 1970s under Denis Healey, a Labour Chancellor of the Exchequer.

That does not mean, in the catchy sounding title of a book by Ken Livingstone, the left-wing Labour MP and populist leader of the Greater London Council in the 1980s, that 'If voting changed anything, they'd abolish it'. For instance, while the at times shaky foundations for the economic policies of the Thatcher government had been laid by Labour before 1979, only the Conservatives would have pushed through either the privatisation of state-run industries on the scale that developed during the 1980s or the series of changes in trade union law. What mattered in both cases was the combination of a succession of Conservative election victories and external circumstances creating the right circumstances for the type of measures then put forward. For instance, while the Heath government failed in the early 1970s in its attempt to reform industrial relations law, the Thatcher government succeeded a decade later in large part because the unions were weaker and had made themselves unpopular. While before 1979 advisers to Margaret Thatcher had discussed the possibility of privatisation, official policy statements remained tentative and few even of her most zealous supporters believed it would be possible to sell off the main monopoly utilities, such as gas, electricity and water. Indeed, privatisation was only gradually extended to these industries during the 1980s in response to the frustrations experienced by ministers in managing the old nationalised industries, and following the success of the early flotations.

Government policies are not solely determined by the outcome of elections. Parties, even ones with the huge majorities which Margaret Thatcher commanded during the 1980s, are constrained by many external factors – from the pressures of global financial markets, via membership of the European Union, to the weight of received opinion and inherited policies. The interdependence of economies and the absence of controls on capital flows have increasingly limited the freedom of manoeuvre of national governments not only over their exchange rates and interest rates but also over the levels of public borrowing, taxes and public spending. Significant differences, of course, remain between countries on levels of spending, but it is now impossible for any sizeable industrial country like Britain to pursue, say, a markedly more expansionist policy than its trading partners without facing unfavourable consequences in the financial markets. This happened in the early 1980s in France when President Mitterrand had abruptly to abandon his attempt to create socialism on a unilateral basis. Left of centre, as well as right of centre, parties now accept that marginal rates of income tax cannot be penal and have to be much lower than in the 1960s and 1970s if highly skilled professionals and businessmen are to be attracted and retained. And Britain's membership of the European Union has meant a transfer of control over many key areas such as trade policy, farming and fishing from London to Brussels. The limits on the power of the British government have been highlighted by the arguments over the rights of fishermen in the south-west and over the export of British beef products in the light of BSE fears in 1996.

Richard Rose and Phillip Davies (1995) have highlighted the importance of the inheritance of past programmes. They calculated that in 1989, after ten years of the Thatcher premiership, only a third of government programmes had been introduced by her, and two-fifths dated from before 1945. The contrast is even larger when programmes are measured in money terms: three-quarters date from before 1945 and a mere tenth from the 1980s. They concluded:

At no point in time did any administration decide how many or what kind of programmes government ought to undertake, or make an ex ante decision about how much money should be spent, or how it should be allocated. The record of each successive administration is largely a record of more of the same; the great bulk of the programmes it administers and finances are inherited from the more or less distant past.

Rose and Davies have a point, though they exaggerate it. Significant changes can be made to a long-established framework of policy, as the Conservatives, for example, did in trimming some social security entitlements from the mid-1980s onwards. But incoming ministers face long-established views, often a consensus, on particular issues formed by civil servants, think tanks, implementers of policies such as local authorities and pressure groups. Some political scientists see ministers less as giants pulling levers than as members of large interconnected policy networks. Parties are best seen as important, but by no means the sole, players in determining policy within tight limits set by a wide range of domestic and international factors.

The role of parties has also changed since they are no longer monolithic representatives of competing class interests. Of course, the Conservatives have always had a sizeable number of working-class supporters – otherwise they would never have won power – but during the middle two quarters of the twentieth century there was a clear class polarisation. That has altered because of changes in the labour market with the decline, for example, in the number of manufacturing jobs in large factories and a growth in middle-class services jobs. That has not only resulted in a sharp decline in membership of trade unions, but has also reduced feelings of class solidarity, with a reduction in partisan identification. Fewer people identify strongly with either of the main parties.

Increased affluence and changes in leisure time have also meant that both working- and middle-class people are less likely to regard membership of the Labour or Conservative parties as a natural, even semi-automatic, part of their lives. The political and social were linked – whether the Tory coffee morning or the Labour working men's club. The audience laughed in 1961 when Tony Hancock remarked in that immortal episode of British television comedy, 'The Blood Donor':

Something for the benefit of the country as whole. What should it be I thought? Become a blood donor or join the Young Conservatives? But as I'm not looking for a wife and can't play table tennis, here I am.

In the 1990s, many, if not most, of the audience would never have heard of the Young Conservatives. These famous lines were quoted by Jeremy Richardson (1995) in an article about the market for political activism, in which he discussed the growth of interest groups as a challenge to political parties. There are many other opportunities available for political activism – from involvement in non-partisan civic organisations to single-issue pressure groups, particularly those on the environment. The Royal Society for the Protection of Birds had a membership in the mid-1990s almost as large as the Conservative and Labour parties combined. In the early 1990s, Greenpeace had a membership of 400,000, substantially higher than Labour at the time, though it then fell sharply, reflecting the high turnover of some of these groups. In some cases, membership of organisations has merely involved sending a cheque or signing a direct debit form rather than direct personal activisim.

Robert Putnam (1996), an American political scientist, has argued that there has been a broad civic disengagement from group activities. He has symbolised this by the contrast between the sharp decline in organised ten-pin bowling leagues in the USA and the rise in individual bowling. His 'bowling alone' thesis has been challenged by those who say there has not been a decline in joining, but rather a shift from old, collective workplace groups and social clubs to sports and single issue groups. Thus membership of political parties, trade unions and bodies such as the British Legion has fallen while membership of environmental groups, civic bodies and health clubs has risen.

Accurate statistics on party membership are almost impossible to obtain because of the absence

of national figures in the Conservative Party and in view of a shift in the Labour Party from nominal affiliation by local parties to a national membership scheme. According to the figures that are available and some surveys, the total membership of the main national political parties declined from around 13 per cent of the electorate in the early 1950s to 9.5 per cent in the mid-1960s and to little more than 2 per cent in the early 1990s. This probably exaggerates the true decline. But Conservative membership may be a quarter or less than its early 1950s' peak, while the Labour total is probably under half its peak – even after its membership rose by roughly a half from a very low base in the two-and-a-half years after Tony Blair was elected Labour leader in 1994. It is unclear whether the revival in Labour's membership is merely a cyclical phenomenon generated by the early enthusiasm for Tony Blair's leadership of the party after his election as Labour leader in July 1994, or whether it represents the start of an underlying reversal of the long-term decline in membership of parties. The rise in Labour membership has been linked with an attempt to involve ordinary members more, both at a local level and in a series of ballots for electing the leader, deputy leader and National Executive Committee, and in approving the draft manifesto. Blair has anyway sought to strengthen the say of individual party members compared with the trade unions and local activists. The unions' share of the vote at Labour's conferences and their relative contribution to the party's finances have also declined, forcing the party to raise more from wealthy donors and from individual members. Similarly, in the Conservative Party, the big drop in membership and a decline in the real, inflation-adjusted level of political contributions by big public companies has forced the party to raise more from wealthy businesspeople, both at home and abroad. The two main parties have yet to reach a new balance between the declining contribution of their long-term institutional backers, their dependence on wealthy donors and their desire, particularly in the case of Labour, to increase the number of individual party members.

The main function of the parties is to select and nurture competing teams of political leaders – who are increasingly committed full-time politicians with little experience of the outside world, as I have argued (1996). If the parties no longer represent the bulk of the middle and working classes, they are more bodies to advance the careers and views of relatively small numbers of activists and full-time politicians who succeed in becoming candidates. Conservative candidates and MPs come heavily from the private sector middle class, small business-people and professionals, while Labour ones come from the public sector middle class, teachers of various kinds, local authority and health service workers and those dependent on political activity for their livelihoods.

These trends qualify the primacy usually given to the main parties in the political process. Parties are one among a range of interests competing for the public's attention and for influence over policy-making. Nonetheless, since virtually all ministers are members of either the Commons or the Lords, and most that matter come from the former, the parties remain the sole ladder to ministerial office. And, judging by the continued high turnout of voters in general elections, parties can still mobilise the support, albeit sometimes grudging, of a majority of the population. The retention of the first-past-the-post system for elections to the House of Commons has helped the Conservatives and Labour retain their dominant positions. But their combined market share has never been above three-quarters to four-fifths of the total since the early 1970s in face of the success of the Liberal Democrats and their predecessors in attracting the support of between a nearly a fifth and a quarter of those voting since the early 1980s. These calculations would, of course, change if Britain moved to a system of proportional representation as in most of the rest of Europe. Following the long period of single-party rule by the Conservatives, support for electoral reform did grow in the Labour Party after its defeat in the 1992 election. But electoral reform is more likely for the proposed Scottish Parliament and regional assemblies and for elections to the European Parliament. This would force the parties to temper their traditional adversarial approaches and to cooperate, as has happened during the 1990s on many county and district councils where no one party has had overall control.

This analysis also suggests that too much emphasis is given to the make-or-break character of elections. The differences in policies likely to be followed – and therefore the impact on voters – are invariably much less than the parties claim during election campaigns. Perversely, however, the pressures to make television less elitist and the intense competition among the broadsheet, as well as the popular, newspapers have heightened differences by focusing on the more dramatic aspects of politics at the expense of rational discussion of policy options. That means every event, every indiscretion tends to be exaggerated. There is a tendency, for instance, on tax to exaggerate half-promises or hints by party spokespersons as having a large importance for voters. In practice, changes in what people pay in taxes have little relationship with what politicians promised before the last election and are affected mainly by the state of the public finances, and other external pressures, whichever party is in office.

Similarly, there is a tendency to overestimate the importance of the election campaign itself. Certainly, the intensity of a campaign can force voters normally uninterested in politics to focus on the choice. Undecideds make up their minds and some change their views. But it is unclear whether the campaigns themselves are decisive in most cases as opposed to the events of the preceeding four or five years. Hence, there is a danger of exaggerating and over-interpreting events which happen during a campaign. Slight movements in the voting shares of parties in opinion polls are often presented as representing big shifts of opinion when they may say more about minor statistical fluctuations than the views of voters. It is, however, a virtue of the democratic process than even politicians as resolute and determined as Margaret Thatcher were nervous at times about the result of elections which the Conservatives looked certain from the start to win, as in 1983 and 1987.

But if parties themselves are no longer mass organisations reflecting a unified class view and the policy choices facing any team of ministers are constrained, then the significance of elections is less. The choice is narrower, and individual elections matter less. The lasting imprint of Thatcherism depended on the Conservatives winning several victories, and on the weakness of Labour for most of the 1980s. This produced much soul-searching after the Conservatives' fourth win in a row in 1992 about whether Britain now had a single- or dominant-party system though after Labour's landslide win in May 1997 some perceive an indefinite period of Labour dominance, especially if the voting system is reformed. That talk proved to be short-lived. Of course, there are differences between the parties: over levels of taxation and spending at the margin, and over the precise balance between the public and private sectors. It is, however, significant that, reluctantly and on a piecemeal basis, the parties have accepted that the electorate as a whole, rather than just their representatives in the Commons, should have a say via referendums on major constitutional issues. When a question really matters – say over devolution or membership of European monetary union – then the electorate is decisive, even though formal sovereignty lies with Parliament. The real role of parties now lies in choosing and presenting alternative teams of leaders rather than in advocating vastly different ideologies. The electorate does have a choice, but within a narrower range than the parties claim.

References

Butler, D. (1995) *British General Elections since 1945* Institute of Contemporary British History.

Putnam, R. (1996) 'The strange death of civic America', *Prospect*, March.

Richardson, J. (1995) 'The market for political activism: interest groups as a challenge to political parties', *West European Politics*, January.

Riddell, P. (1996) *Honest Opportunism*, expanded paper back edn (Indigo; originally published 1993).

Rose R. and Davies, P. (1995) *Inheritance in Public Policy: Change without Choice in Britain* (Yale University Press).

The legislative process

Introduction

Bill Jones

So far this book has addressed the non-institutional elements of British politics; the remainder of the volume deals with the institutional aspect together with specific policy areas. Often institutions can seem confusing to students who tend to study them individually and find it difficult to grasp how they relate to and interact with each other. Accordingly this short section gives two contrasting overviews of how the system works.

Two overviews of the British political system

The functions of government

It is helpful to contrast the British political system with that of the USA. It is well known that the eighteenth-century framers of the constitution wrote into their 1787 document a strict separation of powers. The legislature (Congress) and the executive (the Presidency) were to be separately elected for terms of differing length with the judiciary (the Supreme Court) appointed by the President for life. In diagrammatic form the functions can be represented by three separate and independent circles (see Figure 1).

The purpose of this arrangement was to disperse power to institutions which would check each other

and ensure that no branch of government became overmighty. In Britain, however, there never was such a separation. The three functions overlap significantly. To change or re-elect a government there is only one election and that is to the legislative chamber, the House of Commons. After the election the majority party in that chamber invariably forms the executive. The crucial overlap between the legislative and executive spheres therefore comprises

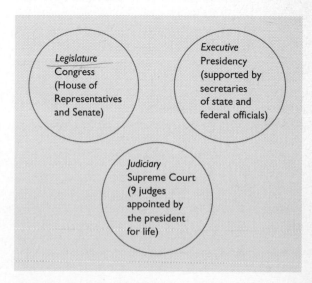

Figure I Functions of government: USA

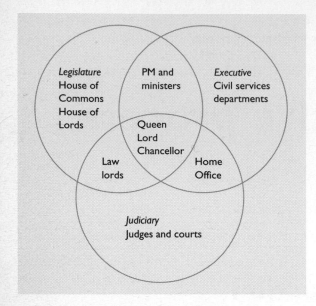

Figure 2   Functions of government: UK

means the President cannot regularly command congressional support for his policies; indeed, like Presidents Bush and Clinton, his party may be in the minority in Congress. The British Prime Minister, in contrast, has relatively more power: provided the support of the majority party is sustained he or she leads both the executive and legislative arms of government. However, loss of significant party support can bring down the British Prime Minister, as it did Chamberlain in May 1940 and Thatcher in 1990. This possibility clearly acts as a constraint upon potential prime ministerial action, but the fact is that parties in government very rarely even threaten to unseat their leaders because they fear the electoral consequences of apparent disunity.

The executive's power is further reinforced by the doctrine of parliamentary sovereignty, which enables it to overrule any law – constitutional or otherwise – with a simple majority vote; and considerable residual powers of the monarch via the royal prerogative. The House of Lords' power of legislative delay only, and local government's essentially subservient relationship to Westminster, complete the picture of an unusually powerful executive arm of government for a representative democracy.

Representative and responsible government

Represented in a different way the British political system can be seen as a circuit of representation and responsibility. Parliament represents the electorate but is also responsible to it via elections. In their turn ministers represent majority opinion in the

Prime Minister, Cabinet and the other seventy or so junior ministers. The judiciary is similarly appointed by the executive; not by the Prime Minister, but by the Lord Chancellor, the government's chief law officer, who sits in the Cabinet and presides over the House of Lords. It is he who sits at the centre of the three-circled web, together with the monarch – who once dominated all three spheres but now merely decorates them (see Figure 2).

The US constitution ensures that the President cannot be overthrown by Congress – except through impeachment – but looser party discipline

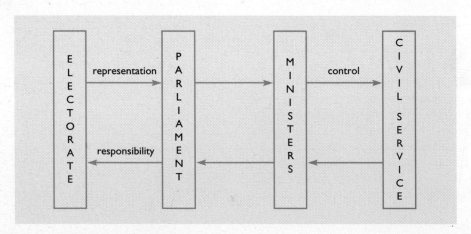

Figure 3   Representative and responsible government

legislature (though they are appointed by the Prime Minister, not elected) and are responsible to it for their actions in leading the executive. Civil servants are not representatives but as part of the executive are controlled by ministers and are responsible to them. Figure 3 illustrates the relationship.

This, of course, is a very simplistic view, but it does express the underlying theory of how British government should work. The reality of how the system operates is infinitely more complex, as Figure 4 – itself highly simplified – seeks to illustrate. Earlier chapters have explained how the different elements of British government operate in practice.

1. Parliament provides the forum, the 'playing field' on which the ordered competition of democratic government is publicly conducted.
2. Political parties dominate the system, organising the electorate, taking over Parliament and providing the ministers who run the civil service.

3. The Prime Minister as leader of the majority party can exercise considerable personal power and in recent years has become more akin to a presidential figure.
4. The judiciary performs the important task of interpreting legislation and calling ministers and officials to account if they act without statutory authority.
5. Civil servants serve ministers but their permanence and their professionalism, their vested interests in searching for consensus and defending departmental interests raise suspicions that they occasionally or even regularly outflank their ministerial masters.
6. Pressure groups infiltrate the whole gamut of government institutions, the most powerful bypassing Parliament and choosing to deal direct with ministers and civil servants.
7. The media have increasingly usurped the role of Parliament in informing the public and

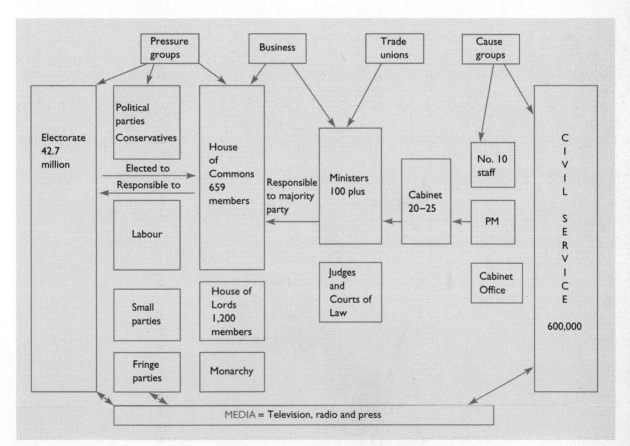

Figure 4 Elements of UK central government

providing a forum for public debate. Television is a potent new influence, the impact of which is still to be fully felt.

Does the reality invalidate the theory? It all depends upon how drastically we believe Figure 4 distorts 3. Indeed, Marxists would declare both to be irrelevant in that business pressure groups call the shots that matter, operating behind the scenes and within the supportive context of a system in which all the major actors subscribe to their values. Tony Benn would argue that the executive has become so dominant at the expense of the legislature that the PM's power can be compared with that of a medieval monarch. As we have seen, Britain's constitutional arrangements have always allowed great potential power – potential which strong Prime Ministers like Margaret Thatcher have been keen

and able to realise when given the time. But I would maintain, and cite in support the analyses offered by the authors of this book, that the essential features of the democratic system portrayed in Figure 3 just about survive in that:

1. party-dominated governments are removable;
2. Parliament still applies watchdog controls (and just occasionally reminds the executive by biting);
3. the electorate has a choice between parties;
4. civil servants will obey their political masters;
5. pressure groups influence but do not dictate.

Part IV explains how the legislative system works; Part V explains the executive process; Part VI the judiciary; and Part VII looks in detail at a number of policy areas.

CHAPTER FIFTEEN

The changing constitution

PHILIP NORTON

LEARNING OBJECTIVES

- To identify the sources and key components of the British constitution.

- To analyse the major changes and modifications made to the constitution in recent decades, and assess different approaches to constitutional change in the 1990s.

- To detail the arguments for and against some of the major changes proposed to the constitution, including electoral reform and devolution.

INTRODUCTION

In the quarter-century following the Second World War, the constitution rarely figured in political debate. It was seen as the preserve more of lawyers than of politicians. Since the mid-1970s it has become an issue of political controversy. Not only has the constitution changed, it has been subject to demands for more radical change. Some commentators now demand a new constitution. Others defend the existing one. For much of the period, though, the debate has been marked by a lack of clarity. What, then, is a constitution? What is distinctive about the British constitution? How is it changed? What are its essential constituents? What changes have been made to it in recent years? And what are the different views now put forward about it?

The constitution: definition and sources

What is a constitution? A constitution can be defined as the system of laws, customs and conventions which defines the composition and powers of organs of the state (such as government, Parliament and the courts), and regulates the relations of the various state organs to one another and of those state organs to the private citizen.

Constitutions vary considerably in nature. Most, but not all, are drawn up in a single, codified document. Some are short; others remarkably long. Some embody provisions that exhort citizens to act in a certain way ('It shall be the duty of every citizen . . . '); others confine themselves to stipulating the formal structures and powers of state bodies. Processes of interpretation and amendment vary. Most, but not all, have entrenched provisions: i.e. they can only be amended by an extraordinary process beyond that normally employed for amending the law.

The British constitution differs from most in that it is not drawn up in a single codified document. As such, it is often described as an 'unwritten' constitution. However, much of the constitution does exist in 'written' form. Many Acts of Parliament – such as the Parliament Acts of 1911 and 1949, and the European Communities (Amendment) Act 1993, ratifying the Maastricht Treaty – are clearly measures of constitutional law. Those Acts constitute formal, written – and binding – documents. To describe the constitution as unwritten is thus misleading. Rather, what Britain has is a part written and uncodified constitution.

Even in countries with a formal, written document, 'the constitution' constitutes more than the simple words of the document. Those words have to be interpreted. Practices develop, and laws are passed, which help give meaning to those words. To understand the contemporary constitution of the United States, for example, one has to look beyond the document to interpretations of that document by the courts in the USA, principally the US Supreme Court, and to various acts of Congress and to practices developed over the past two hundred years. The constitutions of most countries thus have what may be termed a primary source (the written document) and secondary sources (judicial interpretation, legislative acts, established practice). The UK, without a written document, lacks the equivalent primary source. Instead, the constitution derives from four sources which elsewhere would constitute secondary sources of the constitution. Those four sources (see Figure 15.1) are:

1. **statute law**, comprising Acts of Parliament and subordinate legislation made under the authority of the parent Act;

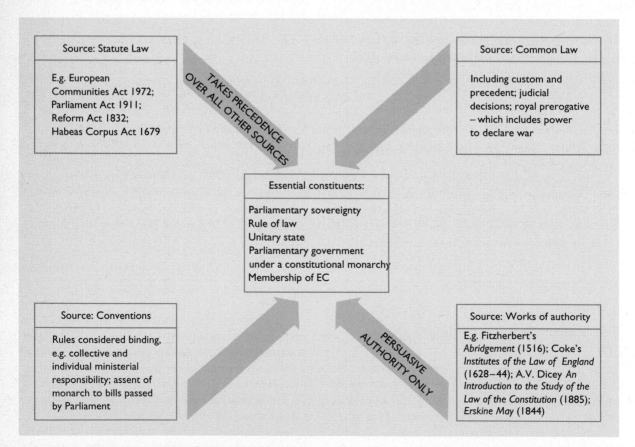

Figure 15.1 *The British constitution: sources and constituents*
Source: Norton, 1986

2. *common law*, comprising legal principles developed and applied by the courts, and encompassing the prerogative powers of the crown and the law and practice of Parliament;
3. *conventions*, constituting rules of behaviour which are considered binding by and upon those who operate the constitution but which are not enforced by the courts or by the presiding officers in the Houses of Parliament;
4. *works of authority*, comprising various written works – often but not always accorded authority by reason of their age – which provide guidance and interpretation on uncertain aspects of the constitution. Such works have persuasive authority only.

Statute law is the pre-eminent of the four sources and occupies such a position because of the doctrine of parliamentary sovereignty. Under this judicially self-imposed concept, the courts recognise only the authority of Parliament (formally the Queen-in-Parliament) to make law, with no body other than Parliament itself having the authority to set aside that law. The courts cannot strike down a law as being contrary to the provisions of the constitution. Statute law, then, is supreme and it can be used to override common law.

Amendment

No extraordinary features are laid down in Parliament for the passage or amendment of measures of constitutional law. All bills go through the same stages and are subject to simple majority voting. As such, the constitution is, formally, a flexible one. There are provisions that would be very difficult to change for political and practical reasons. A measure repealing an Act giving independence to a former colony, for example, would be unenforceable. Parliament is not likely ever to pass such a measure, but there is no formal limitation on its power to do so.

The only significant development that challenges the flexibility of the constitution is membership of the European Community/Union. That has added a new dimension to the constitution. Under the 1972 European Communities Act, European law takes precedence over any conflicting Act of Parliament, with interpretation of European law being undertaken by the courts, ultimately the European Court of Justice. European law may thus be deemed to enjoy some degree of entrenchment, albeit an entrenchment provided by Act of Parliament.

Essential constituents

The main elements of the constitution are shown in Figure 15.1. In combination, they render the UK constitution unique. Holland shares four of the five features, but is not a unitary state.

1. *Parliamentary sovereignty* has been described as the cornerstone of the British constitution. As we have seen, it stipulates that the outputs of the Parliament are binding and cannot be set aside by any body other than Parliament itself. The doctrine was confirmed by the Glorious Revolution of 1688 and 1689, when the common lawyers combined with Parliament against the King. Since the Settlement of 1689 established that the King was bound by the law of Parliament, it followed that his courts were also so bound.
2. *The rule of law* was identified by the nineteenth-century constitutional lawyer A.V. Dicey as one of the twin pillars of the constitution, and is generally accepted as one of the essential features of a free society. However, it is logically subordinate to the first pillar – parliamentary sovereignty – since Parliament could pass a measure undermining or destroying the rule of law. It is also a matter of dispute as to what the term encompasses. In terms of the law passed by Parliament, it is essentially a procedural doctrine. Laws must be interpreted and applied by an impartial and independent judiciary, those charged under the law are entitled to a fair trial, and no one can be imprisoned other than through the due process of law. There is some dispute, however, as to how far the doctrine extends beyond this, not least in defining the extent of the power of the state to regulate the affairs of citizens.
3. *A unitary state* is one in which formal power resides exclusively in the national authority, with no autonomous powers being vested in any other body. In federal systems, power is shared between national and regional or state

governments, each enjoying an autonomous existence and exercising powers granted by the constitution. In the UK, state power resides centrally, with the Queen-in-Parliament being omnicompetent. Parliament can create and confer certain powers in other bodies – such as regional and local councils – but those bodies remain subordinate to Parliament and can be restricted, even abolished, by it.

4. *A parliamentary government under a constitutional monarchy* refers to the form of government established by, and developed since, the Glorious Revolution of 1688 and 1689. That revolution established the supremacy of Parliament over the King. The greater acceptance of democratic principles in the nineteenth and twentieth centuries has resulted in the enlargement of the franchise and a pre-eminent role in the triumvirate of Queen-in-Parliament (monarch, Commons, Lords) for the elected chamber, the House of Commons. 'Parliament' thus means predominantly – though not exclusively – the House of Commons, while 'parliamentary government' refers not to government *by* Parliament but to government *through* Parliament. Ministers are legally answerable to the crown but politically answerable to Parliament, that political relationship being governed by the conventions of collective and individual ministerial responsibility. A government is returned in a general election and between elections depends on the confidence of a majority of Members of Parliament both for the passage of its measures and for its continuance in office.

5. *Membership of the European Community/ Union:* The United Kingdom became a member of the European Community on 1 January 1973, with membership introducing a new layer of supranational law-making institutions. In certain sectors, law is now made by European institutions and that law has binding applicability in the UK under the provisions of the 1972 European Communities Act. Under the terms of the Act, European law takes precedence over any municipal – that is, UK – law that conflicts with it. Any dispute over the European treaties, and laws made under them, has to be treated as a matter of law, with any cases that reach the highest domestic court of appeal (the House of Lords) having to be referred to the European Court of Justice in Luxembourg for a definitive ruling.

Membership of the EC/EU has raised fundamental questions about the continuing relevance of the doctrine of parliamentary sovereignty. Law passed by Parliament can be deemed by the courts to be in contravention of a superior law. In 1990, in the *Factortame* case (see Chapter 22), the Court of Justice ruled that the UK courts could suspend the provisions of an Act of Parliament – if they appeared to breach European law – until such time as a definitive ruling was given. However, the doctrine is deemed to remain extant in that the powers given the courts derive from an Act of Parliament and Parliament retains the power to repeal or amend that Act. Furthermore, if Parliament was to pass an Act expressly overriding a provision of European law, it is presumed that the British courts would enforce the Act under the doctrine of parliamentary sovereignty.

Recent changes

Constitutions are essentially dynamic. Practices change and new conventions develop. The provisions of a codified constitution may be amended. In the British case, the absence of a codified document with entrenched provisions has facilitated significant changes. Recent years have seen what may be described as additions to the constitution and several amendments to existing relationships.

Additions

There have been two principal additions. The first has been *membership of the European Community/ Union*. That, as we have seen, now constitutes one of the essential features of the constitution. The Community itself has undergone major constitutional changes since 1973. The Single European Act, which came into force in 1987, effected a significant shift in the power relationship between the institutions of the Community and the institutions of the member states, strengthening EC institutions, especially through the extension of weighted majority voting in the Council of Ministers. The Act also effected a shift in the power relationships within the institutions of the Community, strengthening the European Parliament through the extension of the cooperation procedure, a procedure that provides a greater role for the Parliament in Community law-making. Further shifts in both levels of power relationship were embodied in the Treaty on European Union (the Maastricht Treaty) which took effect in November 1993. This established a European Union with three pillars (the European Community, common foreign and security policy, justice and home affairs), extended the sectors of public policy falling within the competence of the European Community, and established a new codecision procedure for making law in certain areas, a procedure that strengthened again the position of the European Parliament.

The other addition has been *the use of referendums* (Box 15.1). Referendums are novel constitutional devices through which citizens are asked to express an opinion on a particular issue. Though occasionally advocated in the UK, their use was unknown before the 1970s. In order to overcome serious divisions within the ranks of the Labour Party in 1974, the Labour leadership committed the party to renegotiating the terms of membership of the European Community and to submitting those terms to approval by the people in a referendum. After Labour was returned to power in 1974, the terms of membership were renegotiated. On 5 June 1975 a referendum was held throughout the UK in which citizens were asked 'Do you think that the United Kingdom should stay in the European Community (the Common Market)?' In response 17,378,581 people voted yes, and 8,470,073 voted no. It was the first UK-wide referendum. Other referendums have been held on a country basis, on the issue of the border in Northern Ireland in 1973 and on devolution of powers to elected assemblies in Scotland and Wales in 1979.

The use of referendums has been challenged as undermining the legitimising function of Parliament, with the final say being in the hands of the electorate directly rather than its elected representatives. Against that must be set the formal position that referendums can be held only on the authority of Parliament – they are provided for by statute – and are advisory. Parliament retains the final say.

Furthermore, Parliament has only provided for specific referendums. There is no statutory provision that would allow for any more to be held.

Both additions have significantly affected the constitution, membership of the EC/EU doing so on a fundamental and continuing basis. The use of referendums has been limited, but has none the less created a precedent. Calls for referendums on a number of issues are now variously heard. Such calls have been made to try to resolve disputes that split parties internally. By the end of 1996, both main parties had made commitments to hold them. Prime Minister John Major announced that if the Conservative Party was returned to office in 1997 and the government decided that the UK should participate in a single European currency, then the electorate would be asked to approve that decision in a referendum. Labour leader Tony Blair continued the commitment of his predecessor, John Smith, to hold a referendum on electoral reform and in 1996 announced that a Labour government would hold a referendum in Scotland on whether or not the country wanted its own elected assembly and, if so, if it should have tax-raising powers.

Amendments

The past two decades have seen several changes to existing constitutional relationships. These amendments follow no neat pattern, but are rather the product of different political pressures.

Executive–legislative relations

Recognition of the fact that the relationship between Parliament and the executive was becoming too heavily oriented in favour of the latter led to various structural and procedural changes. Foremost among the structural changes in the House of Commons has been the creation of a series of departmental select committees (see Chapter 16). Government is now subject to more specific questioning by MPs than it has been before in the twentieth century. These various changes were preceded, and facilitated, by changes in attitude and behaviour by many MPs and, indeed, peers. Though party cohesion has remained a marked feature of voting in both Houses, no government since 1970 has been able to take its majority in every vote as guaranteed.

BOX 15.1   REFERENDUMS   DEBATE

The case for

- A referendum is an educational tool – it informs citizens about the issue.

- Holding a referendum encourages people to be more involved in political activity.

- A referendum helps resolve major issues – it gives a chance for the voters to decide.

- The final outcome of a referendum is more likely to enjoy public support than if the decision is taken solely by Parliament – it is difficult to challenge a decision if all voters have a chance to take part.

- The use of referendums increases support for the political system – voters know they are being consulted on the big issues. Even if they don't take part, they know they have an opportunity to do so. The issue is not being decided by politicians in Westminster.

The case against

- Referendums are blunt weapons that usually allow only a simple answer to a very general question. They do not permit of explanations of why voters want something done nor the particular way in which they want it done.

- Referendums undermine the position of Parliament as the deliberative body of the nation.

- There is no obvious limit on when referendums should be held – if one is conceded on the issue of Europe, why not also have referendums on capital punishment, immigration and trade union reform? With no obvious limit, there is the potential for 'government by referendum'.

- Referendums can be used as majoritarian weapons – being used by the majority to restrict minorities.

- There is the difficulty of ensuring a balanced debate – one side may (indeed, is likely to) have more money and resources.

- There is the difficulty of formulating, and agreeing, a clear and objective question.

- Research shows that turnout in referendums tends to be lower than that in elections for parliamentary and other public elections.

- Referendums are expensive to hold and are often expensive ways of *not* deciding issues – if government does not like the result it calls another referendum (as happened in Denmark over ratification of the Maastricht Treaty in 1992).

Centre–local relations

The structure of local government was changed in London in 1963, in Scotland in 1973 and in England and Wales (other than London) in 1974. There have been further changes since. When a

Conservative government was elected in 1979, the perceived need of the government to enforce limits on public expenditure and a concomitant antagonistic relationship between a Conservative administration and many Labour-controlled local councils resulted in greater controls on local government. This has encompassed the abolition in 1986 of the Greater London Council and metropolitan county councils, the limiting of council revenue-raising powers, and requirements for competitive tendering for the provision of local services. A further reform of the structure of local government was begun in 1993. The Conservative government placed greater emphasis on power being given to people locally through other means (health trusts, housing associations, grant-maintained schools). The Labour Party is committed to restoring some power to local councils.

Centre–local changes have also been significant in the context of Northern Ireland. Prior to 1972, the province had its own devolved assembly, with legislative and executive powers, at Stormont. In 1972, following the civil unrest in the province and the refusal of the Northern Ireland government to accept the transfer of responsibility for law and order from Stormont to Westminster, the UK government intervened to govern the province directly from London. Direct rule was seen as a necessary but temporary expedient. Since 1972, successive governments have sought a new constitutional settlement for the province.

Minister–civil service relations

A number of disparate pressures have weakened the convention of individual ministerial responsibility. Under the convention, ministers determine and are answerable to Parliament for departmental policy, while civil servants advise them, carry out their wishes and remain publicly anonymous. The convention has also been taken to entail ministers accepting blame for fault on the part of civil servants. The convention has been eroded by the sheer workload of ministers, with a growing recognition that they cannot be held culpable for every action of officials. It has also been eroded by the actions of a number of civil servants who, disagreeing with a minister's policy or objecting to the withholding or distortion of information, have leaked material to MPs or the press. The most celebrated case in the 1980s was that of Defence civil servant Clive Ponting, who leaked material that his minister did not wish to be disclosed. Civil service anonymity has also been eroded by the appearance of civil servants before parliamentary select committees.

However, the biggest change in minister–civil servant relations has taken place recently with the creation of 'Next Steps' agencies, semi-autonomous units within departments. These agencies are clearly defined, with their own personnel and with particular objectives. Each is headed by a chief executive, employed in most cases on a fixed-term contract, who is responsible to the minister but who none the less deals directly with MPs. When MPs table parliamentary questions about a particular agency, the question is sent to and answered by the chief executive.

Cabinet–minister relations

Under the convention of collective ministerial responsibility, ministers abide by and do not publicly dissent from decisions of Cabinet. The convention has been suspended three times this century and has been undermined by semi-public and sometimes public disputes between ministers. The convention was suspended once in the 1930s in order to allow ministers to express differing views and then twice in the 1970s so that ministers could express different views on the issue of Europe, most notably during the 1975 referendum campaign. More pervasively, ministers under successive governments have been prone to reveal continuing disagreements. Several ministers during the premiership of Margaret Thatcher variously signalled their opposition to policy, including on at least one occasion the Prime Minister herself – encouraging supporters in the Lords to amend a government bill on trade union reform to make it tougher than her Cabinet wanted.

Government–group relations

The increasing dependence of government on outside groups for advice, information and cooperation in implementing policy produced a trend throughout most of this century for the greater cooption of groups into the policy-making process. A number of groups were given representation, sometimes by statute, on a range of advisory and some executive bodies. By the 1970s, the incorporation of groups was extensive, with peak economic organisations such as the TUC and CBI enjoying representation on bodies such as the National Economic Development

Council, the Manpower Services Commission, the Health and Safety Executive, and the Advisory, Conciliation and Arbitration Service (ACAS). However, the return of a Conservative government in 1979 favouring a free market economy saw a marked reversal of this approach, with government seeking autonomy in policy-making and hence adopting an arm's length relationship with groups, especially bodies such as the TUC, which were effectively frozen out of public policy-making. The attempt was not altogether successful – many groups retained close links with departments – but it signalled a greater independence on the part of government. The change was not supported initially by the Labour Party, but neither was it totally rejected, especially under the leadership of Tony Blair. He sought to achieve some distance from the trade unions, the traditional supporters of the party.

State–citizen relations

Relations between the state and the individual have also been variously modified. Civil liberties, in particular, have been variously amended, limited and extended. This has been in part the product of the actions of the British government, decisions by the European Court on Human Rights (see Chapter 23) and the outcome of free votes in Parliament.

In the period from 1979 to 1997, the Conservative government introduced measures that encompassed the franchise, data protection, public demonstrations, trade union powers, immigration, police powers, the activities of the security services and broadcasting. In many of these measures, and in various actions taken by government – and other public agencies – against different groups in society, various civil libertarians asserted a clear trend in the restriction of civil liberties (see Ewing and Gearty, 1990). The actions ranged from limiting the travel of striking miners during the 1984–5 miners' strike to seeking to ban the broadcast of certain television programmes. Ministers for their part argued that rights had been extended, not least through the introduction of a Citizen's Charter, stipulating the service the citizen can expect from public agencies, and through the extension of the rights to different groups or sections of society, including children in court cases, parents in the field of education,

women (in terms of taxation) and suspects under the 1984 Police and Criminal Evidence Act.

To comply with international obligations, especially as a result of decisions by the European Court on Human Rights, the government also introduced a number of measures. These included extending the provisions of the 1967 Sexual Offences Act (allowing homosexual relations between consenting adults) to Northern Ireland. Other changes were brought about – independent of government – by decisions of British courts, including a decision to recognise that it was possible for a husband to be charged with raping his wife.

Recent years have also seen a number of issues affecting the citizen being left to the House of Commons to resolve through free votes. These have included the subjects of embryo fertilisation, war crimes, Sunday trading, and the age of consent for male homosexual activity.

The relationship between the citizen and the state has thus been subject to various changes in past years as a result of decisions taken by different bodies. The changes are notable for their extent rather than their direction.

Government–party relations

Finally, developments within political parties also have some constitutional significance. In 1975, the parliamentary Conservative party introduced provision for the annual election of the leader. When returned to office in 1979, Margaret Thatcher became the first Conservative Prime Minister to be subject to election each year as party leader. She was challenged for the leadership – and, in effect, the premiership – in 1989 (unsuccessfully) and 1990 (successfully). John Major resigned the leadership to force an election in 1995. Had he lost that party leadership election, he would have resigned as Prime Minister. The Labour Party in 1981 changed its rules for the election of the party leader, the electoral power being transferred from the parliamentary Labour party to an electoral college comprising the parliamentary party, the trade unions and the constituency parties. Three leaders have been elected under this system (Neil Kinnock, John Smith and Tony Blair). Some Conservative activists have also called for party members to take part in the election of the Conservative leader.

The British constitution has thus undergone numerous changes over the past twenty-five years. It is remarkable for the extent of those changes. It is remarkable also for the challenges mounted to it, with demands made for further change.

Constitutional reform

During the 1950s and 1960s, the constitution was taken largely for granted. The country was enjoying an increase in economic prosperity. Living standards were increasing. The system of government appeared to be delivering the goods expected of it.

There thus seemed little reason to change the system. Indeed, it seemed a system worthy of emulation, rather than criticism. It was flexible and it appeared to facilitate effective government, unlike some systems – such as that of the USA – which seemed to encourage conflict and stalemate. In the United States, some advocates of constitutional reform took the British system as the basis of their proposals.

Adulation of the constitution increasingly gave way from the late 1960s onwards to criticism and demands for reform. The system of government no longer appeared to be delivering what was expected

---

BOX 15.2 DEVOLUTION   **DEBATE**

The case for

- Devolving powers to elected assemblies in Scotland, Wales and the English regions would be advantageous because:
  - government would be closer to the people;
  - decisions could be geared to the particular needs of the area;
  - elected assemblies could prevent economic and political encroachment by national government.

- Assemblies representing the nation or region would encourage a sense of identity.

- There is popular support for an elected assembly among Scots and to introduce assemblies would bolster confidence in the political system.

The case against

- Devolution would result in a new and expensive layer of government.

- It would introduce the potential for stalemate and clashes between the assemblies and government at Westminster.

- It would introduce the potential for stalemate and clashes between the assemblies and local councils.

- It would have the potential to increase, rather than reduce, regional disparities, the richer regions using their powers to retain as much of their wealth as possible.

- It could help entrench local prejudices, with predominant groups using their power in an assembly to discriminate against minorities.

- In most parts of England there is no clear regional identity and no strong support for elected assemblies.

- Introducing an elected assembly with legislative powers in Scotland would create an imbalance in the political structure of the UK – including at Westminster, where Scottish MPs could vote on English legislation but English MPs could not vote on Scottish legislation – and would need to be approved not just by the Scots but by all UK citizens.

of it. The country faced economic, political and social problems. There was evidence of alienation at the periphery of the UK, with increased support for Nationalist parties in Scotland and Wales. Troops were committed to Northern Ireland. Economic indicators worsened, with unemployment and inflation both rising. There was industrial unrest. The indeterminate results of two general elections in 1974 called into question the capacity of the electoral system to produce strong government. The decade of the 1980s saw serious riots in a number of towns and cities, especially Bristol, Liverpool, Birmingham and London.

For some observers, government was not only not able to deal with these problems but was itself part of the problem. Changing the personnel of government – replacing one party in office with another – was not seen as sufficient to deal with the nation's problems. Instead, it was argued that a change was needed in the very system of government.

Demands for change in the nation's constitution began to be made in the 1970s by various politicians, jurists and academics. Liberals were long-standing advocates of reform but began to be joined by some on the right, and later the left, of the political spectrum. The increase in nationalist support in Scotland and Wales led a number of politicians to accept the need for the devolution of powers to elected assemblies in the two countries, as a way of stemming the demands for full independence. The capacity of a Labour government elected in 1974 on less than 40 per cent of the votes cast to introduce and achieve passage of major and radical policies led some Conservatives to press the case for certain rights to be put beyond the control of a simple majority in Parliament. Lord Hailsham was among those putting the case for a new Bill of Rights. Others argued that a reform of the electoral system was necessary to prevent the return of a radical socialist government. The period also saw the publication of a seminal work, *Adversary Politics and Electoral Reform*, edited by Professor S.E. Finer, which contended that electoral reform was necessary to prevent the condition of adversary politics, in which two parties competed for the all or nothing spoils of electoral victory and, once in office, reversed the policies introduced by their predecessors.

The return of a Conservative government in 1979 and then in successive general elections stilled some of the Conservative demands for change, but encouraged many on the left to consider the case for change. Government was increasingly seen as too powerful, unchecked by other bodies in the political system. Charter '88, a constitutional reform movement founded in 1988 (the tercentenary year of the Glorious Revolution), brought together reformers of the left with long-standing reformers of the political centre. The movement advocated a new constitutional settlement, replacing that of 1688, and one embodied in a written constitution. Among its specific proposals were a new Bill of Rights, a new electoral system, an elected second chamber, a reformed judiciary, open government and an 'equitable distribution' of power between local, regional and national government.

Approaches to reform

The debate has thus become more pronounced. It has also acquired a discernible profile. Initially, the debate lacked shape. There was little familiarity with discussing constitutional issues as constitutional issues. What shape there was to the debate could be seen in terms of political expediency. Political considerations clearly coloured the perceptions of advocates. However, the correlation between party and attitudes on reform was far from complete. The debate, rather, was marked by several approaches to constitutional change. Those approaches became increasingly discernible in the 1980s (Norton 1982, 1993). Seven principal approaches can be identified (Figure 15.2). All had, and retain, advocates, but the debate in the 1990s has polarised around two of their number.

High Tory

This approach contends that the constitution has evolved organically and that change, artificial change, is neither necessary nor desirable. In its pure form, it is opposed not only to major reforms – such as electoral reform, a Bill of Rights, and an elected second chamber – but also to modifications to existing arrangements, such as the introduction of departmental select committees in the House of Commons. Its stance on any proposed reform is thus predictable: it is against it.

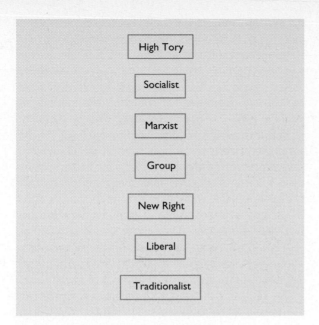

Figure 15.2 *Approaches to constitutional change*
Source: Norton, 1993

Socialist

This approach favours reform, but a particular type of reform. It seeks strong government, but a party-dominated strong government, with adherence to the principle of intra-party democracy and the concept of the mandate. It wants to shift power from the existing 'top-down' form of control (government to people) to a 'bottom-up' form (people to government), with party acting as the channel for the exercise of that control. It favours sweeping away the monarchy and the House of Lords and the use of more elective processes, both for public offices as well as within the Labour Party. It wants, for example, the election of members of a Labour Cabinet by Labour MPs. It is wary of, or opposed to, reforms that might prevent the return of a socialist government and the implementation of a socialist programme. It is thus sceptical or opposed to electoral reform (potential for coalition government), a Bill of Rights (constraining government autonomy, giving power to judges) and membership of the European Union (constraining influence, sometimes viewed as a capitalists' club). For government to carry through socialist policies, it has to be free of constitutional constraints that favour or are dominated by its opponents.

Marxist

This approach sees the restructuring of the political system as largely irrelevant, certainly in the long run, serving merely to delay the collapse of capitalist society. Government, any government, is forced to act in the interests of finance capital. Changes to the constitutional arrangements may serve to protect those interests in the short term but will not stave off collapse in the long term. Whatever the structures, government will be constrained by external elites, and those elites will themselves be forced to follow rather than determine events. The clash between the imperatives of capitalism and decreasing profit rates in the meso-economy determine what capitalists do. Constitutional reform, in consequence, is not advocated but rather taken as demonstrating tensions within the international capitalist economy.

Group

This approach – sometimes called the functionalist approach – seeks the greater incorporation of groups into the process of policy-making in order to achieve a more consensual approach to public policy. The interdependence of government and interest groups – especially sectional interest groups – is such that it should be recognised and accommodated. A more integrated process, it is contended, can facilitate a more stable economic and industrial system. Supporters of this approach look to other countries, such as Germany, as examples of what can be achieved.

This approach thus favours the representation of labour and business on executive and advisory bodies and, in its pure form, the creation of a functionalist second chamber. It is opposed to referendums (weapons that can be used against particular groups, such as trade unions) and is wary of a Bill of Rights (potential to interfere with the free interplay between groups and government, and between unions and employers); on electoral reform and devolution it is more ambivalent – devolution offering the prospect of a new layer of government to influence and a new electoral system the possibility of a form of government more amenable to consensual policy-making.

New Right

This approach is motivated by the economic philosophy of the free market. State intervention in economic affairs is viewed as illegitimate and dangerous, distorting the natural forces of the market and denying the consumer the freedom to choose. The state should therefore withdraw from economic activity. This viewpoint entails a contraction of the public sector, with state-owned industries being returned to the private sector. If institutions need reforming in order to facilitate the free market, then so be it: under this approach, no institution is deemed sacrosanct. Frank Vipert, the former deputy director of the free market think-tank the Institute of Economic Affairs, has advocated a 'free market written constitution'.

Liberal

Like the New Right approach, this is a radical approach to constitutional change. It derives from traditional liberal theory and emphasises the centrality of the individual, limited government, the neutrality of the state in resolving conflict, and consensual decision-making. It views the individual as increasingly isolated in decision-making, being elbowed aside by powerful interests and divorced from a governmental process that is centralised and distorted by partisan preferences. Against an increasingly overmighty state, the individual has no means of protection. Hence, it is argued, the need for radical constitutional change.

The Liberal approach favours a new, written constitution, embodying the various reforms advocated by Charter '88, including devolution, a Bill of Rights, a system of proportional representation for elections, a new second chamber, and a reformed judiciary and House of Commons. These, it believes, will serve to shift power from government to the individual. The only reform about which it is ambivalent is the use of referendums, some Liberals seeing the referendum as a device for majority oppression.

Traditionalist

This is a very British approach and derives from a perception of the existing arrangements as fundamentally sound, offering a balanced system of government. It draws on Tory theory in its emphasis on the need for strong government and on Whig theory in stressing the importance of Parliament as

the agent for setting the limits within which government may act. These emphases coalesce in the Westminster model of government, a model that is part descriptive (what is) and part prescriptive (what should be). Government, in this model, must be able to formulate a coherent programme of public policy – the initiative rests with government – with Parliament, as the deliberative body of the nation, subjecting the actions and the programme of government to rigorous scrutiny and providing the limits within which government may govern.

This approach recognises the importance of the House of Commons as the elected chamber and the fact that the citizen has neither the time nor the inclination to engage in continuous political debate. There is thus a certain deference, but a contingent deference, to the deliberative wisdom of Parliament.

The fact that the Westminster model is prescriptive means that traditionalists – unlike high Tories – will entertain change if it is designed to move present arrangements towards the realisation of that model. They also recognise with Edmund Burke that 'a state without the means of some change is without the means of its conservation' and are therefore prepared to consider change in order to maintain and strengthen the existing constitutional framework. Over the years, therefore, traditionalists have supported a range of incremental reforms, such as the introduction of departmental select committees in the House of Commons, but have opposed radical reforms – such as a Bill of Rights and electoral reform – which threaten the existing framework. There is a wariness about membership of the European Union, with involvement accepted as long as it does not threaten the existing domestic arrangements for decision-making.

The current debate

Each of these approaches has its advocates and in the 1980s they vied for support. However, the debate in the 1990s has largely polarised around two of them: the Liberal and the traditionalist.

Five of the approaches either have become or are becoming the 'outs' in constitutional debate. The high Tory approach was already a minority one in the 1980s. Its supporters were a declining breed and unable to resist the changes that took place. They suffered in any event from an inherent flaw in their

BOX 15.3   **DEBATE**

Electoral reform (proportional representation)

The case for

- Every vote would count, producing seats in proportion to votes.

- It would get rid of the phenomenon of the 'wasted vote'

- It would be fairer to third parties, ensuring they got seats in proportion to their percentage of the poll.

- On existing voting patterns, it would result usually in no one party having an overall majority – thus encouraging a coalition and moderate policies.

- A coalition enjoying majority support is more likely to ensure continuity of policy than changes in government under the existing first-past-the-post system.

- A coalition enjoying majority support enjoys a greater popular legitimacy than a single-party government elected by a minority of voters.

- Coalitions resulting from election by proportional representation can prove stable and effective.

- There is popular support for change.

The case against

- Very few systems, except national list systems, are exactly proportional. Little case to change to a relatively more proportional system than the existing system unless other advantages are clear.

- A system of proportional representation would give an unfair advantage to small parties which would be likely hold the balance of power.

- The government would most likely be chosen as a result of bargaining by parties after a general election and not as a deliberate choice of the electors.

- It would be difficult to ensure accountability to electors in the event of a multi-party coalition being formed.

- Coalitions cobbled together after an election lack the legitimacy of clear electoral approval.

- There is no link between electoral systems and economic performance.

- Coalitions resulting from election under a system of proportional representation can lead to uncertainty and a change of coalition partners – as happened in West Germany in 1982 and Ireland in 1994.

- There is popular support for the consequences of the existing electoral system – notably a single party being returned to govern the country.

- 'Proportional representation' is a generic term for a large number of electoral systems: there is no agreement on what precise system should replace the existing one.

approach: contending that the constitution was evolutionary (as opposed to static) while opposing any change at all. The Marxist approach has lost much of its appeal as a result of events in Eastern and Central Europe. Having been abandoned by its principal proponents, it has become difficult for its small band of supporters to make much of the running in debate. The socialist approach achieved some prominence in the early 1980s, exerting notable influence within the Labour Party. The demise of socialism in Europe, combined with the pragmatic approach adopted towards party policy and constitution by Labour leaders Neil Kinnock, John Smith and – most notably – Tony Blair, would appear to have taken much of the wind out of its sails. The group approach was prominent in the 1970s but was marginalised in the 1980s by the New Right approach, with tripartism being notably out of fashion. The New Right approach enjoyed a prominent place in the debate of the 1980s, finding expression in many of the policies of the Thatcher government. Though still influential in Conservative circles, it lost much of its cutting edge following the departure of Margaret Thatcher from Downing Street. Her successor was to be found squarely in the traditionalists' camp.

Recent years have witnessed a marshalling of forces behind the Liberal and traditionalist approaches. Many on the left rallied in the late 1980s and early 1990s behind the Liberal reform agenda. The signatories of Charter '88 included a former editor of *Marxism Today* and Marxist or radical writers such as Ralph Miliband and Anthony Arblaster. By 1991, the Charter had attracted 25,000 signatories. Elements of the Liberal agenda proved increasingly attractive to Labour MPs. In 1993, the Plant Commission – a party body set up by Labour leader Neil Kinnock to review the existing electoral system – came out in favour of a reformed electoral system (advocating the supplementary vote, a variant of the alternative vote); a growing number of Labour MPs, led by Shadow Cabinet member Robin Cook, wanted to go further and introduce a system of proportional representation. Party leader John Smith committed himself to a referendum on the issue. Though traditionally opposed to a new Bill of Rights, the party in its 1992 manifesto committed itself to a 'charter of rights', constituting a large number of bills designed to protect the rights of the individual. On the issue of the House of Lords, the party shifted from a socialist stance in favour of the Liberal position. In the 1983 election, the party advocated the abolition of the upper House. In the 1992 election, it committed itself to an elected second chamber. Over the same period, it also shifted from a socialist to a Liberal position on the issue of the European Community: it favoured

withdrawal from the EC in 1983 and involvement in 1992. The extent to which the Liberal agenda has been embraced by many on the left was shown by the publication of a draft written constitution by the left-wing think-thank the Institute of Public Policy Research (IPPR) in September 1991.

The initial response of traditionalists to the demands for a new constitution was to ignore them. However, as the Liberal approach became more dominant in debate, they began to marshal their forces. Several on the right who had previously supported electoral reform either renounced their support (among them, in 1991, the then Conservative Party Chairman Chris Patten) or kept their heads below the parapet. Leading ministers also weighed into the debate. One minister, John Patten, proved to be an especially ardent advocate of the traditionalists' position, supported by both the Prime Minister, John Major and Foreign Secretary Douglas Hurd. In 1996 the Prime Minister put a member of the Cabinet (Health Secretary Stephen Dorrell) in charge of coordinating the government's traditionalist position on constitutional issues. The case for retention of the existing framework, however, has not been confined to Conservative ranks. Traditionalists have made common purpose across the party divide. The growing support within Labour's ranks for electoral reform galvanised those Labour MPs who supported existing arrangements into forming the First-Past-the-Post Group, led by the MP for Leeds Central, Derek Fatchett.

Advocates of the other approaches still make their case. In 1993, for example, Labour MP Tony Benn – the leading exponent of the socialist approach – published a draft socialist constitution. The group approach appeared to be making a reappearance in July 1993 when the Employment Secretary spoke of the need for a 'new partnership between government and industry'. However, the running in debate continues to be made by the Liberal and traditionalist approaches. The shift in emphasis over the past decade has been reflected in the parties' election manifestos. In 1983, electors were offered a socialist, New Right and Liberal choice. In 1992, the choice was between the Liberal approach of the Liberal Democrats and, to a lesser extent, that of the Labour Party, and the traditionalist approach of the Conservatives. That choice was to be repeated in the 1997 general election (see Table 15.1).

Table 15.1 Stance of parties on constitutional issues, 1997 general election

	Voting system	House of Lords	Devolution	Regional/local government	Protection of rights	House of Commons
Liberal Democrat	Introduce PR at local, national, European levels	Reform: have a predominantly elected chamber	Home Rule with elected Scottish and Welsh parliaments	Regional assemblies in England Strategic authority for London	Bill of Rights preceded by incorporation of ECHR	Fixed-term parliaments; reduce number of MPs to 200
Conservative	Against PR	No mention, but against wholesale reform	Committed to Union. Sees Home Rule and devolution as leading to break-up of the UK	Against regional assemblies	Against a Bill of Rights	Two-year rolling parliamentary programme
Labour	Referendum on electoral reform	Remove hereditary peers	Elected Scottish and Welsh assemblies preceded by referendums	New Greater London Authority; elected mayors	Incorporation of ECHR	Select committee on modernisation of the House

The debate is thus clearer than in the 1970s and more apparent than in the 1960s. The constitution has become, and remains, an issue of political debate. The significance of that debate is part of the debate itself. Those advocating the Liberal approach point to popular support for many of the reforms they advocate. Traditionalists counter that most people accord no priority to such change. Opinion polls suggest support for some reform is broad but not deep. For electors, economic and social issues take priority.

Where to from here? The return of a Conservative government in 1992 ensured that the traditional approach held sway. The return of a Labour government in 1997 moved the focus to a largely, but not wholly, liberal agenda. In terms of *advocacy*, the high point of the liberal approach was the 1992 general election, when it was to the fore in the manifesto of the Liberal Democratic Party and achieved prominence in the Labour manifesto. In terms of likely *implementation*, the high point was the 1997 general election. Constitutional reform was not at the front of the Liberal Democratic manifesto and the measures in the Labour manifesto were not as extensive as in 1992. However, the Labour Party was returned to office

and thus in a position to deliver on its proposals for constitutional reform. At the beginning of the new Parliament in 1997, the Labour government brought forward its proposals for referendums in Scotland and Wales on the issue of devolution. The prospect of a significant change to the British constitution was under way.

Chapter summary

The British constitution remains distinctive for not being codified in a single document. It is drawn from several sources and retains the main components that it has developed over several centuries. Though little debated in the years between 1945 and 1970, it has not remained static, being subject in recent decades to major changes – most notably as a consequence of British membership of the EC/EU – and some adjustments in relationships between different parts of the body politic (e.g. between government and Parliament). It has been the subject of growing debate, with some demands being made for the sweeping away of existing constitutional arrangements and introduction of a written constitution. Supporters of change have become more vocal and rallied behind this banner of the Charter

'88 reform movement. The period up to 1997 saw debate rather than significant change, the supporters of the traditional approach holding sway in government. The return of a Labour government in 1997 opened the way to constitutional change. Advocates of the liberal approach could call in aid opinion polls showing majority support for many of the proposals for constitutional change. The election of a government with a commitment to constitutional reform appeared to bolster the case for change. Those in the traditionalist camp were able to argue that support was broad rather than deep and that respondents gave no priority to constitutional reform. The prospects were of some constitutional change by the turn of the century – and continuing debate.

Discussion points

- How does the constitution of the United Kingdom differ from that of other countries? What does it have in common with them?

- Which approach to constitutional change do you find most persuasive, and why?

- Should Britain have a written constitution?

- What are the principal arguments against holding referendums?

- What are the main obstacles to achieving major constitutional change in the United Kingdom?

Further reading

A useful overview of constitutional issues is to be found in Norton (1982). Other general works – designed more for the undergraduate than the sixth-former – include Harlow (1986), Brazier (1994) and Jowell and Oliver (1994).

For the case for constitutional reform, see the dated but seminal work of Finer (1975). More recent critiques of existing constitutional arrangements include Thornton (1989), Ewing and Gearty (1990), Marr (1995) and Hutton (1995). For literature advocating particular changes, or a new constitution, see the Institute for Public Policy Research (1992), Benn (1993) and Barnett *et al.* (1993). Mount (1992) offers a reformist view from

the perspective of the political right. The Constitution Unit, based at University College, London, has produced a number of publications on the implementation of constitutional reform. All published in 1996, they cover *Scotland's Parliament*, *An Assembly for Wales*, *Regional Government in England*, *Reform of the House of Lords* and – more generally – *Delivering Constitutional Reform*.

The principal arguments in favour of the existing constitutional arrangements are to be found in Patten (1991, 1995) and Norton (1991, 1992, 1996).

References

Barnett, A., Ellis, C. and Hirst, P. (eds) (1993) *Debating the Constitution* (Polity Press).

Benn, T. (1993) *Common Sense* (Hutchinson).

Brazier, R. (1994) *Constitutional Practice*, 2nd edn (Oxford University Press).

Ewing, K.D. and Gearty, C.A. (1990) *Freedom Under Thatcher* (Oxford University Press).

Finer, S.E. (ed.) (1975) *Adversary Politics and Electoral Reform* (Wigram).

Harlow, C. (ed.) (1986) *Public Law and Politics* (Sweet and Maxwell).

Hutton, W. (1995) *The State We're In* (Jonathan Cape).

Institute for Public Policy Research (1992) *A New Constitution for the United Kingdom* (Mansell).

Jowell, R. and Oliver, D. (1994) *The Changing Constitution*, 3rd edn (Oxford University Press).

Marr, A. (1995) *Ruling Britannia* (Michael Joseph).

Mount, F. (1992) *The British Constitution Now* (Heinemann).

Norton, P. (1982) *The Constitution in Flux* (Blackwell).

Norton, P. (1991) 'In defence of the constitution', in P. Norton (ed.), *New Directions in British Politics?* (Edward Elgar).

Norton, P. (1992) *The Constitution: The Conservative Way Forward* (Conservative Political Centre).

Norton, P. (1993) 'The constitution: approaches to reform', *Politics Review*, Vol. 3, No. 1.

Norton, P. (1996) 'In defence of the constitution: A response to Elcock', *Talking Politics*, Vol. 9, No. 1.

Patten, J. (1991) *Political Culture, Conservatism and Rolling Constitutional Change* (Conservative Political Centre).

Patten, J. (1995) *Things to Come* (Sinclair-Stevenson).

Thornton, P. (1989) *Decade of Decline* (Liberty).

CHAPTER SIXTEEN

The crown

PHILIP NORTON

LEARNING OBJECTIVES

- To identify the place of the monarchy in British constitutional history.

- To outline the roles the citizens expect the monarch to fulfil today.

- To consider the extent to which they are carried out.

- To outline criticisms made of the monarchy – and the royal family – in recent years.

- To look at proposals for change.

INTRODUCTION

It is an extraordinary fact, often overlooked, that Britain's representative democracy evolved over a thousand years out of an all-encompassing monarchy underpinned by the religious notion of the divine right of kings. The monarchical shell remains intact but the inner workings have been taken over by party political leaders and civil servants. The shell itself has been the subject of critical comment, especially in recent years. This chapter analyses the emergence of the modern monarchy and considers its still important functions together with the arguments of the critics.

The crown is the symbol of all executive authority. It is conferred on the monarch. The monarchy is the oldest secular institution in England and dates back at least to the ninth century. In Anglo-Saxon and Norman times, the formal power that the crown conferred – executive, legislative and judicial – was exercised personally by the monarch. The King had a court to advise him and, as the task of government became more demanding, so the various functions were exercised on the King's behalf by other bodies. Those bodies now exercise powers independent of the control of the monarch, but they remain formally the instruments of the crown. The courts are Her Majesty's courts and the government Her Majesty's government. Parliament is summoned and prorogued by royal decree. Civil servants are crown appointees. Many powers – prerogative powers – are still exercised in the name of the crown, including the power to declare war. The monarch exercises few powers personally, but those powers remain important. However, the importance of the monarchy in the twentieth century derives more from what it stands for than from what it does.

The monarchy has been eclipsed as a major political institution not only by the sheer demands of governing a growing kingdom but also by changes in the popular perception of what form of government is legitimate. The policy-making power exercised by an hereditary monarch has given way to the exercise of power by institutions deemed more representative. However, the monarchy has retained a claim to be a representative institution in one particular definition of the term. It is this claim that largely defines the activities of the monarch today.

The monarchy pre-dates by several centuries the emergence of the concept of representation. The term 'representation' entered the English language through French derivatives of the Latin *repraesentare*, and did not assume a political meaning until the sixteenth century. It permits at least four separate usages (see Birch, 1964; Pitkin, 1967):

1. It may denote acting on behalf of some individual or group, seeking to defend and promote the interests of the person or persons 'represented'.
2. It may denote persons or assemblies that have been freely elected. Though it is not always the case that persons so elected will act to defend and pursue the interests of electors, they will normally be expected to do so.
3. It may be used to signify a person or persons typical of a particular class or group of persons. It is this sense in which it is used when opinion pollsters identify a representative sample. A representative assembly, under this definition, would be one in which the members reflected proportionally the socio-economic and other characteristics of the population as a whole.
4. It may be used in a symbolic sense. Thus, individuals or objects may 'stand for' something: for example, a flag symbolising the unity of the nation.

The belief that free election was a prerequisite for someone to claim to act on behalf of others grew in the nineteenth century. Before then, the concept of 'virtual representation' held great sway. This concept was well expressed by Edmund Burke. It

was a form of representation, he wrote, 'in which there is a communion of interests, and a sympathy in feelings and desires, between those who act in the name of any description of people, and the people in whose name they act, though the trustees are not actually chosen by them'. It was a concept challenged by the perception that the claim to speak on behalf of a particular body of individuals could not be sustained unless those individuals had signified their agreement, and the way to signify that agreement was through the ballot box. This challenge proved increasingly successful, with the extension of the franchise and, to ensure elections free of coercion, changes in the method of election (the introduction of secret ballots, for example). By the end of the 1880s, the majority of working men had the vote. By Acts of 1918 and 1928, the vote was given to women.

The extension of the franchise in the nineteenth and early twentieth centuries meant that the House of Commons could claim to be a representative institution under the first and second definitions of the term. The unelected House of Lords could not make such a claim. The result, as we shall see (Chapter 17), was a significant shift in the relationship between the two Houses. However, it was not only the unelected upper House that could not make such a claim. Nor could the unelected monarch. Nor could the monarch make a claim to be representative of the nation under the third definition. The claim of the monarch to be 'representative' derives solely from the fourth definition. The monarch stands as a symbol. The strength of the monarch as symbol has been earned at the expense of exercising political powers. To symbolise the unity of the nation, the monarch has had to stand apart from the partisan fray. The monarch has also had to stand aloof from controversy. When controversy has struck – as during the abdication crisis in 1936 and during periods of marital rift between members of the royal family in the 1990s – it has undermined support for the institution of monarchy and called into question its very purpose.

Development of the monarchy

The present monarch, despite some breaks in the direct line of succession, can trace her descent from King Egbert, who united England under his rule in

AD 829. Only once has the continuity of the monarchy been broken, during the period of rule by the Council of State and Oliver Cromwell (1642–60), though the line of succession was restored with the accession of Charles II. The principle of heredity has been preserved since at least the eleventh century. The succession is now governed by statute and common law, the throne descending to the eldest son or, in the absence of a son, the eldest daughter. If the monarch is under 18 years of age, a regent is appointed.

Though all power was initially exercised by the monarch, it was never an absolute power. In the coronation oath, the King promised to 'forbid all rapine and injustice to men of all conditions', and he was expected to consult with the leading men of his realm, both lay and clerical, in order to discover and declare the law and also before the levying of any extraordinary measures of taxation. Such an expectation was to find documented expression in Magna Carta, to which King John affixed his seal in 1215 and which is now recognised as a document of critical constitutional significance. At the time, it was seen by the barons as an expression of existing rights, not a novel departure from them.

The expectation that the King would consult with the leading men of the realm gradually expanded to encompass knights and burgesses, summoned to assent on behalf of local communities to the raising of more money to meet the King's growing expenses. From the summoning of these local dignitaries to court there developed a Parliament – the term was first used in the thirteenth century – and the emergence of two separate Houses, the Commons and the Lords.

The relationship of crown and Parliament was, for several centuries, one of struggle. Though formally the King's Parliament, the King depended on the institution for the grant of supply (money) and increasingly for assent to new laws. Parliament made the grant of supply dependent on the King granting a redress of grievances. Tudor monarchs turned to Parliament for support and usually got it; but the effect of their actions was to acknowledge the growing importance of the body. Stuart kings were less appreciative. James I and his successor, Charles I, upheld the doctrine of the divine right of kings: that is, that the position and powers of the King are given by God and the position and privileges of Parliament derive therefore from the King's grace. Charles' pursuit of the doctrine led to an attempt to rule without the assent of Parliament and ultimately to civil war and the beheading of the King in 1649. The period of republican government that followed was a failure and consequently short-lived. The monarchy was restored in 1660, only to produce another clash a few years later.

James II adhered to the divine right of kings and to the Roman Catholic faith. Both produced a clash with Parliament and James attempted to rule by royal prerogative alone. A second civil war was averted when James fled the country following the arrival of William of Orange (James's Protestant son-in-law), who had been invited by leading politicians and churchmen. At the invitation of a new Parliament, William and his wife Mary (James's daughter) jointly assumed the throne. However, the offer of the crown had been conditional on their acceptance of the Declaration of Right – embodied in statute as the 1689 Bill of Rights – which declared the suspending of laws and the levying of taxation without the approval of Parliament to be illegal. As the historian G.M. Trevelyan observed, James II had forced the country to choose between royal absolutism and parliamentary government (Trevelyan, 1938, p. 245). It chose parliamentary government.

The dependence of the monarch on Parliament was thus established and the years since have witnessed the gradual withdrawal of the sovereign from the personal exercise of executive authority. Increasingly, the monarch became dependent on ministers, both for the exercise of executive duties and in order to manage parliamentary business. This dependence was all the greater when Queen Anne died in 1714 without an heir and yet another monarch was imported from the continent – this time George, Elector of Hanover. George I of Britain was not especially interested in politics and in any case did not speak English, so the task of chairing the Cabinet, traditionally the King's job, fell to the First Lord of the Treasury. Under Robert Walpole, this role was assiduously developed and Walpole became the most important of the king's ministers: he became 'prime minister'. Anne's inability to produce an heir and George's poor language skills facilitated the emergence of an office that is now at the heart of British politics.

George III succeeded in winning back some of the monarchy's power later on in the eighteenth century. It was still the King, after all, who appointed ministers and by skilfully using his patronage he could influence who sat in the House of Commons. This power, though, was undermined early in the nineteenth century. In 1832, the Great Reform Act introduced a uniform electoral system and subsequent reform acts further extended the franchise. The age of a representative democracy, displacing the concept of virtual representation, had arrived. The effect was to marginalise the monarch as a political actor. To win votes in Parliament, parties quickly organised themselves into coherent and highly structured movements and the leader of the majority party following a general election became Prime Minister. The choice of Prime Minister and government – what Bagehot referred to as 'the elective function' – remained formally in the hands of the monarch, but in practice the selection came to be made on a regular basis by the electorate.

Queen Victoria was the last monarch seriously to consider vetoing legislation (the last monarch actually to do so was Queen Anne, who withheld Royal Assent from the Scottish Militia Bill in 1707). The year 1834 was the last occasion that the ministry fell for want of the sovereign's confidence; thereafter, it was the confidence of the House of Commons that counted. Victoria was also the last monarch to exercise a personal preference in the choice of Prime Minister (later monarchs, where a choice existed, acted under advice), and the last to be instrumental in pushing successfully for the enactment of particular legislative measures (Hardie, 1970, p. 67). By the end of her reign, it was clear that the monarch, whatever the formal powers vested by the constitution, was constrained politically by a representative assembly elected by the adult male population, the government being formed largely by members drawn from that assembly. Victoria could no longer exercise the choices she had been able to do when she first ascended the throne.

The monarch by the beginning of the twentieth century sat largely on the sidelines of the political system, unable to control Parliament, unable to exercise a real choice in the appointment of ministers, unable to exercise a choice in appointing judges. The extensive power once exercised by the King had now passed largely to the people. However, the elective power was only exercised on election day: in between elections it was the Prime Minister who exercised many of the powers formally vested in the monarch. By controlling government appointments, the Prime Minister was able to dominate the executive side of government. And as long as he could command the support of the majority party in Parliament he was able to dominate the legislative side of government. Power thus shifted from an unelected monarch to what one writer later dubbed an 'elected monarch' (Benemy, 1965) – the occupant not of Buckingham Palace but of 10 Downing Street.

The shift to the position above the partisan fray of politics, and above the actual exercise of executive power, has been confirmed in the twentieth century. 'Since 1901 the trend towards a real political neutrality, not merely a matter of appearances, has been steady, reign by reign' (Hardie, 1970, p. 188). The transition has been facilitated by no great constitutional act. Several statutes have impinged on the prerogative power but many of the legal powers remain. There is nothing in law that prevents the monarch from vetoing a bill or from exercising personal choice in the invitation to form a government. The monarch is instead bound by conventions of the constitution (see Chapter 15). Thus, it is a convention that the monarch gives her assent to bills passed by Parliament and that she summons the leader of the largest party following a general election to form a government. Such conventions mean that the actions of the monarch are predictable – no personal choice is involved – and they have helped ease the passage of the monarch from one important constitutional position to another.

The contemporary role of the monarchy

What, then, is the contemporary role of the monarch? Two primary tasks can be identified. One is essentially a representative task: that is, symbolising the unity and traditional standards of the nation. The second is to fulfil certain political functions. The weakness of the monarch in being able to exercise independent decisions in the latter task underpins the strength of the monarchy in fulfilling the former. If the monarch were to engage in partisan activity, it would undermine her claim to symbolise the unity of the nation.

Symbolic role

The functions fulfilled by the monarch under the first heading are several. A majority of respondents in a poll in 1988 considered six functions to be 'very' or 'quite' important. As we shall see, the extent to which these functions are actually fulfilled by members of the royal family has become a matter of considerable debate. Two functions – preserving the class system and distracting people from problems affecting the country – were considered by most respondents as 'not very' or 'not at all' important.

Representing the UK at home or abroad

More than nine out of every ten people questioned in the 1988 poll considered this to be very or quite important. As a symbolic function, it is a task normally ascribed to any head of state. Because no partisan connotations attach to her activities, the sovereign is able to engage the public commitment of citizens in a way that politicians cannot. When the President of the United States travels within the USA or goes abroad he does so both as head of state and as head of government; as head of government, he is a practising politician. When the Queen attends the Commonwealth prime ministers' conference, she does so as symbolic head of the Commonwealth. The British government is represented by the Prime Minister, who is then able to engage in friendly or not so friendly discussions with fellow heads of government. The Queen stays above the fray. Similarly, at home, when opening a hospital or attending a major public event, the Queen is able to stand as a symbol of the nation. Invitations to the Prime Minister or leader of an opposition party to perform such tasks run the risk of attracting partisan objection.

At least two practical benefits are believed to derive from this non-partisan role, one political, the other economic. Like many of her predecessors, the Queen has amassed considerable experience by virtue of her monarchical longevity. In 1993, she celebrated her fortieth year on the throne. During those forty years, she had been served by nine separate prime ministers. Her experience, coupled with her neutrality, has meant that she has been able to offer prime ministers detached and informed observations. (The Prime Minister has an audience with the Queen each week.) As an informed figure who offers no political challenge to the premier, she also offers an informed ear to an embattled premier who may feel he or she cannot unburden him- or herself to anyone else. The value of the Queen's role to premiers has been variously attested by successive occupants of Downing Street, notably in the 1970s by the two Labour prime ministers of her reign, Harold Wilson and James Callaghan. Her relations with both were reputedly much better than with Conservative premiers Edward Heath and Margaret Thatcher (Blackburn, 1992, p. 6; Hibbert, 1979, pp. 151–2).

The political benefit has also been seen in the international arena. By virtue of her experience and neutral position, the Queen enjoys the respect of international leaders, not least those gathered in the Commonwealth. During the 1980s, when relations between the British government of Margaret Thatcher and a number of Commonwealth governments were sometimes acrimonious (on the issue of sanctions against South Africa, for example), various Commonwealth heads attested to the unifying influence of the Queen. There were fears that, without her emollient influence, the Commonwealth would have broken up or that Britain would have been expelled from it.

In terms of economic benefit, some observers claim – though a number of critics dispute it – that the Queen and leading members of the royal family (such as the Prince of Wales) are good for British trade. The symbolism, the history and the pageantry that surround the monarchy serve to make the Queen and her immediate family a potent source of media and public interest abroad. Royal visits are often geared to export promotions, though critics claim the visits do not have the impact claimed or are not followed up adequately by the exporters themselves. Such visits, though, normally draw crowds that would not be attracted by a visiting politician or industrialist.

Setting standards of citizenship and family life

This in 1988 remained an important task in the eyes of all but a small percentage of those questioned.

The Queen in particular, and members of her family in general, are expected to lead by example in maintaining standards of citizenship and family life. As head of state and secular head of the established church, the Queen is expected to be above criticism. She applies herself assiduously to her duties; even her most ardent critics concede that she is diligent (Wilson, 1989, p. 190). She lends her name to charities and voluntary organisations. Other members of her family also involve themselves in charitable activities. The Princess Royal (Princess Anne) is president of the Save the Children Fund. The Prince of Wales sponsors several charitable trusts.

During the 1980s, the Queen was held to epitomise family life in a way that others could both empathise with and emulate. (Queen Elizabeth, the Queen Mother – widow of George VI – was, and remains, popularly portrayed as 'the nation's grandmother'.) Significantly, during the national miners' strike in 1984, the wives of striking miners petitioned the Queen for help. However, the extent to which this role is fulfilled by the Queen has been the subject of debate in the 1990s. By 1992, the Queen was head of a family that had not sustained one successful lasting marriage. As we shall see, this has proved an important element in contemporary debate about the role and future of the British monarchy.

Uniting people despite differences

The monarch symbolises the unity of the nation. The Queen is head of state. Various public functions are carried out in the name of the crown, notably public prosecutions, and as the person in whom the crown vests the monarch's name attaches to the various organs of the state: the government, courts and armed services. The crown, in effect, substitutes for the concept of the state (a concept not well understood or utilised in Britain) and the monarch serves as the personification of the crown. Nowhere is the extent of this personification better demonstrated than on British postage stamps. These are unique: British stamps alone carry the monarch's head with no mention of the name of the nation. The monarch provides a clear, living focal point for the expression of national unity, national pride and, if necessary, national grief.

The effectiveness of this role is facilitated by the monarch transcending political activity. Citizens' loyalties can flow to the crown without being hindered by political considerations. The Queen's role as head of the Commonwealth may also have helped create a 'colour-blind' monarchy, in which the welfare of everyone, regardless of race, is taken seriously. At different points this century, members of the royal family have also shown concern for the economically underprivileged and those who have lost their livelihoods – ranging from Edward VIII's 'something must be done' remark in the 1930s to the Prince of Wales's attempt to help disadvantaged youths in the 1980s and 1990s. The extent to which this role is effectively fulfilled, though, does not go unquestioned. Critics, as we shall see, claim that the royal family occupies a socially privileged position that symbolises not so much unity but rather the social divisions of the nation; and they also draw attention to the fact that the royal family itself employs few black workers or employees from other minority groups.

Allegiance of the armed forces

Ensuring that the armed forces give their allegiance to the crown rather than to the government is an important function, though it is interesting – and perhaps surprising – that respondents to the 1988 poll accorded it the importance they did; more than 75 per cent judged it to be very or quite important, ahead of maintaining continuity of tradition and preserving a Christian morality. The armed services are in the service of the crown. Loyalty is owed to the crown, not least by virtue of the oath taken by all members of the armed forces. It is also encouraged by the close links maintained by the royal family with the various services. Members of the royal family have variously served in (usually) the Royal Navy or the Army. Most hold ceremonial ranks, such as colonel-in-chief of a particular regiment. The Queen takes a particular interest in military matters, including awards for service. 'With the outbreak of the troubles in Ulster in the late 1960s she was a moving force in getting a medal created for services there, and she reads personally all the citations for gallantry there – as she had always done for medals of any sort' (Lacey, 1977, p. 222). Such a relationship helps emphasise the apolitical role of the military and also provides a barrier should the military, or more probably sections of it, seek to overthrow or threaten the elected government. (In the 1970s, there were rumours – retailed in the press and on a number of television programmes – that a number of retired officers favoured a coup to topple the Labour government returned in 1974.) In the event of an attempted military coup, the prevailing view – though not universally shared – is that the monarch would serve as the most effective bulwark to its realisation, the Queen being in a position to exercise the same role as that of King Juan Carlos of Spain in 1981, when he forestalled a right-wing military takeover by making a public appeal to the loyalty of his army commanders.

Maintaining continuity of British traditions

The monarch symbolises continuity in affairs of state. Many of the duties traditionally performed by her have symbolic relevance: for example, the state opening of Parliament and – important in the context of the previous point – the annual ceremony of trooping the colour. Other traditions serve a psychological function, helping maintain a sense of belonging to the nation, and also a social function. The awarding of honours and royal garden parties are viewed by critics as socially elitist but by supporters as helping break down social barriers, rewarding those – regardless of class – who have contributed significantly to the community. Hierarchy of awards, on this argument, is deemed less important than the effect on the recipients. The award of an MBE to a local health worker may mean far more to the recipient, who may never have expected it, than the award of a knighthood to an MP after twenty years' service in Parliament who may regard such an award as a natural reward for services rendered. Investiture is often as important as the actual award. 'To some it is a rather tiresome ordeal but to most a moving and memorable occasion. A fire brigade officer, who was presented with the British Empire Medal, spoke for many when he said: "I thought it would be just another ceremony. But now that I've been, it's something I'll remember for the rest of my days"' (Hibbert, 1979, p. 205). Each year 30,000 people are invited to royal garden parties. Few decline the invitation.

Preserving a Christian morality

The Queen is supreme governor of the Church of England and the links between the monarch and the church are close and visible. The monarch is required by the Act of Settlement of 1701 to 'joyn in communion with the Church of England as by law established'. After the monarch, the most significant participant in a coronation ceremony is the Archbishop of Canterbury, who both crowns and anoints the new sovereign. Bishops are appointed by the crown, albeit acting on advice. National celebrations led by the Queen will usually entail a religious service, more often than not held in St Paul's Cathedral or Westminster Abbey. The Queen is known to take seriously her religious duties and is looked to, largely by way of example, as a symbol of a basically Christian morality.

Preserving what are deemed to be high standards of Christian morality has been important since the nineteenth century, though not necessarily much before that: earlier monarchs were keener to protect the Church of England than they were to practise its morality. The attempts to preserve that morality this century have resulted in some notable sacrifices. Edward VIII was forced to abdicate in 1936 because of his insistence on marrying a twice-married and twice-divorced woman. In 1955 the Queen's sister, Princess Margaret, decided not to marry Group Captain Peter Townsend because he was divorced. She announced that 'mindful of the Church's teaching that Christian marriage is indissoluble, and conscious of my duty to the Commonwealth, I have resolved to put these considerations before others'. However, two decades later, with attitudes having changed to some degree, the Princess herself was divorced. Her divorce was followed by that of Princess Anne and Captain Mark Phillips and later by that of the Duke and Duchess of York and the Prince and Princess of Wales. Though attitudes towards divorce may have changed, divorces and separations in the royal family have none the less raised questions about the royal family's capacity to maintain a Christian morality. This applies particularly in the event of Prince Charles becoming king and seeking to remarry.

Exercise of formal powers

Underpinning the monarch's capacity to fulfil a unifying role, and indeed underpinning the other functions deemed important, is the fact that she stands above and beyond the arena of partisan debate. This also affects significantly the monarch's other primary task: that of fulfilling her formal duties as head of state. Major powers still remain with the monarch: the choice of Prime Minister, the right to withhold assent to legislation, the dispensing of ministerial portfolios, the dissolution of Parliament, and the declaring of war being among the most obvious. All such prerogative powers are now, as far as possible, governed by convention. We have already noted two examples: by convention, the monarch assents to all legislation passed by the two Houses of Parliament; by convention, she calls the leader of the party with an overall majority in Parliament to form a government. Where there is no clear convention governing what to do, the Queen acts in accordance with precedent (where one exists) and, where a choice is involved, acts on advice. By thus avoiding any personal choice – and being seen not to exercise any personal choice – in the exercise of powers vested in the crown, the monarch is able to remain 'above politics'. Hence the characterisation of the monarch as enjoying strength through weakness. The denial of personal discretion in the exercise of inherently political powers strengthens the capacity of the monarch to fulfil a representative – that is, symbolic – role.

However, could it not be argued that the exercise of prerogative powers is, by virtue of the absence of personal choice, a waste of time and something of which the monarch should be shorn? (Why not, for example, vest the power of dissolution in the Speaker of the House of Commons?) There are two principal reasons why the powers remain vested in the sovereign.

Firstly, the combination of the symbolic role and the powers vested in the crown enable the monarch to stand as a constitutional safeguard. A similar role is ascribed to the House of Lords, but that – as we shall see – is principally in a situation where the government seeks to extend its own life without recourse to an election. What if the government sought to dispense with Parliament? To return to an earlier example, what if there was an attempted military coup? The House of Lords could not effectively act to prevent it. It is doubtful if a Speaker vested with formal powers could do much to prevent it. The monarch could. As head of state

and as commander-in-chief of the armed forces, the monarch could deny both legitimacy and support to the insurgents. This may or may not be sufficient ultimately to prevent a coup, but the monarch is at least in a stronger position than other bodies to prevent it succeeding. Thus, ironically, the unelected monarch – successor to earlier monarchs who tried to dispense with Parliament – serves as an ultimate protector of the political institutions which have displaced the monarchy as the governing authority (see Bogdanor, 1995).

Secondly, retention of the prerogative powers serves as a reminder to ministers and other servants of the crown that they owe a responsibility to a higher authority than a transient politician. Ministers are Her Majesty's ministers; the Prime Minister is invited by the sovereign to form an administration. The responsibility may, on the face of it, appear purely formal. However, though the monarch is precluded from calling the Prime Minister (or any minister) to account publicly, she is able to require a private explanation. In *The English Constitution*, Walter Bagehot offered his classic definition of the monarch's power as being 'the right to be consulted, the right to encourage, the right to warn'. The Queen is known to be an assiduous reader of her official papers – she receives all Cabinet papers and important Foreign Office communications – and is known often to question the Prime Minister closely and, on other occasions, the relevant departmental ministers. Harold Wilson recorded when in his early days as Prime Minister he was caught on the hop as a result of the Queen having read Cabinet papers which he had not yet got round to reading. 'Very interesting, this idea of a new town in the Bletchley area', commented the Queen. It was the first Wilson knew of the idea. More significantly, there are occasions when the Queen is believed to have made her displeasure known. In 1986, for example, it was reported – though not confirmed – that the Queen was distressed at the strain that the Prime Minister, Margaret Thatcher, was placing on the Commonwealth as a result of her refusal to endorse sanctions against South Africa; she was also reported to have expressed her displeasure in 1983 following the US invasion of Grenada, a Commonwealth country (Cannon and Griffiths, 1988, p. 620). Indeed, relations between the Queen and her first female

Prime Minister were rumoured to be correct rather than close. Mostly, as we have seen, the Queen is a considerable help rather than a hindrance to prime ministers – offering a private and experienced audience – but she none the less serves as a reminder of their responsibility to some other authority than political party. She also stands as the ultimate deterrent. Though her actions are governed predominantly by convention, she still has the legal right to exercise them. When the government of John Major sought a vote of confidence from the House of Commons on 23 July 1993 (following the loss of an important vote the previous evening), the prime minister made it clear that in the event of the government losing the vote, the consequence would be a general election. (By convention, a government losing a vote of confidence either resigns or requests a dissolution.) However, the government took the precaution of checking in advance that the Queen would agree to a dissolution.

Criticisms of the monarchy

Various functions are thus fulfilled by the monarch and other members of the royal family. There has tended to be a high level of support for the monarchy and popular satisfaction with the way those functions are carried out. However, a high level of support for the institution of monarchy has not been a constant in British political history. It dropped during the reign of Queen Victoria, when she hid herself away from public gaze following the death of Prince Albert. It dropped again in the 1930s as a result of the abdication crisis, which divided the nation. It increased significantly during the Second World War because of the conduct of the royal family and remained high in post-war decades. It dipped again at the beginning of the 1990s; 1992 was described by the Queen as her *annus horribilis* (horrible year). The monarchy was no longer the revered institution of preceding decades and its future became an issue of topical debate. Even at times of high popular support, it has never been free of criticism. In recent years, the criticisms have been fuelled by the activities of various members of the royal family.

Four principal criticisms can be identified: that an unelected monarch has the power to exercise certain political powers; that, by virtue of being neither elected nor socially typical, the monarchy is unrepresentative; that maintaining the royal family costs too much; and that the institution of monarchy is now unnecessary. The last three criticisms have become more pronounced in recent years.

Potential for political involvement

The actions of the sovereign as head of state are governed predominantly by convention. However, not all actions she may be called upon to take are covered by convention. This is most notably the case in respect of the power to appoint a Prime Minister and to dissolve Parliament. Usually, there is no problem. As long as one party is returned with an overall majority, the leader of that party will be summoned to Buckingham Palace (or, if already Prime Minister, will remain in office). But what if there is a 'hung' Parliament, with no one party enjoying an overall majority, and the leader of the third largest party makes it clear that his or her party will be prepared to sustain the second largest party in office, but not the party with the largest number of seats? Whom should the Queen summon? What if she summons the leader of the largest party, the leader of that party then attempts to form a government but is defeated on a vote of confidence and requests a dissolution? Should the Queen grant the request or instead ask the leader of the second largest party to try to form a government? There is no clear convention to govern the Queen's response in such circumstances and the opinions of constitutional experts as to what she should do are divided. Similarly, what if the Prime Minister was isolated in Cabinet and requested a dissolution, a majority of the Cabinet making it clear that it was opposed to such a move, would the Queen be obliged to grant her Prime Minister's request?

These are instances of problems that admit of no clear solution and they pose a threat to the value that currently derives from the sovereign being, and being seen to be, above politics. She is dependent on circumstances and the goodwill of politicians in order to avoid such a difficult situation arising. When the Queen was drawn into partisan controversy in 1957 and 1963 in the choice of a Conservative Prime Minister, the obvious embarrassment to the monarchy spurred the party to change its method of selecting the leader. There remains the danger that circumstances may conspire again to make involvement in real – as opposed to formal – decision-making unavoidable.

Given this potential, some critics contend that the powers vested in the monarch should be transferred elsewhere. Labour MP Tony Benn and a number of other critics would like to see the vesting of the formal powers of a head of state in an elected president and some existing prerogative powers, such as those over appointments to public office, in other, publicly accountable bodies. In 1996, a Fabian Society pamphlet by a Labour parliamentary candidate Paul Richards put the case for transferring all the prerogative powers exercised by the Queen to the Speaker of the House of Commons. Defenders of the existing arrangements contend that the retention of prerogative powers by the crown has created no major problems to date – one constitutional historian, Peter Hennessy, in a 1994 lecture, recorded only five 'real or near real contingencies' since 1949 when the Queen's reserve powers were relevant (Marr, 1995, p. 234; see also Bogdanor, 1995) – and serves as a valuable constitutional longstop. Giving certain powers to other public figures such as the Speaker of the Commons would create the potential for those figures to be dragged into partisan controversy, and an elected president would be likely to lack the capacity to engage the loyalty of the armed forces to the same extent as the monarch.

Unrepresentative

The monarchy cannot make a claim to be representative in the second meaning of the term (freely elected). Critics also point out that it cannot make a claim to be representative in the third meaning (socially typical). The monarchy is a hereditary institution, based on the principle of primogeniture: that is, the crown passes to the eldest son. By the nature of the position, it is of necessity socially atypical. Critics contend that social hierarchy is reinforced by virtue of the monarch's personal wealth. The Queen is believed to be among the world's richest women, and may possibly be the richest. Many of the functions patronised by the Queen and members of the royal family, from formal functions to sporting events, are also criticised for being socially elitist. Those who surround the royal family

in official positions (the Lord Chamberlain, ladies-in-waiting and other senior members of the royal household), and those with whom members of the royal family choose to surround themselves in positions of friendship, are also notably if not exclusively drawn from a social elite. In the 1950s, Lord Altrincham criticised the Queen's entourage for constituting 'a tight little enclave of British "ladies and gentlemen"' (Altrincham, 1958, p. 115). Various changes were made in the wake of such criticism – the royal family became more publicly visible, the presentation of debutantes to the monarch at society balls was abolished – but royalty remains largely detached from the rest of society. Even at Buckingham Palace garden parties, members of the royal family take tea in a tent reserved for them and leading dignitaries, other guests being excluded. Pressures continue for the institution to be more open in terms of the social background of the Queen's entourage and, indeed, in terms of the activities and background of members of the royal family itself. The 1988 Gallup poll found that 64 per cent of respondents believed that royal children should spend at least part of their education in the state system; 49 per cent believed that the Prince of Wales should have a job; and 68 per cent thought that other members of the royal family should also have one. Defenders of the status quo argue that it is, by definition, impossible for the royal family to be socially typical – since they would cease to be the royal family – and that to be too close to everyday activity would rob the institution of monarchy of its aura and charm.

Overly expensive

The cost of the monarchy has been the subject of criticism for several years. This criticism has become more pronounced in the 1990s. Much but not all the costs of the monarchy have traditionally been met from the civil list. The civil list constitutes a sum paid regularly by the state to the monarch to cover the cost of staff, upkeep of royal residences, holding official functions, and of public duties undertaken by other members of the royal family. (The Prince of Wales is not included: as Duke of Cornwall his income derives from revenue-generating estates owned by the Duchy of Cornwall.) Other costs of monarchy – such as the upkeep of royal castles and the royal yacht *Britannia* – are met by government departments. In 1990, to avoid an annual public row over the figure, agreement was reached between the government and the Queen that the civil list should be set at £7.9 million a year for ten years. When the other costs of the monarchy – maintaining castles and the like – are added to this figure, the annual public expenditure on the monarchy was estimated in 1991 to exceed £57 million.

In the 1970s and 1980s, accusations were variously heard that the expenditure was not justified, in part because some members of the royal family did very little to justify the sums given to them and in part because the Queen was independently wealthy, having a private fortune on which she paid no tax. (When income tax was introduced in the nineteenth century, Queen Victoria voluntarily paid tax. In the twentieth century, the voluntary commitment was whittled down and had disappeared by the time the Queen ascended the throne in 1952.) These criticisms found various manifestations. In 1988, 40 per cent of respondents to a Gallup poll expressed the view that the monarchy 'cost too much'. In a MORI poll in 1990, three out of every four people questioned believed that the Queen should pay income tax; half of those questioned thought the royal family was receiving too much money from the taxpayer. Certain members of the royal family became targets of particular criticism.

These criticisms became much louder in 1991 and 1992. They were fuelled by a number of unrelated developments. The most notable were the separation of the Duke and Duchess of York and – in December 1992 – of the Prince and Princess of Wales, accompanied by newspaper stories about their private lives. (Pictures of a topless Duchess of York relaxing with a Texan described as her 'financial adviser' were published in the tabloid press.) The result was that members of the royal family became central figures of controversy and gossip. In November 1992 fire destroyed St George's Hall of Windsor Castle and the government announced it would meet the cost of repairs, estimated at more than £50 million. The public reaction to the announcement was strongly negative. At a time of recession, public money was to be spent restoring a royal castle, while the Queen continued to pay no income tax and members of the royal family pursued other than restrained lifestyles at public expense. A Harris poll found three out of every four respondents believing that ways should be found to cut the cost of the royal family.

Six days after the fire at Windsor Castle, the Prime Minister informed the House of Commons that the Queen had initiated discussions 'some months ago' on changing her tax-free status and on removing all members of the royal family from the civil list, other than herself, the Duke of Edinburgh and the Queen Mother. The expenditure of other members of the royal family would be met by the Queen herself. The Queen announced the following year that Buckingham Palace was to be opened to the public, with money raised from entrance fees being used to pay the cost of repairs to Windsor Castle. These announcements served to meet much of the criticism, but the controversy undermined the prestige of the royal family. Critics continued to point out that most of the costs of the monarchy remained unchanged, funded by public money, and drew attention to the fact that the Queen was using novel devices of taking money from the public (entrance fees to the Palace) in order to fund Windsor Castle repairs rather than drawing on her own private wealth.

Controversy was again stirred in January 1997 when Defence Secretary Michael Portillo announced plans for a new royal yacht, to replace *Britannia*, at a cost of £60 million. Public reaction was largely unfavourable and Buckingham Palace let it be known that the government had not consulted members of the royal family before making the announcement.

Defenders of the royal family contend that the country obtains good value for money from the royal family, the costs of monarchy being offset by income from crown lands (land formerly owned by the crown but given to the state in return for the civil list) and by income from tourism and trade generated by the presence and activities of the Queen and members of her family. They also point out that much if not most of the money spent on maintaining castles and other parts of the national heritage would still have to be spent even if there was no royal family. When such money is taken out of the equation, the public activities of the Queen and leading royals such as Princess Anne are deemed to represent good value for public money.

Unnecessary

Those who criticise the monarchy on grounds of its unrepresentative nature and its cost are not necessarily opposed to the institution itself. A more open and less costly monarchy – based on the Scandinavian model, with the monarch mixing more freely with citizens and without excessive trappings – would be acceptable to many. However, some take the opposite view. They see the monarchy as an unnecessary institution; the cost and social elitism of the monarchy are seen as merely illustrative of the nature of the institution. The most recent advocates of this view have been Tom Nairn in *The Enchanted Glass: Britain and its Monarchy* (1988) and Edgar Wilson in *The Myth of the British Monarchy* (1989). Wilson contends that the various arguments advanced in favour of the monarchy – its popularity, impartiality, productivity, capacity to unite, to protect democratic institutions of state, and its ability to generate trade – are all myths, generated in order to justify the existing order. To him and Nairn, the monarchy forms part of a conservative establishment that has little rationale in a democratic society. They would prefer to see the monarchy abolished. 'The constitutional case for abolishing the Monarchy is based mainly on the facts that it is arbitrary, unrepresentative, unaccountable, partial, socially divisive, and exercises a pernicious influence and privileged prerogative powers' (Wilson, 1989, p. 178). Necessary functions of state carried out by the monarch could be equally well fulfilled, so critics contend, by an elected president. Most countries in the world have a head of state not chosen on the basis of heredity. So why not Britain? In May 1991, Tony Benn introduced a Commonwealth of Britain Bill in the House of Commons (the bill stood no chance of passage), designed to replace the monarch with such a president, chosen from Parliament.

Supporters of the institution of monarchy argue that, despite recent criticisms, the Queen continues to do a good job – a view which, according to opinion polls, enjoys majority support – and that the monarchy is distinctive by virtue of the functions it is able to fulfil. It is considered doubtful that an appointed or elected head of state would be able to carry out to the same extent the symbolic role, representing the unity of the nation. For a head of state not involved in the partisan operation of government, it is this role (representative in the fourth sense of the term) that is more important than that of being an elected leader. Indeed, election could jeopardise the head of state's claim to be representative in the first sense of the term (acting on behalf of a particular body or group). The monarch has a duty to represent all subjects; an elected head of state may have a bias, subconscious or otherwise, in favour of those who vote for him or her, or in favour of those – presumably politicians – who were responsible for arranging the nomination. The Queen enjoys a stature not likely to be matched by an elected figurehead in engaging the loyalty of the armed forces; and by virtue of her longevity and experience can assist successive prime ministers in a way not possible by a person appointed or elected for a fixed term. Hence, by virtue of these assets particular to the Queen, the monarch is deemed unique and not capable of emulation by an elected president. Though these assets may have been partially tarnished in recent years, it is argued that they remain of value to the nation.

Proposals for change

The arguments advanced by critics in the 1980s – and even when Tony Benn introduced his bill in 1991 – were regarded as fairly marginal to political debate. Since then, their arguments have appeared less marginal. Those most responsible for this change are, ironically, members of the royal family themselves. The various marital splits, the antics of various royals, the failure of the Queen to fund the restoration of Windsor Castle herself, have contributed to a popular mood less supportive of the monarchy than before. As Table 16.1 shows, the decline in popular support for the royal family has been substantial.

Criticism of the monarchy and, more especially, members of the royal family, has led to several demands for change. Future options for the monarchy can be grouped under three heads: abolition, reform, and leave alone.

Abolition

Until the middle of 1992, less than 15 per cent of people questioned in various polls wanted to see the monarchy abolished. A Gallup poll in May 1992

Table 16.1   Attitudes towards the royal family (per cent)

Q. Has your personal opinion of the Royal Family gone up or gone down over the past year?

	April 1996	Nov. 1995	Oct. 1994	Nov. 1993
Gone up	1	4	2	5
Gone down	57	49	54	46
Same	39	44	43	48
Don't know	2	3	1	1

Source: GALLUP, Political and Economic Index, April 1996

found 13 per cent of respondents giving such a response. By the end of the year, the figure had increased to 24 per cent.

These figures show an increase in those wanting to get rid of the monarchy, but they mask an increasing agnosticism among the wider population. In 1987, 77 per cent of respondents in a MORI poll thought that Britain would be worse off if the monarchy was abolished. In 1989, the figure was down to 58 per cent. By May 1992, it had slipped a little further, to 55 per cent. Other polls showed a growing scepticism among citizens as to whether the monarchy would survive another fifty years.

However, those who argue the case for the retention of the monarchy appear still to have a considerable edge over those demanding abolition. As Table 16.2 shows, of those questioned in a Gallup poll in November 1995 on their own preferences about the monarchy – whether to abolish, reform, or leave alone – the option of abolition was the least favoured. The high point of those favouring abolition was achieved in 1992, and support for such a radical option has slipped since.

Though there has been some dip in the proportion who believe that the monarchy will not survive, most people questioned in a Gallup poll at the end of 1995 believed that the monarchy and the royal family 'will still exist in the next century': 60 per cent thought that it would, against 20 per cent who believed that it would not. In January 1997, Granada TV held a debate with a 3,000-strong audience, on the future of the monarchy, in Birmingham's National Exhibition Centre, and followed it with a national telephone poll. More than 2.6 million people took part in the poll, with 66 per cent voting to retain the monarchy.

Reform

Recent years have seen a growing body of support for some change in the nature of the monarchy and especially in the royal family. The preference is for a more open and less ostentatious monarchy, with the Queen spending more time meeting members of the public and with other members of the royal family, especially the 'minor royals', taking up paid employment (as some have) and blending into the community. A Granada TV deliberative poll in 1996, which involved interviewing people before and after discussing the subject with experts, found that the biggest percentage of affirmative responses was for the statement that 'Members of the royal family should mix more with ordinary people'. The percentage agreeing was initially 66 per cent and, after discussion, it increased to 75 per cent.

There is also some support for a change in the order of succession. A small number of people favour the Queen abdicating in favour of Prince Charles, but the number is declining: it reached a peak at 29 per cent in a 1994 Gallup poll, but was down to 16 per cent in March 1996. A larger percentage support 'skipping a generation' and allowing Prince William, Prince Charles's eldest son, to succeed to the throne in place of his father: in March 1996, 39 per cent of respondents in a Gallup poll favoured that option, against 46 per cent who did not. These proposals not only do not enjoy majority support, they would also require a change in the law. A decision by the Queen, or by Prince Charles upon or at the time of his succession to the throne, to abdicate is not one that can be taken unilaterally. Under the Act of Succession, Prince Charles will become king automatically on

Table 16.2   Future of the monarchy (per cent)

Q. Which of these three statements comes closest to your own view?

	Nov. 1995	Sept. 1994	Nov. 1993
The Monarchy and the Royal Family should stay pretty much as they are now	26	36	30
The Monarchy and the Royal Family should continue to exist but should become more democratic and approachable, rather like the Monarchy and Royal Family in the Netherlands	54	49	56
The Monarchy should be abolished and replaced by a non-executive figurehead president like the ones they have in some continental countries	15	12	10
Don't know	5	3	4

Source: GALLUP, Political and Economic Index, December 1995

the death of his mother. There is no formal power to abdicate. That would require – as it did in 1936 – an Act of Parliament.

Another change that has variously been discussed, but which has less immediate relevance, is that of allowing the eldest child to succeed, regardless of gender. (Given that Prince Charles is the eldest child of the sovereign and his eldest child is a male, it will be two generations before any change becomes relevant.) In 1996 it emerged that the senior members of the royal family, prompted apparently by Prince Charles, had formed a small group (the 'Way Ahead Group' composed of senior royals and Buckingham Palace officials) to meet twice a year to consider various changes to existing arrangements. One proposal considered by the group has been to allow the eldest child to succeed to the throne; another is to end the ban on anyone married to a Roman Catholic succeeding to the throne.

The measures taken by the Queen in recent years – notably the decision to pay income tax and to limit the civil list – appear to enjoy popular support. More steps designed to make the monarchy and the royal family more open – yet at the same time less open to personal criticism – would appear likely to bolster support for the institution. The deliberations of the 'Way Ahead Group' have been designed in part to bring the institution up to date and enhance such support.

Leave alone

The monarchy as it stands has some ardent admirers. Conservative MPs have generally moved quickly to defend the monarchy from criticism. 'The monarchy', declared Conservative MP John Stokes in the House of Commons in 1981, 'appeals to our sense of history, tradition and pageantry. There is no spectacle in the world to surpass the ceremony of the Queen opening Parliament.... Long may those marvellous ceremonies remain.' When a Fabian Society pamphlet, *Long to Reign Over Us?* was published in August 1996 (Richards 1996) advocating a referendum on the monarchy, a Conservative Cabinet minister, Michael Portillo, immediately portrayed it as an attack on the institution of monarchy. 'New Labour should be warned that they meddle with the monarchy at the nation's peril', he declared.

Though almost 30 per cent of respondents in the 1996 Gallup poll (Table 16.2) are content for the monarchy to stay as it is, this constitutes a decline in the percentage giving a similar response in earlier years (it was 36 per cent in September 1994, for example) and is obviously outweighed by those who wish to see modest changes made. As is clear from Table 16.2, 68 per cent of respondents want to see some change, be it modest or radical.

Chapter summary

The monarchy remains an important institution in British political life. The monarch's transition from directing the affairs of state to a neutral non-executive role has been a gradual and not always smooth one, but a move necessary to justify the monarch's continuing existence.

Transcending partisan activity is a necessary condition for fulfilling the monarch's symbolic ('standing for') role and hence a necessary condition for the strength and continuity of the monarchy. The dedication of the present monarch has served to sustain popular support for the institution. That support has dropped in the 1990s, criticism of the activities of members of the royal family rubbing off on the institution of monarchy itself. Popular support for the institution remains, but not at the same level of preceding decades. Most people when questioned want to see some change, with the monarchy and royal family being more democratic and approachable. Both main parties appear content to leave it to the monarch to undertake those changes.

Discussion points

- What is the point in having a monarchy?

- In what circumstances could the Queen become involved in making political decisions? Can and should such occasions be avoided?

- What are the most important roles fulfilled by the Queen in contemporary society?

- What public role, if any, should be played by members of the royal family, other than the Queen?

- Should the monarchy be left alone, reformed or abolished?

Further reading

There are a large number of biographies of members of the royal family and chronicles of royal activity – the book that sparked media interest in the state of the Prince of Wales's marriage was Morton (1992) – but few analyses of the role of the crown in political activity. The most recent – that by Bogdanor (1995) – seeks to transcend recent controversy. The book provides a good historical perspective on the role of the monarchy as well as offering a defence of the institution. Hardie (1970) provides a useful guide to the transition from political involvement to neutrality; Hibbert (1979) also offers a useful overview. In terms of the debate about the future of the monarchy, the most recent reform tract is that by Richards (1996). The principal works arguing for abolition are Nairn (1988) and Wilson (1989).

References

Altrincham, Lord *et al.* (1958) *Is the Monarchy Perfect?* (John Calder).

Benemy, F.W.G. (1965) *The Elected Monarch* (Harrap).

Birch, A.H. (1964) *Representative and Responsible Government* (Allen and Unwin).

Blackburn, R. (1992) 'The Future of the British Monarchy', in R. Blackburn (ed.), *Constitutional Studies* (Mansell).

Bogdanor, V. (1995) *The Monarchy and the Constitution* (Oxford University Press).

Cannon, J. and Griffiths, R. (1988) *The Oxford Illustrated History of the British Monarchy* (Oxford University Press).

Hardie, F. (1970) *The Political Influences of the British Monarchy 1868–1952* (Batsford).

Hibbert, C. (1979) *The Court of St James* (Weidenfeld and Nicolson).

Lacey, R. (1977) *Majesty* (Hutchinson).

Marr, A. (1995) *Ruling Britannica* (Michael Joseph).

Morton, A. (1992) *Diana: Her True Story* (Michael O'Mara Books).

Nairn, T. (1988) *The Enchanted Glass: Britain and its Monarchy* (Century Hutchinson Radius).

Pitkin, H.G. (1967) *The Concept of Representation* (University of California Press).

Richards, P. (1996) *Long to Reign Over Us?* (The Fabian Society).

Trevelyan, G.M. (1938) *The English Revolution 1688–9* (Thornton Butterworth).

Wilson, E. (1989) *The Myth of the British Monarchy* (Journeyman/Republic).

CHAPTER SEVENTEEN

The House of Commons

PHILIP NORTON

- To explain the importance of the House of Commons in terms of its historical development and current functions.

- To identify and assess the means available to Members of Parliament to fulfil those functions.

- To outline recent developments in the House and current proposals for reform.

INTRODUCTION

The House of Commons has evolved over seven centuries. At various times, it has played a powerful role in the affairs of the nation. Its most consistent activity has been to check the executive power. Its power has been limited by royal patronage and, more recently, by the growth of parties. It none the less remains an important part of the political process. It constitutes the only nationally elected body. It has to give its assent to measures of public policy. Ministers appear before it to justify their actions. It remains an arena for national debate and the clash of competing party views.

Origins of Parliament

Parliament has its origins in the thirteenth century. It was derived not from first principles or some grand design but from the King's need to raise more money. Its subsequent development may be ascribed to the actions and philosophies of different monarchs, the ambitions and attitudes of its members, external political pressures and prevailing assumptions as to the most appropriate form of government. Its functions and political significance have been moulded, though not in any consistent manner, over several hundred years.

Despite the rich and varied history of the institution, two broad generalisations are possible. The first concerns Parliament's position in relation to the executive. Parliament is not, and never has been on any continuous basis, a part of that executive. Though the Glorious Revolution of 1688 may have confirmed the form of government as that of 'parliamentary government', the phrase, as we have seen already (Chapter 14), means government through Parliament, not government by Parliament. There have been periods when Parliament has been an important actor in the making of public policy, not least for a period in the nineteenth century, but its essential and historically established position has been that of a reactive, or policy-influencing, assembly (Box 17.1; see Mezey, 1979; Norton, 1993); that is, public policy is formulated by the executive and then presented to Parliament for discussion and approval. Parliament has the power to amend or reject that which is placed before it, but it has not the capacity to substitute on any regular basis a policy of its own. Parliament has looked to the executive to take the initiative in the formulation of public policy and it continues to do so.

The second generalisation concerns the various tasks, or functions, fulfilled by Parliament. Parliament is a multi-functional body. It not only serves as a reactive body in the process of law-making, it carries out several other tasks as well. Its principal

tasks were established within the first two centuries of its development. In the fourteenth century, the King accepted that taxes should not be levied without the assent of Parliament. The giving of such assent was variously withheld until the King responded to petitions requesting a redress of grievances. At the same time, Parliament began to take an interest in how money was spent and began to look at the actions of public servants. It became, in a rather haphazard way, a body for the critical scrutiny of government.

The development of Parliament

Knights and burgesses were summoned in the thirteenth century in order to give assent to the King's decision to raise extra taxes. They joined the King's court, comprising the barons and leading churchmen of the realm. In the fourteenth century, the summoning of knights and burgesses became a regular feature of those occasions when the King summoned a 'parliament'. At various times during the century, the knights and burgesses sat separately from the barons and churchmen, and so there developed two chambers – the Commons and the Lords.

The House of Commons became more significant in subsequent centuries. It was a significant political actor during the Tudor reigns of the sixteenth century and a powerful opponent of the Stuart monarchs who asserted the divine right of kings to rule in the seventeenth. Clashes occurred between Parliament and Charles I and, later, James II. The fleeing of James II in 1688 allowed leading parliamentarians to offer the throne to James's daughter and son-in-law (Mary and William) on Parliament's terms and the supremacy of Parliament was established. Henceforth, the King could not legislate – or suspend laws – without the assent of Parliament.

Parliament none the less continued to look to the executive power – initially the King, and later the King's ministers assembled in Cabinet – to take the initiative in formulating measures of public policy. When measures were laid before Parliament, assent was normally forthcoming. In the eighteenth century, royal influence was employed, either directly or through the aristocratic patrons of 'rotten boroughs', to ensure the return of a House

BOX 17.1

Types of legislature

Policy-making legislatures: These are legislatures that can not only modify or reject measures brought by the executive but can also formulate and substitute policy of their own (e.g. the US Congress).

Policy-influencing legislatures: These are legislatures that can modify and sometimes reject measures brought forward by the executive but cannot formulate and substitute policy of their own (e.g. UK Parliament, German Bundestag).

Legislatures with little or no policy effect: These are legislatures than can neither modify or reject measures brought forward by the executive nor formulate and substitute policies of their own. They typically meet for only a few days each year to give formal approval to whatever is placed before them (e.g. former legislatures of Eastern European communist states, such as East Germany).

favourable to the ministry. This influence was broken in the nineteenth century. The 1832 Reform Act enlarged the electorate by 49 per cent and abolished many, though not all, rotten boroughs. The effect of the measure was to loosen the grip of the aristocracy on the House of Commons and to loosen the grip of the monarch on the choice of government. The last time a government fell for want of the monarch's confidence was in 1834. MPs entered a period when they were relatively independent in their behaviour, being prepared on occasion to oust ministers and sometimes governments (as in 1852, 1855, 1856 and 1866) and to amend and variously reject legislation. Except for the years from 1841 to 1846, party ties were extremely loose.

This 'golden age' was to prove short-lived. At that time, there was little public business to transact. That business was reasonably easy to comprehend. Members were not tied overly to party and could make a judgement on the business before them. The consequence of the 1867 Reform Act, enlarging the electorate by 88 per cent, and of later Acts reducing corrupt practices, was to create an electorate too large, and too protected, to be 'bought' by individual candidates. Extensive organisation was necessary to reach the new voters and organised political parties soon came to dominate elections. For promises made by parties to be carried out, a cohesive party in the House of Commons was necessary and by the end of the century cohesive party voting was a feature of parliamentary life. Party influence thus succeeded royal patronage in ensuring the assent of MPs for measures brought forward by ministers of the crown.

The effect on Parliament of the rise of a mass electorate was profound. Governments came to be chosen by the electorate, not – as in the preceding years – by the House of Commons. Popular demands on government engendered not only more measures of public policy, but more extensive and complex measures. By the turn of the century, Parliament lacked the political will and the institutional resources necessary to subject increasingly detailed government bills to sustained and effective scrutiny. Albeit in a somewhat different form to earlier centuries, executive dominance had returned.

For the House of Commons, though, the developments of the nineteenth century served to confirm it as the pre-eminent component of the King-in-Parliament. The Glorious Revolution had established Parliament's supremacy over the King. The rise of the democratic principle in the nineteenth century established the supremacy of the elected House over the unelected. The House of Commons was clearly a representative chamber in that it was freely elected and in that its members were returned to defend and pursue the interests of electors (see Chapter 16). The House of Lords could claim to be representative in neither sense. The subordinate position of the House of Lords was confirmed by statute in the Parliament Act of 1911.

The position so established in the nineteenth century continued into the twentieth. The House of Commons remained – and remains – the dominant chamber in a Parliament dominated by party, with the initiative for measures of public policy resting with the Cabinet and with a party majority in the House ensuring the passage of those measures.

That sets the historical context. What, then, is the contemporary position of the House of Commons? What are the essential characteristics of the House – its members and its procedures? What functions does it fulfil? What tools does it have at its disposal to fulfil them? And to what extent have developments in recent years strengthened or weakened its capacity to carry out those functions?

The House of Commons

The House of Commons now has 659 members. The number has varied, ranging in the twentieth century from a high of 707 (1918–22) to a low of 615 (1922–45). The number was reduced in 1922 because of the loss of (most) Irish seats; it has varied in post-war years and from 1945 to 1974 stood at 630; because of the increase in the size of the population, it was increased in 1974 to 635, in 1983 to 650, in 1992 to 651 and in 1997 to 659.

Elections

The maximum life of a Parliament is five years. Between 1715 and 1911, it was seven years.

Members (MPs) are returned for single-member constituencies. These have been the norm since the Reform Act of 1885, though twelve double-member constituencies survived until the general

BOX 17.2

The atmosphere of the house

Anyone entering the gothic splendour of the Houses of Parliament begins to experience its special atmosphere. The Speaker's procession which opens every day's proceedings at 2.25 p.m. (the House only sits in the morning on Wednesdays and Fridays) is almost a parody of solemnity. The peculiar archaic forms of address also amuse foreign visitors: MPs must not refer to others by name but as 'honourable members' for the constituency they represent. But the atmosphere is anything but formal on other occasions. Ministers sometimes lounge on the benches with feet resting on the table in front of the Speaker's Chair. Members do not by convention applaud but they often cheer loudly or wave their order papers: conversely they can heckle relentlessly and when roused make so much noise the Speaker's calls of 'order, order' often resemble the feeble cries of a schoolmaster who has completely lost control of his class.

The former Speaker, George Thomas, defended this behaviour as evidence of the House's life and vigour: a quiet legislature, he suggested, is invariably a lifeless one. Others argue that the noisy barracking of speakers is a necessary test of the person and their arguments: if MPs cannot defend their arguments in the face of such pressure they lack the mettle for higher office. This adversarial atmosphere is enhanced by two factors: the

Chamber of the House of Commons is very small – on big occasions MPs crowd onto the benches and many spill over into the galleries – and its rectangular shape encourages confrontation between government and opposition (Figure 17.1). Unlike many legislatures the government of the day is obliged to explain its actions continually and open itself to constant criticism. The US President does not face a critical Congress and can even hide away from the press if he so chooses. The British Prime Minister, however, has to face the leader of the opposition once a week over the dispatch box. The tension of such occasions and their theatricality imparts a drama to certain debates which compels interest and often gives birth to genuine oratory. British politicians, trained in the House of Commons, are often excellent debaters, used to thinking on their feet and experts in the use of wit to decorate their own arguments or demolish those of their opponents.

The special atmosphere of the House is therefore a product of its intimate geography combined with its robust debating traditions. This is what causes new members to quail as they stand to deliver their maiden speeches and which often exerts such an addictive hold upon MPs that election defeat assumes for them the status of tragedy.

election of 1950. The method of election employed is the 'first-past-the-post' system with the candidate receiving the largest number of votes being declared the winner. This again has been the norm since 1885, though not until the general election of 1950 (with the abolition of university seats, for which a system of proportional representation was used) did it become universal. Since 1951, the practice has been for all seats to be contested. In elections

before 1945 a significant fraction of Members – an average of 13 per cent – had been returned unopposed. As late as the 1951 election, four Ulster Unionist MPs were returned in uncontested elections.

Each constituency comprises a defined geographical area and the MP is returned to represent all citizens living within that area. (University seats were exceptional: the constituencies comprised

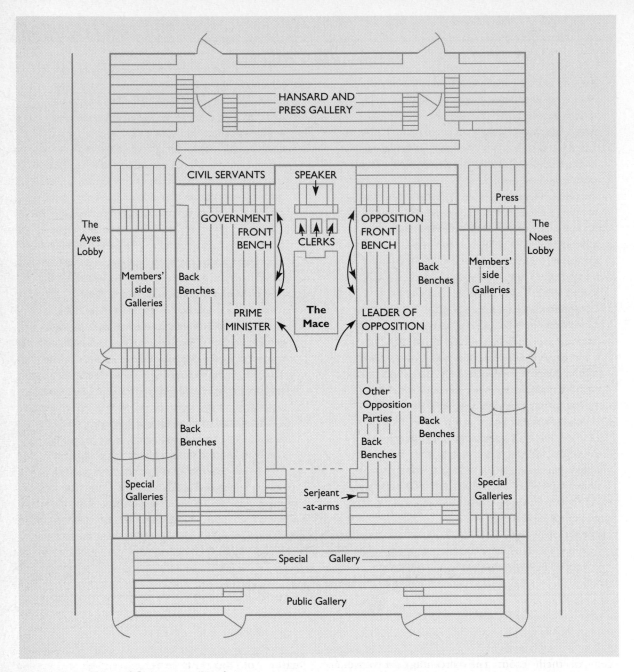

Figure 17.1   *House of Commons seating plan*

graduates of the universities, regardless of where they were living.) Constituency boundaries are drawn up and revised regularly by independent Boundary Commissions (one covering each country – England, Scotland, Wales and Northern Ireland); each Commission is chaired formally by the

Speaker of the House of Commons, though the essential work of leadership is undertaken by a deputy, who is a judge. Under existing legislation, boundary reviews are required every ten to fifteen years. The Commissions are enjoined to produce constituencies within each country of roughly equal size (in terms of the number of electors), though as far as possible retaining existing county and natural boundaries.

Members

Though the House may constitute a representative assembly in that it is freely elected and MPs are returned to defend and pursue the interests of constituents, it is not a representative assembly in being typical of the socio-economic population that elects it. The Members returned to the House are generally male, middle-class and white. These characteristics have been marked throughout the twentieth century. The House has tended to become even more middle class in the years since 1945. Before 1945, and especially in the early years of the century, the Conservative ranks contained a significant number of upper- and upper-middle class men of private means, while the parliamentary Labour party (the PLP) was notable for the number of MPs from manual-working backgrounds: they comprised a little over half of the PLP from 1922 to 1935 and before that had been in an overwhelming majority (Rush, 1979, pp. 69–123). Since 1945, the number of businesspeople on the Conservative benches has increased, as has the number of graduates, often journalists and lecturers, on the Labour benches.

The shift in the background of Conservative MPs since 1945 is reflected in education as well as occupation. In 1945, just over 83 per cent of Conservative MPs had been educated at public schools – 27 per cent at Eton. Almost two-thirds – 65 per cent – had been to university, with half having gone to Oxford or Cambridge. Over the next thirty years, the percentage of those educated at public school showed a decline but not a dramatic one. Of the Conservative MPs elected in October 1974, almost 75 per cent were products of public schools, 17 per cent of them Eton. The percentage of university graduates showed little change: just under 68 per cent, a 3 per cent increase on the 1945 figure. Oxbridge graduates accounted for just under 48 per cent of the total.

However, subsequent general elections – those of 1979 onwards – have shown a marked change in educational background. Of Conservative MPs elected for the first time in 1979, only just over half

had been to public school (13 per cent to Eton) and just over one-third (36 per cent) to Oxbridge. This trend was maintained in 1983. For the first time, less than half the new intake (47 per cent) had public school backgrounds (6 per cent Eton); again only just over a third (35 per cent) had been to Oxbridge. The percentage of those from public schools increased in 1987 – to 61 per cent of the new intake – but receded to just over 55 per cent in 1992. The proportion of old Etonians declined in each succeeding election. The new intake was displacing longer serving MPs with Eton and Oxbridge backgrounds. The percentage of public school educated MPs in 1992 was down to 62 per cent. The percentage of old Etonians was down to 10 per cent. University graduates constituted almost three-quarters of the party (73 per cent), but those who had been to Oxbridge were only 45 per cent of the total.

The changing patterns in education reflect a change in occupational background, with new Conservative MPs now being drawn as much from business backgrounds as the more traditional professional backgrounds. Within the business category, MPs are more likely to be drawn from the ranks of executives rather than from the ranks of directors.

On the Labour side, the notable change in educational background has been the rise in the number of graduates. In 1945, just over one-third of Labour MPs (34 per cent) had been to university. By 1970, just over half of the PLP were university graduates. By 1983, the figure was 54 per cent and in 1992 it had increased to 61 per cent. Most of these were graduates of universities other than Oxford and Cambridge. The percentage of Oxbridge-educated Labour MPs increased only marginally, from almost 15 per cent in 1945 to just over 16 per cent in 1992.

These figures reflect the growing middle-class nature of the PLP. The percentage of manual workers in the party declined in each successive Parliament until 1974, increased in 1979 and 1983, but then dropped back in 1987 and 1992. Only 17 per cent of new Labour MPs in 1992 were drawn from manual backgrounds. Fewer than one in four of Labour MPs in the 1992 Parliament could claim any form of manual background. 'Increasingly Labour MPs were defined by white collar public

Table 17.1 University education of candidates

	All parties' MPs, 1992	New MPs, 1997
Labour	61%	75%
Conservative	73%	90%
Liberal Democrat	75%	74%

Table 17.2 New MPs 1997: characteristics of MPs elected for first time in the 1997 general election, expressed as percentage of the new intake of each party

	Labour	Conservative	Liberal Democrat
Political staffers	20%	40%	32%
Councillors	64%	25%	70%
Women	35%	12%	7%

Source: *Financial Times*, 3 May 1997

sector employment, whether in education, politics or as officials in public sector unions; very small numbers of Labour candidates had any experience of either manual work or business' (Criddle, 1992, p. 225).

Indeed, there is something of a convergence between Members on both sides in terms of education and background. Of new MPs elected to the House of Commons, the vast majority – whether Conservative or Labour – are university educated (Table 17.1) and a large proportion are not only drawn from some middle-class occupation but an occupation that is in the domain of politics or communication.

Of MPs elected for the first time in the 1997 general election, more than three out of every four were university educated. Of new Conservative MPs, 90 per cent had been to university. Of the 178 new Labour MPs, 75 per cent had a university education. For new Liberal Democrat MPs, the proportion was 74 per cent. Of the new intake in 1997, teachers, journalists and political staffers were notable on the Labour benches and the last category – those who had worked in political positions such as advisers and researchers – were very much to the fore on the Conservative benches. Of the newly-elected Members, four out of every ten Conservatives, one in five Labour Members and one in three Liberal Democrats had previously been employed in political posts (see Table 17.2).

Where there is a difference between the two sides is in terms of council experience and in terms of gender. Labour MPs are more likely to have served as local councillors. As shown in Table 17.2, of the new MPs elected in 1997, almost two-thirds of Labour MPs had served as councillors, compared to one-quarter of Conservative MPs. There are also many more women sitting on the Labour benches

than on the Conservative (and Liberal Democrat) benches.

Women only became eligible to sit in the House in 1918. The number elected since then has been small. Between 1918 and 1974, the total number of women elected to the House was only 112 (including Countess Markievicz, the first woman elected but who did not take her seat). In the 1983 general election, twenty-three women were elected to the House, in 1987 the figure was forty-one, and in 1992 it was sixty, an all-time high. The Labour Party in 1993 adopted a policy of all-women short-lists in a number of constituencies in order to boost the number of female Labour MPs. Though the policy was struck down by an employment tribunal in 1996 (see Chapter 22) on the grounds that it breached sex discrimination legislation, it did not affect seats where female candidates had already been selected. As a result, a record number of female Labour MPs were elected in 1997: no less than 101, 64 of them elected for the first time. Though Conservative leaders encouraged local parties to adopt female candidates, very few did so. With a number of female Conservative MPs retiring in 1997, the result was a notable disparity between the two parties (see Table 17.2). The percentage of women MPs in the House of Commons in recent Parliaments remains low by international comparison (see Table 17.3), but it is less marked than before. The percentage of women MPs in the House is now 18 per cent.

The number of non-white MPs remains very small. For most of the twentieth century there were none at all. The first non-white MP was elected in 1892: Dadabhai Naoroji, an Indian, was elected as Liberal MP for Finsbury Central. Another Indian

Table 17.3 Women in national legislatures

Country	Women as % of total membership		
	1975	1985	1994
Sweden	21	31	41
Iceland	5	15	24
New Zealand	5	13	21
China	23	21	21
United States	4	5	11
Soviet Union/Russia	32	34	10
United Kingdom	4	4	9
India	4	8	7
Brazil	0	1	6
France	2	5	6
Japan	1	2	3
Turkey	8	3	2

Note: In bicameral legislatures, the figure refers to the elected lower chamber

Table 17.4 Average length of legislative service, 1994

Country	Average length of service (years)
Canada	6.5
France	7
Denmark	7.8
Germany	8.2
Israel	11
USA (Senate)	11.1
USA (House)	12.2
New Zealand	13.1
Japan	15
United Kingdom	20

Source: Somit and Roemmele, 1995

was elected as a Conservative three years later. A third sat from 1922 to 1929. There was then a fifty-eight-year gap. In 1987, four non-white MPs were elected. In 1992, the number increased to six – five Labour and one Conservative – and reached an all-time high in 1997. No less than nine were elected, including the first Muslim MP and two Sikhs. Even so, the number represents only a little more than 1 percent of the membership of the House.

One reason for the persistence of white, male MPs is the length of time that MPs typically serve in the House. Some MPs sit for thirty or forty years. The Father of the House of Commons (the longest continuously serving MP), Sir Edward Heath, was first elected in 1950. A typical Member sits for about twenty years. Even if parties are keen to replace existing MPs with candidates from a wider range of backgrounds, the opportunity to replace them does not necessarily come up very quickly. The length of service of legislators is a particular feature of the British House of Commons: MPs tend to serve as members longer than legislators in other comparable legislatures (see Table 17.4). Even in the 1997 general election, which – as a result of a massive swing to the

Labour party – brought in a record number of new MPs (no less than 253), more than 60 per cent of MPs had served in the previous Parliament. More than 30 MPs had been first elected to Parliament in 1970 or earlier.

Members are paid an annual salary. Until 1912 MPs received no payment at all. Since then, they have been paid, but on a relatively modest basis. In 1954, for example, the salary was £1,250 and in 1964 it was increased to £3,250. In January 1996, an MP's salary was £34,086, fairly modest in international comparison – legislators in Italy, the USA, France and Germany were all paid considerably more (more than twice as much in Italy and the USA) – and by comparison with higher levels of management in the UK. (Ministers receive higher salaries but retain part of their salaries as MPs.) In July 1996, MPs voted to increase their salaries by 26 per cent, to £43,000. The increase was controversial, and unpopular, but still left MPs lagging behind the salaries of members of other comparable legislatures.

Since the 1960s, parliamentary facilities have also improved. In the mid-1960s, an MP was guaranteed only a locker in which to keep papers and received no allowance, either for hiring a secretary or even to cover the cost of telephone calls. In 1969 a secretarial allowance was introduced. That allowance has evolved into an office cost allowance, allowing an MP to hire one and sometimes two secretaries and in most cases a (more often than not part-time) research assistant. In 1996, the office cost allowance stood at just over £40,000. Each Member now has desk space and, in most cases, an individual office. Offices are scattered about the Palace of Westminster and adjacent buildings. A new office complex has just been completed in Bridge Street (opposite the Palace of Westminster) and a second one is planned. By the turn of the century, every MP should have an office.

Sittings of the House

The House to which Members are returned meets annually, each parliamentary session running usually from October to October (or early November). There is a long summer adjournment, but the session is not prorogued (formally closed) until shortly after the House returns in the autumn; that allows the House to meet and deal with bills which have not completed their passage. The effect of prorogation is to kill off all unfinished public business; any bills which have not received the Royal Assent have to be reintroduced and go through all their stages again in the new session.

The House usually sits for more than 150 days a year, a not unusual number compared with some other legislatures, such as those of the USA, Canada and France, though considerably more than most other legislatures. What makes it distinctive is the number of hours for which it sits: it is not uncommon for it to sit more than 1,500 hours a year (see Table 17.5), more than any of the other legislatures mentioned.

Table 17.5 The House of Commons: length of sittings, 1987–92

Session	Number of sitting days	Number of hours sat	Average length on sitting day
1987–8[a]	218	1,978	9 hrs
1988–9	176	1,581	9 hrs 4 mins
1989–90	167	1,468	8 hrs 48 mins
1990–1	160	1,374	8 hrs 35 mins
1991–2[b]	83	696	8 hrs 23 mins

Note: [a] Long session
[b] Short session, because of the calling of the 1992 general election
Source: House of Commons Sessional Information Digests, 1987–92

The House meets at 2.30 p.m. on Mondays, Tuesdays and Thursdays and at 9.30 a.m. on Wednesdays and Fridays. It rises at 10.30 p.m. on the first four days of the week, though sittings may continue beyond that time in order to transact business. Late or all-night sittings may be held to get through the remaining stages of a bill, though such sittings are now very rare. (If the House has an all-night sitting and is still sitting at 2.30 p.m. the following day, the business for that next day falls.) On Fridays, the House rises at 3.00 p.m.

Functions

The principal function of the House is often seen as being that of being involved in law-making. It is, after all, classified as a legislature and the name means carrier, or giver, of law. In practice, much of the time of the House is given over to business that has nothing directly to do with legislation. Question Time is now an established feature of the House. It is not part of the legislative process. When the House debates the economy or the government's industrial policy, those debates again are not part of the formal legislative process. Some of the most notable speeches made in the House in the 1990s – not least the resignation speech of Sir Geoffrey Howe in 1990 – attracted considerable media attention, but again had nothing to do with the legislative process. The House has an important role to play in the legislative process, but it is clearly not its only role.

The principal functions of the House can be grouped under four headings: those of legitimisation, recruitment, scrutiny and influence, and expression. Several other functions can be identified (see Norton, 1993, Chapter 13) but these can largely be subsumed under these four broad headings.

Legitimisation

The primary purpose for which the representatives of the counties and boroughs (the communes) were first summoned was to assent to the King's demand for additional taxes. Subsequently, their assent also came to be necessary for legislation. The House has thus been, since its inception, a legitimising body. It fulfils what Robert Packenham has termed the function of 'latent legitimisation'. This derives from the fact that 'simply by meeting regularly and uninterruptedly, the legislature produces, among the relevant populace and elites, a wider and deeper sense of the government's moral right to rule than would otherwise have obtained' (Packenham, in Norton, 1990, p. 87). Given that Parliament not only sits regularly but has done so without interruption since the seventeenth century, it is arguably a much stronger agent of latent legitimisation that many other legislatures. It would seem plausible to hypothesise that the function is weaker in a political system in which the legislature is a recent and conscious creation of resuscitation by the prevailing regime. In Britain, legitimisation may also be reinforced by the fact that members of the government are drawn from, and govern through, Parliament – ministers remaining and fulfilling functions as Members of Parliament.

The House also fulfils the task of manifest legitimisation, that is, the overt, conscious giving of assent. This encompasses not only the giving of assent to bills – and requests for supply – laid before the House but also the giving of assent to the government itself. The government depends upon the confidence of the House of Commons for its continuance in office. If the House withdraws its confidence, then by convention the government resigns or requests a dissolution.

The House proceeds on the basis of motions laid before it: for example, to give a bill a second reading or to express confidence in the government. By approving such motions, the House gives its formal – manifest – assent. Members may vote on motions. The Speaker of the House asks those supporting the motion to say 'aye', those opposing to say 'no'. If no dissenting voices are heard, the motion is declared to be carried. If some MPs shout 'no' and persist then Members divide (that is, vote). A simple majority is all that is necessary. (Subject to two basic requirements: that at least forty MPs – a quorum – are shown by the division to be present and that, in voting on a closure motion, at least a hundred MPs have voted in favour.) Members vote by trooping through two lobbies – the division lobbies – where their names are recorded. The result of the vote is then announced in the chamber.

It is this accepted need for assent – for the House to confer legitimacy – that constitutes the basic power of the House in relation to government. Initially, the knights and burgesses summoned to the King's court were called to give assent, but with no recognition of any capacity to deny assent. Gradually, members began to realise that they could, as a body, deny assent to supply and later to legislation. This formed the basis on which they could ensure the effective fulfilment of other functions. It remains the basis of the power of the House of Commons. Without the assent of the House, no measure can become an Act of Parliament. The contemporary point of contention is the extent to which the House is prepared to use its power to deny assent. Critics contend that the effect of the growth of party and hence party cohesion has largely nullified the willingness of the House to employ it.

Recruitment

Ministers are normally drawn from, and remain within, Parliament. The situation is governed solely by convention. There is no legal requirement that a minister has to be an MP or peer.

The practice of appointing ministers from those who sit in Parliament derives from expediency. Historically, it was to the King's benefit to have his ministers in Parliament, where they could influence, lead and marshal support for the crown. It was to the benefit of Parliament to have ministers who could answer for their conduct. An attempt was made early in the eighteenth century to prevent ministers from sitting in Parliament, but the legislation was superseded by another law allowing the practice to continue (Norton, 1993, p. 34).

The convention that ministers be drawn from and remain within Parliament – predominantly now, by convention, the House of Commons – is a strong one inasmuch as virtually all ministers are MPs or peers. It is extremely rare for a minister to be appointed who does not sit in either House and even rarer for that person to remain outside Parliament while in office: the person is either elevated to the peerage (nowadays the most used route) or found a safe seat to contest in a by-election. Occasionally, one of the Scottish law officers – the Solicitor General for Scotland – is appointed from the ranks of Scottish lawyers and remains outside Parliament (this happened in both the 1987 and 1992 Parliaments, for example), but it is the exception that proves the rule.

The relationship between the House and ministers is governed by convention. Under the convention of individual ministerial responsibility, ministers are answerable to the House for their own conduct and that of their particular departments. Under the convention of collective ministerial responsibility, the Cabinet is responsible to the House for government policy as a whole. It is this latter convention that requires a request for a dissolution or the resignation of the government in the event of the House passing a motion of no confidence in the government.

The fact that ministers remain in Parliament clearly has a number of advantages to government. Things have not changed that much from earlier centuries in that ministers can use their positions to lead and marshal their supporters. Ministers themselves add notably to the voting strength of the government, the so-called 'payroll vote' in the House. In 1996, just over eighty ministers served in the Commons and just over twenty in the Lords. With ministers' unpaid helpers – parliamentary private secretaries – added to the number, the number swelled to over a hundred. The government thus has a sizeable guaranteed vote to begin with. Party loyalty – and ambition for office – usually ensures that the votes of back-benchers follow those of ministers.

The convention that ministers be drawn from the ranks of parliamentarians has certain advantages for Parliament. It ensures that members are proximate to ministers, both formally and informally. Ministers can be questioned on the floor of the House; they can be waylaid for private conversations and pleadings by Members in the corridors and division lobbies of the House. The fact that they remain as Members of the House means they retain some affinity with other Members. MPs elevated to ministerial office still retain their constituency duties.

Above all, though, the convention renders the House of Commons powerful as a recruiting agent. The route to ministerial office is through Parliament. In some other systems, the legislature is but one route to the top. In the USA, for example,

there are multiple routes: Cabinet ministers – and presidents – can be drawn from the ranks of business executives, academics, state governors, army officers and lawyers. The US Congress enjoys no monopoly on recruitment. In the UK, Parliament does have such a monopoly. Parliament is thus the exclusive route for those intending to reach the top of the political ladder. Those aspiring to ministerial office thus have to seek election to the House of Commons (or hope – usually in vain – for a peerage) and have to make their mark in the House. The House serves also as an important testing ground for potential ministers and, indeed, for those on the ministerial ladder. A poor performance at the dispatch box can harm a minister's chances of further promotion. A consistently poor performance can result in the minister losing office.

Scrutiny and influence

Scrutiny and influence are essentially conjoined functions. The House subjects both the measures and the actions of government to scrutiny. It does so through various means: debate, questioning and committee deliberations. If it does not like what is before it, it can influence the bill or the policy under consideration. It may influence solely by the force of argument. It may influence by threatening to deny assent (that is, by threatening to defeat the government). Ultimately, it may actually refuse its assent, denying the government a majority in the division lobbies.

These two functions are central to the activity of the House, and absorb most of its time. Government business enjoys precedence on most days. The House spends most of its time discussing legislation and the policy and actions of ministers. Though the growth of party has ensured that government is normally assured a majority in divisions, the party system helps ensure that government is subject to critical scrutiny from opposition parties in the House. The procedures of the House are premised on the existence of two principal parties, with each having the opportunity to be heard. Membership of all committees of the House replicates party strength on the floor of the House, thus ensuring the opposition has an opportunity to offer critical comments and to force government to respond at all stages of the parliamentary process.

Furthermore, scrutiny and influence may also take place outside, or despite, the context of party. MPs sit for particular constituencies. Though elected on a party label, they are none the less expected to ensure that government policy does not damage constituency interests. They may also be influenced by moral and religious views that ensure they pay careful attention to bills and government policies that run counter to their personal convictions.

However, the extent to which the House actually fulfils these functions is a matter of dispute. Critics contend that the government stranglehold, via its party majority, ensures that the House is denied the means for sustained and effective scrutiny, and that inasmuch as it may exert some limited scrutiny, that scrutiny is not matched by the capacity to influence government. MPs may consider and find fault with a particular measure, but not then prove willing to use their power to amend or reject it.

Expression

The House serves not one, but several expressive functions. Members serve to express the particular views and demands of constituents. An individual constituent or a group of constituents may be adversely affected by some particular policy or by the actions of some public officials. Constituents may feel that a particular policy is bad for the constituency or for the country. Contacting the local MP will usually result in the MP passing on the views to the relevant minister and may even result in the Member raising the issue on the floor of the House. The pursuit of such cases by MPs ensures that they are heard and considered by ministers.

MPs also express the views of different groups in society as a whole. A range of issues that do not fall within the ambit of party politics are taken up and pursued by private Members. MPs may express the views of organised interests, such as particular industries or occupations. They may express the views of different sectors of society, such as the elderly. Many will give voice to the concerns of

particular charitable, religious or moral groups. Some MPs press, for example, for reform of the laws governing abortion, some want to liberalise the laws concerning homosexuality, some want to ban hunting. These issues can be pursued by MPs through a number of parliamentary procedures. In some cases, Members table amendments to government bills. Another route is through the use of private Members' bills. Though the more contentious the issue, the less likely the bill is to be passed, the debate on the bill serves an important function: it allows the different views to be expressed in an authoritative public forum, heard by the relevant minister and open to coverage by the mass media.

MPs, then, serve to express the views of constituents and different groups to the House and to government. MPs may also serve to express the views of the House and of government to constituents and organised groups. The House may reach a decision on a particular topic. Members may then fulfil an important role in explaining why that decision was taken. Members individually may explain decisions to constituents. Select committees of the House may, in effect, explain particular policies through their reports which are read not just by government but by groups with a particular interest in the committee's area of inquiry. The House thus has a tremendous potential to serve several expressive functions. The extent to which it does so is a matter of considerable debate. MPs have limited time and resources to pursue all the matters brought to their attention. The attention given to their activities by the media and by government may be slight. Many groups may bypass Parliament in order to express their views directly to ministers. Furthermore, it is argued, the views expressed by MPs on behalf of others are drowned out by the noise of party battle. By limiting the resources of the House and by keeping information to itself, the government has limited the capacity of the House to arm itself with the knowledge necessary to raise support for public policies.

These are the most important functions that may be ascribed to the House. The list is not an exhaustive one. Other tasks are carried out by the House. These include, for example, a disciplinary role (punishing breaches of privilege and contempt) and a small quasi-judicial role, primarily in dealing with private legislation (legislation affecting private interests and not to be confused with private Members' legislation). Other functions often ascribed to the House can, as we have explained, be subsumed under the four main headings we have provided. However, two other functions, identified by Walter Bagehot in *The English Constitution* in 1867, have been lost by the House. One, the 'elective' function – that is, choosing the government – was held only briefly during the nineteenth century. Before then it was a function exercised by the monarch. Since then, it has passed largely, though not quite exclusively, to the electorate. The electorate chooses a government on a regular basis at general elections. The House retains the power to turn a government out through passing a motion of no confidence; but it is not a power it has regularly exercised.

The other function is that of 'legislation'. Initially, the need for the House to give its assent was transformed by Members into the power to initiate measures, first through the presentation of petitions to the crown and later through the introduction of bills. This power was important during the 'golden age' of Parliament in the nineteenth century, when the House could be described as sharing the legislative power with government. Even so, its exercise was limited. Most legislation introduced into the House was private legislation. Since then, public legislation has expanded as party has become more powerful. Party has ensured that the power to formulate – to 'make' – legislation rests with government, with the House then giving its assent. Insofar as the House has retained a residual legislative power, it is exercised through the medium of private Members' legislation. Even that legislative power, however, can be described now as one shared with government. Since 1959, no private Member's bill which has been the subject of a vote at second reading has made it to the statute book without government providing time for it.

Scrutiny and influence

The functions that the House retains can be described as modest but appropriate to a reactive legislature. They have developed over time. But how

Table 17.6 Time spent on the floor of the House 1994–5

Business	%
Addresses, including debate on Queen's Speech	3.0
Government bills	
Second reading	8.8
Committee of the Whole House	2.2
Report	7.6
Third Reading	1.0
Lords amendments	1.0
Allocation of time orders	0.0
Private Members' bills	4.9
Private business	1.1
Government motions	
EC documents	1.0
Business motions	0.0
General	3.3
Opposition motions	
Opposition days	9.6
Opposition motions in government time	0.0
Private Members' motions	1.2
Adjournment	
Government debates	10.7
Back-bench	16.6
Estimates	1.3
Money resolutions	0.1
Ways and means resolutions (including budget debate)	2.8
Statutory instruments	6.6
Question Time	9.1
Statements etc.	6.0
Miscellaneous	0.6
Daily prayers	0.6

Source: Figures calculated from *House of Commons Sessional Information Digest 1994–95*

well are they presently carried out? The principal functions of the House in relation to the executive are those of scrutiny and influence. The means available to the House to fulfil those functions are also at the disposal of Members for expressing the views of their constituents and of wider interests.

Table 17.7   Legislative stages

Stage	Where taken	Comments
First reading	On the floor of the House	Formal introduction: no debate
Second reading	On the floor of the House[a]	Debate on the principle
[Money resolution: Commons	On the floor of the House]	
Committee	In standing committee in the Commons unless House votes otherwise (certain bills taken on the floor of the House); almost invariably on the floor of the House in the Lords	Considered clause by clause; amendments may be made
Report	On the floor of the House	Bill reported back to House; amendments may be made
Third reading	On the floor of the House[b]	Final approval: no amendments possible in the Commons
Lords (or Commons) amendments	On the floor of the House	Consideration of amendments made by other House

Notes: [a] In the Commons, non-contentious bills may be referred to a committee
[b] If a bill is taken in committee of the whole House and no amendments are made, there is no report stage

They can be grouped under two headings: legislation and executive actions.

Legislation

When legislation is introduced, it has to go through a well-established process involving debate and consideration in committee. About one-third of the time of the House is taken up with debate on bills, the bulk of it on government bills. (Private Members' legislation occupies just under 5 per cent of time on the floor of the House: see Table 17.6.) Every bill has to go through three 'readings' plus a committee and (usually) a report stage. The stages are shown in Table 17.7.

The first reading marks the formal introduction. No debate takes place. Indeed, at this stage there is not even a printed bill. All that is read out is the bill's title. Following first reading, the bill is printed. Second reading comprises a debate on the principle of the measure. Most government bills

will be allocated a half or a full day's debate for second reading. Major bills, especially of constitutional significance, may be given two or more days for debate. In 1992, for example, the European Communities (Amendment) Bill – to ratify the Maastricht Treaty – was given a two-day debate.

The debate itself follows a standard pattern: the minister responsible for the bill opens the debate, explaining the provisions of the bill and justifying its introduction. The relevant shadow minister then makes a speech from the opposition front bench, outlining the stance of the opposition on the bill. After these two front-bench speeches, most Members present tend to leave the chamber, leaving usually a small number of MPs to listen to the remaining speeches. Back-benchers from both sides of the House are then called alternately, plus usually a Member from one or more of the minor parties, and the debate is then wound up with speeches from the opposition and government front benches.

(The House tends to fill up again for the winding-up speeches.) If the bill is contested, the House then divides. Debates, though not predictable in content, are generally so in outcome: only three times this century has the government lost a vote on second reading (in 1924, 1977 and 1986). Speeches on occasion may influence some votes, even whole debates, but they are exceptional. A government sometimes loses the argument but not usually the vote.

Once approved in principle, the bill is then sent to committee for detailed scrutiny. Some bills, because of their constitutional significance or because of the need for a speedy passage, will have their committee stage on the floor of the House. The European Communities (Amendment) Bill in 1992, for example, was taken in committee of the whole House (CWH). The majority of bills, though, are sent to a standing committee, the standard practice since 1907. The name 'standing committee' is a misnomer: there is nothing permanent, or 'standing', about it. Each committee is appointed afresh for each bill. The committees are identified by letters of the alphabet: standing committee A, standing committee B, and so on. One committee (standing committee C) normally deals with private Members' legislation. Once standing committee A has completed consideration of a bill, a new standing committee A – that is, with a different membership – is appointed to consider another bill. Because of the number of bills introduced each session, it is common for five or more standing committees to be in existence at any one time. Each committee comprises between sixteen and fifty members (for most bills, eighteen is the standard), reflecting proportionately the party strength in the House as a whole. The purpose of the committee is to render a bill 'more generally acceptable' through scrutinising it and, if necessary, amending it. (It cannot reject it or make any amendment that runs counter to the principle of the bill which has been approved by the House on second reading.) Each bill is considered clause by clause, the committee discussing and deciding on any amendments tabled to a clause before approving (or rejecting) the motion 'that the clause stand part of the bill'.

Committee stage constitutes the most criticised stage of the legislative process. Discussion in committee will often follow the adversarial lines adopted in the second reading debate. Traditionally, a great deal of time has been taken up with the earlier and more controversial clauses of a bill. If debate on the early clauses drags on, the government may resort to a timetable (guillotine) motion. This can result in later clauses getting little or no attention. Each committee resembles the House in miniature, with a minister and a whip appointed on the government side, and the minister's opposite number and a whip serving on the opposition side. Both sides face one another and the whips operate to marshal their members. Though cross-voting by government back-benchers can result in some defeats for the government, such occurrences are rare. The government is able to call on its supporters who constitute not only a majority but often a fairly silent majority on the committee. In order not to delay proceedings, government back-benchers are encouraged to keep as quiet as possible. In consequence, service on standing committees is often not popular, government back-benchers treating it as a chore and using the opportunity to read and sometimes write replies to correspondence.

Because of criticism of the whole process, the two principal parties in the House agreed in 1994 to a voluntary timetabling of bills. This meant that each bill was subject to an agreed timetable, thus avoiding the need for a guillotine to be introduced. There is, as we shall see, pressure for such timetabling to be a compulsory feature of the legislative process.

After committee stage, a bill returns to the House for report stage. This provides an opportunity for the House to decide whether it wishes to make any further amendments and is often used by the government to introduce amendments promised during committee stage, as well as any last-minute (sometimes numerous) amendments of its own. There is, though, no report stage if a bill has been taken for its committee stage on the floor of the House and been passed unamended.

There then follows the bill's third reading, when the House gives its final approval to the measure. Such debates are often short. If the bill is not contentious, there may be no debate at all. On completion of third reading, the bill then goes to the House of Lords and, if the Lords makes any amendments, the bill then returns to the Commons for it to consider the amendments. In most cases, the amendments are accepted. If not, the Lords usually gives way. Once both Houses have approved the bill, it then goes to the Queen for the Royal Assent.

All bills, with certain exceptions, go through this procedure. There are some variations: some uncontentious bills, for example, can be sent to a second reading committee, thus avoiding taking up valuable debating time on the floor of the House. There is also provision for bills to be considered at committee stage by a special standing committee, the committee being empowered to take evidence from witnesses. This power, though, has only been used sparingly, a total of seven times since 1981. Private Members' bills are also treated differently, primarily in terms of timetabling. They have to go through all the stages listed, but time for their consideration on the floor of the House is extremely limited. Each session a ballot is held, and the names of twenty private Members drawn. They are then entitled to introduce bills during the Fridays allocated to such bills, but only about the top half-dozen are likely to achieve full debates.

Bills constitute primary legislation. They often contain powers for regulations to be made under their authority once enacted. These regulations – known as delegated legislation – may be made subject to parliamentary approval. (Under the affirmative resolution procedure, the regulation must be approved by Parliament in order to come into force; under the negative resolution procedure it comes into force unless Parliament disapproves it.) Some regulations, though, only have to be laid before the House and others do not even have to be laid.

Given the growth of delegated legislation in post-war years, the House has sought to undertake scrutiny of it. Detailed, and essentially technical, scrutiny is undertaken by a Select Committee on Statutory Instruments. However, there is no requirement that the government has to wait for the committee to report on a regulation before bringing it before the House for approval, and on occasion – though not frequently – the government will seek approval before a regulation has been considered by the committee. Time for debate is also extremely limited and

much delegated legislation is hived off for discussion in a standing committee on delegated legislation. Similar procedures are adopted for draft European Community legislation: it is considered by a committee and, if recommended for debate, is discussed by one of two European standing committees.

Executive actions

There are various means employed to scrutinise and to influence the actions of government. These same means can be and usually are employed by MPs to express the views of constituents and different interests in society. The means essentially are those available on the floor of the House (debates and Question Time); those available on the committee corridor (select committees); and those available off the floor of the House (early day motions, correspondence, the parliamentary commissioner for administration, party committees and all-party groups). Some individually are of limited use. It is their use in combination that can be effective in influencing government.

Debates and Question Time

Most of the time of the House is taken up debating or questioning the actions of government. **Debates** take different forms. They can be on a substantive motion (for example, congratulating or condemning the policy of the government on a particular issue) or, in order to allow wide-ranging discussion (especially on a topic on which the government may have no fixed position), on an adjournment motion ('That this House do now adjourn'). For example, prior to the Gulf War at the beginning of 1991, the situation in the Gulf was debated on an adjournment motion. After military action had begun, the House debated a substantive motion approving the action. Adjournment debates under this heading can be described as full-scale adjournment debates. They are distinct from the half-hour adjournment debates which take place at the end of every sitting of the House. These half-hour debates take the form of a back-bencher raising a particular issue and the relevant minister then responding. After exactly half an hour, the debate concludes and the House adjourns.

Debates are initiated by different bodies in the House. Most motions initiated by government are to approve legislation. However, government will occasionally initiate debates on particular policies. More frequently, debates are started by opposition parties. There are twenty days each year which are designated as opposition days. On seventeen of these twenty days, the motion (or motions – a day's debate can be split into two) is chosen by the leader of the opposition. On the remaining three days, the topic is chosen by the leader of the third largest party in the House (the Liberal Democrats), though at least one day is usually given over to the other minor parties. There are also three estimates days each session, the choice of estimate for debate being made by a select committee of the House: the Liaison Committee, comprising primarily the MPs who chair other select committees. Three Wednesday mornings are now given over to debate on select committee reports and the other Wednesday mornings are given over to debate on topics raised by private Members. Private Members are also responsible for initiating the topics in the daily half-hour adjournment debates: on four days a week, Members are selected by ballot and on one the Speaker chooses the Member. These back-benchers' occasions provide opportunities to raise essentially non-partisan issues, especially those of concern to constituents. Though such debates are poorly attended, they allow Members to put an issue on the public record and elicit a response from government.

The half-hour adjournment debates involve a back-bencher raising an issue, sometimes one or two other back-benchers making quick contributions, and then a response from a minister. Wednesday morning debates involve several such mini-debates. Full-scale half-day or full-day debates initiated by government or opposition resemble instead the practice adopted in second reading debates. There are speeches from the two front benches, followed by back-bench speeches alternating between the two sides of the House, followed by winding-up speeches from the front benches, and then, if necessary, a vote. The term 'debate' is itself a misnomer. Members rarely debate but rather deliver prepared speeches which often fail to take up the points made by preceding speakers. Members wishing to take part usually inform the Speaker in advance and can usually obtain some indication from the Speaker if and when are they are likely to be called. There is a tendency for Members not to stay for the whole debate after they have spoken. Members, especially back-benchers, frequently address a very small audience – sometimes no more than half-a-dozen MPs. There is a prevailing view in the House that attendance has dropped over recent years. MPs now have offices they can spend time in. There are competing demands on their time and as the outcome of most votes is predictable – and Members know perfectly well how they intend to vote – there appears often little incentive to spend time in the chamber. Major set-piece debates – as on a motion of confidence – and a debate in which the outcome is uncertain can still attract a crowded chamber, some Members having to sit on the floor or at the bar of the House in order to listen to the proceedings. Such debates are exceptional. On most days, MPs addressing the House do so to rows of empty green benches.

Debates take place on motions. However, there is one form of business taken on the floor of the House which departs from the rule requiring a motion to be before the House. That is *Question Time*. This takes place on four days of the week – Monday to Thursday – when the House is sitting. It starts shortly after 2.30 p.m. (some minor business is transacted – announcements from the Speaker, certain non-debatable motions concerning private legislation – before it gets under way) and it concludes at 3.30 p.m. Speaker Betty Boothroyd has adopted the practice of ending Question Time with the words 'time's up'!

Question Time itself is of relatively recent origin (see Franklin and Norton, 1993). The first recorded instance of a question being asked was in the House of Lords in 1721 and the first printed notice of questions to ministers was issued in 1835. The institution of a dedicated slot for Prime Minister's questions is of even more recent origin, dating from July 1961. From 1961 to 1997, the Prime Minister answered questions for fifteen minutes on two days of the week. In May 1997, the new Labour Prime Minister, Tony Blair, changed the procedure, answering questions for thirty minutes once a week.

The practice of asking questions is popular with MPs and demand to ask questions exceeds the time available. Members are thus restricted in the number they can put on the order paper: no more than eight in every ten sitting days and no more than two on any one day. (If two are are on the order paper on the same day, they may not be to the same minister.) Questions must be precisely that – that is, questions (statements and expressions of opinion are inadmissible) – and each must be on a matter for which the minister has responsibility. There is also an extensive list of topics (including arms sales, budgetary forecasts, and purchasing contracts) on which government will not answer questions.

Ministers answer questions on a rota basis, most ministries coming up on the rota every four weeks. Some of the smaller ministries have slots in Question Time from 3.10 p.m. onwards. All questions tabled by Members used to be printed on the order paper, a practice that was costly and largely pointless. The number tabled often ran into three figures but the number that were actually answered in the time available was usually fewer than twenty. Following changes approved by the House in 1990, only the top thirty or so – chosen in advance by random selection – are now printed.

The MP with the first question rises and says 'Question Number One, Madam Speaker' and then sits down. The minister rises and replies to the question. The MP is then called to put a follow up – or 'supplementary' – question, to which the minister responds. Another Member may then be permitted by the Speaker to put another supplementary. If an opposition front-bencher rises, he or she has priority. During Prime Minister's Question Time, the leader of the opposition is frequently at the dispatch box. The Speaker decides when to move on to the next question.

Question Time is not the only opportunity afforded MPs to put questions to ministers. Members can also table questions for written answer. The questions, along with ministers' answers, are published in *Hansard*, the official record of parliamentary proceedings. There is no limit on the number of questions that an MP can table – some table several hundred in a session – and they can be answered at greater length than is possible during Question Time.

Question Time itself remains an important opportunity for back-benchers to raise issues of concern to constituents and to question ministers on differing aspects of their policies and intentions. However, it has become increasingly adversarial in nature, with opposition front-benchers participating regularly – a practice that has developed over the past thirty years – and with questions and supplementaries often being partisan in content. Some Members view the proceedings, especially Prime Minister's Question Time, as a farce. However, it remains an occasion for keeping ministers on their toes (figuratively as well as literally) and it ensures that a whole range of issues are brought to the attention of ministers. It also ensures that much material is put on the public record that would not otherwise be available.

Select committees

The House has made greater use in recent years of select committees, appointed not to consider the particular details of bills (the role of standing committees) but to consider particular subjects assigned by the House. Historically, they are well-established features of parliamentary scrutiny. They were frequently used in Tudor and Stuart Parliaments. Their use declined in the latter half of the nineteenth century, the government – with its party majority – not looking too favourably on bodies that could subject it to critical scrutiny. For most of the twentieth century, the use of such committees has been very limited. The position changed in the 1960s and, more dramatically, in the 1970s.

The House has a number of long-standing select committees concerned with its privileges and internal arrangements. However, for the first half of the twentieth century, the House only had two major select committees for investigating the policy or actions of government: the Public Accounts Committee (the PAC) and the Estimates Committee. Founded in 1861, the PAC remains in existence and is the doyen of investigative select committees. It undertakes *post hoc* (i.e. after the event) scrutiny of public expenditure, checking to ensure that it has been properly incurred for the purpose for which it was voted. The Estimates Committee was first appointed in 1912 for the purpose of examining ways in which policies could be carried out cost-effectively. In abeyance from 1914 to 1921 and again during the Second World War, it fulfilled a useful but limited role. It was abolished in 1971 and replaced by an Expenditure Committee with wider terms of reference.

The PAC and Estimates Committees were supplemented in the 1940s by a Select Committee on Statutory Instruments and in the 1950s by one on nationalised industries. There was a more deliberate and extensive use of select committees in the latter half of the 1960s. The Labour Leader of the House, Richard Crossman, introduced several reforms to try to increase the efficiency and influence of the House, and the more extensive use of select committees was a central feature of the Crossman reforms. Select committees on agriculture and on science and technology were established, followed by committees on education, overseas development, race relations and immigration and Scottish affairs. (One was also appointed with responsibility for the parliamentary commissioner for administration, the ombudsman.) However, the experience of the committees did not meet the expectations of their supporters. They suffered from limited resources, limited attention (from back-benchers, government and the media), limited powers (they could only send for 'persons, papers and records' and make recommendations), the absence of any effective linkage between their activities and the floor of the House, and the lack of a coherent approach to, and coverage of, government policy. The agriculture committee was wound up after it clashed with the Ministry of Agriculture and Foreign Office over its attempts to investigate European Community policy. Two other committees were wound up after the creation of the Expenditure Committee, their areas of interest being covered by subcommittees of the new committee. The result was a patchwork quilt of committees, with limited coverage of public policy.

Recognition of these problems led to the appointment in 1976 of a Procedure Select Committee, which reported in 1978. It recommended the appointment of a series of select committees, covering all the main departments of state, with wide terms of reference, and with power to appoint specialist advisers as the committees deemed appropriate. It also recommended that committee members be selected independently of the whips, the task to be undertaken by the Select Committee of Selection, the body formally responsible for nominating members. At the beginning of the new Parliament in 1979, the Conservative Leader of the House, Norman St John-Stevas, brought forward motions to give effect to the Procedure Committee recommendations. By a vote of 248 to 12, the House approved the creation of the new committees. Initially, twelve were appointed, soon joined by committees covering Scottish and Welsh affairs. In the light of their appointment, various other committees were wound up. The PAC and the Committee on the Parliamentary Commissioner were retained. In 1980, a Liaison Select Committee, comprising predominantly select committee chairmen, was appointed to coordinate the work of the committees.

The fourteen new committees began work effectively in 1980. Their number has fluctuated since, reflecting usually changes in departmental structure. Committees were also added to cover sectors or departments not previously covered, notably science and technology and, in 1994, Northern Ireland. By 1996 no fewer than seventeen departmental select committees were in existence, the largest number ever to be appointed. Thirteen non-departmental select committees were also appointed, most of them 'domestic' committees (administration, catering and selection, for example) but also including the PAC, Statutory Instruments and European Legislation Committees.

The seventeen departmental select committees appointed in 1996 are listed in Table 17.8. Each committee (except for Northern Ireland and Education and Employment) has eleven members and is established 'to examine the expenditure, administration and policy' of the department or departments it covers and of associated public bodies. The chairmanships of the committees are shared between the parties though the committee members are responsible for electing one of their own number from the relevant party to the chair. This power vested in committee members has variously resulted in the election of independent-minded chairmen who have been thorns in the flesh of government ministers: for example, in the 1992 Parliament, Sir Malcolm Thornton (education) and, from 1992 until his death in 1993, Robert Adley (transport), both critics of government policy in the areas covered by their committees.

Table 17.8 Departmental select committees, 1996

Committee	Chairman
Agriculture	Sir Jerry Wiggin (Con.)
Defence	Michael Colvin (Con.)
Education and Employment	Sir Malcolm Thornton (Con.)
Environment	Andrew Bennett (Lab.)
Foreign Affairs	Rt Hon. David Howell (Con.)
Health	Marion Roe (Con.)
Home Affairs	Sir Ivan Lawrence (Con.)
National Heritage	Rt Hon. Gerald Kaufman (Lab.)
Northern Ireland	Clive Soley (Lab.)
Public Service	Giles Radice (Lab.)
Science and Technology	Sir Giles Shaw (Con.)
Scottish Affairs	William McKelvey (Lab.)
Social Security	Frank Field (Lab.)
Trade and Industry	Martin O'Neill (Lab.)
Transport	Rt Hon. Paul Channon (Con.)
Treasury	Matthew Carrington (Con.)
Welsh Affairs	Gareth Wardell (Lab.)

Each committee has control of its own agenda and decides what to investigate. Unlike standing committees, they have power to take evidence and much of their time is spent questioning witnesses. Each committee normally meets once a week – for most committees, on Wednesday – when the House is sitting in order to hold a public, evidence-taking session. Unlike standing committees, the committees are not arranged in adversarial format, government supporters facing opposition MPs, but instead sit in a horseshoe shape, MPs sitting around the horseshoe – not necessarily grouped according to party – with the witness or witnesses seated in the gap of the horseshoe. Each session will normally last between sixty and ninety minutes.

Committee practices vary (see Drewry, 1989). Some hold long-term inquiries. Some go for short-term inquiries and some adopt a mixture of the two approaches. Some will also summon senior ministers for a single session just to review present policy and not as part of a continuing inquiry. The Chancellor of the Exchequer, for example, appears each year before the Treasury Committee for a wide-ranging session on economic policy. Though committees cannot force ministers to attend, the attendance of the appropriate minister is normally easily arranged.

So, too, is the attendance of civil servants, though they cannot divulge information on advice offered to ministers or express opinions on policy: that is left to ministers. Attendance by ministers and civil servants before committees is regular and frequent, though most witnesses called by committees represent outside bodies. In investigating a particular subject, a committee will call as witnesses representatives of bodies working in the area or with a particular expertise or interest in it. Figure 17.2 shows but part of the agenda of select committee meetings and witnesses in a typical week.

At the conclusion of an inquiry, a committee draws up a report. The report is normally drafted by the committee clerk – a full-time officer of the House – under the guidance of the chairman. It is then discussed in private session by the committee. Amendments are variously made, though it is relatively rare for committees to divide along party lines. Once agreed, the report is published. The committees are prolific in their output. Between 1979 and 1992, they issued just over 900 substantive reports (see Norton, 1993, p. 100). Most reports embody recommendations for government action. A proportion, but far from all, of the recommendations are accepted by government. In one year in the 1980s, the government acknowledged that in that year it had accepted 150 recommendations emanating from select committees. The number, though, constituted a minority of the recommendations made.

The departmental select committees, like the House itself, are multi-functional. They serve several purposes. They have added considerably to the store of knowledge of the House. They provide an important means for specialisation by Members. They serve an important expressive function. By calling witnesses from outside groups, they allow those groups to get their views on the public record. The evidence from witnesses is published. The committees may take up the cases espoused by some of the groups, ensuring that the issue is brought on to the political agenda. The reports from the committees are read and digested by the groups, thus providing the committees with the potential to serve as important agents for mobilising support. Above all, though, the committees serve as important means for scrutinising and influencing government, especially the former. Ministers and civil servants

	Time	Room/Place
MONDAY 19 JULY		
DEFENCE	2.45	15
Subject: Statement on the Defence Estimates 1993		
Witness: Rt Hon Malcolm Rifkind QC MP, Secretary of State for Defence		
SCOTTISH AFFAIRS	10.45	Crown
Subject: Drug abuse in Scotland		Office
Witnesses: Greater Glasgow Health Board: Lothian Health Board (at 11.30 am		Building,
approx); Tayside Health Board (at 12.15 pm approx)		Edinburgh
TUESDAY 20 JULY		
NATIONAL HERITAGE	10.30	15
Subject: Future of the BBC		
Witnesses: Classic FM; Association of Independent Radio Companies;		
BBC Network Radio and BBC Regional Broadcasting		

Figure 17.2   *Meetings of select committees*

know they may be called before committees to account for their actions. Committee sessions allow MPs to put questions to ministers in greater detail than is possible on the floor of the House. It gives MPs the only opportunity they have to ask questions of officials. Not only will poor performances be noted – not least by the media present – but poor answers may attract critical comment in the committee's report. No minister or official wishes to be seen squirming in the face of difficult questions.

Select committees have thus developed as a major feature of parliamentary activity, with most MPs viewing that activity in a positive light. None the less, limitations remain. The committees have limited powers and limited resources. They have only the time and resources to investigate a small number of issues. The number of reports they issue massively exceeds the time available on the floor of the House to debate them. Most reports will not be mentioned on the floor of the House or even read by most MPs. Government is committed to providing a written response to committee reports but under no obligation to take action on the recom-

mendations made in those reports. And although ministers and officials appear before committees, they do not necessarily reveal as much as the committees would like. Though the committees constitute a major step forward for the House of Commons, many MPs would like to see them strengthened.

Early day motions

Of the other devices available to Members, early day motions (EDMs) are increasingly popular, though of limited impact. A Member may table a motion for debate 'on an early day'. In practice, there is invariably no time to debate such motions. However, they are printed and other MPs can add their names to them. Consequently, they are used as a form of parliamentary noticeboard. If a motion attracts several hundred signatures, it may induce the government to take some action. This occasionally happens. Motions tabled by Conservative MPs are believed to have influenced the Conservative government in the 1980s to move quicker than it planned to abolish the Inner London Education

Authority and to ensure that compulsory membership of student unions was ended. Such occasions, though, are rare. EDMs are more often used for fulfilling an expressive function, allowing Members to make clear their views on a range of issues, often reflecting representations made to them by people and groups outside the House. Examples of such EDMs are illustrated in Figure 17.3. The range of topics is extremely broad and the number of motions tabled an increasingly large one. In the 1970s and 1980s, three or four hundred a year were tabled. In the 1990s, the number each year exceeds one thousand. The consequence is that their use as a means of indicating strength of opinion on an issue of political significance is devalued. Their utility, which was always limited, is thus marginal, though not non-existent. They still give MPs the opportunity to put issues of concern on the public record.

Correspondence

The means so far considered have been public means by which MPs can scrutinise government and

---

No. 135	Notices of Motions: 10th March 1993	6303

1089   *PARLIAMENTARY SCRUTINY OF THE SECURITY SERVICE*   15:12:92

    Mr David Winnick
    Mr Tony Worthington
    Mr Mike Gapes
    Mr Clive Soley
    Dr Norman A. Godman
    Mr Calum Macdonald

        ★ 112

      Mr Doug Hoyle   Mr Llew Smith   Mr Ieuan Wyn Jones
     That this House is strongly of the opinion that the security services should be subject to Parliamentary scrutiny; and moreover is opposed to a committee composed only of privy counsellors being established, which would be outside the normal Select Committee structure.

1092   *ACCOUNTABILITY OF THE WORLD BANK*   15:12:92

    Mr Mike Watson
    Mr John Denham
    Mr Derek Enright
    Mr Ernie Ross
    Mr John Battle
    Mr Jim Dowd

        ★ 65

      Mr D. N. Campbell-Savours   Mr Llew Smith
     That this House notes that an internal World Bank report concluded that 35 per cent of its projects are 'unsuccessful'; further notes that as a result of this high failure rate, British taxpayers could be throwing as much as £50 million down the drain annually; believes that new British funding to the Bank's concessionary lending wing, the International Development Association, must be linked to greater accountability; and calls on the Government to ensure that this matter is pursued as a matter of urgency.

Figure 17.3   These examples of early day motions show how MPs use this device to draw attention to particular issues.

make representations to it. However, a number of private means exist, two official, and two unofficial. One official means is through corresponding with ministers. Since the 1950s, the flow of letters from constituents to MPs has grown enormously. The flow increased significantly in the 1960s and increased dramatically in subsequent decades. The typical MP in the 1990s receives in one day the amount of mail that the typical MP used to receive in one week in the 1960s. The usual method for an MP to pursue a matter raised by a constituent is by writing to the relevant minister, usually forwarding the letter from the constituent. At least 10,000 to 15,000 letters a month are written by MPs to ministers.

For an MP, writing to a minister is one of the most cost-effective ways of pursuing constituency casework (see Norton and Wood, 1993, Chapter 3). A letter invites a considered, often detailed response, usually free of the party pressures that prevail in the chamber; by being a private communication, it avoids putting a minister publicly on the defensive. Ministers are thus more likely to respond sympathetically in the use of their discretion than is the case if faced with demands on the floor of the House. Furthermore, there is no limit on the number of letters an MP can write and those letters can be dictated usually at a time of the Member's choosing. Letters from MPs to ministers are accorded priority in a department – each is circulated in a special yellow folder – and have to be replied to by a minister. If a letter fails to obtain the desired response, the Member has the option of then taking the matter further, either by seeing the minister or by raising the matter publicly on the floor of the House.

Correspondence is a valuable and efficient means of ensuring a matter is considered by a minister. A great many letters on a particular problem can alert a minister to the scale of that problem and produce action. Letter writing is also a valuable means of fulfilling an expressive function. Most constituents who write do so to express a particular viewpoint or in order to obtain an authoritative explanation of why some action was or was not taken; only a minority write to try to have a particular decision changed. Writing to the MP is a long-established, and now much used,

means for citizens to have some input into the political process. None the less, corresponding with ministers has a number of limitations. MPs are not always well versed in the subjects raised with them by constituents. Some lack sufficient interest, or knowledge of the political system, to pursue cases effectively. Increasingly, they have difficulty finding the time to deal with all the matters raised with them.

Parliamentary commissioner for admlinistration

Since the late 1960s, MPs have had another option at their disposal in pursuing particular issues raised by constituents. The parliamentary commissioner for administration – or ombudsman – was established under an Act of 1967 to investigate cases of maladministration within government. He (never yet a she) considers only complaints referred to him by MPs. (A citizen cannot complain directly.) The commissioner labours under a number of limitations: limited remit, limited resources, limited access to files (he has no formal powers to see Cabinet papers), and no formal powers of enforcement. If he reports that officials have acted improperly or unjustly in the exercise of their administrative duties (the commissioner has no power to consider policy), it is then up to government to decide what action to take in response; if it fails to act, the only remaining means available to achieve action is through parliamentary pressure. The commissioner constitutes something of a limited last resort for most Members. They prefer to keep casework in their own hands and pursue it with government directly. A few years after the commissioner was first appointed, one survey of MPs found that more than 10 per cent of MPs never referred cases to him. Less than 10 per cent 'often' referred cases. For the vast majority of Members, the preferred device for pursuing a matter with a minister remains that of direct correspondence.

Party committees

An important unofficial means of scrutinising and influencing government is that of party committees. These are unofficial in that they are committees of the parliamentary parties and not officially constituted committees of the House.

Each parliamentary party has some form of organisation, usually with weekly meetings of the parliamentary party. The two largest parties – Conservative and Labour – have a sufficient number of members to sustain a series of committees. The principal committees mirror the topics covered by departments, have elected officers, and tend to meet regularly in order to discuss forthcoming business (for example, a bill within their area of interest), listen to invited speakers, and consider topics of interest. The invited speakers will include relevant ministers (or opposition front-benchers in the case of opposition back-bench committees) as well as outside speakers.

There are twenty-four Conservative subject committees and fourteen Labour committees. (Each party also has eight regional groups, each comprising the party MPs from a particular region.) The Conservative committees have a longer history than Labour committees and have a reputation for being the more politically powerful (Norton, 1994a). Conservative committees have no fixed membership – any Conservative MP can attend a meeting – and a large attendance can signal to the whips that there may be a problem with a particular issue. Most meetings will attract a handful of Members – sometimes half a dozen or even less – but if a contentious issue is discussed it can swell to three figures. Meetings are confidential and provide MPs with a means of expressing their views fully to their leaders, usually through the whips: a whip normally attends each meeting. Any disquiet is reported to the chief whip and relevant frontbencher. They constitute important channels of influence: a Conservative minister may have second thoughts if a particular policy encounters opposition in the relevant party committee. The committees also provide important means of specialisation for back-benchers and being elected to officership of a committee is seen as a good means of achieving experience and getting noticed for elevation to the front bench.

However, despite their influence within party ranks, the committees have to compete for the attention of Members – there are many other demands on Members' time – and in recent years attendance has declined, especially on the Conservative side of the House (Norton, 1994a).

All-party groups

All-party groups, like party committees, are not formally constituted committees of the House. They are formed on a cross-party basis, with officerships being shared among members of different parties. There are just under one hundred such groups, each formed to consider a particular topic. (There are also just over one hundred all party country groups, each bringing together MPs – and peers – with a special interest in the country concerned.) Some of the groups are confined to a parliamentary membership; some – known as 'registered groups' – include non-parliamentarians. The subjects covered by these groups are diverse, including industrial safety, children, social science, the Boys Brigade and AIDS. Some exist in name only. Others are active in discussing and promoting a particular cause, some pressing the government for action. Among the more influential are the disablement group, the long-established parliamentary and scientific committee, and more recently the football group. The all-party football group (with over a hundred members) has been active in influencing policy on such issues as safety in sports grounds (see Norton, 1993, p. 64). Many of the all-party groups have links with relevant outside bodies and can act as useful means of access to the political process for such groups. Like party committees, all-party groups have to compete with the other demands made on MPs' time.

In combination, then, there are a variety of means available to MPs to scrutinise and influence government and through which they can serve to make known the views of citizens. The means vary in effectiveness and viewed in isolation may appear of little use. However, they are not mutually exclusive and MPs will often use several of them in order to pursue a particular issue. An MP may write privately to a minister and, if not satisfied with the response, may table a question or seek an half-hour adjournment debate. In order to give prominence to an issue, a Member may table an EDM, speak in debate, and bombard the minister with a series of written questions. The most effective MPs are those who know how to use these means in combination and – on occasion – which ones to avoid.

Recent developments

The House has seen major changes in recent years. A number have served to reinforce its capacity to fulfil its various functions. Other changes – largely external to Parliament – have challenged its capacity to influence government and public policy.

Reinforcements

Over the past twenty-five years, the House has been reinforced as a body for scrutinising and influencing government. It has become relatively more independent in behaviour and more professional in its structures and procedures. There has been a shift from the floor of the House to committees in terms of scrutiny. It has also become more open and accessible, not least to constituents and pressure groups.

More independent behaviour

Before 1970, party voting was almost total in the division lobbies. No post-war government had lost a vote because some of its own supporters had voted with opposition parties. Since 1970, MPs have been relatively more independent in their voting behaviour. Cohesion remains the norm, but dissension is no longer so exceptional. Government cannot always take its majority for granted.

In the Parliament of 1970–4, the abrasive prime ministerial leadership of Edward Heath served as a triggering mechanism for Conservative MPs worried by government policy (Norton, 1978). Conservative back-benchers voted against their own side on more occasions than ever before, in greater numbers, and with more effect. The government suffered six defeats in the division lobbies, three of them on three-line whips (Norton, 1975). The defeats set a precedent for later Parliaments. The subsequent Labour government of 1974–9 experienced significant cross-voting by its back-benchers, on twenty-three occasions being defeated as a result (Norton, 1980). Some of the defeats were on important

issues, including economic policy. The more defeats that were imposed, the more the MPs responsible for them realised they were affecting policy without suffering any dire retribution.

This greater willingness to vote against one's own side continued in subsequent Parliaments of Conservative government. The willingness of MPs to vote against their own side after 1979 was on a scale similar to that of the 1970s, in terms of both breadth (the number of votes in which MPs voted against their own side) and depth (the number of MPs willing to vote against on each occasion) (Norton, 1995, 1996). Where it differed was in terms of significance (the effect of cross-voting on the government's majority) (Norton, 1996). Because of the size of the government's overall majorities, especially in the period from 1983 to 1992, cross-voting was less obvious and had less effect: most dissension could be absorbed by the government's large majority. However, not all could; there were occasional defeats – notably but not only on the second reading of the Shops Bill in 1986 – and there were occasions when government backtracked under the threat of defeat (see Norton, 1985, 1993). The return of a government with a relatively small overall majority in 1992 highlighted again the capacity of a small number of government back-benchers to influence the outcome of votes. The government ran into particular difficulty on its policies on pit closure and ratification of the Maastricht Treaty. Analysis of dissent within the ranks of the parliamentary Labour party also showed that a Labour government could expect problems from its own back-benchers (Cowley and Norton, 1996).

More professional

The House has become more professional, with a shift of emphasis from the floor of the House to the use of committees for detailed scrutiny of government.

The most important structural change to take place has been the creation of the departmental select committees. Their introduction in 1979 constituted the most important reform for more than seventy years. They have, as we have seen, been expanded in number and are now comprehensive in their coverage of government departments.

They have been supplemented by a number of other structural and procedural changes. The House in the 1980s introduced new structures for its own internal administration – including the establishment of a House of Commons commission – and new structures for auditing government spending. The National Audit Office (NAO) was established in 1983 to replace the old Exchequer and Audit Department and a parliamentary Public Accounts Commission (not to be confused with the Public Accounts Committee) set up to control its expenses.

Further changes have taken place in the 1990s. The 1992–7 Parliament saw the appointment of new committees on deregulation and on standards and privileges. A statutory committee for the security services, comprising senior parliamentarians, was also established. New powers were given to the Scottish Grand Committee, which discusses matters affecting Scotland, to question ministers other than Scottish Office ministers.

At the same time as committees are becoming central mechanisms of scrutiny, so less time is being devoted to activities on the floor of the House. In 1992 a special committee set up by the House (the Jopling Committee) recommended that the hours of sitting be reformed, with fewer late-night sittings, fewer Friday sittings and with morning sittings taking place on a Wednesday. The implementation of these reforms in 1994 provided a somewhat more rational timetable for plenary meetings and reduced the pressure on the floor.

The House has thus become somewhat more organised and specialised in its scrutiny of government. It has also adopted more professional standards in the conduct of its own members. Following criticism of some MPs for accepting money from outside sources (including two in 1994 who did not decline money when it was offered to them to table parliamentary questions), the House accepted in 1995 the recommendations of a committee (the Nolan Committee), set up by the Prime Minister, regarding payment from outside sources. MPs went further than the committee recommended in deciding to ban any paid advocacy by MPs (they cannot advocate a particular cause in Parliament in return for payment) and have to disclose income received from outside bodies that is paid to them

because they are MPs (for example, income as a result of working as a barrister or dentist does not have to be disclosed, money from a company for advice on how to present a case to government does). The House also approved the recommendation to establish a Code of Conduct and appoint a Parliamentary Commissioner for Standards to ensure that the rules are followed.

Table 17.9 lists the changes that have taken place in a two-year period (1994–6). Apart from those mentioned already, they include changes to select committees resulting from reforms in the structure of government departments. These various changes in themselves may not appear to affect significantly the relationship between the House and government but in combination they have changed the nature of the House as a body of scrutiny.

More open and accessible

The House is now more open in that more citizens can see what is happening. In 1988 the House voted

Table 17.9 The changing face of the House of Commons: structural and procedural changes 1994–6

Implementation of the Jopling reforms:
  Wednesday morning sittings
  House rises by 10.30 p.m. (Mon.–Thurs.)
  Ten non-sitting Fridays
  (Voluntary) timetabling of bills

Committee changes:
  Appointment of Deregulation Committee
  Appointment of Select Committee on Public Service
  New powers for the Scottish Grand Committee
  Select Committee on Education and Employment
    (replacing two committees)

Implementation of the Nolan Report:
  New Select Committee on Standards and Privileges
  Ban on paid advocacy by MPs
  Disclosure of income from parliamentary activity
  Code of Conduct
  Appointment of a Parliamentary Commissioner for
    Standards

to allow television coverage of proceedings. The first broadcast of a parliamentary debate occurred on 21 November 1989. The televised coverage was experimental but the House soon voted to make it permanent. Televised coverage quickly established itself and is now an accepted feature of parliamentary life.

MPs are also increasingly active in fulfilling their expressive functions. As we have seen, constituents make greater use of their MPs, writing to them on an unprecedented scale. Pressure groups also make greater use of MPs. Since 1979, pressure groups have, in effect, 'discovered' Parliament. Government has adopted something of an arm's length relationship with many groups, especially peak sectional groups. Groups have therefore turned their attention toward Parliament (Norton, 1993; Rush, 1990). In the Commons, the departmental select committees provide a focus for their attention. The relative increase in back-bench independence means MPs may be willing to act independently on behalf of a persuasive cause. Consequently, MPs are busier than ever before listening to, and expressing to government, the views and demands of their constituents and of myriad organised interests.

Challenges

In recent decades, the House has also faced a number of important challenges, both to its formal position and to its capacity to fulfil its various functions.

Centralisation of power

Some critics have identified a process of power centralisation in government as limiting Parliament's capacity to influence government. Some have pointed to the more recent creation of executive agencies within departments. These agencies have semi-autonomous status and the lines of answerability to Parliament are not clearly established. Ministers do not answer parliamentary questions about their activities. Instead, such questions are passed to the chief executive concerned who then replies directly to the MP. (As a result of parliamentary pressure, these replies are

now published in *Hansard*.) As was noted in Chapter 15, the development has important implications for the doctrine of individual ministerial responsibility and hence for the relationship of government to Parliament.

Membership of the EC/EU

A major challenge has come from membership of the European Community/Union. This has had the effect of moving policy-making competence in certain sectors from national institutions to the institutions of the Community. In 1972, Parliament passed the European Communities Act. This gave the force of law not only to existing EC legislation but also to all future EC legislation. Consequently, when European law is promulgated by the EC Commission and approved by the Council of Ministers it has binding applicability in the UK. The assent of Parliament is not required. It has been given in advance under the terms of the 1972 Act. Membership of the EC thus has significant implications for the legitimising function of Parliament. As we have seen in Chapter 15, it also has important constitutional implications for the doctrine of parliamentary sovereignty.

The House has sought to meet the challenge of EC/EU membership by the appointment of a committee that scrutinises all draft European law, prior to it going to the Council of Ministers, and identifies those measures which have political or legal significance. If the committee identifies an important proposal which it believes should be considered by the House, that proposal is now referred for debate in one of two European standing committees. In the committee, the relevant minister can be questioned for up to one hour about the proposal.

Though the House has some mechanism for scrutinising draft European legislation, the only means by which the House can actually affect the outcome of the European legislative process is by persuading the relevant minister to take a particular stance in the Council of Ministers. The House itself – in common with other national legislatures – has no formal standing in the process. Even if the minister accepts the point made by the House, that minister may be out-voted in the Council of Ministers if qualified majority voting (QMV) is employed. The more policy sectors that are transferred to the compet-ence of the EC, as occurred under the 1987 Single European Act and the 1993 Treaty on European Union, the less the formal power of the House of Commons to determine outcomes of public policy.

The House thus faces important challenges from changes within government at a national and supranational level. The House faces another important challenge because of more disparate changes. In large measure, the challenge derives from its very success as an expressive body. So many demands are now made of MPs by constitu-ents and pressure groups that they are having difficulty in coping with them. MPs already have to cope with growing demands of public business. The increase in the number of career-oriented MPs means they are also creating more pressures for themselves: they want to be seen to be active and so make use of the parliamentary opportunities avail-able in order to be seen. The result is that the demands made on MPs are now close to exceeding the time available to deal with them. The resources at the disposal of Members have not kept pace with the demands. MPs are in danger of being overloaded with work (Norton, 1992). The greater the over-load, the less able MPs are to attend to the task of scrutinising government. Members of select commit-tees find it difficult to find the time to read all the papers prepared for their meetings. Many Members cannot find the time to attend party back-bench committee meetings. The pressures in the 1990s are becoming greater.

The Member of Parliament is thus better resour-ced than ever before. The House has more extensive means than ever before to subject government to regular scrutiny. MPs are fulfilling their expressive functions to a greater degree than ever before. Yet the House and its Members are under great pres-sure. For some Members, the pressures can be contained. For others – and for many outside observers – the House is not able to cope effec-tively. As a result, there is pressure for reform of the House.

Pressure for change

There are three principal approaches to reform. Each derives from a particular perception of the role of the House of Commons in the political system. They can be related very roughly to the three types of legislature identified at the beginning of the chapter.

1. *Radical*: The radical approach wants to see the House of Commons as a policy-making legislature. To achieve this, the radical not only supports major reform within the institution but also wants major reform of the constitution in order to change fundamentally the relationship between Parliament and government. Such change would include a new electoral system. The most extreme form of this view advocates a separation of powers, with the executive elected separately from the House of Commons.

2. *Reform*: This approach wants to strengthen the House of Commons as a policy-influencing body, the onus for policy-'making' resting with government but with the House of Commons having the opportunity to consider policy proposals in detail and to influence their content. Reformers thus favour structural and procedural changes within the House that will facilitate the fulfilment of this particular role. Reformers thus welcome the changes made in recent years, especially the emphasis on committees, and want to see them taken further.

3. *Conservative*: This approach opposes change. The conservative stresses the importance of the chamber as the place where the great issues of the day are debated. Committees and greater specialisation detract from the fulfilment of this historic role, allowing MPs to get bogged down in the detail rather than the principle of what is proposed by government. Providing MPs with offices takes them away from the chamber. Though not quite envisaging a House with little or no policy affect, advocates of this approach see the role of the House as one of supporting government.

The conservative approach has been an important influence in the House for much of this century. However, in recent years the reform approach has come more to the fore and, as we have seen, achieved various changes. Advocates of this approach put forward several proposals for further reform and have been able to draw on a reforming mood in the House and one that is not confined to a particular party.

A mood of dissatisfaction was tapped among MPs in the late 1980s and early 1990s (Norton, 1994b). Various surveys revealed dissatisfaction with working conditions and with various aspects of parliamentary procedures. In the 1992 general election the three main party manifestos – Conservative, Labour and Liberal Democrat – committed themselves to parliamentary reform in order to ensure a more effective House of Commons. There is support among MPs in all three parties for further changes to be made that build on those of the 1992–7 Parliament.

The reforms that are advocated are several. If MPs are to carry out their several tasks effectively and efficiently, it is argued that they need the following:

1. *Better working conditions*, with every MP having not just an office but a well-resourced office and with the capacity to communicate quickly and effectively with the outside world, including the constituency and offices of the EC.
2. *Better resources for MPs*, in terms of their office cost allowance and, if necessary, with extra allowances for those involved in extensive committee work, allowing them to buy in extra help to cope with mundane tasks and basic research.
3. *Better resources for the House and its committees*, in particular increasing the staff and research resource of select committees and even, under some reform proposals, giving committees dedicated offices.
4. *More efficient and strengthened procedures*, especially in relation to the legislative process, with standing committees being reformed, with provision for special standing committees (which can take evidence from witnesses) more extensively used, and with major bills being automatically timetabled. There is also a growing body of support for an end to the sessional cut-off, under which a bill falls if not passed by the end of the session. A particularly radical proposal is for a bill to be taken for its second reading after it has been to committee, and not before.
5. *A smaller House of Commons*. This is the most radical proposal of all and has been put forward by a number of MPs. A few MPs started to advocate it in 1996 and it has achieved some attention since. A smaller House, it is argued, would allow for a more professional House, with each MP having more resources.

These proposals are not mutually exclusive. Some reformers advance a package of reforms. In 1993, a Commission on the Legislative Process set up by the Hansard Society recommended a comprehensive series of changes to the whole legislative process, including timetabling of bills, the standard use of special standing committees, and an ending of the sessional cut-off. The Constitution Unit in 1996 also put forward a similar package.

There is thus no shortage of proposals for strengthening Parliament as an agent of scrutiny and of influence. By improving the resources of MPs it is also argued that Members will be better able to fulfil their expressive functions.

Chapter summary

The principal role of the House of Commons is one of scrutinising government. Various means are available to MPs to undertake this role. Those means have been strengthened in recent years but have made only a modest contribution to improved scrutiny. There are demands for further reforms. Reform is a political issue, though not one that divides the parties. With effective leadership, parliamentary support could be mobilised behind some further change. However, those who press for change have to unite on the changes they are prepared to push for and they have to contend with those – in and outside the House – who argue either that they have gone too far in their demands or that they have not gone far enough.

Discussion points

- What are the most important functions of the House of Commons?

- Should ministers remain as members of Parliament once appointed to office?

- What purpose is served by select committees? Should they be strengthened?

- Should, and can, the House of Commons improve its scrutiny of government legislation?

- Should Question Time be abolished?

- What would you do with the House of Commons – and why?

Further reading

The most recent student texts on the House of Commons – and also covering the House of Lords – are Norton (1993) and Silk and Walters (1995). Griffith and Ryle (1989) provide a useful and broad-ranging compendium of material on Parliament. The departmental select committees are covered most extensively in Drewry (1989), though much useful data are also to be found in the report from the Select Committee on Procedure (1990).

There have been a number of books recently analysing different aspects of parliamentary behaviour previously neglected or not covered in recent decades. Parliamentary questions, not covered in any detail since Chester and Bowring's book on the subject in 1962, are now covered thoroughly in Franklin and Norton (1993). Brand (1992) deals with the influence of parliamentary parties. The largely neglected relationship of Parliament to pressure groups is the subject of Rush (1990). MPs' constituency service is covered in Norton and Wood (1993). On reform of the House of Commons, much useful material is contained in the report from the Hansard Society (1993) and the Constitution Unit (1996).

References

Brand, J. (1992) *British Parliamentary Parties* (Oxford University Press).

Constitution Unit (1996) *Delivering Constitutional Reform* (The Constitution Unit).

Cowley, P. and Norton, P. (1996) *Blair's Bastards* (Centre for Legislative Studies).

Criddle, B. (1992) 'MPs and candidates', in D. Butler and D. Kavanagh (eds), *The British General Election of 1992* (Macmillan).

Drewry, G. (ed.) (1989) *The New Select Committees*, rev. edn (Oxford University Press).

Franklin, M. and Norton, P. (eds) (1993) *Parliamentary Questions* (Oxford University Press).

Griffith, J.A.G. and Ryle, M. (1989) *Parliament* (Sweet and Maxwell).

Hansard Society (1993) *Making the Law: Report of the Commission on the Legislative Process* (Hansard Society).

Mezey, M. (1979) *Comparative Legislatures* (Duke University Press).

Norton, P. (1975) *Dissension in the House of Commons 1945–74* (Macmillan).

Norton, P. (1978) *Conservative Dissidents* (Temple Smith).

Norton, P. (1980) *Dissension in the House of Commons 1974–1979* (Oxford University Press).

Norton, P. (ed.) (1985) *Parliament in the 1980s* (Blackwell).

Norton, P. (ed.) (1990) *Legislatures* (Oxford University Press).

Norton, P. (1992), 'The House of Commons: from overlooked to overworked', in B. Jones and L. Robins (eds), *Two Decades in British Politics* (Manchester University Press).

Norton, P. (1993) *Does Parliament Matter?* (Harvester Wheatsheaf).

Norton, P. (1994a) 'The parliamentary party and party committees', in A. Seldon and S. Ball (eds), *Conservative Century: The Conservative Party since 1900* (Oxford University Press).

Norton, P. (1994b) 'Reform of the House of Commons', in B. Jones (ed), *Issues in British Politics* (Manchester University Press).

Norton, P. (1995) 'Parliamentary behaviour since 1945', *Talking Politics*, Vol. 8, No. 2.

Norton, P. (1996) 'Are MPs Revolting? Dissension in the House of Commons 1979–92', paper presented at the Second Workshop of Parliamentary Scholars and Parliamentarians, Wroxton, UK

Norton, P. and Wood, D. (1993) *Back from Westminster* (University Press of Kentucky).

Rush, M. (1979), 'Members of Parliament', in S.A. Walkland (ed.), *The House of Commons in the Twentieth Century* (Oxford University Press).

Rush, M. (1990) *Pressure Politics* (Oxford University Press).

Select Committee on Procedure (1990) *The Working of the Select Committee System*, Session 1989–90, HC 19 (HMSO).

Silk, P. and Walters, R. (1995) *How Parliament Works*, 3rd edn (Longman).

Somit, A. and Roemmele, A. (1995) 'The victorious legislative incumbent as a threat to democracy: a nine nation Study', *American Political Science Association: Legislative Studies Section Newsletter*, Vol. 18, No. 2, July.

CHAPTER EIGHTEEN

The House of Lords

PHILIP NORTON

LEARNING OBJECTIVES

■ To outline the historical development of the House of Lords, the functions ascribed to it in the 1990s and the means available to it to fulfil those functions.

■ To consider recent changes in the House and the debate about the future of the chamber.

INTRODUCTION

The House of Lords remains an enduring part of the political system. It carries out a number of roles. In recent years, this predominantly Conservative House has demonstrated its independence of Conservative governments. It has become more active and has deployed an expertise in a number of areas unmatched by the elected House of Commons. The 1911 Parliament Act envisaged an elected second chamber. That goal has yet to be realised. This chapter examines the various roles and operation of the House of Lords, and the different demands for reform.

The House of Lords is generally viewed by historians as having its origins in the Anglo-Saxon *Witenagemot* and more especially its Norman successor, the *Curia Regis* (Court of the King). Indeed, two basic features of the King's *Curia* of the twelfth and thirteenth centuries are still to be found in the House of Lords. One is the basic composition, comprising the Lords Spiritual and the Lords Temporal. At the time of the Magna Carta, the *Curia* comprised earls and the chief barons as well as the leading prelates of the kingdom (archbishops, bishops and abbots). The main change, historically, has been in the shift in balance between the two: the churchmen – the Lords Spiritual – now comprise a small part of the House. The other significant feature is the basis on which members were summoned. The King's tenants-in-chief attended court because of their position. Various minor barons were summoned because the King wished them to attend. 'From the beginning the will of the king was an element in determining its make up' (White, 1908, p. 299). If a baron regularly received a summons to court the presumption grew that the summons would be issued to his heir. There thus grew a body which peers attended on the basis of a strictly hereditary dignity without reference to tenure. The result was to be a House of Lords based on the principle of heredity, with writs of summons being personal to the recipients. Members of the House have never been subject to election. They are not summoned to speak on behalf of some other individuals or bodies. Any notion of representativeness has been squeezed out. Even the Lords Spiritual – who serve by reason of their position in the established church – are summoned to take part in a personal capacity.

The lack of any representative capacity has led to the House occupying a position of political – and now legal – inferiority to the House of Commons. As early as the fifteenth century, the privilege of initiating measures of taxation was conceded to the lower House. The most significant shift, though, took place in the nineteenth century. As we have seen (Chapter 17), the effect of the Reform Acts was to consign the Lords to a recognisably subordinate role to that of the Commons, though not until the passage of the Parliament Act of 1911 was that role confirmed by statute. Under the terms of the Act, the House could delay a non-money bill for no more than two sessions, and money bills (those dealing exclusively with money, and so certified by the Speaker) were to become law one month after leaving the Commons whether approved by the House of Lords or not. Bills to prolong the life of a Parliament, along with delegated legislation and provisional order bills, were excluded from the provisions of the Act. The two-session veto over non-money bills was further reduced, to one session, by the Parliament Act of 1949.

What, then, constitutes the contemporary House of Lords? What functions can be ascribed to it? What means does it have to carry them out? And what are the demands made for reform?

The House in the 1990s

The House of Lords has more than a thousand members, making it the largest regularly sitting legislative chamber in the world. (Russia and China have bigger legislative assemblies but they do not meet regularly throughout the year.) Its size is hardly surprising given the number of peers created over the centuries by each succeeding monarch, although the largest increase has been in the twentieth century. In 1906, the House had a membership of 602. The number is now almost double that. Of the 1,192 members of the House at the beginning of

1996, 769 were hereditary peers. The remainder comprised 377 life peers, 20 law lords (a category of peer created by the Appellate Jurisdiction Act of 1876, to help the House fulfil its judicial function) and the Lords Spiritual: the two archbishops of the Church of England, the Bishops of London, Durham and Winchester and twenty-one other bishops according to their seniority of appointment. Life peerages – held solely during the lifetime of the holder – were introduced in 1958 and have been the main form of creation since that time. No hereditary peerages were created in the period between 1964 and 1983: two were created in 1983, one in 1984, and none since then. Under the Peerages Act of 1963, hereditary peers may disclaim their peerages for their own lifetime: in 1996, there were eleven (excluded from the foregoing figures) who had done so.

In the 1950s, the House met at a leisurely pace and was poorly attended. Peers have never been paid a salary and many members, like the minor barons in the thirteenth century, found attending to be a chore, sometimes an expensive one: the practice, as in the thirteenth century, was to stay away. The House rarely met for more than three days a week and each sitting was usually no more than three or four hours in length. For most of the decade, the average daily attendance did not reach three figures. There was little interest shown in its activities by most of its own members; not surprisingly, there was little interest shown by those outside the House.

This was to change significantly in each succeeding decade (see Table 18.1). Peers attended in ever greater numbers and the House sat for longer. Late-night sittings, virtually unknown in the 1950s and for much of the 1960s, have been regular features since the 1970s. By the mid-1970s, the average daily attendance was 275. In the 1980s, the figure climbed to exceed 300. By the end of the decade, more than 800 peers – two-thirds of the membership – attended one or more sittings each year and, of those, more than 500 contributed to debate. The House also became more visible to the outside world. In 1985, television cameras were allowed to broadcast proceedings. There was a four-year gap before the televising of Commons' proceedings began: in those four years, the House of Lords enjoyed unprecedented television coverage.

Table 18.1   Growth in activity in the House of Lords

	1959–60	1971–2	1981–2	1988–9
Peers on roll	907	1,073	1,174	1,183
Peers who attended at least once	542	698	713	816
Peers who spoke at least once	283	419	503	537
Average daily attendance	136	250	284	316
Total hours House sat	450	813	930	1,077
Average length of sitting	4 hrs. 0 m.	5 hrs. 45 m.	6 hrs. 20 m.	7 hrs. 4 m.
Sittings after 10 p.m.	1	28	41	67
Number of starred questions	264	494	531	572
Number of questions for written answer	48	315	1,098	1,202
Number of amendments to government bills	na	924	1,309	2,359
Number of divisions	16	171	146	189

Source: Shell and Beamish, 1993, p. 10

Politically, the House remains – as it has been since the end of the eighteenth century – a predominantly Conservative assembly. Of peers with a known political affiliation, Conservative peers outnumber Labour peers by four to one (Table 18.2). In terms of peers who put in an appearance in the House, the Conservative dominance is less marked (Table 18.3). Though Conservative peers are in a plurality among regular attenders, they do not enjoy an absolute majority. They can be outvoted by a combination of Labour, Liberal Democrat and cross-bench peers. Cross-benchers are more likely to vote with the Conservatives but they do not always do so, and the House between 1979 and 1997 proved willing to defeat a Conservative government on numerous occasions. During that period, the government suffered more than 200 defeats at the hands of their Lordships.

The House differs significantly from the Commons not only in its size, composition and remuneration (peers can claim allowances, but still receive no salary) but also in its procedures. Though the Lord Chancellor is the presiding officer of the House, he has no powers to call peers to speak, nor to enforce order. (Given that, and the demands arising from his duties as head of the judiciary, his place on the Woolsack is normally taken by a deputy.) The maintenance of the rules of order is the responsibility of the House itself, though peers usually look to the Leader of the House to give a lead. Peers wishing to speak in a debate submit their names in advance and a list of speakers is then circulated. If two peers rise at the same time, one is expected to give way. (If neither does so, other peers are expected to make clear their preference as to who should speak.) If a speaker strays from what is permissible, other peers shout 'Order'. If a speaker goes on for too long, it is always open to another peer to rise and move the motion 'That the noble peer be no longer heard', but it is a device rarely employed. The Lords remains a more chamber-oriented institution than the Commons, though – as we shall see – it is making more use of committees than before. There are also fewer divisions in the Lords than in the Commons. This in part reflects the recognition by peers of the political predominance of the elected chamber. Peers are often reluctant to press issues to a vote and rarely do so on the principle of a measure. By agreement reached between the two party leaders in the Lords

Table 18.2   Party strength in the House of Lords, 1996

Declared party affiliation	
Conservative	476
Labour	108
Liberal Democrat	53
Cross-bencher	287
Others	116

Source: Dod's Parliamentary Companion, 1996

Table 18.3   Changing party strength in the House of Lords

Session		Conservative	Labour	Liberal/ Alliance	Cross-bench/ Independent
1967–8	Attending	314	113	37	215
	Regular	125	95	19	52
1975–6	Attending	292	149	30	281
	Regular	141	104	24	60
1984–5	Attending	376	122	76	245
	Regular	168	91	51	68
1988–9	Attending	393	108	71	241
	Regular	185	86	59	63

Note: Attending: all who attended on one or more days during the session. Regular: all who attended on one-third or more of the days during the session.
Source: Shell and Beamish, 1993, p. 24

in the 1945–50 Parliament – the Salisbury–Addison agreement, which has remained in place since – the House does not divide on the second reading of any bill promised in the government's election manifesto and, by extension now, any bill appearing in the government's programme for the session.

Functions

The functions of the House – the tasks which it carries out – are broadly similar to those of the Commons but not as extensive. The extent to which they differ derives from the fact that politically the House is no longer co-equal with the Commons.

Legitimisation

The House fulfils the functions of both manifest and latent legitimisation, but on a modest scale. It is called upon to give the seal of approval to bills but, if it fails to give that approval, it can be overridden later by the House of Commons under the provisions of the Parliament Acts. Only in very rare circumstances – as in the case of a bill to lengthen the life of a Parliament – is its veto absolute. By virtue of being one of the two chambers of Parliament and by meeting regularly and uninterruptedly, the House may have a limited claim to fulfilling a function of latent legitimisation. However, such a

claim is largely offset by the House having no claim to being a representative assembly and by its limited legislative authority.

Recruitment

The House provides some of the personnel of government. As we have seen (Chapter 17), ministers are drawn from Parliament and, by convention, predominantly now from the elected House.

The government recruits a number of ministers from the upper House primarily for political and managerial reasons. Though the government is normally assured of getting its bills through the House, it is not necessarily guaranteed getting them through in the form it wants them. It is therefore prudent to have ministers in the Lords in order to explain bills and to marshal support. In addition, the House provides a pool from which the Prime Minister can draw in order to supplement ministers drawn from the Commons. The advantage offered by peers is that, with no constituency responsibilities, they are able to devote more time to ministerial duties than is the case with ministers who have constituency duties to attend to.

However, the supply of ministers is a limited one. A minimum of two peers serve in the Cabinet (Lord Chancellor and Leader of the House) but usually no more than four. (Four is a rarity and two, in recent years, the norm.) About ten to fifteen other ministers are drawn from the Lords, supplemented by seven whips (including the Chief Whip). The number of ministers does not match the number of ministries, with the result that the whips have to take on responsibility for answering for particular departments – another difference from the House of Commons, where the whips have no responsibility for appearing at the dispatch box. Even with a small number of posts to be filled, the government still has difficulty on occasion in finding suitable peers for ministerial office. The problem under Conservative governments has been that many of the regular attenders are too old to serve or have outside interests they wish to pursue. As a result, the government has had to draw on occasion on peers who are young and relatively new to the House. For Labour, the problem is one of numbers. As is clear from Table 18.2, there are relatively few Labour peers.

Scrutiny and influence

It is in its remaining functions that the House of Lords is significant. The House performs an important role as an agent of scrutiny and influence, especially the former. The House does not undertake the task of scrutiny on behalf of constituents, as peers have none. Rather, the House undertakes a more general task of scrutiny. Three features of the House render it particularly suitable for the detailed scrutiny of legislation. Firstly, as an unelected House, it cannot claim the legitimacy to reject the principle of measures agreed by the elected House. Thus, basically by default, it focuses on the detail rather than the principle. Secondly, its membership includes people who have distinguished themselves in particular fields – such as the sciences, the law, education, industry, industrial relations – who can look at relevant legislation from the perspective of practitioners in the field rather than from the perspective of elected party politicians. And, thirdly, the House has the time to debate non-money bills in more detail than is usually possible in the Commons – unlike in the Commons, there is no provision for a guillotine and all amendments are discussed. The House thus serves as an important revising chamber, trying to ensure that a bill is well drafted and internally coherent. In order to improve the bill, it will suggest amendments, most of which will be accepted by the Commons. In terms of legislative

scrutiny, the House has thus developed a role which is viewed as complementary to, rather than one competing with (or identical to), that of the Commons.

The House also scrutinises, and occasionally influences, government policy. Peers can debate policy in a less partisan atmosphere than the Commons and are not subject to the constituency and party influences that dominate in the elected House. They are therefore in a position to debate issues of public policy that may not be at the heart of the partisan battle and which, consequently, receive little attention in the Commons. Given their backgrounds, peers are also often – though not always – able to debate public policy from the perspective of those engaged in the subject. The House, for example, is able to debate science policy with an authority denied the lower House. The Lords contains several distinguished scientists; the Commons does not. When discussing education, the House will normally hear from peers who are professors, university chancellors, vice-chancellors, and former secretaries of state for education. The Commons has members who used to be, but are no longer, lecturers and teachers.

Expression

The House, like the Commons, also fulfils a number of expressive functions. It can bring issues on to the political agenda in a way not always possible in the Commons. MPs are wary of raising issues that may not be popular with constituents and which have little salience in terms of party politics. Peers are answerable to no one but themselves. They can raise whatever they feel needs raising. The House may thus debate issues of concern to particular groups in society which MPs are not willing to address. Formally, it is not a function the House is expected to fulfil. Indeed, according to *Erskine May*, the parliamentary 'bible' on procedure, Lords may indicate that an outside body agrees with the substance of their views, but they should avoid creating an impression that they are speaking as representatives of outside bodies. Thus, not only is the House not a representative assembly, it should avoid giving the impression of being one! In practice, peers take up issues that concern them, often alerted to the issue by outside bodies. Sometimes the issues raised are esoteric – one peer in the 1980s initiated a debate on unidentified flying objects (UFOs) – but some are of great concern to particular groups: the Lords, for example, helped put the issue of homosexual law reform on the political agenda in the 1960s.

The House also has the potential, only marginally realised, to express views to citizens and influence their stance on public policy. The function is limited by the absence of any democratic legitimacy, the capacity to influence deriving from the longevity of the House and its place as one of the two chambers of Parliament, as well as from the authority of the individual peers who may be involved. The scope to fulfil this function has increased slightly as a result of the introduction of the television cameras (greater visibility with which to mobilise support) and the limited use of committees (issuing reports that may mobilise support among affected groups), but the opportunities remain limited.

Other functions

To these functions may be added a number of others, some of which are peculiar to the upper House. Foremost among these is a *judicial function*. The House constitutes the highest court of appeal within the United Kingdom. Though formally a function residing in the House as a whole, in practice it is carried out by a judicial committee comprising the Lord Chancellor, ex-lords chancellor, the law lords and peers who have held high judicial office. Between five and ten will normally sit to hear a case. Hearings take place in a committee room, though the decision is delivered in the chamber. By convention, other peers do not take part in judicial proceedings. One peer earlier this century did try to participate but was ignored by the other peers on the committee until he went away.

Like the Commons, the House also retains a small *legislative role*, primarily in the form of private Members' legislation. In the 1960s, several major measures of social reform – on divorce, abortion, and homosexuality – passed through both Houses as private Members' bills. Peers can introduce private Members' bills and a small number achieve passage, but it is small – even compared to the number of such bills promoted by MPs. In 1990–1, for example, eighteen private Members'

bills introduced by MPs were passed, but only one introduced by a peer. The introduction of such bills by peers is more important in fulfilling an expressive function – allowing views on the subject to be aired – than it is in fulfilling a legislative role. In the 1995–6 session, for example, a Sexual Orientation Discrimination Bill was introduced which, even though it stood little chance of passage (there was no time in the Commons), got the problem of discrimination against homosexuals discussed. The time given to private Members' legislation is important but not extensive: it occupies usually less than 3 per cent of the time of the House.

The House is also ascribed a distinct role, that of a *constitutional safeguard*. This is reflected in the provisions of the Parliament Acts. The House, as we have noted, retains a veto over bills to extend the life of a Parliament. It is considered a potential brake on a government that seeks to act in a dictatorial or generally unacceptable manner: hence it may use its limited power to amend or, more significantly, to delay a bill. In practice, though, the power is a limited one. The House lacks a legitimate elected base of its own that would allow it to act, on a substantial and sustained basis, contrary to the wishes of an elected government.

In combination, these various functions render the House a useful body – especially as a revising chamber and for raising and debating issues on which peers are well informed – but one that is clearly subordinate to the elected chamber. The fact that the House is not elected explains its limited functions; it is also the reason why it is considered particularly suited to fulfil the functions it does retain.

Scrutiny and influence

The means available to the House to fulfil the tasks of scrutiny and influence can be considered, as with the Commons, under two heads: legislation and executive actions. The means available to the House are also those available to fulfil its expressive functions.

Legislation

Legislation occupies an increasing proportion of the time of the House, with almost two-thirds of the time of the House given over to it (Norton, 1993, p. 85; Shell and Beamish, 1993, p. 16). Bills in the Lords have to go through stages analogous to those in the House of Commons. There are, though, differences in procedure. First readings are normally taken formally, but there have been rare occasions when they have been debated: on four occasions (in 1888, 1933, 1943 and 1969) first readings were actually opposed. Second readings, as in the Commons, constitute debates on the principle of the measure. The significant difference occurs at committee stage.

For some bills, the committee stage is actually dispensed with. After second reading, a motion may be moved 'That this Bill be not committed' and, if agreed to, the bill then awaits third reading. This procedure is usually employed for supply and money bills when there is no desire to present amendments. For those bills that do receive a committee stage, it is usually taken on the floor of the House. Furthermore, all amendments tabled are debated. The less crowded timetable of the House allows such a procedure. It has the advantage of allowing all peers with an interest or expertise in a measure to take part and ensures consideration of any amendments they believe to be relevant. There is thus the potential for a more thorough consideration than is possible in the Commons. The emphasis, as we have seen, is on ensuring that the bill is well drafted and coherent. Most Lords' amendments are accepted by the Commons. This is not surprising given the nature of most amendments (tidying up language and meaning) and the fact that many are actually introduced by the government. On some bills, though, the government proves resistant to demands for change. This resistance has usually been sufficient to prevent amendments being made. However, as we shall see, the House has also proved notably willing in recent years to carry amendments moved by back-bench peers.

Since 1968, the House has been able to refer bills for committee consideration in the equivalent of standing committees, known as public bill committees, though there is growing pressure for its more regular employment. More recently, the House has experimented with sending a bill to a special procedure public bill committee, which is empowered to take oral and written evidence. Of longer standing is the power to refer a bill, or indeed any proposal, to a select committee for detailed investigation. It is a power which has been utilised when it has been considered necessary or desirable to examine witnesses and evidence from outside bodies. Between 1972 and 1991, seven bills were sent to select committees. All bar one of the bills were private Members' bills. In future, bills considered in need of detailed scrutiny are likely to be sent to a special procedure public bill committee.

Report and third reading provide further opportunities for consideration. Report may be used by government to bring forward amendments promised at committee stage and also to offer new amendments of its own. It is possible also for amendments to be made at third reading and this opportunity is variously employed.

Executive actions

As in the House of Commons, there are various means available for scrutinising the actions of the executive. The principal means available on the floor of the House are those of debate and questions. Off the floor of the House, there are select committees and, at the unofficial level, party meetings.

Debates

Debates, as in the Commons, take place on motions. These may express a particular view or they may be take the form either of 'take note' motions or motions calling for papers. 'Take note' motions are employed in order to allow the House to debate reports from select committees or to discuss topics on which the government wishes to hear peers' views: ministers use 'take note' motions rather than motions calling for papers because – with the latter – they are responsible for supplying the papers being called for. Motions calling for papers are used by back-benchers to call attention to a particular issue; at the end of the debate it is customary to withdraw the motion, the purpose for which it was tabled – to ensure a debate – having been achieved.

All peers who wish to speak in debate do so and there is a greater likelihood than in the Commons that such proceedings will constitute what they purport to be: that is, debates. Party ties are less rigid than in the Commons (though none the less still strong) and peers are more likely to consider and respond to points made by other peers. Though the order in which peers speak is determined beforehand, it is common practice for a peer who is speaking to give way to interventions. Within the context of the chamber, the chances of a speech having an impact on the thought and even the votes of others are considerably greater than in the more predictable lower House.

These debates are also supplemented by short debates. One day each month, usually a Wednesday, is set aside for two short debates, each of up to two-and-a-half hours in length. These are occasions for issues to be raised by back-benchers or cross-benchers, and the choice of subject is made by ballot. The purpose of each short debate is to allow peers to discuss a particular topic rather than to come to a conclusion about it. Topics discussed tend to be non-partisan and the range is broad. Thus, for example, on 27 January 1993, the Viscount of Oxfuird initiated a debate on the pollution of city centres by road traffic and Lord Pearson of Rannoch initiated one on government policies on the recruitment and training of those entrusted with the residential care of children. Both motions provided the opportunity for interested peers to offer their views and for ministers to explain the government's position and to reveal what proposals were under consideration by the relevant department.

Questions

Questions in the Lords are of two types: starred and unstarred. The meanings are different to those employed in the Commons. In the Commons, starred questions are oral questions and unstarred questions are written questions. In the Lords, starred questions are non-debatable questions and unstarred questions are questions on which a short debate may take place. (Lords may also table questions for written answer, though the number tabled is not numerous: about half-a-dozen on any particular day.) At the beginning of each day's sitting, up to four 'starred' questions may be asked. These are similar to those tabled for oral answer in the Commons, though – unlike in the Commons – they are addressed to Her Majesty's Government and not to a particular minister (see Figure 18.1). A peer rises to ask the question appearing in his or her

name on the order paper, the relevant minister (or whip) replies for the government, and then supplementary questions – confined to the subject of the original question – follow. This procedure, assuming as many as four questions are tabled (they usually are), is expected to last no more than twenty minutes. This allows for perhaps as many as four or five supplementaries on each question to be asked, the peer who tabled the motion by tradition being allowed to ask the first supplementary. Hence, though a shorter question time than in the Commons, the concentration on a particular question is much greater and allows for more probing. At the end of the day's sitting, there is also usually an 'unstarred' question: that is, one which may be debated (as, for example, Lord Henderson's, Figure 18.1).

Peers who wish to speak do so and the appropriate minister then responds. The advantages of such unstarred questions are similar to those of the half-hour adjournment debates in the Commons, except that in this case there is a much greater opportunity for other members to participate. For example, when the Earl of Perth on 28 January 1993 asked what action the government proposed to take on the devastation in Perthshire caused by the River Tay, no fewer than seven peers spoke – in addition to Lord Perth – before the minister rose to reply. The debate lasted more than one-and-a-quarter hours.

Committees

Though the House remains a chamber-oriented institution, it has made greater use in recent years of committees. Apart from a number of established committees dealing, for example, with privilege and the judicial function of the House, it has variously made use of *ad hoc* select committees. Some *ad hoc* committees have been appointed, as we have seen, to consider the desirability of certain legislative measures. A number have been appointed to consider issues of public policy. The House has also made use of its power to create sessional select committees, i.e. committees appointed regularly from session to session rather than for the purpose of one particular inquiry. Two of these committees enjoy reputations as high-powered committees of scrutiny.

NOTICES AND ORDERS OF THE DAY

Items marked † are new or have been altered.

WEDNESDAY THE 23RD of JUNE

At half past two o'clock

* **The Lord Hylton**–To ask Her Majesty's Government whether they will publish the evidence given to, and the conclusions of, Sir John May's enquiry into miscarriages of justice, and if not, why not.

* **The Earl Russell**–To ask Her Majesty's Government whether before implementing any cuts in the social security budget they will attempt to calculate their effects on the budgets of other ministries, and therefore on the total level of public spending.

* **The Lord Boyd-Carpenter**–To ask Her Majesty's Government what action they are taking in the light of the reports by auditors on the operations of Lambeth Borough Council.

* **The Lord Taylor of Gryfe**–To ask Her Majesty's Government whether, in the light of the British Medical Association's report "The Boxing Debate", they will consider setting up an independent enquiry into the risks of brain injury associated with boxing.

† **European Communities (Amendment) Bill**–House to be again in Committee.
[THE BARONESS CHALKER OF WALLASEY]

The Lord Henderson of Brompton–To ask her Majesty's Government what is their view of the report entitled "Four Years' Severe Hardship" published by Barnardo's and Youthaid, and what is their estimate of the number of young people aged 16 or 17 who are not in full-time education, employment or training.

[It is expected that the above question will be asked during the 1 hour dinner adjournment]

Figure 18.1 In the House of Lords, questions are addressed to Her Majesty's Government and not to a particular minister.

The most prominent is the *European Communities Committee*. Established in 1974, it undertakes scrutiny of draft European legislation, seeking to identify those proposals which raise important questions of principle or policy and which deserve consideration by the House. Working through six subcommittees, the committees draw on the services of sixty to seventy peers. Each subcommittee, after having had EC documents referred to it, calls in evidence from government departments and outside bodies. Written evidence may be supplemented by oral evidence and, on occasion (though not often), a minister may be invited to give evidence in person. The subcommittees prepare reports for the House (in total, about twenty to thirty a year), including recommendations as to whether the documents should be debated by the House. (About 2 to 4 per cent of the time of the House is taken up debating EC documents, usually on 'take note' motions.) The EC Committee has built up an impressive reputation as a thorough and informed body, issuing reports which are more extensive than its counterpart in the Commons, and which are considered authoritative both within Whitehall and the institutions of the EC. The House, like the chambers of other national legislatures, has no formal role in the EC legislative process (see Norton, 1996), and so has no power, other than that of persuasion, to affect outcomes. The significance of the reports, therefore, has tended to lie in informing debate rather than in changing particular decisions (Norton, 1993, p. 126).

The *Select Committee on Science and Technology* was appointed in 1979 following the demise of the equivalent committee in the Commons. The remit of the committee – 'to consider science and technology' – is wide and its inquiries have covered a broad range. The committee is essentially non-partisan in approach and benefits from a number of peers with an expertise in the subject. In 1988–9, for example, its members – both appointed and coopted – included a professor of cell physiology, five engineers, a former professor of physics, a professor of pharmacology, and the chairman of the University of Wales Institute of Science and Technology. Between 1979 and 1991, the committee carried out thirty-four principal inquiries, covering topics such as science and government, hazardous waste disposal, space policy, the greenhouse effect, and systematic biology research. The committee has raised issues which otherwise might have been neglected by government – and certainly not considered in any depth by the Commons – and a number of its reports have proved influential (see Grantham, 1993; Hayter, 1992). Its 1986 report on civil research and development, for example, led to the Prime Minister, Margaret Thatcher, taking charge of the government's consideration of priorities on science and technology and the appointment of a council to advise the premier. In 1992, the committee was joined by a sister committee, the Commons deciding to establish again a committee on the subject. However, the Lords retains the advantage of expertise denied to the Commons.

These committees are supplemented now by a *Delegated Powers and Deregulation Scrutiny Committee*, which looks at whether powers of delegated legislation in a bill are appropriate and makes recommendations to the House accordingly (Himsworth, 1995). These permanent committees are variously supplemented by *ad hoc* committees, appointed to consider particular issues. In 1995, for example, the House appointed a Committee on Relations Between Central and Local Government.

The use of committees thus constitutes a modest but valuable supplement to the work undertaken on the floor of the House. They allow the House to specialise to some degree and to draw on the expertise of its membership, an expertise that cannot be matched by the elected House of Commons. They also fulfil an important expressive function. The committees take evidence from interested bodies – the submission of written evidence is extensive – thus allowing groups an opportunity to get their views on the public record. Given the expertise on the committees, committee reports are treated as weighty documents by interested groups; consequently, the committees enjoy some capacity to raise support for particular measures of public policy.

Party meetings

The parties in the Lords are organised, with their own leaders and whips. Even the cross-benchers, allied to no party, have their own elected leader and circulate a whip. However, neither the Conservative nor the Labour Party in the Lords has a committee structure. Instead, peers are able to attend the Commons' back-bench committees and a number do so. Any attempt at influence through the party structure in the Lords, therefore, takes the form of talking to the whips or of raising the issue at the weekly party meeting.

The Conservative Party, not surprisingly given its strength among peers, has the better attended meetings. The Association of Conservative Peers (the ACP), as it is now known (until the 1980s, it was called the Association of Independent Unionist Peers), meets at 2.15 on a Thursday afternoon. Paralleling the increase in attendance in the House, the number of peers attending meetings has gone up over the decades. By the end of the 1980s, between fifty and seventy peers usually attended each meeting, the number rising in the event of an important topic or speaker. The occasion is used to discuss a particular issue or (in government) to listen to a minister. If a government bill is coming up for its second reading in the House, the relevant Cabinet minister will usually attend, often accompanied by the junior minister responsible for the day-to-day handling of the bill. On other occasions, outside guests are invited to speak.

Often the meetings, despite the sizeable attendance, have the characteristics of a specialist committee, since often peers with an expertise in the topic will attend and question the speaker. For a minister, the occasion may be a testing one, having to justify a measure before an often well-informed audience. As one senior figure in the Association noted, it can be daunting for a minister to be faced not just with experts in the subject but also with his (or her) immediate predecessors in office.

Party meetings are useful as two-way channels of communication between leaders and led in the Lords and, in a wider context, between a party's supporters in the Lords and the leadership of the whole party. Given the problems of ensuring structured and regular contact between whips and their party's peers, the party meetings provide a useful means of gauging the mood of the regular attenders.

Recent developments

Over the past twenty-five years, the House of Lords has changed significantly, the changes largely paralleling those of the House of Commons. It has seen changes in attitude, behaviour and structures.

In the 1940s and 1950s, the House met at a leisurely pace and with few peers being actively involved in daily business. All this was soon to change. Peers became more active: they began to attend in greater numbers, sit for more days and spend more time on each day's sitting. The extent of that change we have seen already. Peers also became more independent in their voting behaviour. In the 1950s and early 1960s, Conservative governments had little difficulty with a Conservative-dominated House that did not vote often and which, when it did, voted along party lines. Labour governments fared less well at the hands of a Conservative House. That was especially so in the period of Labour government from 1974 to 1979: the government was defeated no less than 347 times in the Lords. Given the Conservative dominance in the House, this is explicable in party terms. What is surprising is the number of defeats imposed on Conservative governments since 1970. In the period of Conservative government from 1970 to 1974, the Lords defeated the government in twenty-four votes. More remarkable was the number of defeats between 1979 and 1997. As we have already noted, the government was defeated more than 200 times. A typical session would witness ten or more defeats. In the 1992–7 Parliament, for example, the government suffered nineteen defeats in the first session (1992–3), sixteen defeats in the second session (1993–4), seven in the third (1994–5), and ten in the fourth (1995–6).

The overwhelming majority of these defeats were on amendments to legislation (167 of the 173 defeats from 1979 to 1991 were on amendments or clauses to bills). Some of the defeats were on important or politically contentious issues, and took place on a broad range of bills. In the 1989–90 session, for example, they included defeats on the Courts and Legal Services, Education (Student Loans), Coal Industry, and NHS and Community Care Bills. The extent of the defeats became such that the government's business managers became more inclined to anticipate reaction in the Lords before proceeding with measures. 'There is clear evidence that Conservative government concern over not being able to secure the passage of particular items of legislation in a particular session has been at least a factor in persuading ministers to accept unpalatable amendments and to reach compromises on a number of occasions during the post-1979 period' (Baldwin, 1985, p. 101; see also Drewry and Brock, 1993, pp. 87–8). The House also demonstrated a willingness to challenge the view of the House of Commons in 1990 when it rejected the War Crimes Bill, a bill to allow alleged Nazi war criminals domiciled in the UK to be prosecuted. The bill had been passed in the Commons on a free vote by 273 votes to 60. The Lords rejected it by 207 votes to 74. (As it was a free vote, the Lords were able to vote on the second reading.) The bill was passed in the following session under the provisions of the 1949 Parliament Act.

Ironically, as a result of their Lordships' greater independence, going against the wishes of the government more often than the elected House, the House of Lords at times has appeared more responsive to public disquiet and has become a target for lobbying by interest groups. As such, it has been become more significant as a chamber for expressing the views of different groups in society, offering an outlet for views that sometimes fail to find an outlet in the lower House.

The reasons for this significant behavioural change have been identified by Nicholas Baldwin as twofold: a combination of an influx of life peers and a change of attitude (Baldwin, 1985, pp. 96–113). The provision for the creation of life peers under the 1958 Life Peerages Act allowed the injection of considerable new blood into the chamber. This resulted not only in more peers, but also more active peers and more peers active on the opposition benches. Life peers came to provide –

and continue to provide – the bulk of Labour's ranks in the Lords. The collapse in 1969 of the Parliament (No. 2) Bill, designed to reform the upper House, led many peers to adopt a new attitude toward the work of the House. They realised that reform of the House was not likely in the near future – there was no agreement among parties or among MPs as to what reform should take place – and so they felt they may as well get on with the job of scrutinising government and making the chamber as effective a revising body as possible, as no one else was likely to take their place to do it. The juxtaposition of these two developments helped revitalise the House. Two further developments may also have contributed to the change. One was the nature of the government returned in 1979. Although a Conservative government, it pursued radical neo-liberal policies that were not always congenial to Conservative peers. 'Thatcherism' was not in the ascendancy among Conservative peers and the government was not able to wield any sanctions that would force peers to support it. The introduction of television cameras may also have served to reinforce peers' willingness to be involved in the affairs of the House, though the initial novelty has worn off. The House was given a greater public visibility – especially in the four years before the proceedings of the Commons were televised – thus providing a more attractive platform for peers with a point to make.

The changes in the behaviour and attitude of peers have underpinned the structural changes, with peers being willing and able to sustain the sessional committees – such as European Communities and Science and Technology – and the various *ad hoc* committees that are appointed. The work of the EC Committee, for example, is made possible by life peers, who substantially outnumber hereditary peers on the subcommittees. Though the creation of the committees may seem a modest development, relative to what existed before it constitutes a significant advance. It has also proved a cost-effective change, the select committees having allowed the Lords to mobilise considerable expertise at virtually no expense to investigate and report on matters of parliamentary concern (Shell, 1983, p. 102). The fact that the matters investigated have also been of wider concern has helped enhance the reputation of the House among a wide range of affected groups.

The work of the committees has also helped concentrate minds in Whitehall on topics that otherwise might be neglected.

The committees of the House have thus provided an important channel for what Baldwin has termed the 'new professionalism' and independence exhibited by peers and, in combination, these developments have equipped the House with a facility to scrutinise and influence government. The extent to which it is able to do so is limited but none the less significant; and some members of the House would like to see its scrutinising capacity further extended. Compared to thirty years ago, the contemporary House of Lords is physically and politically a much more active body, far better able to fulfil functions of scrutiny, influence and expression.

Pressure for change

Although the Lords has changed in recent decades, demands continue to be made for it to be further reformed or even abolished. Critics contend that there is no case for maintaining a legislative chamber in which the composition is determined predominantly by accident of birth. It is not a representative chamber in any of the four definitions of the term (other, arguably, than in a symbolic sense, representing entrenched wealth and privilege) and therefore, it is argued, has no legitimacy to challenge the decisions of the elected House of Commons. Furthermore, critics contend that the upper House is not such an effective chamber for scrutinising and influencing government as its defenders claim. The government can usually employ its majority in the Commons to reverse a defeat in the Lords. Where it agrees to change a measure in the face of pressure from the Lords, the change is often cosmetic rather than substantive. And on vital issues, the Conservatives can bring in those peers who do not normally attend but will come when urgently pressed to do so. These 'backwoodsmen' are brought in on rare occasions under Conservative governments to overcome opposition on contentious issues, most notably in recent years on the poll tax in 1988 and the issue of a referendum on the Maastricht Treaty in 1993. Under a Labour government, the threat of being overwhelmed by Conservative peers is ever-present.

Critics therefore press for reform, even abolition, of the upper House.

Demands for reform are nothing new. As the democratic principle became more widely accepted in the nineteenth century, so calls for the reform of the unelected House of Lords became more strident. Conservative obstruction of Liberal bills in the 1880s led the Liberal Lord Morley to demand that the upper House 'mend or end', an approach adopted as Liberal policy in 1891. In 1894, the Liberal conference voted in favour of abolishing the Lords' power of veto. When the Lords rejected the Budget of the Liberal government in 1909, the government introduced the Parliament Bill. Passed in 1911, the preamble envisaged an elected House. Schemes of reform have peppered the decades since. They have not been confined to politicians of the left. Various Conservatives have advocated change and it was a Conservative government that was responsible for the Life Peerages Act in 1958 and the Peerages Act – allowing peers to renounce their titles – in 1963. However, the more radical demands for change have generally emanated from Labour politicians. In 1969, the Parliament (No. 2) Bill, introduced by the Labour government of Harold Wilson, sought to phase out the hereditary element. The bill foundered after encountering opposition from Conservative MPs, led by Enoch Powell, who felt it went too far, and from Labour MPs, led by Michael Foot, who believed it did not go far enough. In 1983, the Labour Party manifesto committed the party to abolition of the upper House. In its election manifesto in 1992, the party advocated instead an elected second chamber. This was later amended under Tony Blair's leadership to a two-stage reform: first, the elimination of the hereditary element and, second and in a later Parliament, the introduction of an elected second chamber. The Liberal Democrats also favour a reformed second chamber – a senate – as part of a wider package of constitutional reform. Charter '88, the constitutional reform movement created in 1988 (see Chapter 15), includes reform of the upper House 'to establish a democratic, non-hereditary second chamber' as a fundamental part of its reform programme.

Reform of the House of Lords is thus an issue on the political agenda. Should the present chamber be reformed? Should it be done away with altogether?

There are four separate approaches to reform that can be identified (Norton, 1982, pp. 119–29). They constitute the four Rs – retain, reform, replace or remove altogether.

Retain

This approach favours leaving the House alone. The House, it is argued, does a good job. It complements the elected House and provides a degree of detached expertise that would be lost if the House was elected. Furthermore, the hereditary element provides members who are beholden to no one and can make judgements independent of vested interests. They can also raise important issues which elected politicians may be reluctant to raise. If the House was elected, it would have the same claim to democratic legitimacy as the Commons and would either be the same as the Commons – thus constituting a rubber-stamping body and achieving nothing – or, if elected by a different method or at different times, would have the potential to clash with the Commons and create stalemate in the political system.

Defenders of the present House also point out that there is no strong demand for reform among citizens. The debate takes place principally at an elite, not a mass, level. As reformers cannot agree among themselves on what reform to support, the House is likely to remain as it is – and defenders would like it to stay that way.

Reform

This approach favours a reform to the existing House, retaining its present strengths in terms of expertise and work as a revising chamber while getting rid of the hereditary basis of its membership. This approach was embodied in the 1969 Parliament (No. 2) Bill, which provided for voting peers and non-voting peers. Those peers who had succeeded to their titles were to retain their right to sit in the House but not to vote, and the right to sit was not to pass to their successors. Hereditary peers would thus be phased out, leaving a chamber based on the principle of appointment. The fact that the House was appointed rather than elected would mean that it would lack the legitimacy to challenge the elected House. It would thus retain its existing powers and continue to complement, and not compete with, the Commons. Furthermore, as an appointed chamber it would not be unique, an appointed second chamber being a feature of several legislatures, including, for example, the Canadian federal parliament.

Replace

This approach favours doing away with the House of Lords and replacing it with a new second chamber. Several reformers favour an elected second chamber. Election, it is contended, would give the House a legitimacy which presently it lacks. That greater legitimacy would allow the House to serve as a more effective check on government, knowing that it was not open to accusations of being undemocratic. If members were elected on a national and regional basis, this – it is argued – would allow the different parts of the United Kingdom (Scotland, Wales and the English regions) to have a more distinct voice in the political process.

Others who favour doing away with the House of Lords want to replace it not with an elected chamber but with a chamber composed of representatives of different organised interests – a functional chamber. This, it is claimed, would ensure that the different groups in society – trade unions, charities, industry, consumer bodies – had a direct input into the political process, instead of having to lobby MPs and peers in the hope of getting a hearing. The problem with this proposal is that it would prove difficult to agree on which groups should enjoy representation in the House. Defenders of the existing House point out that there is extensive *de facto* functional representation in any event, with leading figures in a great many groups having been ennobled.

Remove altogether

Under this approach, the House of Lords would be abolished and not replaced at all. Instead, the UK would have a unicameral legislature, the legislative burden being shouldered by a reformed House of Commons. Supporters of this approach argue that there is no case for an unelected second chamber, since it has no legitimacy to challenge an elected chamber, and that there is no case for an elected

second chamber, since this would result in either imitation or conflict. Parliament should therefore constitute a single chamber, like legislatures in Scandinavia and New Zealand. The House of Commons should be reformed in order that it may fulfil all the functions presently carried out by the two chambers.

Opponents of this approach argue that a single chamber would not be able to carry the burden, not least given the volume of public business in a country with a population of 57 million, many times larger than New Zealand and the Scandinavian countries with unicameral legislatures. Furthermore, they contend, the House of Commons could not fulfil the task of a constitutional safeguard, since it would essentially be acting as a safeguard against itself. Nor would it be an appropriate body to undertake a second look at legislation since it would not be able to bring to bear a different point of view and different experience to that brought to bear the first time round.

Chapter summary

The House of Lords now constitutes an increasingly active second chamber, operating as a notable body of scrutiny – both of legislation and of public policy – and as a body for giving expression to views that otherwise would not be put on the public record. The fact that it is not elected means that it has limited significance as a body for legitimising government and measures of public policy and as a body through which politicians are recruited to ministerial office. The fact that it is not elected also makes it a target of demands for reform.

Reform of the House of Lords remains on the political agenda. There are frequent, and differing, calls for a new chamber or no second chamber at all. Though there is more support among political elites for some change than there is for leaving the House as it is, there is no agreement on what form that change should take. The position was well expressed by a leading peer: 'Put four people in a room to discuss reform of the House of Lords', he said, 'and you will end up with five separate solutions.' Even within parties, there is not always agreement. The Labour Party has moved from supporting abolition to favouring the removal of hereditary peers and, in the longer term, having an elected second chamber. The absence of agreement, and the absence of any strong popular pressure for reform, has militated against any major reform being carried through. At least it has so far....

Discussion points

- What are the principal functions of the House of Lords?

- Does the House of Lords do a better job than the House of Commons in scrutinising government legislation? If so, why?

- Should the government pay attention to the House of Lords?

- Should the institutions of the European Union pay attention to the House of Lords?

- To what extent, and why, is the House of Lords more active than it used to be?

- What would you do with the House of Lords – and why?

Further reading

The two main works on the House of Lords are the second edition of Shell (1992) and the edited volume by Shell and Beamish (1993), providing a thorough analysis of the House in one particular session (that of 1988–9). Shell also provides a useful chapter on questions in the Lords in Franklin and Norton (1993). On Lords reform, see Norton (1982) – delineating the four Rs – and the Constitution Unit publication, *Reform of the House of Lords* (1996), as well as the works by Shell.

References

Baldwin, N. (1985) 'The House of Lords: behavioural changes', in P. Norton (ed.), *Parliament in the 1980s* (Blackwell).

Constitution Unit (1996) *Reform of the House of Lords* (The Constitution Unit).

Drewry, G. and Brock, J. (1993) 'Government legislation: an overview', in D. Shell and D. Beamish (eds), *The House of Lords at Work* (Oxford University Press).

Franklin, M. and Norton, P. (eds) (1993) *Parliamentary Questions* (Oxford University Press).

Grantham, C. (1993), 'Select committees', in D. Shell and D. Beamish (eds), *The House of Lords at Work* (Oxford University Press).

Hayter, P.D.G. (1992) 'The parliamentary monitoring of science and technology', *Government and Opposition*, Vol. 26.

Himsworth, C.M.G. (1995) 'The Delegated Powers Scrutiny Committee', *Public Law*, Spring.

Norton, P. (1982) *The Constitution in Flux* (Basil Blackwell).

Norton, P. (1993) *Does Parliament Matter?* (Harvester Wheatsheaf).

Norton, P. (ed.) (1996) *National Parliaments and the European Union* (Frank Cass).

Shell, D. (1983) 'The House of Lords', in D. Judge (ed.), *The Politics of Parliamentary Reform* (Heinemann).

Shell, D. (1992) *The House of Lords* 2nd edn (Harvester Wheatsheaf).

Shell, D. and Beamish, D. (eds) (1993) *The House of Lords at Work* (Oxford University Press).

White, A.B. (1908) *The Making of the English Constitution 1449–1485* (G.P. Putnam).

Constitutional reform

THE RT HON. LORD BIFFEN

The British have never relished large doses of constitutional reform, although they have accepted the drip-feed of frequent, unpalatable and ill-fated local government changes. Ambivalence to reform was reinforced in recent decades. The 1974 Labour government proposed an ambitious programme of devolution for Scotland and Wales. It was a luckless policy, not least because of Labour's divisions. The bill was mangled at the hands of George Cunningham and Tam Dalyell. They helped contribute to Callaghan's defeat in 1979. The Tories then took up the baton of office, but Margaret Thatcher, an undoubted economic radical, was a stern opponent of constitutional change. Her Cabinet loyally followed suit.

Now all is different. The case for Scottish devolution is being argued with renewed vigour. Its consideration is linked with proportional representation for a Scottish Assembly. PR is also on the agenda for the Euro-constituencies. These proposals will not satisfy the Liberals, and it will only be a matter of time before familiarity with PR at Strasbourg and Edinburgh will lead to its serious consideration for Westminster.

That mature chestnut, reform of the House of Lords, is now part of the debate. The arguments are extending beyond the letter columns of *The Times*. It is also suggested we incorporate in our domestic legislation the provisions of the European Court of Human Rights. Finally – particularly from the Tory benches – there is the widespread belief that the balance of authority between national parliaments and Brussels will lead to conflict and not partnership. There is a growing demand for reform, at Westminster if not at Strasbourg.

These constitutional challenges exceed even the ambitions of Asquith and Lloyd George before the First War. Charter '88 can be justly proud of this success in setting so much of the political agenda, The revised edition of *Politics UK* outlines the political background to this situation with enviable academic skill. I will add my own modest remarks as an essentially street politician. I have watched the constitutional argument for some years now, largely as a 'soft' reformer with three objectives. Firstly, I seek a European partnership which reflects Charles de Gaulle's belief that it should rest upon national institutions to make and enforce the law. I hope this can be resolved within the framework of the European Union, but Britain may have to set its terms unilaterally. Over the next decade this could be the most profound constitutional clash, making Lords reform by comparison the small change of conflict. I also believe that as we redesign our European relationships, so we will find it convenient to make major reforms in our national institutions.

Secondly, I would like to see the dominance of the domestic executive over the legislature modified. I concede that there must be strong and decisive government, but I believe the numerical dominance of the payroll and growth of career politicians over the recent generation have clipped the wings of nonconformity. Happily the Maastricht debate has shown that parliamentary independence has not been wholly trodden underfoot.

Thirdly – a vain hope – I would like a seminal

Local Government Act. This would define those responsibilities of local government which could be covered by local revenue resources. It would be based upon Councils that were recognisable to the public. The unitary character of Britain would have been confirmed by this law; and local government, albeit reduced in scale, would have greater independence.

I must confess that my reforming priorities do not coincide with those of Charter '88 and I am once more on the margins of fashionable constitutional change. On the other hand I do think that many of today's avant-garde reformers are a good deal closer to fashion than they are to the public. It is highly questionable if there is great enthusiasm for a Welsh Assembly, particularly if it has to be financed locally. There is even less enthusiasm for English regional government – with the possible exception of the north-east. The prospect of European Union money could, of course, lead to contrived regional sentiment based upon cash considerations. I cannot believe this would lead to well-rooted loyalties, and that is what a functioning society needs.

Clearly Scotland makes the strongest case for constitutional change. A tax-raising assembly is probably a necessary development before the fundamental choice has to be taken between independence or otherwise integration in the union. Any devolution legislation in the late 1990s will not prove as politically fatal as it was in the mid-1970s. On the other hand, the financial relationships between a Scottish Assembly and a suspicious England will win no votes. Possibly it might lead to enduring resentment.

The House of Lords has been promised reform for generations. It seems churlish to disparage the tentative plans now on offer. Yet the present Lords seem to be one of the least objectionable aspects of our government. It has an excellent and highly informed select committee system (ahead of the Commons in my view), and it rarely provocatively challenges the government, and then predictably from a low-key liberal stand point. It is modest, mildly useful and represents no point of likely constitutional conflict. All these virtues are as likely to be maintained by the present membership as by tinkering with it.

I accept there will be an increasingly sharp debate upon the principle of reform. At least it is an achievement for there now to be recognition that the constitution no less than the economy is at the heart of the British debate. My instinct is that the European issue involving the role of national government will eventually be the centre-point of the controversy. It is the accountability of law-makers and tax-raisers that will dominate public anxiety. Law and taxation recycled through European Union institutions and returned to burden the British will be increasingly resented. The response to this state of affairs can be a critical debate in the best British political tradition. Alternatively the situation could be exploited by rabid populism. True friends of reform will seek to avert such an impending danger. This does not involve rejigging English regions or the House of Lords. It means starting a dialogue with Brussels to assert the authority of our own institutions as well as their reform.

PART FIVE

The executive process

CHAPTER NINETEEN

The Cabinet and Prime Minister

DENNIS KAVANAGH AND ANTHONY SELDON

LEARNING OBJECTIVES

- To provide a full analysis of the role of Prime Minister.

- To assess the importance of John Major.

- To examine the role of Cabinet ministers.

- To evaluate the possibilities for reform at the centre of British government.

INTRODUCTION

This chapter examines the work of the Prime Minister and Cabinet. It examines the role and powers of the Prime Minister and the structure of the office, and assesses the impact of John Major on the office. It discusses the factors which influence Cabinet's size and composition, then analyses the structure of the Cabinet and its committees and evaluates proposals for improving the coordination of policies. The Cabinet system, like much of the political system, has been subject to much discussion in recent years. The final section reviews some of these criticisms and suggestions which have been made for reform.

The Prime Minister

The Prime Minister's office in No. 10

No. 10 Downing Street, despite its modest outside appearance, is in fact a fair-sized office block, in which about one hundred people, including secretaries and security staff, work. Its upper floors contain a private flat for the Prime Minister and his or her family, although some prime ministers, notably Wilson in 1974–6, chose to live elsewhere. Staff at No. 10 are grouped into several offices, each with a specialised function. The divide between 'political' and 'official' is a good way of analysing the Prime Minister's different staff.

Political No. 10 comprises the Policy Unit and the Political Office. To this could be added, from 1971 to 1983, the *Central Policy Review Staff* (CPRS, or 'think-tank'), which, while technically working for the Cabinet as a whole, had considerable direct dealings with the Prime Minister. The *Policy Unit* was created in 1974 as a more personal resource for the Prime Minister. It was felt that, lacking a department or a team of personal advisers, the

Prime Minister was finding it difficult to take a strategic view of where the government as a whole was going. The first head of the Policy Unit was Bernard Donoughue, who served Labour prime ministers Wilson and Callaghan. New prime ministers appoint their own head of the Policy Unit, who becomes one of their closest advisers. The Policy Unit consists of no more than eight appointees, a mix of secondment from the civil service and from party politics or business who are classified as temporary civil servants for their stay in the Unit. Different prime ministers have used the Policy Unit to a greater or lesser extent: Thatcher wound down its importance after John Hoskyns (1979–82) departed. The peak of its influence since has been under John Major, with successive heads Sarah Hogg (1990–5) and Norman Blackwell (1995–7) giving key direction to government thinking. In 1990–2 Sarah Hogg's Policy Unit defined a distinctive agenda for Major's government and wrote the election manifesto.

The *Political Office* deals with communication between the Prime Minister and the party organisation, both at the centre with party professionals and in dealing with letters and events of a party political nature. The political secretary also deals with ministerial special advisers and has a general remit to keep the political wheels turning. The Political Office is paid for out of party rather than public funds. The first and most celebrated political secretary was Marcia Williams (1964–70 and 1974–6), whose influence on Wilson was second to none. Douglas Hurd was an important political secretary to Heath (1970–4) though he had a considerably reduced role in comparison to Marcia Williams. Jonathan Hill (1992–4) and Howell James (1995–7) have been important recent incumbents of the office.

The Prime Minister, like other ministers, has a *parliamentary private secretary* (PPS) – an MP whose job it is to keep the Prime Minister in contact with back-bench opinion at Westminster. Since 1994 John Major also had a PPS in the House of Lords. The PPS position is usually only of secondary importance, although some holders of the job have achieved positions of high influence, notably Ian Gow (1979–83) on Thatcher.

The *official* institutions of No. 10 are older than the political ones. The core of Downing Street is the *Private Office*, headed by the principal private secretary. This consists of civil servants usually in their forties, often the most impressive high fliers of their generation, on three-year loan from their departments. Because of the day-to-day contact with the Prime Minister, the job is the third most influential in the civil service, after the head of the home civil service/Cabinet secretary and permanent secretary to the Treasury. Recent influential incumbents have been for Heath Robert Armstrong (1970–4) and for Major Alex Allan (1992–7). There are in addition private secretaries for parliamentary affairs, home affairs, economic affairs, and two (since 1994) for foreign affairs. Within their remit, they handle all official papers destined for the Prime Minister from other government departments, foreign governments and others having official business. Private secretaries quickly learn how to regulate the flow of papers to the Prime Minister, and the best can second-guess with great accuracy what interests the Prime Minister and what he or she will decide.

The *Press Office* regulates the Prime Minister's relations with journalists, including the broadcast media, and covers a range of concerns from issuing government statements to arranging interview appointments. A job of this kind has existed since 1931. The job is a civil service post, usually filled from the professional press officers of the government information service, although different prime ministers and press secretaries have taken different approaches to the obvious political aspects of press relations. Some press secretaries have been drawn not from the civil service but from journalism (Joe Haines, 1969–70 and 1974–6, and Alistair Campbell 1997–). The most noted press secretary was Bernard Ingham (1979–90), who became heavily – too heavily in the eyes of some – politically identified with Thatcher.

The *Appointments Office* deals with the various Church of England, university and a whole range of other appointments outside politics for which the Prime Minister is responsible. The last incumbent was John Holroyd.

The Prime Minister's roles

The Prime Minister has various roles in the British governmental system, which coincide to some extent

Table 19.1   The Prime Minister's roles

Function	Supporting office
Head of the executive	Cabinet secretariat
	Private Office
Head of government policy	Policy Unit
	Press Office (communication)
Party leader	Political secretary (party outside Parliament)
	Parliamentary private secretary
Head appointing officer	Appointments secretary (crown appointments)
	Cabinet secretary (senior civil service)
	Principal private secretary (ministers)
Leader of party in Parliament	Parliamentary private secretary
	Private secretary – parliamentary affairs
Senior British representative overseas	Cabinet secretary (Commonwealth)
	Principal private secretary
	Private Secretary–Foreign affairs

with the administrative divisions of the No. 10 office (see Table 19.1):

1. *Head of the executive*:   The Prime Minister is in charge of overseeing the civil service and government agencies, and is ultimately answerable for all its decisions.
2. *Head of government policy*:   Though most policy is produced through the departments and the party's own policy-making apparatus, the Prime Minister has a key influence over the party's election manifesto and the annual Queen's Speech outlining government legislation for the coming year, and more generally can choose which policies he or she wishes to highlight or play down. Prime ministers traditionally are particularly influential in economic and foreign policy decisions.
3. *Party leader*:   The Prime Minister is not only in organisational charge of the party as well as the government, but is also the figure who personifies that party to the public at large.
4. *Head appointing officer*:   For posts throughout the political and administrative executive

branch, as well as the various appointing powers in the church and academia exercised on behalf of the monarch.

5. *Party leader in Parliament*:   The Prime Minister is the principal figure in the House of Commons, above all in weekly Question Time when the Prime Minister's performance has the greatest effect on party morale and public perception. Since the televising of the Commons in 1989, PM's Questions every Tuesday and Thursday have assumed even greater importance.
6. *Senior UK representative overseas*:   Since the 1970s prime ministers have been involved in increasing amounts of travel and meetings with foreign heads of government. There are several regular engagements per year (the G7, UN, and up to four European Councils) and several less frequent regular events such as the biannual Commonwealth Heads of Government Meeting as well as other less structured summits, most frequently with Ireland and the USA.

Prime Ministers' styles

Prime ministers naturally bring their own personal contributions to the office, and have all demonstrated different approaches to policy, politics and relations with the Cabinet, from Balfour's diffidence (1902–5) through Eden's impulsiveness (1955–7) to Major's striving for unity. It is a truism that each occupant is a different person, but the most important influences on the role and style of particular prime ministers are, however, contingent on factors subject to limited or no control from Downing Street. Prime ministerial power may well have been boosted in the run up to the general election as in 1970, 1987 and 1992 (though in each case this factor was demonstrably only operating for short periods). To a lesser extent, the fluctuations in *party support* in interim elections (by-elections, European and local), in polls and approval ratings for the Prime Minister also create conditions for weak or strong prime ministerial leadership. The state of the economy is a key variable factor: if strong, the Prime Minister's position will be enhanced. As a general election draws near, the Cabinet and party also rally to the Prime Minister, in the realisation that they will prosper or falter depending on how united they are behind the leadership. Prime ministers are constrained in their styles by other political actors – the extent of willing support that can be gathered from the Cabinet, the attractiveness of the parliamentary opposition, and the possibility that there are alternative leaders waiting in the wings, as with Kenneth Clarke and Michael Heseltine in 1993–4, and John Redwood between 1995 and 1997. Britain's standing in the world is also significant, particularly in wartime when the Prime Minister's roles of speaking for the nation as a whole, and direct communication with foreign heads of government, enhance his or her stature and profile, as seen in both the Falklands (1982) and Gulf (1991) wars.

Margaret Thatcher as Prime Minister

The reasons why Margaret Thatcher became more dominant provide important insights into the source of prime ministerial power. They seem to be as follows:

1. Her *successful use of Cabinet reshuffles* – or the power to hire and fire – over time to produce a more loyal team. She had originally appointed her supporters to the key economic departments in 1979. During 1981 she gradually dismissed a number of dissenters from her Cabinet, including Soames, Gilmour, Carlisle and St John-Stevas, and moved James Prior to the office of Northern Ireland. Later she dismissed Francis Pym from the Foreign Office and David Howell. She appointed newcomers like Parkinson, Brittan, King, Lord Young and Lawson, who were more supportive of her policies and owed their promotion to her.
2. She gained from *policy successes*, particularly the down-turn in inflation in 1982 then, decisively, the recapture of the Falklands, the steady rise in the living standards of those in work and, of course, from general election victories in 1983 and 1987.
3. She simply held fewer Cabinet meetings – Peter Hennessy suggests half as many as her Labour predecessors. Ex-Defence Minister John Nott reckoned full Cabinet meetings were more often occasions when decisions reached elsewhere were formally endorsed.

4. She *bypassed the Cabinet* on occasions, relying heavily upon her Policy Unit and making decisions either in Cabinet committees (see above), bilateral meetings between herself and her advisers and the departmental minister, or high-powered interdepartmental task forces of able civil servants reporting direct to No. 10. Peter Hennessy describes a typical example of this way of working:

   Mrs Thatcher will ask a particular Cabinet colleague to prepare a paper on a particular issue just for her, not for the Cabinet or her Cabinet Committee. The Minister is summoned to Number Ten with his back-up team. He sits across the table from Mrs Thatcher and her team which can be a blend of people from the Downing Street Private Office, the Policy Unit, the Cabinet Office and one or two personal advisers. She then, in the words of one Minister, proceeds to 'act as a judge and jury to her own cause'. (Hennessy, 1986, p. 289)

5. She also *interfered energetically in departments*, following up initiatives and taking an unprecedentedly close interest in the promotion of senior civil servants.

John Major as prime minister

Several factors remained consistent throughout John Major's prime ministership, namely a collegial approach to Cabinet decisions, autonomy for most secretaries of state in managing their departments, and a low-key approach to national leadership. Major was most definitely a 'stabiliser', without an overriding political project (save perhaps his consensus-seeking desire for 'a country at ease with itself') rather than a 'mobiliser' like Thatcher or Gladstone, who sought radical changes. Rather like Gladstone, however, he became increasingly concerned with Ireland and sought to leave his mark on history by producing lasting peace.

Different viewpoints on Major

" John is virtually unknown, too vulnerable to the subtle charge of 'not yet ready for it'. He has personal handicaps, not of his own making. The product, indeed of his virtues. He is not at all *flash* … and he is not classy, which doesn't worry me in the slightest, but worse, he doesn't (like Mrs T) even *aspire* to be classy.

Alan Clark, Diaries, 17 November 1993.

The coming year will witness the end, I predict and hope, of the Major Government, the most disreputable of my lifetime. To some extent its awfulness simply reflects changes for the worse in our society, and so within Conservatism, our only national party. [But] John Major, who seems to stand for no principle, belief or ideal of any description, has given his own twist to this downward spiral.   *Paul Johnson, The Spectator, 1 January 1994*

John Major is a master of ambiguity, a man who is not afraid to hesitate, and a man who knows the art of compromise.

Matthew Parris, The Times, 3 March 1995

In other matters the Major years saw several distinct periods, in which prime ministerial power, relations with Cabinet colleagues and perceived

policy success shifted. The first was from *November 1990 to the summer of 1992*. This was a broadly successful period of prime ministerial strength, but of a different kind from that demonstrated by Thatcher in the late 1980s. Major inherited the prime ministership after a particularly brutal demonstration of the limits of prime ministerial power, with a deeply divided Cabinet and party. He could do no other than take a more collegiate approach to his Cabinet, and his personal preferences militated for this as well. Cabinet became a forum for more general discussion than had taken place since the days of Callaghan, and suffered no acrimonious arguments. Major's leadership was strong and successful, in that he held the party together, performed several necessary policy

---

BOX 19.1   JOHN MAJOR (1943–)   **BIOGRAPHY**

By courtesy of Popperfoto

John Major was born into a lower-middle-class family in Worcester Park, a south London suburb. A decline in family fortunes led to a move to

Brixton in 1955, and John Major leaving school at 16 with meagre qualifications for a succession of dead-end jobs. His career took a better turn in 1966 when he joined Standard Bank, rising through the ranks to become head of public relations for Standard Charter in 1976. From an early age he was an active Conservative, winning election to Lambeth council in 1968, and becoming chairman of housing in 1970. After two unsuccessful attempts in a London seat in 1974, he entered Parliament as MP for Huntingdon in 1979.

Major became a whip in 1983, and served as a junior minister in the Department of Health and Social Security 1985–7. In these roles he attracted the interest of Prime Minister Margaret Thatcher as quiet, personable and competent. He continued to impress her as Chief Secretary to the Treasury (1987–July 1989) and was surprisingly promoted to Foreign Secretary, where he served a short and unhappy tenure before returning to the Treasury as Chancellor in October 1989. His term as Chancellor was notable for the start of a recession and sterling's entry into the ERM. In November 1990, after a professional leadership campaign, he became Prime Minister as Thatcher's favoured successor.

BOX 19.2

IDEAS AND PERSPECTIVES

'Majorism': the Citizen's Charter

As a back-bench MP, and as a Cabinet minister, John Major had expressed interest in making public services more 'user friendly'. When he became Prime Minister, he faced the need to develop a policy agenda distinct from – but not a rejection of – Thatcherism. He held discussions with his Policy Unit in early 1991 on contracting out some, and reforming other, public services, and the result was a series of speeches. He announced the Citizen's Charter in March, and it was published as a White Paper – after much Policy Unit prodding of Whitehall – in July. The initiative was consolidated by the establishment of an Advisory Panel and a Charter Unit in 1991 and the Office of Public Service and Science in 1992.

The Charter was much criticised for its apparent concern with trivia, and exposed to ridicule by the 'cones hotline'; rail privatisation, foreshadowed in the Charter, was also controversial. Yet changes caused by the Charter, such as performance targets for the public services, have improved services from the Passport Office to London bus stops. In its low profile, openness to mockery, and subtle but permanent changes to public life, Major's 'big idea' reflects much of his premiership.

changes (abandoning the poll tax, new agendas in education and the public services), won a close election and proved an asset to the government in public opinion terms. In early 1991 his personal ratings were the highest recorded since Churchill and his reassuring national leadership, particularly during the Gulf War, suited the mood better than Thatcher's triumphalism. All of these features mark a sharp departure from Thatcher's premiership. Despite severe recession, the opposition never opened up a commanding lead in the polls.

The second phase lasted from *summer 1992 until early 1995*. Growing turmoil over Europe, plus the devaluation on 'Black Wednesday', the day when Britain withdrew from the exchange rate mechanism, and a series of policy errors and reverses thereafter, gravely weakened the Prime Minister's position. The initial general election majority of twenty-one had dwindled to single figures by 1994, inhibiting freedom of manoeuvre. Existing Cabinet divisions over Europe proved difficult to manage; some ministers, notably John Redwood and Michael Portillo, engaged in more or less open acts of defiance that would have resulted in dismissal during the 1980s. As the popularity of the government fell to record depths, Major's power to

enforce collective discipline eroded. Characteristics acclaimed as Major virtues in the first phase were widely dismissed as weaknesses in the second. Major was unable to articulate a strong sense of where the government was going, and policy appeared to be a mix of scrapings of the barrel of Thatcherism (rail privatisation) with attempts to return to basic values in education and public order. He lost much of his ability to speak for the nation, being treated by the media and the public alike as a target for ridicule and abuse. Progress in Northern Ireland was the principal prime ministerial achievement in this difficult period.

The third phase has been one of irregular recovery of prime ministerial leadership between early 1995 and early 1997. Policy took on more direction as the general election approached and a new team of advisers came to Downing Street. The most considerable act of assertion was Major's decision to flush out his critics by resigning the Conservative leadership and challenging them to oppose him in the summer of 1995. The defeat of John Redwood removed one of the factors systematically weakening Major, the constant speculation that he would resign or be removed in the not too distant future. The subsequent reshuffle produced a Cabinet that was more inclined to accept, and effectively promote, Major's leadership. A key change was the appointment of Heseltine as Deputy Prime Minister, giving him a wide-ranging brief over Cabinet committees and presentation of government policy.

Possible reforms

Several reforms have been suggested as ways of improving the operation of the office of Prime Minister:

1. A *Prime Minister's department*:   This would involve a larger executive office than No. 10, on the lines of chancellors in Germany and in Taoiseach's Ireland. It would have a civil servant as permanent secretary, a bevy of other senior officials, and several junior ministers to oversee it. The advantages would be that there would be greater clarity, and the Prime Minister would be allowed to plan his or her time in a more rational way than currently. The disadvantages would be in fitting it into the hierarchy of Cabinet – could junior Prime Minister's department ministers issue orders to Cabinet ministers? Would it cut the Prime Minister off and act as a buffer between him or her and the

rest of government? In some ways the Cabinet Office already performs many of the functions usually associated with a Prime Minister's department. In a single-party government, the interests of the Prime Minister are supposedly synonymous with those of the government as a whole, unlike in Ireland or Germany.

2. A *regularised Deputy Prime Minister*, with his or her own department. There is no fixed office of this kind in Britain. The title has been used for two purposes: buying off a dangerous political rival with a title (Howe, 1989–90), or appointing a senior figure to coordinate other Cabinet ministers and adjudicate in disputes (Whitelaw, 1983–88) – or indeed both (Heseltine, 1995–7). The position would be akin to the Vice-President in the United States.

3. *Direct election*:   This would resolve conflicts of authority decisively in favour of the Prime Minister and add to his or her status as national leader. It is, however, difficult to reconcile with a parliamentary system (how would one deal with a Prime Minister of one party and a Parliament dominated by the other?) and would probably entail more extensive constitutional reform.

BOX 19.3   **IDEAS AND PERSPECTIVES**

Should Prime Ministers have their own department?

It is possible to envisage a revamped Cabinet Office providing the basis of a Prime Minister's department, but there are many obstacles in the way of such a development. It is difficult to reconcile with the doctrine of collective responsibility and the principle of collegial decision-making. Some Cabinet ministers would also be concerned that their positions in their departments might be undermined by the Prime Minister having access to independent assessments of their policies. The case for a Prime Minister's department may be more pressing if the PM clearly had different political interests and a different political

agenda from that of the Cabinet. But if he or she feels blocked, then it would be simpler to reshuffle the Cabinet, as Thatcher did in 1981. It is still the case that prime ministers who are thought to ride roughshod over Cabinet colleagues or ignore them take political risks and generally get a bad press. This aspect of Thatcher's political style was devastatingly criticised in Sir Geoffrey Howe's resignation speech in November 1990 and was a major factor in her subsequent downfall. The fact that most Cabinet members told her she would lose a second ballot is an indication that many had lost confidence in her.

BOX 19.4

Dimensions of prime ministerial power

I. Prime Minister and government: the power of appointment

Sources

1. Appoints all ministers and subsequently promotes, demotes, dismisses.
2. Decides who does what in Cabinet.
3. Appoints chairmen of Cabinet committees (now increasingly important)
4. Approves choice of ministers' parliamentary private secretaries.
5. Other patronage powers, e.g. appoints chairmen of commissions, recommends knighthoods, peerages and sundry other awards.

Constraints

1. Seniority of colleagues demands their inclusion and sometimes in particular posts
2. Availability for office – experience, talent, willingness to serve.
3. Need for balance:
   (a) Ideological, left + right.
   (b) Regional.
   (c) Occupational.
   (d) Lords.
4. Debts to loyal supporters.
5. Shadow Cabinet expectations.

II. Prime Minister and Cabinet direction

Sources

1. Summons meetings.
2. Determines agenda.
3. Sums up 'mood' of meeting.
4. Approves minutes.
5. Spokesman for Cabinet to outside world.
6. Existence of inner Cabinet (intimate advisers).

Constraints

1. Needs Cabinet approval for controversial measures.
2. Determination of groups of ministers to press a case or oppose a particular policy.
3. Power of vested departmental interests backed up by senior civil servants.
4. Convention dictates certain items will appear regularly on Cabinet agenda.

III. Prime Minister and Parliament

Sources

1. Commands a majority in House (usually).
2. Spokesman for government.
3. Weekly Question Time provides platform upon which PM can usually excel.

Constraints

1. Activities of opposition.
2. Parliamentary party meetings.
3. Question Time: not always a happy experience.

IV. Prime Minister and party

Sources

1. 'Brand image' of party, especially at election time: PM's 'style' is that of the party.
2. Control over appointments.
3. Natural loyalty of party members to their leader and their government.
4. Threat of dissolution (seldom a credible threat, though).
5. Fear of party members that opposition will exploit public disagreements.

Constraints

1. Danger of election defeat: can lead to loss of party leadership.
2. Existence of ambitious alternative leaders.
3. Need to command support of parliamentary party, particularly when majority is thin or non-existent.
4. For Labour premiers, some constraints from party outside Parliament, e.g. National Executive Committee and party conference.

BOX 19.4   (continued)

V. Prime Minister and administration

Sources

1. Appoints permanent secretaries.
2. Cabinet Office: acts as PM's own staff to some extent.
3. High-powered policy unit in No. 10.
4. Traditional loyalty of civil servants to political masters.
5. Is not constrained by departmental responsibilities.

Constraints

1. Sheer volume of work: limit to the amount a PM can read.
2. Power of departmental interests.
3. Treasury: exerts financial constraints over whole of government.

VI. Prime Minister and the country

Sources

1. The most prestigious and publicly visible politician in the country.
2. Access to instant media coverage for whatever purpose.
3. Access to top decision-makers in all walks of public life.
4. Ability to mount high-prestige meetings with foreign leaders, trips abroad, etc.

Constraints

1. Those vested interests – especially economic – represented by powerful pressure groups, e.g. business and trade unions.
2. The public's potential for boredom with the same leader.
3. The tendency of the public to blame the PM for failure beyond the control of No. 10.
4. Failure of the economy.
5. Events abroad, e.g. wars, terrorism, changes of government, etc.

Cabinet

Functions of Cabinet

The functions of the Cabinet may be considered under various headings:

1. Although it does not actually decide many policies (though all ministers may be collectively responsible for the policies of the government), *it is the arena in which most important decisions are taken.* Often the Cabinet receives reports or ratifies recommendations from its committees; with the annual budget – an important influence on the economic policy of the government – Cabinet ministers merely hear the Chancellor of the Exchequer's main recommendations shortly before his statement to the House of Commons. The most fraught day for Cabinet in the 1990s was on 22 July 1993, when three Cabinet meetings were held at the final crisis point in the passage of the Maastricht Bill.

2. *It plans the business of Parliament,* usually a week or so in advance, making decisions about the timetabling of legislation and choosing major government speakers.

3. *It arbitrates in cases of disputes between departments.* A Cabinet adjudication is regularly occasioned when some departments fail to agree with the Treasury about their spending totals. Dramatic cases were the confrontations between the Treasury and the Department of Transport over the form of rail privatisation, or between the Department of Environment and Treasury over the replacement for the poll tax, both in the 1990s.
4. *It provides for oversight and coordination in government policies* (for further discussion of this, see below).
5. *It provides political leadership for the party* in Parliament and in the country.

The Cabinet meets weekly on Thursdays for two hours or so and less frequently during holiday periods, unless in emergencies when summoned by the Prime Minister. It meets usually in the Cabinet Room in No. 10, and about forty Cabinet meetings are held a year. A good part of its business is fairly predictable. Regular items include a review of foreign and European Community affairs and a parliamentary business report from the Leader of the House of Commons. In addition issues which are politically sensitive or highly topical are usually considered.

An item is usually introduced by the departmental minister in charge of the subject under discussion. In chairing the Cabinet the Prime Minister may wish to promote a particular line but more often wants to establish how much agreement there is about a proposed course of action. At the end of the discussion the Prime Minister sums up the mood of the meeting. Once the summary is written in the minutes it becomes a decision of the Cabinet. Votes are not taken; they advertise divisions, may fail to reflect the different political weight and experience of ministers and detract from Cabinet's role as a deliberative body. But the Prime Minister is very aware of the balance of opinion within Cabinet when summing up and reaching his or her own decision.

The Cabinet occupies a central position in the political system, *vis-à-vis* Parliament, the civil service and the public. Government ministers and whips have come to ensure they have a majority in the House of Commons for it is the Commons which sustains and may unseat them as a government. The decisions of Cabinet are instructions for civil servants to translate into laws and policies. Finally, the Cabinet has to gain the consent of the public, represented by interest groups and public opinion. Peter Hennessy describes this mix of pressures:

Ministers must look constantly in three directions: inward to the civil service machine, across Whitehall to Parliament, and outward to the party beyond Westminster, to institutions, professions, the country as a whole and to other nations. (Hennessy, 1988, p. 432).

Who serves in the Cabinet?

In a 1985 article Martin Burch and Michael Moran examined Cabinet personnel from 1916 onwards. Their findings (see Table 19.2) challenged the widely held view that grammar-school-educated meritocrats like Heath, Thatcher and Major have come to the fore in Conservative Cabinets. During the period 1955–84 a *higher* percentage of public-school-educated Cabinet members served than during the 1916–55 period, together with a higher percentage of Oxbridge graduates and people from working-class backgrounds. However, the proportion of Eton- and Harrow-educated Cabinet ministers has fallen from nearly half to a (still quite remarkable) third and those with aristocratic origins from just under a third to less than one-fifth.

Examination of the years 1970–84 reveals the maintenance of public school and Oxbridge percentages at former levels and a continuing decline of aristocrats, Etonians and Harrovians. Heath and Thatcher therefore represent no revolution: they are the exceptions rather than the rule. For all the media talk of John Major's 'classless' society, over 70 per cent of his post-election 1992 Cabinet were from Oxbridge and private school.

The Labour pattern is rather more complex. Their small number of aristocrats has virtually disappeared but big increases were registered in university- and especially Oxbridge-educated members. Ex-public school boys also increased from just over one-quarter in the earlier period to about one-third in the later period. But these increases are put into a different perspective when class origins are examined: over 60 per cent of Labour Cabinet

Table 19.2   Social background of Cabinet ministers (per cent)

| | 1916–55 | | 1955–84 | |
	Conservative	Labour	Conservative	Labour
All public schools	76.5	26.1	87.1	32.1
Eton/Harrow	45.9	7.6	36.3	3.5
Oxbridge	63.2	27.6	72.8	42.8
Elementary/secondary only	4.0	50.7	2.5	37.5
All universities	71.4	44.6	81.6	62.5
Aristocrat	31.6	6.1	18.1	1.8
Middle class	65.3	38.4	74.0	44.0
Working class	3.0	55.3	2.6	41.0
No data	–	–	4.0	12.6
Number	98	65	77	56

Source: Burch and Moran, 1985

ministers were working class in the later period and of the nineteen new entrants between 1974 and 1979 no fewer than eight were from manual working backgrounds. In the later period it is clear that working-class recruitment to Labour Cabinets was still substantial but improved educational opportunities explained why an increased proportion had enjoyed a university education. The Labour Party has experienced an embourgeoisement process to some extent, but on the basis of these figures Burch and Moran argue that it is less than is widely supposed.

Size

Peacetime Cabinets in the twentieth century have varied in size between sixteen (Bonar Law in 1922) and twenty-four (Wilson in 1964). The average size of Cabinets in the twentieth century has been twenty. The wartime Cabinets of Lloyd George and Winston Churchill have been much praised and both contained fewer than ten members. Both Thatcher and Major experimented with small war Cabinets for the short Falklands and Gulf campaigns. It is important to note, however, that in war very different considerations operate from peacetime politics.

Decisions about the Cabinet size and composition have to balance the needs of decision-making and deliberation against those of representatives. The Cabinet is a committee which has to be small enough to allow ministers the opportunities to discuss, deliberate and coordinate policies. Yet at the same time it must be large enough to include heads of major departments and accommodate different political groups in the party. Lobbies for different interests, e.g. education, Scotland or health, expect to have 'their' minister represented in Cabinet.

Prime ministers have frequently expressed their wish for small or smaller Cabinets. Some commentators have advocated a Cabinet of six or so non-departmental ministers, which would concentrate on strategy and coordination and be supported by standing and *ad hoc* committees of other departmental ministers. The growing burden of work on ministers and the tendencies for some ministers gradually to acquire a departmental perspective do pose problems of oversight and stategy in the Cabinet. On his return to 10 Downing Street in 1951 Winston Churchill appointed a number of so-called 'overlords', ministers who sat in the House of Lords, were free from departmental and constituency duties, and were charged with coordinating policies in related departments. The experiment was not, however, a success. It was difficult to separate the coordinating responsibilities of the 'overlords' in the Lords from the ministerial duties of ministers who were formally answerable to the House of Commons. More generally, it is difficult to separate

BOX 19.5

Ministerial committees of the cabinet

Economic and domestic policy (EDP)
Terms of reference: 'To consider strategic issues relating to the Government's economic and domestic policies.'

Defence and overseas policy (OPD)
Terms of reference: 'To keep under review the Government's Defence and Overseas policy.'

The Gulf (OPDG)
Terms of reference: 'To keep under review developments in the Gulf region and to co-ordinate any necessary action.'

Nuclear defence policy (OPDN)
Terms of reference: 'To keep under review the Government's policy on nuclear defence.'

European security (OPDSE)
Terms of reference: 'To keep under review arrangements for defence and security in Europe.'

Hong Kong and other dependent territories (OPDK)
Terms of reference: 'To keep under review the implementation of the agreement with the Chinese on the future of Hong Kong and the implications of that agreement for the Government of Hong Kong and the wellbeing of its people; and to keep under review as necessary the Government's policy towards other Dependent Territories.'

Northern Ireland (NI)
Terms of reference: 'To oversee the Government's policy on Northern Ireland issues and relations with the Republic of Ireland on these matters.'

Science and technology (EDS)
Terms of reference: 'To review science and technology policy.'

The intelligence services (IS)
Terms of reference: 'To keep under review policy on the security and intelligence services.'

Industrial, commercial and consumer affairs (EDI)
Terms of reference: 'To consider industrial, commercial, and consumer issues including questions of competition and deregulation.'

The environment (EDE)
Terms of reference: 'To consider questions of environmental policy.'

Home and social affairs (EDH)
Terms of reference: 'To consider home and social policy issues.'

Local government (EDL)
Terms of reference: 'To consider issues affecting local government, including the annual allocation of resources.'

Regeneration (EDR)
Terms of reference: 'To consider regeneration policies and their coordination.'

Public expenditure (EDX)
Terms of reference: 'To consider the allocation of the public expenditure control totals and make recommendations to the Cabinet.'

The Queen's Speeches and future legislation (FLG)
Terms of reference: 'To prepare and submit to the Cabinet drafts of the Queen's Speeches to Parliament, and proposals for the Government's legislative programme for each Session of Parliament.'

Legislation (LG)
Terms of reference: 'To examine all draft Bills; to consider the Parliamentary handling of Government Bills, European Community documents and Private Members' business, and such other related matters as may be necessary; and to keep under review the Government's policy in relation to issues of Parliamentary procedures.'

BOX 19.5 (continued)

Subcommittee on health strategy (EDH(H))

Terms of reference: 'To oversee the development, implementation and monitoring of the Government's health strategy, to coordinate the Government's policies on United Kingdom-wide issues affecting health, and report as necessary to the Ministerial Committee on Home and Social Affairs.'

Subcommittee on public sector pay (EDI(P))

Terms of reference: 'To coordinate the handling of pay issues in the public sector, and report as necessary to the Ministerial Committee on Industrial, Commercial and Consumer Affairs.'

Subcommittee on European questions (OPD(E))

Terms of reference: 'To consider questions relating to the United Kingdom's membership of the European Community and to report as necessary to the Ministerial Committee on Defence and Overseas Policy.'

Subcommittee on Eastern Europe (OPD(AE))

Terms of reference: 'To consider questions relating to Britain's policy of assisting change in the former Soviet republics and other former Communist countries in Europe and report as necessary to the Ministerial Committee on Defence and Overseas Policy.'

Subcommittee on terrorism (OPD(T))

Terms of reference: 'To keep under review the arrangements for countering terrorism and for dealing with terrorist incidents and their consequences and to report as necessary to the Ministerial Committee on Defence and Overseas Policy.'

Subcommittee on London (EDL(L))

Terms of reference: 'To coordinate the Government's policies on London.'

Subcommittee on drug misuse (EDH(D))

Terms of reference: 'To coordinate the Government's national and international policies for tackling drugs misuse, and report as necessary to the Ministerial Committee on Home and Social Affairs.'

Subcommittee on women's issues (EDH(W))

Terms of reference: 'To review and develop the Government's policy and strategy on issues of special concern to women: to oversee their implementation; and to report as necessary to the Ministerial Committee on Home and Social Affairs.'

Group on refugees from former Yugoslavia (GEN 24)

Terms of reference: 'To consider whether a visa regime should be instituted for citizens of former Yugoslavia in the context of the Government's overall policy towards that region and to review the practical arrangements for the reception and subsequent support of those arriving in the United Kingdom from this area taking account of the implications for the treatment of refugees from other parts of the world, and to report to Cabinet.'

Group on sanctions against the Federal Republic of Yugoslavia (GEN 27)

Terms of reference: 'To keep under review the implementation of the sanctions against the Federal Republic of Yugoslavia imposed under United Nations Security Council Resolutions 757, 787 and 820, and to report to the Ministerial Committee on Overseas and Defence Policy as necessary.'

the tasks of coordination and strategy from those of the day-to-day running of a department. Separating policy from administration is easier in theory than in practice. In opposition before 1964 Harold Wilson implied that the large size (twenty-three) of Sir Alec Douglas-Home's Cabinet (1963–4) reflected the weakness of Sir Alec as a Prime Minister. He was implying that he would have had a much smaller one. In the event he ended up with one of twenty-four, the largest in the century. Thatcher's Cabinets in 1983 and 1987 had twenty-two members, as did John Major's in 1992.

Cabinet committees

The system of Cabinet committees is a practical response to the increasing workload of Cabinet and the need for some specialisation and greater time in considering most issues. In 1992, as part of Major's drive for greater openness in government, the names and members of Cabinet committees were made public. As part of the Cabinet system deliberations of the committees are bound by secrecy and served by the Cabinet secretariat. There are various types of Cabinet committee. *Standing committees* are permanent for the duration of the prime minister's term in office, while miscellaneous or *ad hoc committees* are set up to deal with particular issues. A third category is *official committees*, which consist only of civil servants.

A number of critics have seen the development of the committee system as a means for the Prime Minister to bypass the full Cabinet and expand his or her own power. It is the Prime Minister who decides to set up committees and appoint their members, chairmen and terms of reference. Scope for prime ministerial influence is enhanced by the *ad hoc* committees, since the PM has more discretion to define their terms of reference than those of the standing committees, such as defence and foreign affairs. Supporters of the system observe that it is the only way a modern Cabinet can cope with the volume of work facing it. The committee system is a sign of the adaptability of Cabinet. Ministers can appeal against a committee's conclusion to the full Cabinet but only with the approval of the committee chairman.

Thatcher was more reluctant than her predecessors to set up Cabinet committees. She preferred to hold 'bilateral' meetings with the minister and officials in a department or 'working parties' to tackle a problem. Under Major the Cabinet and Cabinet committee system reverted to the normal pattern, after the battering of the Thatcher years. Major was exceedingly keen to bind his ministers into decisions, and to ensure that the widest group of relevant ministers was party to key decisions. The only occasion on which big decisions were taken on core government policy outside the Cabinet and committee system was on leaving the ERM on 16 September 1992, but even then Major took care to consult in an *ad hoc* way all his most senior ministers – Norman Lamont, Kenneth Clarke, Douglas Hurd and Michael Heseltine.

The Cabinet machine

Until 1916 there were no formal procedures for keeping minutes of Cabinet meetings or records of decisions. In that year, however, the Cabinet Office or secretariat was established by Lloyd George. Today the Cabinet Office is at the heart of the government machine. Its main tasks in relation to Cabinet and the committees are: to prepare the agenda of the Cabinet by circulating relevant papers to ministers beforehand; to record Cabinet proceedings and decisions; and to follow up and coordinate the decisions by informing the departments of decisions and checking that appropriate action has been taken. The Cabinet secretary is also the prime minister's secretary. Sir Robert Armstrong, a previous Cabinet secretary, was sent by Thatcher to answer questions by the House of Commons select committee in 1986 when it investigated Westland, and he also answered for the government in the Australian courts when the government tried to prevent publication of the *Spycatcher* memoirs of an ex-MI5 officer.

Coordination

Some observers have suggested that British government resembles a medieval system in which the departments operate as relatively independent fiefdoms. Bruce Headey (1974) interviewed a number of former and present Cabinet ministers and found that most of them regarded themselves primarily as *representatives* or spokesmen for the department *vis-à-vis* Parliament, the Cabinet and the public. Others emphasised the internal aspect of their work, *managing* and organising the department. Only one in six regarded themselves as *initiators* of policies, in the sense of defining the department's policy options. The departmental pressures on many ministers tended to limit their opportunities to contribute to the formation of government policy-making in general. Thus Headey argued that *Britain had departmental rather than Cabinet government.*

How, therefore, is government policy coordinated? How do ministers have a sense of strategy, a sense of *where*, collectively, they are going?

1. On a financial level Treasury controls public spending and the annual spending reviews.
2. There are informal consultations between senior officials of departments.
3. Formal interdepartmental meetings also provide the opportunity for coordination.
4. The role of the Cabinet Office in servicing the Cabinet and its committees, preparing and circulating papers and following up Cabinet decisions is relevant.
5. The system of Cabinet committees itself helps to coordinate policy.
6. The Prime Minister, and No. 10 office, take an overview across all government policy.

Many argue that Cabinet itself does not coordinate very efficiently. In part, this is a problem of sheer overload of work which results in ministers lacking sufficient time to read and digest papers on many matters outside their departmental responsibilities. The Cabinet does many things other than coordinating policy (see above). In part it is also a consequence of so much of ministers' time being spent on running and representing their own departments. A number of ministers have remarked upon how rare it was for them to comment on other issues before the Cabinet. Many illustrations of these pressures are to be found in the published diaries of Richard Crossman and Barbara Castle: ministers, for example, arrived at Cabinet having only glanced at papers which did not concern their own departments.

It is worth considering the views of two experienced observers on the 'overload' problem. Sir Frank Cooper, a senior civil servant throughout much of the post-war period, commented:

I think the whole idea of collective responsibility, in relation to twenty-odd people, has had diminished force, quite frankly, over the years, coupled with the fact that to deal with the modern world … with the very, very complex problems that government have to deal with, it's inevitable that they should move into a situation where four or five are gathered together. (Cited in Hennessy, 1986, p. 164)

David Howell, who served as a minister under Heath and Thatcher, commented:

The Cabinet is not a place where decisions can be formulated. It's bound to be a place where decisions that have been formulated by smaller groups, maybe of ministers, and party people together, or maybe parliamentary groups outside and then to put to ministers or maybe the Prime Minister and her advisers quite separately, are then tested and validated and argued about. (Cited in Hennessy, 1986, p. 164)

Reforms of Cabinet

Among reforms of the Cabinet which have been canvassed in recent years are the following:

1. *The creation of a body which can help the Cabinet deal with strategy*: This may include the re-creation of something along the lines of the Central Policy Review Staff, which existed between 1970 and 1983. A number of observers claim that even if the original CPRS did not fill the need, there is still scope for a body which can brief the Cabinet as a collective body.
2. *The creation of a Prime Minister's department* (see above).
3. *An increase in the number of political aides or advisers for ministers*: Since 1974 between twenty and thirty political or special advisers have worked in Whitehall, under the oversight of the political secretary at No. 10. It is often argued that this system should be extended and strengthened, as in France and the USA. This is urged on the grounds of strengthening ministerial influence in the department rather than enhancing the collective role of the Cabinet.
4. *A reduction in the power of the Prime Minister,* so developing what Tony Benn, in 1979, called

a constitutional premiership. Benn objected to the scale of the Prime Minister's patronage as well as other fixed powers. He advocated the election of Cabinet ministers and allocation of their duties by Labour MPs and the confirmation of public appointments by Parliament. The demand for limits on the PM's powers grew under Thatcher, but declined with Major at No. 10.

5. Taking steps to *improve the quality of policy-making in opposition*:   It is striking how total the divorce between government and opposition is in the British system. It is possible for a government to take office with many of its members having little or no executive experience. This was largely the case with Ramsay MacDonald's first Labour government in 1924 and Wilson's 1964 government. Neil Kinnock never held even a junior ministerial post. In the first post-war Labour government a minister, Emmanuel Shinwell, confessed that for many years he had talked about nationalising the coal industry but when he came to implement the manifesto pledge in 1945 he found no plans existed.

Measures which might improve the transition between opposition and government include the following:

1. Relaxation of secrecy so that the documents and options considered by ministers and civil servants are opened to public discussion.
2. The temporary appointment of a few high-flying civil servants to the opposition to assist the policy-making process.
3. An increase in the budgets and research expenses of political parties.
4. Greater use of the Douglas-Home rules (1963) which allow opposition spokesmen to have contacts with senior civil servants in the relevant departments. The Conservatives made some use of this facility before 1979 but Labour did not before 1983.

The Blair team, in anticipation of election victory, held several meetings with senior civil servants and undertook extensive briefings and seminars with those familiar with the problems Labour face in office.

Ministers

Appointments

If the size of the Cabinet has hardly grown in the twentieth century, that of the government certainly has. The major increase since 1900 has been in government appointments outside the Cabinet – non-Cabinet ministers of state, junior ministers and parliamentary private secretaries (PPSs) in the House of Commons. In 1900 forty-two MPs were in involved in government; today, *the number is well over a hundred, well over a third of government MPs*. Although the PPSs are unpaid they are still bound by the doctrine of collective responsibility.

The increase in patronage is obviously an advantage for prime ministers. They can use it to reward or punish colleagues and perhaps to promote policies. It is, however, a power which is exercised subject to several administrative and political limitations. One is that *ministers must sit in Parliament and most of them must be members of the House of Commons*. A few Cabinet ministers have been appointed shortly after their election to the House of Commons. The trade union leader Ernest Bevin, at the Ministry of Labour in 1940, was a success, but another trade unionist, Frank Cousins, Minister of Technology (1964–7), and a businessman, Sir John Davies, at Trade and Industry (1970–4) were less effective. A Cabinet must also contain at least two peers, the Lord Chancellor and the Leader of the House of Lords. The parliamentary background increases the likelihood that ministers will be skilled in debate and able to handle parliamentary questions competently. Thatcher was willing to reach out and appoint to the Cabinet peers who have had a short party political career, for example Lord Young of Graffham, Secretary of State for Employment (1985–7) and then at the Department of Trade and Industry (1987–9), and Lord Cockfield, Department of Trade and then Duchy of Lancaster, before becoming a commissioner with the European Economic Community. Major similarly elevated Lord Waddington in November 1990 direct into the post of Leader of the Lords. Elevating laypeople to the peerage and then giving them office is a useful way of utilising extra-parliamentary talent, but it can cause resentments in the government's parliamentary party.

A second limitation is that *appointments also need to take account of a person's political skill and administrative competence*. In any Cabinet there are at least half a dozen ministers whose seniority and reputation are such that it is unthinkable to exclude them. In 1964 Harold Wilson 'had' to give senior posts to James Callaghan and George Brown, his rivals for the leadership. In 1974 there was little doubt that posts would be found for Barbara Castle, Roy Jenkins, Anthony Crosland, Denis Healey, Tony Benn and Jim Callaghan. Margaret Thatcher's Cabinet in 1979 contained hardly any surprises: Sir Keith Joseph, William Whitelaw, James Prior and Lord Carrington were all expected to hold senior posts.

The qualifications appropriate for particular posts are not always obvious and this is suggested by the apparently haphazard movement of ministers between departments: Major from the Foreign Office to the Treasury after a few months in 1989, and Kenneth Clarke from Health (1988) to Education (1990) to the Home Office (1992), and to the Treasury (1993). On the other hand, appointments to legal officers (Lord Chancellor, Attorney General and Solicitor General) must be made from lawyers in the party. The Chancellor of the Exchequer is expected to be competent in economic matters; Nigel Lawson (Thatcher's Chancellor for the six years before he resigned in October 1989) took a degree in politics, philosophy and economics and was a financial journalist before he went into politics. The Secretaries of State for Scotland and Wales are expected to sit for Scottish and Welsh seats, respectively, and if possible be nationals of the country concerned.

In general, however, ministers are expected to have skills in managing Parliament and conducting meetings, reading papers quickly, and making decisions. If we exclude as effectively 'ineligible' for office MPs who are very young or inexperienced, too old or who suffer from political or personal deficiencies, the Prime Minister may actually be giving government appointments to about one half of 'eligible' MPs in his party.

Prime ministers usually make some appointments to reward loyalty and limit dissent or outright opposition. Thatcher pointedly excluded Heath from her Cabinet in 1979 and Heath excluded Powell in 1970. Both were powerful figures but had been at odds with so many aspects of the party's policies and with the party leader personally that their presence would have made the Cabinet a divisive body. The Cabinets of Wilson in 1964 and Thatcher in 1979 contained majorities who had almost certainly voted against them at the first stage of the leadership elections in 1963 and 1976 respectively, but both prime ministers had to take account of administrative talent and political weight. Benn was a prominent left-wing dissenter from the Labour leadership in the 1970s but both Wilson and Callaghan thought it safer to keep him in the Cabinet rather than act as a focus for opposition on the back benches. In November 1990, Major gave the difficult job of Environment Secretary to the man who had precipitated Thatcher's downfall, Michael Heseltine. The appointment both recognised Heseltine's strength in the party and promised to keep him absorbed with fulfilling his claims over reforming the poll tax.

A final constraint is that *prime ministers want their Cabinet to be representative of the main elements in the party*. This is particularly the case with the Labour Party which has had well defined left- and right-wing factions. Thatcher was less tolerant of the 'wets' in her early Cabinets and set about weeding them out one by one and breaking their influence in the party. Major felt bound to include in his Cabinet opponents of his European policy, including Michael Howard, Peter Lilley, Michael Portillo and, until 1995, John Redwood.

There is no adequate preparation for being a Cabinet minister. The British tradition has been to rely on a form of on-the-job learning in which ministers, like civil servants, pick up the skills as they settle into the job. Three background features which most ministers have and which probably shape the way they work are:

1. *Lengthy tenure in the House of Commons*:
   Since 1945 the average length of time spent in the House of Commons, prior to becoming a Cabinet minister, has been fourteen years, a sufficient period of time to acquire parliamentary skills.
2. *Experience on the ladder of promotion*, or ministerial hierarchy, which most politicians ascend. In an ideal world they would start off as parliamentary private secretaries and move

through the ranks of junior minister, minister outside the Cabinet, and then through some of the Cabinet positions, ending with the most senior ones like Chancellor of the Exchequer or Foreign Secretary and then perhaps prime minister.

3. *Preparation in opposition*:   In 1955 the Labour leader Clement Attlee formalised the arrangements of a Shadow Cabinet in opposition, in which a front-bench spokesman 'shadows' a Cabinet minister. Both Heath and Thatcher used the opportunity of making appointments in opposition in order to prepare for office. For example, all but two of Heath's appointments in the consultative committee (the Conservative front-bench team in opposition) in 1969 went to similar Cabinet postings. Over 80 per cent of Thatcher's opposition front-bench appointments went directly to similar Cabinet postings in 1979. Blair similarly made his Shadow Cabinet appointments with ministerial office in mind.

Ministerial roles

If the work of ministers varies with the department, so minister–civil servant relationships also vary according to personalities, departments and the nature of issues. Bruce Headey (1974) in his study of Cabinet ministers has usefully distinguished three broad types of ministerial role. One is *the ambassador*, who sells the policies of the government to bodies outside Westminster and Whitehall and even abroad. In particular this describes the case of a Foreign Secretary who spends a good deal of time representing the position of the British government to other states. A second is *the executive*, who is concerned to promote legislation and take decisions. He or she thus focuses on winning Cabinet battles (for approval of policy, legislation or money) and getting parliamentary time for his legislation. For example, in 1988, Kenneth Baker's education bill (the Education Reform Act) covered a large number of educational issues and dominated the parliamentary agenda. Finally, there is *the key issues minister*, who selects a few policy areas and tries to initiate policy. This means that he or she has to delegate much of his or her other work to junior ministers and departmental officials.

A surprising amount of time is spent on public relations activities by ministers, including the Prime Minister. A typical minister will spend a good deal of time attending functions, making speeches and making official visits and inspections.

Ministerial responsibility

According to this doctrine, each minister is responsible to Parliament for his or her own personal conduct, the general conduct of his or her department, and the policy-related actions or omissions of his or her civil servants. The most important consequence of the convention is that the minister is answerable to Parliament for the work of his or her department. Another interpretation is that Parliament can actually force the resignation of a minister who has been thought to be negligent. The outstanding resignation on grounds of policy in recent years was that of the Foreign Secretary, Lord Carrington (and two other ministers), in April 1982, following the widespread criticism of his department's policy when Argentina captured the Falklands. There are, however, two difficulties in the way of the Commons forcing the dismissal of a minister. One is that MPs in the majority party can usually be counted upon to support a minister under pressure. In addition, the Cabinet is also responsible for policy and a Prime Minister knows that a minister's resignation often reflects badly on the work of the government. Collective responsibility may therefore weaken a minister's individual responsibility (for a longer discussion see Chapter 20). This surely was a reason which reduced pressure on Norman Lamont to resign from the Treasury in September 1992. He had frequently defended Britain's membership of the ERM, excluded the possibility of withdrawal, and claimed that it was the basis of Britain's anti-inflationary strategy. The forced departure from the ERM was, by any standards, a failure of policy. But nobody resigned. Neither did any minister resign – with William Waldegrave and Nicholas Lyell the two tipped figures – following the 1996 Scott Report on the 'arms to Iraq affair'. Indeed, resignations are now so rare that the notion of resignation as part of the responsibility convention has virtually disappeared.

Collective responsibility

According to the convention of collective responsibility Cabinet ministers assume responsibility for all Cabinet decisions and a minister who refuses to accept, or opposes, a decision is expected to resign. In more recent years the convention of collective responsibility has been extended to incorporate all junior government ministers, including even the unpaid and unofficial parliamentary secretaries. The doctrine is supported by the secrecy of the Cabinet proceedings: the refusal to make public the differences of opinion which precede or follow a Cabinet decision assists the presentation of a united front to Parliament and the country. Another aspect of the convention is that the government is expected to resign or seek a dissolution if it is defeated on a vote of confidence in the House of Commons. In other words the Cabinet is collectively responsible for policy to the Commons. (See Chapter 20 on individual accountability of ministers.)

In recent years, however, both aspects of the convention have come under pressure. The 1974–9 Labour government relaxed the principle of collective responsibility over the referendum on Britain's membership of the EEC in 1975 and the vote on the European Assembly Elections Bill in 1977. On both issues the Cabinet was divided. The myth of Cabinet unity has also been exploded by the increase in the leaks to the news media of Cabinet procedures in recent years. In 1969 the opposition of James Callaghan, then Home Secretary, to the Labour Cabinet's decision to proceed with an industrial relations bill was widely known because of his leaks to the media and his open vote against the government's policy on the party's National Executive Committee. Wilson responded by reminding all Cabinet ministers that acceptance of collective responsibility applied at all times and in all places. He did not, however, dismiss Callaghan, presumably because of the latter's powerful political backing from the unions. In 1974 some ministers voted against the Labour government policies on the party's National Executive Committee and similar warnings were given.

There was also a good deal of leaking Cabinet proceedings under Thatcher. In 1981 a number of Cabinet ministers made known their disagreement with the Chancellor's Budget strategy and the Leader of the House, Francis Pym, disagreed publicly with the Chancellor over economic policy. Thatcher herself also publicly indicated her disagreement with Nigel Lawson's economic strategy. The tendency of Thatcher to depart from agreed Cabinet positions, particularly on the European Community, and to make policy on the hoof was a key charge in Sir Geoffrey Howe's resignation speech. He said:

The task has become futile … of trying to pretend there was a common policy when every step forward risked being subverted by some casual comment or impulsive answer [by Thatcher]. (Howe, 1994, p. 667)

Under Major, collective responsibility had reasserted itself to the extent that the Prime Minister was adamant that the principal decisions of his government were agreed by all relevant ministers in Cabinet committee, and subsequently endorsed by full Cabinet. But equally, collective responsibility had been undermined by the bitterness in his post-1992 Cabinet principally over Europe, and more generally over his style and quality of leadership, judged by those on the right to be insufficiently strong. Peter Lilley, Michael Howard, Michael Portillo and John Redwood were the principal critics on both issues. Leaking rose to unprecedented proportions, but some harmony was restored after Redwood's resignation after his leadership challenge in June–July 1995, and with the coming of the general election.

Conclusion

Reforms

There are a number of steps which might promote coordination and the quality of British government, including the following:

1. The creation of a *small Cabinet*, including some *non-departmental ministers*. The model often advanced is that of the wartime Cabinets of Lloyd George (1916–18), Churchill (1940–5) or Thatcher during the Falklands War and Major during the Gulf War. But many are not convinced that the wartime model is suitable for peacetime and there are political and

administrative problems involved in divorcing coordination from policy-making.

2. The creation of *small groups*, or *'inner' Cabinets*, of senior figures, to impart a greater sense of direction to Cabinet. After 1945 Clement Attlee regularly consulted with the senior ministers, Morrison, Bevin and Cripps. In 1968 Wilson created a parliamentary committee which was supposed to operate like an inner Cabinet. In fact, Crossman's diaries confirm that Wilson was not keen on developing a strategy and the group never played such a role. Most prime ministers have had groups of colleagues with whom they informally discussed matters before they reached the full Cabinet. But such behaviour may be more a recognition that ministers are not equal in political weight and experience than evidence of attempts to develop an inner Cabinet.

3. *The amalgamation of departments:*   Of major departments today those of Defence, Foreign and Commonwealth Office, Environment, Health and Social Security, Education and Employment, and Trade and Industry have all resulted from amalgamations in the past twenty years of previously autonomous departments. It has been argued that the creation of giant departments provides the opportunity for coordination of policies within the enlarged departments and allows for the creation of a smaller Cabinet. Heath introduced two of the giant departments, Environment and Trade and Industry, and also had the smallest (eighteen) post-war Cabinet.

4. The creation of *a central analytical body*, not attached to a department but serving the Cabinet as a whole. Heath had this in mind in 1970 when he set up the Central Policy Review Staff, or 'think-tank' as it was called, located in the Cabinet Office. Its task was to present briefing papers on issues, free from any departmental perspective, and to undertake research and suggest ideas which did not fall within the responsibility of any particular department. It also provided periodic reviews on how the government and departments were performing in relation to the strategies set out in the party's 1970 manifesto.

5. The creation of *a Prime Minister's Department*

(as discussed above). In spite of the Prime Minister's Private Office and Policy Unit it is doubtful whether he or she has sufficient resources to monitor and coordinate the policies of departments. The development of a strong prime ministerial office would probably move Britain into a more presidential style of leadership and might face resistance in departments.

Quality of Cabinet government

Dissatisfaction with the structure and performance of Cabinet government is not surprising in view of the criticisms of Britain's economic performance in the post-war period. Among criticisms which have been advanced are the following:

1. Ministers are too frequently *generalists* and appointed to posts for reasons which may have little to do with their presumed expertise. For example, Richard Crossman, having shadowed education in opposition before 1964, was surprised to learn that he would become Minister of Housing and Local Government in the new Labour government. In the 1979 Conservative government Francis Pym started off in Defence, moved to the Leadership of the House of Commons and then became Foreign Secretary, all in the period of three years. In 1995, Malcolm Rifkind replaced Douglas Hurd, who had had a lifetime's experience of foreign affairs, as Foreign Secretary. In cases of routine policy-making – with ministers lacking the time and often the experience to become versed in the detail – it is perhaps not surprising that civil servants may often determine policy and the principle of ministerial responsibility may provide a shield behind which the civil service dominate the policy process.

2. *The frequent turnover of ministers*, who last an average of some two years in each department, a rate of change exceeding that in most other Western states. Such turnover means that at any one time a number of ministers are actually learning their jobs. Under Harold Wilson (1964–70) the average ministerial tenure was less than two years. In his 1966–70 government

only Denis Healey at Defence, Lord Gardiner as Lord Chancellor, William Ross, Minister of State for Scotland and Wilson himself held the same office for the duration of the government, and in the lifetime of Thatcher's 1979 government only six ministers held the same office. Some commentators have claimed that ministers need a period of two years or so to actually master a department. On the other hand, it is often claimed that if a minister spends too long in a department he or she may 'go native' and perhaps become too closely identified with its interests. The case for introducing a new minister is that he or she is likely to provide a stimulus to the policy routine. But many reshuffles of ministers are made for reasons which have little to do with policy but may have more to do with public opinion or party management.

3. *Ministers are often so overloaded with work* that the functions of oversight and discussion are neglected. In his revealing book *Inside the Treasury* (1982), the former Labour minister Joel Barnett commented on how 'the system' can defeat ministers:

The sheer volume of decisions, many of them extremely complex, means that by the time even a fairly modest analysis of a problem is done, and the various options considered, you find yourself coming up against time constraints. Consequently ministers often find themselves making hasty decisions, either late at night or at an odd moment during a day full of meetings. (Barnett, 1982, p. 20)

Nigel Lawson (1992) caustically described the Cabinet meeting as the most restful and relaxing event of the week. He also claims that the Cabinet showed no interest in or support for his criticisms of the proposed poll tax (pp. 562–3). If the Prime Minister and relevant departmental minister had agreed a line, then it was very difficult for another minister to intervene.

4. *Decisions are taken for short-term political gain*, as instanced in Barnett's book, as well as in the Castle and Crossman Diaries. Barnett (1982, p. 17) criticised the ways in which decisions were taken by his 1974–9 Cabinet colleagues 'for some other reason which has nothing to do with the merits of the case'. About priorities in public expenditure he commented:

expenditure priorities were generally decided on often outdated, and ill-considered plans made in Opposition, barely thought through as to their real value, and never as to their relative priority in social, socialist, industrial or economic terms. More often they were decided on the strength of a particular spending minister and the extent of the support he or she would get from the Prime Minister.

Secrecy

British government has traditionally been amongst the most secretive in the world. Fairly routine official documents tend to have been given classifications that restrict access even to canteen menus – and, famously, a paper produced in the late 1970s on improving access to government papers. The amendment to the Official Secrets Act passed in 1989 restricted criminal liabilities to a very broad list of categories, a liberalisation from the previous 'catch all' clauses. The efficiency of the Act, however, came through the effective removal of the public interest defence claimed by Ponting. Under the 'thirty-year rule' most official documents, including Cabinet papers, are released to the Public Record Office. However, some documents are held back for longer periods.

The activities of the security and intelligence services have long been subject to particular secrecy, even to the extent of refusing to admit the existence of these agencies.

Major's premiership saw a cautious liberalisation of official secrecy rules. In 1992, the Cabinet Office published membership lists and terms of reference for Cabinet committees, and *Questions of Procedure for Ministers*, the official guidance on conduct expected of ministers. A bill to put MI5 and MI6 on a statutory footing was in that year's Queen's Speech. In July 1993 the government published a White Paper on *Open Government*, which covered a variety of secrecy issues. For the first time a Code of Practice on information – monitored by the parliamentary commissioner for administration – was established, giving access to information about the facts and analysis behind government policy, and internal guidance papers. The number of official documents kept secret for longer than thirty years was cut back. But it fell some way short of granting

BOX 19.6 SECRECY IN BRITISH GOVERNMENT DEBATE

Debates about official secrecy in the 1990s have become considerably more subtle than a polarised confrontation between secretive mandarins and freedom of information campaigners.

For increasing openness
- A greater incentive for good decision-making; the 1996 Scott Report showed the perils of secrecy.

- Makes government more accessible and therefore accountable to citizens.

- Reduces the risk of corruption.

- Corresponds better with practice in other countries, especially in the EU.

- Enhances study of government, and therefore its efficiency.

- Reduces influence of secretive pressure group lobbyists.

For maintaining secrecy
- Decision-making would be worsened because civil servants and ministers would be more reluctant to speak out during internal debates.

- Cabinet collective responsibility would be diminished.

- Civil servants would become associated with policies and lose their tradition of impartial service.

- Pressure group influence would increase because campaigning would take place within the government.

citizens rights equivalent to those in the USA under the Freedom of Information Act.

Chapter summary

The Prime Minister is the most powerful figure in British government, but his or her power is not fixed: it depends not least upon the personality and style of the incumbent, and the strength of the Cabinet he or she faces. Cabinet itself has undergone major changes in the last twenty-five years, and is now substantially run by a series of committees which do the detailed work. The heart of British government, the Prime Minister and Cabinet, is under closer scrutiny now than possibly ever before, and a wide number of proposals of reform are examined.

Discussion points

- Is the Prime minister (still) too powerful?

- What if anything does Cabinet government mean today?

- Is power still too centralised around Cabinet and No. 10?

- Should government be made less secretive?

- Should there be a Prime Minister's department?

- Is Britain an oligarchy or a democracy?

Further reading

On the Cabinet Mackintosh (1962) is still the best guide. Hennessy (1986) is a lively analysis of more recent developments. Donoughue (1987), Barnett (1982), Lawson (1992), Thatcher (1993) and Howe (1994) are perceptive insider accounts. King (1985) is an excellent collection of articles. On the Major years, the best account so far is Hogg and Hill (1995).

References

Barnett, J. (1982) *Inside the Treasury* (Deutsch).
Burch, M. and Moran, M. (1985) 'The changing British parliamentary elite', *Parliamentary Affairs*, Vol. 38, No. 1.

Clark, A. (1993) *Diaries* (Weidenfeld and Nicolson).

Donoughue, B. (1987) *Prime Minister* (Cape).

Headey, B. (1974) *British Cabinet Ministers* (Allen and Unwin).

Hennessy, P. (1986) *Cabinet* (Blackwell).

Hennessy, P. (1988) *Whitehall* (Secker and Warburg).

Hogg, S. and Hill, J. (1995) *Two Close to Call* (Little, Brown).

Howe, G. (1994) *Conflict of Loyalty* (Macmillan).

Jones, B. and Kavanagh, D. (1989) *British Politics Today: A Student's Guide*, 3rd edn (Manchester University Press).

King, A. (ed.) (1985) *The British Prime Minister*, 2nd edn (Macmillan).

Lawson, N. (1992) *The View from Number 11* (Cape).

Mackintosh, J. (1962) *The British Cabinet* (Stevens).

Thatcher, M. (1993) *Thatcher: The Downing Street Years* (HarperCollins).

CHAPTER TWENTY

Ministers, departments and civil servants

ANDREW GRAY AND BILL JENKINS

LEARNING OBJECTIVES

- To promote an understanding of the essential features of central government departments and the role of ministers and civil servants within them.

INTRODUCTION

The chapter aims to: elaborate the major functions of the central administrative system; characterise its organisational properties by investigating the structures and processes of the central departments; and characterise its political properties by examining the way that different interests can be promoted and defended in departments and affect the relationships between ministers and civil servants.

John Major's victory over John Redwood in the Conservative Party leadership election in the summer of 1995 heralded some important changes to the machinery of government. The Department of Employment was dissolved and its functions reallocated to Education and several other departments and the position of Deputy Prime Minister was resurrected for Michael Heseltine with wide-ranging powers and responsibilities (and possibly the most spacious and impressively furnished office in Whitehall). Part of Heseltine's new brief was to coordinate the government's responses to the draft report of the Scott Inquiry into the Matrix Churchill affair and the first report of the Committee on Standards in Public Life (the Nolan Committee, Cm 2850, 1995). In different ways these inquiries questioned the transparency and substance of the Whitehall departments and the relationship between ministers

and civil servants during a period of considerable upheaval in central government.

Many of these issues emerged in the autumn of 1995 when the Home Secretary, Michael Howard, reacted to a highly critical report on the breakout from Parkhurst Prison in January 1995 (the Learmont Report, Cm 3020, 1995) by sacking the Director General of the service, Derek Lewis. Lewis, who refused to resign when requested to do so by the Home Secretary, claimed his job had been made impossible by Howard and his officials' excessive interference. Howard, however, took the view that while he was responsible for policy, Lewis was responsible for operations, including those meant to prevent the Parkhurst escape.

The stories of Howard and Lewis as well as Scott and Nolan and the changing departmental arrangements reveal an important characteristic of politics in the United Kingdom, i.e. that the structure of central government, no less than its policies, reflects the changing political preferences of prime ministers and colleagues. Moreover, the resulting departments are the mechanisms by which ministers formulate and implement their policies and thus, to a considerable extent, make their political fortunes.

Together these realities help to explain why the pattern of central departments lacks coherence and why the relationship between ministers (the temporary politicians) and civil servants (the permanent managers of their departments) is so important for the character of British politics. As with so much else in British political life, both the variety of central government organisations and the nature of minister–civil servant relationships have developed rather haphazardly over the years. A chronological rather than logical development, it is not governed by any single set of principles, let alone a body of law. As Bagehot remarked:

Ministers, departments and civil servants: a view from the past

> A friend once told me that an intelligent Italian asked him about the principal English officers [of government] and that he was very puzzled to explain their duties … the unsystematic and casual arrangement of our public offices is not more striking than their difference of arrangement for the one purpose they all have in common [serving ministers] … Yet there are almost no two offices which are exactly alike in the defined relations of the permanent official to the Parliamentary chief.
>
> *Walter Bagehot, The English Constitution, 1964*
> *[1867], p. 210*

Question: Is Bagehot's description still apt at the end of the 1990s?

Nevertheless, there are functions which governments wish to perform and there are principles which may be used to organise departments in their service. Similarly, there are established constitutional conventions by which civil servants serve ministers who in turn serve the monarch as head of state (thus the terms *ministers of the crown* and *Her Majesty's Government*). Even so, it is not surprising that what is thought to be good administration in government is as much a political matter

as a managerial one or that what is good policy is an administrative issue as much as a political one. Thus, this chapter will be addressing these two features of central departments, the political and the organisational, throughout its discussions.

The organisation of central departments

The state has been a pioneer in using organisation as the principal mechanism by which its decisions and orders are translated into effects; the epithet 'bureaucratic' is still, if mistakenly, associated more with government than with private business. Thus, we cannot account for the administration of government without an examination of those of its features which derive from the existence of organisations within it.

A variety of organisations

The principal organisation of central government is the ministry or (much more commonly these days) *department* (see Table 20.1). Each is responsible for providing a service or function and is headed by or directly accountable to a minister or secretary of state in the Cabinet. This link between the department and Parliament is crucial. Through it policies are formulated, decisions taken, programmes and services implemented and accountability exercised. Among these departments are the great offices of state (the Foreign and Commonwealth Office, the Home Office and Her Majesty's Treasury) and others still retaining the title of office (e.g. Northern Ireland, Scottish and Welsh) and ministry (as in Defence and Agriculture). Of those now called departments, many are well known because of the services they provide directly to the public (e.g. the departments of Health and Social Security). Some departments, however, are very small and hardly impose themselves on the public in a visible way. These include the Lord Chancellor's Department, which administers the system of justice through the courts.

Departments have been the mainstay of central administration for centuries. Over the past fifty and particularly the last ten years, however, some of their functions have been delegated internally to semi-independent but still departmental *agencies*

Table 20.1 Principal central departments

Departments	Ministries	Offices	Others
Education and Employment	Agriculture	Cabinet	HM Treasury
Environment	Defence	Foreign and Commonwealth	(includes:
Health		Home	Inland Revenue
Lord Chancellor's		Northern Ireland	Customs and Excise)
National Heritage		Scottish	
Social Security		Welsh	
Trade and Industry			
Transport			

(see Table 20.2). These bodies are responsible mainly for clearly defined executive operations without a significant public policy implication. The Driver and Vehicle Licence Agency, for example, registers and issues motor licences for the Department of Transport, and the Training Agency is responsible for government training programmes on behalf of the Department for Education and Employment. Each agency has a director or chief executive responsible to the permanent secretary of the parent department or directly to the minister. Their advantages include the flexibility available in creating and dissolving them and the way day-to-day management is relatively free from ministerial interference.

In 1988 the government announced the Next Steps programme to transform most of the central departments into agencies. By the spring of 1997, about four-fifths of all civil servants were employed in nearly 200 agencies. This radical development will be discussed in more detail in Chapter 21. In theory it should allow the remaining cores of departments to devote more attention to general policy formulation and resource management, thus improving the quality of both policy and service.

Another feature of the period since the Second World War, and associated particularly with the Labour government of 1945–51, is the development of *public corporations*. They are accountable to Parliament through specified departments and ministers. The latter set policy for standards of service, pricing, and financial targets, but day-to-day operations are the responsibility of their managements. The purpose of such corporations is to ensure that activities which contribute strategically to the national infrastructure should be guided by the public interest while operating on a commercial basis free from detailed departmental interference. However, most of these have been sold to private investors under the privatisation programme of the Conservative government from 1979. As a result only the BBC and the Post Office survive. We shall discuss the implications of this development in more detail in Chapter 21.

Distaste by Conservatives and others for public corporations has been based in part at least on the economic and especially tax burdens they place on government and their ambiguous accountability. However, there remain activities which are more suitably performed through organisational arrangements only loosely connected to ministers. These are functions associated with the rules of the political game (e.g. setting the boundaries of parliamentary constituencies), civil rights (e.g. race relations and

Table 20.2 Executive agencies: facts and figures

	No.	Agency staff[a]	Civil servants
Agencies at 1 September 1996	126	337,620	314,985
HM Customs and Excise Executive Units	24	23,185	23,185
Inland Revenue	27	52,150	52,150
Totals	177	412,955	390,320
Agency candidates	33	37,655	31,295

Note: [a] includes military personnel and other non-civil servants. For examples of agencies see Chapter 21 Table 21.3
Source: Next Steps Team (1996)

equal opportunities) or aspects of regulation (e.g. in the newly privatised utilities). There have always been *ad hoc* bodies to perform these functions but over the past twenty years they have been subject to some dispute as to what they are called, how many there are and where they fit into the administrative structure.

Although governments have tried to describe these as *non-departmental bodies*, the political debate about their number and function has created a new, and more wide-ranging term, *quango*, or quasi-autonomous non-governmental organisation. Strictly the term was coined for those organisations which were legally private (i.e. non-government) but which performed often statutory functions for government in a semi-independent way. Current examples include the General Medical Council,

which supervises the training, registration and professional conduct of medical practitioners, and the Jockey Club, which runs horse racing. Other organisations which were indeed government but set up deliberately at arm's length or semi-independently were labelled quagos, i.e. quasi-autonomous government organisations. Current examples include the Equal Opportunities Commission, the Higher Education Funding Council, health service trusts and regulators of privatised utilities (e.g. Oftel, the regulator of the telecommunications industry). Over time, however, politicians, ever the enemies of exactitude, have conspired with journalists to use the term quango to embrace both groups of organisation and thus obscure their distinct legal and political relationships with government. The government group, in which members are appointed

---

BOX 20.1

Quangos: government facts, figures and issues

Numbers: Just over 2,000 (Hall and Weir, 1996, counted 6,424!).

Biggest budgets: Legal Aid Board £1.28 bn; Medical Research Council £288m; English Arts Council £225m.

Smallest budgets (all under £2,000): UK Polar Medal Assessment Committee; Welsh Office Place Names Advisory Committee.

Accounts audited by National Audit Office: About two-thirds.

Members: Over 42,000 of whom 28 per cent were women and 2 per cent from ethnic minorities

Appointments: The 8,000 or so made directly by ministers have been subject since July 1996 to a code of appointment supervised by the Commissioner for Public Appointments. The code stresses appointment by merit.

Payments: 37 per cent receive remuneration other than expenses

Best-paid heads (over £95,000 in 1996): Monopolies and Mergers Commission, Law

Commission, Scottish Law Commission, Horserace Totalisator Board.

Source: Government statistics published in 1995

In 1994 the Nolan Committee on Standards of Public Life argued that there were two areas of concern in all this: appointment and standards of conduct of members and senior officers. The Committee therefore asked:

- Should appointments be politically neutral or has the government the right to make senior appointments to support its policies?

- Should key appointments be advertised and the recruitment process be made transparent?

- What controls are there on propriety of members and procedures?

Question: What are the advantages and disadvantages of public bodies of this kind?

by ministers, has expanded rapidly since the late 1960s, and has been notable for including an increase in bodies such as in the health service which were formerly subject to some form of elected representation. This has raised concerns about ministerial patronage and accountability.

A variety of civil servants

It is common to regard the civil service as simply a small core of top administrators at the centre of Whitehall. The reality is rather different. It employs nearly half a million people in a host of occupations, such as customs officers, social security clerks, tax inspectors and veterinary surgeons, located in offices throughout the country. Moreover, the service has never been very unified. Rather, it has resembled the armed services in the First World War with an officer corps (the higher or senior civil servants) separate from the non-commissioned officers (the executive groups who translate decisions into action) and the 'poor bloody infantry' (the clerical and manual operatives). The task of the senior elite has been to assist ministers and advise on policy; that of the rank and file to administer decisions and policies imposed from above. The strata have had little in common and few (indeed very few) have moved from the lower echelons to senior positions.

The principles of the civil service developed from the 1854 Northcote–Trevelyan Report (named after its major authors), which reacted against the nepotism and corruption of the times and sought to place the service on a professional and neutral footing. It advocated appointments and promotions on merit, and a structure of administrative, executive and clerical 'classes' to deal with the different intellectual, operational and clerical tasks. In practice, the changes evolved gradually over half a century. The emerging model had its heyday from the last decades of the nineteenth century to the middle of the twentieth.

However, even as it evolved, voices began to be raised against it. In particular, the higher civil service was thought to be isolated from the changing world around it, favouring continuity in personnel and activities in the face of the need for change. This form of complaint was sharpened by the experiences of the Second World War, when a variety of outsiders, such as economists, scientists and statisticians, were drafted into senior positions for the duration of hostilities. Often their role was to solve particular problems such as intelligence cyphers or weaponry, and not surprisingly, they were far from the traditional civil service mould. But, however unorthodox, they were generally successful. Yet, their sojourn was brief and, after their departure at the end of the war, the civil service returned to business as usual.

As earlier chapters have shown, however, the business of government then underwent a revolution. The role of the state widened swiftly with the creation of the National Health Service, a massive nationalisation programme and generally increased state-provided services. By the late 1950s and early 1960s some questioned the appropriateness of classical civil service model to cope with all this. The most critical was the report of the Fulton Committee on the Civil Service, set up by the new Labour government in 1965 (Cmnd 3638, 1968). It was scathing on the emphasis on generalist administrators (rather than specialist professionals), its recruitment to the administrative class of a narrow social elite, and the lack of management and training. Its recommendations included a greater preference for subject relevance in recruitment (i.e. more economists and scientists), an enhancement of training, and a greater degree of accountable management by which civil servants would have greater responsibility (and accountability) for discrete activities and resources.

As we shall see later in this chapter and the next, much of the general direction of the Fulton proposals and ethos can be seen emerging in today's civil service, 30 years later. The White Paper *The Civil Service: Continuity and Change* (Cm 2627, 1994) and its successor, *The Civil Service: Taking Forward Continuity and Change* (Cm 2748, 1995), established a new senior civil service (grades 1–5, see Table 20.3) which by the end of the century will be recruited from outside as well as inside the service on the basis of specialist and managerial qualifications, be appointed on personal contracts and rewarded though systems designed to reflect performance and marketability. The resulting increase in the variety of civil servant will reflect not just Conservative Party philosophy but the functions of the administrative process in British government under almost any party.

Table 20.3 Senior grades in the home civil service

0	Head of the Home Civil Service	
1	Permanent Secretary	Permanent head of a government department
1A	2nd Permanent Secretary	Head of distinct and major areas of policy within departments
2	Deputy Secretary	Heads of small departments or large executive agencies; heads of professions or substantial areas of policy within departments
3	Under Secretary	Comparable to board members in major companies; most common level for holders of non-executive directorships
4		Generally senior professional civil servants
5	Assistant Secretary	Heads of discrete areas of policy

The functions of the administrative process

Despite the attempts since 1979 to reduce the role of the state, and former Prime Minister Lady Thatcher's contention that there is no such thing as 'society' only 'individuals', government departments in the UK contribute economic, social and political management to the *development of society*. In economic management the administrative process supports the development of the economy. This varies with governments and particular ministers, but it has always been the government's job to manage the economy and facilitate trade. Similarly, the administrative system provides a machinery of political and social management by which government can assimilate and satisfy political forces. Pressure-group representations on current political and social issues, for example, are made directly to departments, which then assist in registering and managing the interests involved.

Policy management conceals a host of different functions, from those providing supporting services for policy-making and implementation, through research and advisory tasks, to promotional or even obstructive roles. Much of this is hidden from public view. To the citizen, however, departments are important because they provide a wide range of **public services** to society. Each has its own scope, technical complexity, resource requirements and client group which give it its character. However, developments over the past few years may be having the effect of shifting the emphasis away from this function towards the core functions (i.e. from the outer ring to the inner and centre of Figure 20.1).

Many of those who seek to join the higher ranks of the civil service are aware of these functions. Almost all recognise the potential power and influence which arises from close proximity to the centre of government. Few, at least until recently, however, have made much of the managerial scope which is offered by departments. Yet their scope and scale of operation means that in government there are some of the most rewarding challenges found anywhere in the organisational world. It is this combination of the organisational and the political which gives central administration its character, significance and appeal.

The structure of central administration

The importance of departments as organisations has been recognised increasingly over the past twenty years as more attention has been paid to the managerial quality of government and thus to its structures and processes. Structure refers to the allocation of authority, the division of labour, formalisation, and different aspects of size and complexity of organisations. Processes are the dynamic mechanisms by which the executive organisations maintain themselves (e.g. staffing, decision-making, implementation and control). Moreover, organisations do not exist in a vacuum but relate to the world outside (i.e. their environments). The forces in this environment can push and pull organisations or in turn be influenced by them. The environment and organisation are thus always in a state of change. Managing this changing relationship is a vital part of administration in government.

It was suggested at the beginning of this chapter that not only is the machinery and management of central government subject to political whim but in general its overall development has lacked a set of guiding principles. In fact, it is not so much the

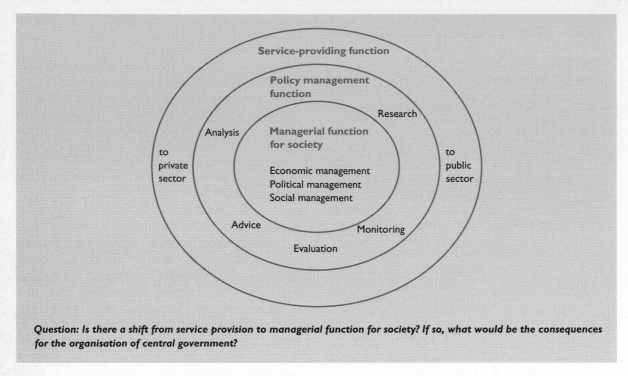

Question: *Is there a shift from service provision to managerial function for society? If so, what would be the consequences for the organisation of central government?*

Figure 20.1   Issue: functions of the administrative process

shortage of underlying principles as their multiple and perhaps inconsistent use which is striking. This is not simply the fault of those responsible for the structures and processes which have evolved. The differentiation of tasks, functions and contexts is both a cause as well as an effect of administering central government.

Why are there these different central government organisations and how are functions allocated between them? There is no golden rule by which these matters are regulated. Rather, different factors are influential in different times and contexts. However, this does not mean there cannot be *any* underlying principles. The justification for having different types of central organisation, for example, lies in the fact that government tasks and functions vary and thus one form would not be suitable for all of them. Some may be essentially commercial in nature (and thus can be left to the disciplines that entails), while others are intrinsically political and require ministerial involvement. Similarly, dividing up functions helps to develop specialisation in the performance of tasks, while encouraging discipline and quality in the provision of services. Yet these advantages also bring their problems; each separation of function brings a

potential for those who work in them to identify with their functional interests rather than with the general interest of government as a whole.

Authority

Government organisations are designed to serve ministers and their authority. This legal authority complements the political and comes from their position within the government and in turn from Parliament. Each department may be seen as a bureaucracy, i.e. an organisation in which there are fixed areas of jurisdiction, activities governed by rules, and authority allocated through a hierarchy of positions; in short an organisation governed by office. But other authorities are also exercised in departments. Expertise, for example, is an authority in its own right. Thus lawyers, accountants, doctors, engineers and other professions are recognised as holding their own authority based on expertise and ethical standards.

Government organisations are therefore characterised by many authorities, often reflected in the structures which separate the responsibilities of generalist administrators (i.e. those representing the main line of ministerial authority) and specialist professionals. Nowadays this distinction is less obvious in the formal structures of departments but is still important for day-to-day operations. Moreover, this professional authority can challenge the ministerial authority in a department, such as in the case of the military in the Ministry of Defence or civil engineers in the Department of Transport. That is why, as we shall see below, the civil service's professional expertise in running government can be such a powerful force in the relations between ministers and their civil servants.

Objectives

These issues arise notably in the extent to which central departments have objectives. In practice such objectives can be multiple and conflicting. Yet the obvious appeal of departments with purposive activities has led to a steady stream of developments which have placed an increasing emphasis on objectives and their achievement in the management of government departments. The Conservative government's Financial Management Initiative (FMI), for example, sought from 1982 to provide departmental managers with 'a clear view of objectives and performance' (Cmnd 8616, 1982, Appendix 3, para. 5), departmental annual reports have since 1989 systematically set out aims and goals, and the framework documents under which new executive agencies are set up also oblige departments to set out targets for their agencies to achieve.

At first departments found it hard to articulate their intended achievements. Under the FMI, for example, they were better at telling us what they did. This may have been because departments are themselves federations of divisions and sections all with their own varied purposes and goals. Expressing all these in other than a general bland statement was difficult. But, under the new climate in which resources are linked increasingly to the achievement of targets and with the development of marketing skills, departmental presentations became more articulate (see Box 20.2) and significant.

Allocation of functions

Government organisations are not, however, simply structures of authority and objectives; they are also mechanisms by which functions in government are allocated and provided for. Here, at last, there some principles which we can identify as being usable. Faced with the multiplicity of functions of modern government, an administration (i.e. a Prime Minister) can allocate them in at least four distinct ways: by purpose, by process, by client group or by territory.

An allocation by *purpose* takes us back to goals or objectives. Traditional governmental tasks such as law and order, defence and foreign relations, and the facilitating of trade, are supplemented in modern government by a range of welfare and related services such as social security, health, housing and education. Departments and other agencies based on allocation by purpose will be based on these services. Often, however, these services or purposes depend on particular working methods or *process* and the skills which they call for. Where these processes (e.g. medicine, finance, engineering) have distinctive characteristics requiring separate organisational forms, we can expect to find organisations based on them.

Departments or agencies based on purpose or process may well contribute beneficially to the development of specialised service provision by integrating effort around a particular purpose or skill. There is a danger in such an arrangement, however, which lies in the way that the needs of the *clientele* of these services rarely if ever neatly coincide with these purposes or skills themselves. Indeed, clients tend to have conditions which require integrated rather than separate treatments. This can apply especially to those who are socially disadvantaged, as one condition can often be associated with another; the poorly housed, for example, tend to suffer more sickness. Over the past hundred years or so this has led to demands for services to be provided by organisations which bring together the needs of clients rather than the needs of the service or process. In principle, this could mean agencies dealing with the elderly, the young or the unemployed.

It is also possible to see an integration of services or processes in relation to the needs of *territories* as well as clients. If different areas of the country have their own topographical, cultural, economic or political characteristics, it may be advantageous to bring services together to serve the resulting distinctive needs. In the recession which began in the late

BOX 20.2

Aim, mission and objectives of Her Majesty's Treasury

AIM
The Treasury's overall aim is to promote rising prosperity based on sustained economic growth

Mission

In seeking to meet this aim we will:

- maintain a stable macroeconomic environment;
- strengthen the long-term performance of the economy and the outlook for jobs, in strategic partnership with others;
- maintain a professional, well motivated and outward-looking. organisation, committed to continuous improvement.

Objectives

In seeking to meet this aim we will:
maintain a stable macroeconomic environment, by

1. delivering permanently low inflation
2. maintaining sound public finances
3. keeping public expenditure to a level that is affordable
4. pursuing tax policies which generate sufficient revenue, while doing the least damage to the economy and encouraging enterprise

strengthen the long-term performance of the economy and the outlook for jobs, in strategic partnership with others, by

5. promoting policies and public expenditure priorities which improve the use of resources and the efficiency of markets throughout the economy, within an affordable level of total public expenditure
6. maintaining a financial control system which delivers continuing improvements in the efficiency of government
7. maintaining a framework for government accounting which makes clear how resources are used and provides effective accountability to Parliament
8. promoting greater use of private finance in support of services currently provided by the public sector and the privatisation of those parts of the public sector which do not need to remain in public ownership
9. maintaining a regime for the regulation of financial services which preserves a stable financial system, honest markets and the confidence of investors and depositors, while promoting an open, efficient and competitive financial services sector

In carrying out all these responsibilities we will:

10. keep abreast of developments in other countries and promote UK economic interests and ideas abroad
11. ensure that the Parliament and the public are well informed about the objectives and effects of the Government's economic and financial policies

and maintain a professional, well motivated and outward-looking organisation, committed to continuous improvement, by

12. ensuring that the Treasury is resourced, staffed and managed to deliver its objectives as effectively and efficiently as possible.

Source: HM Treasury, 1996

1980s, for example, it was noticeable how the traditional heavy industries were hit hardest. These tended to be in a few parts of the UK (the north-east, Clydeside and Northern Ireland, for example). Where such characteristics are reinforced by the need to acknowledge distinctive political traditions (as in the case of Scotland, Wales or Northern Ireland), this makes an even stronger case for agencies based on these territories so that their development can be tackled in a coherent way consistent with their character and local wishes. Thus the creation of the Northern Ireland, Scottish and Welsh Offices.

It is clear that these principles are not mutually consistent. This implies a problem for British central government because, as Table 20.4 shows, it uses all of them simultaneously. But the problem goes deeper, for even these departments represent combinations of these principles. In practice, however, allocation by purpose has been the most persistent influence, even if other factors have been important enough to have frequently overruled it. The explanation of the variety (or you may think it an inconsistency) is of course that circumstances and political pressures change. Thus at one moment an economic recession may lead a government to attend (or wish to show it is attending) to hardship in certain areas, at another to a particular client group's needs, and at another to the development of a particular service. We must also remember that a government has to accommodate a number of political forces often by particular ministers all using the machinery of government as the means of advancing their own political careers. Thus all these factors exert competing pressures on the allocation of functions to government organisations.

A structure of disintegration?

One of the major problems arising from all these separated structures is the potential disintegration of departments. Governments can overcome this with coordinating institutional arrangements. These include some of the central departments and other agencies which have functions across central government (e.g. the Treasury through its management of public expenditure and the economy, and various offices of ministers for the civil service through their responsibility for personnel matters). There are also Cabinet and interdepartmental committees which work to coordinate activities in areas covered by more than one department.

The Conservative government after 1979, however, dismantled a number of these integrative arrangements, including the Civil Service Department (which was the personnel department for the civil service) and the Central Policy Review Staff (a corporate policy planning unit). As a result, more coordinating responsibility has fallen on the Treasury and the Cabinet Office. In particular, the Treasury's role as guardian of public expenditure has been enhanced by the increased emphasis on cash control and public finances since the mid-1970s and by changes to the system of public expenditure planning which have reduced departmental flexibility. However, cases such as the government's energy policy decisions in 1992–3 and their effects on pit closures by British Coal suggest that the integration of government is difficult to achieve. It is a picture reinforced by Sir Richard Scott's Inquiry into *The Export of Defence Equipment and Dual-Use Goods to Iraq and Related Prosecutions* (HC 115, 1995–6). From the Report we gain a glimpse of the way the Ministry of Defence, the Department of Trade and Industry and the Foreign and Commonwealth Office all had responsibilities connected with selling arms to overseas countries and all had distinct interests which they pursued more or less vigorously. In such circumstances, and in the increasing complex business that is modern government this may be frequent, the corresponding integrating burden on the structures of

Table 20.4 Allocation of functions: some examples by department

Purpose principle	Process principle	Client principle	Territory principle
Health, Social Security	Foreign and Commonwealth	Agriculture	Northern Ireland Office
Education and Employment	Board of Inland Revenue		Scottish Office
Environment	Lord Chancellor's Department		Welsh Office

central administration is increased but perhaps less than adequately dealt with. A belated attempt to tackle the problem may have been behind the creation of an extensive portfolio for Michael Heseltine as Deputy Prime Minister. Whether such an integrating structure will work remains to be seen.

The processes of central departments

The processes of central departments are those systematic activities designed to help facilitate the delivery of government. This section will examine only a few of the main processes but from them you should be able to understand not only how they operate but also the contribution they make to the effectiveness of government. These are the systems which give government its management style.

The increasing recognition since 1979 of the importance of the management of central departments has led to a more systematic approach to the definition of problems, the setting of goals, the making of choices, and the implementation and control of programmes of activity. The following sections will explore some of these aspects to see whether they do represent a shift to a more coherent *management* of central government.

Staffing

Although the Conservative government after 1979 has made a few changes to the responsibilities of these departments (it separated Social Security and Health, and incorporated Energy into Trade and Industry and Employment into Education), its emphasis was on reducing the *size* and latterly the recruitment of the civil service, i.e. the permanent staff in the departments. Figure 20.2 traces the changes since the Second World War. The Conservative government achieved a reduction of over 150,000 between 1979 and 1987, about one-fifth of what it inherited, and by April 1996 the numbers had fallen to 494,300. Official statistics suggest that about a third of the reduction has been due to the transfer of functions to non-civil service or private sector organisations or the ending of services and about a half to increases in efficiency.

These numbers are managed through *staffing*, i.e. those processes of recruitment, training and personnel review which are designed to promote a social and technical homogeneity in the management of government. Because central government is a massive undertaking, much of the responsibility for the content and design of staffing processes rests with the departments themselves, a feature reinforced by Conservative government reforms in the 1980s and 1990s. However, in the central departments and associated agencies there is a common policy and, especially in the new senior civil service (see Table 20.3 above), a central implementation as well. Thus, the Civil Service Commission is responsible for *recruitment* policy for the higher grades of the service while other recruitment is the direct responsibility of the individual departments. Both the Commission and the departments have been using

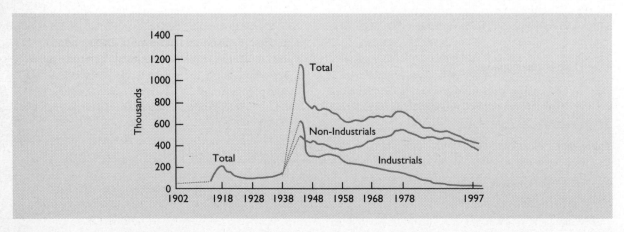

Figure 20.2 Civil service numbers
Source: Office of Public Service

the Recruitment and Assessment Services Agency, a government executive agency which has now been privatised.

The main instrument of selection of recruits to senior grades is the Civil Service Selection Board. Its procedure is based on certain minimum academic qualifications and involves a series of tests combining simulations, analytical exercises and interviews. In the past some criticism has been made of the validity of the tests employed for the way successful candidates came very largely from arts-based subjects studied at Oxford and Cambridge. Over the years this pattern has become gradually less marked but still few scientists and technologists come through the procedures. Of course, this may be as much the result of the predisposition of persons from these disciplines towards civil service work as a reflection of any distortion in the selection process itself.

Following the White Paper *The Civil Service: Continuity and Change* (Cm 2627, 1994), the recruitment to the senior civil service has more often been through open advertising. Box 20.3 concerns the advertisement for the first such appointment, that of the Permanent Secretary to the Department of Employment. Note that this shows not only the willingness to advertise openly but also the use of head-hunting agencies (in this case, the consulting firm Price Waterhouse). The successful candidate,

Michael Bichard, who came from an executive agency, soon found that his department had been absorbed into that for education, but he later became that department's permanent secretary too.

Training in central government is carried out largely by the organisations themselves. Especially in the larger departments, there are extensive training divisions which cater for the varied technical needs of functional performance. But under the plans announced in the first ever White Paper on training (Cm 3321, 1996), the Cabinet Office is providing direction through its training targets for departments. By the end of the century, for example, all departments are expected to be recognised as Investors in People (a national accreditation scheme for human resource management) and to be operating action plans for training and career development.

Central to this effort is the Civil Service College, an executive agency reprieved in 1995 from imminent privatisation (see Box 20.4). Part of the original intention in 1970 was to develop a staff college on similar lines to the Military Staff College at Sandhurst. Under such a scheme, officials would undergo regular training programmes, some of which would be required for promotion. There has never been the government commitment to the training function nor to the College itself necessary to give this idea any chance of being realised. Indeed,

---

BOX 20.3　　　　　　　　⒠.ℊ.　　　　　　　　**EXAMPLE**

Who wants to be a permanent secretary?

It was intended to be a breakthrough. For the first time the job of heading a Whitehall department – the Department of Employment – has been publicly advertised to external, as well as internal, applicants. It nearly ended in farce, with Price Waterhouse, the headhunters, struggling to find high-calibre outsiders for the shortlist, from which a choice is imminent.

The reason is the salary, advertised at £95,000 although the job could pay up to 20% more to an exceptional candidate. This is simply not competitive. By coincidence, the Department of Employment's expenditure of £4.6 billion is

almost precisely the turnover of Cable and Wireless, the telecommunications company run by Lord Young, a former secretary of state for employment. Lord Young was paid £777,163 last year. So it is hardly surprising that Price Waterhouse was not knocked over by a stampede of qualified applicants.

Source: The Economist, 18 February 1995

Question: Should permanent secretaries of central departments be recruited in this way? Should they be paid the same as chief executives of large companies?

BOX 20.4 **EXAMPLE**

Civil Service College: management training for mandarins?

Set in handsome grounds in leafy Surrey, the old college was set also in its ways: a genteel, peeling institution, dishing out long, slow courses to young, fast-stream civil servants and offering remedial treatment to the older, slower ones. Now it resembles a business school. Signs point to the jogging track; the swimming pool is newly heated; the bedrooms are at last 'en suite', and outside caterers provide appropriately up-market food.

More importantly, the college has been reorganised as a business. Indeed its wholesale adoption of business language and methods borders on pastiche. The college has a strategic plan. Courses on offer are 'products', organised in seven 'market business groups'. Performance is ruthlessly measured against targets, and consultants have been brought in to advise on how to reward it in pay. 'Market testing' is embraced with enthusiasm.

One aim is to get rid of the college's old remedial image. Civil servants used to be sent to it because they were failing. Now it wants them to come to be taught to succeed. It invites Whitehall's top managers – those in grades 1 to 3, the top 600 – to undertake leadership training. Nearly half have said 'yes, please'. They come because they want to: they have to sign themselves up for courses, and the cost comes out of their own slice of their departmental budgets. If the college does not deliver, it will die …

Some things have been lost in the change. The college is now too busy getting on with its work to think much about the role of the civil service. It knows a lot about public administration, but never finds time to write it down. But the staff mind less about what they have lost than what they might lose in future. Profit making, marketable and adaptable, the college could easily be privatised. Its senior staff believe that, if it were, something irreplaceable would be lost: a relationship of trust with Whitehall which allows the new techniques of public management to be taught without destroying the old ethos of public service.

Source: The Economist, 31 October 1992

Question: Should the college be privatised and government obtain its training from the private sector?

---

paradoxically, the College has gained a reputation for considerable competence in routine training programmes at the same time as its capacity for innovation and development has been reduced. The introduction in the mid-1980s of the Top Management Programme, a three-week course which is designed for ascending under secretaries, is one of very few programmes which fits the original conception. However, the training White Paper provides a new opportunity for the College to adopt a central role up to the millennium.

Departmental management

Since 1979, the government has initiated a number of management reforms designed to promote econ-

omy, efficiency and effectiveness. Although these terms are often confused by ministers, they represent a rallying call to the new managers and, more significantly, a philosophy for ministerial decision-making and control. What are its elements?

Theories of decision-making popular in the private sector and business schools point to the need to identify problems, specify objectives, search for and select options, implement choices and review effects. In reality decisions are never as straightforward as this rational exposition implies. Objectives and means tend to become merged in government, especially where there is a need to move forward on an agreed basis. If Margaret Thatcher attempted to edge closer to the popular model, in particular by seeking to separate the choice of values and objectives from the management of means, John Major saw decisions as more a matter of consensus management. Both, however, believe that setting values and policies is the preserve of ministers, who are supposed to have some very clear ideas about what these are. It is the job of civil servants to manage the implementation of the chosen policies. It is this idea which is central to the development of departmental agencies (more on this in Chapter 21).

There have been various developments in the government's programme to managerialise central government, some of which relate principally to the management of the core of departments (others will be discussed in Chapter 21). *Efficiency reviews* were originally established in 1979 under Sir Derek (later Lord) Rayner, who until 1983 was the Prime Minister's adviser on efficiency and head of the Efficiency Unit. Sir Derek, then a senior executive with the retailers Marks and Spencer, had worked previously for government in the Ministry of Defence during the early 1970s. He had established a reputation as a management expert in both private and public sectors.

Under Sir Derek and his successors, including Sir Peter Levene, the current efficiency adviser, the strategy has sought to combine attempts to reduce operating costs with the identification of more deeply seated obstacles to good management in government. Thus the reviews (still called 'Rayner Scrutinies' in some quarters) have identified problems with the collection of government statistics, systems for paying benefits, and those caused to members of the public and managers alike by unwieldy and incomprehensible forms. Over the years, the reviews have led to considerable savings in the costs of services.

Whether these savings have been at the expense of service effectiveness is another matter. But the

---

BOX 20.5

Managing the Ministry of Defence

1996–7 Facts and figures:

Annual spending: £22.13 bn.

Staff: 116,000 (down from 240,000 in 1980).

Executive agencies: 48 (over 80,000 staff).

Private finance: Projects in process attracting £1.5 bn of private funding.

Competition: £1 bn worth of activity (40,000 jobs) tested against the private sector.

Headquarters: Employs less than 5% of MoD civil servants (45% reduction since 1990) in two London buildings (reduced from 45 in 1990), with functions dispersed to regions (e.g. Procurement Executive to Bristol).

Fundamental review: 'Front Line First' – impetus of many of the changes.

Resource accounting: Biggest change in financial management for 50 years and will require recruitment of over 300 qualified accountants.

Human resource management: Seeking Investors in People recognition.

Issues until 2000:

The major issue: Establishing and sustaining core values in new devolved, decentralised and dispersed ministry.

Career development: More individual and less ministry responsibility for careers resulting in more career mobility including in and out of the Ministry.

Professionals: Less reliance on generalist civil servants and more on specialists, including accountants for resource accounting and lawyers for contracted out work, in addition to MoD's existing very large groups of scientists and engineers.

Bureaucracy: Breaking down of hierarchical ways of working on the civilian side has to be harmonised with military hierarchies.

Source: Discussions with MoD officials

success of the reviews in producing action has encouraged the development of more wide-ranging reviews of departments' major programmes. These *fundamental reviews* have forced departments to consider whether activities can be dispensed with altogether, privatised, contracted out or reorganised into agencies, and what structures and resources are appropriate to their future provision. Results have included a reduction in the Treasury's core staff by 25 per cent, a rationalisation of the services provided by the Department of Social Security, and a reorganisation of the Ministry of Defence (see Box 20.5).

Another significant development of the 1980s was the *Financial Management Initiative* (FMI).

Announced in 1982, the FMI set out to make managers responsible for specific blocks of resources and activities, give them the means for executing those responsibilities and hold them to account for their discharge. The emphasis was on formalising top management structures and information systems, installing procedures for measuring performance of activities, and developing management accounting systems that stress the delegated management of resources.

There has been considerable progress in these respects. Most departments, driven by their own senior managements, put a great deal of effort into institutionalising this reform so that its elements have become established as part of the normal way

---

BOX 20.6

Principles of departmental management – or are they?

The Conservative government after 1979 made much of the 3 Es of management:

Economy	*Minimisation of resource consumption*
Efficiency	*Ratio of resources consumed to outputs gained*
Effectiveness	*Maximisation of outputs*

But other E principles apply as well and they can be contradictory:

Efficacy	*Maximisation of beneficial impacts for community*
Equity	*Equality of treatment for equal cases*
Excellence	*Maximisation of quality of process and product*
Enterprise	*Maximisation of profit-making initiative*
Electability	*Maximisation of electoral gain*

The Harvard management writer Rosbeth Kanter (cited in Alimo-Metcalfe, 1993) has suggested some F principles as well:

Focused	*Concentration on the core business objectives*
Flexible	*Less rigid structures to adapt to change*
Friendly	*Openness to employees and customers*
Fun	*Stimulation, challenge and reward*

However, sceptics (e.g. Alimo-Metcalfe 1993) argue that 'F' can stand for less complimentary characteristics:

Façade	*form over substance*
Fear	*of the future*
Fragility	*of new structures and processes as they face the future*
Fire	*as in the sack*
Feudal	*as in management style*

Question: Is this all just a game or is there real substance in the terms?

of managing. Officials in Whitehall as well as in the operational outposts of central department (which have always been more managerially minded), talk now of budgets, cost centres, financial responsibility and performance indicators.

Now this language as well as practice faces another challenge, that of *resource accounting*. Until recently, departments have accounted for themselves on a purely cash basis, reporting at the end of the year on how they spent the cash allocated to them by Parliament. By the end of the century, however, resource accounting will have obliged each central government organisation to present its annual financial statements on an accruals basis as though it were a business. This will involve a much more systematic account of revenue and expenditure and, in particular, a balance sheet expressing values for its assets (buildings, equipment and reserves) and liabilities (its creditors and obligations).

Underlying both the new vocabulary and practice of management in central departments has been a government concern with *value for money* and *organisational fitness*. This began with the government's three Es of economy, efficiency and effectiveness. As Box 20.6 shows, there are other 'E' principles in public management. The illustration also suggests that there are also 'F' principles of departmental change. No doubt this exercise could be extended to most of the alphabet (and keep a few management consultants in good money!). Even if these principles tend to contradict each other and there is disagreement over priorities, they do at least indicate that there is a commitment to developing effective organisations and management. Historically, management of departments was notable by its absence. In short, this is more than simply a new way of talking; it represents a new way of administering. And that, as we shall see, raises political issues of its own.

The politics of central departments

According to the Cabinet Office in December 1994, Derek Lewis, then Chief Executive of the Prison Service, was the UK's highest paid civil servant, earning £160,000 (including £35,000 in performance bonuses) per annum. This was considerably more than Sir Robin Butler, Cabinet Secretary, and the Prime Minister. The Home Secretary, Michael

Howard, defended Lewis's salary and later, in April 1995, with the Prison Service under fierce criticism following escapes from Whitemore and Parkhurst prisons, renewed his contract for two more years. However, by the end of October, following the publication of the Learmont Report on the Parkhurst affair, Howard abruptly sacked him.

Given that he was the chief beneficiary of the new performance culture in Whitehall, Lewis might be seen to have got what he deserved. He was paid well for success but had to take the responsibility for failure. However, a close reading of the Learmont Report on the prison breakouts (Cm 3020, 1995) raises other issues. The author, a former quartermaster general in the Army, was suspicious of Lewis's modern management techniques but even more scathing on the interference in the agency by the Home Office ministers. Although the Prison Service as an agency was meant to be free to manage its operations within a framework agreed with ministers every three years, the report revealed that over a random period of eighty-three days, the correspondence between the agency and ministers amounted to more than 1,000 documents. Further, when Sir John's investigating team tried to interview Lewis he was constantly interrupted by calls from the Home Office. As Sir John wearily noted, 'there were many hands on the tiller on this voyage to disaster'.

A few years earlier, when he was appointed Chancellor of the Exchequer in John Major's first administration (1990), Norman Lamont vacated his private residence in favour of the official home at 11 Downing Street. Part of his private residence was let out as a flat to a lady later discovered to be known professionally as Miss Whiplash. When Lamont became aware of the nature of her business he used due legal process to evict her. It was an expensive process, so much so that, as a later inquiry by the government's auditor of expenditure, the National Audit Office, revealed, it required a contribution of several thousand pounds from the Treasury to sustain it. Some asked what the administration was doing supporting the minister in this way.

These are by no means the only recent cases where politics and administration have become confused. But they raise the question of how there can be politics in administration. It is a question which has intrigued many for a long time. Some have made its answer their life's work. Their answers are emphatic: politics do not stop at the entrances to departments. On the contrary, they are often played out most actively within the corridors of Whitehall. So, what is the relationship between them?

In public ministers are fond of distinguishing between politics and administration; they are involved in the former and civil servants the latter. Civil servants are usually at pains also to point out that they are merely the servants of their political masters, the ministers. This highlights what political scientists call a normative/descriptive problem. What the distinction between politics and administration *should* be (i.e. the normative part of the problem) varies with writers and contexts. However, in general it seeks a separation of administration from politics, often with a view to preventing a type of pollution of the former by the latter. The premise is, of course, that politicians make policy and officials implement it.

In practice (i.e. the descriptive part of the problem), the distinction is not as simple as this (see Box 20.7). Despite the attractiveness of the idea that only politicians engage in politics, the latter are found wherever differences between people affect their interests. In central departments, these internal politics come principally from the way administrative structures divide up functions and responsibilities and help to form interests and loyalties. One of the reasons often given for moving civil servants from post to post is to prevent the officers identifying themselves too closely with the activity they are responsible for. Nevertheless, it is human nature and organisationally functional to develop such attachments, especially when resources are in short supply.

This is all part of the political dimension of the administrative process which derives from the wider political system and, as we have seen, from within the process itself. Civil servants and ministers alike have views about the system of representative democracy, the role of the state or the conduct of the individual in government, views which provide a climate in which the administrative process operates. Moreover, the workings of our representative and responsible government (a term borrowed from Birch, 1964) provide the context to which administration must necessarily adapt. Thus, the nature of participation in the system, the elective method of appointment, and the extent to which government reflects the population over which it rules are political qualities which embrace administration. Similarly, the administration is expected to be responsive, rational and accountable, all qualities of responsible government.

BOX 20.7   **IDEAS AND PERSPECTIVES**

Politics and administration: separate or fused?

Peter Riddell on politics
This distinction between policy and operations sounds neat but is unconvincing. Executive agencies were supposed to produce clearer and more open lines of responsibility, but it is impossible in practice to separate the policy decisions of ministers from the operational decisions of chief executives. Ministers cannot distance themselves from sensitive events such as prison breakouts, and they inevitably become involved in giving explanations. The Learmont report makes clear that ministers did not leave Mr

Lewis and his senior officials to get on with administering the prisons, but intervened all the time with initiatives and requests. In that respect, responsibility as well as accountability was confused.

Source: The Times, 17 October 1995

Question: Is Riddell correct to argue that the distinction between policy and administration is inherently unworkable, or is his argument based too much on the idiosyncrasy of one minister's megalomania?

Thus, although there might be a theoretical distinction between politics and administration, it is very difficult to sustain in practice. Politics arise when differences affect interests. Administration necessarily has political implications because it raises issues which affect interested parties. Thus politics can be found not only at the ministerial or parliamentary level, through parties and interest groups, but within the administrative process itself, including in the relations between ministers and civil servants.

Ministers and civil servants

It was said that Margaret Thatcher's favourite television programmes were the series *Yes Minister* and *Yes Prime Minister*. These humorous and perceptive programmes gained an almost cult following in the 1980s both in this country and abroad. Indeed, one of this chapter's authors was once kept waiting in the Malaysian Ministry of Education while a minister and senior officials discussed the previous evening's episode!

The series, repeated by the BBC in the mid-1990s, featured the way the enthusiastic but often naive politician, Jim Hacker, was served by his permanent secretary, Sir Humphrey Appleby, and private secretary, Bernard Woolley. How far Hacker was ever in command was the underlying issue. As he came gradually to realise, 'yes minister' often meant 'perhaps minister' and even 'no minister', while Sir Humphrey's claim that his job was merely 'to serve' was often far from credible.

The programmes were written up by the script writers as ministerial memoirs (Lynn and Jay, 1981). In them, Sir Humphrey is a composite character of all that many have seen as the best and worst of the traditional British higher civil service: well educated and with a lifetime of experience moving up slowly through its higher grades, he is master of the spoken and written word and expert in the ways of Whitehall. He is the ultimate career civil servant: permanent, neutral and professional, well able not only to serve politicians of any political colour but also his own interests.

The great constitutional textbooks of the early and mid-twentieth century which set out the minister–civil servant relationship since the nineteenth century would have recognised only part of this description of the higher civil servant. They hinted at nothing of the politician in the official, only the servant of the minister and public interest (essentially the same thing). Were they misleading their readers or have practices changed?

If we were to follow a minister and his principal officials through a typical week, we would see that although perceptions of this relationship have changed, the reality has retained its essential and inevitable character. A day might begin with the minister being briefed by officials on the main business and meetings of the day and a discussion of major items coming up. These sessions are often called 'prayers' by those involved, perhaps reflecting the need for the Almighty to give inspiration, not to mention some help with the workload. Meetings with outside organisations concerned with policy proposals or visits to sites of departmental activity may precede an afternoon in the House of Commons answering questions, making statements on government policy or contributing to debates on departmental measures. Throughout, the officials will sit to the rear of the Speaker's chair (i.e. technically outside the Chamber), from where they keep the minister informed and advised by passing notes.

All this necessarily brings a political character to the work of officials. Of course, this is not to suggest that they seek to usurp the policy process. But it does reflect the differentiation of interests and values in the administrative process and the way that, in the service of government, civil servants come to be involved in the political game. An examination of responsibility and accountability in British central departments shows how this arises.

Responsibility and accountability

The precise *responsibility* of ministers and officials is far from clear. At least in part this derives from the absence of a constitutional law on the matter and the reliance on (necessarily changing) custom and practice. This became evident during the trial in 1985 of Clive Ponting, an official who was acquitted of passing classified information to an unauthorised person, an MP, under the Official Secrets Acts. The trial confirmed the confusion over exactly what the obligations of a civil servant were to a minister, particularly whether obedience should extend to matters of doubtful legality or propriety. In what some saw as an attempt to restrict the implications of the acquittal (i.e. that an official might be able to disclose confidential information in the public interest), Sir Robert Armstrong, then Cabinet Secretary and Head of the Civil Service, issued a note reasserting that the responsibilities of civil servants were to their ministers (see Box 20.8).

The Armstrong note is a classic formal statement of principle. It articulates a distinction between policy (the sphere of ministers) and administration (that of civil servants). What the note fails to elaborate, however, is the complex and varied interplay of these distinctions in practice.

In pointing to the central function of officials as serving ministers, the note portrays the heart of the relationship. However, it also alludes to a policy responsibility which, although formally the preserve of ministers, cannot be carried out in practice without civil servants. As we saw earlier, officials can research, advise, support and refute policy options. In effect this points to a distinction between the *making* and the *taking* of decisions.

Ministers often like to think that they take decisions; here not only constitutional doctrine but the practical reality suggests that they do. On the other hand, the basis on which they so take them and the extent of their choice may be severely constrained.

BOX 20.8   **IDEAS AND PERSPECTIVES**

Responsibility and accountability: minister or civil servant?

Memorandum from Sir Robert Armstrong, Cabinet Secretary (February 1985) on the duties of civil servants:

The duty of the individual civil servant is first and foremost to the minister of the crown who is in charge of the department in which he or she is serving. ... The determination of policy is the responsibility of the minister. ... In the determination of policy the civil servant has no constitutional responsibility or role distinct from that of the minister. ... When, having given all the relevant information and advice, the minister has taken the decision, it is the duty of civil servants loyally to carry out that decision. ... Civil servants are under an obligation to keep the confidences to which they become privy in the course of their official duties. ...

The Scott Report on the distinction between responsibility and accountability as elaborated by Sir Robin Butler, Cabinet Secretary (HC 115, 1995–6):

The Minister must always answer questions and give an account to Parliament for the actions of his department. ... It does not necessarily, however, require blame to be accepted by a Minister in whose department

some blameworthy error or failure has occurred ... unless he has some personal responsibility for or some personal involvement in what has occurred. The kernel of Sir Robin's point, I think, is that the conduct of government has become so complex and the need for ministerial delegation of responsibilities to and reliance on the advice of officials has become so inevitable as to render unreal the attaching of blame to a Minister simply because something has gone wrong in the department. ... For my part, I find it difficult to disagree. ... If Ministers are to be excused blame and personal criticism on the basis of the absence of personal knowledge or involvement, the corollary ought to be an acceptance of the obligation to be forthcoming with information about the incident in question. Otherwise Parliament (and the public) will not be in a position to judge whether the absence of personal knowledge and involvement is fairly claimed or to judge on whom the responsibility for what has occurred ought to be placed.

Source: (HC.115, 1995/6, K8 pp. 1801–6)

Question: Do you agree with this distinction between responsibility and accountability?

Events may seem to suggest a particular course of action. So too might the way the issues, options and potential outcomes come to be identified, researched and presented. In these ways civil servants may come in a real sense to make the decisions which ministers then take.

The relationship between ministers and civil servants is not limited to matters of departmental programmes or policy. Just as officials necessarily contribute to policy, so ministers have views about administration and management. Often these arise from the implications of administrative developments for wider government policy or the more recent emphases in government on the management of resources and the delivery of departmental services. Since governments became in the mid-1970s much more concerned with government expenditure, ministers have become much more active, for example, in managing the resource allocation and cost profiles of their departments.

This explains why a minister such as Peter Lilley as Secretary of State for Social Security was keen to establish a profile of administrative costs for his huge spending department. It also explains how in the pursuit of the management reforms described earlier, some officials come up against what they see as ministerial interference in matters managerial. Thus, for example, a manager of a tax collection who is able to show that the cost of employing two more inspectors would be recovered perhaps ten times by the extra revenue gained (an argument which in a private business would lead to extra recruitment) might find this blocked by a minister committed to a reduction rather than an expansion of the civil service. Thus, just as the administrative influences the political, so the political itself comes to constrain the administrative.

Ministers and civil servants therefore share varying responsibilities for the policy and administration of their departments, programmes and services. With these responsibilities, moreover, comes *accountability*, i.e. the liability to present accounts of, and answer for, their execution. Indeed, accountability is one of the cornerstones of our representative and responsible system of government. The doctrine of individual ministerial accountability governs the way individual ministers are obliged to present accounts to and answer questions in Parliament in respect of the policy and conduct of themselves as ministers and of their departments.

Some have seen a sinister development in the way increasing accountable management (as in executive agencies) is undermining this chain of responsibility by separating out the accountability of officials from that of ministers (and thus exposing the former, who have previously remained anonymous and impartial). But the constitutional doctrine which holds that a minister is accountable for *every* action of a department has now, however, passed into disuse. Sir Robin Butler's evidence to the Scott Inquiry (see Box 20.8) sets out the view that while ministers have to account for and submit to examination on the conduct of themselves and their departments, they are not deemed to be held culpable for the actions and inactions of their officials unless they were committed with the authority and cognisance of the minister. After the Vehicle and General insurance company went bankrupt in 1971 an inquiry found that the Department of Trade and Industry had acted negligently in monitoring and acting on the company. The section and officials involved were identified but the Secretary of State for Trade and Industry, John Davies, although giving an account of the situation and the remedial action, faced no censure. On the other hand, during a dispute in 1985–6 between Leon Brittan, Secretary of State for Trade and Industry, and Michael Heseltine, Secretary of State for Defence, over the sale of Westland Engineering, a major defence contractor, Brittan arranged for one of his officials to leak to the press extracts unfavourable to Heseltine of a letter from the Solicitor General. Brittan resigned when it became clear that he had lost the confidence of the House of Commons not only over his account of this affair, but also over the impropriety of his actions.

That ministers should be held accountable but not directly culpable for the actions of their officials is realistic. The business of central administration is now so vast, complex and professionalised that a minister cannot effectively be held ultimately responsible for it. But the process of accountability is itself more complex than this. It implies an obligation on the minister first to give accounts of his or her departmental activities, second to answer questions on this account, and only then to be judged on these accounts. As accountable management becomes institutionalised in Whitehall, government managers themselves will become increasingly obliged within their departments to present accounts of and answer to the discharge of their responsibilities. It is only a small step then for civil servants rather than ministers to be liable in public (such as select committees of the House of Commons) to present accounts and answer for the execution of their responsibilities. Some argue that this may lead to a minister's being able to avoid this accountability him- or herself.

Two fundamental issues arise from this developing relationship between responsibility and accountability: the factors which determine whether a culpable minister resigns and the protection of civil servants from the arbitrariness of ministers.

Box 20.9 shows the occasions of ministerial resignations since 1945. Apart from the cases of public scandal, especially those enhanced by hypocrisy, these do not seem to reveal a clear set of factors leading to resignation. More intriguing, but much more difficult to catalogue, are those occasions when ministers, although apparently culpable, managed to evade resignation. However, if we were to speculate on why a minister is forced to resign or manages to stay, we might offer a number of factors: personal determination, public and mass media commentary, parliamentary opinion, support of governmental colleagues, and, perhaps most telling of all, the attitude of the Prime Minister. But if these are the ingredients of outcome, the recipe always

---

BOX 20.9   (e.g.)   **EXAMPLE**

Individual ministerial accountability: resignations since 1970

	Edward Heath 1970–4	Harold Wilson 1974–6	Jim Callaghan 1976–9	Margaret Thatcher 1979–90	John Major 1990–97
Sex scandal	2	0	0	1	4
Financial scandal	2	0	0	0	3
Failure	0	0	0	3	0
Political principle	2	5	4	7	4
Public criticism	0	0	0	3	1
TOTAL	6	5	4	14	11

Examples:

Sex scandal: Tim Yeo, Environment Minister, resigned 1993. In the middle of John Major's back to basics campaign he admitted that he had recently fathered an illegitimate child.

Financial scandal: Reginald Maudling, Conservative Home Secretary, resigned 1972. Unwisely became president of the troubled Real Estate Fund of America and linked himself with the business of architect John Poulson, who was under investigation for corruption.

Failure: Lord Carrington, Conservative Foreign Secretary, resigned 1982. His conduct of British relations with Argentina was judged to have led to war in the Falklands.

Political principle: Michael Heseltine, Defence Secretary, resigned 1986 over way Cabinet decisions were made, specifically those allowing the sale of Westland Engineering (a helicopter manufacturer) to a US firm.

Public criticism: Nicholas Ridley, Conservative Trade and Industry Secretary, resigned 1990 after describing the European exchange rate mechanism as a 'German racket to take over Europe' and said Britain might just as well have given in to Hitler.

Source: The Independent, 18 October 1995, drawing on Butler and Butler, 1995

BOX 20.10   **EXAMPLE**

The Scott Report: Should Waldegrave and Lyell have resigned?

Of the many attempts to provide the absent summary to Sir Richard Scott's Report on *The Export of Arms and Dual-Use Goods to Iraq and Other Prosecutions* (HC 115, 1995–6) that by William Rees-Mogg in *The Times* on 26 February 1996 was one of the clearest. These extracts discuss the cases of Lyell and Waldegrave, two ministers criticised in the report:

There seemed to be 12 separate charges which might be regarded as potential resigning matters...

1. Were arms exported to Iraq during the period of the arms guidelines? *Finding*: They were not.
2. Were items of arms-making equipment exported? *Finding*: They were.
3. Did the Government know of these exports? *Finding*: It did.
4. Were these exports a change in the Howe guidelines of 1984? *Finding*: They were.
5. Was this change in the guidelines reported to Parliament? *Finding*: It was not.
6. Was there a failure to keep Parliament properly informed about the supergun case? *Finding*: There was, but as a result of officials failing to inform ministers.
7. Was William Waldegrave particularly responsible for the failure to inform Parliament of the changes in the guidelines? *Finding*: He was.
8. Was there a wrongful prosecution in the Matrix Churchill case? *Finding*: There was.
9. Can the Attorney-General be held responsible for the errors of this prosecution? *Finding*: He can.
10. Did the Attorney-General mislead Michael Heseltine, the President of the Board of Trade, on the law on public interest immunity certificates? *Finding*: He did.
11. Did the ministers who signed PII [public interest immunity] certificates do so recklessly or wrongfully? *Finding*: In the light of the Attorney-General's advice, they did not.
12. Did the Government conspire to cover up its own conduct by using PIIs to send innocent men to prison? *Finding*: It did not ...

This leaves two groups of issues which are in dispute. These groups could be called the Waldegrave and the Lyell issues. There is an important difference....William Waldegrave was at the time Minister of State of the Foreign Office. The government policy on arms for Iraq, right or wrong, open or duplicitous, was not his personal policy. During the relevant period, there were two Prime Ministers, three Foreign Secretaries, several Secretaries of Trade and Secretaries of Defence. All of these were senior to him in Government, and the policy was undoubtedly a collective one. ... It would, whatever view one takes, have been quite wrong for Waldegrave to resign and the Government to remain.

That is not the case with the Attorney-General, since his particular responsibility for the administration of justice is personal to him. He probably did mislead Michael Heseltine on the law on PII certificates. Yet bad legal advice, honestly given, is not a resigning matter. What should be a resigning matter is Sir Nicholas Lyell's general maladministration of the prosecution, his failure to supervise it, his failure to see that the instructions to prosecuting counsel were properly drawn, his failure to pass on the President of the Board of Trade's reservations to the trial judge, as he had said he would do, his failure even to read Michael Heseltine's letter of September 11, 1992, for three or perhaps even seven weeks. ... The Attorney-General treated this obviously difficult and sensitive prosecution as a routine matter, and negligently at that. ... He should have resigned long ago.

seems to vary case by case. Some of the occasions appear relatively trivial but they lead to resignation because they represent an accumulated lack of confidence by members of the government. On the other hand, the case of Nicholas Lyell (and some may say William Waldegrave) in various aspects of the arms to Iraq policies of the Conservative government appear much more grave and yet neither resigned (see Box 20.10).

The Scott Inquiry on the arms to Iraq saga also revealed unease about the role of civil servants both in assisting ministers in their dealings with Parliament and in being asked to draft inaccurate press releases indicating that ministers had been cleared of impropriety. This is of course an inherent difficulty in a system of parliamentary government and that it should be recognised is a healthy democratic sign in itself. Recent concerns began to be aired publicly after the Westland dispute of 1985–6. As we have noted, Leon Brittan, then Secretary of State for Trade and Industry, with the apparent approval of the Prime Minister's office, ordered one of his officials to disclose part of a letter from the Solicitor General which questioned the validity of arguments used by Heseltine (then Secretary of State for Defence) in opposition to the sale of the company to an American firm. Apart from the malfeasance of using a law officer's letter in this way, the case demonstrated the problem for officials if ministers order actions or inactions of doubtful propriety. Although appellate procedures were set up for officials, the development of executive agencies with its implicit distinction (made much of by Michael Howard in his sacking of Derek Lewis for the prison escapes referred to earlier) of policy from administration made it more rather than less likely that civil servants could be made the scapegoats for policy failure. Eventually the government, largely it seems at the Prime Minister's insistence, accepted the call most forcefully expressed in a report from the Treasury and Civil Service Subcommittee of the House of Commons (HC 27, 1994–5), that a Civil Service Code should be elaborated. This came into force in January 1996 and was issued to all officials in the form of a laminated pocket leaflet (see Box 20.11).

The code reaffirms the constitutional duty of civil servants to assist the government of the day and lays down the qualities required: integrity, honesty, impartiality, objectivity and confidentiality. But it also lays down the duties of ministers to Parliament and to their officials, including not asking the latter to act illegally or improperly. In some ways, therefore, the code is more than a civil service code; it seeks to define the relationship between civil servants and ministers.

Whether the code will contribute to the clearer accountability of ministers and to the determination of ministerial resignation remains to be seen. The code is not law and as with much else you have learnt about in this book it is subject to the pushes and pulls of practice. On the other hand its very publication and its reference to *Questions of Procedure for Ministers* suggests an increase in the openness of governmental administration.

Secrecy and freedom of information

Among the implied criticisms of government made by the Scott Report was that of the ministerial reticence, not to say deception, in providing information to Parliament about the policy and practice of the export of arms and arms-related material. If such practices fuel an argument that British government is the most secretive of the developed world, the response is that secrecy is often necessary for good government. Yet it can be argued that all the matters discussed so far in this section on the politics of the administrative process share a requirement for information. The extent to which this is freely available to inform decisions, accountability or redress, will determine the extent to which the administrative process can function effectively. Perhaps, then, open government and secrecy present an inherent dilemma.

The year 1988 was the year of the tercentenary of the Bill of Rights. It was also the year in which the government introduced a new set of proposals to reform the Official Secrets Acts, i.e. the legislation governing official secrecy and freedom of information. A variety of incidents led to the government's desire for reform. They included two prosecutions of Ministry of Defence officials brought by the government in 1984 and the Westland dispute of 1985–6 described above.

These were followed by the embarrassment caused by *Spycatcher*, the published memoirs of a former intelligence officer, Peter Wright. Wright

BOX 20.11

The Civil Service Code

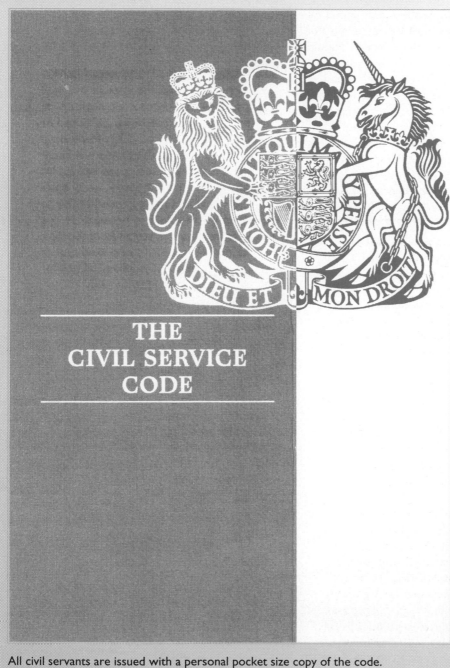

THE
CIVIL SERVICE
CODE

All civil servants are issued with a personal pocket size copy of the code.

held a grievance against his employers over his pension rights. Publication was intended to compensate him. He succeeded admirably thanks to the free publicity generated by the British government's single-minded attempts to prevent publication. The government's argument was very properly based on the need to maintain the oath of confidentiality of its MI5 employees. The argument, which should have been about what was fit for disclosure, became diverted by a series of steamy civil court cases in Britain and overseas featuring government witnesses later found, by the admission of one of them, to have been 'economical with the truth'.

These events turn on fundamental qualities of the administrative process much in need of serious examination and reform. They also go some way to explaining how the government came to realise that the Official Secrets Acts were probably unworkable. The primary aim of the new legislation, the Official Secrets Act 1989, is to clarify the grounds for non-disclosure to include defence, security, intelligence (including international cooperation) and information relating to criminal investigations. Some important former classifications have been liberalised, reinforced by developments announced by William Waldegrave in 1993 and 1994.

Yet very little appears to have changed. The government reported that 2,600 requests were made in the first eight months of the government's new scheme (in Australia the annual rate is about 30,000!). *The Independent* (15 March 1995) complained that only half of its enquiries were

---

BOX 20.12

None of your business?

The prevailing assumption in Whitehall is not that the public have a right to information, but that the government has every right to decide what it discloses, and what form such disclosure should take. Secrecy is deeply embedded in the system. For example:

– The government has failed to honour its promise (in a White Paper of July 1993) to introduce a new legal right of access to health and safety information. Though the public has the right to examine personal records held on computers, the government has also failed to legislate for a separate right of access to manually held personal records... .

– Ministers refuse to publish reports prepared by a joint Whitehall–industry committee indicating whether tobacco manufacturers have infringed restrictions on tobacco advertising... .

– British port health authorities inspect cruise ships for safety and hygiene, but their findings are never published... .

– The Royal Air Force refuses to publish a list of places in Britain which its pilots are instructed to avoid on environmental grounds during low-flying exercises, because the government claims such information is a matter of national security... .

– The government refuses to disclose the scientific advice it gets from the expert committee which advises it on the risks of cancer from chemicals in food and consumer products. Even those companies whose products are banned are not allowed to see the advice... .

– Results of fire brigade inspections at British Rail stations are never disclosed, although similar reports at London Underground stations are now made public following the recommendations of the Fennell report into the 1987 King's Cross fire... .

– The Ministry of Agriculture refuses to identify British slaughterhouses which have lost their export licences because of poor hygiene. The reason: it would be detrimental to their trading position. Many of these slaughterhouses continue to supply meat to British consumers.

Source: *The Economist*, 20 January 1996

Question: Is government right to withhold any of this information? If so, why?

responded to within the time suggested by the government (twenty days), and *The Economist* (20 January 1996) reported that one health enquirer faced a bill of £2,000 for providing information and another was charged over £100 a page for photocopying. More telling, however, are the areas still protected from enquiries (Box 20.12). The changes of the past few years have made little difference to the essential characteristics of the relationship between ministers and civil servants (the advice of the latter to the former is still confidential). Information is the fuel of that process, serving both the activity and its proper audit. However, the Conservative government's changes were introduced as a result (so it seems) of a fear of embarrassment. The Labour Party is committed to a proactive Freedom of Information Act, a prospect which could have beneficial effects not only on the administrative process (e.g. in the information relating to decision-making), but on the ability of citizens to gain access to information held about them as individuals. Whether Labour will deliver on such a commitment remains to be seen.

Conclusion: the centralisation and politicisation of administration?

On Thursday 9 January 1986, Michael Heseltine, then Secretary of State for Defence, walked out of a Cabinet meeting after tendering his resignation. Later that day he read out a statement relating a series of events involving the government, Westland Engineering and various other parties, and attacking the demise of collective Cabinet government.

The Westland affair was essentially a minor dispute between two central government departments and their ministers over the future of a small helicopter company which wished to restore its financial stability by linking up with one of its American competitors. As such it demonstrated how structures in administration can shape politics: the Ministry of Defence sought to promote the interests of the defence community, the Department of Trade and Industry those of industrial competition. The story escalated into two resignations (the other, as we have seen, was that of Leon Brittan, the Secretary of State for Trade and Industry) and questions about the direction of the government itself.

On the role of Cabinet Heseltine argued that government had become more centralised and that ministers needed support if they were to restore their constitutional roles. This argument was taken up by a range of commentators. Sir John Hoskyns, once Margaret Thatcher's policy adviser, saw Whitehall and Westminster as an 'embattled culture' which could only be improved by serious attention to the machinery of government (*The Financial Times*, 11 April 86). Two books and a series of television documentaries by one of the most respected of Whitehall commentators, Peter Hennessy, also postulated that Cabinet government was overloaded and the civil service incapacitated (Hennessy, 1986, 1990). Both these critiques came to similar conclusions, i.e. that ministers needed their own cabinets in their departments in order to restore some balance at the centre of government.

How interesting then that in the summer of 1995, after John Major's re-election as Conservative Party leader, Michael Heseltine should find himself not just back in the Cabinet (he had returned to office in Major's first administration) but as Deputy Prime Minister and with a pivotal brief to provide coherence in the centre of government. Heseltine immediately gathered to him a number of strategically important functions in the running of the government machine, so much so that he could have been likened to a company chief executive reporting to the chairman (John Major) (see Figure 20.3).

Some of Michael Heseltine's first tasks were related to exactly those issues about which he complained in 1986. The Scott Report revealed the enduring and unmanaged factional interests of Whitehall as the Department of Trade and Industry, the Foreign and Commonwealth Office and the Ministry of Defence each pursued their own interests in the export of arms-related materials to Iraq. It was an account incidentally in which the Deputy Prime Minister came out not only unscathed (achievement enough in the circumstances) but actually smelling of political propriety! At the same time, various aspects of the Nolan Committee's investigations of standards in public life, including political appointments, demanded attention at the centre of government.

Meanwhile, the Treasury and Civil Service Committee and the Public Services Committee of the House of Commons pursued more detailed issues

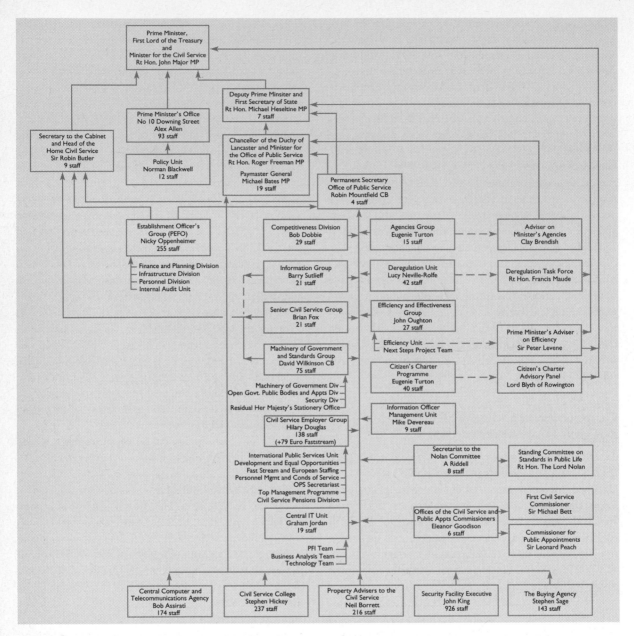

Figure 20.3 The jurisdiction of the Deputy Prime Minister
Source: Finance and Planning Division, Cabinet Office, January 1997

such as the tasks, values and constitutional position of the civil service, its political impartiality, policy advice and support for ministers, the mechanisms of responsibility and accountability, and the processes of recruitment (including the appointment of senior officials), pay, grading, equal opportunity and other personnel management issues. Although, as

this chapter has tried to point out, administration is inherently political, the Committee, as others, is keen to investigate whether there have been changes to the organisation of central government which have intensified the politicisation of administration. Of particular interest here are the roles of the Cabinet secretary as Head of the Civil Service. The problem lies in the way that the duties of the former to a Prime Minister and Cabinet may conflict with the responsibilities of the latter to the civil service as a whole. Yet other senior officials have been perhaps forced into political roles as more responsibility and power have been taken on by the centre, specifically through the Prime Minister and a few trusted official aides.

These worries over centralisation and confusion in the roles at the centre of government organisation and process were treated with scepticism by the Conservative government. But the issue continues to cause concern. Such a centralising tendency has been observed in other aspects of central administration, including within departmental management (see Chapter 21) and in the relations between central and local government (see Chapter 22). Despite the explicit decentralising ethic of the executive agencies and associated developments, the arrangements appear to have replaced one type of centralisation with another. Removed certainly have been the detailed controls over individual activities, but in their place have appeared systemic (especially financial) mechanisms which so regulate and constrain operations as to prevent much freedom in practice, even assuming this is desirable (see Miller, 1995).

Perhaps these illustrations of a centralising and politicising force in the administrative process are coincidental. After all we would not expect a Conservative government committed to a reduced role for the state to be party to such a contradictory tendency. On the other hand, perhaps there are deeper and more powerful centralising forces.

Nevertheless, the two Conservative governments of Margaret Thatcher and John Major made some remarkable changes to the civil service between 1979 and 1997. Not only was the number of officials significantly reduced, but early on the civil service leadership was replaced and the departments at the centre of government streamlined. Although some of the changes were not as great as some in the government would have wished, they were the result of a political commitment. There was undoubtedly waste which the government could cut out. Similarly, Margaret Thatcher's administration was fortunate that so many of the highest ranking officials, many of whom she regarded as obstacles to civil service change, came up for retirement. Some of the replacements were unexpected, giving

rise to accusations of political interference in the appointments process. Under John Major, however, fewer eyebrows were raised.

Other obstacles which were removed included the Civil Service Department (CSD), which was responsible for personnel functions, and the central formal machinery of policy advice. The CSD's pay functions were allocated to the Treasury and other personnel responsibilities to the Cabinet Office (Office of Public Service). Similarly the Central Policy Review Staff, a small team of officials, businessmen and academics charged with reviewing long-term policy in the Cabinet Office, was disbanded in 1983. This allowed the enhancement of the Prime Minister's own Policy Unit, an even smaller group of hand-picked policy advisers, which in turn had the ear of a number of think-tanks sympathetic to radical Conservative thinking.

Does all this amount to a politicisation of Whitehall, as some have claimed? Although there have been accusations that Margaret Thatcher filled the vacated senior official positions with those who were 'one of us', there is no evidence that she systematically appointed those sympathetic to her Conservative vision. However, she (and Major also) most certainly made the most of the opportunity to advance those who impressed as being able to get things done. Similarly, there is really little to quibble within the changes to the machinery of central policy advice. Governments have done this as a matter of course.

There is some evidence, however, that some officials have been used to bolster or rubbish the policy or personal claims of members of the government. Certainly there have been some confused roles and consciences, especially amongst the press offices of No. 10 and the departments. Margaret Thatcher's press officer, Bernard Ingham, in particular came under a good deal of criticism for his mode of operating, and during the Westland affair of 1986, Colette Bowe, the press officer in the Department of Trade and Industry, found herself unwillingly acting as the stooge for her minister, Leon Brittan, in his campaign against the Defence Secretary. Although Brittan's subsequent resignation left matters no clearer, the eventual publication of the Civil Service Code ten years later has helped to allay fears, even it is too early to say if it will make a difference to practice.

Changes to policy planning have been less easy to accept, especially when they have included a downplaying of the importance of consensus management in policy-making, leading officials to assume that only certain types of options should be presented to ministers, and even less prominence to policy evaluation. Certainly under Margaret Thatcher all this may have reduced the possibility of considering some viable and even desirable policy changes or instruments. But, under the less confident times of John Major's regime, this was less marked. If anything, these were characterised more by indecisiveness rather than a ruthless political credo insinuating itself in Whitehall.

It would be hard to argue, therefore, that all this has politicised the administration of government beyond what one might expect, even wish, of an elected government in the pursuit of its programme. Perhaps more telling, however, is the exposure of public services to the disciplines and challenges of what some refer to as free market economics. This is a change of quite a different order, for it implies that our public services are to be governed less by conceptions of public good and social need, as represented through the political process, than the forces of supply, demand and the ability to pay. How much truth there is in this claim will be examined in the next chapter.

Chapter summary

This chapter has sought to contribute to an understanding of the executive process in British government by elaborating the major functions of the central administrative system and characterising its organisational and political properties. In the tradition of the British constitution, the resulting picture lacks definition but displays great variety. The features of central government departments and the role of ministers and civil servants within them suggest not so much a lack of principle as a plethora of competing values, traditions and doctrines.

Discussion points

- How do you explain the variety of British central government institutions and personnel?

- Is a distinction between policy and administration sustainable in British government?

- Has the idea of a permanent neutral, career-based civil service outlived its usefulness?

- Have changes in British central departments improved or weakened the capacity to produce high-quality policy ideas and analysis?

- If a minister does not resign when something goes wrong in the department, does this mean that accountability is weak?

- Do you agree with Lord Nolan, Chairman of the Committee on Standards on Public Life, that there are 'the remains of a continuing cult of secrecy which persists to a greater or lesser extent in different government departments' (speech to Chartered Association of Certified Accountants, 14 March 1996)?

Further reading

The main difficulty with books on this subject is that they are out of date soon after they are published. References to already published volumes must run an even greater risk of offending the present let alone the future. Therefore, in some ways, our encouragement is to read quality newspapers and periodicals (*The Economist* has a consistently good coverage). But books are still valuable for the thought they can offer. Our account is consistent with that you will find in most texts (e.g. James, 1992; Jordan, 1994; Pyper, 1992, Theakston, 1995). More readable on the development and operation of central government departments and the civil service is Hennessy (1990, 1995). Drier but more focused is Fry (1995). Barberis (1996) brings together extracts of both official documents and commentaries in an effective mix. Do not overlook official documents themselves. Indeed, some of the best reads of all are the transcripts of evidence taken before the Public Services Committees of the House of Commons, the Scott Inquiry (HC 115, 1995–6) and the Nolan Committee (Cm 2850, 1995). Hennessy's evidence on 15 February 1995 to the Nolan Committee, for example, is a vignette which, apart from other qualities, suggests that even undergraduates can change the Constitution, (Cm 2850–11, 1995)!

References

Alimo-Metcalfe, B. (1993) 'The F Words', *Health Services Journal*, 1 July.

Bagehot, W. (1964) *The English Constitution* (Watt; originally published 1867).

Barberis, P. (ed.) (1996) *The Whitehall Reader* (Open University Press).

Birch, A.H. (1964) *Representative and Responsible Government* (Allen and Unwin).

Butler, D. and Butler, G. (1995) *British Political Facts* (Macmillan).

Cm 2627 (1994) *The Civil Service: Continuity and Change* (HMSO).

Cm 2748 (1995) *The Civil Service: Taking Forward Continuity and Change* (HMSO).

Cm 2850 (1995) *Standards in Public Life*, First Report of the Committee on Standards on Public Life (The Nolan Committee) (HMSO).

Cm 3020 (1995) *Review of Prison Security in England and Wales and the Escape from Parkhurst Prison on 3 January 1995* (The Learmont Report) (HMSO).

Cm 3321 (1996) *Development and Training for Civil Servants: A Framework for Action* (HMSO).

Cmnd 3638 (1968) *The Civil Service* (The Report of the Committee on the Civil Service, chairman Lord Fulton) (HMSO).

Cmnd 8616 (1982) *Efficiency and Effectiveness in the Civil Service* (HMSO).

Fry, G.K. (1995) *Policy and Management in the British Civil Service* (Prentice Hall/Harvester Wheatsheaf).

Hall, W. and Weir, S. (1996) *The Untouchables: Power and Accountability in the Quango State* (Democratic Audit of the UK and Charter '88).

Hennessy, P. (1986) *The Cabinet* (Blackwell).

Hennessy, P. (1990) *Whitehall*, rev. edn (Fontana).

Hennessy, P. (1995) *The Hidden Wiring: Unearthing the British Constitution* (Victor Gollancz).

HC 27 (1994–5) *The Civil Service* (Report of House of Commons Treasury and Civil Service Subcommittee) (HMSO).

HC 115 (1995–6) *The Export of Defence and Dual-Use Goods to Iraq and Related Prosecutions* (The Scott Report) (HMSO).

James, S. (1992) *British Cabinet Government* (Routledge).

Jordan, G. (1994) *The British Administrative System* (Routledge).

Lynn, J. and Jay, A. (1981) *Yes Minister* (BBC).

Miller, W.L. (ed.) (1995) *Alternatives to Freedom* (Longman).

Next Steps Team (1996) *Next Steps Review* (HMSO).

Pyper, R. (1992) *The Evolving Civil Service* (Longman).

Theakston, K. (1995) *The Civil Service since 1945* (Blackwell).

The management of central government services

ANDREW GRAY AND BILL JENKINS

LEARNING OBJECTIVES

- To promote an understanding of the essential features of the changing way in which central government services are being delivered and the issues which arise for the nature of the modern service state.

INTRODUCTION

The chapter aims to: identify principal changes in service delivery, e.g. privatisation, agencies, market testing and the Citizen's Charter; and to discuss the implications for the public services and for central government itself.

In the summer of 1996 an internal Treasury document was leaked to the BBC. It was the sort of paper we might expect any well-managed department to produce. It speculated on different futures in public services and tried to work through the options for the Treasury itself. Catching the eye of editors in the BBC was a portrait of a world in which central government provided very few services itself, relying not only on further privatisations and contracting out, but on considerable reductions in the scope of those services traditionally considered central to the welfare state.

Questioned on the *Today* programme on Radio 4, Kenneth Clarke, the Chancellor of the Exchequer, the Cabinet minister responsible for the Treasury, was in typically pugnacious mood. Rather surpris-

ingly he dismissed the paper as an analytical exercise for 'kids in the Treasury', by which he meant presumably the younger officials in his department. Yet, for many, the ideas of the paper could be seen as an extension of what had been in train for the previous seventeen years. After all, in 1979 not many could have foreseen that by 1996:

1. the provision of water, one of the country's most essential commodities, would be provided by private companies, one of which, having aggravated a drought for its customers by its preference for paying dividends rather than investing in the underground infrastructure, would have been fined by something called Ofwat, a regulator;

2. the prisons would have been run by a businessman formerly employed in the mass media;
3. and the child benefit work of the Benefits Agency, one of the central institutions in delivering social welfare, would not only have been rewarded for its quality of service with something called a charter mark but then been offered for sale by the government.

These examples illustrate some central features of the changing world of the management of public services in central government in the United Kingdom. In a wide range of services the talk is now of privatisation, regulation, private finance initiatives, market testing, executive agencies and citizens' charters. Some ask whether as a result central government services are provided increasingly by fragmented little businesses with an emphasis on cost management, marketing and customers rather than public services with an emphasis on equality of provision and equity of access to citizens. The following sections will describe some of the most important elements of this development before assessing their impact on the current and future provision of public services in central government.

Privatisation: private ownership of public goods?

In the summer of 1996, Nuclear Electric, the British government's nuclear generating industry, was offered for sale on the stock market. Although it attracted sufficient buyers, the share price quickly suffered something close to a 'melt-down', helped on its way by the company's reporting, conveniently just after the sale, a pair of accidents at two of its generators.

The sale followed a bad two or three years of publicity for the chiefs of the other companies which had been nationalised industries before they had been privatised (i.e. sold to private investors). Cedric Brown, chief executive of British Gas, had kept the newspapers provided with plenty of copy with the annual leaps in his salary or bonuses at the same time as announcing that the company would not apply for a renewal of its charter mark award for public service. Usually along the lines of 'fat cats getting fatter', the newspapers reported on a series

of other executives voting themselves pay and benefit rises while they were at the same time making large parts of their workforces redundant.

How had many of these once central government services come to such a state of affairs? The story goes back at least to the 1970s when the received wisdom both within and outside Whitehall was that previous attempts to improve the quality of public services had failed. Management remained neglected, financial control weak and many, if not most, government activities were inefficient. When Margaret Thatcher became Prime Minister in 1979, she clearly shared this view and was convinced that the scale of the state needed to be reduced to allow the private sector of the economy more scope to flourish. A central element in this mission was and remains privatisation, i.e. the selling of nationalised industries, utilities and related entities to private investors.

For some, this policy's rationale has been simply to provide revenue for the Exchequer to offset its spending and allow tax reductions. The former Prime Minister, the late Harold Macmillan, likened this to selling off the family silver. This conceals, however, a more fundamental issue. The theory behind the public ownership of what economists call public goods is to prevent private ownership developing them in ways inconsistent with the requirements of society as a whole. Power supplies, communication services and other contributions to the infrastructure of the country are critical to our progress as a nation. The issue, therefore, is how to secure them.

In fact, privatisation has been about more than just selling off state industries: it has embraced the wider issues of deregulation (e.g. of the buses), contracting out of services (e.g. catering in the health service), and the opening up of the public sector generally to market forces. The whole debate raises issues about natural monopolies in private hands, the measurement of the efficiency of nationalised undertakings, and the type of management and regulation required to promote the public interest.

There has been no consistent way of resolving these issues. As a result, some of the one-time public corporations have had very varied histories. What is now BT plc, for example, began life as part of the General Post Office (a government department), was then established as part of the Post Office Corporation, and later set up separately as a public corporation (British Telecom) before being sold to the private sector. Others, such as the Rover Group (formerly British Leyland), were private companies rescued by government and then resold to the private sector once profitable. For the Conservative government, however, the privatisation solution was sought throughout a very considerable range of its activities, even to areas such as defence, and the resulting sales have brought considerable benefits, at least for the Treasury (see Table 21.1).

The Conservative government's public argument for privatisation was that private ownership improves efficiency and customer service. In reality what brought specific organisations up for sale was the more immediate prospect of cash flows to ease government borrowing. To be fair, some in the government, or at least among its advisers, realised that it was not public or private ownership which affected efficiency and quality of service but competition. There were therefore attempts to create quasi-competitive markets, either by selling off the industry in separate entities (e.g. National Power and Powergen are both generators of electricity), or allowing the emergence of new private competitors against the privatised corporations (e.g. licensing Mercury to compete with BT). Where a competitive market was not possible, e.g. in some of the public utilities, new mechanisms were set up to regulate their activities, especially pricing.

This regulation of industry could be seen as one of the fastest growing parts of the public sector. Of course, regulation and inspection are traditional government activities. Auditing bodies, such as the National Audit Office and the Audit Commission, examine not only the financial regularity of central and local government bodies respectively but also their value for money. The Monopolies and Mergers Commission and the Office of Fair Trading investigate industrial competition and trading practices. There are also inspectorates for many government services such as education, where there is also a new Office of Educational Standards in Schools (Ofsted), and housing, where the Housing Corporation, amongst its other duties, sets the standards for over 2,500 voluntary housing associations.

Perhaps the most public of the new regulators, however, are those of the former gas, electricity,

Table 21.1 Principal privatisations, 1977–96

Company	Date	Sale value (£m)
Amersham International	1982	64
Associated British Ports	1983–4	97
Belfast City Airport	1994–5	47
British Aerospace	1981–6	390
British Airports Authority	1987–8	1,223
British Airways	1986–8	854
British Coal	1994–5	811
British Gas	1986–92	5,291
British Petroleum	1977–87	284
British Rail	1995–	not yet known
British Steel	1988–90	2,425
British Sugar Corporation	1979–82	44
British Telecom	1984–95	14,187
Britoil	1982–6	1,053
BTG	1991–2	25
Cable & Wireless	1981	1,021
Electricity generating and distribution companies	1990–6	13,078
Enterprise Oil	1984–5	384
Forestry Commission	1982–5	192
General Practice Finance Corp.	1988–9	67
Motorway Service Leases	1982–93	24
National Enterprise Holdings	1979–88	1,375
National Seed Development Corp.	1987–8	65
National Transcommunications	1991–2	70
Privatised companies debt	192–3	3,471
Royal Ordnance	1986–8	19
Rolls-Royce	1987–9	1,032
Rover Group	1988–90	150
Short Brothers	1989–90	30
Water and sewerage companies	1989–92	3,395
Wych Farm (oil)	1986–91	148

Source: based on Cm 3201 1996

water and telecommunications utilities which together constitute more than 20 per cent of the economy. Each of these has its own regulator (see Box 21.1). These mechanisms are necessary because although direct control by government on these services has been relaxed there remains a need to maintain a national service at an acceptable standard and price. The pressure of competition for

The regulators

Who are they and what do they do? The following are the regulatory offices of the principal privatised utilities with their telephone numbers. If you call their libraries they will send you material about their functions.

	Telephone
Offer: electricity	0121 456 6378
Ofgas: gas	0171 828 0898
Oftel: telecommunications	0171 634 8700
Ofwat: water	0121 625 1300

Remember that the regulators also help with complaints:

Source: Ofwat leaflet March 1995

shareholders' investment would lead the companies to exploit their customer monopolies if they were not restrained. The result of the application of pricing regulations which have kept rises below the rate of inflation (though not in water services) has indeed been to remove waste, although some would argue at the expense of a truly public service.

Perhaps, and despite the 'kids from the Treasury' cited earlier, there are some government services which cannot be privatised. Even Margaret Thatcher doubted that the Post Office could be taken out of the public sector. She found it unlikely that the public would accept the idea of the Royal Mail being in private hands and the threat to thousands of rural post offices. However, as we shall see below, there have been and remain other ways in which central government services can be made more business-like: they can be explicitly contracted out to private companies for fixed periods; they can be tested against external suppliers to check their efficiency; they can be set up as mini-businesses within central departments within frameworks which emphasise cost and customer. The rest of this chapter looks at these arrangements in more detail.

The private finance initiative

For a variety of reasons, many of them of successive governments' own making, public services have been experiencing chronic capital famine since the early 1970s. As part of an attempt to alleviate the situation within its own public expenditure targets, the Conservative government encouraged private investment in those public services which are remaining in government hands. The most recent scheme, known as the Private Finance Initiative (PFI), was announced in 1992. At its simplest, the initiative allows public authorities to contract with private sector entities for the provision of capital finance and an acceptance of some of the venture's risks in return for an operator's licence to provide specified services. The contractor makes its return on the investment through the revenue stream arising from its service operation. Examples have included the Channel Tunnel and high-speed link, toll bridges (e.g. Isle of Skye), hospitals (St James' in Leeds), prisons (Rochdale), museums (Royal Armouries, see Box 21.2), community care and even student accommodation (if you are a student at the University of Greenwich you may be reading this in a PFI project). Contractors, usually in consortia, have included construction firms, banks and companies in the housing, health care, security and welfare industries.

BOX 21.2   EXAMPLE

Example of PFI in practice: the Royal Armouries

Background

- Tower of London able to display only 12 per cent of the amouries collection.
- Leeds chosen as new home: city centre site, bounded by water, excellent infrastructure, with catchment population greater than London's by 1.5 m.
- Public sector funding: Department of National Heritage £20m, Leeds City Council £3.5m, Development Corporation £5.0m: total £28.5m.
- Private sector consortium investment £14m.

Public and private sector roles

- Partnership based on coincidence of interest in creating a successful visitor attraction of national and international standing.

- Royal Armouries (the government agency) retains responsibility for the collection, together with all curatorial, interpretative, education and conservation matters.
- Royal Armouries (International) plc takes the financial risk but will control and operate all commercial activities and receive all of the revenues.

Some benefits to date

- Significant urban regeneration and employment both through the construction and operation (about 300 people).
- Boost to local economy through tourism.
- Tower of London able to redisplay and develop commercial facilities.

Source: Royal Armouries documents

The commissioning by public agencies of private contractors to build and even design their capital projects is not new. Nor is it unknown for contractors in capital projects to accept some of the venture risk; penalty provisions for delays are common and contractors usually have to absorb cost overruns. The significance of the PFI, however, lies in:

1. the provision by the contractor of the capital investment;
2. the transfer to the contractor of some of the venture's operating risks as well as those of construction; and
3. the awarding of an operator's licence for the capital facility along with associated services.

Although originally conceived as a means of attracting private investment into capital-intensive policy sectors with traditions of public–private partnerships (particularly transport), the scope of the PFI has been gradually extended into services such as health, social services, prisons and housing. Perhaps because the attraction of such investment is less than obvious to private companies, progress has

not been rapid. Alistair Morton, outgoing chairman of the PFI panel of Treasury advisers, commented that there were 'plenty of ideas going in at one end but little coming out at the other'. By 31 March 1996 £4.8 billion had been agreed, of which £1.3 billion was for the high-speed Channel Tunnel link in Kent. Nevertheless, as with many budgetary projections in times of revenue shortage, better days are claimed to be just around the corner. Treasury forecasts, for example, provide for a further £7.2 billion to be agreed by 1998/9 (see Table 21.2).

Attractions and disadvantages

The attraction of the scheme to the government lies in the value for money offered, specifically the cost advantages of capital projects being funded by private investment and operated by contractors specialist in their businesses. Such advantages may be offset, however, by concessions which may have to be made to attract private contractors as well as public commissioners (e.g. removing value-added tax liability to reduce the costs). Moreover, to

Table 21.2 Planned PFI spending in major departments (£ million)

	1997/8	1998/9	1999/00	Total	%
Transport	1,140	1,330	1,420	3,790	36
Scotland	260	560	690	1,510	14
Local govt	100	350	500	950	9
Health	170	310	420	900	9
Defence	120	230	320	670	6
Home Office	200	130	120	450	4
Social Security	100	170	110	380	4
Wales	70	120	150	340	3
Others	440	450	540	1,430	14
Total	2,500	3,650	4,270	10,420	100

Source: HM Treasury

employ a scheme for capital projects which is based on their attraction of private investment might be thought unacceptable as a public policy, not least for its implication that the government is abandoning its traditional role as guardian of the public infrastructure.

Yet there can be attractions to a public agency in need of capital investment. Its capital programme does not have to be constrained by its access to government sources of capital finance and the limits of the public sector borrowing requirement (PSBR); it can exploit the additional value which specialist private sector providers can bring through innovation, notably in design, and quality of service; and some of the long-term operating risk, such as higher maintenance costs for the facility or a less than predicted working life, can be transferred to the contractor, who is still obliged to hand back the facility in working condition at the end of the (perhaps thirty-year) contract.

Perhaps the lack of significant progress reflects the inevitable time taken for a breakthrough in very complex and speculative initiatives in which there is a long learning process to manage and resource. Nevertheless, the Conservatives are committed to extending the PFI, including into higher education and local government, and the Labour Party has indicated that it regards the initiative as a transferable technology and even one to be made more widely applicable (such as to all local education authority schools).

Market testing

This fusion (some say *con*fusion) between collectivist values of public service and the individual values of the marketplace can be seen even more clearly in the new enthusiasm for 'market testing'. The idea is an extension of privatisation in that discrete activities provided by a government organisation should be tested for cost and effectiveness by subjecting the in-house provision against competitive bids from outside. In the early days of Margaret Thatcher's reign it was introduced into local government and the national health service as compulsory competitive tendering (CCT) and applied to the likes of refuse collection and hospital catering services. The aim was to improve efficiency and customer responsiveness by breaking the control on services by monopoly suppliers, cushioned from outside pressures and often in the grip of strong unions or associations.

Yet it was not until 1991 that central government applied the discipline to itself with any vigour. The White Paper on *Competing for Quality* (Cm 1730) announced that 'Public Services will increasingly move to a culture where relationships are contractual rather than bureaucratic.' The objective was to apply market pressure to even professional services (e.g. financial or statistical) and other core activities within the civil service. The argument is that the very process of tendering forces activities to be costed and shakes out waste and restrictive practices. Hence, a slimmer, fitter and more efficient organisation emerges.

Although the government sought savings of 25 per cent from market-tested services involving about 130,000 jobs, it claimed in 1996 that it had saved £720 million annually from a total expenditure of £3.6 billion (about 20 per cent) and had reduced staff by over 30,000 (see Figure 21.1). In-house bids were not made in half of the work tested (they were often excluded) although they won nearly three-quarters of the contracts for which they tendered. Nevertheless, once the skill and know-how to mount an in-house bid has been lost to the government domain, a service is likely to stay out-sourced.

This language of the health farm is attractive but conceals important issues. Should contracts go to the lowest bidder irrespective of quality or should there be a quality threshold (as used, though some-what idiosyncratically, in the last round of independent television franchises)? (See the quota-tion by Ruskin.) Are there some activities that need to be kept in state control (security, control of major penal establishments, financial manage-ment)? When the services in question have been waste collection and street cleaning, secretarial and messenger services, these issues have not been critical. However, when the work put out to tender includes fisheries surveillance (Ministry of Agricul-ture, Fisheries and Food), resettlement centres

(Social Security), and the management of prisons (Home Office), they become crucial.

Ruskin on a danger in market testing

> It's unwise to pay too much, but it is worse to pay too little. When you pay too much, you lose a little money – that is all. When you pay too little, you sometimes lose everything, because the thing you bought was incapable of doing the things it was bought to do.
>
> *Attributed to John Ruskin, Victorian philosopher*

Question: Is there a danger that market testing will lead to services which are economical but ineffective?

If on the surface progress appears to have been smooth if slow, there is clearly an underlying dis-trust, if not hostility, among many ranks of the civil service. Some of the objections are based on techni-cal and legal complications inherent in the process (the contract state requires very considerable disci-plines and capabilities of its own); others are concerned with the effects of uncertainty on civil service morale, a concern which has aggravated some of the impacts of departmental executive agencies, a parallel reform which attempts to put most of what remains of direct departmental provi-sion under a business-like regime.

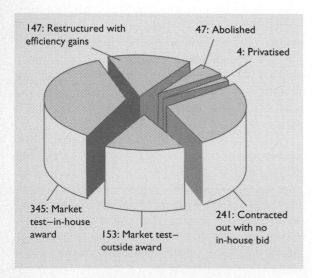

Figure 21.1 Market testing: Competing for Quality Initiative facts and figures
Source: Government Opportunities, 27 June 1995

Executive agencies in central departments

The story of early attempts in the 1980s to change the management of the UK civil service are described in Chapter 20. These included the creation in 1979 of the Prime Minister's Efficiency Unit and the launch in 1982 of the Financial Management Initiative (FMI). Headed by a succession of indus-trialists and one retired civil servant, the Unit has been a catalyst for initiating managerial change in government through its programme of departmental efficiency scrutinies. In the mind of Lord Rayner, the founding head, its task was not only to detect and drive out waste but also to change the culture of the civil service by making good management a valued and well-rewarded activity.

The FMI promulgated Rayner's values on a broader scale. Its instruments were delegated bud-gets, the creation of information systems and a regime of accountable management under which managers were given a certain amount of operational freedom so long as they met resource and performance targets. By the late 1980s, however, sections of opinion in Whitehall were concerned that progress in the efficiency strategy and the FMI was not as fast and substantial as required. Indeed, there was a suspicion that it was being blocked in some quarters. As a result the Efficiency Unit, then headed by Sir Robin Ibbs, formerly of ICI, carried out an evaluation of the reforms. As with all efficiency scrutinies, the study was conducted in ninety working days, during which the team talked to ministers, permanent secretaries and former civil servants. It also visited regional and local offices of departments and a number of private sector organisations.

In its report, *Improving Management in Government: The Next Steps* (Efficiency Unit, 1988), the team observed that:

1. the civil service was too large to be managed as a single organisation;
2. ministerial overload diverted attention from management matters;
3. the freedom of middle managers was being frustrated by hierarchical controls; and
4. there was little emphasis on the achievement of results, especially in the quality of service.

These fundamental problems demanded radical changes in the delivery of government services, in the departments themselves and at the centre of government. Departments needed to focus on the work to be done and ways in which to sustain continuous improvement in the delivery of policy and services. The team's principal proposals were:

1. the designation of discrete operational areas of activity;
2. the establishment of departmental executive agency for each designated activity;
3. the appointment of agency chief executives who would be free, within policy and resources frameworks set by departments, to manage their 'businesses'; and
4. the removal of detailed management from direct ministerial responsibility and accountability.

The idea of agencies was not new, even in the UK. A number, including the Crown Agents and the Property Services Agency, both of which had very chequered histories, had existed for many years. The report's prescription of agencies, however, caught the mood of the government. When Margaret Thatcher told the House of Commons in February 1988 that the report's major recommendations had been accepted and that from then on the executive or service delivery functions of government would be, to the greatest extent practicable, carried out by 'Next Steps' agencies, she also announced that the implementation of the programme would be directed by a senior-level project manager with her full backing.

The development of agencies

Seasoned observers of UK government responded to the Prime Minister's announcement with a degree of cynicism. True, the Rayner efficiency strategy and the FMI had been implemented more successfully than many expected, but the track record of lasting structural change in Whitehall was poor. Given the experience of the nationalised industries (e.g. coal, steel, railways), the idea of ministers adopting an arm's length approach to important parts of their departmental empire seemed especially fanciful.

In many respects such a reaction appears to have been confounded by the implementation of the Next Steps. The project team, headed initially by Peter Kemp (from the Treasury) and attached to the Cabinet Office, set out to encourage departments to establish their agencies. At first, however, the pace was steady rather than spectacular. Of the first eight to be created by the summer of 1989, most were already *de facto* agencies with well-defined businesses and a commercial outlook, e.g. Her Majesty's Stationery Office (HM Treasury). However, undeterred by a mixed reaction in Whitehall and supported by the House of Commons Treasury and Civil Service Committee and a second Efficiency Unit investigation (*Making the Most of the Next Steps* (1991)), the team gathered momentum. By spring of 1997 the task of establishing the agencies had all but been completed, resulting in 80 per cent of all civil servants working in over 170 agencies or units based on agency principles (examples are listed in Table 21.3). By any standards, this has been an implementation success story. But what of the value of agencies in the delivery of public services?

Table 21.3 Some examples of departmental executive agencies

	Staff
Building Research Establishment	625
Cadw (Welsh historic monuments)	190
Central Office of Information[a]	420
Civil Service College	240
Defence Evaluation and Research Agency[a]	12,445
Driver and Vehicle Licensing Agency	3,535
Employment Service	31,305
Forensic Science Service	1,175
Government Property Lawyers	105
Highways Agency	1,645
Her Majesty's Prison Service	38,235
Insolvency Service	1,285
Meat Hygiene Service	890
Medicines Control Agency[a]	350
Meteorological Office[a]	2,155
National Savings	4,580
Ordnance Survey	1,820
Patent Office[a]	720
Public Record Office	435
Registrars of Scotland[a]	1,075
Royal Mint[a]	980
Social Security Benefits Agency	74,925
Social Security Child Support Agency	7,170
United Kingdom Passport Agency	1,515
Vehicle Inspectorate[a]	1,485
Wilton Park Conference Centre	35

Note: [a] Denotes Trading Fund status
Source: Adapted from Next Steps Team, 1997

Making an agency

The process of establishing an agency has a number of stages. It begins with the so-called 'prior options' examination by the Next Steps Unit, the department and the Treasury to determine whether the activities identified should be privatised, their work contracted out, market tested or dispensed with altogether. Agencies are, therefore, a choice *after* the privatisation option has been rejected, at least for the time being. If, however, the agency form is deemed appropriate (taking account of the political sensitivity of the activity and potential improvement in the quality of management and service), work proceeds on the design of a policy

and resources framework document, within which the agency will operate, and the appointment of the chief executive.

The framework document is not a corporate plan, nor is it a contract in law. Rather, it sets out the parameters in which the agency is to be managed. Although they differ in content as well as presentation, they all contain:

1. an outline of the agency's objectives and targets against which performance can be measured;
2. details of the financial and human resource management regimes; and
3. details of department–agency relations.

The document emerges after negotiations between the Next Steps Units, the Treasury and the parent department and is reviewed normally after five years. Some changes, e.g. in targets, can be made at any time.

The issue of targets illustrates the departmental and wider political context of agencies. Although technically set by ministers, targets are proposed in practice by chief executives and then negotiated. However, according to Sir Peter Kemp, the former project manager, chief executives have few options if faced with ministerial fiat: 'They can buckle down and do what the minister has asked them to do; or they can resign' (HC 496, 1990–1, p. 106).

But who are the chief executives, how are they appointed and how are they rewarded? In the early days most chief executives were drawn from inside the civil service and posts were not necessarily openly advertised. However, pressed on by the Treasury and Civil Service Committee, about two-thirds of chief executive posts (other than possibly sensitive areas such as defence) are now openly advertised and a quarter are recruited from outside the civil service from a variety of backgrounds, including local government, the NHS and the private sector. These individuals are on fixed-term contracts and salaries that have performance-related elements linked to agency targets. They also have direct access to ministers.

Managing agencies

One of the most frequent complaints of managers in the UK civil service has been of the hierarchical financial regimes in which they have had to operate.

Purchasing, appointing temporary staff and even painting the office often seemed impossible without reference to principal finance officers. More fundamentally, the annual limits on the budget and controls over capital investment decisions hampered efficiency and effectiveness. The Financial Management Initiative with its philosophy of accountable management was intended to move departments from this position and the Next Steps to take these changes in delegation and financial freedom even further.

There is no doubt that these developments are crucial in shaping the management regimes negotiated in framework documents. An increasing number of agencies, for example, are now treated as trading funds, i.e. as commercial businesses with concomitant accounting practices and financial freedoms over capital investment. Such bodies are those with identifiable products and markets (e.g. the Royal Mint and the Vehicle Inspectorate). However, financial freedoms are not the only management systems of importance. Encouraged by the Treasury's policy of local rather than national pay bargaining, agencies are developing their own personnel management regimes. Thus, since April 1994, all agencies with over 2,000 staff have had responsibility for their own pay bargaining and the Civil Service (Management Functions) Act, passed in December 1992, has given scope for the Treasury to delegate to agencies powers to alter the terms and conditions of staff without further reference to the centre. All this, and the Treasury's preference for all new systems to link pay with performance, has been endorsed by government White Papers, especially *The Civil Service: Change and Continuity* (Cm 2627, 1994).

The Next Steps programme also assumes that good management requires a discipline of targets both to focus and motivate managers and to assess performance. This is consistent with the wider use of performance indicators in the public expenditure review process and in the financial regimes that departments can negotiate with the Treasury. Although agency targets are officially set by ministers, the reality is more complex, with chief executives suggesting programme targets which ministers may or may not accept. The Treasury also takes a close interest, not least since pressure on targets may be one way of squeezing budgets or

pressurising ministers to produce savings. This explains at least partly why the take-up rate for welfare benefits is not an agency target.

Examinations of published targets show the predominance of financial (e.g. staying in budget or breaking even) or turnover targets (e.g. 95 per cent of driving licences to be issued within eleven days, passport applications to be processed within a maximum of ten working days). Even if these suggest that agencies are not yet fully addressing quality of service, such efforts should not be belittled, especially where agencies are complementing the ministerial targets with their own customer surveys. The target regime acts as a discipline for those running the organisation while offering a guide to agency clients and others of what can be expected.

These controls on target setting as well as those which limit entrepreneurial activity (e.g. bidding for private sector business) may constrain managerial development and innovation in the agencies, but they are legitimate politically. They emphasise, however, the way chief executives operate within a political as much as a managerial world and suggests that the distinction on which the whole idea is based, i.e. between policy (the domain of the core of the department) and management (that of the

---

BOX 21.3 **EXAMPLE**

Agency annual reports

The *Next Steps Review* is published by The Stationery Office Ltd at the beginning of each year. It contains details of individual agencies and their performance against targets and summarises achievements for agencies as a whole. Have you got your copy? Only £56!

(Question: should public information about government activities be subject to commercial pricing policy?)

Not as glossy but informative and free of charge, the *Next Steps Briefing Note* is available from the Next Steps Team in the Cabinet Office (tel. 0171 270 6282; fax 0171 270 6136).

agency), is not as feasible in practice as the rhetoric suggests. Nevertheless, there is a greater commitment to more structured management processes and to increasing competition and the quality of service to customers.

Evidence of agency success

Any assessment of agency success is necessarily speculative. This holds for the performance of individual agencies as well as for the initiative as a whole. The House of Commons Treasury and Civil Service Select Committee and its successor the Public Services Committee have made persistent efforts to have Next Steps evaluated, only to be resisted by the government on the grounds that the range of different agencies make any large-scale evaluation unfeasible. However, the Next Steps Team does publish annual aggregate statistics of agency performance against ministerially imposed targets. Figure 21.2 shows this performance to have improved steadily over the last few years.

At the level of individual agencies, however, the Conservative government was also keen to highlight how agencies could lead to improved performance and better service to customers. These included a procedure for social security claimants to lodge any complaints through any office of their choice regardless of the benefit received and the integration by the Employment Service of 90 per cent of benefit payment and job placing services in single job centres.

All this is interesting but, inevitably, difficult to assess as external audits of client effectiveness are rarely conducted and independent inspectorates are not involved. However, the National Audit Office (NAO) does investigate the value for money of agencies. Its assessments have generally been favourable, even if it has noted that the understandable restrictions on agencies to expand their businesses are likely to exhaust the scope for improvements (HC 249, 1991–2, p. 5).

Nevertheless in July 1996 the Deputy Prime Minister, Michael Heseltine, announced that the

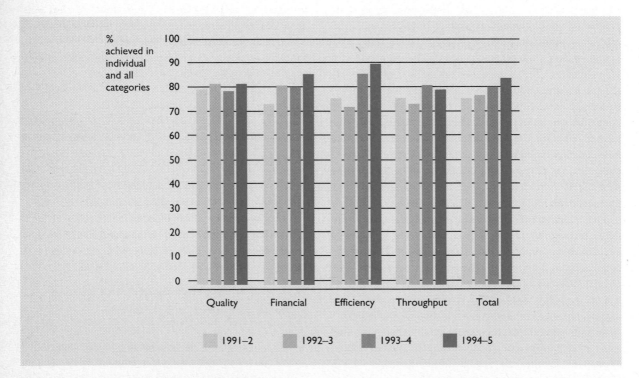

Figure 21.2 Agency performance against targets

Source: Next Steps Team, 1996 Figure 2. Note that these data say nothing about how hard or easy the targets are. See Next Steps Team, 1997, Figures 2 and 3, for information on this.

search for improvement would be sustained. He had awarded a contract to the British Quality Foundation to carry out a benchmarking exercise of agency performance. Another mouthful of management mantra, benchmarking is a device for comparing the performance of entities against an industry standard. By the end of 1996 a sample of thirty agencies had been subjected to a self-assessment model and each had been required to develop an improvement action plan. The aim of the exercise was to not only help the sample agencies improve their own performance but to identify generic examples of best practice which could be disseminated through all agencies (Next Steps Team, 1997).

All this indicates the continuing commitment to the development of departmental agencies, potentially the most significant of all the Conservative government reforms of the civil service. It has implications for the accountability of ministers and their officials because it seems to separate responsibility for administration and management from that for policy. It also affects the way in which government services are provided, not least in the emphasis placed on securing value for money and serving customer needs, an emphasis reinforced by the Citizen's Charter, under which sixty-two agencies have won charter marks.

The Citizen's Charter

Towards the end of 1987, in a once elegant room looking out on the autumnal colours of Regent's Park, a gathering of civil servants, management experts, MPs and even a couple of academics discussed the changing nature of the management of central government. To help address the consumer dimension of the change, a manager from the then recently privatised British Airways gave a presentation on the company's 'customer first' policy. Video screens, transparency projections, soundtracks and voice-overs bombarded the audience to announce the change in customer satisfaction with the company's service and how all this had come about. It was quite a show, certainly an antidote to the post-lunch dip in attention spans! At the close, a few of those not dumbstruck uttered their reactions: 'the art of illusion', muttered one; 'how come only after privatisation are customers important?', questioned another.

Others, perhaps, merely marvelled at the success of British Airways (which once had a reputation rather like that of British Rail) in finding anyone in the company sufficiently skilled in electronics to make such a presentation work!

That such a customer focus was not just an overnight wonder but has become a feature of the public services in the 1990s owes a considerable amount to the personal commitment of John Major as Prime Minister. His personal initiative, the Citizen's Charter announced in 1991 (Cm 1599), aims to provide 'a revolution in public services' by emphasising and raising the quality of service delivery. The scheme covers all government departments, the National Health Service, nationalised industries, privatised utilities, local government and universities. The programme is managed by the Citizen's Charter Unit in the Cabinet Office and a prime ministerial adviser from the private sector (at the time of writing, Boots plc).

Under this direction, organisations are encouraged to apply for their service to be assessed against criteria which emphasise standards of performance, information and openness, choice and consultation, courtesy and helpfulness, an ability to put things right when they go wrong, and overall value for money. If they pass the test they are awarded a charter mark of excellence for three years (see Box 21.4).

Yet progress has not been unproblematic. In its first year there appeared to be strong resistance in Whitehall to some of its recommendations (e.g. compensation for aggrieved clients). As a result, the initiative was relaunched both before and after the 1992 general election, with the promise of more mini-charters and increased rights of customer redress throughout the public sector and increased powers to William Waldegrave (the minister in charge of the programme) to force departments into action.

Five years or more later, however, the Citizen's Charter has become an established part of the public service scene. Applications, only 300 or so for the 1992 awards (thirty-six winners), rose to 740 (223 awards) for 1995 and came from all manner of public services. Winners included even schools and university libraries (see Box 21.5)! But the Citizen's Charter is more than about the charter awards. At its heart, this is about the 'empowerment' of

BOX 21.4

The principles of public service

The Charter Mark, a new award for excellence in delivering public services.

Standards

Setting, monitoring and publication of explicit standards for the services that individual users can reasonably expect. Publication of actual performance against these standards.

Information and openness

Full, accurate information readily available in plain language about how public service are run, what they cost, how well they perform and who is in charge.

Choice and consultation

The public sector should provide choice wherever practicable. There should be regular and systematic consultation with those who use services. Users' views about services, and their priorities for improving them, to be taken into account in final decisions on standards.

Courtesy and helpfulness

Courteous and helpful service from public servants who will normally wear name badges. Services available equally to all who are entitled to them and run to suit their convenience.

The Charter Mark, a new award for excellence in delivering public services

Putting things right

If things go wrong, an apology, a full explanation and a swift and effective remedy. Well publicised and easy to use complaints procedures with independent review wherever possible.

Value for money

Efficient and economical delivery of public services within the resources the nation can afford. And independent validation of performance against standards.

Source: Cm 2101, 1992

---

customers (a new piece of public sector jargon), i.e. the freedoms and rights of parents, patients, passengers and passport applicants. It seeks to give consumers clear statements of the standards of service they can expect from public organisations and explain the procedures for gaining redress when practice falls short.

Certainly there has been a noticeable publication of charters. A tourist arriving at London's Heathrow Airport may be amazed to be received by immigration, customs, London Transport, British Rail (in various guises), and all sorts of tourist attractions in the capital all sporting their charters. Yet, admirable as all this is, it poses plenty of problems for public service management. Do the performance standards match the real needs of customers? Who are the customers anyway? How are they different from citizens? How far should the demands of citizens and customers be met? For example, should all schools remain open if parents so wish and should all patients be treated on demand? What, therefore, are the criteria on which public services should be provided? The problem lies with the tension between the good of the collectivity and that of the individual consumer, a tension which derives from the attempt to fuse public service collective values with the individual values of the free market. How this will be resolved remains to be seen.

BOX 21.5

Charter Mark Winners 1995 – and a loser

Some winners

The Victoria Infirmary NHS Trust Cardiac Rehabilitation Centre (Scotland)

Royal Ulster Constabulary Child Abuse & Rape Enquiry Unit (Northern Ireland)

The Dell Primary School (Wales)

Sunderland Eye Infirmary (England)

Trafford MBC Leisure Management Division (England)

Benefits Agency Family Credit Unit (England)

Moseley School (Birmingham)

Coventry Technical College

Newcastle University Library

London Borough of Ealing W13 Social Club for Young People

Dover Harbour Board Police

Legislation Office, Foreign & Commonwealth Office

Renewed awards

Preston Disablement Services Centre

South Yorkshire Police

And you might wish to award the Charter Unit itself a wooden spoon for the following:

Important Note
Please note that the four paragraphs that appear on page 31 under the heading 'The criteria' relate to the section on the criteria (pages 20–29) and not the section on the user and staff suggestion awards (pages 30–31).

Source: The Charter Mark Awards Scheme 1996: Guide for Applicants

Conclusion: a new public service?

One organisational consequence of John Major's re-election as Conservative Party leader in the summer of 1995 was the revamping and strenghtening under the new Deputy Prime Minister and First Secretary of State, Michael Heseltine, of the Office of Public Service. In encompassing the Efficiency Unit, Next Steps, the Citizen's Charter and the market testing programme (and its links to privatisation), the Office has responsibility for all the current major managerial initiatives in British central government.

Are these initiatives ends in themselves or the means to a wider objective? The creators might respond that their aim was to facilitate the better management of central government services. What does this mean? After all, the good delivery of bad policy is hardly the measure of a healthy state, nor, perhaps, is a system which, while speaking the language of empowerment, choice and citizen's rights, acts in a consistently centralist way with regard to the making of policy decisions.

It can be argued that to a considerable extent these innovations have been successful managerially. Through them a large section of the UK civil service has been structurally and culturally reformed. Real improvements in service delivery have been achieved and organisations have began to relate to clients in a different way. These have been important gains, fulfilling the hopes of those who designed them.

Yet there are also important concerns, including on the impact on the structure and morale of the civil service and what has been called the democratic deficit, i.e. the loss of democratic control and accountability in public services.

The changing civil service

The logic of the new public service management encourages a world of delegated provision in which control and responsibility are pushed down the central government machinery. This raises the question of what compensating integrating mechanisms are required and how government itself copes with and manages such changes. Moreover, following a period in which the civil service was subjected to considerable verbal and procedural abuse by ministers collectively and individually, there are real concerns over its morale.

Integration and managerial freedom

The original Efficiency Unit report on the Next Steps (1988) stated that the home civil service was too large to manage as one unit. Few would disagree. Indeed, it could be argued that the concept of a uniform service has been untenable in such a highly differentiated system of central government. The changes noted earlier in the chapter have reinforced this pattern of differentiation between and within departments. Privatisation and market testing have reclassified many public servants as private employees, Next Steps agencies have produced local personnel management arrangements, and charters are helping to fragment identification with the public service as a whole. The consequence is an even more federated, some would

say disintegrated, service (see Table 21.4). As the First Division Association (the union for senior ranks of the UK civil service) noted, the new climate is characterised by 'a shift away from a uniform, centralised system of civil service pay and conditions' and its replacement by 'legislation enabling divergent departmental and agency recruitment practices, and the use of short term contracts for civil servants' (First Division Association in HC 390, 1992–3).

We have seen, however, that many of these changes are the functional responsibility of the Office of Public Service (see Figure 20.3 in Chapter 20, p. 344). This offers the prospect of an integrated strategy for the changing management of central government services Yet the omens are not good. The delegation of detailed service provision away from the policy core of departments, for example, has not been followed by a visible improvement in the coherence of strategy in different policy areas (e.g. energy, transport and welfare) and there has been little attempt even to address let alone resolve the ambiguity of what managerial freedom means for the new civil service managers. Agencies, charters and market testing may all be seen as legitimate attempts to decentralise government and yield freedoms to managers along with greater responsibility for service delivery. However, as many of the discussions on decentralisation indicate, true freedom to manage demands a yielding of power by the centre. Thus, decentralised management is a *political* as much as an *organisational* strategy.

It would be unrealistic and probably against the democratic tradition to contemplate managerial freedoms akin to those in the private sector. It is not hard, however, to sympathise with managers whose attempts to improve public service through meeting the demands of the Citizen's Charter are constrained by the frameworks within which they work as well as the constant threat that their operations will be subjected to market testing. Again, this suggests that there is no real integrated coherent strategy for the development of the management of central government services. Rather there is a series of disjointed initiatives with various degrees of ministerial commitment. Not surprisingly, this has had an effect on civil service morale.

Table 21.4 The old and the new civil service?

	The classical model	The new civil service
The task	Managing ministers	Managing services and resources
Focus	Public interest	Customer interest
Criteria of service supply	The public good (as politically interpreted)	Market demand
Recruitment	Generalist administrators	Specialist managers
Career	Life-long department-based	Less than life periods in outposts, even outside civil service
Values	Politically neutral, detached administrators	Politically neutral, committed managers
Conditions	Nationally determined, uniform	Locally negotiated, varied
Structure	Uniform	Federated

Questions: How far is the above a valid portrayal? What are its implications?

Morale

Privatisation, market testing and agencies are, of course, just part of a long-running debate over the structure and function of the civil service and the appropriate roles of civil servants in the business of management. The issues involved have been invigorated by a squeeze on civil service manpower and pay since 1979 (see Chapter 20) and the general climate of bureaucracy baiting.

Many issues in the current debate over pay, motivation and morale concern all levels of the service and are linked to those of politicisation and neutrality discussed in Chapter 20. Behind these is the question of what constitutes appropriate structures and processes for achieving both policy and management objectives within the constraints of parlimentary accountability and the requirements of good government. Governments have not generally been willing or capable of addressing these systematically. This is not unexpected given that ministers' prime concerns are with their own salvations in the short term. Nevertheless, in the core of departments and the agencies, the morale and commitment of civil servants have been low. Some have expressed their frustrations by leaving the service altogether. The exit from Whitehall to companies in the private sector, many of which gain an advantage in their dealings with government by their employment of such ex-officials, has even included senior officials from the Treasury's privatisation programme, the Efficiency Unit and the Inner Cities Directorate.

These are the very managers which any government should hope to retain. Nevertheless, their departures could be seen as beneficial if they were part of an orchestrated interchange of staff between government and the outside world. But they are not. Rather they are symptomatic of a wider loss of morale associated not only with politicisation and the hostile attitude of government but also with contracts, pay and general conditions of service.

The latter are important. Many of those in private industry are appalled by the facilities, for example, which many public officials have to contend with: outdated, ill-equipped and under-maintained offices and public reception areas designed to do anything but make clients feel at ease. The irony of the development of agencies may well be that managers will be given the chance to run services like businesses but, having proved that they can, will expect to be rewarded accordingly, i.e. as their counterparts in the private sector.

These last few paragraphs should not be taken as criticism of the changes as such in the management of central government services. Indeed, many are making contributions to a more professional approach to public services and an improvement in the quality of government. However, change management needs to be planned and implemented through comprehensive, coherent and properly resourced programmes. Perhaps it is unreasonable to expect ministers to act like professional managers themselves. But as many of their role models come from the private business sector, ministers could do well to recognise that one of the ingredients of successful companies is the proper attention to the management of employees' morale.

A democratic deficit?

The year 1992 saw the publication in the USA of a public managament text which attracted something of a cult following. Osborne and Gaeblar's *Reinventing Government* went into its fourth edition within a year and, on the cover of the paperback edition, contained a ringing endorsement by President Clinton. The cult soon crossed the Atlantic. In autumn 1992 the text was commended to public administration academics by Sir Robin Butler and endorsed by William Waldegrave (1993), then Chancellor of the Duchy of Lancaster and minister responsible for the Office of Public Service.

Osborne and Gaeblar's message is simple if supported by anecdote rather than evidence. It commends entrepreneurial government, i.e. a government that anticipates problems rather than reacts to them, encourages competition, expands consumer choice, and measures and publicises service achievements. Like the ten commandments the wisdom is distilled into ten principles. These include the empowerment of citizens, the treatment of clients as customers, a focus on outputs not inputs, the decentralisation of authority and a preference for market rather than bureaucratic mechanisms. Even though the authors recognise that 'governments and business are fundamentally different institutions' and 'government cannot be run like a business', for a government moving rapidly down the road of market testing and developing the purchaser–provider split, the attraction of the dictum that government's primary role is 'steering rather than rowing' is clear.

Coinciding with the book's publication and dissemination, however, various British academics have argued that the Conservative government's pursuit of a public sector characterised by entrepreneurship and quasi-economic markets distanced public services from the regular processes of responsibility and accountability. The reference here is to the world of privatised utilities and regulation, departmental executive agencies and health service trusts, and the contracting out to the private sector of parts of public services.

The critics have been concerned by the fragmentation of elected institutions and their replacement by a complex hotch-potch of arrangements with no clear focus or responsibility. Jones and Stewart, for example, argued that:

instead of giving powers to individual citizens, the government has acquired powers for itself or conferred them on the new magistracy to act as agents, or set up government regulated quasi-markets in which individuals have little or no power. Everyone but the government sees this as centralisation and the reason is clear. It is centralisation. (Jones and Stewart, 1993, p. 13)

Vernon Bogdanor reinforced these arguments by drawing attention to the way the new magistracy had led to a 'democratic deficit' in domestic politics (*The Guardian*, 14 June 1993).

This attack clearly found out the Conservative government's sore spots. Ministers such as Kenneth Clarke, the usual combatant for the government on such occasions, and others were very public in their rejection of this criticism. In July 1993, for example, William Waldegrave set out a vigorous defence of central government reforms. In a public lecture, later published in various forms in newspapers and public sector journals, he named and castigated the critics and argued that, on the contrary, the government's development of the contracting role (what it calls the 'purchaser–provider split') within Whitehall departments and the National Health Service was enhancing both the quality of public service and the information consumers receive. Moreover, this had increased the accountability of public services and strengthened citizens' rights.

Yet how far have such freedoms and their development threatened traditional public sector accountability? Is there an inherent contradiction between accountability and managerial freedom? How far is the risk-taking, entrepreneurial world of devolved government compatible with detailed legislative scrutiny, audit and accountability?

For students of politics and practising politicians alike the problem starts with the fact that while the term 'accountability' is in universal currency it is often defined in very different ways. This has not helped the clarification of parliamentary accountability, as a 1996 House of Commons Public Service Committee inquiry has discovered (HC 313, 1995–6). Ministers are clearly responsible for and accountable to Parliament for the activities of their departments. But accountability can become more obscure as the responsibilities are devolved through executive agencies with their own chief executives, and on to private organisations which have contracted to undertake specific services. Ministers are no fonder than the rest of us of accepting failure as well as success (we remember Margaret Thatcher as Prime Minister jubilantly announcing the Falklands War successes herself while leaving the bad news to the official Ministry of Defence spokesman). Thus they may not be too bothered by this diffusion of accountability.

There are signs that the traditional mechanisms by which governments are called to account (and, by the way, learn about the relative success or failure of their activities) are straining under the new arrangements. The ballot box, for example, is necessarily a clumsy instrument. Select committees of the House of Commons can certainly cause embarrassment but are ultimately manageable by the government majority in the House. A citizen seeking redress against a government wrong-doing can approach a Member of Parliament who, in a necessarily remote and lenthy process, may write letters to ministers or refer the matter to one of the parliamentary commissioners for administration or ombudsmen. An offending agency or minister may be taken to court, but this is so expensive as to be out of reach of ordinary mortals.

Undoubtedly, however, the reforms to central government services have made some responsibilities for services clearer to the citizen as consumer and have established some effective mechanisms of redress which deal directly with the organisation responsible. Yet, desirable as these are, they are related to the protection of the individual in the receipt of a service, not the decisions about the level and quality of service appropriate in a societal context. It is these matters which are of concern to the critics of the democratic deficit, for, just as there may be appearing a strategic vacuum for the development of government policy as a whole, so there may be developing an accountability vacuum in public services.

Two of the most distinctive features which emerge from this examination of central government services are, therefore, the intrinsically political character of the management process and the variety of structures and arrangements by which it is carried out. The first is intrinsic to the governmental process. The latter, however, is both a reflection of the nature of the tasks of government and the result of decades of *ad hoc* development without any systematic thinking about the implications for our system of government. Is this in the interests of good government?

Chapter summary

This chapter has identified the principal changes in service delivery, e.g. privatisation, the Private Finance Initiative, market testing, executive agencies and the Citizen's Charter, and has discussed their implications for the public services and for central government itself. The aim has been to promote an understanding of the essential features of the changing provision of central government services and an awareness of the issues they raise in the modern service state.

Discussion points

■ What is a public service?

■ Are there core parts of government which should never be privatised?

■ What are the gains or losses from contracting private companies to provide public services on behalf of government organisations?

■ Have executive agencies been a success?

■ Is there a difference between a citizen and a customer? Does this matter for public services?

Further reading

A general textbook on public sector service management is Flynn (1997) and a more reflective analysis can be found in Pollitt (1992). Good accounts of the development and issues of privatisation and regulation in the UK can be found in Veljanovski (1987, 1991) and more recently in Moran and Prosser (1994). Many of the British central government reforms are discussed in Campbell and Wilson (1995) and Theakston (1995) and contrasted with those in Australia in Zifcak (1994). But as this is a field in which change is rapid, the books can become dated fairly quickly. Therefore it is worth using journals of which the most relevant and readable are *Public Money and Management* (the 1996–7 issues cover almost everything discussed in this chapter), *Politics Review* and *Talking Politics*.

References

Campbell, C. and Wilson, G.K. (1995) *The End of Whitehall: Death of a Paradigm?* (Blackwell).

Cm 1599 (1991) *The Citizen's Charter: Raising the Standard* (HMSO).

Cm 1730 (1991) *Competing for Quality* (HMSO).

Cm 2101 (1992) *The Citizen's Charter: First Report* (HMSO).

Cm 2627 (1994) *The Civil Service: Change and Continuity* (HMSO).

Cm 3201 (1996) *Public Expenditure Statistical Anaylsis* (HMSO).

Efficiency Unit (1988) *Improving Management in Government: The Next Steps* (HMSO).

Efficiency Unit (1991) *Making the Most of Next Steps: The Management of Ministers' Departments and their Executive Agencies* (HMSO).

Flynn, N. (1997) *Public Sector Management*, 3rd edn (Harvester Wheatsheaf).

HC 249 (1991–2) Report by the National Audit Office, *The Vehicle Inspectorate: Progress as an Executive Agency* (HMSO).

HC 313 (1995–6) Report by House of Commons Public Service Committee, *Ministerial Accountability and Responsibility* (HMSO).

HC 390 (1992–3) Report by the House of Commons Treasury and Civil Service Committee, *The Civil Service* (HMSO).

HC 496 (1990–1), House of Commons Treasury and Civil Service Committee, 7th Report, *The Next Steps Initiative* (HMSO).

Jones, G. and Stewart, I. (1993) 'A law unto themselves', *Local Government Chronicle*, 14 May.

Moran, M. and Prosser, T. (1994) *Privatization and Regulatory Change in Europe* (Oxford University Press).

Next Steps Team (1996) *Next Steps Review 1995* (HMSO).

Next Steps Team (1997) *Next Steps Review 1996* (The Stationery Office).

Osborne, D. and Gaeblar, T. (1992) *Reinventing Government* (Addison-Wesley).

Pollitt, C. (1992) *Managerialism and the Public Services* (Blackwell).

Theakston, K. (1995) *The Civil Service Since 1945* (Blackwell).

Veljanovski, C. (1987) *Selling the State: Privatisation in Britain* (Weidenfeld and Nicolson).

Veljanovski, C. (ed.) (1991) *Regulators and the Market: An Assessment of the Growth of Regulation in the UK* (Institute of Economic Affairs).

Waldegrave, W. (1993) *The Public Service* (Public Finance Foundation).

Zifcak, S. (1994) *New Managerialism: Administrative Reform in Whitehall and Canberra* (Open University Press).

Local government

ANDREW GRAY AND BILL JENKINS

LEARNING OBJECTIVES

- To understand the development and current state of local government in the UK.

INTRODUCTION

This chapter will examine: the history, structure, and politics of UK local government; the internal management and organisation of local authorities; the development of and tensions in central–local government relations, particularly in the area of local government finance; the changing nature of local government in the 1990s; and recent proposals to reform and revitalise local government and local politics.

On 1 April 1996 the local government map of England, Wales and Scotland was changed for the umpteenth time in the past twenty-five years. The English counties of Avon, Cleveland, Humberside and North Yorkshire (themselves creations of the 1974 reorganisation) were replaced by a raft of new unitary authorities including Bristol, Hull, Middlesbrough, Redcar and Cleveland and York. In Wales and Scotland change was even more dramatic, with the whole local government structure converting to a system of unitary authorities, i.e. those providing the full range of local government functions in its area. The Conservative government proclaimed the changes as promoting the delivery of local services more efficiently and responsively. Critics argued that the whole reorganisation process had been mishandled and unions condemned the loss of 7,000 jobs.

These changes in the *external structure* of English local government were programmed to continue over a period of at least two years (1996–8) as other counties and districts were reorganised. Moreover, its *internal structure* is also being re-shaped by a series of government initiatives designed to expose its major activities to competition. Indeed, just two months after the 1996 reorganisations, Sir Paul Beresford, former Conservative local government leader in the London Borough of Wandsworth and junior minister in the Department of the Environment, announced draconian measures to force the authorities 'frustrating competition by any means at their disposal' to put out to tender increasing proportions of services such as finance, information technology, personnel and housing management (*Public Finance*, 24 May 1996). Such a vision would leave little for the new unitary authorities to manage directly other than the awarding and monitoring of contracts with private sector suppliers.

What, then, is the purpose of local government, and would anyone miss it if it disappeared? On this, the Commission for Local Democracy (an independent think-tank not to be confused with the government Local Government Commission) argued:

While global or national issues may require global or national action, local issues are for local decision. The centre cannot control everything nor impose uniform standards upon everyone. A modern nation state must share a common constitution and a common economic and social framework. ...But a national body of elected representatives cannot scrutinize local administration with the rigor demanded by an alert democracy. (Commission for Local Democracy, 1995, pp. 4–5)

Moreover, the requirement of good local government was that 'it be democratic, not that it be efficient' (p. 3).

Local government can arouse a variety of intense passions. Its *structure* raises deep issues of territorialism that cut across party political lines, and its *financing* and *cost* reveal tensions in central government control of local authority spending, and the wider issue of local taxation. Some have argued that political difficulties over the community charge (known as the poll tax) made a significant contribution to the fall of Margaret Thatcher as Prime Minister in 1990. Certainly, one of the first acts of the new Major government was to abolish the charge and to replace it with the new council tax in April 1993. However, relations between central and local government remained tense, aggravated by the *capping* (i.e. limiting with penalties) of local government expenditure and financial crises in many services (e.g. education and the sacking of teachers).

Meanwhile, less publicly, some traditional local government functions, such as education, housing and social services, have been removed in part or in whole from local authority control and given to other providers. The government sees these moves as leading to the creation of the *enabling authority*, i.e. one in which a council is the purchaser of services from a competitive marketplace of providers and citizens are empowered as customers of services. By these means efficiency, accountability and democracy will be enhanced and bureaucracy and monopoly reduced.

Not everyone sees these changes as beneficial. Some argue that all this is leading to an erosion of elected local government and its replacement by systems of quasi-markets and unelected organisations suppressing accountability and democracy. They point out that whereas in its dealings with the European Community the Conservative government expressed enthusiasm for the idea of subsidiarity, i.e. devolution to lower levels of government authority, it eschewed it in its own domain. Thus a new 'nationalisation' of Britain has taken place: central powers have been increased and those of elected local government substituted by the creation of a system of extra-governmental organisations or quangos (see Chapter 20) who are 'accountable to none' (Jenkins, 1996).

Local government therefore illustrates a fundamental issue for students of politics, the tensions inherent in a polity between *centralism* and *localism*. Local government is a form of decentralisation. The case for its existence can be made in terms of democratic theory and the efficient delivery of a range of services. Central to this argument is the

---

BOX 22.1

The characteristics of local government

Local government is distinguished from many organisations because it:

- is based on local election;

- is subject to public accountability enforced through the electoral process;

- has the right to tax;

- is a multi-purpose organisation;

- is constituted by statute;

- gains its identity directly from its area;

- is a multi-contact organisation (i.e. impacts on the public in a way unmatched by any other organisation).

Source: Leach *et al.* 1994, pp. 6–7

idea that there exist identifiable areas that have specific local needs best dealt with by a local political system, i.e. one close to individuals, responsive to their demands, democratic and accountable.

Yet Britain does not have a political system in which a written constitution enshrines decentralised units with specific rights and defined areas of autonomy. It is a unitary system in which the autonomy of local government is constrained by ordinary statute and can do only what Parliament permits. So how should local government be structured and organised? On grounds of efficiency (the most cost-effective way to deliver local services), communities (the slippery concept of local identity) or politics (where the votes are and even where the money is)? This chapter will attempt to deal with these questions by explaining local government's changing structures and functions, internal management, politics, finance and relations with central government. It will conclude with a discussion of the nature of local government in the 1990s and its prospects as we approach the twenty-first century.

The structure of local government

Local government in Britain is as old as the parish church and the parish pump. Its historical legacy was a vast maze of structures and authorities. However, these were incapable of coping with the effects of the industrial revolution and during the 1880s a sustained programme of legislation dragged local government from 'ad hocism' to an integrated system of territorial and jurisdictional authorities. What emerged was a mixed system with a three-tier structure of counties, districts and non-county boroughs, and parishes and a separate system of all-purpose county boroughs for large towns. The pattern thus provided characteristics still debated today: the number of *tiers* (or levels) of government, in which the higher levels, the counties, were responsible for functions such as planning, education and police, and the lower units housing, public health and local amenities etc.; the *unitary authorities*, the county boroughs, which carried out all or most functions themselves; and the concept of authorities based on local communities.

Although the system survived in England and Wales (the organisation of Scottish local government was a little more complex) for nearly a

century, problems with both the structure and the allocation of functions arose as early as the 1920s and 1930s. The strains were demographic, economic and political. Suburbanisation (the flight from the cities) eroded the financial base of many of the county boroughs and caused problems for the efficient delivery of services. Moreover, the increase in welfare services after 1945 made the authorities financially more dependent on central government.

The problem for post-1945 reformers was how to reconcile the need for larger authorities to cope with the financial and administrative costs of effective service provision with democratic localism. The first attempt to deal with this dilemma was in the Herbert Commission Report on London (Cmnd 1164, 1960). This led in 1965 to the replacement of the London County Council (LCC) by the Greater London Council (GLC) as the strategic planning authority with thirty-three boroughs providing day-to-day services.

Encouraged by Herbert's demonstration that local government reform was feasible, the Labour government set up a Royal Commission on Local Government in England (1966) and separate enquiries to examine local government in Scotland and Wales. The various reports and the government's reactions to them are responsible not only for the basic framework of the local government system we now have but for raising most of the issues still debated today.

The Royal Commission's report (Cmnd 4040, 1969) accepted the case for the existence of local government in the UK. It argued that ideally this should:

1. provide services efficiently;
2. attract and hold public interest;
3. be able to deal with other parts of national government; and
4. adapt to changing circumstances.

The Commission believed there were too many small units and fragmented and inefficient operations, but could not agree fully on how to maximise efficiency and democracy, and fit demographic trends. The Commission's majority report recommended a unitary solution for areas outside London with fifty-eight authorities providing all functions. But a minority report argued strongly for a two-tier structure based on city regions.

The majority report was accepted by the Labour government in 1969, but its Conservative successor the following year came forward with a two-tier system that was the basis of the Local Government Act (1972). The resulting structure taking effect in 1974 separated the metropolitan conurbations from the counties. Thirty-six metropolitan districts were created within six metropolitan counties. In the shire counties the system was based to a large extent on existing counties, although incorporating the old county boroughs who lost status, functions and financial independence in the new system. They were not the only casualties. The counties were slimmed from fifty-eight to forty-seven (England and Wales) and the districts from 1,249 to 333 (see Figure 22.1). At the same time the structure of local government in Scotland was also reorganised following the proposals of the Wheatley Commission (Cmnd 4159, 1969). Here the acceptance of the Commission's recommendations led in 1975 to the creation of a two-tier system of local government in Scotland comprising nine regions (each with elected regional councils such as Strathclyde) linked with fifty-three district councils and three 'island' authorities. Beneath the districts were over 1,000 'community councils', although these had little real power or influence.

Local government structure in the 1980s and 1990s

The 1974 reorganisation certainly accelerated the politicisation of local government. The increase in size of many units was accompanied by an increase in the importance of the major political parties in local politics and the organisation of many councils in a mirror image of Westminster with stronger party control over elected members and council processes. Although this strengthened the organisation of many councils, the growth of political activity in the 1980s, especially amongst Labour-controlled urban local authorities, drew central and local government into intense ideological conflict.

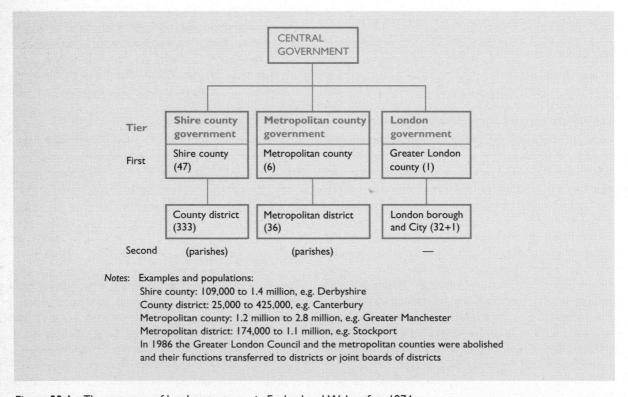

Notes: Examples and populations:
    Shire county: 109,000 to 1.4 million, e.g. Derbyshire
    County district: 25,000 to 425,000, e.g. Canterbury
    Metropolitan county: 1.2 million to 2.8 million, e.g. Greater Manchester
    Metropolitan district: 174,000 to 1.1 million, e.g. Stockport
    In 1986 the Greater London Council and the metropolitan counties were abolished
    and their functions transferred to districts or joint boards of districts

Figure 22.1 The structure of local government in England and Wales after 1974
Source: Adapted from Gray, 1979

In its election manifesto of 1983 Margaret Thatcher's Conservative government committed itself to abolishing the largest of these authorities. After a White Paper entitled *Streamlining the Cities* (Cmnd 9063, 1983), the Greater London Council (GLC) and the six metropolitan counties created by the 1974 reorganisation (Greater Manchester, Merseyside, South Yorkshire, Tyne and Wear, West Midlands and West Yorkshire) were abolished in 1986. Their functions either passed down directly to lower tier boroughs or were made the responsibility of joint boards comprising representatives of the combining boroughs.

Proponents of these changes argued that they increased accountability and empowered and widened the scope of district authorities. Yet the removal of the upper tier authorities was at the expense of strategic planning in education, transport, and economic development. It left London as one of the few major capital cities in Europe without an overarching directly local elected authority to represent the interests of its citizens.

In 1990, Margaret Thatcher was replaced as Prime Minister by John Major, who had begun his political career as a Conservative councillor in the London Borough of Lambeth. Further, the unpopularity of the poll tax put pressure on the new government to take a strong interest in local authority matters. The responsibility for local government went to Michael Heseltine, who returned to the Cabinet as Secretary of State for the Environment. Together with his colleagues the Secretaries of State for Scotland and Wales, Heseltine announced a rethink of local government.

In England, the Local Government Commission was established to make proposals for the reorganisation in England excluding London and the metropolitan districts. It began in 1992, with Sir John Banham (former Director of Audit for the Audit Commission and Director General of the Confederation of British Industries) as its chairman. Government guidance to the Commission stressed the criteria of *efficiency*, *accountability*, *responsiveness* and *localness*, favoured the creation of unitary authorities as a single tier of local government and intimated that any new structures should not cost more than the old.

Meanwhile, the Welsh Office's review resulted in the replacement of eight county councils and thirty-seven district councils by twenty-one new unitary authorities providing all local government services in their areas (Figure 22.2) (Cm 2155, 1993). Scottish Office proposals (Cm 2267, 1993) similarly replaced sixty-eight regional and district councils with a new system of twenty-eight single-tier unitary authorities. The government's argument was that the new structures would (a) promote local democracy, (b) reduce administrative costs, and (c) improve the quality of local services. Moreover, in line with the idea of *enabling authorities*, the government expressed a strong preference for the new authorities to seek out and implement new and innovative ways of service delivery, especially in terms of partnership with the private sector.

If the government hoped for a smooth and uncontroversial reorganisation programme in England it was to be disappointed, first, because the Commission under Sir John Banham pursued an independent and often controversial course and, second, because the process of considering reorganisation stirred up conflict between sectional interests in English local government, most noticeably between the counties (who fought to survive), and the districts (who sought to expand and take over the counties' functions). The tensions between the Commission and the government appeared as early as 1993 when a progress report of the Commission stated that it was not its job to sell the idea of unitary local government and warned against seeing reorganisation as a cost-cutting exercise. At the same time it began to issue a series of initial recommendations that in some cases proposed the creation of new unitary authorities but in others retained either the old two-tier system intact or in a slightly modified fashion. These recommendations, varying between the structure favoured by the government and the status quo, were justified by the Commission on the basis of its analysis of costs, community identity and local geography specific to each case. A consequence of these diverse proposals was further 'guidance' from the government to the Commission, seen as unwelcome by Sir John and challenged in the High Court by some local authorities.

During 1994–5 the Commission continued to recommend differing structural solutions for various parts of England (e.g. the abolition of the counties of Cleveland and Avon but the retention of counties such as Kent and Wiltshire). The differences were

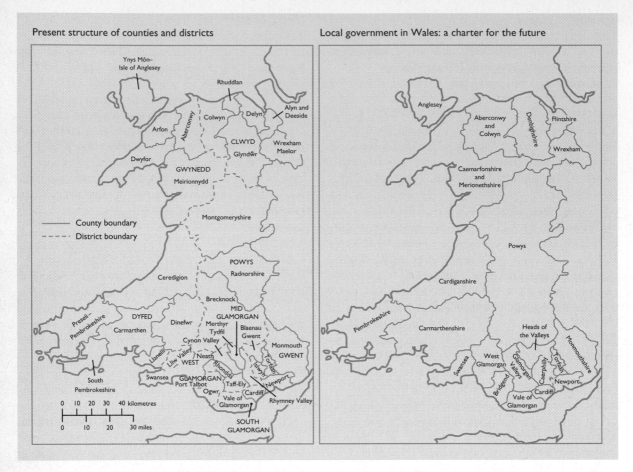

Present structure of counties and districts

Ynys Môn–
Isle of Anglesey

Rhuddlan

Alyn and
Deeside

Colwyn   Delyn

Arfon   Aberconwy

CLWYD

Wrexham
Maelor

Dwyfor   Glyndŵr

GWYNEDD

Meirionnydd

—— County boundary
---- District boundary

Montgomeryshire

POWYS

Ceredigion   Radnorshire

Brecknock

MID
GLAMORGAN

Preseli-
Pembrokeshire   DYFED   Dinefwr   Merthyr
Tydfil   Blaenau
Gwent

Carmarthen   Cynon Valley   Monmouth

Llanelli   Neath   GWENT

Llyw Valley   WEST   Rhondda

South
Pembrokeshire   Swansea   GLAMORGAN
Port Talbot   Taff-Ely   Cardiff   Newport

Ogwr   Vale of
Glamorgan   Rhymney Valley

0 10 20 30 40 kilometres

0   10   20   30 miles

SOUTH
GLAMORGAN

Local government in Wales: a charter for the future

Anglesey

Aberconwy
and
Colwyn   Denbighshire   Flintshire

Wrexham

Caernarfonshire
and
Merionethshire

Powys

Cardiganshire

Pembrokeshire   Carmarthenshire   Heads of
the Valleys   Monmouthshire

Swansea   West
Glamorgan   Glamorgan
Valleys   Caerphilly   Torfaen

Bridgend   Newport

Vale of
Glamorgan   Cardiff

Figure 22.2 Proposals for restructuring local government in Wales into unitary authorities, 1993
Source: Cm 2155, 1993

justified on the grounds of demography, financial costs and the degree of local support for change (measured by opinion poll surveys conducted by the Commission). Meanwhile the acrimonious exchanges between the government and Sir John continued and in 1995 he was effectively sacked by the Secretary of State for the Environment, John Gummer, who told the House of Commons that he intended to reopen the cases of several towns and cities as well as plans for a number of counties. Sir John, characteristically, went out fighting, informing Gummer that there 'is simply no point in having an independent Commission and you seeking to manage the process for us' (*The Guardian* 4 March 1995).

The reorganised Commission under Sir David Cooksey, the retiring Chairman of the Audit Com-

mission, reconsidered a number of cases for unitary status including towns such as Blackburn, Basildon and Warrington and district councils such as Huntingdonshire (John Major's own locality) and Rochester/Gillingham in Kent. In the event the number of recommendations for unitary status was increased but not by a great number.

When contrasted with earlier efforts to reorganise English local government the saga of the Local Government Commission for England reveals deep and significant problems both in terms of the objectives of the exercise and how it was managed. Although the Commission was continually at pains to point out that its initial recommendations should be seen as the basis for further consultation and that in all cases other options could still be considered, many critics were quick to attack the apparent governmental assumption that the two-tier form had failed and to question the limited evidence on which the case for unitary authorities was based. Faults were also found with the Commission's methodology, its costings, and its failure to ask what functions local government was intended to serve and what structures were best suited to these.

In Wales and Scotland the proposals for reorganisation led to acrimonious debate but little or no change from the system of unitary authorities proposed by the government's original White Papers. On 1 April 1996 these changes were duly implemented. In England, however, change was more gradual and piece-meal. In 1994 the Isle of Wight became the first English unitary authority and on 1 April 1996 the counties of Cleveland, Avon, Humberside and North Yorkshire were replaced by a system of unitary authorities. Further unitary authorities are due to emerge between 1997–8 making a total of forty-six in all (see Table 22.1). When these are in place the new structure of English local government will be a patchwork of two-tier and unitary authorities representing the old 1974 structure, an amended 1974 structure and the new unitaries. Whether this ends the restructuring remains an open question. As the *Local Government Chronicle* noted, it can only be a matter of time before someone asks why Rutland (population 36,900) can run its schools and social services while Northampton (population 186,100) cannot (5 January 1996). But how will this new world of unitary authorities and two-tier authorities be organised and managed? To answer this question we need to turn to an examination of the changing internal structures and government of local authorities.

Councils, councillors and officers

In cities such as Paris and New York the role of mayor is an important one. Often elected by direct franchise, mayors of such cities are generally powerful figures with a high public and political profile. In contrast, mayors of UK local authorities, elected

Table 22.1 List of new unitary authorities (start date 1 April)

Bath and North East Somerset	1996	North West Somerset	1996
Blackburn	1998	Nottingham	1998
Blackpool	1998	Peterborough	1998
Bournemouth	1997	Plymouth	1998
Bracknell Forest	1998	Poole	1997
Brighton and Hove	1997	Portsmouth	1997
Bristol	1996	Reading	1998
Darlington	1997	Redcar and Cleveland	1995
Derby	1997	Rutland	1998
East Riding of Yorkshire	1996	Slough	1998
Gillingham and Rochester	1988	Southampton	1997
Halton	1998	Southend	1998
Hartlepool	1996	South Gloucestershire	1996
Herefordshire	1998	Stockton-on-Tees	1996
Hull	1996	Stoke	1997
Isle of Wight	1994	Thamesdown	1997
Leicester	1998	Torbay	1998
Luton	1997	The Wrekin	1998
Middlesbrough	1996	Thurrock	1998
Milton Keynes	1997	Warrington	1998
Newbury	1998	Windsor and Maidenhead	1998
North East Lincolnshire	1996	Wokingham	1998
North Lincolnshire	1996	York	1996

Source: Local Government Chronicle, 22 March 1996

by their fellow councillors, are often relatively unknown to local voters and spend most of their time in office presiding at civic and charitable functions. When a sample of the UK public was asked (in 1996) whether they would welcome the idea of directly elected mayors, 70 per cent said yes, yet in the same survey this idea was supported by only 16 per cent of elected councillors (*Municipal Journal*, 14 June 1996).

The question of the role of mayor is one element in a wider debate over civil leadership and the visibility and importance of local government and local politics. In its 1995 report the independent Commission on Local Democracy put forward a major recommendation that the leader/mayor of each local authority should be elected by a ballot of all citizens in a council area using a proportional representation system of voting. The Commission argued that this and associated proposals would tackle head on problems such as low turnout in local elections and citizen ignorance of local politics and leadership, as well as highlighting who would be accountable for decisions.

Similar ideas have also engaged the political interest of the Labour leader, Tony Blair, and the Conservative deputy leader, Michael Heseltine. Worried by public disenchantment with politics, Blair has proposed that new forms of political leadership, including directly elected mayors, be given serious consideration. Mr Heseltine's enthusiasms, first given prominence in the early 1990s following his return to the Department of the Environment (DOE), were part of a wider interest in reforming the internal management of authorities. For some time Heseltine had been an advocate of city managers and elected mayors (as found in other parts of Europe and the USA), not least since he believed this would lead to a more entrepreneurial style of local government management more suited to the age of enabling authorities in a competitive world.

BOX 22.2

Mayoral models

1. **Council selection of leader**
   (a) **Present British System**
   - Councillors appoint political leader.
   - Party/Group constantly holds political leader to account.
   - No formal role or powers for the leader.

   (b) **Cabinet system**
   - Elected councillors appoint or elect a cabinet of political leaders.
   - These leaders have portfolios.

   (c) **Single leaders**
   - Elected councillors 'appoint' or elect the political leader for a fixed term (i.e. they are protected against internal challenge).
   - Powers vary along a strong mayor – strong council continuum.

2. **Electorate selects the leader**
   (a) **Head of list**
   - Electorate selects (votes for) a list of candidates put forward by political party with head of list becoming leader.

   (b) **Elected multi-person executive**
   - Electorate chooses a small cabinet.
   - These leaders have portfolios.

   (c) **Elected single person executive**
   - Electorate chooses the political leader.
   - Political powers vary along a strong mayor to strong council continuum.

   Source: Based on Hambleton, 1996

Question: Would elected mayors be beneficial to local government?

Hence while Blair and Heseltine may differ in their prescriptions for the internal reform of local government, they share a concern that local authorities often have low visibility to a public which generally demonstrates little active interest in local politics and its consequences (unless this directly involves the voter in question). Part of the problem here is seen to lie with the internal organisation and management of local authorities and, in 1991, Heseltine published a consultation paper proposing to:

1. promote more effective, rapid and business-like decision-making;
2. increase the scope for the public to take an interest in local government; and
3. make more effective use of councillors' time (Department of the Environment, 1991a).

A working party was established to consider the reform of the council committee system, the appointment of council managers and directly elected mayors. Its report, *Community Leadership and Representation: Unlocking the Potential*, indicated a widely shared concern about the political relevance and administrative effectiveness of local government and the roles of councillors and officials as we approach the twenty-first century (Department of the Environment, 1993).

Councillors and officers

Traditionally each UK local authority comprises a representative system of elected members and an administrative system staffed at the most senior level by professional officers. This system delivers a variety of services (e.g. education, social services, housing and highways) to its local area on which it is dependent for political and some financial support. Such a system is complex and interdependent. Members need officers to develop and implement policy while officers need members to give political legitimacy to their activity. In theory at least, both need the public whom they are supposed to serve! Perhaps failure to achieve such a system has led to the low public interest in local government and engendered some of the current concern articulated above.

Given certain residential qualifications, any adult can seek election to a council, though such an achievement may be difficult without the help of a political party. But who are the councillors? Surveys conducted between 1970 and 1990 appeared to show that they were white, middle class, middle aged and male. In 1977, 50 per cent were over the age of 54, 83 per cent were male, 76 per cent were owner-occupiers and fewer than 25 per cent had a background in manual work (Robinson Committee, 1977). Ten years later, research for the Widdicombe Committee revealed little change, although in urban areas Labour and Liberal councillors were more likely to be younger than the average (Cmnd 9799, 1986). The latter survey also found strong links between party and employment or economic status. Not surprisingly perhaps, Labour councillors are more likely to have a background in manual occupations and to have lower incomes. However, even in the Labour Party, male domination persisted and no major party registered more than 20 per cent of women as councillors.

This picture has continued into the 1990s with the Commission for Local Democracy reporting survey research indicating that nearly 80 per cent were over 45 years old, a third had retired and only 25 per cent were women. Further evidence submitted to the Commission indicated a rapid turnover of councillors of between 40 and 50 per cent, leading to a situation where one in four councillors had less than three years' experience (Commission for Local Democracy, 1995, p. 12). If this is true then local government faces serious problems of representation, recruitment and organisational continuity.

In recent years there has been much talk of the politicisation of local government and, in particular, the role of political parties. However, for almost all aspiring councillors, the political party is the way on to the council and on to groups which shape policy and make major decisions. Following its election, the major party takes control, elects its leaders and chairs the powerful committees.

So what power does an individual councillor have? As executive authority is exercisable only by the council operating as a corporate body, the legal answer is: very little. Further, councillors are normally part-time, unpaid (apart from attendance allowances and expenses) and untrained. As indicated above, many have seen this as a cause for concern, leading to calls for proper remuneration for elected members together with an increase in support such as that of office, secretarial and other facilities (Commission for Local Democracy, 1995, p. 29; Labour Party, 1995, p. 16). Yet such matters cannot be separated from the problem of what the job of a councillor comprises, an issue linked to wider questions on the role and function of local government. For example, would a different system require full-time councillors or, in a world dominated by unitary authorities and compulsory competitive tendering, is a new type of representative required?

But what of the permanent local bureaucracy, the local government officers? Traditionally the permanent officials of local authorities constituted a career service rooted in the local government professions (law, highway engineering, education, etc.). Consequently in the 1970s and early 1980s it was rare to find departmental heads in local authorities who did not have a professional qualification and an extensive background in their particular field. Local government for many years therefore differed from the civil service in being more specialist, with greater mobility between authorities, all of whom are employers in their own right.

The service is further differentiated between senior officers, middle management and what might be termed field operatives (e.g. teachers, social workers and office staff). As with senior civil servants, the formal role of the senior local government officer is policy advice, implementation and the management of services. Also like civil servants, they are formally politically neutral. However, for a variety of reasons the above model is changing as since the 1980s chief executives and non-professional chief officers have begun to appear in many of the larger urban and metropolitan authorities. Such officers, including some without any prior experience of local government, have often been hired on short-term contracts and high salaries to implement as swiftly as possible programmes of political and administrative change.

This redesign of senior appointments has often been associated with the election of councils with radical mandates committed to changing previous or established practices, e.g. the London boroughs of Wandsworth and Westminster (both Conservative-controlled) and Tower Hamlets (under the Liberal Democrats). However, this erosion of the career service has also been fuelled by changes in local authority functions, in particular the development of compulsory competitive tendering (CCT), that have led to the reorganisation and reordering of many traditional local authority functions. This in turn has led to wider questions regarding the roles of officers and members in the current local government world, some of which were on the agenda of the investigation in 1996 by the (Nolan) Committee on Standards in Public Life.

Councils and committees

The structure of a typical local authority, apparently simple (see Figure 22.3), hides a more complex reality. The council itself is the supreme decision-making body, acting as a corporate entity arriving at its decisions through a series of regular meetings held throughout the year. However, since it would be impossible to conduct all business in full council much is delegated to committees (usually service-based) whose operations are then keyed in to the cycle of full council meetings. There are some powers that cannot be delegated (e.g. setting the council tax), but many can be, with the result that

---

BOX 22.3

A councillor's job description

The aims and purposes of the job of a councillor might be said to be:

■ to represent and be accountable to the electorate;

■ to assist in formulating policies and practices for the authority;

■ to monitor the effectiveness of policies and practices;

■ to provide leadership for the community.

Source: Based on Wilson and Game, 1994, p. 216

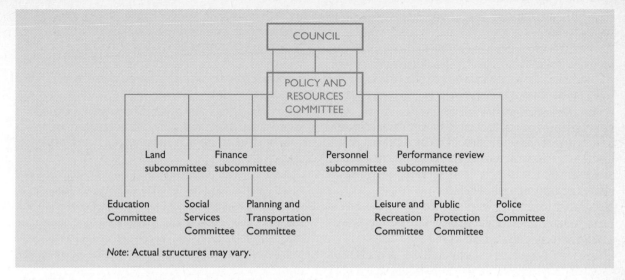

Figure 22.3 Local authority committee structure (shire county)

fully delegated issues may be only reported back to full council and never debated.

Committees consist of elected members served by officers. The major council committees are traditionally functionally based (housing, social services, education, etc.) with others devoted to areas such as personnel and finance. Traditionally local government operations have been dominated by the service-committee relationship: councils relate to matters of detail through their committees and the committees relate directly to the departments. The relationship between the council and its activities is, therefore, filtered through committees. This has many advantages but it also has a number of serious weaknesses, not least in the strategic coordination and management of council business. It is also now thought to be a process that consumes far too much of a councillor's time to little real effect (Audit Commission, 1990), focusing councillors' attention on the detail of service management rather than issues of strategy and failing to address crucial questions such as the *performance* of council activities and the impact of service delivery on citizens.

Moreover, as will be discussed in more detail below, traditional local government structures and processes have come under increasing pressure from a variety of factors, including changing financial and economic circumstances and continual government legislation. In response some councils have

reorganised their committee structure to reflect a greater emphasis on:

1. policy and strategy;
2. delegated service management;
3. performance review, and
4. the public.

This, in turn, can lead to a greater emphasis on the corporate management of the authority with 'boards' replacing committees. It should be emphasised that such changes may currently be the exception rather than the rule and changes from traditional political structures are often resisted for reasons of internal politics and self-interest. However, at a time when local authorities are being subjected to continual pressures to change, the need to introduce new forms of political management may be difficult to resist.

Politicisation and management reform

The roles and organisation of councillors and officials have been the focus of a number of attempts since the 1960s to reform the internal workings of local authorities. The early thrust of these efforts has been concerned with (a) the *politicisation* of local authorities and (b) the *efficiency and effectiveness* of their internal structures. To this should now be added initiatives to restructure the internal management of local authorities to cope with an *enabling* role and to relate more closely to its electorate.

The traditional model of council life assumes that political differences can be accommodated within traditional council structures and processes. As we have seen, these assumptions came under strain during the 1970s and, by the early 1980s, were causing the Conservative government some concern. This led to the appointment of a committee in 1985, under the chairmanship of David Widdicombe QC, which examined the rights and responsibilities of elected members and the roles of officers. It was also asked to suggest ways to strengthen the democratic process, although finance and structure were excluded from the scope of its inquiry.

The Widdicombe Committee's investigation resulted in a comprehensive report, backed up by four substantial research volumes (Cmnd 9797, 1986). Its eighty-eight recommendations were essentially modest. It argued that local government was characterised by diversity, with citadels of the left and right the exceptions rather than the rule. Undoubtedly, in some councils tensions had increased, and at its worst local politics had become a malign influence. Yet political organisation in local government was inevitable and had to be accommodated.

The report came out strongly for elected local people making decisions, for consolidating the role of councillors and for councils operating in a political framework. It acknowledged the role and importance of central government in setting the framework for local politics, but argued that, if local government was really *local*, it would give rise to local as opposed to national demands, and if it was really *government*, then political tensions with the centre would be inevitable.

The Widdicombe findings also had implications for the internal structures and processes of local government. For many years the debate on these had been dominated by a number of consistent themes: (a) the quality, competence and effectiveness of elected members to carry out their tasks; (b) the efficiency of local government internal organisations and procedures; and (c) the capacity of local authorities to manage and make effective policy. There had been earlier attempts by the Maud Report (1967) and the Bains Report (1972) to correct these perceived weaknesses. Maud focused on the councillors and the committee system. Bains' message was corporate management: the power of functional departments should be weakened and the minds of officers and members focused on the corporate good. Parts of both messages were heeded in the organisation and operation of local authorities in the 1980s and early 1990s, although talk of strategic management often evaporated in an era of continual centrally imposed change and financial crisis.

Since the early 1990s the pressure on many if not most local authorities to change their internal management structures (and in some cases their political organisation as well) has become almost irresistible (see Figure 22.4). As Leach *et al.* (1994) have argued, this has been the consequence both of the challenges of a changing society and the consistent pressures of government legislation. In terms of societal pressures many authorities now operate in areas characterised by high unemployment, changing demographic profiles and a multi-ethnic environment. In such a world traditional service delivery solutions may no longer work while public attitudes to service provision have often also changed. Such factors are exacerbated by financial pressures, in particular resource availability and the inability of authorities to raise money for either current or capital expenditure (see below). Further, the fragmentation of local authority responsibilities in areas such as education, housing and social services has eroded the jurisdiction of local government and weakened its capacity for strategic control. Finally, and perhaps most importantly, the demands of legislation on CCT have meant that authorities have had to rethink their purpose and restructure their activities. Consequently, while the traditional local government assumptions of self-sufficiency, bureaucracy, professionalism and central control have by no means disappeared, they have often been radically reinterpreted.

Indeed, the real issue now is what internal arrangements are appropriate to the new concept of the *enabling authority*, characterised by contracting out services to a mixture of internal council organisations and external providers, and the avoiding of financial penalties or capping (see below). This puts pressure on traditional structures and processes, on officers and on members themselves.

This was part of the brief of Michael Heseltine's review of the internal management noted above. Reporting in July 1993, the working party made a number of proposals for experiment (i.e. they did not offer one universal model) (Department of the Environment, 1993). The thrust of the recommendations was to empower and reward councillors more effectively and to streamline decision-making. Thus, local authorities should have discretion over payment of members and could streamline by (a) replacing the existing committee system by an executive made up of key councillors from the majority party, (b) establishing single-party committees that would advise the executive, and (c) decentralising decision-making. Perhaps surprisingly, Heseltine's predilection for elected mayors did not feature in the report.

In the period 1993–6 the public debate on the internal management of local authorities became somewhat lost in the acrimonious discussions over the activities of the Local Government Commission and the 1996 structural reorganisation in Wales and Scotland (see above). However, for bodies such as the Commission for Local Democracy and the Audit Commission this is a serious mistake. Quoting research evidence to support its claim that both councillors and officers were resistant to change the Commission for Local Democracy concluded that:

> the present system of local government in Britain is seriously inadequate to meet the requirements of a mature democracy. It obscures and distorts what should be open and lively political activity for the majority of citizens and it fails to supply clear lines of local accountability. The system encourages political parties to continue the private informal management of councils and grants them inordinate power. The basis of local administration is secretive in itself and confusing for the bulk of local people. From that confusion arises apathy and cynicism towards local democracy. (Commission for Local Democracy, 1995, pp. 16–17)

Such strong views would perhaps not be shared by the Audit Commission and other commentators, who would argue that many local authorities have indeed been innovative in attempting to adapt their structures to changing circumstances. Nevertheless, the role of authorities has become increasingly complex in a changing world. Thus as Leach *et al.* (1994, pp. 94–6) have argued, local authorities do not simply 'provide' services; rather they (a) promote activities (e.g. tourism), (b) regulate the activities of the private sector (e.g. environmental health) and the public at large (e.g. planning controls) and (c) develop strate-

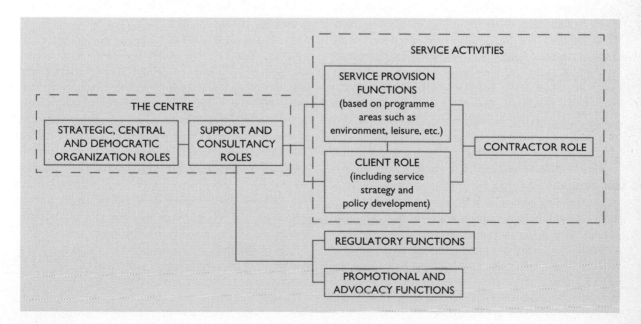

Figure 22.4 Organisation of a local authority based on functional roles
Source: Leach *et al.*, 1994, p. 96

gies to guide a range of public and private sector agencies (e.g. strategic plans). Given this multiplicity of functions and the impact of changes such as CCT, a functional rather than professional structure may help to focus on strategy and the relationship of activities to the public (see Figure 22.4). If this is the case then some serious rethinking of the traditional roles and operations of both officers and members would appear necessary.

Local government and local politics

In the local government elections of May 1996, Tunbridge Wells, traditional home of shire counties Conservatism, was won by the Liberal Democrats from a previous position of no overall control. In the same elections, Basildon, home of 'Essex man' (and woman) and bedrock of the 1992 Tory general election triumph, fell to the control of the Labour Party, leaving only one Conservative councillor surviving in a council of forty-two members.

Perversely, although they lost over 500 council seats in the 1996 local elections, the scale of the 1996 defeat was seen as a minor success for the Conservative Party, which, over a period of four years, had seen its influence over elected local government in the UK steadily ebb away to the extent that very few English local authorities (either county or districts) were left in overall Tory control. Moreover, as a result of successive elections, many councils were 'hung', i.e. no party held overall control. New councillors had to strike deals over how the council was run often by forming local coalitions. This was greeted by most Conservatives as the end of strong local government, while others, mainly Liberal Democrats, welcomed it as a sign of the realities of political life and the wishes of citizens. But does it matter? Why should local politics be governed by national politics and national parties? Is there really a distinctive Conservative, Labour or Liberal Democrat way to provide education, social services, highways and allotments? Are not the agendas of national and local government different? These questions have been a matter of contention for many years but parties have become a fixture even as the nature of local and national politics has itself changed.

In its examination of the alleged *politicisation* of local government the Widdicombe Committee (see above) pointed out that to assume an apolitical form of government was a contradiction in terms. Government, by definition, involves the resolution of conflicting interests, values and aspirations. Perhaps it is the *form* that local politics take that is important, and whether the changing role of the major political parties in UK local politics has strengthened or weakened local government or, indeed, is now adequate for the system of local government required for the twenty-first century.

Although the development of the major parties in local politics was identifiable in the nineteenth century, it has been largely a twentieth-century phenomenon (see Gyford *et al.,* 1989). Indeed, the nationalisation of local parties really took effect only after the Second World War and the development of the welfare state. During this period national political issues were expressed in local politics even though the local parties still retained a good deal of autonomy from their national headquarters. However, the 1974 reorganisation provided a watershed as the national organisation of the Labour and Conservative parties sought to tighten their grip on the newly created larger councils. This led to a sharp decline in so-called 'independent' councillors not aligned to major political parties and groups. Yet these changes have been accompanied by ideological shifts between and within the parties.

Pressures on councillors intensified and polarised as party groups came under the control of leaders and subject to whipping procedures to toe the party line. Members also became more involved in matters of council detail and procedure, thus straining their relationships with officers. Such changes reflect the effects of the 1974 reorganisation and the broader changes in British politics of the 1970s and 1980s, including the breakdown of consensus politics nationally. In the Conservative Party, the eclipse of Heath saw the rise of the radical right under Thatcher. On the Labour left the world of traditional socialism was disturbed by the emergence of a more explicitly radical left, the splitting of the party via the Social Democrats (SDP) and a call for a return of power to the grassroots of the movement.

These changes were mirrored in local politics, where new political movements emerged. The former Liberal Party promoted *community politics*, i.e. local action on community issues. This idea of using a local base to fashion political commitment was followed in a different way by Labour in *local socialism*, especially in the cities. Here the old Labour political organisations, seen as corrupt, inefficient and little interested in electors, were challenged, broken up and replaced by the radical left in cities such as London, Sheffield and, most spectacularly, Liverpool. But the Tory party was also changing its face in the counties, and even in the cities (Wandsworth) traditional loyalists were replaced by a new breed of accountants and businesspeople who talked of managing new *internal markets* in local government and reducing its overloaded functions.

This change in local politics is of considerable importance since it reflects different attempts to revitalise the UK political system and to raise political awareness and consciousness. It has also been charactised by an increased flexing of muscles by individual local authorities over central government spending controls and general tensions in central–local relations over restrictions on local autonomy and attempts to bypass local government altogether (e.g. in local economic development).

Perhaps particularly galling to central government has been the way local government has been so innovative. The local socialism of the Greater London Council (before abolition), London boroughs such as Islington and Labour cities such as Sheffield and York has attempted to reinvigorate urban areas with policies that sought both to provide a wider range of services, to raise the position of what are seen as disadvantaged groups and to heighten political awareness by citizen involvement. Meanwhile, the Liberal Democrats followed a similar though distinctive path in, for example, the London Borough of Tower Hamlets in the early 1990s, where they decentralised most decision-making and service delivery to a set of seven traditional East End neighbourhoods (e.g. Bow, Stepney and Bethnal Green), each with its own budget, chief executive and elected members. This *neighbourhood* focus was accompanied by a further decentralisation of council central services, including legal advice and finance, leaving only a small central core.

Both the Labour and Liberal strategies involved decentralisation and the empowerment of groups and localities. In contrast, but equally innovative,

the Conservative New Right in local government has followed a market-driven ideology based on the belief that the major concerns of local electors focus on low local taxes and value for money sources. This model assumes that citizens wish to receive a quality service but care little who the provider is. Such an approach has been exemplified by the London Borough of Wandsworth, whose community charge and now council tax have for many years been one of the lowest in London and whose strategy has been to reassess what it should provide, privatise as much as possible, and drive down administrative costs. Hence, from the Conservative Party's viewpoint, Wandsworth is the exemplar of the *enabling authority*.

What characterises all these innovations is a rejection of traditional local government models of internal organisation and management and a search for new forms. This search is clearly directed by political ideology to the extent that Conservative authorities are most likely to adopt market-based solutions with the citizen as customer while Labour and Liberal councils maintain a public service ethos and direct themselves to consumer-based reforms. In all cases, however, the old traditional local government structure run in a paternalistic way by councillors of polarised parties is under pressure. The ideas of enabling and internal markets, for example, operate on the premise of the citizen as customer or consumer who can or should make informed choices on the basis of information. Hence, recent Conservative governments have encouraged and cajoled local authorities via devices such as the Citizen's Charter (further see Chapter 21) to provide the public with more and better information on a regular basis, as well as to publish league tables of performance indicators covering local authority services such as housing, social services and environmental health. These and other league tables for schools and the police services were claimed both to inform and to empower the public in their dealings with public bodies such as local authorities.

This idea of more and better information as the main instrument of 'empowerment' would be rejected out of hand by many of those who advocate the rejuvenation of local government by decentralisation and increased citizen participation. However, if the disillusionment and apathy of the public are to be addressed, then a proactive council stance of informing and consulting citizens is a move in the right direction. Indeed in the mid-1990s many councils already provide citizens with extensive, well-presented and better targeted information on activities, services and performance. In some instances (e.g. Islington) this is disseminated via electronic media such as the Internet.

For those interested in rejuvenating local democracy this is only a start. Local government needs to move beyond the three- to five-year electoral cycle to explore different ways of involving local citizens directly and indirectly in the political process. Hence, for the Commission for Local Democracy (1995, pp. 32–3), the involvement of citizens in decision-making should be a 'fundamental principle' of any new system of local government achieved by a variety of innovative methods ranging from 'citizens' juries' through community involvement in service development to officer support for community groups (further see Box. 22.4).

Such ideas may appear fanciful, but some of them, like citizens' juries, are already being explored on a pilot basis in some UK local authorities. More importantly, such schemes may also appear inherently destabilising to both the accepted and established political and administrative order at both the central and local level. Such effects may not in themselves be unwelcome but whatever local system emerges will still have to grapple with the thorny problems of local government finance.

Local government finance and central–local relations

In July 1996 Tony Blair, leader of the Labour Party, addressing the new Local Government Association (formed to coincide with the local government reorganisation of the 1990s), informed his audience of councillors and officers that any new Labour Government would not be able to offer local government any extra money. Instead they would have to survive by becoming more efficient. This news was unsurprising to his audience, for whom the last decade or more has seen central controls over local finance increase to an unprecedented degree. Nevertheless, spurred on by Labour's previous commitments to make councils responsible 'locally for a much higher proportion of the money they invest and spend' (Labour Party, 1995, p. 18), they no doubt hoped for some promise of assistance in a hostile and demanding financial world.

To understand local finance it is necessary to understand how local government spends and raises its money. This may seem merely technical. In fact, the structural nature of the financial system together with the way it has developed has resulted in a number of fundamental political problems. At its simplest, local authority expenditure is divided

---

BOX 22.4

New methods of involving the public in local authority decision-making

- Citizens' juries and other forms of deliberative assembly.

- Electronic networks.

- The use of 'phone-ins'.

- Standing panels of citizens to monitor the delivery of services.

- Innovation in public meetings to make them less confrontational and more deliberative.

- Mediation groups to deal with conflicting interests.

- Citizens as monitors to report on the democratic failings of the council and other agencies.

- User involvement in the development of service plans and priorities.

- Community development.

- Direct officer support to community groups in deprived areas.

Source: Commission for Local Democracy, 1995, p.33

Question: Are these just gimmicks or would any really make a difference to public involvement?

between revenue and capital: *revenue* refers to matters of a short-lived nature (salaries, office supplies, etc.) while *capital* relates to longer-term projects such as school building. This money is required primarily to finance services. As Figure 22.5 shows, the biggest consumer of resources is education, followed by personal social services and police.

Revenue expenditure is paid for out of current income, capital from borrowing, including from the money markets or the issuing of bonds. Because it has implications for economic policy, governments have kept a careful eye on borrowing, restricting its size and bringing it into line with macro-economic objectives. This has resulted in a range of controls that have, in turn, strained relations.

To fund its current expenditure, local government has relied traditionally on three main sources of income: charges, central government grants and local taxes. *Charges* are paid directly by clients for services (e.g. rents), *grants* come as a subsidy from the central government, and *local taxes* are locally determined levies on personal property or income. After 1945, grants increased so that by the mid-

1970s they contributed over 60 per cent of total local government income, implying an increasing financial dependence of local authorities on the centre. In such a world, if grants were cut back (as they were) and if charges failed to rise (as they did), then the choice for local government was either to raise rates or to cut services. Since 1990, local government's autonomous revenue-raising capacity has been reduced sharply with the centralisation of the business or non-domestic rate (see below) and the reduction in chargeable stock, especially in housing. Recent statistics (Figure 22.6) indicate that less than 20 per cent of local authority income will come from local sources.

Originally, grants tended to be specific (i.e. awarded for the financing of specific services). More recently, however, and especially since 1958, many of these were replaced by a *block grant* (for many years, the Rate Support Grant (RSG)), the use of which was not specified by central government but left to a local authority to spend according to its needs. After 1965, the RSG was designed to allow each authority to provide a given standard of service to citizens and compensate for differences in

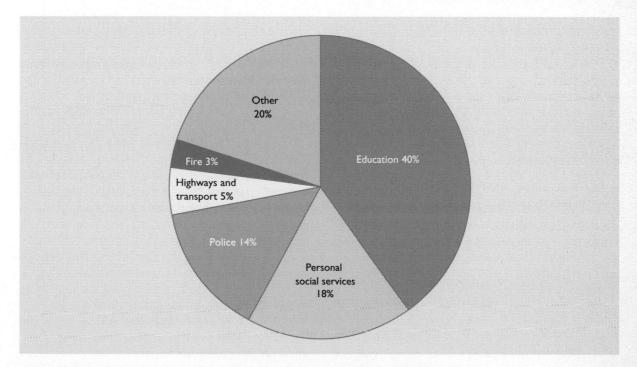

Figure 22.5 Local government in England and Wales: service expenditure 1995–6
Source: CIPFA, 1996

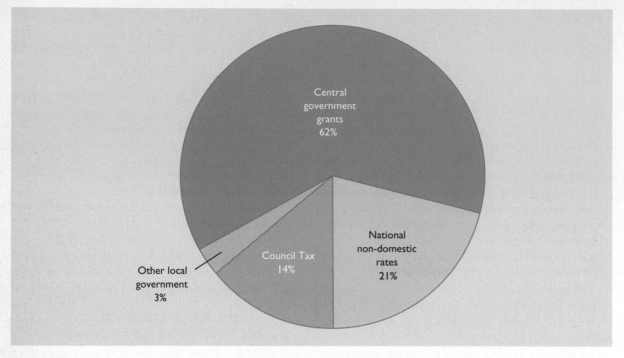

Figure 22.6 Sources of local government funding in England and Wales, 1995–6
Source: CIPFA, 1996

its revenue-raising capacity, a principle known as equalisation. In addition, it included an element to subsidise domestic ratepayers who would otherwise have had to face huge increases in bills. But a succession of formulae, often weighted by the political preferences of the different governments, meant that by the mid 1970s the credibility of the grant system was severely undermined.

Rates were a property tax of ancient origin and the one independent source of revenue available to local authorities. The rating system allowed authorities to raise taxes on domestic and commercial properties subject to certain exemptions. This was done by giving each property a rateable value to reflect the rent it would raise on a commercial basis. The intention was to update these values frequently but for administrative and political reasons re-evaluations were often postponed or cancelled. As a consequence, even by the mid-1970s, the traditional rating system was in serious difficulties.

As a tax, rates had a number of strengths: they were simple to administer, difficult to evade and cheap to collect. They were also local in nature, supplying a reliable source of income on a regular basis. However, they were also regressive, taking little or no account of an individual's ability to pay. For domestic ratepayers this effect was cushioned in the 1960s and 1970s by measures such as rebates for lower income groups and by the subsidies in the RSG. However, this meant more of the rates bill was forced onto the increasingly complaining business ratepayers.

Rates should not, however, be seen in isolation. They were part of a system of local government finance which by the mid-1970s was displaying structural weaknesses. In particular, high grant levels led to a situation where small fluctuations in grant and price inflation could result in wild and large surges in rate demands. This effect, known as gearing, remains a problem into the 1990s, demonstrating how the level of local tax demands are in fact often less a consequence of local decisions than of central government allocation formulae.

In 1974 a series of rate rises led to what the government described as a 'crisis' in local government finance. To examine this it set up a committee of enquiry, the Layfield Committee. The Committee's report (Cmnd 6453, 1976) argued that the local government financial system was characterised by confused responsibilities and weakened local accountability. Neither the government nor the local authorities appeared willing to accept responsibility for spending levels. For Layfield, the way out of this muddle was to increase either central control or local accountability. The majority of the committee favoured local solutions including a greater range of income-raising sources for local authorities. These included a local income tax together with a simplification and reduction of the grant system.

Layfield's proposals met with a chilly response from the Labour government which advocated instead the retention (with some minor changes) of the status quo (Cmnd 6813, 1977). However, the tone of the Green Paper signalled other changes that were soon to gather pace, namely, 'that, whatever happened, the Government wanted greater central control over local government spending' (Travers, 1986, p. 77). The arrival in 1979 of Margaret Thatcher's first administration coincided with the Treasury's determination to introduce such controls.

The ideas of the Layfield Committee therefore fell by the wayside. However, the importance of its arguments and perspective should be neither ignored nor forgotten. For Layfield it was crucial for decisions on local government finance and local government structure to be considered *together*, not least since such decisions had a direct bearing on accountability. That such an approach has rarely been adopted since by governments of either political persuasion has undoubtedly contributed to the current confusion in central–local government relations.

Financial control in the 1980s

The first foray of the new Conservative government of 1979 into the world of local government spending was its Act of 1981 which reorganised the grant system (the RSG was replaced by a new block grant based on grant-related expenditures (GREs)) and linked it with specific controls to enable high spenders to be identified and financially penalised. As Box 22.5 shows, this move was part of a continuing saga of attempted financial reform that continued into the 1990s. The Government's objectives were to offer a fairer and more comprehensible allocation system, enhance local authority accountability and discourage high spenders. This was done by comparing local authorities' projected expenditure with what the centre calculated it should spend (its grant-related expenditure (or GRE)). The more the former exceeded the latter the more grant would be lost.

	BOX 22.5	CHRONOLOGY

Grant systems since 1958

1993	Council tax replaces the community charge.	**1981**	Needs and resources elements consolidated into block grant. Grant-related expenditure assessments introduced.
1992	Expenditure capping applies to all local authorities.	**1974**	Needs element of rate support grant calculated via regression analysis of actual spending.
1990	Introduction of community charge and national non-domestic rates. Block and domestic rate relief grant replaced by revenue support grant, based on standard spending assessment.	**1967**	Rate support grant introduced including the first direct subsidy for domestic ratepayers.
1985	Expenditure limitation through rate capping, initially for selected authorities.	**1958**	Many specific grants consolidated into a total grant which councils could choose how to allocate.

Source: Audit Commission, 1993a

The new system differed from earlier regimes in its detailed central government intervention. Previously the centre influenced authorities by altering the totals of the RSG. Under the new arrangements the theory was that controls would be exerted selectively on classes of local authorities. If grant was cut back, these authorities would either have to reduce spending or raise money via the rates. This would force overspenders to account for themselves to local electors and ratepayers.

Following the local elections of May 1981, many of the new Labour urban authorities began to implement their commitments to extend local services and subsidise local transport. As authorities attempted to meet financial shortfalls by circumnavigating the restrictions, so the government intensified the pressure by announcing proposals to *rate-cap* (i.e. place a ceiling on) overspending authorities. This new legislation allowed the Secretary of State at the Department of the Environment to designate local authorities whose spending was considered 'excessive'. Once designated, the local authority could appeal to have its capping limit increased, but if this appeal was turned down the Secretary of State's mandate was absolute. This regime of capping, which gave the government almost absolute control over a local authority's finances, was refined and extended over the next decade precipitating what Simon Jenkins (1996, p. 64) has termed 'the biggest single act of nationalisation' since the Second World War.

The introduction of the community charge

The main thrust of government policy regarding local government finance in the early 1980s was, therefore, almost wholly directed at controlling spending totals via the grant system. Although Margaret Thatcher, whilst in opposition, had promised to 'abolish the rates', no more than lip service was paid to local taxation reform. However, in 1985 the threat of the political repercussions from a rate revaluation in Scotland sent shudders through the Conservative Party. Suddenly, the commitment to do something about the rates was finally acted on.

A Green Paper, *Paying for Local Government* (Cmnd 9714, 1986), argued that existing arrangements for local finance had long-standing flaws, not least the limited connection between voting and paying for local services and the operational complexity of the grant system. It argued that the Conservative government had a duty (linked to its goals of macro-economic management) to control the totals of local authority spending. Given this mandate, it wished to replace the old arrangements with a simpler, more efficient and more accountable system. In particular it recommended:

1. the abolition of domestic rates and their replacement with a per capita *community charge* (the so-called *poll tax* as it was essentially a tax on each of an authority's electors);
2. non domestic (business rates) to be taken away from local authority control and to be set, collected and distributed by central government; and
3. a simplification of the grant system with part to be allocated on a per capita basis and part allocated according to need (this resulted in the introduction of standard spending assessments (SSAs) as the basis for calculating local authority grants).

There was intense debate over these proposals, particularly the community charge. The government claimed that its introduction would increase local accountability and raise interest in local politics. It would also be easy to understand and was fair when linked to systems of rebates and to general levels of taxation. The issue of accountability was of great importance. In the government's view, low interest in local politics and the ability of many authorities to generate high levels of expenditure without electoral penalty arose from the fact that many electors either did not pay or escaped from rates. Such a system was also cushioned by the system of business rates, which could be increased without electoral consequences. The community charge, coupled with the removal of business rates from local authority control was intended to counter this. By making nearly all adults liable for the charge it was argued that authorities would be forced to account for their spending and that excesses would be immediately visible and felt by electors. The community charge was therefore advocated as introducing a much needed strengthening of local accountability.

There was, however, considerable criticism of the community charge. This came not only from local authorities themselves and opposition parties but also from many of the government's own back-benchers. It was argued that the charge was unfair (it was not linked to ability to pay), would involve substantial administrative costs, threaten individual freedom and liberties and was based on a spurious idea of accountability. As a consequence, there were hints from MPs during the passage of the legislation that the community charge could only cause trouble. In the event the darkest fears of the critics came true.

From community charge to council tax

In the autumn of 1991 Michael Portillo, then junior minister in charge of local government, told the Conservative Party conference that he was proud to be responsible for the community charge: 'with your help', he announced 'it will be a vote winner and launch us on our fourth term'. Several months and one Prime Minister later, he told potential voters in the Ribble Valley by-election much the same thing. The Tories duly lost one of their safest seats.

The story of the community charge has now passed into UK political history as one of the classic policy failures of the last twenty years (and now well documented; see Butler *et al.*, 1994; Jenkins 1996, Chapter 3; Lawson, 1992, Chapters 45 and 46). Its introduction and demise indicated what *The Economist* saw as the 'first law of political dynamics, the law of gainers and losers. Those to whom the government gives offer no thanks; those from whom the government takes scream like mad.' As a taxation innovation the charge perhaps holds a record for the brevity of its life. Formally introduced in April 1990, it disappeared, to the day, three years later. With hindsight, it was perhaps a triumph of ideology over experience and pragmatic politics. It engendered polarised emotions even within the Conservative Party: detractors such as former Chancellor Nigel Lawson claimed after leaving office that he and the Treasury had always been against it, (see quotation), while the late Nicholas Ridley (former Secretary of State for the Environment) believed that the idea was sound but had been poorly implemented and abandoned before it had settled in.

The case against the poll tax

"Whatever theoretical arguments may be advanced in its support no new tax can be introduced and sustained that is not broadly acceptable to the majority of the British people. The Poll Tax failed this basic test in the most fundamental way imaginable. ...What was insupportable was the anguish it caused to millions of ordinary people, with no political axe to grind, up and down the land. In all my years as a Member of Parliament, I had never encountered anything like it. Constituents of modest means would come to me, asking why they should suddenly be faced with this huge increase in their local tax bills and there was no convincing answer I could possibly give them.   *Lawson, 1992, pp. 583–4*"

Question: Why was the poll tax so unpopular?

Certainly the introduction of the charge raised the political temperature of the country. Effects ranged from rumbles of discontent amongst solid Tory voters in the shire counties to riots on the streets of London and magistrates' courts clogged with hordes of non-payers. The charge was undoubtedly highly unpopular, especially in terms of its perceived unfairness. It was also a bureaucratic nightmare to collect. For local authorities, collecting the rates had been relatively simple. Now they found themselves involved with a host of new payers who had to be logged and traced (including all students who were due to pay 20 per cent). By early 1991 it was estimated that over £1 billion (almost 10 per cent of the total due) remained unpaid.

These difficulties were magnified by other problems. In the legislation that established the charge, the government had retained its rate-capping powers in the form of 'charge-capping' and proceeded to use these to restrain what it termed 'overspending' local authorities. It was pointed out that this flew against the logic of the community charge, which was meant to promote local accountability. Further complaints were levelled against the block grant assessment formulae and the new system of business rates.

The resistance to payment, and the protests of those who had paid it, made clear that the legitimacy of the tax was unworkably low. Since many of the worst-affected areas were also Tory marginal seats, pressure built up in the Commons for something to be done. Suggestions for improvement ranged from cash relief from the Treasury, through removal of education from local authority budgets, to the total restructuring of local government and central financing of all its functions. Under Margaret Thatcher, the Tory leadership resisted these pressures. Her departure in November 1990 changed all this. All leadership contenders pledged themselves to the reform of local government finance and John Major gave his defeated rival, Michael Heseltine, the opportunity to come up with a new solution.

Heseltine launched a wide-ranging review and offered other major parties the chance to join him. They declined. Instead, the Labour Party pursued its own solution of a reformed rating system linked to capital values of properties and changes in the benefits system ('fair rates') while the Liberal Democrats, in the spirit of Layfield (see above), championed the cause of a local income tax. Meanwhile the Conservatives trawled through a host of alternatives, including a floor tax (based on a house's floor space), a bedroom tax (number of bedrooms) and a capital value tax (market price).

In the spring of 1991 Michael Heseltine told the House of Commons that the community charge would be abolished with effect from April 1993 and would be replaced by a new form of local taxation, the council tax. As a consequence, the community charge began its descent into the dustbin of history, mourned by some although not by many. Its advocates saw it as a good idea badly implemented, critics as a political disaster from conception to execution. There is strong evidence that this initiative was fundamentally flawed in terms of policy design and implementation. It contained conflicting objectives, neglected the confused state of central–local government relations and ignored the political psychology of the electorate. All this led to damaging political and administrative difficulties that split the Conservative Party and contributed to Margaret Thatcher's fall. As importantly, however, the legislation that accompanied it and in which it was embedded (e.g. centralisation of the business rates etc.) accelerated the increase in central control over local government finance and severely eroded what little remained of local financial autonomy.

The council tax

Details of the *council tax* were announced by the Department of Environment in a 1991 consultation paper (Department of the Environment, 1991b). The new tax would involve one bill per household. This would be calculated using two elements: a property element based on the market value of the house, with a banding system dictating the tax burden, and a second element that assumed at least two adults per household with a 25 per cent discount for single persons. In addition there would be a system of discounts (similar to the community charge) and certain categories of individuals would be exempted (e.g. students). The grant system, the centralised system of business rates and charge-capping (to become council tax capping) would be retained.

These proposals were welcomed by the embattled Tory Party with some relief and between 1991 and 1993 work was done on putting them into operation. This involved the valuation of all properties in local authority areas to create a register of properties and then the organisation by the authority to move from a community charge to a council tax base. This process appears to have worked smoothly, aside from some debate over the way valuations were made in a falling property market.

The calculation of an individual council tax, however, is undoubtedly more complex than either the rates or the community charge. The first step, *valuation*, is designed to place each property into a valuation band as determined by the government. This task is the responsibility of the Valuation Branch of the Inland Revenue, although in practice it may be subcontracted to firms of estate agents. According to this scheme, properties are placed in a range of valuation bands of rising value from Band A (the lowest) to Band H (the highest). The government designated Band D (range of property values £68,000–£88,000 in England) as the average. Owners of properties in other bands then pay more or less tax in relation to Band D (e.g. Band A 67 per cent of D, Band H 200 per cent). Thus owners of larger properties pay proportionately more than owners of smaller properties. However, the actual size of the *bill* that any property owner then receives depends on the tax base of individual local authorities (calculated on the basis of the total value of properties in an area) and the expenditure requirement for the authority. In 1996 the results of these calculations produced an average council tax for a Band D property in England of £638.26. On this basis a dwelling with two adults is likely to make a financial saving over the community charge. The same would not be true for one-person households (even with discount) and owners of large properties. In the world of the council tax these are the new losers.

Introducing the tax, the Department of the Environment stated that grant distribution would take account of the spread and value of properties in a local authority area. In theory, therefore, there should be a direct link between council tax levels and authority spending However, this would only be the case if grant formulae are valid and realistic.

When the council tax took effect in April 1993 there were few if any protests (aside from a number of appeals against property valuations). Authorities themselves also seemed happier with the introduction of the tax than they had been with the community charge. These impressions were also confirmed by independent research (see Keen and Travers, 1994). However, what continued to unite most authorities against the government was the mechanics and application of the grant system, in particular the design and operation of the standard spending assessments (SSAs), the application of capping and the total grant level itself.

Standard spending assessments and capping

The introduction of the SSA system in 1990 was meant to simplify and improve the grant system. In this it has not been a total success. Complaints have been made by local authorities regarding both the way calculations are made within it and its use by central government to castigate authorities as 'overspenders' in a particular area. It has also been perceived as the device used by the centre to cut council budgets. In a study of the SSA system the independent Audit Commission (1993a) noted its weaknesses. Setting out its recommended criteria for a good grant system, the Commission gave SSAs only two marks out of twelve. On the negative side the system's relation to accountability was considered weak, while, like much to do with local government finance, the system was thought to be poorly understood by both politicians and local authority members (and some officers) alike.

Debate over SSAs has continued through the mid-1990s, not least since the system is inexorably linked with the *capping* regime used by the government to keep local authority spending under 'control'. Initiated in the early 1980s when it was applied selectively to a small number of authorities, capping has gradually widened to become a fundamental instrument in central control of local authority spending. This has been achieved since 1992/3 by extending capping criteria to all councils, thus using the capping regime as a threat to force councils to accept central grant settlements (calculated via the SSA system). This 'is probably more offensive than was the imposition of the community charge. It amounts to government's setting a ceiling for every council in the country, leaving locally elected politicians in the position of having the framework for their budgets, if not the detailed content, determined for them' (Wilson and Game, 1994, pp. 152–3). This position is further compounded by rigorous central controls on council capital budgets both via strict borrowing limits enforced by the Treasury and by draconian limits on local authorities' freedom to spend their capital receipts, for example from the sale of council houses.

This tightening of central financial controls on local authority spending has led to protests not only from local government but also from groups of politicians within all major parties. For local government the case is continually made that not only has financial autonomy been almost totally eroded but in many cases tight government settlements have made it difficult to set legal budgets without eroding services (e.g. schools and social services). Some politicians argue that as a result it is no longer possible to identify who is responsible for service delivery and quality. Indeed, in 1995, Michael Forsythe, then Secretary of State for Scotland, promised to include capping in a review of 'unnecessary interference' by the Scottish Office into local government affairs.

Yet is there anything better? For many years the government position has been that local government must play its part in the restraint of public expenditure. Even the opposition Labour Party, in asserting that the current capping regime was 'a clumsy instrument' and wrong 'in principle or in practice', also accepted that it would need to be retained to be

Suggested reforms to local government finance

■ There should be a new settlement establishing the financial relationship between central government and local authorities.

■ The dependence of local government on central government grant should be reduced.

■ The non-domestic (i.e. business) rate should be restored to local authorities

■ The capping of local authority expenditure

should be ended but not controls on their borrowing.

■ Local authorities should be able to examine other forms of taxation.

■ Restrictions on the use of capital receipts should be relaxed to allow local authorities freedom to invest their own resources for the long term benefit of their area.

Source: Commission for Local Democracy, 1995, pp. 40–43 and 56

used 'in exceptional circumstances' by the Secretary of State (Labour Party, 1995, pp. 20–1).

If there is a consensus that, in a world where public expenditure is under pressure and local government consumes a good slice of this, some degree of central control must be exercised, must this be achieved at the expense of local autonomy and accountability? In considering the possibilities for changing current arrangements, the Audit Commission (1993a) offered a number of options, ranging from enhancing local control by increasing revenue-raising power to more centralisation by removing services from local government. In considering these suggestions, the independent Commission for Local Democracy (1995, p. 42) argued that the capping of budgets, revenue and expenditure was 'wholly incompatible with democratic accountability. It is as offensive to local government as capping by Brussels would be to a national government.' The Commission therefore suggested a series of financial reforms ranging from greater local revenue discretion to, in the longer term, the availability of a wider range of local taxing options over and above the council tax (see Box 22.6). However, given the earlier rejection of Layfield, how far any government (Conservative or Labour) will be willing to go down this road remains an open question.

Local government in the 1990s: from professional bureaucracy to enabling authority

It was reported that in the aftermath of Margaret Thatcher and the poll tax débâcle the Conservative Cabinet under John Major gave serious consideration to the total abolition of local government in the UK. Some ministers argued that the time had come to shift responsibility for many of its main functions (e.g. education, police) and powers to Whitehall (Jenkins, 1996, p. 60). Such views, while perhaps extreme, were by no means new or isolated. Nicholas Ridley (1988), one time Secretary of State for the Environment, idealised a local authority as a body that met once a year to award contracts. In a similar vein the Adam Smith Institute (1989) argued that local authorities should become private limited companies known as 'community companies', with a Cabinet style of government pursuing policies of charging and contracting out to an increasing variety of private providers. It was claimed that this model would be wholly compatible with principles of local democracy.

In a decade when local government's powers and functions have been eroded, these views no longer seem so far-fetched. But is the world they envision acceptable?

The changing council: redefinition and loss of functions

Up to the 1980s the underlying assumption of local government as a major service provider was rarely if ever questioned. But with the election of the Conservative government in 1979 came challenges even to core services such as housing and education. One of the Conservative Party's first initiatives was the 'right to buy' legislation, whereby the tenants of council houses were given the right to buy the property they lived in. This electorally popular move was opposed by some on the grounds that it would dilute the stock of public housing and thereby damage housing policy. Yet, 'right to buy' was only the first in a series of initiatives that questioned the assumption that the state, let alone local government, should be a major provider of public housing. From 1986 Conservative government policy focused on privatising the housing service and reducing local authority involvement. In the 1988 Housing Act, the government stated that its aim was to create a more 'businesslike' framework for the management of council housing in which local authorities were to adopt a 'strategic role' in housing provision rather than be the providers. The Act therefore proposed to (a) open up the private rented sector by removing restrictions from private landlords, (b) allow tenants to choose a landlord (a housing association, trust or private landlord), and (c) create bodies called Housing Action Trusts (HATs) that would take over some of the worst council estates, renovate them and sell them off.

These proposals all met with strong opposition, not least from suspicious council tenants, and some of the initiatives (e.g. HATs and 'tenants choice') proceeded only slowly with considerable dilution of the original policy. However, driven by an ever tighter regime for housing finance, a significant number of local authorities have voluntarily transferred their entire housing stock to newly established housing associations, sometimes of the authority's own creation. This at least allowed an evasion of central government restrictions on building and redevelopment. Further legislation in the 1990s has accelerated this process and financial regulations on housing investment have tightened. The official language now talks of the provision of 'social housing' in which councils design 'cost-

effective' and 'realistic' strategies for themselves and other providers (Department of the Environment, 1992). A major consequence of this is that local authorities' role in the provision of social housing has been marginalised with many of their traditional tasks passing to bodies such as housing associations. This policy drift was enhanced more recently by further Conservative government proposals set out in the White Paper *Our Future Homes: Opportunity, Choice and Responsibility* (Cm 2901, 1995), which sought to boost the private rented sector, strengthen owner-occupation and offer incentives to private organisations to participate in the privatisation of council estates.

The last decade has also seen major changes in education functions. Of particular importance have been the provisions for schools to opt out of local authority control (subject to Secretary of State approval) and take on delegated financial management. These initiatives were core parts of the Education Act (1989). In the case of opting out it was argued that it was important to create an internal market that would be parent (consumer)-driven, offer greater choice and raise standards. This was followed by the 1993 Education Act which threw local authority educational responsibility further into question by seeking to create more grant-maintained schools, removing all schools from local authority control in areas where opting out becomes the norm, encouraging more financial delegation to schools remaining in local authority control and creating bodies known as Education Associations to take over designated 'failing schools' from local authority hands. This package, presented as a strategy to improve education and secure value for money, was criticised as bypassing local government provision of education, with a consequent danger of instability and lack of strategic focus for the service.

Since 1994 education policy has continued to move in these directions, with different initiatives in turn seeking to increase the freedoms of schools to recruit pupils on a selective basis, to introduce voucher schemes for nursery education and to increase the powers of central educational inspection and audit in terms of setting and imposing standards. These policies (said to be stimulated in part by John Major's vision of reintroducing a grammar school in every town) were justified by the

Conservative government as strategies to maximise educational diversity and choice. However, in the view of many commentators, these moves have not only failed in their own terms but have 'centralized power over the content and organization of education in a way that seemed the antithesis of everything for which the Conservatives traditionally stood' (Jenkins, 1996, p. 134).

Yet not all central government initiatives have stripped away or eroded functions. In April 1993 local government gained a major role in the new community care initiative set out in the National Health Service and Community Care Act (1990). Community care is concerned with the care of individuals who are frail, elderly, mentally ill or otherwise vulnerable, and who traditionally have been looked after in institutions such as specialised hospitals or residential homes. For a decade or more the main thrust of policy has been to close such institutions and replace them by care arrangements in the community, where a more normal and independent existence can be encouraged. After extensive debate, it was decided that local authorities should have the lead role in community care and in 1993 funds were transferred from social security to facilitate this. Local authorities, however, have claimed that the funding is seriously inadequate for what is by definition an expensive programme. Further, even here, the local authority is seen as an enabler having a commissioning role to ensure care is delivered not necessarily by itself but by a mixture of public and private sector agencies in a 'mixed economy' of care.

Thus in different, but significant and substantial ways, local authorities have found their functions redefined or in certain cases removed. The Conservative government argued that these moves would increase efficiency and choice, for example for parents and council tenants. However, these developments also led to an increasing concern as the functions of elected bodies passed to unelected organisations and boards often referred to as 'quangos' (i.e. quasi-autonomous non-governmental organisations).

As we saw in Chapter 20, the issue of quangos is wide and diverse. In local government, however, the typical quango is an organisation responsible for the management and spending of public funds whose members are appointed rather than elected and whose activities are often open to only limited scrutiny by the public or by other official organisations (e.g. audit bodies, ombudsmen). The idea of such bodies is by no means new, but they do now appear to have taken over many of the functions of local government. Indeed in some parts of the UK it is argued that quango members currently outnumber elected local authority councillors, raising concern over the criteria for the appointment of board members, relationships with the public and client groups, sleaze, assessment of performance and openness, and in particular accountability. This has led Stewart and others (Stewart and Stoker, 1995; Stewart *et al.*, 1995) to talk of a developing 'democratic deficit' in local government.

Examining the quango phenomenon, the Commission for Local Democracy registered its concern with the lack of accountability and the way conduct usually fell far short of the standards of openness and deliberation expected of local authorities past and present. More fundamentally, the Commission (1995, p. 45) also argued that the onus on all such bodies should be to prove why they should not be governed by elected representatives and indeed went on to suggest that with regard to Training and Education Councils (TECs), health trusts and police authorities, a reformed local government system might simply assume responsibility for their functions and absorb their staff.

The changing council: competitive tendering and market testing

As will be seen from the previous section, the loss of functions via waves of successive legislation has dramatically changed the situation of local government in the 1990s. However, over and above these changes, the internal management and often the political organisation and capacity of local authorities have been reshaped and redefined by the introduction and extension of *compulsory competitve tendering (CCT)*.

The first landmark in the development of CCT was the Local Government Planning and Land Act (1980). This compelled local authorities to put out to tender highway repair, building construction and maintenance work. The issue of compulsion is of central importance since local authorities must comply with CCT directives whatever their own views (political or managerial) of how services should be provided. This initiative was justified by the government in terms of efficiency. It was also the first major attempt to promote the view that the client or *purchaser* (the local authority) and the contractor or *provider* need not be part of the same organisational structure or, if they were, then there were good efficiency reasons that they should be organisationally split (see Figure 22.7). Again this conception of organisation and service management was to have fundamental and wide-ranging effects.

There is little doubt that there were also wider ideological reasons behind this move. Many free-marketeers and others associated with the Conservative Party hold the view that local government services have been monopolies protected from competition and thus under no pressure to improve quality or reduce costs. Hence the introduction of CCT.

The CCT initiative started slowly but picked up pace in the 1980s and rapidly gathered substantial momentum in the 1990s (see Box 22.7). Initially extended by the 1988 Local Government Act, CCT does not necessarily mean that a local authority will no longer continue to provide the service. But it obliges internal providers to bid for this work in competition with outside contractors knowing that the contract will generally go to the lowest bidder. As a consequence, the process of contracting is considered to improve efficiency by forcing down internal costs and questioning established practices. Further, as a precursor to the tendering process, it forces local authorities to fragment their organisational activities in the areas concerned so that the purchaser (customer) and provider (contractor) roles are organisationally and financially separate.

Not surprisingly, the introduction of CCT was controversial. Its critics claimed that its consequences included lower quality of service and cash savings at the expense of employment and poorer working conditions. None the less, the volume of local government work under contract rose steadily to be worth nearly £2 billion by August 1992. However, for the Conservative government, this represented only a stepping stone and in 1991 part of the White Paper *Competing for Quality* (Cm 1730, 1991) sought to extend CCT to core local government professional services.

Competing for Quality was accompanied by suggestions from the Department of the Environment (1991c) that local authorities should immediately market test activities such as arts and theatre management, and architectural, engineering and property management services. More controversially, it was also proposed that a percentage of local authorities' core administrative activities (central administration, legal work, personnel, finance and later housing management) should also be put out to annual competition.

These proposals met with strong opposition from local authority associations and professional bodies on the grounds that they would damage the corporate management capacity of authorities as well as destabilise their administrative structures. However, the Conservatives remained firm in their intentions arguing for a phased introduction of CCT. In connection with this the Audit Commission issued a number of papers analysing the pressures these developments were placing on local authorities and offering a guide to good practice in dealing with the trauma of CCT and the consequent reorganisation of central services (Audit Commission, 1994, 1995a, 1995b).

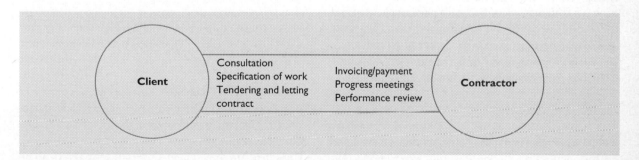

Figure 22.7 The client–contractor split
Source: Audit Commission, 1993b

BOX 22.7   **CHRONOLOGY**

Developments in Compulsory Competitive Tendering (CCT) in UK Local Government

1980 Local Government Planning and Land Bill (instructions to tender out highway repair, building construction and maintenance work)	services, also in future to percentage of white-collar services (e.g. finance, personnel, central administration and legal work)
1985 Green Paper on Extension of CCT	**1992** Housing management added to above
1988 Local Government Act 1988 (compulsory tendering of building cleaning, ground maintenance, school meals, other catering, refuse collection, street cleaning)	**1993** Consultation paper on legal services
	1994 Consultation papers on housing management, construction-related services, information technology and personnel services
1989 Sports and leisure management added to above	**1995** Tendering exercises for white-collar services commence
1991 White Paper *Competing for Quality* (Cm 1730) proposes extending immediately CCT to arts and theatre management, architectural, engineering and property	**1996** Consultation paper (May) sets out to redefine rules and raise percentages on white-collar CCT

Sources: Local Government Chronicle, 8 March 1996 and Wilson and Game, 1994, Chapter 19

In general, local authorities complied with the letter of the law. However, in the eyes of the private sector striving to win contracts and the Department of the Environment seeking to widen the CCT process, they did not comply with its spirit. Hence in late 1995 the DOE asked eighty councils to explain why they had awarded contracts in-house in the first round of white-collar competition and in May 1996 draconian changes to the CCT regime were proposed in a government consultative paper. This set much higher targets of work to be contracted out in areas such as financial services and personnel, changed previously negotiated ground rules and generally sought to speed up the overall process. Commenting on these proposals the *Local Government Chronicle* (24 May 1996) remarked that many local authorities would consider it little short of scandalous that a regime constructed over five years of consultation was to be chopped down in a consultation exercise lasting a mere five weeks, while another professional journal gloomily announced the news under the headline 'Apocalypse now...' (*Public Finance*, 24 May 1996).

CCT is a major political issue in terms of increasing tension between local authorities and central government, in particular since its implementation is based on the central imposition of a uniform set of regimes on a set of widely differing organisations. In its 1995 draft policy document for Local Government the Labour Party committed itself to ending the 'compulsory' element in the CCT process, arguing that the choice should be returned to local councils, leaving them to decide whether they wished functions to be carried out in-house or not. The same paper also argued that the criteria on which contracts should be awarded should reflect quality as well as cost (Labour Party, 1995, p. 5).

Whatever the future, it cannot be denied that the CCT process has had a fundamental effect on the organisation, management and political control of local government. As noted earlier, CCT has obliged many local authorities to restructure, whether or not they wish to retain work in-house. This, in turn, has led to different systems of management (personnel, financial) that have in turn fragmented local authority structures, e.g. the separation of housing policy from housing management, social service policy from welfare delivery. In many instances this has also affected the political role and responsibility of members, perhaps even changing the 'culture' of authorities at both the political and officer level.

So is CCT a success? Its enthusiastic supporters claim cost savings, greater efficiency, incentives for entrepreneurial behaviour on the part of contractors and an erosion of the power of the public sector unions. Against this its critics argue that the evidence of cost savings is patchy and varies with activity and area, that cost reduction is often championed over quality and that a uniform prescription for the contracting process does little to grapple with the differentiated needs and circumstances of different local authorities. Over and above this, however, they argue that these changes redefine local government as a political force. But is the *enabling* authority of necessity the *disempowered* authority? In the last section of this paper we address this question in terms of the possible need for, and role of, local government as we approach the twenty-first century.

Local government in the twenty-first century?

In 1995 *The Economist* ran a series of articles arguing for the reform of the British constitution. One of these was a stinging attack on the relentless concentration of power in London that had 'left Britain's government centralized and undemocratic'. It went on to argue that the case for strengthening local government was simple: 'decisions ought to be made more often by local people and politicians, who know more about particular local issues and have more stake in the final outcome' (11 November). It also added that any efforts to reform the system should involve three elements: more *accountability*, more *efficiency* and more *democracy*.

The Economist's analysis would undoubtedly not be accepted by those Conservatives who have claimed that, far from removing freedom and powers from localities, recent changes in central–local relations have enhanced the role and power of citizens, giving them more choice and freeing them from the dead hand of local politics. It is hard to deny that the recent decade or more of reform has

---

BOX 22.8 **IDEAS AND PERSPECTIVES**

Does anybody really want local government any more?

Imagine this. It is the year 2010 and a few thousand civil servants are arriving for work at UK Government Building 2 (local) in Victoria Street, London. From one building stuffed with computers they run all our public services: street cleaning, rubbish collection, schools, health, social services, public transport and planning. Compared with the messy, scattered town hall system of the 20th century it is efficient and cheap. The services are of high quality and steadily improving.

What do people think about this? The answer is that they are happy. True, there is a small, noisy faction organised around a group called Charter 2008, which argues that the system is desperately undemocratic, but for most citizens the most

important test is whether the service is of the required standard.

What is wrong with this fantasy is that it is impossible. In reality no central body can comprehend and react to those in central Newcastle, west Wales and Canterbury. Services would not be good without an effective channel of communication between citizen-consumer and service provider.

It is worth stating this blindingly obvious point because we seem to need to remind ourselves just why we need democracy at the local as well as at the national and international level.

Source: The Independent (Editorial), 23 October 1995

Question: Well, do we want it?

not led to the fragmentation of local government, the decline of accountability and a narrowing of local choice.

Yet what cannot be refuted is that recent major external and internal forces have redefined local government's role and purpose and reshaped its structures and processes. In particular, as Leach *et al.* (1994) point out, a decade of change and instability has raised important questions over how local authorities organise and conduct themselves and exposed them to new and fundamental choices. In particular their view is that this debate has been influenced by three key issues relating to the *economic, governmental* and *democratic* roles of local government. In economic terms choices may have to be made between a market emphasis and public sector emphasis, in governmental terms between a weak (narrow range of functions, low level of self-determination) or strong (wide range of functions, high autonomy) role for local government and in democratic terms between an emphasis on representative democracy (regular elections) and participatory democracy (use of wider democratic forums).

This analysis led Leach *et al.* (1994) to suggest a range of future models of local authority that spell out these choices in a sharper fashion and also reveal some of the main arguments relating to the past and future role of local government. These are as follows:

1. *Traditional bureaucratic authority:* A hierarchical, professionally based administrative and political body with an emphasis on service delivery and the conduct of statutory duties where the public are seen as clients in a passive sense.
2. *Residual enabling authority:* The authority is the provider of the last resort with most of the limited services offered contracted out. Here the key relationship is an individual one between the authority and the local taxpayer while notions of 'community' in any sense are insignificant (e.g. as outlined by the Adam Smith Institute, 1989).
3. *Market-oriented enabling authority:* As with the residual enabler, the market would be important but the emphasis different. Here the authority is a key force in terms of a planning and coordination agency and any contracting would seek to maximise benefit and quality

rather than decrease cost. This model might be seen as the vision of 'one nation' Conservatives (such as Michael Heseltine (1987)).

4. *Commununity-oriented enabler:* This model, drawing on the writings of Clarke and Stewart (1989), is one based on a vision of an authority whose prime purpose is to serve its community by the most appropriate means available. Here the emphasis is on mechanisms of participatory democracy and accountability and the recognition of resident as citizen.

So what is the utility of such an analysis? Leach *et al.* (1994) argue that these models indicate the range of choices available to local authorities seeking to respond to the pressures indicated above, and that empirical research on local authority behaviour indicates that in many, if not most, cases authorities are actively responding to the forces of change by seeking to relocate themselves along the dimensions indicated above. Thus, as indicated in Figure 22.8, the direction of change is generally away from traditional bureaucratic structures to more market-oriented bodies. How far and how fast local government organisations move in this direction are influenced by their values and in particular whether they seek (a) to pursue a *business* orientation, (b) are more concerned with *responsiveness* to customers/clients or (c) organise themselves to promote *citizenship*. These values may overlap. However, drawing on their empirical work Leach *et al.* (1994) argue that the values expressed by authorities as a starting point are often directly linked to their main perception of their role, i.e. the residual authority emphasises business values, market enablers customers and community enablers citizens.

So where should local authorities locate themselves? Leach *et al.* (1994) suggest that many of the signals from the Conservative government, such as the erosion of functions, expansion of quangos and extension of CCT, implied a residual role but other initiatives placing greater emphasis on openness, citizen's charters and more participation could stimulate different responses. Whatever choices are made, it is clear that as we approach the twenty-first century traditional systems of internal management and political organisation and representation in local government are not likely to survive intact.

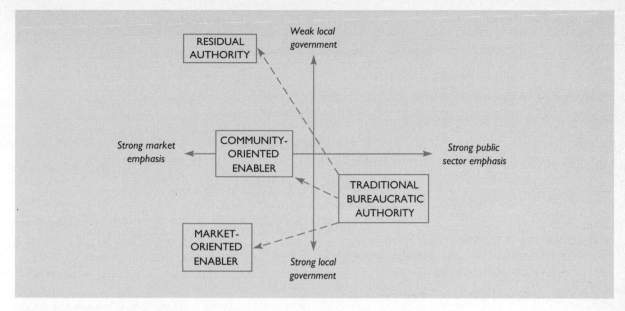

Figure 22.8   Local government: directions of change
Source: Leach *et al.*, 1994, p. 244

This perspective would undoubtedly be accepted by the independent Commission for Local Democracy (1995), whose analysis and recommendations have been referred to frequently in this chapter. The Commission's *raison d'être* was a perception that the local element in British politics has withered and is in danger of disappearing. Further, when compared with other countries in Europe and North America, Britain appears unique in proceeding down a central-ist path. The Commission found this alarming for a number of reasons, but particularly since

local administration delegated by ministers cannot adequately reflect local citizenship. Nor can citizenship be traded as consumption goods in the market place. Individualised choice over privatised services is no substitute for collective influence over those services.

It went on to argue:

We do not believe that the present state of local government in Britain can be improved merely by tinkering with the relation-ship between centre and localities. This relationship is deeply flawed, its flaws contributing to the emasculation of local democracy since the war. This has diminished turnout at local elections; made local councils less representative of their communities; reduced the local taxation base and eased the removal of discretion and power from local authorities to unelected agencies. Local government has itself been weak in remedying its own defects. (p. 2)

The thrust of this argument is that local govern-ment itself is partly to blame for its erosion as a political force in the latter half of the twentieth century. Consequently efforts need to be made to re-establish local government in our system of governance specifically by enhancing local demo-cracy. For the Commission this requires radical change to the internal structure of local government and the relationship between localities and the centre. It also implies a rediscovery and reestablish-ment of citizenship at a local level (see Box 22.9). Such an agenda is initially attractive but it is also threatening to a political system that has for decades shrunk from devolving power and responsibility away from the centre. Thus, as with Europe, nationalist feelings in Scotland and Wales and other issues such as national electoral reform and open government, any re-engineering of local government requires not simply tinkering with the existing machinery of British government but also by a more fundamental assessment and restructuring of the political and constitutional status quo.

Reforms to reinvigorate local government and democracy in the UK

- Directly elected councils and directly elected leaders/mayors.

- Local elections to be conducted by proportional representation.

- Development of methods to improve voter turnout and facilitate balloting.

- Increased remuneration and support for councillors.

- Mechanisms to increase citizen participation (e.g. via referendums and single-issue ballot questions) to be encouraged.

- Increased powers and authority for local government *vis-à-vis* central government.

- Increased functional responsibility for local services.

- Renegotiated financial settlement for local government.

- Direct elections to extra-governmental organisations (quangos) such as health authorities and police authorities.

- Mechanisms to allow decentralisation and local autonomy to be encouraged.

Source: Commission for Local Democracy, 1995, pp. 54–7

Question: What are the strengths and weaknesses of these proposals?

Chapter summary

The development and current organisation of local government in the UK cannot be understood without an appreciation of its development over the last century as a provider of services such as housing, education and recreation and its political evolution as the only elected subnational tier of government in a unitary state. The supporters of local government emphasise its democratic political role as a guard against an over-centralised state. Against this opponents argue that it has become inefficient and irrelevant to the needs of the late twentieth century. Stated in this form this debate is too simplistic, but, as the chapter has indicated, the search for an appropriate structure for local government and agreement over its powers and autonomy have raged over most of the period since the Second World War.

These issues have become sharper over the last two decades, especially with regard to the financing of local government, the erosion of its traditional functions and the development of quasi-markets and the contracting out of services. At the same time, but in a different way, many commentators inside and outside local government have become concerned with increasing both its relevance and visibility to the general public and public involvement and participation in local government's operations and activities. The final sections of this chapter have sought to address these issues with regard to the role and purpose of local government as we approach the twenty-first century. In particular this debate has been explored in terms of the case made for the development of local democracy in the UK and the associated fear of the growing centralising powers of central government with a consequent loss of accountability. In many ways local government is at a cross-roads in search of a role and an identity in a rapidly changing world. Whether it will be able to find one and what form this could, and should, take are questions that lie at the heart of the current debate over its future.

Discussion points

- Is there a need for local government in Britain? If so, what form should it take?

- What do you understand by an 'enabling' local authority? What are the strengths and weaknesses of this concept as a model for the future organisation and functioning of local government?

- Ask your local authority for details of its committee structure. Does it have a clear rationale? How does it differ from that in Figure 22.3?

- Why has it proved so difficult to reform local government finance?

- Can compulsory competitive tendering (CCT) improve the delivery of local government services?

- Do you have any ambition to become a local councillor. Is so, why? If not, why not?

- Do you support the idea of local councils being headed by directly elected mayors?

- Do party politics have any place in local government?

Further reading

An excellent and generally up-to-date text on the structure, organisation and operation of UK local government is Wilson and Game (1994). For a more factual account of local government structures and procedures, see Byrne (1992). Developments in the 1980s and early 1990s are well covered in Stewart and Stoker (1995).

For discussions on the internal operation of local government and the work of the Widdicombe Committee (Cm 9797, 1986), see Gyford *et al.* (1989). Gyford has also written on local politics and local socialism (1984, 1985) and on consumers in local government (1991). For an account of recent changes in the organisation and management of local authorities, see Leach *et al.* (1994) and more specifically on decentralisation experiments see Burns *et al.* (1994). On the complex subject of local government finance, see Travers (1986), and see Butler *et al.* (1994) for a detailed discussion of

the development and implementation of the community charge. Brief discussions of changes in traditional local government services such as education and housing are in Taylor-Gooby and Lawson (1993).

Ideas for local government reform can be found in the final report of the Commission for Local Democracy (1995). Further, for a readable and challenging account of some of the issues investigated by the Commission, as well as his view of wider developments, see the book by the Commission's Chairman, Simon Jenkins (1996).

For students wishing to keep up with contemporary events, see *Local Government Chronicle* and *Municipal Journal*, while another weekly publication, *Public Finance*, covers areas such as local government finance and changes in the operation and financing of services such as housing, education and social services.

References

Adam Smith Institute (1989) *Wiser Counsels*.

Audit Commission (1990) *We Can't Go On Meeting Like This: The Changing Role of Local Authority Members*, Management Paper No. 8.

Audit Commission (1993a) *Passing the Bucks: The Impact of Standard Spending Assessments on Economy, Efficiency and Effectiveness*.

Audit Commission (1993b) *Realising the Benefits of Competition: The Client Role for Contracted Services*.

Audit Commission (1994) *Behind Closed Doors: the Revolution in Central Support Services*.

Audit Commission (1995a) *Calling the Tune: Performance Management in Local Government*.

Audit Commission (1995b) *Making Markets: A Review of the Audits of the Client Role for Contracted Services*.

Bains Committee (1972) *The New Local Authorities: Management and Structure* (HMSO).

Burns, D., Hambleton, R and Hoggett, P. (1994) *The Politics of Decentralisation: Revitalising Local Democracy* (Macmillan).

Butler, D., Adonis, A. and Travers, T. (1994) *Failure in British Government: The Politics of the Poll Tax* (Oxford University Press).

Byrne, T. (1992) *Local Government in Britain*, 5th edn (Penguin).

CIPFA (1996) *Finance and General Statistics 1996 97* (CIPFA).

Clarke, M. and Stewart, J. (1989) *Challenging Old Assumptions* (Local Government Management Board).

Cm 1730 (1991) *Competing for Quality* (HMSO).

Cm 2155 (1993) *Local Government in Wales: A Charter for the Future* (HMSO).

Cm 2267 (1993) *The Structure of Local Government: Shaping the Future – the New Councils* (HMSO).

Cm 2901 (1995) *Our Future Homes: Opportunity, Choice and Responsibility* (HMSO).

Cmnd 1164 (1960) *Royal Commission on Local Government in Greater London 1957–60* (The Herbert Commission) (HMSO).

Cmnd 4040 (1969) *Report of the Royal Commission on Local Government in England* (The Redcliffe Maud Report) (HMSO).

Cmnd 4159 (1969) *Royal Commission on Local Government in Scotland* (The Wheatley Commission) (HMSO).

Cmnd 6453 (1977) *Report of the Committee on Local Government Finance* (The Layfield Committee) (HMSO).

Cmnd 6813 (1977) *Local Government Finance* (HMSO).

Cmnd 9063 (1983) *Streamlining the Cities* (HMSO).

Cmnd 9714 (1986) *Paying for Local Government* (HMSO).

Cmnd 9797 (1986) *The Conduct of Local Authority Business* (The Widdicombe Report) (HMSO).

Cmnd 9799 (1986) *The Conduct of Local Authority Business, Research Volume II: The Local Government Councillor* (HMSO).

Commission for Local Democracy (1995) *Taking Charge: The Rebirth of Local Democracy* (Municipal Journal Books).

Committee on Standards in Public Life (The Nolan Committee) (1996) *Third Investigation: Conduct in Local Government: Issues and Questions* (HMSO).

Department of the Environment (1991a) *The Internal Management of the Local Authorities in England: A Consultation Paper.*

Department of the Environment (1991b) *A New Tax for Local Government: A Consultation Paper.*

Department of the Environment (1991c) *Competing for Quality: Competition in the Provision of Local Services.*

Department of the Environment (1992) *The Development of the Local Authority Housing Investment Process.*

Department of the Environment (1993) *Community Leadership and Representation: Unlocking the Potential* (report of the working party on the internal management of local government).

Gray, A.G. (1979) 'Local government in England and Wales', in W.D.A. Jones and D. Kavanagh (eds), *British Politics Today* (Manchester University Press).

Gyford, J. (1984) *Local Politics in Britain*, 2nd edn (Croom Helm).

Gyford, J. (1985) *The Politics of Local Socialism* (Allen and Unwin).

Gyford, J. (1991) *Consumers, Citizens and Local Politics* (Macmillan).

Gyford, J., Leach, S. and Game, C. (1989) *The Changing Politics of Local Government* (Unwin Hyman).

Hambleton, R. (1996) 'Why Blair's mayors have centre stage', *Local Government Chronicle*, 24 June.

Heseltine, M. (1987) *Where There's a Will* (Hutchinson)

Jenkins, S. (1996) *Accountable to None: The Tory Nationalisation of Britain* (Penguin).

Keen, P. and Travers, T. (1994) *Implementing the Council Tax* (Joseph Rowntree Foundation).

Labour Party (1995) *Renewing Democracy, Rebuilding Communities.*

Lawson, N. (1992) *The View from Number 11* (Corgi Books).

Leach, S., Stewart, J. and Game, C. (1994) *The Changing Organisation and Management of Local Government* (Macmillan).

Maud Committee (1967) *Report of the Committee on the Management of Local Government* (HMSO).

Ridley, N. (1988) *The Local Right* (Centre for Policy Studies).

Robinson Committee (1977) *The Remuneration of Councillors*, Vol. 2 (HMSO).

Stewart, J. and Stoker, G. (eds) (1995) *Local Government in the 1990s* (Macmillan).

Stewart, J., Greer, A. and Hoggett, P. (1995) *The Quango State: An Alternative Approach*, Commission for Local Democracy, Research Report No. 10.

Taylor-Gooby, P. and Lawson, R. (1993) *Markets and Managers* (Open University Press).

Travers, T. (1986) *The Politics of Local Government Finance* (Allen and Unwin).

Wilson, D. and Game, C. (1994) *Local Government in the United Kingdom* (Macmillan).

The executive process

DAVID WALKER

When Sir David Ramsbottom, former adjutant-general of the British Army, became HM Inspector of Prisons in December 1995, the tabloid newspapers greeted his appointment with headlines predicting 'Rambo' would toughen the penal regime.

Within weeks the inspector was refusing to inspect. Holloway jail in London, he said, was 'not decent'. It had to be improved before he would visit. Politically this was embarrassing. The Home Secretary (Michael Howard) had dispensed with the previous Inspector, Sir Stephen Tumim, because of his outspokenness. Now his replacement, a military man habituated to good order and discipline, was proving obstreperous.

Or is the word *independent*? HM Inspector of Prisons is a crown appointee who reports to Parliament. However the textbooks parse them, neither of those terms, 'crown' or 'parliament', tell us much, in an operational sense. Crown appointments are made by ministers on the basis of (private) civil service advice. Parliamentary reports are received, in the first instance, by the executive in the House of Commons, which in turn means the majority party's ministers relying on (private) civil service advice.

Yet that formula crown and Parliament is one treasured by the occupants of many offices of state. Sir David Ramsbottom located it within his military experience when I interviewed him (for the *Independent on Sunday*, 28 July 1996, p. 11). Within twenty-four hours, in 1979, Roy Mason was replaced as Secretary of State for Northern Ireland by Humphrey Atkin: different man, different party. 'I was still commanding Belfast.' In other words, his public service extended beneath and beyond the passage of individual ministers.

That points us towards a definition of that notion of 'independence' which is so widely used within British public administration. It usually means not entirely beholden to the minister/councillor/possessor of political authority. It means occupants of offices of state see themselves – in their ideal personalities at least – taking decisions on a basis broader than the interests (party or personal) of the minister.

The idea of independence is the cornerstone of what constitutes the ethos of the British public servant. If civil or other public servants see themselves, as the prevailing Whitehall doctrine has it, as mere servants of incumbent political leaders, then it is hard to see why they should worry about politicisation or become demoralised in the way the Association of First Division Civil Servants (FDA) claims they are. (The FDA, representing senior grades, released the results of a survey of its members in summer 1996 confirming its previous assertions.)

In Britain the public service ethos rests on an idea of public interest wider than the service offered by any given set of ministers. It requires belief in an entity existing in time or space ... usually taking the form of monarchy crossed with social democracy. In the British political and intellectual context we hesitate to talk about the state (in case it takes on Hegelian colours), so the exact location of 'wider interest' is far from clear. However, it does seem there is a close relationship between the public service ethos and political pluralism.

This discussion is only taking place because of the lack of executive pluralism caused by the maintenance in power of the Conservatives from 1979 to 1997 and, in local government, a sense that the Conservatives sought to squash opposition and difference. We could sketch the history of public administrators during the past few years as an effort by them and other custodians of the British state on their behalf to circumvent those facts of party political life.

Absence of political change has encouraged allegations that the public service ethos is in danger. Reporting in January 1994 in extraordinarily coloured language – not justified by the evidence – the Public Accounts Committee evoked a crisis in standards of probity. With even greater exaggeration John Sheldon of the National Union of Civil and Public Servants spied the Italianisation of the public services. Admittedly, 1994 was a bad year: in the autumn allegations of widespread 'sleaze' (a handy portmanteau not a quantification) forced Prime Minister John Major to appoint Lord Nolan to conduct an ethical workshop to carry out running repairs on standards in public life. Commentators such as Professor Vernon Bogdanor of Oxford University have used heated language to describe what they see as a breakdown in norms of integrity and impartiality previously observed in Whitehall.

But how much of this hyperbole about the public service ethos is justified? In the absence of democratic change, it turns out there are self-correcting mechanisms in the British governing system (though the use of such language could encourage a sort of Oakeshottian/conservative mysticism, which would be wrong).

Conventional wisdom says the British public service ethos has been hurt or etiolated during the Conservative era. That may be true. But we need also to acknowledge ways in which the ethos has been strengthened and burnished. For example, new expressions of public service commitment have grown up in recent years, some aided and abetted by the very Conservative reforms other public officials have found so demoralising. Head teachers of grant-maintained schools, vice-chancellors of new universities, health service managers, certain local

authority chief executives, heads of civil service executive agencies: they have all, empirically, been seeking to refine a new and revised ethos of service based on notions of effective management.

In addition, ethos – defined, as above, in terms of emancipating public servants from immediate and absolute obedience to the politicians set in charge of them – has been redefined and strengthened by processes that have uncoiled in response to the phenomena of Thatcherism and Conservative hegemony.

One is the process of 'constitutionalisation'. This involves, simply put, the writing down of the norms that underpin the conduct and beliefs of public servants. Instead of being tacit and closed, these norms are becoming open and contestable.

The main example is the application of the judicial mind to the conduct of officials. In a string of court judgements on decisions taken by ministers old/new principles have been embedded. One is that there is indeed a higher law to which public servants are accountable, be it the common law doctrine of reasonableness or (European-influenced) notions of rights and Roman rectitude. Judicial review is sometimes misinterpreted as diminishing the ambit of the public servant. But if we distinguish officials and ministers, we can see that judges have been inviting the former to adhere to ethical obligations.

What Sir Richard Scott did for the government in his massive report on the sale of defence equipment to Iraq was judicial review *ex post facto*: the narrative testing of umpteen decisions against implicit norms of due process and fair dealing. Sir Richard's report is, if nothing else, a critical commentary on the public service ethos.

In a similar vein, the reports coming from Lord Nolan's Committee on Standards of Conduct in Public Life operate (a) to check and confine the area of political discretion (which is the enemy of the public service ethos); (b) to affirm certain principles of official life, such as appointment on merit.

This kind of affirmation of the ethics of public service has not just been carried by judges. Auditors, too, have buttressed both the idea and the practice of ethos-driven service, while attacking the idea and practice of illimitable political discretion. Michael Power (1994) of the London School of Economics identified an 'audit explosion'. He was critical. However, we might observe how auditors have time and again emphasised procedure and the need to pay attention to principles that supersede the immediate concern of politicians.

The District Auditor for the City of Westminster, John Magill, reported on allegations against Conservative councillors and officials and found they surrendered their moral and statutory duties to the council as a whole to their service of incumbent leaders. What more cogent expression of the (British) public service ethos could there be? No wonder audit has been interpreted as an attack on democratic politics: at an inaugural meeting of the Local Government Association we read of the critical reception given the controller of the Audit Commission, Andrew Foster, for arguing that elected politicians were sometimes the enemies of good management (*Local Government Chronicle*, 26 July 1996, p. 15).

The government itself has succumbed to the process of attempting to codify ethics. Years after its existence was disclosed, the government finally mustered the courage to publish *Questions of Procedure for Ministers* and set down the general conditions governing the relationship of civil servants and ministers.

In response to a report by the House of Commons Treasury and Civil Service Committee advocating a new statement of the duties and responsibilities of civil servants, the government produced just that, updating the Armstrong/Butler doctrine of obedience to ministers. The new code struggled to meet the expectations of the ethos and acknowledge public servants are beholden to norms and considerations outside the department and its minister chieftains. 'The duty of all public officers is to discharge public functions reasonably and according to law ... to comply with the law, including international law and treaty obligations, and to uphold the administration of justice.' The Civil Service Code, in operation from January 1996, gives officials in Whitehall a right of appeal when the ethos is breached – appeals to go up to a new First Civil Service Commissioner with, in theory, the right to make a fuss and ring alarm bells. (Whether the trusted businessman appointed to the post, Sir Michael Bett, would ever tinkle is an open question.)

It would be going too far to argue that the British public service ethos is in fine fettle; but equally it would be wrong to heed the Cassandras who claim it lies in rags and tatters, trampled under the Tories' former triumphant political majority.

Reference

Power, M. (1994) *The Audit Explosion* (Demos).

PART SIX

The judiciary and public order

The judiciary

PHILIP NORTON

LEARNING OBJECTIVES

■ To identify the relationship of the judicial system to other parts of the political process.

■ To describe the basic structure of that system, and how it has changed in recent years as a result of a greater willingness of judges to undertake judicial review and as a consequence of British membership of the EC/EU.

■ To consider demands for change because of perceived weaknesses in the system.

INTRODUCTION

Britain does not have a system like the USA where the Supreme Court acts as ultimate interpreter of the constitution and pronounces upon the constitutionality of federal and state laws together with the actions of public officials. Since 1688, British courts have been bound by the doctrine of parliamentary sovereignty. They have been viewed as subordinate to the Queen-in-Parliament and detached from the political process. However, the perceived wisdom has not always matched the reality and recent years have witnessed a growth in judicial activism. That growth coincided with new powers being vested in the courts as a consequence of British membership of the European Community. Recent years have also seen criticism of the criminal justice system. This chapter explores the nature of the British judicial system and growing concern about its powers and competence.

The literature on the judicial process in Britain is extensive. Significantly, most of it is written by legal scholars: few works on the courts or judges come from the pens of political scientists. To those concerned with the study of British politics, and in particular the process of policy-making, the judicial process is deemed to be of peripheral interest.

That this perception should exist is not surprising. It derives from two features that are considered to be essential characteristics of the judiciary in Britain. Firstly, in the trinity of the executive, legislature and judiciary, it is a subordinate institution. Public policy is made and ratified elsewhere. The courts exist to interpret (within defined limits) and apply that policy once enacted by the legislature; they have no intrinsic power to strike it down. Secondly, it is autonomous. The independence of the judiciary is a much vaunted and essential feature of the rule of law, described by the great nineteenth-century constitutional lawyer A.V. Dicey as one of the twin pillars of the British constitution. The other pillar – parliamentary sovereignty – accounts for the first characteristic, the subordination of the judiciary to Parliament. Allied with autonomy has been the notion of political neutrality. Judges seek to interpret the law according to judicial norms that operate independently of partisan or personal preferences.

Given these characteristics – politically neutral courts separate from, and subordinate to, the central agency of law enactment – a clear demarcation has arisen in recent decades, the study of the policy-making process being the preserve of political scientists, that of the judiciary the preserve of legal scholars. Some scholars – such as J.A.G. Griffith, formerly Professor of Law at the University of London – have sought to bridge the gap, but they have been notable for their rarity. Yet in practice the judiciary in Britain has not been as subordinate or as autonomous as the prevailing wisdom assumes. The dividing line between politics and the law is blurred rather than rigid.

A subordinate branch?

The judiciary is subordinate to Parliament (in legal terms, the Queen-in-Parliament) in that it lacks the intrinsic power to strike down an Act of Parliament as being contrary to the provisions of the constitution or any other superior body of law. It was not always thus. Prior to the Glorious Revolution of 1688, the supremacy of statute law was not clearly established. In *Dr Bonham's Case* in 1610, Chief Justice Coke asserted that 'when an Act of Parliament is against common right and reason, or repugnant, or impossible to be performed, the common law will control it, and adjudge such act to be void'. A few years later, in *Judge* v. *Savadge* (1625), Chief Justice Hobart declared that an Act 'made against natural equity, as to make a man judge in his own case', would be void. Statute law had to compete not only with principles of common law developed by the courts but also with the prerogative power of the King. The courts variously upheld the power of the King to dispense with statutes and to impose taxes without the consent of Parliament.

The Glorious Revolution put an end to this state of affairs. Thereafter, the supremacy of statute law, under the doctrine of parliamentary sovereignty, was established. The doctrine is a judicially self-imposed one. The common lawyers allied themselves with Parliament in its struggle to control the prerogative powers of the King and the prerogative courts through which he sometimes exercised them. The supremacy of Parliament was asserted by the Bill of Rights of 1689. 'For the common lawyers, there was a price to pay, and that was the abandonment of the claim that they had sometimes advanced, that Parliament could not legislate in derogation of the principles of the common law' (Munro, 1987, p. 81). Parliamentary sovereignty – a purely legal doctrine asserting the supremacy of statute law – became the central tenet of the constitution (see Chapter 15). However, the subordination of the common law to law passed by Parliament did not – and does not – entail the subordination of the judiciary to the executive. Courts retain the power of interpreting the precise meaning of the law once passed by Parliament and of reviewing the actions of ministers and other public agents to determine whether those actions are *ultra vires*, that is, beyond the powers granted by statute. The courts cannot strike down Acts of Parliament; but they can quash the actions of ministers which purport to be, but which on the court's interpretation are not, sanctioned by such Acts.

If a government has a particular action struck down as *ultra vires* it may seek parliamentary approval for a bill which gives statutory force to the action taken; in other words, to give legal force to that which the courts have declared as having – on the basis of existing statutes – no such force. But seeking passage of such a bill is not only time-consuming, it can also prove to be politically contentious and publicly damaging. It conveys the impression that the government, having lost a case, is trying to change the rules of the game. Though it is a path that governments have variously taken, it is one they prefer to – and often do – avoid.

The power of judicial review thus provides the judiciary with a potentially significant role in the policy cycle. It is a potential which for much of the past century has not been realised. However, recent years have seen an upsurge in judicial activism, judges being far more willing both to review and to quash ministerial actions. It is an activism which coincides with another development that has enlarged the scope for such activism: British membership of the European Community. The courts, whether they wanted to or not, have found themselves playing a more central role in the determination of public policy.

An autonomous branch?

The judiciary is deemed to be independent of the other two branches of government. Its independence is, in the words of one leading textbook, 'secured by law, by professional and public opinion' (Wade and Bradley, 1993, p. 60). Since the Act of Settlement, senior judges have held office 'during good behaviour' and can be removed only by the Queen following an address by both Houses of Parliament. (Only one judge has been removed by such a process: Jonah Barrington, an Irish judge, was removed in 1830 after it was found he had misappropriated litigants' money and had ceased to perform his judicial duties.) Judges of inferior courts enjoy a lesser degree of statutory protection. (In 1977, a Scottish judge – Sheriff Peter Thomson – was removed by Order in Council after campaigning for a Scottish plebiscite, continuing to do so after being warned about his activities. He had been found guilty of misbehaviour on two occasions by a judges' inquiry and declared unfit for office.) Judges' salaries are a charge upon the consolidated fund: that means that they do not have to be voted upon each year by Parliament. By its own resolution, the House of Commons generally bars any reference made by Members to matters awaiting or under adjudication in criminal and most civil cases. By convention, a similar prohibition is observed by ministers and civil servants.

For their part, judges by convention refrain from politically partisan activity. Indeed, they have generally refrained from commenting on matters of public policy, doing so not only of their own volition but also for many years by the direction of the Lord Chancellor. The Kilmuir Guidelines issued in 1955 enjoined judges to silence since 'every utterance which he [a judge] makes in public, except in the course of the actual performance of his judicial duties, must necessarily bring him within the focus of criticism'. These guidelines were relaxed in the late 1970s but then effectively reimposed by the Lord Chancellor, Lord Hailsham, in 1980. For judges to interfere in a contentious issue of public policy, one that is not under adjudication, would – it was felt – undermine public confidence in the impartiality of the judiciary. Similarly, for politicians to interfere in a matter before the courts would be seen as a challenge to the rule of law. Hence, the perceived self-interests of both in confining themselves to their own spheres of activity.

However, the dividing line between judges and politicians – and, to a lesser extent, between judicial and political decision-making – is not quite as sharp as these various features would suggest. In terms of personnel, memberships of the executive, legislature and judiciary are not mutually exclusive. There is, particularly in the higher reaches, some overlap. The most obvious and outstanding example is to be found in the figure of the Lord Chancellor. He has a judicial role: he is the head of the judiciary and exercises major judicial functions; most judges are either appointed by him or on his advice. He may, if he chooses, take part in judicial proceedings. He has a parliamentary role: he is the presiding officer of the House of Lords, albeit a position entailing no significant powers. He has an executive role: he is a member of the Cabinet. A number of Lord Chancellors have been prominent party politicians, most recently and most notably Lord Hailsham, Lord Chancellor for eleven years (1970–74 and 1979–87) and a contender for the leadership of the Conservative Party in 1963. Other members of the government with judicial appointments are the law officers: the Attorney General, the Solicitor General, the Lord Advocate for Scotland, and the Solicitor General for Scotland. The Attorney General and Solicitor General lead for the crown in major court cases as well as serving as legal advisers to the government. In Scotland, the Lord Advocate and Solicitor General for Scotland perform somewhat broader functions, including the control of public prosecutions.

The highest court of appeal within the United Kingdom is the House of Lords. For judicial purposes, this constitutes a judicial committee of the House, though all members of the committee are peers. Some Members of Parliament serve or have served as recorders (part-time but salaried judges in the Crown Court) and several sit as local magistrates. Judges in the High Court, Court of Appeal and Court of Session are barred by statute from membership of the Commons and any MP appointed to a judgeship becomes ineligible to remain in the House. No such prohibition exists in the case of the House of Lords.

Though those holding political office seek as far as possible to draw a clear dividing line between political and judicial activity, that line cannot always be maintained. At times, they have to take judicial or quasi-judicial decisions. As members of an executive accountable to Parliament, they have regard to public opinion to an extent that judges do not. For instance, a number of judicial decisions or the comments of judges result each year in public controversy. The Lord Chancellor has the power to call for transcripts of proceedings and to issue reprimands. Such power is occasionally employed. In 1988, for example, Lord Chancellor Mackay reprimanded a judge who had given a light sentence to a man convicted of sexually assaulting his 12-year-old stepdaughter, the judge asserting that the man's actions were the likely consequence of his pregnant wife not being able to fulfil his sexual needs.

The Home Secretary, a senior member of the Cabinet, also exercises certain quasi-judicial powers. Until recently he had the power to refer convictions back to the Court of Appeal when new evidence was laid before him. Between 1990 and 1997, several cases were so referred – including those of the 'Birmingham Six' and the 'Guildford Four', to which we shall return, and the 'Bridgewater Four'. (In 1997, the power to refer cases was assumed by a new, independent body.) He also exercises a number of powers over the terms to be served by prisoners. Successive home secretaries have been lobbied by groups and individuals (especially members of the victims' families) not to allow the release on parole of 'Moors murderer' Myra Hindley, sentenced in the 1960s for her part in the murder of several schoolchildren (a demand to which Michael Howard acceded in January 1997).

Nor are the Lord Chancellor and Home Secretary alone in having power to intervene in the judicial process. Certain powers also reside with the Attorney General and his Scottish equivalent. The Attorney General may intervene to prevent prosecu-

tions being proceeded with if he considers such action to be in the public interest. Under powers introduced in 1989, he may refer to the Appeal Court sentences which appear to the prosecuting authorities to be unduly lenient. He also has responsibility in certain cases for initiating proceedings, for example under the Official Secrets Act, and – though he takes decisions in such matters independently of his government colleagues – he remains answerable to Parliament for his decisions.

By the very nature of the powers vested in them, a number of political office-holders thus have to take decisions affecting the judicial process. They are decisions which cannot be avoided and which sometimes entail public controversy. Some home secretaries have attracted criticism for being slow to act (for example, in referring cases to the Appeal Court) and others for exercising their powers, especially over parole, with excessive zeal and an eye to the opinion polls.

Judges themselves do not completely stand apart from public controversy. Because they are detached from political life and can consider issues impartially, they are variously invited to chair public inquiries into the causes of particular disasters or scandals and to make recommendations on future action. This practice has been employed for many years. Recent examples have included the inquiries into safety at sports grounds in 1989 headed by Lord Justice Taylor, into the collapse of the BCCI bank in 1991 (Sir Thomas Bingham), into standards in public life in 1995 (Lord Nolan) and into the sale of arms-making equipment to Iraq in 1996 (Sir Richard Scott). The inquiries or the reports that they issue are often known by the name of the judge who led the inquiry (the Nolan Committee, the Scott Report). The reports are sometimes highly controversial and may lead to criticism of the judge involved. Lord Nolan was berated outside the Palace of Westminster in 1995 by one irate Conservative MP and his report was the subject of heated debate in the House of Commons. Sir Richard Scott was heavily criticised by many Conservative MPs and by a former Foreign Secretary, Lord Howe, for the way he conducted his inquiry.

Judges themselves have also been more willing in recent years to enter public debate of their own volition. The past decade has witnessed a tendency on the part of several judges to justify their actions publicly and in 1988 Lord Chancellor Mackay allowed some relaxation of the Kilmuir rules in order that judges may give interviews. One judge in particular – Judge Pickles – made use of the opportunity to appear frequently on television. A greater willingness to comment on issues of public policy

has also been apparent on the part of the most senior judges. The appointment of Lord Justice Bingham as Master of the Rolls (See Box 23.1), and Lord Justice Taylor as Lord Chief Justice, in 1992 heralded a new era of openness. Both proved willing to express views on public policy, both advocating

---

BOX 23.1 LORD BINGHAM
BIOGRAPHY

THE LORD CHIEF JUSTICE (1933–)

By courtesy of Popperfoto/Reuter

Thomas Bingham was born in Surrey, the son of two doctors. He was head boy of Sedbergh School before going on to read history at Balliol College, Oxford, where he graduated with a first. He studied law and came top in his Bar finals in 1959. He joined the liberal legal chambers of Lord Scarman. In 1972, at the age of 38, he became a Queen's Counsel

and three years later was appointed a Crown Court Recorder.

Bingham achieved public prominence in 1977 when he was appointed by Foreign Secretary David Owen to investigate alleged breaches of sanctions against Rhodesia by UK companies. Three years later he became a High Court judge and was knighted. He was appointed to the Court of Appeal in 1986.

In 1991 he conducted another inquiry, this time into the collapse of the Bank of Credit and Commerce International (BCCI). He attracted criticism for taking evidence in private, while Lord Woolf's investigation the previous year into the Strangeways Prison disturbances had been held in public. The criticism did not dent his reputation or his advancement. The following year he was appointed Master of the Rolls. He achieved a reputation as a reformer. In a debate at the 1992 Bar Conference, he joined with law professor Michael Zander in arguing the case for the incorporation of the European Convention on Human Rights into British law.

On 4 June 1996 he became Lord Chief Justice at the age of 62. His appointment was considered unconventional in that his career was not forged in the criminal courts. *The Times* described him as 'a radical moderniser'. He is keen to cut the costs and delays of the legal system, make courts more accessible, and to change the system by which High Court judges go out on circuit.

Lord Bingham is married with three children; his wife has been politically active, campaigning for the Liberal Democrats in the 1992 general election. He likes modern art and brisk walks.

the incorporation of the European Convention on Human Rights into British law. Taylor not only gave press interviews but also used the floor of the House of Lords to criticise government policy. He retired in 1996 on health grounds to be succeeded by Bingham. Bingham's successor as Master of the Rolls, Lord Justice Woolf, maintained the practice of giving interviews. One of his first acts was to appear on a Sunday lunchtime current affairs programme.

Thus, though the two generalisations that the judiciary constitutes a subordinate and autonomous branch of government – subordinate to the outputs of Parliament (Acts of Parliament) but autonomous in deciding cases – remain broadly correct, both are in need of some qualification. The courts are neither as powerless nor as totally independent as the assertion would imply. For the student of politics, the judiciary is therefore an appropriate subject for study. What, then, is the structure of the judicial system in Britain? Who are the people who occupy it? To what extent has the judiciary become more active in recent years in reviewing the actions of government? What has been the effect of membership of the European Community? And what pressure is there for change?

The courts

Apart from a number of specialised courts and tribunals, the organisational division of courts is that between criminal and civil. The basic structure

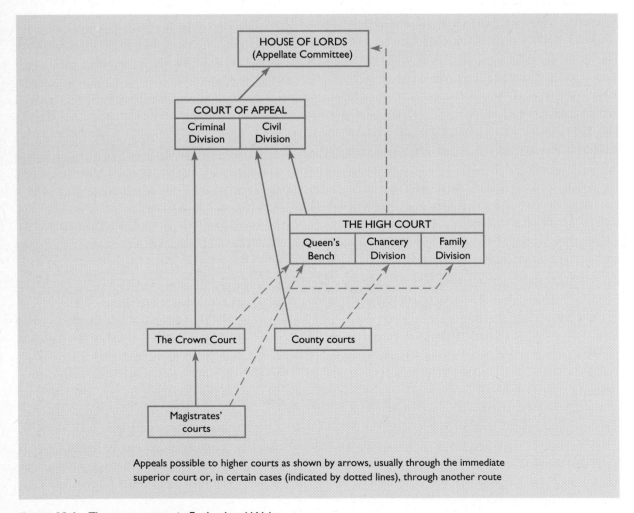

Appeals possible to higher courts as shown by arrows, usually through the immediate superior court or, in certain cases (indicated by dotted lines), through another route

Figure 23.1   The court system in England and Wales

of the court system in England and Wales is shown in Figure 23.1. (Scotland and Northern Ireland have different systems.) Minor criminal cases are tried in the magistrates' courts, minor civil cases in county courts. Figure 23.1 also shows the higher courts which try serious cases and the routes through which appeals may be heard. The higher courts – the Crown Court, the High Court and the Court of Appeal – are known collectively as the Supreme Court. At the head of the system stands the House of Lords.

Criminal cases

About 98 per cent of criminal cases in England and Wales are tried in magistrates' courts. This constitutes each year between one and two million cases. (The number was higher before 1987, but dropped after then following the introduction of fixed penalty fines for summary motoring offences.) The courts have power to levy fines, the amount depending on the offence, and to impose prison sentences not exceeding six months. The largest single number of cases tried by magistrates' courts are motoring offences. Other offences tried by the courts range from allowing animals to stray on a highway and tattooing a minor to burglary, assault, causing cruelty to children and wounding. It takes on average between 100 and 130 days from the offence taking place for it to be tried. Once before a court, a majority of minor offences are each disposed of in a matter of minutes; in some cases, in which the defendant has pleaded guilty, in a matter of seconds. The courts also have a limited civil jurisdiction, primarily in matrimonial proceedings, and have a number of administrative functions in the licensing of public houses, betting shops and clubs.

Magistrates themselves are of two types: stipendiary and lay. Stipendiary magistrates are legally qualified and serve on a full-time basis. They sit alone when hearing cases. Lay magistrates are part-time and, as the name implies, are not legally qualified, though they do receive some training. Lay magistrates are drawn from the ranks of the public, typically those with the time to devote to such public duty (for example, housewives, local professional and retired people), and they sit as a bench of between two and seven in order to hear cases,

advised by a legally qualified clerk. Cities and larger towns tend to have stipendiary magistrates; the rest of England and Wales rely on lay magistrates.

Until 1986, the decision whether to prosecute – and the prosecution itself – was undertaken by the police. Since 1986, the Crown Prosecution Service (CPS), headed by the Director of Public Prosecutions, has been responsible for the independent review and prosecution of all criminal cases instituted by police forces in England and Wales, with certain specified exceptions. In Scotland, responsibility for prosecution rests with the Crown Office and Procurator Fiscal Service. Members of this service – like the CPS in England and Wales – are lawyers.

Appeals from decisions of magistrates' courts may be taken to the Crown Court or, in matrimonial cases, to the Family Division of the High Court, or – on points of law – to the Queen's Bench Division of the High Court. In practice, appeals are rare: less than 1 per cent of those convicted appeal against conviction or sentence. The cost of pursuing an appeal would, in the overwhelming majority of cases, far exceed the fine imposed. The time of the Crown Court is taken up instead with hearing the serious cases – known as indictable offences – which are subject to a jury trial and to penalties beyond those which a magistrates' court may impose. In 1991, just over 117,000 people were committed for trial in the Crown Court.

The Crown Court is divided up into six court circuits and a total of nearly a hundred courts. The most serious cases will be presided over by a High Court judge, the most senior position within the court; other cases will be heard by a circuit judge or a recorder. High Court and circuit judges are full-time, salaried judges; recorders are legally qualified but part-time, pursuing their normal legal practice when not engaged on court duties.

Appeals from conviction in a Crown Court may be taken on a point of law to the Queen's Bench Division of the High Court but usually are taken to the Criminal Division of the Court of Appeal. Appeals against conviction are possible on a point of law and on a point of fact, the former as a matter of right and the latter with the leave of the trial judge or the Court of Appeal. Less than 10 per cent of those convicted in a Crown Court usually appeal. The Appeal Court may quash a conviction, uphold it or vary the sentence imposed by the lower courts. Appeals against sentence – as opposed to the conviction itself – are also possible with the leave of the Appeal Court and, as we have already seen, the Attorney General now has the power to refer to the Court sentences which appear to be unduly lenient. In cases referred by the Attorney General, the court has the power to increase the length of the sentence imposed by the lower court.

The Court of Appeal consists of judges known as Lords Justices of Appeal and five judges who are members *ex officio* (the Lord Chancellor, the Lord Chief Justice, the Master of the Rolls, the President of the Family Division of the High Court and the Vice-Chancellor of the Chancery Division), though the composition varies from the criminal to the civil division. Appeals in criminal cases are usually heard by three judges. Though presided over by the Lord Chief Justice or a Lord Justice, judges of the Queen's Bench may also sit on the court.

From the Court of Appeal, a further appeal is possible to the House of Lords if the Court certifies that a point of law of general public importance is involved and it appears to the Court, or to the Lords, that the point ought to be considered by the highest domestic court of appeal. For the purposes of such an appeal, the House of Lords – as we have seen – does not comprise all members of the House but rather a judicial committee (the Appellate Committee). The work of the committee is undertaken by the Lord Chancellor, law lords known as Lords of Appeal in Ordinary (appointed to the Lords in order to carry out this judicial function) and those members of the Lords who have held high judicial office. Between five and ten will sit to hear a case, the hearing taking place in a committee room of the House of Lords but with the judgement itself being delivered in the chamber. Before 1966, the House considered itself bound by precedent (that is, by its own previous decisions); in 1966, the law lords announced that they would no longer consider themselves bound by their previous decisions, being prepared to depart from them when it seemed right to do so.

Civil cases

In civil proceedings, some minor cases (for example, involving the summary recovery of some debts) are dealt with in magistrates' courts. Most cases involving small sums of money, however, are heard by county courts; more important cases are heard in the High Court.

County courts are presided over by circuit judges. The High Court is divided into three divisions, dealing with common law (the Queen's Bench Division), equity (Chancery Division) and domestic cases (Family Division). The Court comprises the three judges who head each division and just over eighty judges known as puisne (pronounced 'puny') judges. In most cases judges sit alone, though a Divisional Court of two or three may be formed, especially in the Queen's Bench Division, to hear applications for writs of *habeas corpus* and writs requiring a public body to fulfil a particular duty (*mandamus*), to desist from carrying out an action for which it has no legal authority (prohibition) and to quash a decision already taken (*certiorari*). Jury trials are possible in certain cases tried in the Queen's Bench Division (for example, involving malicious prosecution or defamation of character) but are now rare.

Appeals from magistrates' courts and from county courts are heard by Divisional Courts of the High Court: appeals from magistrates' courts on points of law, for example, go to a Divisional Court of the Queen's Bench Division. From the High Court – and certain cases in county courts – appeals are taken to the Civil Division of the Court of Appeal. In the Appeal Court, cases are normally heard by the Master of the Rolls sitting with two Lords Justices of Appeal.

From the Court of Appeal, an appeal may be taken – with the leave of the Court or the House – to the House of Lords. In rare cases, on a point of law of exceptional difficulty calling for a reconsideration of a binding precedent, an appeal may go directly, with the leave of the House, from the High Court to the House of Lords.

Cases brought against ministers or other public bodies for taking actions which are beyond their powers (*ultra vires*) will normally be heard in the Queen's Bench Division of the High Court before being taken – in the event of an appeal – to the Court of Appeal and the House of Lords. Thus, in 1993, when Lord Rees-Mogg brought an action challenging the powers of the government to ratify the Maastricht Treaty (see Box 23.2), the case was

Challenging the Maastricht Treaty

In the United Kingdom, ratification of a treaty is a prerogative power. An Act of Parliament is only necessary where provisions of the treaty are intended to have the force of law in the UK. Thus, the 1972 European Communities Act was not a measure to ratify the treaty of accession to the Community but an Act to give effect to what was described as 'the legal nuts and bolts' necessary for membership.

However, Parliament made a change in 1978 when it passed the European Assembly Elections Act. Section 6 of the Act stipulated that 'No treaty which provides for an increase in the powers of the European Parliament shall be ratified by the United Kingdom unless it has been approved by an Act of Parliament.' In December 1991, heads of government of the member states of the EC negotiated the Maastricht Treaty, designed to achieve economic and monetary union. Part of the Treaty increased the powers of the European Parliament. As a result, ratification in the UK required an Act of Parliament. The European Communities (Amendment) Bill was introduced in 1992 and, after a difficult parliamentary passage, received Royal Assent in July 1993.

Shortly before the bill received Royal Assent, an opponent of the Maastricht Treaty, Lord Rees-Mogg (a former editor of *The Times*) launched a legal challenge to ratification of the treaty. He claimed that the government would be in breach of the 1978 Act if it ratified the treaty because Parliament had approved the Maastricht Treaty but not the protocols attached to it, and the social protocol would increase the power of the European Parliament. He also claimed that the government had no lawful prerogative to ratify the social protocol because it would alter the Treaty of Rome, which, as a fundamental part of domestic law, required parliamentary approval. And he further claimed that the crown had no lawful prerogative to transfer elements of Britain's foreign and security policy to the European Community as the fundamental prerogatives of the crown could not be transferred to some other person.

Lord Rees-Mogg claimed that it was the 'most important constitutional issue to be faced by the courts for 300 years'. He was granted leave to seek a review by the High Court. The action of the courts in giving him leave was then challenged in the House of Commons. Labour MP Tony Benn claimed that it was a breach of privilege as the bill had not yet been passed by Parliament and Lord Rees-Mogg had already been given leave to challenge it. The Speaker Betty Boothroyd ruled that it was not a breach but, unusually, read a statement giving her reasons for so ruling. The sole basis for her decision, she

emphasised, was because the bill had already gone to the House of Lords when Lord Rees-Mogg made his legal challenge. However, she reminded the courts of the Bill of Rights of 1689, stating that the proceedings of Parliament could not be challenged by the courts.

The case of *Regina* v. *Secretary of State for Foreign and Commonwealth Affairs. Ex parte Rees-Mogg* was heard in the High Court by a Divisional Court of the Queen's Bench Division comprising Lord Justice Lloyd, Lord Justice Mann and Mr Justice Auld. On 30 July 1993, Lord Justice Lloyd delivered the twenty-two-page judgement of the court. The court, he said, had heard nothing to support or even suggest that by bringing the proceedings the applicant had trespassed on the privileges of Parliament, and while it was an important case it was an exaggeration to describe it as the most important constitutional case for 300 years. On the three arguments advanced by counsel for Lord Rees-Mogg, the court rejected each one. The fact that the protocols were annexed to the Treaty did not show that they were not also part of the Treaty. The construction of section 2 of the 1993 Act allowed incorporation of the protocols. On the second point, the social protocol was not intended to apply in UK law. The argument that it might have some indirect effect in UK law was too slender a basis on which to hold that Parliament had impliedly excluded or curtailed the crown's prerogative to alter or add to the Treaty of Rome. On the third point, the part of the treaty that established a common foreign and security policy among member states was an intergovernmental agreement which could have no impact on UK domestic law. Title V of the 1993 Act could not be read as a transfer of prerogative powers. It was an exercise of those powers. In the last resort, it would presumably be open to the government to denounce the treaty or fail to comply with its international obligations under Title V. In so far as the point was justiciable, their Lordships ruled that it failed on the merits.

After the judgement was delivered, Lord Rees-Mogg – who was not in court to hear it – said he would give careful thought as to whether to appeal. (A provisional date had been set for such an appeal.) However, given that the judgement of the court had been unanimous and had comprehensively rejected the points advanced by counsel for him, the chances of Lord Rees-Mogg achieving a reversal on appeal appeared slim and he soon announced that he would not be pursuing the case. Consequently, the government – which had said it would not ratify the Maastricht Treaty until the legal challenge was out of the way – moved promptly and ratified it.

heard in the Queen's Bench Division before three Lords Justices.

Tribunals

Many if not most citizens are probably affected by decisions taken by public bodies, for example those determining eligibility for particular benefits (such as social security) or compensation for compulsory purchase. The post-war years have seen the growth of administrative law, providing the legal framework within which such decisions are taken and the procedure by which disputes may be resolved.

To avoid disputes over particular administrative decisions being taken to the existing, highly formalised civil courts – overburdening the courts and creating significant financial burdens for those involved – the law provides for a large number of tribunals to resolve such disputes. There are now tribunals covering a wide range of issues, including unfair dismissal, rents, social security benefits, immigration, mental health, and compensation for compulsory purchase. Those appearing before tribunals will often have the opportunity to present their own case and to call witnesses and cross-examine the other side. The tribunal itself will normally – though not always – comprise three members, though the composition varies from tribunal to tribunal: some have lay members, others have legally (or otherwise professionally qualified) members; some have part-time members, others have full-time members. Industrial tribunals, for example, each comprise an independent chairman and two members drawn from either side of industry.

Tribunals offer the twin advantages of speed and cheapness. As far as possible the formalities of normal courts are avoided. Costs tend to be significant only in the case of an appeal.

The activities of tribunals are normally dull and little noticed. On rare occasions, though, decisions may have political significance. In January 1996, an employment tribunal in Leeds held that the policy of the Labour Party to have women-only short-lists for some parliamentary seats breached sex discrimination legislation. Rather than pursue an appeal, which could take up to twenty months to be heard, the Party decided not to proceed with such short-lists.

The judges

At the apex of the judicial system stands the Lord Chancellor and the law officers. As we have seen, these are political appointments and the holders are members of the government. Below them are the professional judges. The most senior are the law lords, the Lords of Appeal in Ordinary, presently twelve in number. They are appointed by the crown on the advice of the Prime Minister and they must have held high judicial office for at least two years. By virtue of their position they are members of the House of Lords and remain members even after ceasing to hold their judicial position. Indeed, they constitute the earliest form of life peers, the first Lord of Appeal in Ordinary being created under the provisions of the Appellate Jurisdiction Act of 1876.

The other most senior judicial appointments – the Lord Chief Justice (who heads the Queen's Bench Division), Master of the Rolls (head of the Court of Appeal), President of the Family Division and the Lords Justices of Appeal – are also appointed by the crown on the advice of the Prime Minister. In practice, the Prime Minister's scope is restricted. The Lords Justices are drawn either from High Court judges or from barristers of at least fifteen years' standing. Other judges – High Court judges, circuit judges and recorders – are drawn from barristers of at least ten years' standing, though a solicitor of ten years' standing is eligible for consideration for appointment as a recorder and a recorder of five years' standing may be appointed a circuit judge. Magistrates are appointed by the Lord Chancellor.

The attraction in becoming a judge lies only partially in the salary (see Table 23.1) – the very top earners among barristers can achieve annual incomes of several hundred thousand pounds. (In 1996, it was reported that the very top barristers, such as George Carmen QC, could command fees of £2,000 a day.) Rather, the attraction lies in the status that attaches to holding a position at the top of one's profession. For many barristers, the ultimate goal is to become Lord Chief Justice, Master of the Rolls or a law lord.

Judges, by the nature of their calling, are expected to be somewhat detached from the rest of society. However, critics – such as J.A.G. Griffith, in *The Politics of the Judiciary* (1994) – contend that this professional distance is exacerbated by social

Table 23.1 Judicial salaries, 1995

Position	Annual salary (£)
Lord Chief Justice	118,179
Court of Appeal judges	108,922
High Court Judges	95,051
Circuit/County Court judges	69,497
District judges/Stipendiaries	56,974

exclusivity, judges being predominantly elderly upper-class males.

Though statutory retirement ages have been introduced, they are generous in relation to the normal retirement age: High Court judges retire at age 75, circuit judges at 72. All judges bar one are white and less than 5 per cent are female, the proportion declining markedly in the higher echelons (see Table 23.2). All the senior office-holders in the judiciary, and all the law lords, are male. At the beginning of 1996, there was only one female among the thirty-two Lords Justices of Appeal. And as Table 23.2 reveals, of ninety-two judges of the High Court, only eight were women.

In their educational backgrounds, judges are also remarkably similar. The majority went to public school (among law lords and Lords Justices, the proportion exceeds 80 per cent) and the vast majority graduated from Oxford and Cambridge universities; more than 80 per cent of circuit judges did so, and the proportion increases the further one goes up the judicial hierarchy.

Judgeships are almost exclusively the preserve of barristers. It is possible – just – for solicitors to become judges. As we have seen, someone who has

Table 23.2 Gender of senior judges, 1996

Position	Male	Female	Total
Lords of Appeal in Ordinary	12	0	12
Lords Justices of Appeal	31	1	32
High Court:			
Chancery Division	18	1	19
Queen's Bench Division	61	3	64
Family Division	13	3	16
Total	135	8	143

practised as a solicitor for ten years may be considered for appointment as a circuit judge. Few, however, have taken this route: less than 3 per cent of circuit judges have been drawn from the ranks of solicitors.

Judges thus form a socially and professionally exclusive or near-exclusive body. This exclusivity has been attacked for having unfortunate consequences. One is that judges are out of touch with society itself, not being able to understand the habits and terminology of everyday life, reflecting instead the social mores of thirty or forty years ago. The male-oriented nature of the judiciary has led to claims that judges are insufficiently sensitive in cases involving women, especially rape cases. The background of the judges has also led to allegations of in-built bias – towards the government of the day and towards the Conservative Party. Senior judges, according to Griffith (1994), construe the public interest as favouring law and order and upholding the interests of the state.

Though Griffith's claim about political bias has not been pursued by many other writers, the effect of gender and social exclusivity has been a cause of concern among jurists as well as ministers. The narrow professional and social background from which judges have been drawn constitutes, as we shall see, but one cause of concern about the British judiciary in recent years.

Such concern exists at a time when the judiciary has become more active. There has been a greater willingness on the part of judges to review the actions of ministers. There has also been an increased activity arising from a novel departure external to the judiciary: membership of the European Community/Union. In combination, they have raised the courts in Britain to a new level of political activity – and visibility.

Judicial activism

The common law power available to judges to strike down executive actions as being beyond powers granted – *ultra vires* – or as contrary to natural law was not much in evidence in the decades prior to the 1960s. Courts were generally deferential in their stance towards government. This was to change in the period from the mid-1960s onwards. Though the judiciary changed hardly at all in terms of the background of judges – they were usually the same elderly, white, Oxbridge-educated males as before – there was a significant change in attitudes. Apparently worried by the perceived encroachment of government on individual liberties, they proved increasingly willing to use their powers of judicial review.

In four cases in the 1960s, the courts adopted an activist line in reviewing the exercise of powers by administrative bodies and, in two instances, of ministers. In *Conway* v. *Rimmer* in 1968, the House of Lords ruled against a claim of the Home Secretary that the production of certain documents would be contrary to the public interest; previously such a claim would have been treated as definitive. Another case the same year involved the House of Lords considering why, and not just how, a ministerial decision was made. It was a demonstration, noted Lord Scarman (1974, p. 49), that judges were 'ready to take an activist line'.

This activist line has been maintained and, indeed, become more prominent. Successive governments have found ministerial actions overturned by the courts. There were four celebrated cases in the latter half of the 1970s in which the courts found against Labour ministers (Norton, 1982, pp. 138–40), and then several in the 1980s and first half of the 1990s when they found against Conservative ministers.

Perceptions of greater judicial activism derive not just from the cases that have attracted significant media attention. They derive also from the sheer number of applications for judicial review made to the courts. At the beginning of the 1980s, there were about 500 applications a year for judicial review. The figure grew throughout the decade, exceeding 1,000 in 1985, 1,500 in 1987 and 2,000 in 1990. In 1994, there was a record number of applications: 3,208. 'Judicial review was the boom stock of the 1980s', declared Lord Bingham in 1995. 'Unaffected by recession, the boom has roared on into the 1990s.'

Each year, a number of cases have attracted media attention and been politically significant. In 1993, as we have already noted, Lord Rees-Mogg challenged the power of the government to ratify the Maastricht Treaty. His case was rejected by a Divisional Court of the Queen's Bench Division. The same month – July 1993 – saw the House of Lords

find a former Home Secretary, acting in his official ministerial capacity, in contempt of court for failing to comply with a court order in an asylum case. The ruling meant that ministers could not rely on the doctrine of crown immunity to ignore orders of a court. *The Times* reported (28 July 1993):

Five law lords declared yesterday that ministers cannot put themselves above the law as they found the former home secretary Kenneth Baker guilty of contempt of court in an asylum case. The historic ruling on Crown immunity was described as one of the most important constitutional findings for two hundred years and hailed as establishing a key defence against the possible rise of a ruthless government in the future.

Ironically, the case was largely overshadowed by attention given the unsuccessful case pursued by Lord Rees-Mogg. Kenneth Baker's successor as Home Secretary, Michael Howard, also variously ran foul of the courts, the Appeal Court holding that he had acted beyond his powers. Indeed, tension between government and the courts increased notably in 1995 and 1996 as several cases went against the Home Secretary (Woodhouse, 1996). In 1995 a criminal injuries compensation scheme he had introduced was declared unlawful by the House of Lords. A delay in referring parole applications by a number of prisoners serving life sentences was held by the High Court to be unreasonable. In July 1996 the court found that he had acted unlawfully in taking into account a public petition and demands from members of the public in increasing the minimum sentence to be served by two minors who had murdered the 2-year-old Jamie Bulger. These and several other judgements – including a number by European courts – combined to create a new visibility for the judiciary.

The courts, then, are willing to cast a critical eye over decisions of ministers in order to ensure that they comply with the powers granted by statute and are not contrary to natural justice. They are facilitated in this task by the rise in the number of applications made for judicial review and by their power of statutory interpretation. As Drewry (1986) has noted:

Although judges must strictly apply Acts of Parliament, the latter are not always models of clarity and consistency. ... This leaves the judges with considerable scope for the exercise of their creative skills in interpreting what an Act really means.

Some judges, of which Lord Denning was a particularly notable example, have been active and ingenious in inserting their own policy judgments into the loopholes left in legislation. (p. 30)

Judicial activism has thus been a feature of the past thirty years. The courts have been willing to scrutinise government actions, and on occasion strike them down, on a scale not previously witnessed. Some commentators in the 1990s saw it as a consequence of a Conservative government being in government for more than a decade. However, even a number of Labour politicians expressed concern about the activities of the courts, reminding judges of the supremacy of Parliament. 'The judges' job is to judge, the government's job is to govern', declared Labour MP Paul Boateng.

However, the extent and impact of such activism on the part of judges should not be exaggerated. There are three important caveats that have to be entered. Firstly, statutory interpretation allows judges some but not complete leeway. They follow well-established guidelines. Secondly, only a minority of applications for judicial review concern government departments: a larger number are for review of actions taken by local authorities. (Government departments are respondents in about 25 per cent of cases, and local authorities in 35 per cent.) Thirdly, most applications for judicial review fail. In an interview in July 1996, Lord Woolf claimed that for every case that the government lost, there were ten more than it won. The proportion of applications allowed to proceed has also declined in recent years. 'It is becoming more difficult to achieve success in such cases', noted *The Times* (19 July 1993). 'High Court leave for a review is harder to obtain and legal aid is more scarce. Fewer than half of applicants obtain leave to proceed.'

Even so, activism on the part of the courts constitutes a problem for government. Even though the percentage of applications where leave is given to proceed has declined, the absolute number has increased. And even though government may win most of the cases brought against it, it is the cases that it loses that attract the headlines.

Europe and the courts

There are two separate European dimensions to British law. The first, chronologically, is a consequence of Britain's adherence to the European Convention on Human Rights. The second is a consequence of membership of the European Community/Union.

The **European Convention on Human Rights** was signed at Rome in 1950 and was ratified by the United Kingdom the following year. It came into effect in 1953. It declares the rights which should be protected in each state – such as the right to life, freedom of thought and peaceful assembly – and stipulates procedures by which infringements of those rights can be determined. Alleged breaches of the Convention are investigated by the European Commission on Human Rights and may be referred to the European Court of Human Rights (ECHR).

The convention is a treaty under international law. That means its authority derives from the consent of the states who have signed it. It was not incorporated into British law and not until 1966 were individual citizens allowed to petition the Commission. Since then, a large number of petitions have been brought against the British government. Though the British government is not required under British law to comply with the decisions of the ECHR, it does so by virtue of its international obligations and introduces the necessary changes to bring UK law into line with the judgement of the Court. By 1995, over a hundred cases against the UK government had been judged admissible, and thirty-seven cases had been upheld (see Lester, 1994, pp. 42–46). Some of the decisions have been politically controversial, as in 1994 when the Court decided (on a 10–9 vote) that the killing of three IRA suspects in Gibraltar in 1988 by members of the British security forces was a violation of the right to life. In 1996, one case being considered by the Court was that brought by two young gays claiming that UK law which provided a different age of consent for homosexuals and heterosexuals was in breach of the convention.

The decisions of the ECHR have variously resulted in calls from some Conservative MPs for the UK not to renew the right of individuals to petition the European Commission. The move of opinion in Labour ranks has been in the other direction, favouring the incorporation of the Convention into British law.

The second dimension derives from Britain's **membership of the European Community**, now part of the European Union. The United Kingdom signed the treaty of accession to the European Community in 1972. The European Communities Act passed the same year provided the legal provisions necessary for membership. The UK became a member of the EC on 1 January 1973.

The 1972 Act gave legal force not only to existing EC law but also to future law. When law has been promulgated by the Commission and the Council of Ministers, it takes effect within the United Kingdom. Parliamentary assent to the principle is not required. That assent has already been given in advance by virtue of the provisions of the 1972 Act. Furthermore, under the provisions of the Act, questions of law are to be decided by the European Court of Justice (the ECJ), or in accordance with the decisions of that court, and all courts in the United Kingdom are required to take judicial notice of decisions made by the Court of Justice. Cases in the UK which reach the House of Lords must be referred to the European Court for a definitive ruling and requests may be made by lower courts to the Court of Justice for a ruling on the meaning and interpretation of European treaties. In the event of a conflict between the provisions of European law and those of an Act of Parliament, the former are to prevail.

The question that has most exercised writers on constitutional law since Britain's accession to the EC has been what British courts should do in the event of the passage of an Act of Parliament that expressly overrides European law. The question remains a hypothetical one. Though some doubt exists – Lord Denning when Master of the Rolls appeared to imply on occasion that the courts must apply EC law, Acts of Parliament notwithstanding – the generally accepted view among jurists is that courts, by virtue of the doctrine of parliamentary sovereignty, must apply the provisions of the Act of Parliament that expressly overrides European law (see Bradley, 1994, p. 97).

Given the absence of an explicit overriding of European law by statute, the most important question to which the courts have had to address themselves has been how to resolve apparent inconsistencies between European and domestic (known as municipal) law. During debate on the European Communities Bill in 1972, ministers made clear that the Bill essentially provided a rule of construction: that is, that the courts were to construe the provisions of an Act of Parliament, in so far as it was possible to do so, in such a way as to render it consistent with European law. This has been the position that the courts have adopted. However, what if it is not possible to construe an Act of Parliament in such a way? Where the courts have found UK law to fall foul of European law, the UK government has introduced new legislation to bring domestic law into line with EC requirements. But what about the position prior to the passage of such legislation? Do the courts have power to strike down or suspend Acts of Parliament which appear to breach EC law? The presumption until 1990 was that they did not. However, the constitutional waters became muddied in that year in the landmark *Factortame* case. When the owners of some Spanish trawlers challenged the provisions of the 1988 Merchant Shipping Act as being contrary to EC law, the High Court granted interim relief, suspending the relevant parts of the Act. This was then overturned by the House of Lords, which ruled that the courts had no such power. The European Court of Justice, to which the case was then referred, ruled in June 1990 that courts did have the power of injunction and could suspend the application of Acts of Parliament that on their face appeared to breach European law until a final determination was made. The following month, the House of Lords granted orders to the Spanish fishermen preventing the Transport Secretary from withholding or withdrawing their names from the register of British fishing vessels, the orders to remain in place until the Court of Justice had decided the case.

The provisions of an Act of Parliament were thus, in effect, being put into cold storage until it could be determined whether they did breach European law. The doctrine of parliamentary sovereignty formally remained intact in that the courts were acting under authority granted by the provisions of the 1972 Act and Parliament retained the power to amend or repeal that Act; and, furthermore, the assumption that the courts would apply an Act expressly overriding European law remained extant (Munro, 1992, pp. 8–10). None the less, the effect of the *Factortame* case was to give to the courts a new power.

The courts have thus assumed a new role in the interpretation of European law and the court system itself has acquired a new dimension. The ECJ serves not only to hear cases that emanate from British courts but also to consider cases brought directly by or against the EC Commission and the governments of the member states.

There is thus a significant judicial dimension to British membership of the European Community, involving adjudication by a supranational court, and the greater the integration of member states the greater the significance of the courts in applying European law. Furthermore, under the Maastricht Treaty, which took effect in November 1993, the powers of the Court of Justice were strengthened, the court being given the power to fine member states which did not fulfil their legal obligations. Though the cases heard by the European Court of Justice may not appear often of great significance, collectively they produce a substantial – indeed, massive – body of case law that constitutes an important constraint on the actions of the UK government. Each year, that body of case law grows greater.

Again, the effect of this change in the British constitution should not be exaggerated. As we have seen, the doctrine of parliamentary sovereignty remains intact. When Lord Rees-Mogg sought judicial review of the government's power to ratify the Maastricht Treaty, the Speaker of the House of Commons, Betty Boothroyd, issued a stern warning to the courts, reminding them that under the Bill of Rights of 1689 the proceedings of Parliament could not be challenged by the courts. (Lord Rees-Mogg, whose application was rejected, emphasised that no such challenge was intended.) And it was the British government which instigated the provision in the Maastricht Treaty for the Court of Justice to fine member states. The UK has one of the best records in the European Union for complying with European law. Between 1991 and 1995, the UK was referred to the Court of Justice for infringement proceedings on only six occasions – the second lowest number among member states; only Denmark had fewer. There were seventy cases brought against Italy. Even so, the impact of membership of the EC should not be treated lightly. It has introduced a major new judicial dimension to the British constitution. It has profound implications for the role of the courts in influencing public policy in the United Kingdom, a role that is likely to become even more significant in the future.

Demands for change

Recent years have seen various calls for change in the judicial process. Some of those calls have been to strengthen the powers of the courts. Critics of the existing constitution have argued that too much power is vested in the executive, with the consequence that individual liberties are vulnerable to erosion by executive fiat. The way to protect individual liberties, it is argued, is through the introduction of a new bill of rights, codifying basic rights which would then be protected not by Parliament but by the courts (see Box 23.3). On this argument, the courts are thus part of the solution to the problem. However, other calls have been to reform the judicial process itself. Those demanding such change see the courts not so much as part of the solution to a problem, but rather as part of the problem itself.

Most respondents – 54 per cent – in a 1993 MORI poll disagreed with the statement that 'you can have confidence in the legal system'; only 29 per cent agreed with the statement. Fifty-nine per cent said they were 'satisfied with the way my area is being policed'. By January 1994 only 36 per cent gave the same response.

Several developments appear to have contributed to this growing public unease. One has been the activity and policy of the Crown Prosecution Service. The CPS has been largely overworked and has had difficulty since its inception in recruiting a sufficient number of well-qualified lawyers to deal with the large number of cases requiring action. It has also been criticised for failing to prosecute in several highly publicised cases where it has felt that the chances of obtaining a conviction have not been high enough to justify proceeding. In 1993, for example, it decided not to proceed with a case against some white youths in the case of an alleged racially motivated murder of a black youth.

Another criticism is that already touched upon: the insensitivity of some judges in particular cases, notably rape cases. In 1993, for example, the Attorney General referred to the Court of Appeal a lenient sentence handed out by a judge in a case where a teenager had been convicted of the attempted rape of a 9-year-old girl. The judge had said that he received evidence that the girl in the case was 'no angel herself'. The comment attracted

Various proposals have been put forward for the enactment of a new Bill of Rights for the United Kingdom, entrenching fundamental rights in a way that cannot be changed by a simple parliamentary majority. The Labour Party has committed itself to the incorporation of the European Convention of Human Rights into British law. This would give rights some judicial protection but by itself would not provide for any formal entrenchment. The law could be changed by a later Parliament. Those who favour entrenchment wish to see this achieved by means such as extraordinary majorities in both Houses for example, requiring any subsequent amendment to receive a two-thirds majority of those voting.

The issue of an entrenched Bill of Rights has proved politically contentious. The principal arguments put forward both for and against such a Bill are as follows:

THE CASE FOR

■ **It would clarify and protect the rights of the individual:** Citizens would know precisely what their rights were (which at the moment they don't) and those rights would be protected by law.

■ **It would put interpretation in the hands of independent judges:** The rights would be interpreted and protected by judges, who are independent of the political process.

■ **It would prevent encroachment by politicians in government and Parliament:** Entrenchment would put the rights beyond the reach of a simple majority in both Houses of Parliament. Rights could not be treated like a political football, changing with every new government.

■ **It would prevent encroachment by other public bodies, such as the police:** Citizens would know their precise rights in relation to public bodies and would be able to seek judicial redress if those rights were infringed.

■ **It would ensure a greater knowledge of rights:** It would be an educative tool, citizens being much more rights-conscious.

■ **It would bolster confidence in the political system:** By knowing that rights were protected in this way, citizens would feel better protected and as such be more supportive of the political system.

THE CASE AGAINST

■ **It would confuse rather than clarify rights:** Bills of Rights are necessarily drawn in general terms and citizens would therefore have to wait until the courts interpreted the vague language in order to know precisely what is and what is not protected.

■ **It would transfer power from an elected to a non-elected body:** What are essentially political issues (e.g. abortion, capital punishment) would be decided by unelected judges and not by the elected representatives of the people.

■ **It would entrench rights that are the product of a particular generation:** It would entrench the rights of a particular time and make it difficult to get rid of them after their moral validity has been destroyed, as was the case with slavery in the United States.

■ **It would not necessarily prevent encroachment by public bodies:** Rights are better protected by the political culture of a society than by words written on a document.

■ **It would create a false sense of security:** There is a danger that people will believe that rights are fully protected when later interpretation by the courts may prove them wrong. Pursuing cases through the courts can be prohibitively expensive; often only big companies and rich individuals can use the courts to protect their interests.

■ **There is no agreement on the rights to be entrenched:** There is no agreement on the details of what should be included. Though there may be agreement at the most general level (e.g. the right to life), there is disagreement as to what these general rights actually mean — what does 'the right to life' mean in terms of abortion, euthanasia and the death penalty?

widespread and adverse criticism. The Appeal Court, while asserting that the judge had been quoted out of context, none the less condemned the sentence as inappropriate and increased it. An earlier case, in which another judge had awarded a young rape victim £500 to go on holiday to help forget about her experience, attracted even more condemnation. Such cases highlighted a problem that appears pervasive. A survey published in 1993 revealed that 40 per cent of sentences by circuit courts in rape cases were of four years or less, even though Appeal Court guidelines recommend that five years should be the starting point in contested rape cases. (The maximum sentence possible is life imprisonment.) Lenient sentences in a number of cases involving other offences also fuelled popular misgivings about the capacity of the courts to deliver appropriate sentences. In the 1993 MORI poll, 81 per cent of those questioned believed that 'the police are handicapped in the fight against crime by the criminal justice system'.

The courts also came in for challenge as a result of several cases of miscarriages of justice (see Mullin, 1996). In 1989, the 'Guildford Four', convicted in 1975 of bombings in Guildford, were released pending an inquiry into their original conviction; in 1990, the case of the Maguire family, convicted of running an IRA bomb factory, was referred back to the Appeal Court after the Home Secretary received evidence that the convictions could not be upheld; and in 1991, the 'Birmingham Six', convicted of pub bombings in Birmingham in 1974, were released after the Court of Appeal quashed their convictions. In November 1991, Winston Silcott, convicted for the murder of a police officer during a riot in 1985, also had his conviction quashed by the Appeal Court.

The judges involved in the original cases were variously criticised for being too dependent on the good faith of prosecution witnesses – as was the Court of Appeal. The Appeal Court came in for particular criticism for its apparent reluctance even to consider that there may have been miscarriages of justice. As late as 1988, the Court had refused an appeal by the Birmingham Six, doing so in terms that suggested that the Home Secretary should not even have referred the case to the Court. When the Birmingham Six had earlier sought to establish police malpractice by bringing a claim for damages,

the then Master of the Rolls, Lord Denning, had caused controversy by suggesting, in effect, that the exposure of injustice in individual cases was less important than preserving a façade of infallibility (Harlow, 1991, p. 98). By 1991, that façade of infallibility had been destroyed.

The standing both of the courts and of senior judges was impaired by the outcomes of these cases. In 1991, a hundred Labour MPs tabled a motion calling for the dismissal of Lord Lane, the Lord Chief Justice.

Various proposals have been advanced for reform of the judiciary and of the system of criminal justice. In 1992, the Conservative government appointed a Royal Commission on Criminal Justice. The Commission reported in July of the following year. It made 352 recommendations for change, among them for an independent body to refer cases of apparent miscarriages of justice to the Appeal Court. Not all the recommendations were widely welcomed and the government proved hesitant in taking up the proposals. Conservative politicians instead tended to stress the need for changes in judicial culture and a greater emphasis on deterrent sentencing. In 1996, the government introduced a Crime (Sentences) Bill to impose automatic life sentences for serious violent and sexual offenders and minimum mandatory sentences for persistent burglars and drug dealers, in effect restricting the discretion of judges in deciding periods of imprisonment. The Bill precipitated further clashes between the government and the judiciary, the Master of the Rolls, Lord Woolf, denouncing it in the House of Lords as a 'consitutional departure'. Conservatives have also been wary of allowing judges too great a say in public policy and have opposed demands for a Bill of Rights or the incorporation of the ECHR into British law.

The approach of the Labour Party in the early 1990s was to stress structural reforms. In its 1992 manifesto, it proposed the creation of a Department of Legal Administration but the proposal was dropped in 1995. It also favoured a judicial appointments and training commission, a proposal opposed by the judiciary which saw it as a threat to its independence. Given the criticisms of the proposal, it was not pursued. The emphasis has changed instead to sentencing policy – ensuring greater consistency and making sure that people know what sentencing practice is. Left-wing Labour MPs continue to press the case for significant structural reforms.

The Labour Party has also committed itself to the incorporation of the European Convention on Human Rights into British law. 'This will give the courts an increased constitutional role, moving them from the margins of the political process to the centre and increasing the underlying tension between the executive and the judiciary' (Woodhouse, 1996, p. 440). Though tension between courts and the executive in the 1980s and first half of the 1990s was seen by many as a consequence of a Conservative government falling foul of judicial activism, there was growing recognition on the Labour benches that such tension may not prove to be the preserve of a Conservative administration. As we have noted, various leading figures in the Labour Party have variously reminded judges of the supremacy of Parliament over the courts.

Chapter summary

Though not at the heart of the policy-making process in Britain, the courts are none the less actors in the political system. The doctrine of parliamentary sovereignty denies them the intrinsic power to strike down measures as being contrary to the provisions of the constitution, but their task of interpreting the law passed by Parliament – and determining whether public officials are acting within the powers granted by those laws – has ensured that they have a role in the political domain. A combination of growing concern on the part of judges about the powers of government and the constitutional implications of British membership of the European Community/Union has produced an activism on the part of the judiciary in Britain that has thrust the courts far more into that domain. The greater willingness of the courts to concern themselves in the determination of issues affecting public policy has alarmed politicians, fearful that policy-making power may slip from elected politicians to unelected judges. The failures of the courts to hand out sentences deemed appropriate by citizens, and their failure to avoid miscarriages of justice, has variously alarmed a wider community, resulting in a declining faith in the criminal justice system.

Discussion points

- Why should the courts be independent of government?

- What role is now played by judges as a result of Britain's membership of the European Community/Union?

- Can, and should, judges be drawn from a wider social background?

- Is the incorporation of the European Convention on Human Rights into British law a good idea?

Further reading

Basic introductions to the legal system can be found in student texts on constitutional and administrative law. Recent examples include Wade and Bradley (1993) and McEldowney (1994).

Works on the role of judges include Zander (1989), Waldron (1989) and the particularly pungent critique of Griffith (1994). Drewry (1991) addresses the question of judicial independence.

On the impact of the European Convention on Human Rights and membership of the EC/EU on British law, see Lester (1994). On the debate as to whether Britain needs a new Bill of Rights, see Norton (1982, Chapter 13) and the debate between Puddephatt (1995) and Gearty (1996).

References

Bradley, A.W. (1994) 'The sovereignty of Parliament – in perpetuity?', in J. Jowell and D. Oliver (eds), *The Changing Constitution*, 3rd edn (Oxford University Press).

Drewry, G. (1986) 'Judges and politics in Britain', *Social Studies Review*, November.

Drewry, G. (1991) 'Judicial independence in Britain: challenges real and threats imagined', in P. Norton (ed.), *New Directions in British Politics?* (Edward Elgar).

Gearty, C.A. (1996) 'An answer to "Legislating liberty: the case for a Bill of Rights" by Andrew Puddephatt', *The Journal of Legislative Studies*, Vol. 2, No. 2.

Griffith, J.A.G. (1994) *The Politics of the Judiciary*, 5th edn (Fontana).

Harlow, C. (1991) 'The legal system', in P. Catterall (ed.), *Contemporary Britain: An Annual Review* (Blackwell).

Lester, Lord (1994) 'European human rights and the British constitution', in J. Jowell and D. Oliver (eds), *The Changing Constitution*, 3rd edn (Oxford University Press).

McEldowney, J.F. (1994) *Public Law* (Sweet and Maxwell).

Mullin, C. (1996) 'Miscarriages of Justice', *The Journal of Legislative Studies*, Vol. 2, No. 2.

Munro, C. (1987) *Studies in Constitutional Law* (Butterworths).

Munro, C. (1992) '*Factortame* and the constitution', *Inter Alia*, Vol. 1, No. 1.

Norton, P. (1982) *The Constitution in Flux* (Blackwell).

Puddephatt, A. (1995) 'Legislating liberty: the case for a Bill of Rights', *The Journal of Legislative Studies*, Vol. 1, No. 1.

Scarman, Lord (1974) *English Law – The New Dimensions* (Stevens).

Wade, E.C.S. and Bradley, A.W. (1993) *Constitutional and Administrative Law*, 11th edn, ed. by A.W. Bradley and K.D. Ewing (Longman).

Waldron, J. (1989) *The Law* (Routledge).

Woodhouse, D. (1996) 'Politicians and the judges: a conflict of interest', *Parliamentary Affairs*, Vol. 49, No. 3.

Zander, M. (1989) *A Matter of Justice*, rev. edn (Oxford University Press).

CHAPTER TWENTYFOUR

The politics of law and order

BILL JONES

LEARNING OBJECTIVES

- To explain the connection between political ideas and the problem of law and order.

- To chart the extent of the problem and discuss the phenomenon of the 'crime wave' together with claims that it was reversed in the early 1990s.

- To consider the causes of crime.

- To examine responses to crime in the form of policing, penal policy, prisons and vigilantism.

INTRODUCTION

This chapter examines a political issue which affects everyone: crime and punishment. Opinion surveys show that concern on this topic has been steadily rising throughout the 1980s and 1990s as crime figures have soared and in some cases even exceeded American levels. This chapter examines the subject within the context of political ideas; assesses the extent of the current problem; discusses some of the probable causes of crime; looks at the contentious issue of policing and concludes with a look at sentencing, prisons and crime prevention, including vigilantism.

Law, order and political ideas

Ever since humankind began to live together over 9,000 years ago the question of law and order has been of central concern. Solitary cave dwellers did not need a code of law but any group of humans living in a community did. Fundamental to such a code was property. From the earliest times this included food, clothes, homes and utensils, joined later of course, by money, once it became a medium of exchange. Also highly important was physical safety – one of the reasons, after all, why people

lived together in the first place. The Babylonian king Hammurabi (d. 1750 BC) established a body of law famously based on the notion of retribution: 'an eye for an eye, a tooth for a tooth'; Islamic law tends to perpetuate such principles.

Legal systems in Western developed countries still seek to defend property and the person but an infinite variety of considerations have been embodied in pursuit of that elusive concept, 'justice'. Political thinkers have also wrestled with these problems. Aristotle recognised the necessity of law and governments which apply it with wisdom and justice. In the wake of the English Civil War, the philosopher Thomas Hobbes (see Chapter 7) rested his whole justification for the state on its ability to provide physical protection for citizens. Without such protection, he argued, life would be a brutal process of destructive anarchy. Conservative philosophers have always stressed the need for such protection, arguing that humans are inherently weak and unable to resist the lure of evil without the deterrent of strict state-imposed sanctions. Conservative Party policy still reflects this powerful emphasis: 'The Conservative Party has always stood for the protection of the citizen and the defence of the rule of law' (1992 manifesto).

Another group of philosophers approach the problem from a different angle. They argue that people are naturally inclined to be law-abiding and cooperative. They only transgress, so the argument runs, when their social environment damages them and makes deviation both inevitable and understandable. Foremost amongst these thinkers was Karl Marx, who attributed most of what was wrong with society to the corrupting and debilitating effect of a vicious capitalist economic system.

A kind of continuum is therefore recognisable: pessimists who see criminals as victims as well as perpetrators: and optimists who believe crime has roots in society which can be attacked and remedied by social action. In British politics the Tories have tended to occupy a position towards the pessimistic end of the spectrum and Labour the optimistic one.

In 1979 Margaret Thatcher made great play of how hers was the party of law and order. Studies have shown that this benefited her enormously in the election of that year. There is, moreover, reason to believe that most voters tend towards the pessimistic end of the spectrum and respond to tough remedies which harken back to Hammurabi if not the American Wild West. The Thatcherite analysis – still very influential in the Conservative Party – is that humans are basically weak and sinful creatures who need all the support of church, family, school and community to keep them on the straight and narrow. During the 1960s ('that third-rate decade', according to Norman Tebbit) Labour's overliberal approach tipped the balance of socialisation towards an absence of individual responsibility: parents were encouraged to slough off their responsibility in

favour of an insidiously vague concept of 'society' which took the blame for a whole portmanteau of things and destroyed the notion of 'personal accountability', that crucial binding quality in any functioning society. Consequently children grew up expecting and exercising free licence – 'doing their own thing' in the argot of the time – moving on to become juvenile offenders and then hardened criminals. *The Sunday Telegraph* neatly summarises the Thatcherite argument (15 August 1993):

> It is the very beliefs of those theorists [left-wing academics who maintain that crime is caused by social conditions] that are responsible for our present malaise. They preach, in a doctrine which first became prominent during the sixties but stretches back to Rousseau, that man is inherently good, and that he must cast off the chains of conventional behaviour and morality that enslave him.

The unlimited flow of immigrants, the argument continues, caused more tensions and contributed to crime, while the mob rule encouraged by militant trade union leaders further eroded belief in the rule of law.

Labour rejected this view of the world. Their Home Office spokesmen and -women preferred to concentrate on the roots of crime, which they believed lay in poor economic and social conditions. The first element of this is seen as the huge inequality between rich and poor which the free enterprise economic system invariably creates. Such social gulfs create anger and frustration: members of the favoured elite are able to progress smoothly through privileged education to highly paid and influential jobs. Meanwhile poor people face vastly inferior life chances and huge, often insurmountable, challenges if they wish to succeed. They are surrounded by images which equate personal value with certain symbols like expensive cars and clothes: when they cannot acquire them legally it is a small step to break the law to redress the balance. So the system itself causes crime by encouraging people to want things which they have to steal to acquire. When they do not the result is often poverty and hopelessness: the breeding ground of crime for successive generations of people at the bottom of the pile. Left-wingers also point at how the law favours the rich and protects their property, imprisoning petty burglars and letting off city fraudsters with suspended sentences or fines.

Interestingly, the positions of both major parties began to converge in the early 1990s. The Tories had long insisted that social conditions were not connected with crime: how else did figures stay stable during the Depression years of the 1930s? However, the massive increase in crime during the 1980s and early 1990s and a series of studies by the Home Office (especially those of Simon Field, who plotted graphs of property crime and consumption in 1900–88, finding a close correlation between unemployment and theft) encouraged a change of heart. Eventually the government abandoned this untenable position: on 28 October 1992 Home Office minister Michael Jack accepted that recession had played its part in pushing up the crime figures, saying that downturns in the economy were traditionally accompanied by increases in crime.

For its part Labour responded to the spate of fearsome juvenile crime in 1993 by expressing a tougher line on sentencing and the treatment of young offenders. The two big parties, especially with Kenneth Clarke as Home Secretary and Tony Blair as Shadow Home Secretary ('tough on crime – tough on the causes of crime'), found a surprising amount upon which to agree. This is not to say that there are not differences. *The Sunday Telegraph* (15 August 1993) reported a plan by the government to privatise secure homes for young offenders: Labour condemned the plan.

As the 1997 election approached, both parties targeted crime as a campaign priority, adopting tough postures on handguns and combat knives in the autumn of 1996 for example. Indeed Michael Howard, the populist Conservative Home Secretary, sought to play to the right-wing gallery in his own party; what was more surprising was that his Labour shadow, Jack Straw, sought to match him and even exceed him in right-wing zeal, so sensitive had the opposition become to the need to attract floating votes, especially middle-class ones, in order to end eighteen long years out of power.

The extent of the problem

The BBC *Panorama* programme on 2 August 1993 revealed how widespread the perception of crime is in the UK. In a study commissioned by the BBC, majorities were found who had been burgled in the previous year and who expected to be burgled

again. Crime is ubiquitous and all-pervading. Many people can recall a different era when it was safe to leave a car unlocked for half an hour or more or to leave doors unlocked at night. Not now. In 1979 the number of notifiable offences was 2.5 million; by 1993 it had increased to 5.7 million (see Figure 24.1 and Table 24.1): a 128 per cent increase in fourteen years.

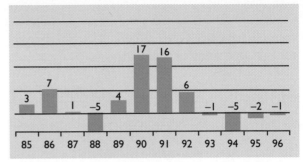

Figure 24.1 Notifiable offences recorded by the police: percentage change from previous year
Source: Home Office data in *The Guardian*, 27 March 1996

Table 24.1 Notifiable offences recorded by the police by offence

England and Wales	Number of offences (thousands) and percentages		
			Changes(1)
Offence group	1995	1996	Percentage
Violence against the person	212.6	239.1	+12.5% (−2.6%)
Sexual offences	30.3	31.2	+3.2% (−5.3%)
Robbery	68.1	74.0	+8.6% (+13.4%)
Total violent crime	*310.9*	*344.3*	*+10.7% (+0.2%)*
Burglary	1,239.5	1,164.4	−6.1% (−1.4%)
Total theft & handling stolen goods	2,452.1	2,383.0	−2.8% (−4.4%)
Vehicle crime	*1,321.5*	*1,292.7*	*−2.2% (−4.5%)*
Fraud and forgery	133.0	135.9	+2.2% (−8.4%)
Criminal damage	914.0	950.7	+4.0% (−1.5%)
Total property crime	*4,738.6*	*4,633.9*	*−2.2% (−3.2%)*
Other notifiable offences	50.7	55.6	+9.6% (+6.2%)
Total all offences	5,100.2	5,033.8	−1.3% (−2.9%)

(1) Change between 1994 and 1995 in brackets.
Source: Home Office Statistics, March 1997

Sex crimes represented only 5 per cent of the total but violent crimes as a whole have displayed a worrying increase over the last decade (up 12 per cent in 1996 on 1995), especially those involving firearms. Over half of all recorded crimes were either thefts of or from vehicles (28 per cent) or burglary (24 per cent) (see Figure 24.2). Indeed, according to the British Crime Survey 1992, 94 per cent of all notified crimes were against property while 5 per cent were crimes of violence. A house in the UK is broken into once every thirty seconds, and even allowing for some reductions in the rate of increase, a 6 per cent annual increase – the current average for the industrialised world – will double the overall crime rate by 2004. At the end of the 1970s the police cleared up 40 per cent of all crime; this rate has fallen to one-quarter. The annual percentage change grew rapidly during the early 1980s, then dipped reassuringly later in the decade, only to take off again in 1989–90. Even worse, the Home Office-sponsored British Crime Surveys in recent years suggest that nearly three times as many crimes are committed as are reported; up to half of all burglaries may not be reported, even more cases of vandalism and sex offences.

Conservative spokesmen are at pains to minimise the rate of crime increase: they do not want voters to think there has been no return for all the money spent on law and order since 1979. The party's *Campaign Guide* in 1997 played the international comparison card:

Since 1945 the general trend in crime in Western countries has been upward. However, in the years 1993–5, England and Wales ... had the largest fall in recorded crime – 8% – of any of the 18 OECD countries .... In Amsterdam there are ... 84 murders per million people; in Stockholm 54 per million; in Berlin 39 per million. The homicide rate for London was 22 murders per million people in 1995.

The 1992 International Crime Survey for England and Wales revealed a lower rate of theft victims

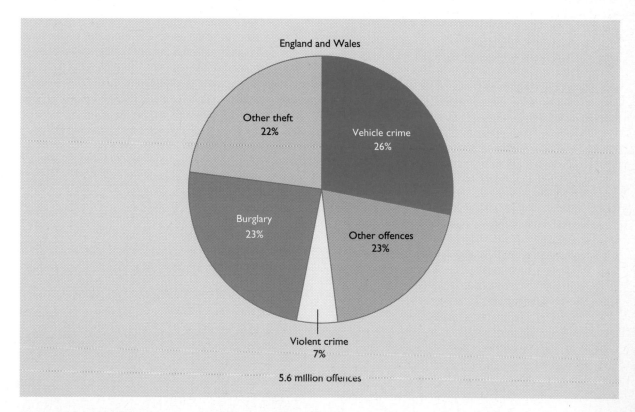

Figure 24.2 Notifiable offences recorded by the police, 1996
Source: Home Office, 1996

than Germany, Switzerland, Finland, the USA and Australia. Moreover, the same survey showed that in terms of violent assault the home figures were well below those of (surprisingly) The Netherlands, Germany, the USA and Australia. Some criminologists point out that the 'crime wave' is a statistical concept and like all statistics can be easily misunderstood:

1. It is not the volume but the proportion of certain crimes being reported which has increased in some cases. More people have reported burglaries because many more people now have property insurance as well as telephones.
2. The majority of crime is very trivial, perhaps involving no damage or derisory sums of a pound or two.
3. Britain used to be much more violent than it is today, as the work of E.G. Dunning from Leicester University has demonstrated. In thirteenth-century Britain, historians estimate there were twenty murders committed for every 100,000 people: seventeen times today's rate.
4. The huge increase in police manpower since 1979 has boosted the ability of the police to record crimes which before might have been omitted.
5. The publicity given to crime figures can mask the fact that Britain is still a country where the chances of being mugged are slightly less than once every five centuries; or sustaining an injury from an assault once every century. In this respect Britain is much safer than Germany, the USA or Australia.

Conservative claims to have reversed the crime wave

Just when the Conservative government must have been despairing of what to do about crime and had seen its lead over Labour of 40–26 reversed to a 23–29 deficit, the crime statistics of 1993–4 came to the rescue. They showed a drop of 5 per cent on the previous year and the 1994–5 figures showed a similar decline, though the 1995 figures registered only a 2.4 per cent fall (see Figure 24.1). Michael Howard claimed jubilantly that his get-tough policies were finally winning through and the 1994 party conference – containing grey-haired old ladies

who want to bring back the birch – applauded him to the echo. *The Economist* (23 September 1995), however, would not believe a word of it. The right-of-centre journal pointed out the following:

1. Unemployment had been falling and even official Home Office studies proved a causal connection between levels of unemployment and crime rates.
2. Most crimes are committed by young men aged between 15 and 24; between 1989 and 1993 their number declined from 4.5 million to 4 million.
3. Some police forces have been targeting groups of hardened criminals, e.g. the Met's pre-emptive Bumblebee and Eagle Eye Operations. It could be they have borne some fruit.
4. Better anti-theft devices on cars could also have had a slowing down effect on vehicle crime, which fell by 10 per cent between 1993 and 1994.

On 23 April 1997 *The Guardian's* feature on crime reported:

The crime figures … have masked a steady rise in crime since 1991. As the British Crime survey [BCS, recording the experiences of victims of crime] shows, fewer than half the crimes committed are reported to the police and only half those that are reported are recorded. This means that even small changes in reporting or recording rates will produce artificial changes in the rates of recorded crime. As [Figure 24.3] shows, the trends in both the BCS – up 83% – and the police figures – up 91% – were almost identical between 1981 and 1995. The BCS trend shows a steady increase over the 15 years. The police figures however show a more rapid rise until 1991 and then a fall. The reason for the rise in the police figures is that the proportion of crime reported to the police rose by 10% from 1981 to 1991.

As the little publicised central finding of the BCS concluded, the reason for the fall is that police recording practices changed: a significantly smaller proportion of crimes reported to the police found their way into recorded police statistics in 1995 than in 1991.

The article concluded that this change was caused not by better policing but by the pressure put on the police to demonstate their effectiveness in politically significant statistical form. This did not stop Michael Howard claiming a 10 per cent drop in crime since 1991 in a campaign statement on 21 April 1997.

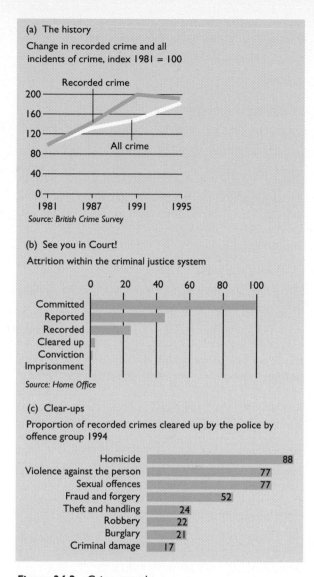

(a) The history

Change in recorded crime and all incidents of crime, index 1981 = 100

Source: British Crime Survey

(b) See you in Court!

Attrition within the criminal justice system

Source: Home Office

(c) Clear-ups

Proportion of recorded crimes cleared up by the police by offence group 1994

Figure 24.3 Crime trends
Source: *The Guardian*, 23 April 1997

The criminal mind

❝ In the long term criminals adapt to the changing environment by concentrating on less detectable offences such as drug abuse and perhaps fraud. What we have to realise is that persistent criminals are entrepreneurial in character. Their antennae are constantly twitching to ensure they can operate in the most profitable manner.

Sir John Smith, deputy head of Metropolitan Police, 1995 ❞

Fear of crime

Considerable concern has been expressed over the fear of crime which so much lurid publicity engenders. Newspapers know that the public has a morbid interest in crime stories and consequently feed it in order to sell copies. The result is that elderly ladies are terrified to go out even though they are the category least at risk from violent crime. Interviews with 10,000 women for the 1994 British Crime Survey revealed that one in five felt 'very unsafe' when walking out at night, even though fewer than seventy claimed to have been attacked in the past year (see Figure 24.4). Paradoxically, young males living in inner city areas are least afraid yet most likely to be the victims of crime. Indeed, the inner cities seem to be the breeding ground of a great deal of crime and their working-class denizens most likely to be the victims. Similarly, a professional person is 50 per cent less likely to be burgled than an unskilled worker.

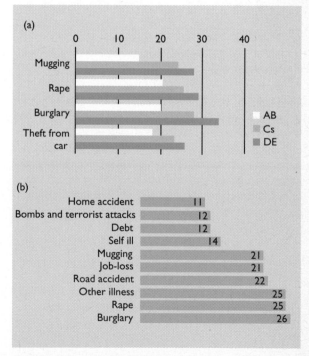

Figure 24.4 Fear of crime
(a) Percentage by social class of people who said they were 'very worried' about crime
(b) Context of crime and other fears: percentage of those 'very worried'
Source: British Crime Survey data in *The Guardian*, 11 January 1996

The position of the inner cities as the headquarters of crime has slipped, however. A report in *The Guardian* (12 December 1992) revealed that the biggest increases since 1979 occurred in the shires: 167 per cent in Gloucestershire; 166 per cent in Leicestershire; 160 per cent in Avon and Somerset; and 146 per cent in Norfolk. In fact more crime is now committed in rural areas (56 per cent) than in urban areas (44 per cent). Nevertheless, the inner areas of the cities are still the most prone to crime. The 1992 British Crime Survey revealed that the poorest council estates face a risk of burglary 2.8 times the average.

Patterns of offending

One longitudinal survey of all people born in 1953 revealed that by the age of 30 one in three men had been convicted of a crime; one in sixteen had been to prison; and, significantly, the 7 per cent who had been convicted six or more times accounted for two-thirds of all offences. The survey also showed violence was on the increase: one in eight men convicted of an offence had committed a crime of violence by the age of 20. For those born in 1963 the proportion had risen to one in five. Certainly young criminals seem to abound. Most crimes are committed by people aged 14 to 20; at a 1993 conference it was revealed that 93 per cent of young offenders are regular drug users. Over 90 per cent of all 15- to 16-year-old offenders reoffend within four years. On 20 November 1996 the Audit Commission reported on juvenile justice. Its document, *Misspent Youth*, revealed that: the 150,000 teenage offenders commit some 7 million crimes every year, of which only 19 per cent are recorded by police and only 5 per cent cleared up with a mere 3 per cent resulting in arrest and action. Moreover, there is a demographic 'crime bomb' in the making as the population begins to bulge in the 18- to 20-year-old age group, now the peak age of offending for young men.

Whatever the qualifications one has to apply to crime figures there is no doubt as to which way they are heading: constantly upwards. All the crime surveys show that the public is highly aware that crime is a ubiquitous threat. As Walter Ellis wrote in *The Sunday Telegraph* (4 July 1993):

For the public ... crime has become a lottery, a prize draw in which the odds of becoming a victim are shortening every day. To those who have been burgled for the fourth time, or seen their car driven off by a 15-year-old, or been mugged for 50p outside a kebab house the ergonomics of policing are only of passing importance. Ordinary people want to feel safe in their own streets.

Causes of crime

Some of the causes of crime have already been touched on. Politicians, it has been shown, argue either that people have become, or have been allowed to become, less law-abiding, more 'evil' even, or that society has become a forcing ground of such deviancy. Inevitably causes are chosen to conform with political prejudices, but there are other possible causes.

The huge gap which exists between rich and poor

One view is that all forms of private property constitute a form of theft, that all property by rights belongs to everyone. According to this view, everyone who is rich has 'appropriated' their property from others, leading to the position espoused by the American radical Angela Davis: 'The real criminals in this society are not the people who populate the prisons across the state but those who have stolen the wealth of the world from the people.' A less articulate version of this justification was offered by a Liverpudlian youth in a *Weekend World* programme broadcast in December 1987: 'Some people have got jobs, they can go out and buy things they want. But we're on the dole, we haven't got the money so we go out robbing to get the money.' It remains a fact that the gap between rich and poor in Britain over the last fifteen years has grown faster than in any other developed Western country.

There are now so many more potential crimes

In the old days family arguments were ignored by police as 'domestics'. Since the law has changed, crimes of violence have registered an increase. Furthermore, the proliferation of consumer goods has increased the opportunity for crime: there are simply more things to steal, especially valuable portable objects.

BOX 24.1 EXAMPLE

Approved training to become a criminal

When Denis was 12, the police found him sitting in a parked stolen car: 'I hadn't nicked it, I had no idea how to drive.' He was sent to an approved school near Dundee, 'a big house which had been converted'. Some of the children were not offenders at all, but the victims of abuse: the youngest, who lived in their own cottage, were only five. There was a little education: basic English and maths, but plenty of sport, including swimming, football and table tennis.

'More often than not, we were left to ourselves in the dorms,' Denis said. 'There was no counselling, no one to talk to about my experiences, what I had witnessed. When I was 10, I saw my stepfather smash a full bottle of Scotch over someone's head and split it open, and stab another person in the eye.

'I was in shock most of the time. I was stuck in a place where all the kids were as fucked up as I was, and these staff had to control us. Yes, we had our activities, our games, our visits to the swimming baths. They gave us merit badges when we were good. But there was no love there, no emotional growth. It was an institution, my first prison.'

The fourteen months Denis spent at approved school laid the foundations for what was to follow. He said: 'I learnt everything about crime there. I did my first burglary one night when I ran away. I learnt how to drive, how to steal a car; how to fight and how to lie and get away with it. It made me what I am, it was where the criminal subculture started. We got together there and formed relationships because we had nothing else.'

After leaving, he went on the run, living rough in squats, before eventually rejoining his mother at her new home near Manchester. 'By then the die was cast. I was a criminal.'

At the age of 15, Denis was arrested for stealing a car, he was sent to DC, a detention centre in Nottinghamshire. It was the 'short, sharp shock'.

'They turned us into little tough guys,' he said. 'There was circuit training every day, and a lot of physical abuse from the staff. And again, you met all the lads, who'd been to approved school, through the courts system, who were already dreaming of a career in the big time.'

'And the more they tell you you're bad, you're a criminal, the more you accept it and get on with it. At DC, kids were already seeing themselves as gangsters. That's where you made your connections, and found out what families from what areas are into what type of crime, and how to sell your goods.'

'Afterwards, it was like the Vietnam syndrome: you're only drawn to those who've suffered the same trauma, the same experience. So your only pals are the people you met in DC.'

Two months after leaving, aged just 15, Denis was in Strangeways for the first time, waiting to be sent for fifteen months to a borstal, convicted of burglary, criminal damage and car theft. 'It was more of the same. You met the lads you'd met in DC, all the same faces.' At 17, after further burglaries, he was back in Strangeways, this time for a year.

Then, for a while, the pattern seemed broken. Denis married and worked as a welder. But it was not easy to build a settled life. 'You were always involved in a bit of "dodge" because you always got phone calls from your pals. The underworld is always there, still thriving.'

He lost one job when a colleague told management he had been to prison. Then his marriage broke up, precipitating a period of drug abuse, and armed robbery seemed like 'a natural progression, the pinnacle of my career'.

Prison education saved him :'It was a route into myself, I discovered my mind and another world. Up to that point I'd been told by my mother, by the courts, by prison, that I was mad, bad.'

Now preparing to begin a law degree at Bristol University, he has a stark message for Mr Major and Mr Clarke [the then Home Secretary]. 'They frighten me to death, because they don't have a clue what they are doing. They need to break the circle, stop the abuse. The prisons are where Great Britain hides from its inner self. They are full of the educational system's mistakes, the mental hospitals' mistakes, the courts' mistakes. That's why I want to practise law.'

Source: The Observer, 28 February 1993

Young people are faced with a difficult world in which to grow up

1. Many of them are increasingly the products of fragmented families and have lacked the emotional security of a proper home.
2. Long-term unemployment has replaced valuable socialisation with despair. As a consequence young people lose out, as American sociologist Charles Murray (1990) observes, on 'acquiring skills and the network of friends and experiences that enable them to establish a place for themselves – not only in the workplace but a vantage point from which they can make sense of themselves and their lives' (p. 25).
3. As a consequence of unemployment, youngsters find life infinitely grey and pointless. Crime can seem like the ultimate rebellion and excitement. John Purves, a solicitor who has defended many young joy-riders in the north-west and the north-east, explains that it 'provides an escape from their humdrum existences. They are thrilled by the speed of these flying machines and the more dangerous it gets the more excited they become. It's an addiction. ... The press call them "deathriders"; that's the real thrill' (*Observer*, 25 June 1994).

Growth of an underclass

Charles Murray, quoted above, has written that he thinks the UK is well on the way to developing its own underclass of disaffected poor living in the inner cities, often in council housing and unemployed, eking out their lives on benefits and crime. Any youngster living in such an area finds it very difficult to resist the allure and rewards of crime and the attractions of drugs, easy living and violence.

Values have declined

This view is especially popular with Conservatives, who harken back to a golden age when it was possible to live without fear of crime. Geoff Pearson's book *Hooligan* disposes of this myth:

Conservatives have enthused about this mythical law abiding society 20 years ago for decades. Twenty years ago, in fact, they were just as worried about crime and disorderly youth as they are now, panicked by hippies in the late sixties and early

seventies, by Teds in the fifties and 'Americanised youth' in the forties.

Responses to crime

Policing

If, as Hobbes asserted, the prime purpose of government is the preservation of law and order, then the police, in modern society, are at the cutting edge of enforcement: they implement the most important thrust of government. Figure 24.5 shows police numbers in the years 1964–93.

The police occupy an ambivalent and politically sensitive role in society. According to classic democratic theory they are the neutral instruments of society, acting, as Sir Robert Mark (Commissioner of the Metropolitan Police in the 1970s) observed, 'not ... at the behest of a minister or any political party, not even the party in government. We act on behalf of the people as a whole.'

However, the police command great power in society and there are plenty of examples of how they have become the creatures of a particular political ideology or the willing instruments of oppression: Nazi Germany, the USSR, Red China and many regimes in South America and elsewhere. In Britain,

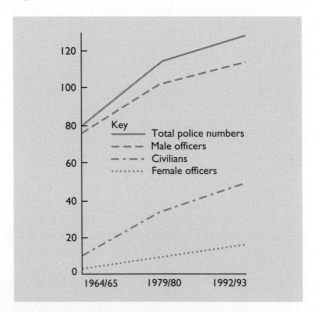

Figure 24.5 Police numbers in England and Wales (thousands)
Source: *The Guardian*, 12 October 1993

the police have traditionally been thought to be a source of national pride: the 'friendly bobby on his beat' being an international symbol of our social stability and consensual style. However, as crime figures rose in the 1970s and the right-wing policies of Thatcherism began to be implemented in the early 1980s, the police became a subject of intense political debate. The left accused Thatcher of using the police to suppress public reaction to her unpopular and socially divisive policies. The police were also seen as willing accomplices, weighed down with right-wing prejudices like contempt for the poor, ethnic minorities and women, and riddled with corruption and criminal inefficiencies of the kind which caused miscarriages of justice like the Guildford Four and the Birmingham Six.

Is there any proof of these left-wing allegations? A report by the Policy Studies Institute (PSI) in the late 1980s revealed widespread racist and sexist attitudes together with frequent drunkenness on duty. Reiner (1993) reports that one of his studies revealed that 80 per cent of officers questioned described themselves as Conservatives, with the remainder equally divided between Labour and Liberals (p. 123). He also cites substantial evidence from the UK and US supporting the contention that police routinely subscribe to racist views (pp. 125–8). However, these research findings should be qualified: British police seem no worse than similar forces in the USA and Canada; and the same PSI report revealed that the large majority of Londoners were satisfied with the service provided.

The right preferred to see the police as staunch defenders of society, beleaguered by attacks from the left and misguided 'do-gooders'. The eccentric chief constable of Greater Manchester, James Anderton, even believed at one time that the left planned to undermine the whole edifice of police neutrality in preparation for the totalitarian state they craved (Reiner, 1993). Throughout the 1980s debate over the police was highly polarised, particularly during the 1984–5 miners' strike when Labour accused the government of trying surreptitiously to establish a national police system antithetical to the notion of community service and accountability. Towards the end of the decade, however, the manifest failure of the police to stem the increase in crime led to a change of heart on the right. This was occasioned partly by the publicity given to miscarriages of justice

and the spate of lawlessness typified by joy-riders operating with apparent impunity while the police seemed to stand idly by. All this helped create an unprecedented fall in public esteem for the apparatus of law enforcement. Writing in *The Sunday Times* (11 February 1989), journalist Simon Jenkins wrote:

> *No area of public policy is in such dire need of reform as crime. … Crime is the Passchendale of Whitehall. The more money wasted on fighting it the more is demanded by the generals for 'just one more push'.*

On 10 February 1989 *The Economist* quoted a disillusioned Tory MP who said: 'In my opinion the police need a jolly good kick up the backside. They get jolly well paid and they're not much good at catching criminals.'

On the value for money criterion so much beloved by the Conservatives, the police had indeed become an embarrassment. Between 1979 and 1993 spending on the police rose by 88 per cent (£5.4 billion per year) and police pay by 70 per cent in real terms (at 127,000, numbers have doubled since 1950) (see Figure 24.6). Yet crime figures have more than doubled and become a national obsession which no politician can ignore. In September 1993, even the chief of the new National Criminal Intelligence Service was moved to describe the entire criminal justice system as 'archaic and irrelevant'.

Figures support the latter contention: in the late 1970s the percentage of crimes cleared up was 40 per cent; by 1993 it had dropped to 25 per cent (see Figure 24.3c, though note the rates vary according to category of crime). For their part the police complain that the demands upon them to be fair to the criminal and to defend civil liberties has placed an excessive burden upon their activities. They complain of a multitude of forms they have to fill in for any offence. On 22 September 1993, *The Guardian* reported a case in which paperwork weighed an astonishing 45 tons. The figures for 1992 reveal that indeed 16 per cent of their time is spent writing reports; 11 per cent on station duties; 5 per cent traffic incidents; 10 per cent each crime incidents and traffic control; 22 per cent preventive patrol; and 26 per cent other duties. In total 75 per cent of police time is spent on non-crime matters.

On 26 June 1993 *The Economist* ran a story that in many parts of London the police had simply 'given up', letting criminals off with a caution

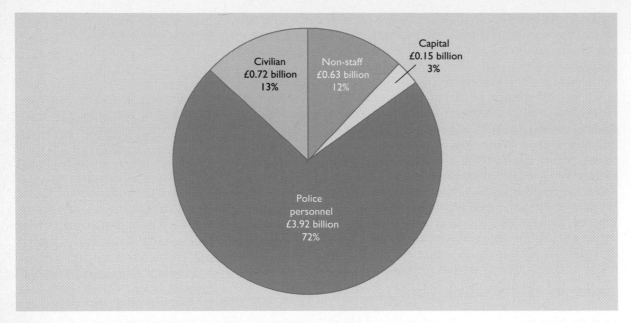

Figure 24.6   Expenditure on the police in England and Wales, 1992–3
Source: The Guardian, 12 October 1993

rather than face the excessive paperwork and the good chance the criminal will get off with a light sentence. Writing in *The Daily Telegraph* on 20 July 1993 Roger Graef observed: 'The net effect of victims not reporting crimes and police not recording or detecting them is that only two out of every hundred crimes are punished in court.' As if to compound these fears, an Audit Commission report leaked to *The Guardian* on 20 September 1993 recommended that police forces should prioritise responses to crime, concentrating on the important ones at the expense of the trivial, handing over the latter to uniformed officers while the CID addressed major crime and criminals.

Following the inner city riots in the early 1980s, the Scarman Report urged closer cooperation with local communities and more bobbies on the beat. Some of these recommendations were implemented and the spirit of Scarman permeated thinking on police policy in the 1980s. However, concern with management structures and value for money led to the production of an even more contentious report in 1993, produced by Sir Patrick Sheehy, a businessman.

The Sheehy Report pointed to a 'top-heavy' rank structure with overlapping responsibilities and 'inefficient' management systems plus a promotion system based on service rather than merit. Recom-

mendations included:

1. The abolition of three senior ranks, including senior inspector, senior superintendent and deputy chief constable. Up to 60 per cent of spending in some forces goes on management; if this change happens, 5,000 officers would lose their jobs over the next three years.
2. The scrapping of linked pay award increases.
3. Fixed-term (possibly ten-year) contracts – police officers currently have jobs for life.
4. Performance-related pay and less generous sick pay arrangements.

The Police Federation was incensed, described the proposals as 'outrageous' and even organised a massive demonstration in July 1993 involving 15,000 officers. It took out an advert featuring former Labour Prime Minister Lord Callaghan (who used to represent the Federation when a back-bench MP) which stated:

The Sheehy Report is a series of dogmatic conclusions backed by very little argument and based on inaccurate analysis of the problem. The attitude of its authors can be guessed from the comment 'the time is ripe for taking on the boys and girls in blue'. Such an attitude will command no respect either in the Police Service or among the public, and rules out the Report as a serious document.

In the light of such criticism, Michael Howard, the Home Secretary, agreed late in 1993 to discount some of the most contentious Sheehy proposals.

Penal policy

Speaking in 1985 Margaret Thatcher told the American Bar Association of the fear of ordinary people that 'too many sentences do not fit the crime'. Given the provenance of her own ideas (see above), it is hardly surprising that she thought sentences should be higher, and indeed between 1984 and 1987 sentences for serious crimes like armed robbery and rape increased markedly (see Table 24.2).

However, despite the invariable rhetoric of Conservative candidates during elections and the well-publicised views of Margaret Thatcher, the death penalty for murder was not reintroduced under the Tories despite several attempts by diehard 'hangers'. On 8 June 1988 the vote went 341 votes (in the traditional free vote on this issue) to 218. The truth seems to be that however hard candidates try to milk the two-thirds majority of the public in favour of the death penalty, when they hear the arguments and statistics coolly explained in parliamentary debates they surrender to reason and vote to sustain abolition. The facts show that, at fewer than 700 a year, Britain has a relatively small number of murders (the USA has over 20,000); there is no evidence to suggest that murders have increased since abolition; reintroduction would impose immense burdens on judges and juries; affairs like the Guildford Four and the Birmingham Six show how easy it is for innocent people to be

Table 24.2 Crown court sentences (average: adult male)

	1984	1987	% increase
Using firearms to resist arrest	3.4	6.7	97
Rape	3.8	6.2	63
Robbery with firearms[a]	5.7	7.0	23
Robbery without firearms	3.1	3.8	23
Indecent assault on a female	2.0	2.3	15
Manslaughter	4.9	5.5	12

Note: [a] Offenders charged with firearm offences at same court appearance.

found guilty of murder, and when they have been executed it is too late to make amends.

Prisons

Since the Strangeways prison riots in 1990, prisons have been at the centre of an intense debate. Denying a malefactor his/her freedom has been a traditional form of punishment ever since law and order was invented. In the early days conditions in prisons were horrendous, with no sanitation and appalling food. Since then conditions have improved immensely but denial of freedom is still a very punitive measure. Some experts argue persuasively that prison is counterproductive. They argue that prison is merely a place where new crimes are learnt and planned and young petty offenders turned into serious criminals – 'the universities of crime'. It is sadly true that 60 per cent of prisoners reoffend within two years. These experts also point out that only a small percentage of those locked up – perhaps 10 per cent – are serious offenders: the majority are there on minor offences against property.

The notion of rehabilitation is sometimes overlooked when we discuss prisons. Punishment is seen as the chief rationale – and we punish more extensively by custodial sentences than any other country in Europe: only South Africa and the USA imprison more. Prison sentences are also expensive: it costs £450 per week (£1.6 billion per year) to keep someone in prison, much more in many cases than has been stolen in the first place.

During the 1980s, it became apparent that our prisons were grossly overcrowded: in one case, a maximum prison capacity of 40,000 prisoners was being forced to accommodate, in the mid-1980s, 55,729, many squeezed two or three to a cell and without any proper sanitation. Even William Whitelaw was moved to describe our prisons as 'an affront to civilised society'. The Strangeways riots, and related riots in other prisons, were to some extent an explosion of pent-up frustration at poor conditions and official indifference. In response came the impressive Woolf Report (600 pages, 204 recommendations) urging a fundamental reform of prison regimes to ensure that they prepared inmates for release by treating them with dignity and respect. The report was endorsed by all three parties in the 1992 general election but has yet to be implemented.

Towards the end of the 1980s the prison population began to decline (45,693 in 1989) as more non-custodial sentences like community service orders were passed, but this did not mean that all was well. A report by Judge Stephen Tumin, the head of the prison service, discovered that in some prisons inmates had to wait ten days for a shower and even longer for clean underwear. Post-Strangeways changes, moreover, did not stop another serious riot breaking out in September 1993 in Wymott prison, Lancashire. Here prisoners ran amok causing £20 million worth of damage to a prison which had been held up as a model regime. Judge Tumin was appointed to investigate, the irony being that in 1991 Tumin had already reported on Wymott discerning widespread drug taking and the permeation of 'a gangland culture'.

The Labour opposition and the Prison Officers' Association heavily criticised the Conservative government and Michael Howard, the Home Secretary, for concentrating all his efforts not on solving present problems but seeking to privatise as many prisons as he could in order, according to his critics, to satisfy the right wing of his own party.

BOX 24.2   **IDEAS AND PERSPECTIVES**

Howard's measures to curb crime

At the 1993 Conservative Party conference in Blackpool, Home Secretary Michael Howard unveiled 'the most comprehensive programme of action against crime' announced in Britain, including: abolition of the right to silence for defendants; new measures against terrorism; tougher penalties for persistent young offenders; building six new prisons; new powers to evict squatters and for police to stop trespassers; automatic custody for anyone convicted of rape, manslaughter or murder or attempting the offence who is subsequently accused of any of these crimes; a review to toughen sentences in the community; accepting all sixteen proposals of review on cutting paperwork to let police do more active duties.

Howard told the conference:

There is a tidal wave of concern about crime in this country. I am not going to ignore it. I am going to take action. Tough action.

The reaction to Howard's line was not, however, as warm outside the conference chamber as it was within. Lord Justice Woolf threw in a firecracker when he said publicly that these 'get tough' policies would not work and were 'short-sighted' and irresponsible'. On 17 October

1993 *The Observer* led with the views of no fewer than seven judges, all of whom attacked the idea asserted by Howard that 'prison works' through taking criminals off the street and providing a deterrent to others.

Lord Ackner said the causes of crime 'lay deep in society, in the deterioration of personal standards, the family and the lack of self-discipline'. Lord Justice Farquharson, chairman of the Judicial Studies Board, said:

I cannot understand why the population of people in prison in this country is greater than in others. I think that's wrong .... My general philosophy is that you should never impose a prison sentence when you can avoid it. The idea that we are building more and more prisons appals me. I have never believed prison rehabilitates anyone.

Lord Bruce Laughland was even more explicit:

The effectiveness of the deterrent diminishes the more an individual goes to prison. People fear hearing the gates shut behind them for the first time. Prison may satisfy public opinion and the victims' understandable feelings, but it has no rehabilitation effect whatsoever ... a great deal of dishonesty is contributed by politicians.

Certainly, he marked a shift towards a more punitive philosophy, urging less recreation and more sewing of mailbags, arguing that 'prisoners enjoy a standard of comfort which taxpayers would find hard to understand'.

In September 1993, a new programme of prison privatisation was announced: twelve contracts to be awarded for new prisons within two years. Howard declared the aim was to 'create a private sector able to secure continuing and lasting improvements in standards, quality and cost efficiency across the whole of the prison system'. Despite encouraging experience of private prisons in the USA (see Windlesham, 1993, pp. 280–6), experience in the UK had been mixed. The success of the in-house bid by Strangeways staff was hailed by the government. But the privately run Wolds prison had been criticised in April 1992 by the Prison Reform Trust for creating a life for inmates which was 'boring and aimless with evidence of widespread violence and drug abuse'. The contracting out of court escort services to Group 4 Security (a director of which embarrassingly turned out to be Sir Norman Fowler, then Chairman of the Conservative Party) became a laughing stock in 1993 when a succession of prisoners escaped.

The Conservatives were not consistent on prison policy in the 1980s. In the early part of the decade they pandered to their activists by being tough and the prisons filled up; towards the end of the decade they supported non-custodial sentences, but as crime grew relentlessly the gut instinct to get tough again could not be resisted and Michael Howard adopted his 'prison works' approach (see boxes 24.2 and 24.3). His policy was much criticised by prison reform groups (but not by police organisations) as likely to increase prison populations by 15,000 new inmates and cost up to £700,000. In April 1996 the population stood at 54,974, rising to nearly 60,000 in only 1997.

Alternatives to prison are often mooted but community service orders are often seen by the public as being too mild a corrective for violent young offenders. Indeed it is young offenders who pose the most intractable problem. It often seems that the problem begins with broken homes, leading to institutionalised children who grow up without any real affection. This often leads to misbehaviour in school with truanting and then petty crime. Once on the elevator of crime and detention centre the child is lost to the alternative values of the criminal world where all means to better oneself are acceptable as long as one is not caught. The Audit Commission's report, cited above, judges that money spent on

---

BOX 24.3 **IDEAS AND PERSPECTIVES**

On the report by Sir David Ramsbottom, Chief Inspector of Prisons

Sir David's report does not finger particular prisons, but the news from one one of London's tougher nicks is that the cuts are affecting the regime. The number of probation officers, who work with prisoners to stop them being anti-social, and to help rehabilitate them, is down from 14 to 3. Funding for education has been cut by 55%. Modern languages have been dropped, as has a vocational course for music technicians, almost all art and half of English and maths. Education is down to basic numeracy and literacy. The annual plays which Wandsworth used to put on for

the general public have been dropped, 'Wandsworth is warehousing prisoners', says one insider.

Mr Howard insists that 'prison works' and that it does not do to be 'soft' on prisoners. But he might note that, according to volumes of research, education works. There are more than 500 pieces of international research on prison regimes. Most of them agree that regimes with more education and more rehabilitation work, produce prisoners less likely to reoffend.

Source: The Economist, 2 November 1996

sending second- and third-time offenders through an extended and ineffective court system could be better spent on tackling the problem at an earlier stage before the cycle of decline has set in. Alternative schemes available include the following:

1. *Caution Plus*: The favoured approach of Northamptonshire diversion unit. The offender is cautioned and agrees to pay compensation to the victim, who has to be met face to face. An 'action plan' is drawn up to prevent further offending. Average cost £640 per case, one-quarter of the present system. Only 35 per cent reoffend after eighteen months.

2. *The Halt Programme*: A Netherlands scheme whereby under 18s can be referred to one of seventy available schemes if they admit guilt and have not been on such a scheme more than twice. Compensation has to be paid and a degree of 'shaming' takes place in which offenders are seen publicly to make amends, for example shoplifting girls had to clean the floors of the supermarket they had stolen from. The scheme claims a 40 per cent reoffending rate compared with 80 per cent of those prosecuted.

3. *New Zealand family group conferences*: Based on a Maori method of settling disputes whereby instead of a court case, the extended family is convened to discuss the offender's actions; reparation and preventive measures are agreed. Fifty per cent of victims say they are satisfied with the outcome.

Crime prevention and the vigilante movement

Many experts argue that spending money on preventing crime is more cost-effective than trying to cope with it once it has occurred. Often proposals centre on alerting the community to be more vigilant. Neighbourhood watch areas are now a common feature, numbering over 40,000 nationwide. Some studies, however, suggest such schemes merely squeeze crime out of the suburbs and back on to the street. Neighbours have also become a little inured to alarms sounding: to some extent they have become merely another ubiquitous urban noise.

In 1993, the Holme Wood estate in Bradford was assigned a special team to look after its interests: the result was a 61 per cent decrease in burglaries. Much more widespread, however, seems to be a growing reliance on 'do it yourself' policing or to use its popular name, vigilantism. This issue came dramatically to public attention in 1993. On 10 August the press reported the case of Alan Hocking, who kidnapped 18-year-old Michael Roberts, whom he suspected of selling LSD to 13 year olds, and drove him on a nightmare thirty-minute journey before attacking him with a wooden club spiked with nails. Duncan Bond and Mark Chapman were given a five-year sentence for kidnapping a well-known local thief in order to teach him a lesson. The huge public response to the sentence helped reduce it on appeal to six months. Public outrage did little, however, in the case of Robert Osborne, a Streatham music teacher and father of two who picked up a wooden mallet and pursued a local ne'er-do-well called Joseph Elliot who he had good reason to believe had been slashing tyres. Once the law-abiding Osborne cornered his quarry he was fatally stabbed in the chest; when the case came to court the jury believed Elliot's story that he had acted in self-defence and he was acquitted.

The fear of legal reprisals has not deterred other groups of residents from making their own arrangements when they feel the police have let them down. In St Anne's, a Bristol suburb, a shopkeeper, Norman Guyatt, was so appalled by a brutal daylight robbery of an old couple that he and his two sons and a few others started patrolling the streets in the small hours to detect and report possible burglaries. A sports groundsman, Stan Claridge, now leads the fight against crime in the same area organising patrols and setting up video cameras in key areas. A local security firm, Knighthawk Security, regularly patrols the streets, being paid a pound a week by each resident. A similar force patrols Sneyd Park in Bristol and in Merseyside and other urban areas. As a result crime has dropped in such areas by as much as three-quarters.

Certainly there are dangers that vigilantes can dispense arbitrary justice to the wrong people, but the press and public reaction have been largely in favour of self-help so far. Even the police, wary of a movement which is by definition a criticism of their ineffectiveness, have given occasional guarded welcomes to such initiatives, although the Police

Federation officially regards private guards as potentially dangerous. In Sedgefield, County Durham the local council has reacted to local crime by setting up its own thirty-strong community force to patrol the streets. The Home Office has responded by exhuming and re-encouraging 'special constables', an idea which has the advantage of giving some legal powers to the police helpers. At least one of the Home Office ministers, David Maclean, regards vigilantes warmly. In a speech he planned to deliver to the Commons he wrote: 'Let us congratulate those who tackle crime and criminals head on. They are examples to us all and I want to find out if there is more we should do to encourage them.' The speech was considered too strong by the Home Secretary, however, and he was apparently forced to excise this section.

It seems obvious that Michael Howard was determined to be seen by the Conservative Party faithful as a vigilant defender of traditional party values. Every Home Secretary soon discovers, however, there are no easy answers to law and order problems. The rank and file thirst for tougher sentences and more police on the streets but hard experience often refutes these cherished certainties. It is the Conservative party conference which annually provides the knee-jerk stimulus to any Home Office minister threatening to go 'soft' on crime. As a result, judges, police and the prison service have been able to ask for what they want and stand a good chance of getting it: in the words of Simon Jenkins (*The Times*, 3 February 1993) they operate a 'union stranglehold on ministers more intense and more costly than anything the TUC attempted in the Wilson/Callaghan years'. But this was before the Runciman Report proposed sweeping changes in the judiciary, the Sheehy Report threatened to shake up the police and the proposed privatisation of prisons threatened to reorganise the whole service.

Chapter summary

Conservative thinkers have tended to base their law and order policies on a pessimistic view of human nature whilst Labour has tended to be more optimistic. However, both views began to converge in the late 1980s and early 1990s. Crime figures suggest a crime wave but there are many qualifi-

cations to bear in mind. It is doubtful if the Conservatives substantially reversed the crime wave in the early 1990s. It seems likely that crime breeds in poor, run-down areas of big cities. Police attempts to control crime have not been very successful and they have received much criticism even from the Conservatives. Tougher prison sentences are favoured by the Conservatives but experience suggests this is no real answer. Vigilante groups have set up in some parts of the country to take the law into their own hands.

Discussion points

- Which analysis of human nature seems closest to the truth, the pessimistic or optimistic version?

- How reliable are crime figures?

- Would more widely spread prosperity solve the crime problem?

- Is vigilantism justified?

Further reading

A slightly longer analysis than the above can be found in Jones (1994). A good discussion of the causes of crime can be found in Lea and Young (1984). The best book on the police is by Robert Reiner (1993). On race riots, Michael Keith (1993) is worth a read; and on penal policy, Windlesham (1993) is authoritative and interesting. *The Economist*'s reports on crime are always well informed and well written, as are those of the quality press whenever crime moves to the top of the political agenda.

References

Jones, B. (1994) 'Crime and punishment', in B. Jones (ed.), *Political Issues in Britain Today* (Manchester University Press).

Keith, M. (1993) *Race Riots and Policing* (UCL Press).

Lea, J. and Young, J. (1984) *What is to be Done About Law and Order* (Penguin).

Murray, C. (1990) *The Emerging British Underclass* (IEA Health and Welfare Unit).

Reiner, R. (1993) *The Politics of the Police*, 2nd edn (Harvester Wheatsheaf).

Windlesham, Lord (1993) *Responses to Crime*, Vol. 2 (Clarendon Press).

Parliament and the judges: a constitutional challenge?

THE RT HON. LORD MACKAY OF CLASHFERN

In the United Kingdom, all power derives ultimately from the crown. Parliament, in the tripartite form of Lords, Commons and the monarch, is the supreme legislative authority. The powers of the crown are also exercised by the judiciary, who apply the law to the cases which come before the courts, and by the executive, in the day-to-day business of government. Under our constitution there is a separation of the powers and responsibilities of these three organs, but this separation is by no means rigid. The legislative and judicial functions may take some rest in parliamentary recesses and judicial vacations, although the amount of rest taken by the judiciary in the judicial vacations can certainly be overestimated. The day-to-day executive government of the country must nevertheless continue to operate around the clock and around the calendar, and in many cases cannot adequately do so unless allowed both to make rules and to decide disputes. When it does so, this may appear to some as an encroachment both on the legislative and on the judicial sphere. In practice, Parliament has found it necessary to delegate legislative powers to members of the executive, and to confer powers of adjudication on ministers and other non-judicial agencies.

This kind of overlap is not only found in the legislative and adjudicative powers conferred on the executive. Under our Cabinet system of government the executive branch is recruited from, located within, and collectively responsible to Parliament. The same overlap with Parliament can be found within the judiciary – the most senior judges serve not only as judges but as legislators in Parliament, since they sit in the House of Lords. The office of Lord Chancellor overlaps all three strands of government by adding a ministerial role to the judicial and legislative functions shared with the other judicial members of the House of Lords.

I believe these arrangements have tremendous advantages in practice. The presence of the most senior members of the judiciary in Parliament enables the legislative process to draw on a tremendous and unique concentration of legal expertise. The benefits of this are to be seen not just in relation to technical law, but in relation to the whole range of legislation that is put before Parliament.

The primary function of making the law rests with Parliament, and Parliament is the supreme law-making body. The government can act only in accordance with the law, and the courts must apply and give effect to the law. The judges therefore have a pivotal role to play, for it falls to them to decide, in the event of challenge to a particular act or decision of the executive, whether the executive has remained within the bounds set for it by Parliament, to which it is accountable. It is therefore an important feature of our constitutional arrangements that the judges are independent of the executive. This appears clearly in the oath taken by each judge on his, or her, appointment to 'do right to all manner of people after the laws and usages of this Realm without fear or favour, affection or ill-will'. I would like to elaborate on four of the elements which make up judicial independence thus defined.

Firstly, a judge must be free of bias, either political or personal: thus judges are excluded, under the Act of Settlement, from the House of Commons, and by convention from speaking in the House of Lords on party political issues. Furthermore, judges must not try cases in which they are personally interested. Secondly, judges must be free from political pressure: they should be appointed solely on merit and for those qualities which best fit them to decide cases, and once appointed should have security of tenure free from political patronage. Thirdly, judges must deliver judgement openly, so that, in Lord Hewart's words, 'Justice must not only be done; it must manifestly be seen to be done.' To this end judges must be free to speak boldly in their judicial capacity, and so may not be sued in respect of their utterances on the bench. Finally, judges are called upon to give decisions only on the facts, and the law applicable to the facts, of each individual case as between actual flesh-and-blood litigants, and not on hypothetical cases put to them by the executive or by anyone else; and in contested cases, they must give reasons for their decisions.

I turn now to the subject of judicial review of executive acts and decisions, a rapidly expanding area of law endorsed by Parliament in the Supreme Court Act of 1981, and reserved to judges of the High Court by the Courts and Legal Services Act. In some judicial review cases the act or decision under review has been that of central government, and has been adjudged to be wrong in law. These questions are not always clear-cut and can be hard for the government and its advisers to predict an outcome with certainty. In these cases, there are often very sharp differences of judicial opinion. The principle, however, is clear: that judicial review in no way undermines the sovereignty of Parliament. Of course, whether a particular decision is in accordance with the will of Parliament is often extremely difficult to determine.

The judges themselves have made it clear, in decided cases, that the more evident it is that a minister is acting with the authority of Parliament, the slower the court should be to find that he had acted unreasonably.

The judges of our highest court acknowledge the importance and the sensitivity of this particular interface between the legislature and the judiciary. In my view it is wise for both judges and legislators to approach it with caution and to be careful and moderate in their language when they do so.

In any event, much care should be taken not to overstate the extent to which the executive is found to have erred. Research on the outcome of judicial reviews carried out by the Public Law Project and the University of Essex suggests that government action is found to be fully justified and lawful in the vast majority of cases. While the number of applications for judicial review has increased in recent years, so has the rate at which the courts have refused leave, and it is precisely those areas where central government is the respondent that the rates of refusal of leave are highest. The outcome is that less than 10 per cent of all applications for judicial review against central government result in a substantive finding against the department or minister concerned.

What, then, of the relationship between the judiciary and Parliament? The proposals in the government's Crime (Sentences) Bill have attracted criticism from some members of the judiciary, including the recently retired Lord Chief Justice, Lord Taylor of Gosforth. I believe it is important to note that there is no suggestion that the structure proposed would, if it became law, not be applied in the courts. Lord Taylor himself said in 1993 in a letter to *The Times*: 'I do not ignore Acts of Parliament', going on to say, 'it is my duty and that of all the judges to apply the law as Parliament has enacted it. That duty we will fulfil.' Statute is therefore the supreme source of law, and in the event of conflict between the common law and the clearly expressed will of the legislature set out in an Act of Parliament, the will of Parliament will prevail. Suggestions by some parts of the media that the judiciary is contemplating refusing to give effect to Parliament's will have recently been described by Lord Wilberforce as a 'health scare, based on exploratory, extra-judicial utterances', and I strongly endorse his assessment.

However, there is a degree of interface and overlap here also. Not only do the most senior judges contribute to the proceedings of the House of Lords in its legislative capacity, but the judges also exercise, and have done for many centuries, a law-making function. This function was not readily acknowledged, and was argued by such authorities as Hale and Blackstone to be no more than a process of expounding, declaring and publishing the law, and the common law likewise to consist of ancient customs and usages made known by the judges, whose decisions were not sources of law but simply evidence of what the law was.

This theory, however, notably fails to explain the fact that the rules of equity are known to have been judge-made, and indeed that the names of the Lord Chancellors responsible are known in many cases. Practically the whole framework of the modern law of tort and contract was constructed by the judges in a conscious process of moulding and adapting the principles of the law in response to the changing usages of society. However, in modern times this process only complements the legislative function of Parliament rather than competing with it.

Lord Reid, who in 1972 described the Blackstonian declaratory theory of the judicial function as being a fairy tale, sought earlier to delimit the boundaries within which judges could change the law. He suggested judges should be restricted to the development and application of fundamental principles, ruling out the introduction of arbitrary conditions or limitations, which must be left to legislation, and limiting change to cases where the decision would produce finality or certainty. Earlier still, Lord Simonds, responding in the negative to an invitation to overrule the long-established doctrine preventing a third party from suing on a contract, stated: 'The law is developed by the application of old principles to new circumstances. Therein lies its genius. Its reform by the abrogation of these principles is the task not of the courts of law but of Parliament.'

The judicial function is first and foremost to do justice between litigants according to the law: judges must hear both sides, assess the facts, apply the law as they find it to those facts and deliver judgement on the basis of the law as applied to those particular facts so as to produce a just outcome in each individual case. As Lord Diplock succinctly put it, the judicial process is directed to three distinct functions. The first is to settle disputes about facts, that is, to find out what really happened. The second is to settle disputes about legal concepts – to decide whether what really happened amounted to a breach of one person's duty towards his or her neighbour. The third is to determine what is the remedy for that breach of duty.

The degree to which judges can change the law which they must apply is constrained not only by the supremacy of the will of Parliament, so that statutes, good or bad, cannot be struck down or ignored, but also by the fact that the court can only decide on the facts of the case which happens to come before it. This means that the court, unlike Parliament, cannot examine the effects of a range of alternative options, having regard to a multiplicity of interests. It also means that the court must frame a judgement between the competing claims of the opposing parties, and is in no position systematically to examine or evaluate the disturbance which a change of course in the case before it may cause in other related areas.

Judicial law-making must therefore operate through the development and application of established fundamental principles to disputes between parties concerned about specific events which have occurred in the past. It is quite possible for this process of development and application to show that a particular rule, although applied in the past, should no longer apply, but that the fundamental principles were always part of the law and that it is therefore justifiable to apply them to the case before the court, taking account of the need for certainty and the impact in other areas and other cases.

The profile of these matters has been raised recently by the response of some commentators to recent lectures by members of the judiciary, which raises the issue of the proper relationship between judges, the public and Parliament in relation to lectures and other public utterances. It has for many years been accepted without question that judges should be able to participate in discussion of developments in the law, and they have done so in innumerable cases through the medium of public lectures. Of course, it may be said that there has been rather more public comment from members of the judiciary in recent years as a result of my action in waiving the Kilmuir Rules. That system, under which judges were required to seek the consent of the Lord Chancellor before taking part in public discussion, seemed to me to be rather artificial and difficult to reconcile with the concept of judicial independence. I believe that judges should have the judgement to decide such matters for themselves.

I and my senior colleagues in the judiciary remain as ever willing to offer advice in particular situations, but I believe it is right that the responsibility of deciding whether to intervene in public discussion should rest on the shoulders of the individual judge concerned. This may of course mean that individual judges may publicly express views disagreeing with the government of the day. In my view, provided that they are able to do so without putting their impartiality at risk in the cases that come before them, or the confidence of the parties concerned in that impartiality, it is proper that they should contribute to debate on subjects where their expertise may be particularly valuable. Once the government has presented legislative proposals to Parliament and Parliament has enacted legislation, either as originally proposed or with such modifications as Parliament thinks fit to incorporate, then the courts will of course proceed to apply that legislation, consistently with the judicial oath and the legislative supremacy of Parliament.

Judicial independence should, however, be firmly distinguished from any hint of judicial supremacism. Just as the independence of the judiciary is fundamental to our constitutional arrangements, so is the idea that the judiciary is bound by an Act of Parliament. I am not convinced by arguments, although eloquently advanced, that there exists a higher order of law comprising basic or fundamental principles against which the judiciary may measure Acts of Parliament, and if necessary strike them down.

I should like to draw to a close, however, by posing the question whether a challenge to our constitutional arrangements, and to the conventions and the thinking underlying them, might arise in connection with the European Convention on Human Rights. That convention does not bind Parliament. The judgements of the European Court of Human Rights do not bind the United Kingdom directly in domestic law, but are rather binding in international law as a matter of agreement, by way of continuing commitment under the convention. It is accordingly for Parliament to consider what should or should not be done in the light of any particular judgement of that court.

It is currently a matter of debate whether the European Convention should be incorporated into domestic law, and it is in this connection that I raise the question. As I have said, the judges presently approach their function on the basis of a collaborative approach with Parliament, employing techniques of adjudication which limit them to the individual case between specific litigants and generally keep them clear of the political arena in which policy issues are discussed. Thus they are selected for their ability to decide individual cases in accordance with the law, and their independence is assured.

Incorporation of the European Convention or a Bill of Rights as the yardstick by which Acts of Parliament are to be measured would inevitably draw judges into making decisions of a far more political nature, measuring policy against abstract principles with possible implications for the development of broad social and economic policy which is and has been accepted by the judiciary to be properly the preserve of Parliament. The question which would then be asked, and to which an answer could not be postponed indefinitely, is whether the introduction of such a political element into the judicial function would require a change in the criteria for appointment of judges, making the political stance of each candidate a matter of importance as much as his or her ability to decide cases on their individual facts and the law applicable to those facts. Following on from that is the question of how confidence in judicial independence and impartiality could be maintained, and whether their appointment should be subjected to political scrutiny of the sort recently seen in the United States.

Those are by no means the only questions to be asked, however. Just as the European Union recognises the concept of subsidiarity, so does the machinery of the European Convention and the European Court of Human Rights, through the concept of the 'margin of appreciation'. This concedes not only that the European Court does not seek to sit in judgement of alleged errors of law made by the domestic court or to substitute its own assessment of facts for that of the domestic court, but also that the national authorities are in a better position than the European supervisory bodies to strike the right balance between the interests of the community at large and the protection of the rights of the individual, and indeed between different rights protected by the Convention.

Thus the Court will concede that a range of ethical standards may be set in different states so that, for example, pornography may be a permitted means of expression in one state but prohibited in another, or a different political balance, for example as between the right to free speech and the right to privacy, without there necessarily being a violation of the Convention. The setting of standards is for 'national authorities' to decide; however, while the United Kingdom's national authority is pre-eminently Parliament, a fundamental question would have to be asked if the Convention were incorporated, namely which authority should be the standard-setter? For example, the Convention in many places permits restriction of the rights pro-tected so far as this is 'necessary in a democratic society'. If the Convention were to be incorporated into domestic law, which body should decide what is so necessary: the courts which are charged with the function of applying the law, or Parliament, which is democratically elected?

For these reasons, I do not agree that the Convention should be incorporated into our domestic law. The nature of these issues underlines once again the need to give close and careful consideration to the established principles on which our constitutional machinery operates before taking up the challenge of changing them.

PART SEVEN

The policy process

The policy-making process

BILL JONES

LEARNING OBJECTIVES

- To define policy in government.

- To encourage familiarity with the most popular models of policy-making.

- To introduce the notion of policy networks.

- To give some examples of policy-making.

INTRODUCTION

This chapter examines the anatomy of policy and policy making in central government, focusing on the stages of policy making together with some theories relating to the process before concluding with a look at the privatisation of British Telecom as a case study.

How policy is made

Policy can be defined as a set of ideas and proposals for action culminating in a government decision. To study policy, therefore, is to study how decisions are made. Government decisions can take many forms: Burch (1978, p. 128) distinguishes between two broad kinds, as follows:

1. rules, regulations and public pronouncements (e.g. Acts of Parliament, Orders in Council, White Papers, ministerial and departmental circulars).
2. public expenditure and its distribution: The government spends over £350 billion per annum mostly on public goods and services (e g.

education, hospitals) and transfer payments (e.g. social security payments and unemployment benefit).

Figure 25.1 portrays the government as a system which has as its input political demands together with resources available and its output as the different kinds of government decisions. The latter impact upon society and influence future inputs. So the process is circular and constant. Students of the policy process disagree as to how policy inputs are fed into government and, once 'inside', how they are processed. Both Burch and Wood (1990) and Jordan and Richardson (1987) review these different analyses as models. Eight of them are summarised below.

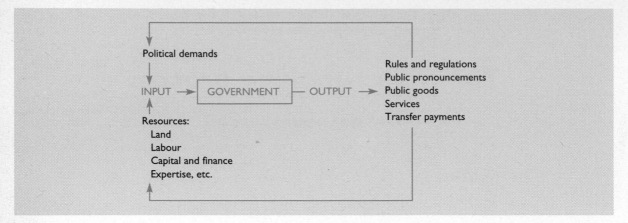

Figure 25.1 The policy process
Source: Burch, 1978

1. *The conventional model*: This is the 'official' (see Figure 3, p. 210) explanation of policy-making found in Central Office of Information publications and the utterances of civil servants in public (though seldom in private). This maintains that Parliament represents and interprets the public will through its representatives, who formulate executive policies which are faithfully implemented by civil servants.

2. *The ruling-class model*: This is effectively the Marxist interpretation, that those empowered with taking key decisions in the state – civil servants and politicians – subscribe consciously or unconsciously to the values of the dominant economic class. According to this view most policy outputs will have the effect of protecting dominant group interests.

Institutional theories

These attribute decisive importance to differing elements within the political system.

3. *The pluralist model*, often associated with the US political scientist Robert Dahl, assumes that power is dispersed within society to the various interest groups which comprise it – business, labour, agriculture, and so forth – and that they can 'make themselves heard effectively at some crucial stage in the process of decision' (Jordan and Richardson, 1987, p. 16). According to this

view, interest groups interact and negotiate policy with each other in a kind of free market, with government acting as a more or less neutral referee.

4. *Corporatism* is associated with the work of Philippe Schmitter and is offered as an alternative to pluralism. This model perceives an alliance between ministers, civil servants and the leaders of pressure groups in which the latter are given a central role in the policy-making process in exchange for exerting pressure upon their members to conform with government decisions. In this view therefore interest groups become an extension – or even a quasi-form – of government. Corporatism has also been used pejoratively by British politicians of the left (Benn), right (Thatcher) and centre (Owen) to describe the decision-making style of the discredited 1975–9 Labour government.

5. *The party government model*: The stress here is on political parties and the assertion that they provide the major channel for policy formulation.

6. *The Whitehall model* contends that civil servants either originate major policy or so alter it as it passes through their hands as to make it substantially theirs – thus making them the key influence on policy.

Nature of decision-making

These theories concentrate upon the way in which decision-makers set about their tasks.

7. *Rational decision-making*: This approach assumes that decision-makers ought to behave in a logical, sequential fashion. Accordingly they will identify their objectives, formulate possible strategies, think through their implications and finally choose the course of action which on balance best achieves their objectives.

8. *Incrementalism*: This approach, associated with the work of Charles Lindblom, denies that policy-makers are so rational and argues that in practice they usually try to cope or 'muddle through'. They tend to start with the status quo and make what adjustments they can to manage or at least accommodate new situations. In other words policy-makers do not solve problems but merely adjust to them. The case of privatisation argues against this approach in that when Nigel Lawson came to consider it in the early 1980s the cupboard, in terms of relevant files and experience, was totally bare. Instead Conservative ministers had to devise wholly new approaches and, whatever one's views on the outcome, it is perhaps to their credit that – even allowing for a determined Prime Minister and a large majority – they succeeded in a government culture so unfriendly to radical innovation.

It is clear that some of these models are basically descriptive while others, like the rational choice or conventional models, are also prescriptive – they offer an ideal approach as to how policies *should* be made. It is also obvious that echoing somewhere within each approach is the ring of truth. It would not be too difficult to find examples in support of any of the above models. The truth is that policy-making is such a protean, dense area of activity that it is extremely difficult to generalise. Nevertheless, the search for valid statements is worthwhile, otherwise our political system will remain incomprehensible. We will therefore look at the process in greater detail in a search for some generally true propositions about it.

The policy cycle

If they agree on nothing else, policy study scholars seem to agree that policy-making can best be understood as a cycle. Analyses of the cycle can be quite sophisticated. Hogwood and Gunn (1984) discern a

number of stages: deciding to decide (issue search and agenda-setting); deciding how to decide; issue definition, forecasting; setting objectives and priorities; options analysis; policy implementation, monitoring and control; evaluation and review; and policy maintenance succession or termination. For our purposes, however, three easily understood stages will suffice: initiation, formulation and implementation.

Policy initiation

Each government decision has a long and complex provenance but all must start somewhere. It is tempting to think they originate, eureka-like, in the minds of single individuals, but they are more often the product of debate or a general climate of opinion involving many minds. Policy initiatives, moreover, can originate in all parts of the political system. Figure 25.2 depicts six groups of policy initiators placed on a continuum starting from the periphery and moving in towards the nerve centre of government in No. 10.

General public

The public's role in policy-making is limited to (the not unimportant function of) voting for a particular policy package at general elections. They do have other occasional opportunities, however, for example the referendums on the EEC and Scottish and Welsh devolution in the 1970s, and pressures which can be built up through lobbying MPs, as when Sir Keith Joseph was forced to withdraw his proposals to charge parents for a proportion of their children's university tuition fees.

Cause groups, media and academic experts

Many *cause groups* operate in the 'wilderness' – their values antithetical to government and not listened to – and many also stay there, but some do influence public opinion and decision-makers and after years of struggle achieve action on issues like abortion, capital punishment and the environment. Others achieve success on specific issues like Des Wilson's campaign to reduce lead in petrol. Certain policy 'environments' will include a bewildering array of pressure groups, all of whom seek to lean on the policy-making tiller. Local government associations, for example, are particularly important in areas like education, housing and social services.

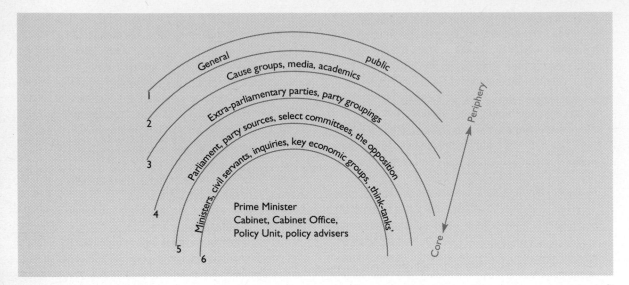

General public

Cause groups, media, academics

Extra-parliamentary parties, party groupings

Parliament, party sources, select committees, the opposition

Ministers, civil servants, inquiries, key economic groups, 'think-tanks'

Prime Minister
Cabinet, Cabinet Office,
Policy Unit, policy advisers

Periphery

Core

1
2
3
4
5
6

Figure 25.2 Policy initiatives

Media coverage heavily affects the climate in which policy is discussed and important policy proposals occasionally emerge from television programmes, newspaper editorials, articles in journals and so forth. One editorial on its own would have little effect but a near consensus in the press might well stimulate action. Occasionally ideas are picked up from individual journalists – *Observer* columnist Alan Watkin's late 1980s proposal that Labour should concentrate on the theme of the Conservatives' 'squalid society' was discussed in Shadow Cabinet, for example – though in the event Neil Kinnock turned it down. Other media figures who used to be consulted regularly on policy matters by Margaret Thatcher included such people as Rupert Murdoch, the press magnate, and journalists Brian Walden and Woodrow Wyatt. Lord (Jeffrey) Archer tells us he used regularly to send around to Margaret Thatcher draft speeches on a range of topics, but there is no confirmation of anything important being picked up and implemented.

Occasionally the *media* provide crucial information. The most surprising example of this was in 1987 when Nigel Lawson, as Chancellor, denied entry to the ERM by prime ministerial veto, had tried to achieve his object by other means, namely shadowing the Deutschmark. When *Financial Times* journalists interviewed Margaret Thatcher they questioned her about this policy. She denied any knowledge of it but when they produced definitive evidence in the form of charts, somewhat surprised, she accepted they were correct and the stage was set for the mammoth argument which resulted in Lawson's damaging resignation two years later and the beginning of the end of her reign in No. 10.

All these agencies in the 'outer rim' (see Figure 25.2) interact to provide that intangible climate of discussion which encourages the emergence of certain proposals and inhibits others. Each policy environment has its own climate created by its specialist press, pressure groups, academics, practitioners and the like who frequently meet in conferences and on advisory committees. An interesting feature of these bodies, however, is that from time to time they are blessed with favour, their arguments listened to, their proposals adopted, their leaders embraced by government and given advisory or even executive status. It is almost as if, God-like, the government has reached down and plucked them up to place them – albeit temporarily – on high.

Part II explained how policy emerged out of an ideological framework and pointed out how *academics, philosophers and other thinkers* had contributed towards these frameworks. The most obvious influences on the left would include Karl Marx, R.H. Tawney, Harold Laski, William Beveridge and, incomparably in the economic sphere,

J.M. Keynes. Right-wing writers would include figures like David Hume and Michael Oakeshott and (on economics) two overseas academics, Friedrich Hayek and Milton Friedman. Academics specialising in specific policy areas like transport, housing, criminology, and so forth, also regularly come up with proposals, some of which are taken up or drawn upon. John Major has welcomed the views of the so-called 'seven wise men' (selected academics) on economic policy. On other occasions academics can be suddenly welcomed in by departments, as when the Foreign Office began to use them extensively when the fall of the Shah of Iran revealed that they had been reading events in that country more accurately than the diplomats. In July 1990 much publicity was given to a seminar of six academics convened at Chequers to discuss the implications of German reunification. Colin Brown (*The Independent*, 17 July 1990) revealed that such seminars were regular features of Margaret Thatcher's policy-making style. They were kept confidential and involved 'sympathetic' academics.

Extra-parliamentary parties and party groupings

Both the Labour and Conservative *extra-parliamentary parties* are more influential in opposition than in government. As Chapter 14 noted, Labour's system of internal democracy gave a substantial policy-making role to the trade unions, the National Executive Committee and the party conference during the 1930s and 1950s. The Conservative Party is far less democratic but conference can set the mood for policy formulation, the research department can initiate important proposals and the Advisory Committee on Policy did much to reformulate the main outlines of Conservative policy in the late 1970s.

Party groupings – many of which have contacts with Parliament – can also exert influence. The Fabian Society has long acted as a kind of left-wing think-tank (see Box 25.2) and in the 1980s the left-wing Labour Coordinating Committee was influential in advising Neil Kinnock as he shifted Labour's policies towards the centre.

Parliament

The role of Parliament in initiating policy can be considered under two headings: party sources and party groups, and non-party sources.

In government parliamentary parties have to work through their back-bench committees though individual MPs seek to use their easy access to ministers to exert influence and press their own solutions. One Conservative MP, David Evans, pulled off the remarkable coup of convincing the Prime Minister that the identity card system introduced by Luton Town Football Club should be compulsorily introduced nationwide. His success was short-lived: the scheme was dropped in January 1990.

The opposition is concerned to prepare its policies for when and if it takes over the reins of government. As we saw in Chapter 14, Kinnock wrested future policy-making out of the party's NEC with his policy review exercise (1987–9), involving leading members of his front-bench team in the process. The opposition, however, also has to make policy 'on the hoof' in reaction to political events. It is their function and in their interests to oppose, to offer alternatives to government – but this is not easy. Opposition spokesmen lack the detailed information and support enjoyed by government; they need to react to events in a way which is consistent with their other policy positions; they need to provide enough detail to offer a credible alternative yet they must avoid closing options should they come to power.

Party groups like the Bow Group, Monday Club, Tribune and Campaign Group can all have peripheral – but rarely direct – influence on policy-making.

The fourteen select committees regularly make reports and recommendations, some of which are adopted. Most of these represent cross-party consensus on specific issues like the successful Home Affairs Committee recommendation that the laws allowing arrest on suspicion (the 'sus' laws) be abolished, but others, like the Social Services Committee, chaired by the much admired Frank Field, have offered a wide-ranging and coherent alternative to government social policy without any major success. Individual MPs probably have a better chance of influencing specific, usually very specific, policy areas through the opportunities available to move private Members' bills (see Chapter 17).

Ministers, departments, official inquiries and 'think-tanks'

Strong-minded ministers will always develop policy ideas of their own either as a reflection of their own

BOX 25.1   **IDEAS AND PERSPECTIVES**

Think-tanks

In the winter of 1979–80 Margaret Thatcher presided over what looked like a crumbling party and a collapsing economy. Tory grandees talked of dumping the leader. Mandarins, muttering 'I told you so', prepared to welcome the consensual 'Mr Butskell' back from retirement.

Mrs Thatcher regained her momentum partly because she discovered Thatcherism: a new set of ideas on getting rid of supply constraints in the economy, privatising nationalised industry and reforming the public sector. They were provided by the intelligentsia of the new right. Where have the visionaries gone, now that the Tories could do with some fresh strategic thinking?

To understand the seriousness of the ideological deficit on the right, visit its pet think-tanks. These institutions were once monuments on the political landscape. The Centre for Policy Studies (CPS) enjoyed close personal links with Mrs Thatcher, its founder and patron. The Adam Smith Institute (ASI) became a specialist in privatisation. The Institute of Economic Affairs (IEA), the oldest of the three, offered views on just about anything. Politicians looked to the think-tanks for instant policies, journalists for instant opinions, and people on the make for instant connections.

Today the think-tanks are all but silent. The CPS has retreated into itself and moved to a drabber address. In its glory days it produced a policy-pamphlet a fortnight: none has appeared from its presses since the [May 1992] general election. The IEA publishes little. The ASI is suffering from a recession in the privatisation business.

There were always going to be problems for the think-tanks after the frenetic 1980s. Many of the Tories' targets – the unions, nationalised industries, health and education – had been 'handbagged'. Some of their policies had misfired or backfired (the poll tax).

Splits were inevitable. The radical right had always been an alliance of convenience. People who were willing to co-operate on trade-union reform fell out over issues like reforming the constitution or legalising drugs. No sooner had Mrs Thatcher packed her bags than the die-hard Thatcherites began to squabble with the give-him-a-chance Majorites. At first the squabble was just about tactics. The die-hards wanted to retreat into their bunker: the Majorites hoped to preserve their contacts with Downing Street. But it quickly developed into a full-blown feud about Europe.

The atmosphere became increasingly fractious. At the IEA, the die-hards denounced Graham Mather, its director, for sucking up to the Tories. He decamped to start a think-tank of his own, the European Policy Forum. At the CPS, the die-hards criticised David Willetts, its director of studies, for a similar thought-crime. He became MP for Havant and a director of a rival think-tank, the Social Market Foundation.

The CPS and the IEA have taken refuge in outraging respectable opinion and annoying government ministers. An IEA pamphlet, published in June, argued, among other things, that laws on equality of opportunity undermine freedom and private property, and that sex roles are genetically determined. At a recent CPS lecture, Virginia Bottomley, the health secretary, was denounced for promoting radical feminism.

Other people are still thinking. The Social Market Foundation, founded in 1989 to develop ideas for the Social Democrats, has survived its progenitor and is producing some interesting work on, for instance, where markets can usefully be applied to the public sector and where they cannot. The Institute of Public Policy Research, a left-leaning think-tank, is beginning to question universal benefits, a heresy once seen as the ranting of the far right. The Labour Party has a small army of academics beavering away on big questions such as social justice and another on the constitution. For the right, though, the larder is bare.

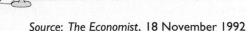

Source: The Economist, 18 November 1992

convictions or to get noticed and further their ambitions. Michael Heseltine, in the wake of the Toxteth troubles, probably shared both motivations when he submitted a paper to the Cabinet called 'It took a riot', proposing a new and un-Thatcherite approach to inner city regeneration: the policy was partially implemented in Merseyside but not elsewhere. Such major initiatives are not the province of civil servants but through their day-to-day involvement in running the country they are constantly proposing detailed improvements and adjustments to existing arrangements. Such initiatives are not necessarily the preserve of senior officials: even junior officers can propose changes which can be taken up and implemented.

A Royal Commission can be the precursor to major policy changes (for example, the Redcliffe Maud Royal Commission on Local Government, 1966–9), but Margaret Thatcher was not well disposed towards such time-consuming, essentially disinterested procedures – she always felt she knew what needed doing – and during the 1980s none was set up. Departments, however, regularly establish their own inquiries, often employing outside experts, which make important policy recommendations. John Major also seems to be more favourably inclined, setting up a number of commissions, including the Royal Commission on Criminal Justice which reported in 1993.

Right-wing 'think-tanks' were especially favoured by Margaret Thatcher (see Box 25.1). *The Economist* (6 May 1989) notes how she spurned Oxbridge dons – the traditional source of advice for No. 10 – and suggests that 'the civil service is constitutionally incapable of generating the policy innovation which the prime minister craves'. Instead, as a reforming premier she instinctively listened to the advice of 'people who have been uncorrupted by the old establishment'. Think-tank advice was often channelled to Margaret Thatcher via the No. 10 Policy Unit. Their radical suggestions acted as a sounding board when published and helped push the climate of debate further to the right. If new ideas are received in a hostile fashion, ministers can easily disavow them – on 8 February 1990 a think-tank suggested that child benefit be abolished: Thatcher told the Commons that her government had no 'immediate' plans to do this. The 'privatisation' of government advice in the form of think-tanks was a striking feature of Margaret Thatcher's impact upon policy-making. John Major was proved less receptive to such influences.

Prime Minister and Cabinet

This is the nerve centre of government, supported by the high-powered network of Cabinet committees, the Cabinet Office, the No. 10 Policy Unit and policy advisers. After a period of ten years in office it is likely that any Prime Minister will dominate policy-making. Chapter 14 made it clear that while many sought to whisper policy suggestions in her ear, Margaret Thatcher's radical beliefs provided her with an apparently full agenda of her own. The evidence of her personal impact on major policy areas is plain to see: privatisation, trade union legislation, the environment, the exchange rate, sanctions against South Africa, the poll tax and Europe – the list could go on. She was also unusual, however, in taking a personal interest in less weighty matters like her (somewhat ill-starred) attempt to clean up litter from Britain's streets following a visit to litter-free Israel.

Harold Wilson saw himself as a 'deep lying halfback feeding the ball forward to the chaps who score the goals'. Thatcher was not content with this role: she wanted to score the goals as well. Wilson also said a Prime Minister governs by 'interest and curiosity': Thatcher had insatiable appetites in both respects and an energy which enabled her to feed them to a remarkable degree. Under her, assisted by her own relentless energy and a constitution which delivers so much power to the executive, the office of Prime Minister took on a policy-initiating role comparable to that of the US President. John Major was also exceptionally hard-working, as premiers must be, but he was happy to delegate more than his predecessor and to listen to voices around the Cabinet table, especially that of his powerful deputy, Michael Heseltine.

From this brief and admittedly selective description it is clear that:

1. Policy can be initiated both at the micro- and macro-levels from within any part of the political system, but the frequency and importance of initiatives grows as one moves from the periphery towards the centre.

2. Even peripheral influences can be swiftly drawn into the centre should the centre wish it.

3. Each policy environment is to some extent a world unto itself with its own distinctive characteristics. Higher education policy-making, for example, will include, just for starters: the Prime Minister, Cabinet, the No. 10 Policy Unit, right-wing think-tanks, numerous parliamentary and party committees, the Departments of Education and Employment, the Treasury, the funding councils for the universities, the Committee of Vice-Chancellors and Principals, the Association of University Teachers and other unions, *The Times Higher Education Supplement*, together with a galaxy of academic experts on any and every aspect of the subject.

Policy formulation

Once a policy idea has received political endorsement it is fed into the system for detailed elaboration. This process involves certain key players from the initiation process, principally civil servants, possibly key pressure group leaders and outside experts (who may also be political sympathisers) and, usually at a later stage, ministers. In the case of a major measure there is often a learning phase in which civil servants and ministers acquaint themselves with the detail of the measure: this may require close consultation with experts and practitioners in the relevant policy environment. The measure, if it requires legislation, then has to chart a course first through the bureaucracy and then the legislature.

The bureaucratic process
This will entail numerous information-gathering and advisory committee meetings and a sequence of coordinating meetings with other ministries, especially the Treasury if finance is involved. Some of these meetings might be coordinated by the Cabinet Office and when ministers become involved the measures will be progressed in Cabinet committees and ultimately full Cabinet before being passed on to parliamentary counsel, the expert drafters of parliamentary bills.

The legislative process
As Chapter 17 explained, this process involves several readings and debates in both chambers. Studies show that most legislation passes through unscathed, but controversial measures will face a number of hazards which may influence their eventual shape. Opposition MPs and Lords may seek to delay and move hostile amendments, but more important are rebellions within the government party: for example, the legislation required to install the community charge, or poll tax, in 1988–9 was amended several times in the face of threatened and actual revolts by Conservative MPs. The task of piloting measures through the legislature falls to ministers closely advised by senior officials and this is often when junior ministers can show their mettle.

From this brief description it is clear that three sets of actors dominate the policy formulation process: ministers, civil servants and pressure group leaders and experts. Some scholars calculate that the key personnel involved in policy formulation might number no more than 3,500. As in policy initiation, Margaret Thatcher also played an unusually interventionist role in this process. Reportedly she regularly called ministers and civil servants into No. 10 to speed things up, shift developments on to the desired track or discourage those with whom she disagreed.

Policy implementation

It is easy to assume that once the government has acted on something or legislated on an issue it is more or less closed. Certainly the record of government action reveals any number of measures which have fulfilled their objectives: for example, the Attlee government wished to establish a National Health Service and did so; in recent years, Conservative governments wished to sell off houses to tenants and did so. But there are always problems which impede or sometimes frustrate implementation or which produce unsought for side-effects. Between legislation and implementation many factors intervene. Jordan and Richardson (1982, pp. 234–5) quote the conditions which Hood suggests need to be fulfilled to achieve perfect implementation:

1. There must be a unitary administrative system rather like a huge army with a single line of

authority. Conflict of authority could weaken control, and all information should be centralised in order to avoid compartmentalism.

2. The norms and rules enforced by the system have to be uniform. Similarly, objectives must be kept uniform if the unitary administrative system is to be really effective.
3. There must be perfect obedience or perfect control.
4. There must be perfect information and perfect communication – as well as perfect coordination.
5. There must be sufficient time for administrative resources to be mobilised.

To fulfil wholly any, let alone all, of those conditions would be rare indeed, so some degree of failure is inevitable with any government programme. Examples are easy to find.

Education

The 1944 Education Act intended that the new grammar, technical and secondary modern schools were to be different but share a 'parity of esteem'. In practice this did not happen: grammar schools became easily the most prestigious and recruited disproportionately from the middle classes. The government could not control parental choice. To remedy this, comprehensive schools were set up in the 1950s and 1960s, but it was the middle-class children who still performed best in examinations. Reformers also neglected one crucial and in retrospect blindingly obvious factor: comprehensive schools recruit from their own hinterlands, so inner city schools are predominantly working class with a tendency for lower standards, while suburban schools are more middle class with higher standards. The government made policy on the basis of inadequate information.

The economy

Burch and Wood (1990, pp. 172–3) record how recent governments have consistently planned on the basis of public expenditure plans which in the event were exceeded: an estimated increase of 12 per cent in 1971 for the year 1975 proved to be 28.6 per cent in practice. The government lacked control over its own spending departments. Following the stock market crash of 1987 Chancellor Nigel

Lawson lowered interest rates to 9.5 per cent to avoid the danger of a recession. This measure, however, led to an explosion of credit, fuelling an inflationary spending boom which required high interest rates to bring it under control. High interest rates in their turn went on to cause economic recession in 1990. The government chose to ignore relevant information offered by advisers in 1988.

Social security payments

Many claimants report that a necessary service to which they have entitlement has been transformed by state employees and the restrictions they have been told to enforce into a humiliating, time-consuming obstacle course.

Inner city policy

In the wake of her 1987 victory Margaret Thatcher resolved to attack the problems of the inner cities. In March 1988 the Action for Cities initiative was launched with considerable fanfare. In January 1990 the National Audit Office reported that it had achieved only 'piecemeal success' (*The Guardian*, 25 January 1990); departments had 'made no overall assessment of inner cities' "special requirements"' and there was 'insufficient information to assess the strategic impact of the various programmes and initiatives involved'.

Poll tax

The euphemistically named 'community charge' – known as the Poll Tax – was the brain-child variously of right-wing think-tanks, Kenneth Baker, William Waldegrave and others (though following its collapse most people were keen to disclaim parentage – political failures, unsurprisingly, are always orphans). The rationale behind it was logical; local taxes – the 'rates' – were based on property but penalised the wealthy, who paid more on big properties. Over half, however, were either exempted or received rebates yet still enjoyed the benefits of local services; consequently they had no reason to vote for lower rates and were not 'accountable' for them in the opinion of Conservatives like Thatcher, a keen supporter of the scheme. The new tax was to be a flat-rate one and payable by all to some degree, even students and the unemployed. The obvious unfairness of taxing the poor as heavily as the rich was widely perceived, even by

Conservative voters. Yet Thatcher's personal support, defiant style and the pusillanimous nature of many MPs and ministers – Michael Portillo informed conference he was not daunted but 'delighted' to be placed in charge of it – let a clearly flawed law on to the statute book. In March 1990 polls showed a huge majority opposed it and on 7 April a riot erupted in London. When John Major succeeded Thatcher he quickly replaced the measure with one more closely resembling the old property-based rates and the heat soon left the issue of local government finance (for more on the poll tax see pp. 386–9).

Programme failure also often results from the operation of constraints which constantly bear upon policy-makers.

Constraints upon policy-makers

Financial resources
Policy-makers have to operate within available financial resources which are a function of the nation's economic health at any particular time, and the willingness of key decision-makers, especially in the Treasury, to make appropriate provision from funds available to government.

Political support
This is initially necessary to gain endorsement for a policy idea, but support is also necessary throughout the often extended and complex policy-making process. Lack of it, for example, characterised the tortured birth of the poll tax, as well as its ignominious demise. Support at the political level is also crucial but it is highly desirable within the bureaucracy and elsewhere in the policy environment. Resistance to policies can kill them off *en route* and anticipated resistance is also important; as Jordan and Richardson (1982, p. 238) hypothesise. 'There are probably more policies which are never introduced because of the anticipation of resistance, than policies which have failed because of resistance.' Some departments now seek to gauge levels of popular support through the use of focus groups, a technique borrowed from political marketing.

Competence of key personnel
An able, energetic minister is likely to push policy measures through: a weak minister is not. Civil servants need to be up to the task of rapidly mastering the detail of new measures: their failure will impede the progress of a measure and limit its efficacy.

Time
New legislative initiatives need to carve space out of a timetable so overcrowded that winners of private Members' ballots are lobbied by departments themselves to adopt bills awaiting parliamentary consideration. The whole system is, moreover, arguably overcentralised and, some would say, chronically overloaded.

Timing
Measures can fail if timing is not propitious. Just after a general election, for example, is a good time to introduce controversial measures. Margaret Thatcher, it will be recalled, was unable to secure the sale of British Leyland to an American company in the spring of 1986 because she had lost so much support over the Westland episode.

Coordination
Whitehall departments divide up the work of government in a particular way: proposals which fall between ministries are often at a disadvantage and the job of coordinating diverse departments is not, in the view of critics, managed with particular efficiency. Burch (1978, p. 133) also notes that:

Too often policy making becomes a conflict between departments for a share of the limited resources available. This is . . . especially true of expenditure politics when departments fight for their own corner at the cost of broader policy objectives.

Personality factors
Key decision-makers are not as rational as perhaps they ought to be. They might have personal objectives – ambition, desire for image and status and rivalries – which lead them to oppose rather than support certain policy objectives. The best recent example of this is the row between Margaret Thatcher and Nigel Lawson in the late 1990s over Britain's proposed entry into the exchange rate mechanism (ERM), which caused policy to drift.

Geographical factors
A bias in favour of the south-east is often detectable in government policies – for example, in the

granting of defence contracts – partly because decision-makers in our centralised system live in the home counties, partly because the south-east has a more buoyant economy and partly due to political factors: this after all is the Conservative heartland. (For a subtle and controversial analysis of territorial politics in the UK, see Bullpitt, 1983.)

International events

The increasing interdependence of the large economies has made events like the quadrupling of oil prices in the early 1970s major constraints upon policy-making. In some cases these constraints are formal, as when the International Monetary Fund attached strict public expenditure conditions to its 1976 loan to Callaghan's Labour government. Political events like the Falklands War can clearly have an enormous impact upon major policy areas, while the 1989 revolutions in the communist countries changed the whole context within which foreign policy is formulated.

The influence of Europe

Treaty obligations and the growing power of Community institutions have imposed increasingly powerful constraints upon the freedom of action which British policy-makers have enjoyed (see Chapter 31).

Policy networks

Jordan and Richardson (1987) argued that policy-making in Britain is not uniform; every aspect has its own specific characteristics. They lay less stress on manifestos or the activities of Parliament but point to the mass of interconnecting bodies which have an interest in the policy area: the 'policy community'.

To some extent this is a theory about how interest groups interact with government to help formulate policy. Access to the policy community is restricted to actors prepared to play the game: act constitutionally; accept that the government has the last word; keep agreements; and make reasonable demands. These rules automatically exclude radical groups with high-profile campaigning styles in most cases, though the accession to power of a radical political message can alter this as in the case of Thatcherism. To exercise real clout, a group has to become an 'insider' (see Chapter 13). Communities have a core and a periphery – rather like that suggested in Figure 25.2 – with the stable core continuously involved in the policy process and a secondary group, less stable in membership, involved from time to time but lacking the resources to be in the core.

Professor Rod Rhodes developed this idea but saw that often the policy community was not

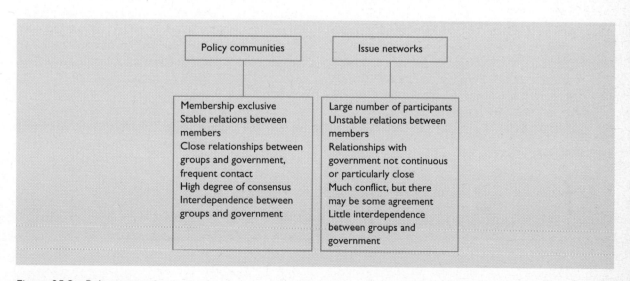

Figure 25.3 Policy networks
Source: Baggott, 1995, p. 24

cohesive or sharply defined; he began to discern a more fragmented and more accessible form: a 'policy network' with a very large and constantly changing membership, often with conflicting views. Baggott's diagram (Figure 25.3) shows the contrast between the two ideas with some clarity. Baggott (1995, p. 26) criticises the approach for not explaining the provenance of the networks and overconcentrating on the group–government nexus to the exclusion of the broader political environment.

The case of the privatisation of British Telecom

This chapter concludes with an examination of policy formulation and implementation in the case of the privatisation of British Telecom (BT) in 1984.

While Conservative ideology had long argued for minimal state interference, official policy on privatisation was very cautious as late as 1978. 'Denationalisation', reported a Conservative policy study group in that year, 'must be pursued cautiously and flexibly, recognizing that major changes may well be out of the question in some industries' (Lee, 1989, p. 139). The 1979 manifesto had spoken only of selling just under a half share in selected industries. On 21 November 1980 a bill was presented separating the postal from the telephone side of the General Post Office. On 27 July 1981 British Telecom came into being. Shortly afterwards Sir Geoffrey Howe inaugurated the age of privatisation with the announcement that several industries were being considered for this treatment: the biggest was British Telecom. Figure 25.4 characterises in a very simplified form the policy process which any measure has to negotiate.

Legislative process

When the bill to privatise BT was introduced it faced great opposition. The Post Office Engineering Union (POEU) had three sponsored MPs in the Commons, led by John Golding, who went on to become its general secretary (under its changed name, the National Communications Union). Golding spoke for eleven hours in the committee stage but it was the general election which caused the bill to lapse in May 1983. Margaret Thatcher

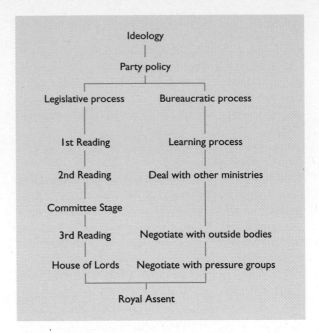

Figure 25.4 Negotiating the policy process
Source: Jones, 1986

was quick to reintroduce an amended form of the bill after the election and, after a speedy progress helped by the guillotine, it became an act on 12 April 1984.

By common consent the second bill was a much more workable piece of legislation. In a Tyne Tees TV programme in August 1986, John Golding claimed some of the credit. Having realised that the large Conservative majority would ensure the bill's eventual success, he decided to cut his losses by pressing for the best possible terms for his members. Most of the important work took place in the corridors and at the committee stage rather than on the floor of the House, which was thinly populated during the debate stages. Golding claims his own advice and expertise was often sought by ministers and civil servants alike as the bill was discussed and amendments moved.

Bureaucratic process

The bureaucratic process in this case to some extent preceded and to some extent continued in parallel with the legislative process. It began with a learning process when civil servants had to negotiate with BT officials and experts. Jason Crisp of *The Financial*

Times, who followed these discussions closely, testified that talks were 'frequent, frantic, often very bad tempered'. Then negotiations with other ministries ensued, especially with the Treasury, which was primarily interested in the huge increases in revenue privatisation would produce. Inevitably, the Department of Trade and Industry was more concerned with achieving a particular kind of settlement, and one which worked, and negotiations with the Treasury were consequently not always smooth.

Next came consultations with the City, where most of the finance was expected to originate. The DTI and the Treasury were clearly determined not to overprice BT's shares. The 1983 election manifesto had listed British Gas, Rolls-Royce, British Steel and others as future candidates for privatisation: they could not afford the failure of such a major test case as BT. The City financiers, like all potential buyers, had an interest in talking the price down, and this they assiduously did.

Finally, negotiations with outside pressure groups took place. In 1980 the British Telecom Union Campaign was formed with the POEU to the fore. With the help of a public relations company and an advertising agency it orchestrated a campaign to frustrate the bill, and, when that failed, to soften its impact upon trade union members. The POEU, in its booklet *The Battle for British Telecom*, tells the story of how it put pressure on 800 key opinion-makers in industry, and in the programme already referred to (Tyne Tees, 1986) John Golding told how the relevant pressure groups were mobilised over rural services, especially the provision of kiosks. The response from the likes of the National Farmers' Union, the local authority associations and the Women's Institutes was so overwhelming that civil servants 'begged' him to call off the campaign because the Department was absolutely inundated by resolutions and letters that came from all those traditionally Conservative supporting bodies. 'But of course we kept the campaign on and . . . The ministers caved in and made certain that they protected the rural services as far as it was possible.'

A number of points can be made about the way in which this decision was made, which also serve as a conclusion to this chapter.

1. *Result differed from intention*: According to party ideology, the main thrust of privatisation is to reintroduce competition and to spread public ownership of shares. At the end of the three-year process, competition seemed to have taken a back seat. (Though Mercury Communications was licensed to compete with BT and in 1990 this duopoly ended and other enterprises were considered as licensed competitors.) And while nearly two million people helped produce the £4 billion flotation (within two years BT doubled in price to about £8 billion), the numbers had decreased to under 1.6 million owning only 12.6 per cent of the BT stock. The result of all the pressures bearing upon the process therefore produced an outcome substantially different from the original intention.

2. *Complexity*: Given the dense complexity of the process, it is small wonder that the public loses touch with all the various twists and turns through Parliament and the corridors of Whitehall. Nor is it surprising that many governments shrink from major initiatives when such mountains of vested interests have to be moved. Margaret Thatcher's governments were indeed unusual in taking so many major initiatives – trade union reform, abolishing the metropolitan counties, privatisation – and succeeding in pushing so many through.

3. *The limits of majority rule*: The case of BT illustrates that a large majority is no substitute for workable legislation. On occasions even opposition MPs have to be called upon to provide the necessary expertise.

4. *The opportunities for influence and consultation are considerable*: Throughout the legislative and bureaucratic processes there are extensive opportunities for individuals and pressure groups to intervene and make their point.

5. *The professionalism of civil servants*: Civil servants are often accused of being generalists – experts on nothing – but in the case of BT they mastered an immensely technical field with remarkable speed. There is no evidence either that they dragged their heels over the privatisation of BT or did anything other than loyally carry out the bidding of their political masters. The irony, however, is that the team which privatised BT dispersed soon afterwards,

lured by private sector employers impressed with the relevant knowhow the privatisation process had bestowed upon them.

Chapter summary

Policy can either be defined as rules and regulations or public expenditure and its distribution. There are various theories about or models of policy-making, including the pluralist corporatist ruling-class and Whitehall models plus the rational choice and incrementalist perspectives on decision-making. Policy can be seen to pass through three stages: initiation, formulation and implementation. 'Core' decision-makers have a constant control of the process but elements from the 'periphery' are brought in from time to time. The concept of policy networks is useful in analysing policy-making. Extra-parliamentary parties and think-tanks can have considerable influence depending on the issue and the situation. Implementation can be very difficult and result in policy objectives being missed or even reversed. Policy-makers face many restraints upon their actions, including timing, coordination and international events.

Discussion points

- Which model of policy-making seems closest to reality?

- Should there be more popular control over policy-making?

- How persuasive is Lindblom's theory of incrementalism?

- What lessons can be learnt from the process whereby BT was privatised?

Further reading

The field of policy studies has spawned a substantial literature over the past ten years or more. Burch and Wood (1990) and Ham and Hill (1993) are good introductions to the denser studies available. Hogwood and Gunn (1984) is a well-written and interesting study, as is Jordan and Richardson (1987). For an up-to-date and penetrating analysis see Smith (1993).

References

Baggott, R. (1995) *Pressure Groups Today* (Manchester University Press).

Bullpitt, J. (1983) *Territory and Power in the United Kingdom* (Manchester University Press).

Burch, M. (1978) 'The policy making process', in B. Jones and D. Kavanagh (eds) *British Politics Today*, Manchester University Press.

Burch, M. and Wood, B. (1990) *Public Policy in Britain*, 2nd edn (Martin Robertson).

Ham, C. and Hill, M. (1993) *The Policy Process in the Modern Capitalist State* (Harvester Wheatsheaf).

Hogwood, B. and Gunn, L.A. (1984) *Policy Analysis in the Real World* (Oxford University Press).

Jones, B. (1986) *Is Democracy Working?* (Tyne Tees TV).

Jordan, G. and Richardson, J.J. (1982) 'The British policy style or the logic of negotiation', in J.J. Richardson (ed.), *Policy Styles in Western Europe* (Allen and Unwin).

Jordan, G. and Richardson, J.J. (1987) *Governing Under Pressure* (Martin Robertson).

Lee, G. (1989) 'Privatisation', in B. Jones (ed.), *Political Issues in Britain Today*, 3rd edn (Manchester University Press).

Smith, M. (1993) *Pressure, Power and Policy* (Harvester Wheatsheaf).

CHAPTER TWENTYSIX

Social policy

MICHAEL MORAN

LEARNING OBJECTIVES

- To define the nature of social policy.

- To identify the main trends in social commitments undertaken by the state in Britain.

- To examine the main issues and debates within the political system produced by those commitments.

INTRODUCTION

Social policy is central to British politics. Guaranteeing entitlements to various social services has become a major responsibility of British governments, but the exact range of those guarantees and how they are to be delivered is a source of political debate. Social policy is also of major importance in the distribution of resources in the community. A market economy like that in Britain is known to have great benefits, especially in assisting individual choice and delivering efficiency. It is also recognised to be a source of inequality, often substantial economic inequality. One of the important historical functions of social policy has been to use the power of government to moderate the inequalities produced by the market.

The nature of social policy

The idea of social policy is linked closely to the existence of the welfare state. The United Kingdom is a 'welfare state'. In other words, a large part of the responsibility of government has to do with paying for, and in some cases directly providing, welfare services for the population. Many of the welfare policies initiated in Britain made the country an international pioneer: for instance, the foundation of the National Health Service in 1948

established a system of largely free health care for everybody paid for mainly out of taxation.

There are two striking features of welfare policy in the United Kingdom. The first is that throughout the present century there has been a long-term growth in the volume of resources given over to spending on welfare. The long-term nature of this trend is illustrated in Figure 26.1; it shows that over the last fifty years in particular the upward pressure has been almost continuous. The second feature is summarised in Figure 26.2, which

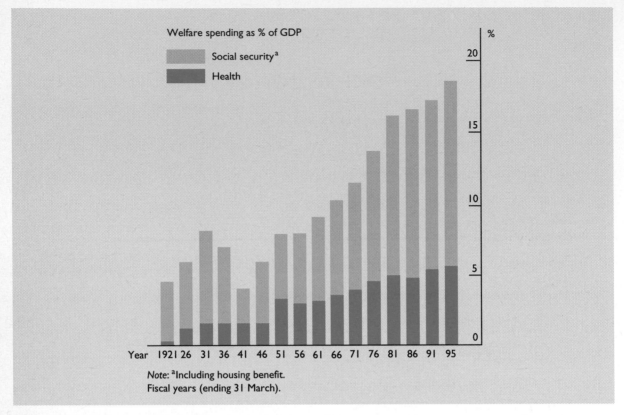

Figure 26.1   Changes in welfare spending, 1921–95
Source: The Economist, 27 April 1996

compares the level of spending on a broad measure of welfare spending in the twelve long-term members of the European Union. The figure shows that, despite the long historical growth, welfare spending in the United Kingdom is comparatively low, set against the record of other advanced industrial countries.

Although the welfare state is commonly spoken of as 'providing services', the reality is that the phrase refers to a wide range of institutions and practices. In the United Kingdom the most important role of the state lies in raising the resources to pay for welfare. It does this in two rather different ways. Firstly, the direct cost of providing some important services – of which health care is the best example – is largely met from the taxes raised by central government. Secondly, the state plays an important role in administering 'transfer payments': it raises money in taxes from one group in the community and 'transfers' it to other groups, in

the form of payments like pensions and unemployment benefit. Thus, eligibility rules for unemployment and social security benefits are settled by central government, and a large administrative apparatus actually processes payments to millions of citizens.

Notice that while we routinely speak of the welfare state as providing welfare services to the population, hardly anything in the description is about direct provision: it is about funding, and about organising systems of provision. Teachers and health care professionals have mostly been paid for out of the public purse, but the role of *central government* in delivering services is limited. Many social services are actually delivered by the 'local state' – in other words, by local government. But much welfare provision goes beyond the institutions of the state completely. Schooling up to the age of 16, for instance, while long compulsory in Britain, has been provided in many cases by

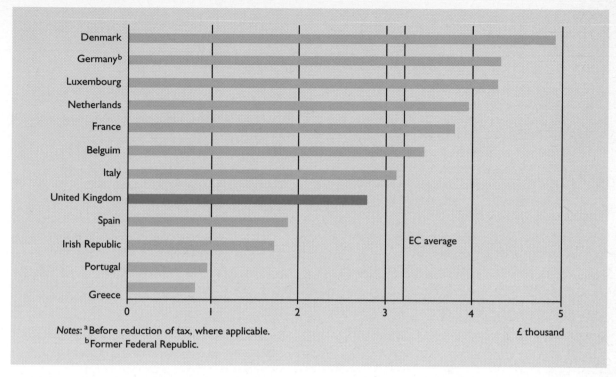

Figure 26.2   Social protection expenditure per head:[a] EC comparison, 1992
Source: Social Trends, 1996, p. 136

church schools. Low-cost housing for rent has in recent years been provided by charities sponsored by government, like housing associations. And many important 'personal social services' – like the care of the handicapped outside hospitals – have been 'contracted out' by the state to voluntary associations and charities. Finally, some important welfare services are contracted out by the state to firms in the marketplace – for instance, care of many old people in privately owned 'residential homes'.

The fact that central government, while predominantly a payer for welfare, is only partly a direct deliverer of services has important consequences for the way welfare policy is made. It means that there is a very wide range of organisations involved in the welfare policy-making process. It is impossible for central departments in Whitehall to make policy without involving these organisations. They include the local authorities and the health authorities responsible for the delivery of so many important services 'on the ground'; the many charities and

voluntary associations likewise involved in service provision; private firms who have contracts with government to deliver services; and professional bodies – representing, for instance, doctors, social workers, teachers – whose members directly deliver the service.

Thus while we speak of the welfare state, welfare services are by by no means produced only, or even mainly, by central government. Indeed, as the political scientist Richard Rose has shown, the state is only one of a number of institutions through which welfare services are delivered. Rose distinguishes three means of providing welfare services: the state; the market, where the service is provided in exchange for cash payments; and the household, where the service is provided within the family unit. He distinguishes seven 'welfare services', arguing that there are differences in the suitable 'mix' by which they can be delivered. The seven are: income, food, housing, personal social services, education, health and transportation. Box 26.1 reproduces Rose's argument.

BOX 26.1   **IDEAS AND PERSPECTIVES**

The welfare mix according to Richard Rose

1. *Household monopoly* (personal social services): Caring for the young and the elderly occurs in the home as a by-product of family relationships The family, rather than institutional or communal care, remains the basic household unit in every OECD nation. Even in Israel, the *kibbutz* ideal of collective communal responsibility for care has been falling by the wayside.

2. *State monopoly* (education): The provision of education came first among the responsibilities assumed by the modern state in the late nineteenth century. Industrialisation and democratisation required a literate population. In the twentieth century the growing complexity of subject matter requires more sophisticated and experienced instructional facilities, reducing the potential input from the household and making marketed education increasingly expensive. Concurrently, secularisation has removed the church, the chief organisational alternative to the state as a source of education.

3. *Household and market* (food): In OECD societies food is sold by the market: it is not treated as a merit good to be supplied without charge by the state. Preparing meals in the household is the norm. The most basic of individual needs, food, is only a primary state responsibility in the very exceptional circumstances of wartime, when the state rations food as part of mobilising resources for total war. Exceptionally, the United States has a Food Stamp program that gives some low-income families vouchers to exchange for specified foods. But this program is more an outgrowth of the need to dispose of surplus crops generated by subsidies to farmers than it is an expression of government intent to regulate diet.

4. *Household and state* (health care): To a substantial extent an individual's health is not a product of social services: it reflects the way in which a person looks after himself or herself. Insofar as health care is provided by others, throughout Europe and Japan there is state provision of specialised medical and hospital services. But care for minor illnesses of children and the elderly is often provided in the home. A person visiting a doctor for treatment is more likely to return home for recuperation than to enter a hospital.

5. *Household, market and state* (income, housing, and transportation). Within OECD societies, families draw income from a mixture of sources. About half of all persons receiving a regular money income are either public employees or else receive an income maintenance grant such as a pension; the other half work in the private sector. Another substantial bloc of the population – children and housewives – receive money through transfers within the household. . . . As for housing, it is bought and sold in the market, but tax subsidies for interest payments affect costs, and some housing may be publicly owned. A substantial fraction of housing maintenance is produced by unpaid do-it-yourself household labour. Transportation too reflects a mix of inputs: the market sells motor cars; the state provides roads and usually operates railways, buses and airlines; and individuals drive themselves about or walk to many destinations.

Source: Rose, 1986

Why is the welfare state so important?

Welfare spending is by far the largest part of public expenditure in the United Kingdom – as it is in most comparable countries. What is more, this has been the case for many decades, and seems likely to continue to be so. Why has the welfare state grown to such an important scale? Four reasons can be identified.

Democratic politics

The welfare state expanded with democracy, because it benefited some of those who were given the vote under democratic politics. Now, the beneficiaries of the welfare state are enormous in number. When we consider the full range of services, from health through education and pensions, we can see that virtually the whole population has a stake in welfare services. Consequently, there are large numbers of votes to be won and lost in the field of welfare policy. What is more, while some of the original motivation for the expansion of welfare services was to help the poor, it has now been demonstrated that many of the services – especially education – also benefit the middle classes (see below). In other words, the educated, prosperous and politically well organised have a big stake in the preservation of many welfare services. This is reinforced by the role of the welfare state as an employer, often of highly educated professionals: for instance, there are over a million people employed in health services in Britain. These occupations amount to a considerable lobby for the preservation of the welfare state.

Political philosophy

Although many of the services of the welfare state are known to benefit the relatively well-off, it is undeniably the case that one motive behind its original development was to provide safeguards against sickness, unemployment and poverty. The philosophies of the political parties which have dominated British politics in this century have all in different ways viewed the state as a source of welfare. Before the First World War important social policy reforms were introduced by the Liberal government which had won office in 1906, and which was dominated by politicians who believed in 'social reform' liberalism – in other words, in using the state as an instrument of social reform. Since the end of the First World War British politics has been dominated by two parties – Labour and Conservative – which in different ways also support welfare provision: the Labour Party because it believes that the purpose of the state is to intervene to ensure that inequalities and deprivations caused by markets should be remedied, especially if they affect manual workers and their families; the Conservative Party because, at least until the 1980s, it was dominated by politicians who believed that government had obligations to ensure that the poorest were cared for by the state. Immediately after the Second World War a reforming Labour government greatly extended the scope of the welfare state. These reforms were accepted, and consolidated, by the Conservative governments in office from 1951 to 1964. In other words, for much of its recent history British politics has been dominated by two parties which, for different reasons, have been committed to a large welfare state.

Economic efficiency

As we shall shortly see, in the 1980s the welfare state had many critics on the grounds that its cost was a 'burden' on the economy. But as Figure 26.2 showed it is striking how many nations with highly advanced economies also have large welfare states. In part, of course, this is because successful economies produce the resources needed to pay for welfare. But it is also because an efficient industrial economy needs the sort of services provided by the welfare state. Industrial economies demand a highly educated workforce. Indeed, one of the commonest criticisms of this part of the British welfare state is that we do not educate the population to as high a level as our main competitors (see Figure 26.3.) An industrial economy also requires a healthy workforce – which in turn demands efficient health care available to all. The most successful economies also function best when workers are willing to be highly adaptable – for instance, to change work practices, and even to accept unemployment, in order to make the best use of the latest technology. Obviously this cooperation is only likely to happen when workers

BOX 26.2   CHRONOLOGY

Landmarks in the history of the welfare state

Income maintenance

1945	Universal flat-rate family allowances for all but first child in the welfare family
1948	National insurance system flat-benefits for retirement, widows, sickness and unemployment, with flat-rate contributions
1948	National Assistance: means-tested social assistance on uniform national scales
1961	Graduated state pension on money purchase basis for workers without occupational pension
1966	Earnings-related supplement for first 6 months of unemployment or sickness benefit
1966	Supplementary benefit, with legal entitlement, replaced national assistance
1971	Invalidity pensions introduced
1974	National insurance contributions earnings-related; pensions uprated annually in line with earnings or prices, whichever greater
1977	Child benefit for all children replaced family allowances and child income tax allowances
1978	State earnings-related pension scheme (SERPS), reflecting increases in earnings and prices, replaced graduated pensions
1980	Pensions indexed to prices only
1982	Earnings-related supplement to sickness and unemployment benefit abolished

Health

1948	National Health Service: free, universal health care, with hospitals managed by central government
1952	Charges for drug prescriptions and optical and dental treatment
1974	Major reorganisation of National Health Services: hospitals, family practitioner and community health services integrated under regional and area boards
1982	Further reorganisation, with area tier abolished

Education

1944	Education Act increased school-leaving age to 15; organised system into primary, secondary and further sectors; selective education according to ability to be the norm for secondary pupils
1965	Government request for local authorities to organise secondary schools on a comprehensive, all-ability basis
1971	School-leaving age increased to 16
1976	Public grants to some independent (direct-grant) schools ended

Housing

1946	New subsidy system for local authority housing, with contributions from central government, local taxations, and rents paid by tenants
1972	National rent rebate system to give means-tested assistance to public and private sector tenants
1980	Right for local authority tenants to buy their house at a discount according to length of residence
1982	Means-tested assistance with rent and rates (Housing Benefit) integrated under local authority administration

Personal social services

1970	Establishment of integrated Social Services Departments in local authorities to provide non-cash residential and home-based services to children, the elderly and others

Source: Parry, 1986

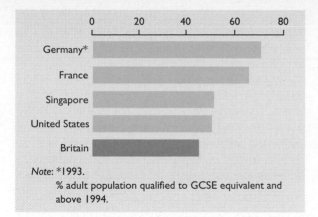

| | 0 | 20 | 40 | 60 | 80 |

Germany*

France

Singapore

United States

Britain

Note: *1993.
% adult population qualified to GCSE equivalent and above 1994.

Figure 26.3 National comparisons of education levels
Source: *The Economist*, 15 June 1996

believe that if they lose their jobs through new technology the state will both retrain them for new work and ensure that while unemployed they, and their families, are guaranteed levels of benefit which will keep them above poverty levels. In other words, economic success demands generous unemployment and other social security benefits.

Market failure

The United Kingdom is a capitalist economy – which means that the chief mechanism for the production and distribution of goods and services is the marketplace, where exchanges are made for money. But in many cases markets will fail to produce goods and services, or will produce them in insufficient amounts. 'Market failure' is one of the most important reasons for state intervention. Goods and services as different as national defence, street lighting or public parks would be difficult to organise if the state did not compel citizens at large to contribute to their upkeep. Similar problems of collective choice undermine the market in areas of welfare provision. For instance, if the state made education entirely voluntary, and relied on parents to buy education for their children, it is undoubtedly the case that some children would not be educated because their parents would be unwilling voluntarily to make the necessary economic sacrifices. Likewise, if the long-term sick and handicapped had to find the resources to pay for the full cost of their own care, they would simply not be

able to raise those resources; there would be great gaps in the care for the sick and the handicapped if the market alone were left to ensure that funds were available. (Notice that this is not at all the same as saying that the state *directly* provides those services; it only suggests that government ensures that the resources are available. Whether the services are then delivered by the state, by charities or by private firms is a separate question.) The issue of how to deliver welfare services is one of the most important facing policy-makers – and is included in the list of key issues which we now examine.

Issues in welfare policy

'Welfare policy-making' is about choices concerning the welfare services in a community: about their range, about how they should be paid for, about how they should be delivered, and about who should benefit from the welfare state. How to make these choices lies at the heart of most debates about the big issues in welfare policy in the Britain.

The absolute level of spending

Although, as we have seen, the welfare state in the United Kingdom is not large by international standards, there has nevertheless been concern about the 'burden' of welfare spending. In part this concern reflects pressures common to all nations which have established generous systems of welfare provision. The expansion of the welfare state across the industrial world took place in the decades after 1945 in a period of international prosperity. In the last twenty years this prosperity has become much less certain, and in most countries questions have been raised about the scope of welfare provision. In the United Kingdom the problem of the level of provision has been especially severe because the UK economy has been particularly unsuccessful in delivering the increased wealth needed to fund welfare services.

In some areas difficulties are made more serious by long-term increases in the demand for services. For instance, although the cost of the National Health Service is by international standards modest, the level of spending on health shows a long-term rise: as a nation we spend £10 billion more on health than we did a decade ago. The pressure of rising costs comes from two areas in particular:

constant improvements in medical technology are widening the range of conditions which can be treated; and the ageing of the population is expanding the numbers of people who live to a great, and sickly, old age.

The issue of how much in total to spend on welfare has become particularly important because of changes in the outlook of the Conservative Party, which of course ruled the country from 1979. After Margaret Thatcher became leader in 1975 the influence of those Conservatives who supported large-scale welfare spending declined within the party. Under Thatcher, and under her successor, John Major, welfare spending was viewed in terms of 'opportunity cost': although often desirable, every pound spent on welfare was viewed as a resource diverted from productive investment, and therefore from wealth creation. These ambitions to cut the size of the welfare state have actually come to little (see Figure 26.1.) They have, however, affected the government's stance on related issues, notably the balance to be struck between different welfare programmes and the means of delivering welfare.

The balance between programmes

The question of the overall size of the welfare state is of course inseparable from the question of the relative size of particular programmes, because it is obvious that cuts in welfare spending can only be made by cutting specific programmes. Cutting programmes has in practice proved very difficult, for two reasons. Firstly, some expensive parts of the welfare state are exceptionally popular. In particular such is the level of support for the National Health Service that even Margaret Thatcher was obliged in the 1983 general election campaign to pledge support for its principles for fear that to do otherwise would damage the Conservative Party electorally. Secondly, the largest proportion of spending on welfare, like public spending as a whole, is not really in the control of governments, at least in the short term: it amounts to obligations inherited from decisions taken by predecessors. This is particularly true of 'income transfers' – cash benefits like pensions and social security – which are based on entitlements usually embodied in law. Sudden changes in the numbers of those entitled to

claim – such as occurs when unemployment rises – force governments to spend more. This is exactly what happened in the recessions at the start and at the end of the 1980s, when government was forced to spend unexpectedly large amounts on social security payments.

As a result of the difficulty of cutting spending across the board, governments have therefore been forced to concentrate on *restructuring* the welfare state – trying to change the balance of spending. As we have just seen, their ability to do this is limited. Nevertheless, in one of the most important programmes of the welfare state – public subsidy for low-cost housing – considerable cuts were made after the Conservatives came back to government in 1979. In the post-war years the provision of low-cost housing for the poor (council housing) was one of the main areas of welfare spending. In the 1980s governments cut investment in new housing virtually to nothing and sold a large part of the public housing stock to sitting tenants: 1.4 million dwellings were disposed of in this way. The attempt to *restructure* the welfare state has been connected to the third issue identified above: how to deliver welfare services.

The means of delivery

Although we often speak of the welfare state as 'providing' welfare services, in fact it is both possible and common for the state to *fund* services rather than directly take on responsibility for delivery.

The issues raised by the means of service delivery can be well illustrated by the case of the National Health Service. In hospital care, for most of the service's history the same public bodies both paid for, and delivered, care. Hospitals were publicly owned institutions. The reforms in the National Health Service introduced since 1989 are intended to separate the funders of care from the providers. Through a system of 'internal markets' public health authorities contract with providers – such as hospitals – to supply health care on agreed terms. A growing number of hospitals, in addition, are now self-governing trusts rather than publicly owned organisations. They are responsible for their own budgets and have some independence in fixing the pay and conditions of staff. The theory behind this system is that providers of care, like hospitals, will have incentives to deliver care more efficiently in order to win and retain contracts from those funding care.

This change in the health service is only part of a wider shift in the organisation of service delivery in British government. There has taken place a general shift in the direction of a 'contract state' – a state where government pays for services, but contracts the job of delivery out to a separate body, usually by some sort of competitive system. Some shifts in this direction took place in the National Health Service even before the important reforms of recent years – contracting out of laundry services in hospitals, for instance, was already well established by the late 1980s. Beyond the particular sphere of welfare, contracting out has spread to a wide range of services, like refuse collection in local authorities.

The contrasting arguments surrounding the shift to contracting out in service delivery are well known. On the one hand, there is nothing new in principle involved in contracting: as we saw in Chapter 4 the government is a 'customer' for a wide range of services, and there is no obvious dividing line between goods and services that ought to be delivered directly, and those that can be 'bought in' from the private sector. It is difficult to imagine anybody seriously defending the proposition that the state should produce everything itself. Competition can extend choice and can create pressures for the delivery of more responsive and more efficient services. On the other hand, the welfare state has been built on the principle of universalism: in other words, on the principle that all citizens should have access to a similar minimum level of service. However, when services are contracted out with the aim of ensuring that providers compete by offering differing levels and kinds of service, this commitment to universalism is compromised.

'Universalism' is also at the centre of the fourth issue identified above: funding.

Who should pay?

Britain is fairly unusual in relying on general taxation to provide the lion's share of the money for welfare. In many other European states, for instance, it is common for programmes to be funded out of insurance contributions levied on workers and employers. These contributions are usually obligatory, though they can be voluntary. This is, for instance, one of the commonest ways of paying for the cost of health care in Europe. The advantages of an insurance system are twofold. Firstly, the contributions guarantee a stream of income for a welfare programme like health care, whereas in the British system welfare programmes have to compete as best they can against other public spending priorities. (This may be why the British welfare state spends rather less than the international average.) A second advantage is that in some circumstances insurance systems may encourage more competition and efficiency, because the insurers can be separated from the providers, and have an incentive to shop around for the most cost-effective forms of delivery. The disadvantage of insurance systems, even of compulsory ones, is that they usually produce inequalities in the service offered. For instance, insurance funds based on the workplace usually end up offering a better deal to the better paid workers. In discussions about funding the National Health Service in the 1980s some advocates of reform expressed interest in shifting to an insurance system, though this has never been pursued.

Arguments about the choice between general taxation or insurance to fund welfare make an important assumption – that there is no charge for services at the point of consumption. Indeed, for the most part this is true of major programmes like education. However, 'user charges' have always existed for some services, and in the 1980s they were considerably expanded. In health care, for instance, in both dental and optical services 'free' services have almost disappeared except for groups exempted on grounds of low income. The case for user charges is twofold: charges, even set at modest levels, can raise money that is badly needed; and charges encourage clients to be prudent in making calls on services, whereas if the service is a 'free good' there is the possibility that it will be used (and abused) thoughtlessly. The most important argument against user charges is that charging even a modest amount risks deterring the poorest from using services – and thus undermines one of the most important functions of the welfare state.

There is in turn a connection between the issue of charges and the final issue examined here: who should benefit from welfare policy?

Who should benefit?

It is in the nature of universal services – like schooling, health care, pensions – that they are available to everybody who meets the appropriate conditions. Thus, to receive free schooling it is necessary only to be of school age, to receive health care only to be judged sick by a doctor, to receive an old age pension to have reached the stipulated age.

This principle of universalism has created two problems, one concerning efficiency and one concerning equality. The efficiency problem exists because, since resources are limited, it can be argued that it is more efficient to 'target' resources on those in most need. This implies a shift away from universalism in the provision of, for instance, pensions and other benefits to a selective targeting on the needy. These 'efficiency' concerns interact with the concern with equality, for it is obviously a principle of universalism that all, regardless of their personal economic circumstances, should be entitled to a benefit. In some circumstances, this can give the wealthy the same entitlement to benefits as the poor. Table 26.1 draws on calculations by Le Grand. He divided services into three categories – pro-poor, equal in their impact on the rich and poor, pro-rich. He measured impact by the ratio of spending on a service between those earning incomes that put them in the top fifth in the community compared with those in the bottom fifth. Thus in the table, the figure of 5.4 for universities means that spending on those from families with high earning is nearly five and a half times as great as spending on those from low-income families. An intuitive way of making sense of these figures is to say that any service with a figure below 1 benefits the poor; any service with a figure of 1 is neutral as between rich and poor; and the higher a figure is above 1, the more the service benefits the rich. The table shows that many welfare services actually advantage the rich.

Why do we get the apparently odd outcome that systems established with the aim of benefiting the poor in the community end up distributing higher levels of benefit to the wealthy? There seem to be two main reasons.

Firstly, in part the outcomes of welfare policy are affected by the ability of particular groups to lobby

Table 26.1 Who benefits from welfare services?

Service	Ratio of expenditure per person in top fifth to that per person in bottom fifth
Pro-poor	
Council housing (general subsidy and rent rebates)[a]	0.3
Rent allowances	na
Equal	
Nursery education	na
Primary education	0.9
Secondary education, pupils over 16	0.9
Pro-rich	
National health service	1.4[b]
Secondary education, pupils over 16	1.8
Non-university higher education[c]	3.5
Bus subsidies	3.7
Universities[c]	5.4
Tax subsidies to owner-occupiers	6.8
Rail subsidies	9.8

Notes: [a] The estimates pre-date the introduction of housing benefit
[b] Per person ill
[c] Colleges of education, technical education and institutions that were polytechnics at the time of calculation
Source: Goodin and Le Grand, 1987, p. 92

government in order to improve the quality of the services available to them. The pattern of welfare spending is not, in other words, a straightforward response to need. In general terms the poor are less well organised in lobbies than are the wealthy, and are less well placed to exert influence over policy outcomes: notice in Table 26.1 the substantial advantages to the better-off from tax subsidies to owner-occupiers.

Secondly, eligibility for some services is not automatic, but depends on achieving success in competition. The most obvious example of this is university education, the overwhelming cost of which is paid for by the state. Admission to university in all cases depends on demonstrating the capacity to benefit from a university education, and in most cases rests on success in examinations (chiefly 'A' levels). We know, however, that success in educational examinations is closely tied to social class. This explains the pattern shown in Figure 26.4, which shows acceptances to university places to be consistently greater for higher than for lower social classes.

Resolving the question of who should benefit from welfare spending depends on arriving at a view about the fundamental purpose of the welfare state. If the point of the welfare state is to ensure that a set of rights are available to all citizens, then there is nothing objectionable in the millionaire having the same rights as, say, an unemployed person, just as we naturally expect the rich and the poor to be treated equally in other spheres – before the courts, for instance. On the other hand, if the purpose of the welfare state is to remove or moderate social inequality created, for instance, by the

market system, then the fact that the rich have some of the same benefit entitlements as the poor becomes a real problem.

Chapter summary

In this chapter we have seen that: the scale of resources committed to social policy is very large, has been growing for a long time, but is still comparatively modest by international standards; the growth of state involvement in the provision of welfare has taken place for a mixture of economic and ideological reasons; there are significant problems of equity and efficiency raised by the way the welfare state is presently organised.

Discussion points

- Why does Britain seem to be so modest by international standards in the the scale of its welfare state?

- Should welfare policy aim at promoting equality?

- How would you explain the long-term growth in social spending by the state in Britain?

Further reading

Esping-Andersen (1990) sets the British welfare state in an international context. Ham (1992) reviews one of the most expensive and contentious sectors. Wilding (1986) reviews and criticises some of the contemporary policy arguments. Mohan (1995) examines a wide range of evidence on distributions and impact. Goodin and Le Grand (1987) examine evidence about the class distributional effect of the welfare state. Deakin (1994) is up-to-date on recent history.

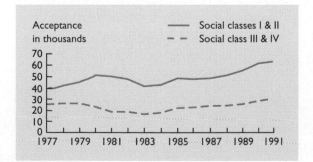

Figure 26.4 Class composition of university acceptances
Source: Times Higher Education Supplement, 4 September 1992

References

Deakin, N. (1994) *The Politics of Welfare* (Harvester Wheatsheaf).

Esping-Andersen, G. (1990) *The Three Worlds of Welfare Capitalism* (Polity Press).

Goodin, R. and Le Grand, J. (1987) *Not Only The Poor: The Middle Classes and the Welfare State* (Allen and Unwin).

Ham, C. (1992) *Health Policy in Britain* (Macmillan).

Mohan, J. (1995) *A National Health Service?* (Macmillan).

Parry, R. (1986) 'United Kingdom', in P. Flora (ed.), *Growth to Limits* (De Gruyter).

Rose, R. (1986) 'Common goals but different roles: the state's contribution to the welfare mix', in R. Rose and R. Shiratori (eds), *The Welfare State East and West* (Oxford University Press).

Wilding, P. (ed) (1986) *In Defence of the Welfare State* (Manchester University Press)

Economic policy

MICHAEL MORAN AND BILL JONES

LEARNING OBJECTIVES

- To identify the nature of economic policy.

- To describe the machinery by which economic policy is made and implemented.

- To outline some of the main political debates that surround economic policy in Britain.

INTRODUCTION

Probably the single most important feature of modern British politics is the extent to which governments are judged by how well they manage the economy. Governments can get lots of things wrong and still win elections if they can deliver what electors perceive as economic success; but no matter how well governments do in other fields, it is almost impossible to be electorally successful if they are economic failures. This simple observation identifies the key place of economic policy in the political system.

The nature of economic policy

It may be thought a simple matter to identify 'economic policy': 'policy' consists in the choices made and rejected by government; 'economic' refers to that set of institutions and activities concerned with the production and distribution of goods and services; economic policy therefore consists in those choices made or rejected by government designed to affect the production of goods and services in the community.

This is, it will be plain, a very broad definition. Many activities of government not commonly thought of as 'economic' become so if we rigorously follow this guideline. Thus policy towards the arts – for instance, the provision of subsidised opera and theatre – is directed to influencing the price at which particular artistic services are provided to the community.

A broad definition of economic policy is revealing, for two reasons. Firstly, it alerts us to the fact that the boundaries of 'economic policy' are moving all the time. For example, in recent years government has increasingly pictured education in economic terms. It conceives the primary purpose of schooling to be the production of one of the community's most valuable economic assets – a competent and educationally adaptable workforce. Thus, to an increasing extent policy towards schools has been conceived as a facet of economic policy. One of the primary features of economic policy is, therefore, that it has wide and constantly changing boundaries.

This connects to a second factor making a 'broad' definition of policy appealing: there is constant struggle and argument over the making and control of policy. British government works in part by a series of conventions which allocate subjects to particular institutions. An issue defined as purely concerned with education, for instance, will be in the domain of the Department for Employment and Education and the teaching profession. Until recently, for example, the content of the school curriculum was thought of as such a purely 'educational' matter. But the growing belief that the quality of education, by affecting the quality of the workforce, in turn shapes the fortunes of the economy has introduced economic considerations into arguments about the curriculum – and has destroyed the idea that choices about what is to be taught in schools are to be made only by those concerned with education. That indeed was the point of adding 'employment' to the education portfolio.

This example shows that in economic policy-making arguments about what is, and what is not, relevant to the economy are of more than definitional significance. They are part of the process by which different groups in government try to gain control over particular areas of decision. If, for instance, the task of reviving the decaying parts of Britain's inner cities is pictured as one concerning the renovation of the physical environment, it will naturally be thought of as the responsibility at national level of the Department of the Environment. If, by contrast, it is pictured as a task of reviving a declining part of the industrial economy, it will more naturally be thought of as the proper responsibility of the Department of Trade and Industry. The 'boundaries' of economic policy are, therefore, uncertain and disputed. But if the boundaries are open to argument, there is nevertheless considerable agreement about where the heart of economic policy lies. The most important parts concern the government's own 'housekeeping', and its wider responsibilities for economic management.

Government has to make choices concerning the raising and distribution of its own resources: it has, in other words, to make choices concerning its budget in the same way as a firm or a family makes choices. But the choices made by government about

how much to spend, where to allocate the money and how to raise it have a special significance. This significance is partly the result of scale: government is the biggest institution in the British economy and has a correspondingly great effect on the rest of society. Decisions by government about how much to spend and how much to tax crucially affect the prosperity or otherwise of the economy at large. But the significance of public spending and taxation choices also lie in their purpose, for they are important *instruments* which government can and does use to influence the course of the economy. This connects to a second 'core' aspect of economic policy.

Complementing its role as a major appropriator and distributor of resources in Britain, government has a second major economic policy responsibility – to 'steer the economy'. The implied comparison with steering a vessel or a vehicle, while not exact, is nevertheless helpful. Like the pilot of a vessel, government possesses *instruments* of control which can be manipulated to guide the economy in a desired direction; and like a pilot it has available a variety of *indicators* telling it how successfully these instruments are working. Among the most important instruments of control used by British government in recent decades are the budgetary instruments to which we have already referred. By varying the total volume of public spending, or the level of taxation, government is able to increase or depress the total amount of activity in the economy. By targeting its spending on particular areas – like education, or the inner cities, or as subsidies to particular industries – government can also try to influence specific groups in the economy.

The image of 'steering the economy' was particularly important in the twenty-five years after the end of the Second World War. Margaret Thatcher's administrations, as we have seen in earlier chapters, denied that government could control the economy in the way that was attempted in the past. During the 1980s 'Thatcherites' asserted that government could only hope to create the right conditions for a freely functioning market economy; competitive forces, for better or worse, would do the rest. Yet the government still does try to 'steer the economy'. It has objectives – like the control of inflation – which it seeks to achieve, and instruments of control which it uses to that end. After the 1970s, therefore, the direction of economic steering and the instruments of control changed; but all governments in post-war Britain have been engaged in steering the economy.

The machinery of economic policy

When we refer to the 'machinery' of something we are usually speaking of more than the mechanical parts of which it is composed; we also mean the process by which those parts combine in movement. So it is with the machinery of economic policy-making: we mean not just the institutions, but the process by which they interact to produce choices.

If we look at a formal organisation chart of British government we will see that it is hierarchical in nature with elected politicians – ministers – at the top. It would be natural to assume, therefore, that the machinery of economic policy-making worked by reserving the power to make policy to a few people at the top of government and reserving the task of carrying out policy to those lower down the hierarchy. But perhaps the single most important feature of policy-making is that there is no simple distinction to be made between a few at the top who 'make' policy and a larger number lower down in government who 'implement' or 'execute' policy. More perhaps than in any other area of public affairs, *economic policy-making* and *policy implementation* are inseparable. Those at the top of government certainly have the potential to make broad decisions about the direction of policy. But the substance of economic policy is determined not only by broad strategic judgements; it is also shaped by the way large numbers of organisations in *both the public and private sectors* translate those into practical reality. The best way of picturing the machinery of economic policy-making, therefore, is not as a hierarchy in which a few take decisions which are then executed by those further down the hierarchy, but rather as a set of institutions in the centre of the machine which negotiate and argue over policy with a wide range of surrounding bodies in both the public and private sectors.

The centre of the machine

The Treasury

At the centre of the machinery of economic policy making is *the Treasury*. At first glance the Treasury looks an insignificant institution. It is tiny by the standards of most central departments. What is more it plays little part in the execution of economic policy. Vital tasks like administering schemes for financial support of industry and regulating the activities of particular sectors and occupations are carried out elsewhere, notably by the Department of Trade and Industry. The Treasury's importance essentially lies in three features.

Firstly, it is universally recognised as a vital source of policy advice about economic management, not only to its political head, the Chancellor of the Exchequer, but also to other senior ministers, notably the Prime Minister. Secondly, it is, as its name implies, in effect the keeper of the public purse: it is the key institution in decisions about the composition and about the volume of public spending. This is organised around a virtually continuous cycle of bargaining between the Treasury and the 'spending departments' to fix both the level of spending commitments and the proportionate allocation of resources between competing claimants.

Thirdly, the Treasury shares with the Bank of England a large measure of control over policy towards financial markets. These matters include the terms on which the government borrows money, intervention to affect the level of interest rates throughout the economy and the 'management of sterling' – in other words intervention in foreign exchange markets to influence the rate at which the pound is exchanged for other foreign currencies. Although in most of these activities the Bank of England acts as the agent of government, it only does this in close, virtually continuous, consultation with the Treasury. These responsibilities are especially important because the management of financial markets has since the mid-1970s become a key task of economic policy. Consequently *the Bank of England* should now be placed alongside the Treasury at the core of the machinery of economic policy, despite the fact that it is not a government department, nor even located in the area around Westminster where most of the major departments have their headquarters.

The Bank of England

The Bank of England is the nation's 'central bank'. This means that it is a publicly owned institution (though it only became so in 1946) with responsibility for managing the national currency. It also has a legal responsibility to oversee and safeguard the stability of the country's banking system and a more general responsibility to oversee the stability of financial markets. It is, as we have already seen, also the Treasury's agent in managing public debt and in interventions to influence levels of interest rates in the economy. The Bank's headquarters are located in the City of London and this symbolises its distinctive character. Although a public body and part of the core of the machinery of policy-making, it retains a tradition of independence. Its Governor, while nominated by the Prime Minister, is usually a considerable and independent figure, in both the City of London and in international gatherings of other 'central bankers'. Likewise employees of the Bank are recruited separately from, and paid more than, civil servants.

The Bank's importance in the machinery of economic decision-making rests on two factors. Firstly, it plays a major part in the execution of decisions increasingly considered to be the heart of economic policy – those concerning the management of conditions in financial markets. Secondly, as a result of its continuous and deep involvement with the markets it has an established position as a source of advice about the policy options best suited to the successful management of these markets.

Describing the Treasury and the Bank of England as the centre of the machinery of economic policy does not amount to the same thing as saying that these two institutions dominate policy. As we will see in a later section, there is considerable room for argument about the extent of Treasury and Bank of England power. However, it is undoubtedly the case that the two have a continuous role in the discussions about the strategic purposes and daily tactics of economic policy which occupy so much of modern government. No other *institution* in government specialises in this activity at such a high level.

The Treasury's and the Bank's positions at the centre of the machine are nevertheless shared with others. All governments in modern times have viewed economic policy as a primary responsibility and as a major influence on their chances of re-election. This means that economic management is never far from the minds of senior ministers. Two departmental members of the Cabinet usually occupy Treasury posts: the Chancellor of the Exchequer; and the Chief Secretary to the Treasury, whose main responsibility is managing at the highest level the negotiations over expenditure plans between the Treasury and the 'spending' departments. Given the importance of economic policy, prime ministerial participation in consideration of strategy and tactics is now customary.

The Prime Minister

'Prime Minister' here partly means the individual who happens to be the occupant of that position at any particular moment. The Prime Minister is both figuratively and physically close to the machinery of economic policy-making: his/her residence and that of the Chancellor adjoin, while the Treasury itself is barely a footstep away from No. 10 Downing Street. However, 'prime ministerial' involvement in economic policy denotes more than the involvement of a particular personality. It happened to be the case in the 1980s that Britain had in Margaret Thatcher an unusually commanding Prime Minister with a particular interest in, and firm grasp of, the mechanics of economic policy. Consequently, she was a central figure in the machinery. Any modern Prime Minister is, however, likely to be an important part of the machine. The precise position will depend on changing factors: the abilities and interests of a particular individual; the personal relations between the Prime Minister and the Chancellor; and the wider popularity and authority which the Prime Minister can command. Prime ministerial involvement need not consist only of personal intervention. It can also take the form of participation by the staff of the Prime Minister's own office and from institutions closely connected to the Prime Minister, notably the Cabinet Office. Prime ministerial economic advisers can also exert considerable influence: in 1989 the Chancellor Nigel Lawson actually resigned over the role performed by Margaret Thatcher's adviser, Sir Alan Walters.

The Cabinet

Prime ministerial participation in the machinery of economic policy-making may now be described as 'institutionalised' – which means that it is part of the established procedures, irrespective of the capacities and outlook of the individual who at any particular moment happens to occupy No. 10 Downing Street. It is less certain that the same can be said of the Cabinet, a body which once was indeed indisputably a dominant participant. It is true that the Cabinet retains a role irrespective of particular circumstances, such as the style of an individual Prime Minister. Thus the weekly meetings of Cabinet will always contain agenda items which bear on central parts of economic strategy. More important still, the network of Cabinet committees which now do much business in place of full Cabinet are important forums for consideration of strategy and tactics. The Cabinet system retains a particularly important role in deciding public spending. Although the process is dominated by direct bargaining between the Treasury and the individual departments, it is still accepted that it is at Cabinet committee level that irreconcilable differences between a department and the Treasury are effectively resolved.

Nevertheless, since the end of the 1970s the extent of collective Cabinet involvement in economic policy-making has been uncertain. The importance of individuals remains: after all, three Cabinet Members – the Prime Minister, the Chancellor and the Chief Secretary to the Treasury – are all indisputably part of the core machinery. But what may have declined is the collective consideration of strategy and tactics by Cabinet institutions – either in full Cabinet or in committee. Whether this is due to the style of leadership practised by Margaret Thatcher, who dominated her Cabinets in the 1980s, and tended to keep economic policy off the Cabinet agenda, or whether it is due to longer-term changes in the significance of the Cabinet, is at present uncertain; but if it is due to long-term changes it is plainly important; and if due to Thatcher's leadership style it is also revealing, since it shows that the Cabinet's place in the machinery is dependent on the style of the particular Prime Minister who happens to be in office. We will need to know more than we presently do about former Prime Minister Major's relations with his Cabinet before we can answer this question.

The observation that the Cabinet's role in the machinery is uncertain should not be taken to mean that Cabinet ministers and their departments are unimportant. Indeed, since we saw earlier that no simple division can be made between the 'making' of policy and its 'implementation', it follows that departments, in the act of executing policy, in effect also 'make' it by shaping what comes out of the government machine. This is manifestly the case with, for instance, the Department of Trade and Industry, which, in its multitude of dealings with individual firms, industries and sectors, plays a large part in deciding what is, in practice, to be the government's policy towards a wide range of industries.

The machinery of economic policy stretches not only beyond the central institutions like the Treasury to other central departments; it also encompasses what is sometimes called 'quasi-government' and even institutions which are in the private sector. It is to these matters that we now turn.

Quasi-government

One of the striking features of British government is the small proportion of the 'public sector' which is actually accounted for by what we conventionally think of as the characteristic public institution – the central department headed by a Cabinet minister located in central London. Most people who work in the public sector are not 'civil servants', and most of the work of the public sector is done by institutions which do not have the status of civil service departments. This is an especially noticeable feature of the machinery of economic policy. It has become conventional to speak of this range of institutions as 'quasi-government' organisations. By this is meant that they have many of the marks of public bodies: they are usually entrusted with the task of carrying out duties prescribed in law; they often draw all, or a proportion of, their funds from the public purse; and the appointment of their leading officers is usually controlled by a minister and his or her department. Yet in their daily operations they normally work with some degree of independence of ministers and are usually less subject than are civil service departments to parliamentary scrutiny. In economic policy it is helpful to distinguish between two categories of quasi-government institution: *nationalised corporations* and a more diverse category best labelled *independent specialised agencies*.

Nationalised corporations are a comparatively standard organisational type. They normally work under a charter prescribing such matters as the constitution and powers of their governing board. The corporation form was used for activities as different as delivering broadcasting services (the BBC) and mining coal (British Coal). They have responsibility for providing particular kinds of goods and services (although the boundaries of their appropriate activities are often unclear). Most nationalised corporations provide goods or services through the market, deriving the bulk of their revenue from sales. But they are also linked to central government. It is common for a corporation to have a 'sponsoring department' in Whitehall. The 'sponsor' will be expected to 'speak for' its corporation inside central government, but it is also an instrument for exercising control over the corporation.

From 1945 to the end of the 1970s the nationalised corporation was a major instrument of government policy – and was itself in turn a major influence over the shape of economic policy. In the 1980s 'privatisation' reduced the size and significance of the nationalised corporation in the machinery of economic policy.

Free-standing, specialised agencies have, if anything, become more important in recent years. They cover a wide range of areas, and take a variety of organised forms. They have become one of the most important means by which economic policy is 'delivered' – and, in being delivered, shaped. For example, the government has established an Urban Regeneration Agency, whose purpose is to bring vacant and derelict land in towns and cities into use. It is worth stressing that bodies like these do not just carry out policy decisions made elsewhere; they shape policy by their control over the details of its execution and their role in policy advice.

There are many reasons why 'quasi-government' is important in the machinery of economic policy, but two are particularly significant. The first is that central government departments simply do not have the resources and knowledge to carry out the full tasks of the public sector; the system would become impossibly overloaded if the effort were made to control everything through a handful of government departments in London. The second reason is that the 'quasi-government' system offers some protection against control by politicians, especially

Members of Parliament. It is much harder for a Member of Parliament to scrutinise and call to account an agency or a nationalised corporation than to do the same thing with a civil service department headed by a minister.

The machinery of economic policy stretches into 'quasi-government'; but it also, we shall now see, reaches into the private sector.

The private sector

It may seem odd to include privately owned institutions like business firms in the machinery of policy. But it will become obvious when we realise two things: that economic policy is made in the process of execution, not just by a few people at the top handing down decisions to be routinely carried out elsewhere; and in executing policy government relies widely on private bodies.

One of the most striking examples of this is provided by the banking system in Britain. Almost all British banks are privately owned; yet without

---

BOX 27.1

Actors in economic policy

Prime Minister
Chancellor
Chief Secretary to the Treasury
Governor of the Bank of England
Senior Treasury Officials
Economic advisers
Cabinet Office
Key Cabinet committees
Secretary of State, Department of Trade and
　Industry
Cabinet

Quasi-government
Nationalised
　corporations
Independent specialised
　agencies

Private sector
Business firms
Banks

the services provided by the banks any government's economic policies would come to nothing. For instance, the whole payments system, on which the economy depends, is administered by the banks. This includes, for example, the circulation of notes and coins throughout the population and the processing of cheques and other forms of payment. In some of the most technologically advanced sectors of the economy, like the nuclear power industry, firms in private ownership work in close partnership with government to implement jointly agreed policies.

Economic policy and public spending

Economic policy comprises a number of very important areas: dealings with foreign economies and international agencies, management of the economy and the raising of revenue. The control and allocation of public expenditure, however, is of particular interest as it affects all of us as consumers of government services. Since the early 1960s this policy area has been the responsibility of the Public Expenditure Survey Committee (PESC), comprising the chief departmental finance officers plus senior Treasury officials.

The lead Cabinet minister on this is the Chief Secretary to the Treasury. It is his job to keep departmental bids under control; the measure of his success used to be, until it lapsed in 1993, how often the Star Chamber – an informal court of appeal for department ministers chaired by a senior Cabinet member – is obliged to meet (during 1988, for instance, it did not meet at all when John Major held this office). The Chancellor also has a big say and inevitably so does the Prime Minister. Other Cabinet and junior ministers are drawn in as necessary, often to advise the Cabinet committee on future economic strategy, which regularly addresses the overall shape of public expenditure plans. Consideration by the full Cabinet is intermittent. By that time most of the major decisions will have been taken and Cabinet has often little more to do than endorse what has been agreed elsewhere. The whole process is highly centralised, therefore, and secretive, in that recipients of government funding – local government, nationalised industries – are consulted beforehand but are informed of the outcome usually without any explanation of how

and why decisions are made. Since 1993 an attempt has been made to unify the cycle of decision on taxation (previously separately announced in the Budget) and the public spending cycle.

This whole process results in policy outcomes with a number of distinguishing features:

1. *Continuity is dominant*: Most changes in spending are gradual, because most public spending is the result of commitments entered into in the past. In the language of administrative theory, the policy process is incremental.
2. *Many factors are beyond government control*: The huge social security bill, for instance, is shaped by demographic factors – in other words, by the age structure of the population. Thus, the fact that Britain has an increasing population of old people means that governments are virtually compelled to spend more on pensions and on health care.

Thus, there is actually little freedom of choice open to governments in making public spending policy. Nevertheless, governments can exercise some marginal influence, and if a government is in office for a sufficiently long time, those marginal influences can affect policy substantially. Among the most important influences are the following:

1. *Party ideology*: For instance, the Conservatives have viewed themselves as the 'law and order' party, and in the 1980s (1980–9) they increased spending on law and order by 53 per cent.
2. *Electoral considerations*: All governments use public spending to create an atmosphere of economic optimism when an election is approaching. Thus it is almost invariably the case that spending controls are tougher immediately after, than immediately before, an election.

These points are illustrated clearly by Figure 27.1 and Table 27.1. Figure 27.1 shows, of course, a rise in the share of national production taken by public spending; but it also shows that this change has been a long-term process, with only two big jumps, both caused by the exceptional circumstances of the two world wars. Table 27.1 presents a picture of gradual change, under governments whose avowed

BOX 27.2　　　　　　　　　　　　　　　　　　　　**EXAMPLE**

The 1996 Budget

The Budget announced by Kenneth Clarke, the Chancellor, on 26 November 1996 was reckoned to be the Conservatives' first major counter-offensive in the campaign to win the 1997 election. Room for manoeuvre was slight as government borrowing was still high at over £30 billion and most commentators believed (Clarke actually said it) voters would not be fooled by a 'bribe' in the form of an unrealistically big tax cut; this had happened in 1991 and then, faced with a subsequent expenditure debt of £50 billion, taxes had been increased, according to Labour, no less than twenty-two times. Clarke opted in the end for a modest (he called it 'virtuous') budget which took 1p off income tax and increased a few allowances but virtually compensated with taxes on tobacco and petrol and other items.

Calculations for 1997–8 anticipated government income would comprise £300 billion (deriving from amongst other sources: £71 billion from income tax; £27 billion corporation tax; £51 billion VAT; and £50 billion social security contributions) and expenditure of £320 billion (including expenditure on: social security [£94 billion]; health [£35 billion]; education [£14 billion] defence [£22 billion] Scotland, Wales and Northern Ireland [£30 billion]; and debt interest [£25 billion]).

Commentators observed Clarke's calculations were based on optimistic projections for economic growth, inflation and tax collection combined with low interest rates. Even popular budgets, according to the experts, only gain governments up to six points in the polls; this one, according to polls the following week, lost it five points.

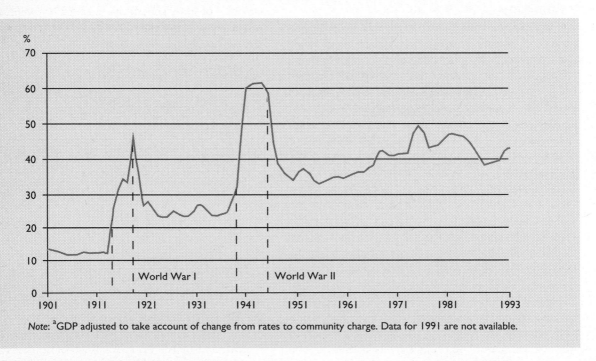

Note: [a]GDP adjusted to take account of change from rates to community charge. Data for 1991 are not available.

Figure 27.1 The trend of government spending (general government expenditure as a percentage of GDP[a])
Source: Social Trends, 1996, p. 112

Table 27.1 The five biggest categories of government spending: continuity and change (per cent of total spending, various dates)

	1981	1986	1993
Defence	10.8	11.7	8.9
Public order and safety	3.7	4.2	5.5
Education	12.2	11.9	12.4
Health	11.4	11.8	13.5
Social security	26.6	30.8	34.2

Note: Percentages do not sum to 100
Source: *Social Trends*, 1996, p. 112

objective was to alter the size and the composition of the public budget. In fact the only dramatic change shown in Table 27.1 – the sharp rise in social security budget – was forced on the government by the unintended rise in unemployment in the 1980s (and the consequential rise in benefits for the unemployed).

Themes and issues in economic policy

Economic policy has been the single most important, and the single most contentious, area of British politics in modern times. Arguments about who runs the economy, about the causes of Britain's economic failures and about the proper way to remedy those failures have been at the heart of political divisions in the country. Understanding economic policy and understanding the political system with which it is so clearly bound up necessarily involves understanding the nature of these debates and issues. In this section, therefore, we look at key areas of debate – who controls policy; why has it been so ineffective in reversing decline; and the impact of 'Thatcherism', the most important ideology in modern politics.

Who controls economic policy?

The argument about who, if anyone, has the decisive influence over the shape of economic policy is an argument about the location of power – a classically political question. It has prompted a variety of answers – many of them in effect critical of the way the economy has been governed. Formally, of course, the

answer to the question is plain: Britain is a constitutional democracy and ultimate control of policy is in the hands of the people's elected representatives. More critical accounts have looked elsewhere – either to parts of the civil service or to powerful organised groups in the wider economy. We examine each of these in turn.

A Treasury elite view

The view that economic policy in Britain is controlled by a Treasury elite does not assert that all important decisions are taken by senior Treasury officials – but it does argue that the shape of economic policy and of arguments about policy are moulded by thinking closely in line with the Treasury's view of the world. Three grounds can be produced for this argument. The first we have already encountered in our previous section. Inside the machinery of policy-making itself the Treasury is uniquely placed to influence the content of decisions: it has formal powers, for instance over spending decisions; it is always led in Cabinet by a major political figure, the Chancellor of the Exchequer; it has traditionally attracted the most able civil servants of each generation, many of whom subsequently carry Treasury views elsewhere when they become heads of lesser departments; and it has historically enjoyed a supreme position inside government as the authoritative source of information for advice about economic policy choices. Secondly, it can be argued that in the decisive crises of recent economic history it is the Treasury's concerns which have been dominant. Thirdly, it has been argued that the Treasury itself is part of a wider alliance of financial interests located in the City of London who have shaped economic policy with an eye on international rather than on domestic interests. In particular, the links between the Bank of England and the Treasury are often seen as ensuring that financial interests control policy.

Against this view three points can be made. Firstly, although the Treasury is undoubtedly powerful and prestigious, as a small department dealing mostly in policy advice, rather than in the actual carrying out of decisions, it is often at a considerable disadvantage. Secondly, while the Treasury has undoubtedly been decisive in many critical events, its record of lost battles is also a long one. For example, during most of the period since the Second World War public spending has been higher than the Treasury would have wished. Finally, it is not obvious that there is a single 'Treasury' view of the world, as distinct from positions on particular problems; it is indeed a department where sharp argument about policy choice is encouraged.

Opponents and supporters of the 'Treasury domination' view tend to argue on the assumption that the critical influences on economic policy lie somewhere inside the machinery of government. By contrast, a 'veto group' account suggests that the shape of economic policy is moulded by forces in the wider economy – usually at the point where it is being put into effect.

The 'veto group' argument

We emphasised at the start of this chapter the extent to which the 'making' and 'implementation' of economic policy were intertwined. The 'veto group' argument stresses the significance of this point. It also points to a feature emphasised in Chapters 3 and 4 on the social and economic context: that because Britain is a market economy, no policy can operate effectively without the cooperation of the institutions which keep a market economy functioning. Different views exist, however, as to which groups in the marketplace have so much power that they can place a veto over the policies of government.

Some observers stress the power of business as a veto group. They argue that the rules of a market economy give to business firms crucial capacities to facilitate or obstruct economic policy. The characteristic long-term economic aims of all governments – the creation of jobs, industrial investment, expansion of production – all depend, in a market economy, on decisions taken largely by private enterprises. They will only take these decisions if induced to do so by the hope of profits. All economic policy, so the argument runs, is ultimately at the mercy of business, which, if not convinced of the rightness of a policy, can exercise a 'veto' by declining to put resources behind that policy. Because the controllers of capital possess this veto they are, even in conditions where they do not use the veto, the decisive influence over the content of

policy. An extension of this argument focuses on the power of financial markets to control what happens to the British or indeed any economy. The occasion when Britain was forced out of the European exchange rate mechanism (ERM) in 1992 – so-called 'Black Wednesday' – is said to have burned deeply into the minds of economic policy-makers the fact that the markets can cripple an economy if they do not like what is going on. For this reason, it is argued, large amounts of government debt will be punished by the markets as will excessive public expenditure. Supporters of Tony Blair maintain this is one of the major reasons why 'socialism' is no longer a viable political objective.

The private ownership of capital is undoubtedly a key to understanding the conduct of economic policy in Britain. But alongside capital as a resource must be set **labour**. It has commonly been argued that labour, especially when organised into trade unions, is actually a more significant veto group than is capital. The most important version of this argument asserts that workers, when organised into unions, are in a position where they can prevent the introduction of a policy, or destroy it in the process of implementation. This is possible because life in a community like Britain is tolerable only if groups of workers voluntarily supply their labour. Through the organised strike weapon, or even its threatened use, teachers, power workers, nurses or any of a host of other groups can veto policy quite as effectively as can a powerful business corporation.

The argument that unions are a powerful veto group was especially popular in the 1970s, when the country's economic crisis was widely associated with industrial disputes which did, indeed, disrupt everyday life. In other words, there exists a connection between arguments about who controls economic policy and arguments about the nature of Britain's economic problems. We now examine, as our second major theme, the debate about the causes of the country's economic decline.

The causes of Britain's economic decline

The long-term purpose of economic policy is to create the conditions for continuing and growing prosperity. Measured by that standard, British economic policy has been a great success. The nation as whole, and almost every social group within it, is now much richer than was the case a generation ago. But another aim of economic policy has been not only to make the country prosperous, but to maintain Britain's place as a leading world economic nation. Nobody disputes that in this respect policy has failed – though as we shall see in the next section some argue that 'Thatcherite' solutions in the 1980s reversed this history of failure. Here we look at three of the most important sets of explanations offered for the inability of policy to stem decline.

An historically inevitable decline

It is appropriate to begin with a view which challenges the notion that economic policy can indeed be described as a failure. The United Kingdom is a small island state which for a brief moment in the nineteenth century led the world economically – just as it led it politically. It is unrealistic, such an argument runs, to expect such domination to endure. For many years after the end of the Second World War the more rapid economic growth rates of other nations were thus viewed as a process of 'catching up' on the lead originally opened by Britain in the nineteenth century. By the early 1960s this was a doubtful argument; in the 1990s it is more doubtful still. Other economies had not only closed Britain's lead; they had accelerated past it. The strikingly greater economic success of states of a similar size to Britain – like Germany and Japan – suggested that there was nothing natural about Britain's condition. Furthermore, while the country continued to grow more prosperous it was plain as long as two decades ago that many of the industries on which this prosperity had been founded were in decay, and were not being replaced by comparably successful new ones. If Britain's economic decline is inevitable, this inevitability must lie in some British characteristics which obstructed the development of appropriate remedial policies. 'Cultural' explanations of failure address this problem.

Cultural explanations of economic policy failure

A 'cultural' explanation traces failure to the attitudes and assumptions of powerful groups in British society. According to this view, a successful economy demands that the ruling groups in a nation promote economic change, technical research and economic and administrative efficiency. These traits have been held to be conspicuously absent among the rulers of Britain. Economic policies have been made in an amateurish and ill-informed manner because competence and efficiency were less highly valued than social connections and the possession of a 'gentlemanly' style. Even more damaging, economic policy has been guided by a set of attitudes unsympathetic to manufacturing industry – the very bedrock of the country's historical economic power. This distaste for the 'ungentlemanly' nature of manufacturing industry spread even to the leaders of business itself, leading to a decay of enterprise as the heirs to industrial fortunes turned to gentlemanly ways of life, instead of pursuing business success.

One of the obvious difficulties with this argument can be expressed as follows. Even if it is indeed the case that crucial interests in the British economy have been unsympathetic to industry and to innovation, why has it proved so hard to dislodge them – as they have indeed been dislodged in other, more successful, economies? One explanation for this may lie in the idea that Britain has a 'weak state'.

A 'weak state' and policy failure

The 'weakness' of a state is quite distinct from its size. Britain has long had a large state sector. 'Weakness' refers rather to the style of policy-making – in other words, to the way in which public policy-makers wield the state power vested in them. Two features have marked the British policy style, especially in the area of economics: it has been 'consensual'; and central government has played a relatively small part in the actual carrying out of policy. By 'consensual' is meant a preference for bargaining and compromise, as an alternative to the imposition by government of its will. This has been connected to the second feature, for it has been usual to rely on a wide range of institutions – local government, nationalised corporations, privately organised pressure groups, corporate bodies like universities and professional associations – to assist in the implementation of policy. This reliance on the cooperation of a wide range of institutions and groups forced a consensual style of policy-making because, obviously, cooperation would not happen if policies were imposed in an atmosphere of hostility. But the price of this arrangement, so the argument runs, has been a weak state: in other words, a policy style which has been forced to accommodate interests in the community, when the creation of an efficient and internationally competitive economy often demanded that these interests be confronted.

There is a twofold objection to the view that economic policy-making has been of poor quality because of the policy style imposed by a 'weak state' arrangement. Firstly, it is not at all clear that a consensual and cooperative policy-making approach are indeed irreconcilable with successful policies: many of Britain's more successful competitors, like Germany and Japan, also have 'consensual' policy-making characteristics. Secondly, the 'weak state' thesis is difficult to reconcile with the policies pursued by central governments since Margaret Thatcher originally came to power in 1979. Central control over education, local government, social services have all grown enormously. The central state in Britain is anything but a weak institution in the 1990s.

The debate about Thatcherite economic policy

'Thatcherism', a short-hand to describe the economic policies pursued throughout the 1980s by Margaret Thatcher's Conservative governments, is now so familiar to political argument that it is necessary to recall that it has quite recent origins. Those origins lie in the policy failures preceding Margaret Thatcher's election to office in 1979, and the debate prompted by those failures – debates sketched earlier in this chapter. Thatcherism had two elements: it was an attempt to introduce historically different policies; and an attempt to replace the 'consensual and cooperative' policy style of British government with a more centralised and directed way of doing things.

The most important features of Thatcherism as economic policy are threefold. The first involves an attempt radically to change the structure of ownership in the community: in the 1980s the government 'privatised' nearly half of what had been publicly owned in 1979. Secondly, Thatcherism attempted to change the structure of rewards: it cut the tax bills

of the very rich, while also reducing the real value of many welfare benefits, especially those to the unemployed. The expectation behind this change was that increasing the rewards of success would stimulate enterprise beneficial to all. Making unemployment more unattractive economically would encourage the unemployed to take jobs at lower wage rates, thus reducing both unemployment and the overall pressure of wage demands. Finally, Thatcherism withdrew or reduced subsidies to many industries, compelling the closure of many concerns and the more efficient operation of the rest in the face of international competition.

These changes in substance were accompanied by a change in the style of economic policy-making. Precisely because Thatcherism involved an attempt radically to alter the substance of policy, it was compelled to break with the consensual and cooperative approach. Many reforms, such as those bearing on trade unions, were imposed upon groups whose cooperation was usually sought in the past. Many policies – such as obliging inefficient manufacturing to reorganise or to close – were pursued in spite of protests from representatives of manufacturing industry.

This break with consensus and cooperation helps explain why, despite its domination of economic policy-making in the 1980s, judgements about the Thatcherite solution remain deeply divided. The case for Thatcherism can be summarised under three headings. The first is that, however painful the experience of closing down large parts of manufacturing industry may have been, it was only the recognition of the inevitable, in conditions where British industries simply were not efficient enough to find markets for goods. Secondly, a change to a more centralised and directive style of policy-making was necessary because the traditional cooperative approach was responsible, at least in part, for the failed policies of the past. Finally, comparison of Britain with other economies shows that Thatcherism is not unique. Across the world governments are, almost regardless of party, introducing economic reforms resembling the Thatcherite programme. This suggests that Thatcherism in Britain was a necessary adjustment to changing patterns in the world economy, without which Britain would lose even its present modest place in the international economic hierarchy.

The alternative, critical judgement of Thatcherite economics can be summarised under two headings. Firstly, the most distinctive consequence of Thatcherite economic policies has been to eliminate important parts of manufacturing industry, in a world where the manufacture and sale of finished goods is still the characteristic sign of an advanced industrial economy. In other words Thatcherism has only hastened what is sometimes called 'deindustrialisation'. Secondly, the shift away from a consensual policy style, combined with a deliberate strategy of increasing the rewards to the rich and enterprising, carries great dangers for social peace and harmony.

Conclusion

Economic policy lies at the heart of British politics. The most important issues dividing parties and groups are economic. The most important individuals and institutions in the government spend the largest part of their time struggling with economic problems. And the range of institutions which can affect economic policy goes well beyond bodies like the Treasury – it extends to the outer reaches of the government, and beyond into the private sector. In the wider society, divisions about economics – about how to manage the economy, and about how to distribute the results of economic production – provide the basis for some of the most important arguments in British politics.

Chapter summary

In this chapter we have: identified the shifting boundaries of economic policy; described the machinery of economic policy-making and implementation; described the role of public spending in economic policy; and summarised the main debates to which the conduct of economic policy in Britain has given rise.

Discussion points

- Where does most power lie in the shaping of British economic policy?

- What are the main problems faced by governments in controlling public spending?

- Is any particular group or institution responsible for the decline of the British economy?

Further reading

Two excellent recent brief surveys of the whole range of the politics of economic policy are Grant (1993) and Thomas (1992). The debates about the nature and cause of economic decline are well described in Gamble (1994). Blank (1979) and Pollard (1982) are examples of the 'Treasury/finance' domination thesis. Barnett (1972) and Weiner (1981) remain standard on the 'cultural' sources of decline. Dyson and Wilks (1983) argue the 'weak state' thesis. Finer (1973) and Brittan (1975) are standard on the 'veto power of labour' thesis. Heclo and Wildavsky (1981), though dated, is a classic on the politics of public spending; the modern successor is Wright and Thain (1995).

References

Barnett, C. (1972) *The Collapse of British Power* (Methuen).

Blank, S. (1979) 'Britain: The politics of foreign economic policy. The domestic economy and the problems of pluralistic stagnation', in P. Katzenstein (ed.), *Between Power and Plenty* (Wisconsin University Press).

Brittan, S. (1975) 'The economic contradictions of democracy', *British Journal of Political Science* Vol. 5.

Dyson, K. and Wilks, S. (eds) (1983) *Industrial Crisis* (Martin Robertson).

Finer, S. (1973) 'The political power of organised labour', *Government and Opposition*, Vol. 8, no. 4.

Gamble, A. (1994) *Britain in Decline*, 4th edn (Macmillan).

Grant, W. (1993) *The Politics of Economic Policy* (Harvester Wheatsheaf).

Heclo, H. and Wildavsky, A. (1981) *The Private Governance of Public Money* (Macmillan).

Pollard, S. (1982) *The Wasting of the British Economy* (Croom Helm).

Thomas, G. (1992) *Economic Policy Today* (Manchester University Press).

Weiner, M. (1981) *English Culture and the Decline of the Industrial Spirit, 1850–1980* (Cambridge University Press).

Wright, M. and Thain, C. (1995) *Treasury and Whitehall: Planning and Control of Public Spending* (Clarendon Press).

Foreign and defence policy

ANTHONY SELDON

LEARNING OBJECTIVES

■ To examine the influences on British foreign and defence policy.

■ To explore the main issues in the 1980s and 1990s.

■ To discuss how foreign and defence policy are made in Britain.

INTRODUCTION

Britain might be a second-rate power, but it is still a major player on the world stage – with a permanent seat on the UN Security Council, membership of the Group of Seven (G7) of leading industrial nations, the possessor of an independent nuclear deterrent, with a leading role in NATO, the European Community/Union, the Commonwealth, and a close and historic relationship with the United States.

The making of foreign policy

Five main groups have an input into policy (see Figure 28.1):

1. *Executive*: This is the most important centre for foreign policy-making. A number of separate bodies compete for power and influence. All civil service departments are involved in foreign policy considerations to some extent, in particular the six departments listed. Of these, the Foreign and Commonwealth Office (FCO) is of course the most closely concerned, and it oversees the diplomatic service and British embassies across the world ('overseas posts'). The Cabinet and in particular its key Defence

and Overseas Policy Committee (OPD) take the main decisions on policy, with the Foreign Secretary and ultimately the Prime Minister dominant. The Prime Minister's private office keeps the PM in touch with the rest of Whitehall and the world, and the Cabinet Office provides the coordination for the different Whitehall departments and the Cabinet. As the Prime Minister and Foreign Secretary are so important in shaping policy, the next section is devoted exclusively to them.

2. *Legislative*: Parliament tends to endorse or ratify policy made by the executive. Unlike the US Congress, Parliament does not *make* policy in Britain. But it can block or amend policy, as it

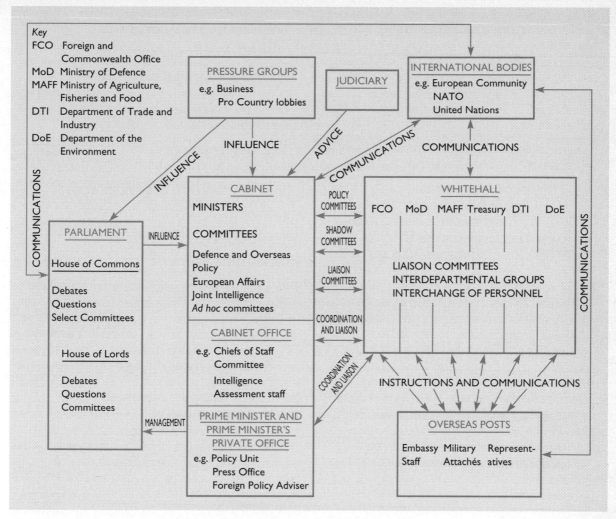

Figure 28.1   Schematic representation of the contemporary British foreign policy-making process

Source: Adapted from Michael Clarke, 'The policy-making process', in Michael Smith, Steve Smith and Brian White (eds), *British Foreign Policy: Tradition, Change and Transformation* (London, Unwin Hyman, 1988), p. 86 (Figure 4.1), reproduced by kind permission of Unwin Hyman Ltd; © M. Smith, S. Smith and B. White 1988

tried to do over European policy in the early/mid-1990s. The executive in turn manages Parliament to ensure it does what it wants.

3. *Judiciary*:   The judges again do not make policy, but the judiciary can and does regularly advise the government on the legality in British, EC or international law of various steps it proposes.

4. *Pressure groups*:   These bodies exercise influence over government policy, and can often affect policy, albeit at a fairly low level. A

pressure group could be a mining company wanting the British government to develop a close relationship with a central American government so it can open up a mine in that country, or a pro-Arab group urging the government to take a hard line on Israel, or a relief organisation pressing for more aid and protection for minorities in former Yugoslavia. The media, with their ability to whip up public opinion, as during the famine in Africa in 1984, are also a potent pressure source on government.

5. *International bodies*:   Britain does not make its policy in a vacuum. It must consider its international obligations to other countries, like the Republic of Ireland over policy on Northern Ireland, as well as to bodies like the UN, NATO and the European Community. Increasingly membership of the last is constraining Britain's freedom to act.

Which of these bodies exercises most influence? It all depends on which type of issue one is considering.

1. Trade and low-level diplomacy see an input from all five actors. Pressure groups and civil servants may be very influential here.
2. High-level policy, such as Britain's policy on the former Yugoslavia, or towards the European Community, sees the weight of policy-making shifting to the executive, and within the executive to the Prime Minister and Cabinet.
3. *National Security matters*:   For the most sensitive matters, the Prime Minister may not even consult the Foreign and Commonwealth Office or the Cabinet. The speed of the decision, and need for strict secrecy, often prevent wider consultation. Instead the Prime Minister may consult just the Foreign Secretary and perhaps one or two other very senior ministers or officials like the Cabinet Secretary or Chief of Defence Staff. An example of a national security issue would be Major's decision in 1991 over deployment of forces in the Gulf War.

Before concluding this section, it is important to note that those who analyse foreign policy-making have produced a number of models to explain the way decisions are made, even though there is not space here to do more than to mention just three of the models.

1. *Rational actor*:   This model sees the decisions made in foreign policy, e.g. to invade the Falkland Islands in 1982, as determined by key individuals who think logically about what end they are trying to achieve, which might be to bolster national pride.
2. *Bureaucratic politics*:   Here the emphasis is more on offices and organisations rather than individuals. The choices made in foreign policy on this reading are the outcome of struggle between different offices and interests struggling to make their perception prevail.
3. *Marxist models*:   These look beyond the actions of individuals or offices to international economic forces which under capitalism constrain the choices of individuals, offices and governments because of the determining logic of capitalist self-interest.

Most observers would agree that individuals and organisations do matter. The next section examines the power and policies of the most important actors in British foreign policy, the Prime Minister and Foreign Secretary.

Prime ministers and foreign policy

Prime ministers habitually like to dominate foreign policy, and hence their foreign secretaries. This tendency was in evidence when Britain was still indisputably a great power, as when Chamberlain (1937–40) and Churchill (1940–5, 1951–5) were prime ministers, and it still held true when Britain had declined to second-power status. Thus Heath (1970–4), Thatcher (1979–90) and Major (1990–97) have all devoted considerable time and energy to Britain's overseas affairs.

Under Heath, Europe was the centrepiece of his administration. Although he possessed a very capable Foreign Secretary in Sir Alec Douglas-Home, it was Heath's will that prevailed on the major issues.

With Thatcher, the tendency to dominate increased with the passing years. She was, of course, prime mover in the conduct of the Falklands War of 1982, but in those early years her attention was absorbed more by domestic affairs. In addition, in Lord Carrington (1979–82), she possessed a strong Foreign Secretary who did not welcome too many interventions from No. 10. Thatcher never trusted Carrington's successor, Francis Pym (1982–3), and after the 1983 general election victory lost no time in replacing him with a man she initially valued much more highly, Geoffrey Howe (1983–9).

Yet over the years she increasingly came to dislike Howe's favoured policies, especially on Europe, and felt that he was becoming far too closely identified with her least favourite of any Whitehall department, the FCO. Tensions rose throughout 1987 and 1988 and culminated in Thatcher, in effect, sacking

Howe as Foreign Secretary in July 1989, replacing him by the relatively young and inexperienced John Major, who many thought at the time would become little more than a mouthpiece for Thatcher's wishes. Major did not last long enough in that office for anyone to draw many conclusions because after three months he was smartly translated into the Treasury to take the place of Nigel Lawson, who had resigned in October 1989 partly due to disputes with Alan Walters, a prime ministerial adviser, over the exchange rate mechanism. Douglas Hurd, Major's successor as Foreign Secretary, was an ex-diplomat possessed of considerable independence and self-assurance, but his freedom for manoeuvre was restricted by the machinery which the Prime Minister had established. The key Cabinet committee was chaired by Thatcher and then Major and they received independent advice upon foreign policy from special advisers (until the post was abolished in 1994) and above all their foreign affairs private secretary, John Holmes.

Although a defeated challenger for the leadership after Thatcher, Hurd's power base at the FCO grew stronger after Major became PM. Hurd's position owed much to his mastery of foreign affairs, his proven competence, and the Prime Minister's own focus on domestic issues. Major delegated some areas to Hurd, such as relations with South America, some areas they shared, such as policy towards the European Community and Bosnia, and other areas Major liked to have almost a free hand on, notably relations with American presidents.

Britain's position in the post-war world

Britain from 1945 liked to see itself as enjoying a special position in international affairs, being uniquely at the centre of three 'overlapping circles' of the Commonwealth, Europe and the Atlantic relationship. Being the only 'member' to belong to each of those three, Britain harboured the partly romantic view that it had a vantage point giving it special weight in world affairs. The reality, however, is that power in international relations is critically dependent upon economic might, and as Britain's economy and the strength of the pound declined post-war, so too did its ability to remain a major actor on the international stage.

The 'special relationship' with the USA

Thatcher and Major, like previous Conservative prime ministers such as Churchill and Macmillan (1957–63), put great value upon the 'Atlantic alliance' with the USA. Like them, they saw the alliance as a vehicle to help maintain Britain's status as one of the world's 'great powers'. Britain, lacking the necessary financial, industrial and military resources, could no longer do this through independent assertion of its power, as it could do before 1945; rather, it liked to see itself as a bridge between the USA and Western Europe and even between the USA and the USSR.

The 'special relationship' with the USA was reinforced in the 1980s by Thatcher's admiration for the policies of US President Ronald Reagan (1981–9). Reagan's economic programme of monetarism, coupled with tax cuts and emphasis on the private sector of production, paralleled the domestic thrust of 'Thatcherism'. In foreign policy, Reagan's anti-Soviet rhetoric in the early 1980s was eagerly backed by the Thatcher government. When Carter (1977–81) had been President, Britain had been the most prominent European supporter of the December 1979 decision by NATO to deploy US Cruise and Pershing II missiles in Western Europe. Despite vocal demonstrations by the Campaign for Nuclear Disarmament (CND) and other anti-nuclear groups against the deployment, the government held its ground. When the USA entered negotiations in November 1981 with the USSR on the reduction of strategic nuclear weapons, Thatcher again gave unwavering support to the position of the Reagan administration, despite complaints by the opposition Labour Party that the USA was trying to impose unreasonable terms upon the USSR. As long as Reagan was in the White House, Anglo-American relations remained arguably closer than at any point since the war. It was a remarkable example of the ability of individual leaders to affect the direction of a nation's foreign policy.

After George Bush (a Republican who shared many of Reagan's policy views, and who had indeed been Reagan's Vice-President) became President in January 1989 relations cooled. Personally, Bush and Thatcher did not enjoy the same warm personal chemistry. Pressure from within the Washington community to take US foreign policy in a less

Anglophile direction gathered pace. The State Department (the US equivalent of the FCO) smartly announced that the US link with Japan was its 'most important bilateral relationship with the world'. Washington under Bush also regarded Thatcher's heel-dragging over closer economic and political union with the European Community with increasing distaste. Within the Community itself, West Germany quickly reasserted itself as the more important ally to the USA. The 'special relationship' was strengthened in her last months, however, by Thatcher's firm support for Bush over the Gulf crisis after Iraq invaded Kuwait in August 1990.

Major initially pleased Washington by his firm support for the Gulf War in early 1991. Major's sympathy for the US over the GATT stalemate, and support for the new North Atlantic Cooperation Council (NACC) also ensured the special relationship stayed cordial during Bush's last months in the White House. Personally, Bush and Major quickly formed a very close bond, every bit as warm as Thatcher's relationship with Reagan. But a shadow was cast over US–UK relations in 1992 by Bill Clinton's veiled criticism of British policy in Northern Ireland, and by the open Conservative support for the Bush re-election campaign. This angered some in the Clinton camp, and resulted in some cooling of relations in 1993 and 1994. Clinton's inconsistent policy – as the British saw it – towards Northern Ireland and Bosnia continued to aggravate relations, but by 1995 relations improved considerably. The claim by former US Secretary of State James Baker during the Republican Convention in August 1996 that US–UK relations were the worst under Clinton for two hundred years were absurd. Even with a Democrat President, and with no great personal warmth between Clinton and Major, the relationship was still one of the most important overseas bonds – for both countries.

Labour and the US Democrats have always felt an ideological bond. During the run up to the 1997 election Labour campaign strategists Philip Gould and Peter Mandelson visited Washington to pick up tips on how to win in the way Bill Clinton did so handsomely in November 1996. What they learnt may well have proved helpful given their huge victory in May 1997.

President Clinton was quick to send warm congratulations to Tony Blair; a man whom he both 'liked' and 'admired'. With Robin Cook as Foreign Secretary, widely regarded as the sharpest mind in Labour's front bench, its supporters feel sure the Special Relationship will be kept in good shape.

Relations with the former Soviet Union

When Thatcher came to power in 1979 the USSR was still ruled by the iron hand of the Communist Brezhnev, and she had little opportunity and no desire to change the hardline policy Britain had followed ever since the start of the Cold War. Brezhnev's death, followed by the deaths in quick succession of Andropov and Chernenko, changed all that. A new climate was soon felt and Thatcher, to her credit, was quick to realise new opportunities.

In the mid-1980s the Thatcher government attempted to become a full-fledged actor in the arms controls discussions between the USA and the USSR. The Prime Minister met Mikhail Gorbachev in 1984, even before he became the new Soviet leader. Subsequently she announced that 'he was a man she could do business with'. While Britain continued to back the US bargaining position, Thatcher had declared her wish to serve as a go-between to speed up the negotiations. After the Reykjavik summit between Reagan and Gorbachev in autumn 1986 ended in apparent failure over arms control, Thatcher again presented herself as a helpful mediator, crowning the effort with a high-profile visit to Moscow in March 1987. The Prime Minister could then claim some of the credit for subsequent progress in American–Soviet negotiations, whose fruits included the December 1987 agreement on reductions in intermediate-range nuclear weapons.

Relations became even warmer after the collapse of communist regimes in Eastern Europe in 1989. Brief visits were exchanged that year between Thatcher and Gorbachev, with the former maintaining her warm support for *glasnost* and *perestroika*.

The break-up of the Soviet Union, and fall of both Thatcher and Gorbachev, temporarily dislocated the warm relations between London and Moscow. But with the assumption to power of Boris Yeltsin, contacts again became close, with regular high-level meetings between Britain and Russia, reminiscent of the cordiality that existed before the 1917 communist revolution. In November 1992, the British–Russian Friendship Treaty was signed during Yeltsin's visit to London, including important military clauses, and a London–Moscow 'hotline', thereby to an extent promoting Britain's position on the world stage. Major worked hard to forge a personal relationship with Yeltsin, though strains were evident throughout the 1990s with differences over policy on the former Yugoslavia and with Russia's apparently insatiable demands for Western financial assistance.

Britain and Europe

Britain's role in the European Community has been the most continually divisive issue in British politics since the early 1960s, blending as it does both domestic and foreign policy issues and alignments. Despite her coolness towards both groupings, Thatcher tried at first to establish a role in both Europe and the Commonwealth which would not only confirm the prominence of British influence in those groupings but also protect British economic and diplomatic interests. She embarked on the task in typically combative fashion. Immediately after her first victory as Prime Minister in May 1979, Thatcher served notice that the EEC would have to reduce the price of Britain's participation in the organisation. She noted that while Britain financed 20 per cent of the EEC budget, it received less than 10 per cent of the receipts of the Community; Britain's net contribution (gross contribution minus receipts) to the EEC would be more than £1 billion in 1980. A particular target of the British was the Common Agricultural Policy (CAP), the subsidy of European farm products financed by two-thirds of the Community's budget. The Prime Minister contended that the CAP was financed by the money of British taxpayers but benefited continental farmers, notably those in France and West Germany.

After a heated clash with leaders of the other EEC countries at the Dublin summit in November 1979, Thatcher obtained a temporary settlement which provided more than £3 billion in budget 'rebates' to Britain between 1980 and 1984. The long-term problem of EEC receipts and the CAP was more difficult to solve. An interim agreement at Copenhagen in 1985 raised contributions by member countries from 1 per cent of value-added tax to 1.4 per cent and established the principle that Britain

would get an annual rebate of two-thirds of its net contribution, but no deal was reached on the CAP. Relations with the EEC remained difficult. Deep divisions opened up within the Conservative Party following the Single European Act coming into operation in 1987, with Thatcher remaining cool towards plans for further economic and monetary union (EMU), and others in her party far less concerned by the apparent threats of an erosion of British sovereignty.

Europe came to be an increasing sore between Thatcher and her once much-trusted lieutenant Howe, who had been appointed Foreign Secretary in 1983. Unhappiness at his and Lawson's pro-European line came to the fore in 1989, at the Madrid summit, at which Thatcher had been forced to compromise. With the more biddable Major as Foreign Secretary (July–October 1989), however, tension between No. 10 and the Foreign Office eased, as it did in Hurd's early months as Foreign Secretary.

The year 1990 saw divisions over Europe dominate both foreign and domestic policies. The Bruges Group within the Conservative Party, formed after Thatcher's celebrated 1988 Bruges speech, campaigned for a slowdown of progress to greater federalism, and were outraged by the successful pressure from the pro-Europeans within the government, which resulted in the much-delayed announcement in October 1990 that Britain could join the exchange rate mechanism (ERM) of the European monetary system. A Community meeting at Rome later that month forced Thatcher into a narrow minority blocking the pace of progress to greater union. The subsequent furore played a major part in the leadership election the following month, and her demise. The year also saw France and Britain move closer together, the product of a united Germany encouraging Paris to look more to London than to the new German capital, Berlin.

The period since has been one of continued turbulence. The departure of Thatcher promised greater harmony within Britain on Europe: the promise proved illusory. The party was quiescent for the eighteen-month run up to the 1992 general election, and appeared happy with the opt-outs on EMU and the Social Chapter secured by Major at the Maastricht conference in December 1991. But when the Danes rejected Maastricht in a referendum in June

1992, it was the trigger for the simmering resentment at Maastricht to break out into the open. All hell was let loose in 1992–3 during the passage of the Maastricht Bill through Parliament, with Conservative Euro-sceptic back-benchers being unprecedentedly rebellious, culminating in a confidence motion in the House of Commons in July 1993. The virtual break-up of the ERM in the summer of 1993 showed the distance to be travelled by the dwindling numbers favouring EMU within the party. Towards mid 1997, Ken Clarke, the Chancellor, remained virtually the only enthusiast in Cabinet for closer European integration. From 1992, Major and the centre ground drifted firmly in the direction of a more Euro-sceptic stance. The desirability of distancing themselves from Labour, which had become increasingly positive about Europe under Kinnock, Smith and Blair, proved a further attraction.

The distancing continued in the run up to the election in May 1997 but came unstuck fatally halfway through the campaign, when over 200 candidates refused to accept the 'wait and see' policy over the single currency which Major had hammered out on pain of Clarke's resignation. Certainly the electorate was not in favour of joining EMU but the issue of Europe was less important than other issues, the most important of which was probably voters' feeling it was time for a change. In any case they were unimpressed by the appearance of division and indiscipline in the Conservative Party. In the ensuing bloodbath for the Tories, 'sceptics' went to the wall as often as the 'philes' leaving the resultant balance similar to that before the election. The Tories lost the election disastrously, but unfortunately for them the issue of Europe will divide them for many more days yet.

The Commonwealth

The third of the three overlapping circles of influence is Britain's relationship with the Commonwealth. The 1980s and early 1990s saw several storms emanating from this once grand connection, which had in earlier days helped confer great power status on Britain.

The Thatcher government obtained a significant victory for British prestige with its negotiation of an agreement for the legal independence of Southern Rhodesia, later renamed Zimbabwe, in 1980. The problem had persisted since the leadership of the white minority in Rhodesia declared independence in 1965 and Britain, under the Labour Prime Minister Harold Wilson, imposed economic sanctions against the country. After April 1979 elections indicated support for a government headed by the leader of the whites, Ian Smith, a leader of one section of the ethnic minorities, Bishop Abel Muzorewa, and many Conservative Members of Parliament wanted recognition of the new regime and the lifting of sanctions. Thatcher hinted that she would support such measures but the Foreign Secretary, Lord Carrington, persuaded her that no government could survive which did not include the rebel leaders Robert Mugabe and Joshua Nkomo.

British diplomacy through the ensuing Lancaster House negotiations provided for representation of all groups in the new state, and British troops ensured that a cease-fire held before elections and the full independence of Zimbabwe in spring 1980.

Commonwealth issues receded in importance until 1985–6 when the problem of South Africa and its policy of racial apartheid threatened to split the group. With tension and internal violence increasing, pressure grew upon the USA and Western European countries to impose economic sanctions against the white minority regime in Pretoria. After prolonged resistance to sanctions, the Reagan administration was pushed by the US Congress and public opinion to take limited measures; European countries like France did likewise, and the EC began to consider joint sanctions. Despite the demands of black African states and other Commonwealth members such as India and West Indian countries for action, the Thatcher government, conscious in part of the high volume of British exports, refused to impose any significant financial or trade restrictions upon South Africa. The imposition of a state of emergency by the South African government, followed by the detention of thousands of blacks and anti-apartheid activists, worsened the situation. Black African and West Indian nations, as well as India, boycotted the Commonwealth Games in Edinburgh in 1986, and a public row arose in Britain when it was reported that the Queen was concerned that Thatcher's intransigence on sanctions would wreck the Commonwealth. Although the immediate British domestic crisis passed and the South African issue had little or no bearing upon the May 1987 elections, reports of black

African resentment against the Thatcher government persisted.

The dispute erupted at the Commonwealth conference of heads of government in October 1987 in Vancouver, Canada. Thatcher accused the banned anti-apartheid movement, the African National Congress, of being 'terrorists', while leaders such as Robert Mugabe of Zimbabwe and Kenneth Kaunda of Zambia accused the Prime Minister of sacrificing all moral interests for the sake of greed and British trade with South Africa. Even non-African leaders such as Brian Mulroney of Canada and Bob Hawke of Australia publicly joined in condemnation of British policy. Tensions reached new peaks when in the summer of 1989 British cricketers announced their intention to take part in a 'rebel' tour of South Africa. In the event, the tour was cancelled in February 1990 in the face of demonstrations which preceded and accompanied the release from prison of the black African ANC leader, Nelson Mandela. Thatcher welcomed his release, but refused to support the maintenance of economic sanctions on the De Klerk regime. In the face of considerable opposition, especially from European partners, she used Mandela's release as a reason for relaxing the economic and cultural sanctions Britain already had in place.

The nadir of Britain's relations with the Commonwealth probably came at the Commonwealth Heads of Government meeting in October 1989, at which Thatcher made it clear that being outvoted 48 to 1 on the question of South Africa did not worry her in the least. In 1990 Thatcher clashed with European Community partners again over easing sanctions against South Africa, though some easing of tension came when she met Nelson Mandela of the ANC in London, albeit on his second visit (he refused to see her on his first trip).

Major's arrival at No. 10 resulted in an easing of tension over South Africa, as did De Klerk's continued movement towards political reform. By the early 1990s Conservative and Labour policies on South Africa had become closer than for many years. Major also made rebuilding relations with the Commonwealth, after the battering of the Thatcher years, a conscious aim of policy, as seen at the Commonwealth Heads of Government meetings in Zimbabwe (1991), Cyprus (1993) and New Zealand (1995).

The final colonial country to preoccupy the British government in the 1980s and 1990s was Hong Kong. Howe signed the Joint Declaration over Hong Kong with the Chinese government in 1984, in which China agreed to maintain Hong Kong's way of life until at least 2047, fifty years after it took over the colony in 1997. The severe repression of the pro-democracy movement by the Beijing government in June 1989 led to great anxieties in the colony and back in Britain that China might try to implement the same heavy-handed tactics in Hong Kong after 1997. It also raised the question of Britain's admission of refugees from the colony, and put severe stress on Sino-British relations.

While the British government debated how many passports to give to inhabitants of the colony, unrest continued in Hong Kong at the spectre of what Beijing rule might mean as 1997 drew nearer. Restoration of contacts between Britain and China in July 1990 did not allay fears in Hong Kong, though the tenure as governor of Hong Kong of Chris Patten, appointed in April 1992, quelled some anxieties, while increasing others because of the tough and, initially at least, inflexible line he adopted towards China. In truth, though, Beijing knew that it merely had to sit tight and block whatever it disapproved of as 1997 approached.

The Falklands War

The most significant crises in foreign policy in the period since 1979, however, happened outside the 'three rings' of Atlantic alliance, Europe and Commonwealth. In April 1982 Argentina, frustrated by decades of inconclusive negotiations, invaded the Falkland Islands, a British territory (population 1,800) in the South Atlantic. The invasion caught the British by surprise and led to the resignation of the Foreign Secretary, Lord Carrington, and the near-resignation of the Defence Secretary, John Nott. Within weeks, however, the Thatcher government was able to turn the disaster into a diplomatic and military victory. Britain obtained United Nations condemnation of the invasion, and EC sanctions against Argentina. A British task force sailed 8,000 miles and, despite tenuous supply lines and numerical inferiority in manpower, inflicted an overwhelming naval, air and land defeat upon the Argentines.

Argentina surrendered in early June and Britain reasserted its sovereignty over the islands.

After the fall of the military government in Argentina and its replacement by an elected civilian regime, many countries, notably the USA, urged Britain to negotiate a long-term settlement with Argentina over the islands. The Thatcher government, however, adamantly refused to discuss the issue, arguing that Argentina had never ended the state of belligerency against Britain and that the sovereignty of the islands was beyond negotiation. Instead, Britain maintained a military garrison of 2–3,000 men and built up the infrastructure of the islands. In January 1987 a new airport with runways suitable for heavy civilian and military aircraft was opened, thirty miles from Port Stanley, the capital of the islands. By the end of the 1986–7 financial year, Britain had spent £2.6 billion, almost £1.5 million per resident, to defend and develop the territory.

The overthrow of the military junta and election in 1989 of a new Argentine government under Carlos Menem, however, led to a softening of stances of both sides, with agreement to leave the question of sovereignty on one side. This new cordiality culminated in the resumption of diplomatic relations between Britain and Argentina in February 1990. Britain agreed to lift its 150-mile exclusion zone, but in the important matter of sovereignty Britain had got its way; a restoration of the position before the war, and no compromise over ownership of the islands.

The Gulf War and the Middle East

Considering the importance of Britain in the Middle East throughout much of this century, it is surprising that the region did not figure more prominently in British foreign policy after 1979. Britain has played very much second fiddle to the USA in trying to bring about rapprochement over the Israeli–Arab contest. Support for US bombing of Libya in 1986 owed as much to a desire to back a favoured ally as dislike of Colonel Gadaffi. Dislike of Libya was fuelled by Libyan involvement in selling arms to the IRA, and suspected Libyan involvement in the Lockerbie plane disaster of December 1988. British hostages in the Lebanon, notably John McCarthy and Terry Waite, kept the region in the public eye in the later 1980s and early

1990s, but British governments staunchly refused to give the hostages a high priority. Dislike of Iran in the 1980s turned to a desire for friendship after the end of the Iran–Iraq war when the ambitions of Saddam Hussein of Iraq became more obvious from the later 1980s. This culminated in the invasion of Kuwait in August 1990, and the Gulf War in early 1991, in which, in its biggest overseas operation since the Korean War (1950–3), British forces served alongside, as a prominent but junior partner of, the US military. Britain subsequently remained in a state of semi-war with Iraq, with the RAF helping to enforce no-fly zones over its land in the policy which Major helped to initiate of Kurdish 'safe-havens'.

Eastern Europe and former Yugoslavia

British foreign policy in Eastern Europe is largely concerned with its potential for causing conflict between the great powers of the time – as the main historical interventions (1878, 1914, 1938–9) demonstrate. From 1945 to 1989 the region was part of the Soviet sphere of interest, and hardly a separate concern, apart from occasional symbolic support for democratic reformers (Poland 1980) or independent foreign policy lines (Romania). Since the revolutions of 1989 policy towards most countries has centred on assistance for economic restructuring, and dismantling of Cold War restrictions on travel and investment.

Traditional British concerns about the Balkans as a crucible of instability surfaced when Yugoslavia started to disintegrate in 1990–1. This coincided with the growing desire among many European Community member states for a common foreign policy and a collective sphere of influence, and US readiness to shed some of the burden of its role as world policeman. Britain was also prepared to let Germany set the agenda by deciding to recognise Croatia and Slovenia's independence from Yugoslavia in December 1991.

War broke out in the multi-ethnic former Yugoslav republic of Bosnia-Herzegovina in April 1992, and by the summer Serb forces had overrun 70 per cent of the republic's territory and driven out or killed non-Serbs in a process known as 'ethnic cleansing'. International involvement in Bosnia began that summer, when 1,800 British troops were sent via the UN to guard aid shipments, and a conference convened in London.

British policy in Bosnia was governed by four factors.

1. The traditional imperative to stop conflict spreading. It was argued that there was a risk of the war dragging in Albania, Greece, Turkey and Russia and becoming a wider Balkan war. This was used to justify British policies such as maintaining the arms embargo that had left the Bosnian government nearly defenceless against Serb (and Croat 1993–4) attack.
2. The nature of the war created a desperate humanitarian crisis, with large numbers of refugees and the risk of starvation of the besieged city of Sarajevo. British forces went to Bosnia under UN auspices to oversee aid deliveries.
3. Once they had arrived, the safety of British UN personnel became the determinant of British policy in Bosnia. This reinforced British reluctance to 'take sides' in the conflict by measures such as lifting the arms embargo or taking military action against Serb forces involved in war crimes.
4. Periodic British interventions in Bosnia were driven to a considerable extent by media coverage. Revelations about Serb concentration camps in 1992, Croat atrocities in 1993 and mortar attacks on Sarajevo in 1994 and 1995 led to demands – including those voiced by Thatcher – for a more hawkish policy against the aggressor. The balance finally shifted in 1995 when Bosnian Serbs murdered 8,000 prisoners after overrunning the so-called UN safe haven of Srebrenica. After an uneasy peace agreement at Dayton, Ohio, in 1995, Britain contributed troops to international implementation forces.

The Bosnian war led to severe strains in British relations with the USA. To many in the US, British policy was destined simply to let Serbia – the aggressor – win. To the British, US policy seemed to be moral grandstanding which, while endangering lightly armed UN forces in Bosnia, contributed no US forces to back up the point. Harmony was only restored in 1995. For the time being, the uneasy peace is destined to hold.

Defence policy developments

The cornerstone of the defence strategy was the commitment to the Atlantic alliance and NATO. Besides supporting the deployment of Cruise and Pershing nuclear missiles in the early 1980s, the Thatcher government maintained its commitment to Britain's independent nuclear deterrent, most notably in the development of the Trident missile system. Opposition to Trident came not only from anti-nuclear protesters but also from those who were concerned at the escalating costs of the project and the possibility that Trident would be rendered obsolete, even before its deployment, by more advanced missile systems.

Conservative victories over Labour, which had favoured unilateral nuclear disarmament in 1983 and 1987, led to the development of Trident despite escalating cost and lukewarm public support. Trident remained the official Conservative policy, and in the 1992 general election even Labour pledged support to its continued development. It was deployed in 1994.

Less publicised but just as significant in Britain's defence policy within NATO was a commitment, made in the late 1970s, to increase real spending on defence by 3 per cent per year through to 1985–6. As a result, British spending on defence increased 27 per cent in real terms between 1978–9 and 1985–6. Britain had sustained its commitment to keep 55,000 troops in West Germany. Planned reductions in naval forces, recommended by the 1981 defence review, were mitigated by Britain's involvement in the Falklands War.

The maintenance of Britain's defence capability in the 1980s had not been unopposed within the government, however. The Treasury, determined to control public expenditure, argued for cutbacks in the defence programme; the conflict led to the move of Francis Pym from Defence Secretary to Leader of the House of Commons in 1981. With the expiration of NATO's commitment to 3 per cent real growth in defence budgets, the Treasury had gained the upper hand in the battle with the Ministry of Defence. Spending on defence decreased from £26.2 billion in 1985–6 to £24 billion in 1989–90 (1991–2 prices).

Even before the end of the Cold War from 1989, constraints on defence spending, combined with the increasing cost of an independent nuclear deterrent, forced difficult choices on British policy-makers. One option was to abandon commitments outside NATO, such as the maintenance of the Falklands garrison. Such a decision, however, would represent a retreat from Britain's attempts to maintain its status as an international power. Another option was to reduce Britain's NATO commitments, but this risked alienating the USA, which has called for a greater European contribution to the organisation, and countries in Western Europe. The option of holding down the salaries of members of the armed forces would aggravate military staffing shortages and would yield only marginal savings.

But it was the collapse of communist regimes, first in Eastern Europe, then in the Soviet Union itself, which fundamentally altered the outlook. Suddenly, the traditional NATO fear of a surprise Warsaw Pact invasion had passed, and coupled with it came breakthroughs in the long-protracted discussions over East–West arms control negotiations.

Debate raged in political and defence circles in 1989 and early 1990 about what shape a post-Cold War British defence policy might take, and how great the yield of the 'peace dividend' might be. In July 1990 Defence Secretary Tom King announced the result of the five-month defence review 'Options for Change', which included cuts of 20 per cent in the Army, and stiff cutbacks also to the RAF and Royal Navy. Defence spending as a proportion of GDP continued to decline, from a high point of 5.3 per cent in 1984–5 to below 4 per cent by the mid-1990s; although even this level is higher than that of comparable countries (France 3.4 per cent, Germany 2.2 per cent, Italy 2 per cent in 1992, to Britain's 4.1 per cent).

The Iraqi invasion of Kuwait on 2 August 1990 caused a pause in the debate and talk of major cutbacks, with the Gulf War in early 1991 and breakdown or threatened breakdown of peace across the Soviet Union and Eastern Europe forcing a rethink. A certain ambivalence became evident in British thinking focusing on the new role Britain wanted to play in the post-Cold War world. The 1993 defence White Paper only further confirmed that Britain lacked an overall and clear defence and foreign policy strategy. It spoke of a wide range of responsibilities from maintaining a nuclear capability to operations against the illicit drugs trade in the Caribbean.

Britain and the world in the late 1990s

Britain's position in the world remains unclear. While clearly less significant than its position in the 1940s, Britain arguably has greater influence and authority than it did in the 1960s and 1970s. Thatcher's strident assertion of British power on the world stage provided the impetus, her courting of Reagan and Gorbachev being paramount. In the post-Cold War world Britain's authority has continued high, after Major became one of the longest-serving heads of government in the West.

In contrast to those arising from NATO obligations, British military operations since the end of the Cold War have been 'voluntary'. By contributing forces to UN operations, Britain was staking a claim to retain its permanent seat on the Security Council and its more diffuse status as a significant actor in world politics. The shift to voluntary operations leaves more degrees of freedom for policy decisions, but also a need for reorienting capability from large standing forces to a more flexible response.

The process of reorienting British defence policy has taken place in the context, since 1992, of heavy downward pressure on public expenditure. Defence was targeted by the Treasury for cuts, arousing levels of opposition among the forces unseen since the 1950s. The 1994 White Paper *Front Line First* was an attempt to answer some of the criticism. The direction of British defence policy in the post-Cold War world remains to be clarified in a definitive manner under Labour after 1997.

Chapter summary

Britain's major standing in the world declined in the 1960s and 1970s with the wind-up of the British Empire and the entry into the European Community. In the 1980s and 1990s Britain has reasserted its position on the world stage in a process aided by the collapse of the Soviet Union and the end of the Cold War. But in the new world order, Britain's future position in the world – as major or minor player – remains uncertain.

Discussion points

■ Is it important or necessary for Britain to remain a nuclear power?

■ Does it matter if Britain becomes a less important player on the world stage?

■ Is party politics relevant to foreign and defence policy? How much has party affected British overseas policy since 1945?

Further reading

For the longer perspective, Reynolds (1991) and Sanders (1990) are both excellent introductions on the foreign policy side, as is Bayliss (1989) on defence policy. The best year-by-year survey on British foreign policy is the relevant chapter on foreign policy in Catterall (1996), which is an annual publication that began in 1990. Partos (1993) gives an excellent account of the Cold War and its ending, and was originally a highly acclaimed radio series. Studies of the 1980s which are still worth examining are Smith *et al.* (1988), Byrd (1988) and Croft (1991). More analytical approaches to foreign policy and its making can be found in Adamthwaite (forthcoming) and Freedman and Clarke (1991).

References

Adamthwaite, A. (forthcoming) *British Foreign Policy since 1945* (Blackwell).

Bayliss, J. (1989) *British Defence Policy: Striking the Right Balance* (Macmillan).

Byrd, P. (ed.) (1988) *British Foreign Policy Under Thatcher* (Philip Allan).

Catterall, P. (ed.) (1996) *Contemporary Britain: An Annual Review 1996* (Blackwell).

Croft, S. (ed.) (1991) *British Security Policy: The Thatcher Years and End of the Cold War* (HarperCollins).

Freedman, L. and Clarke, M. (1991) *Britain in the World* (Cambridge University Press).

Partos, G. (1993) *The World That Came in From the Cold* (BBC).

Reynolds, C. (1991) *Britannia Overruled: British Foreign Policy and World Power in the 20th Century* (Longman).

Sanders, D. (1990) *Losing an Empire. Finding a Role: British Foreign Policy since 1945* (Macmillan).

Smith, M., Smith, S. and White, B. (eds) (1988) *British Foreign Policy: Tradition, Change and Transformation* (Unwin Hyman).

CHAPTER TWENTYNINE

Environmental policy

ANDREW GRAY AND ANDREW FLYNN

LEARNING OBJECTIVES

- To promote an understanding of the institutions and dynamics of policy-making in relation to the protection of the environment.

INTRODUCTION

The chapter aims to: describe the role of key institutions, and the activities and positions of political parties and interest groups; assess the impact of the greening of society (involving both business and consumer behaviour) on the political process; examine some areas of environmental policy.

Where once the environment as an issue was regarded as the preserve of the middle classes or fringe elements in society, today it is the subject of widespread and mounting concern. Throughout the advanced industrial world people are taking their own actions to protect the environment and are demanding higher environmental standards. As we saw in earlier chapters, there is now something of a green ideology and green political parties have developed in a number of countries including in the United Kingdom. Moreover, during the past decade membership of environmental groups has soared. The global significance of environmental issues has been illustrated by the attendance of nearly all governments at the United Nations Conference on Environment and Development (UNCED) (the so-called Earth Summit) in Rio de Janeiro in June 1992. For many, though, the status of the environment in public policy-making is ambiguous. It grabs

the headlines for short periods of time, politicians then make up many fine-sounding phrases but deliver only piecemeal responses before passing on to deal with other issues.

There is undoubtedly an episodic element to environmental policy. Perhaps, however, this is no different from other areas such as social, transport and even economic policy. If so, the environment will keep returning to the forefront of the political agenda. For students of politics the challenge raised by environmental issues to existing administrative structures is of enormous interest. But the nature of the challenge posed by environmentalism goes beyond simply studying bureaucratic structures. It involves questions of how governments respond to environmental issues, how societies articulate their environmental concerns, and how political parties and interest groups seek to represent the environment. In the course of this chapter we will seek to provide answers to these questions, at least in the context of the United Kingdom. We begin by asking what environmental policy might be.

Environmental issues are here to stay

❝Environmental issues are here to stay; they are not just going to fade away so long as serious environmental problems remain unsolved.

. . . More profoundly, they are arguably not simply issues any more; they reflect a more fundamental conflict which is concerned with the very nature of the future development of society as a whole.

Rudig, 1990, p. 2❞

What is environmental policy?

It is easy to suggest that environmental policy was 'discovered' in the 1980s and 1990s. Yet many of the most prominent environmental groups were formed well before then, while Britain has long-standing policies to regulate air quality and land use, two components of any environmental policy. So a first question must be whether the environment is really a new policy area or simply older issues recast in a more fashionable light. In part the answer is determined by the way the environment transcends traditional administrative and policy boundaries leading to, for example, the greening of policies in transport *and* the environment, agriculture *and* the environment, etc., rather than existing as a separate policy sector. Defining, the content of environmental policy, however, is not easy.

Not surprisingly, therefore, many commentators duck the question of what they regard as environmental policy. It is assumed implicitly that everyone knows what it is and is not. Nevertheless, it is possible to distinguish two popular approaches to defining environmental policy. The first is broad in scope and seeks links to the *physical environment*: thus, environmental policy is 'public policy concerned with governing the relationship between people and their natural environment' (McCormick, 1991, p. 7). Unfortunately this definition is both too narrow, in the sense that it seems to exclude urban areas (as these are difficult to classify as a natural environment), and too general, as it would seem difficult in practice to distinguish it from other policy areas such as rural social policy.

The other approach is much narrower in scope and focuses on 'the use of land and the *regulation* of human activities which have an impact on our physical surroundings' (Blowers, 1987, pp. 278–9, our emphasis). This implies a prescriptive element to policy, as politicians should seek a balance in the use of land between its development, conservation and ecological functions. In practice this involves working through two regulatory systems, that of the land use planning system (responsible for development and conservation) and pollution control (the ecological function). Whilst providing a framework against which to assess changes in environmental policy, the regulatory definition ignores the wider political and social backcloth, including the activities of political parties and new social groups, against which environmental decisions are made.

Perhaps, however, we do not need to ask what environmental policy *should* be, but what it *is*. Writing at the end of the 1980s Lowe and Flynn claimed that:

government structures and law relating to environmental protection have been (and largely remain) **an accretion of common law, statutes, agencies, procedures and policies**. *There is no environmental policy other than the sum of these individual elements, most of which have been pragmatic and incremental responses to specific problems and the evolution of relevant scientific knowledge. (Lowe and Flynn 1989, p. 256, our emphasis)*

The 1990 White Paper *This Common Inheritance* (Cm 1200) became the first ever comprehensive statement in Britain of a government's environmental policy. However, it was hardly a coherent strategy for action. Moreover, an understanding of contemporary environmental policy in Britain demands that we go beyond government statements. It may therefore be best to begin, as we have already suggested, with the key elements in the governmental structure and then broaden the analysis to take account of the socio-political phenomena of environmentalism.

Key public institutions

Although the reform of the machinery of central government has been a constant issue since the 1960s, British central government is still organised on self-contained policy sectors (energy, agriculture, transport, etc.). It is widely agreed that the environment should be integrated into all of these. The question is whether this should be carried out within individual departments or whether environmental responsibilities should be centralised within a single department that would then 'look across' government. The latter has been the favoured option because it fits in with the traditional operating style of government, treating the environment as a function and providing a focus for political activity.

The Department of the Environment (DOE)

During the late 1960s and 1970s there was widespread agreement on the need to consolidate related functions of government in order to improve the efficiency and effectiveness of decision-making. This led to giant departments, for example Health was merged with Social Security, and Housing with Local Government. In 1970 the Conservative Party won the general election and soon published a White Paper on *The Reorganisation of Central Government* (Cmnd 4506, 1970). This argued that:

It is increasingly accepted that maintaining a decent environment, improving people's living conditions and providing for adequate transport facilities, all come together in the planning of development. ... Because these functions interact, and because they give rise to acute and conflicting requirements, a new form of organisation is needed at the centre of the administrative system.

This new organisation was the Department of the Environment. Headed by a Secretary of State in the Cabinet, it was an amalgamation of the Ministries of Housing and Local Government, Public Building and Works, and Transport. Whilst narrowing the Heath thinking of integrating environmental and economic decision-making (see the quotation by Heath), the reorganisation did promise much for the environment.

The machinery of government and environmental policy

❝ These decisions [on the machinery of government] do not of course amount to a policy. They do little to guarantee that government departments take account of the environment as one of the necessary dimensions in the making of policy. The environment is by definition inter-disciplinary and all-embracing. Almost all government departments are involved. Almost all proposals for action have an environmental as well as an economic cost ... we are used to looking at the latter but not the former. We must learn to do both.

Edward Heath, as Leader of the Opposition, *The Spectator*, 11 April 1970 ❞

With the benefit of hindsight, however, it is easy to see that whilst the government may have believed that organisational reform was sufficient to deal with environmental problems, the Department of the Environment was more a rearrangement of the machinery of government than the creation of a department with new powers. It was never going to work as a department *of* the environment let alone one *for* the environment because the politics of Whitehall had left key environmental issues with other departments. Thus, responsibility for agriculture and the countryside remained with the Ministry of Agriculture, and energy with the then Department of Energy (now part of the Department of Trade and Industry). Even by 1976, as political priorities shifted, transport was separated from the department.

As interest in the environment increased during the 1970s and 1980s, therefore, the attention of policy-makers centred on other agencies of central and local government.

The Environment Agency

The substance of environmental policy presents enormous challenges to decision makers because it defies their conventional time-scales and functional divisions. Thus, where politicians' horizons may normally be bounded by that of elections, the environment forces them to think on a quite different scale, of generations for which they cannot possibly receive any political payback. Meanwhile, organisations like to do things in their own way with the minimum of external interference. But environmental policy cross-cuts traditional divisions of government and raises, for those concerned, the unwelcome possibility of turf disputes about who gets to do what. Faced with these dilemmas, decision-makers have shown a greater interest in the organisation of environmental protection as a substitute, or at least an alternative focus, for the more challenging issues surrounding the content of policy. Thus recent years have witnessed a flurry of, perhaps, unprecedented organisational reforms. The result has been some grander thinking on structures than is normal and the creation in 1996 of a large, centralised Environment Agency which may fit less easily into Britain's traditional administrative culture. In the past, small, specialised bodies, with for the most part low public profiles, have tended to be favoured.

Demands for the creation of a unified environment body have been long-standing (see Box 29.1). Since the mid-1970s the standing Royal Commission on Environmental Pollution had argued for a greater integration of the functions of what were at the time a set of disparate organisations. By the 1980s, increasing support from environmental groups, such as Friends of the Earth, and latterly the Labour and Liberal Democrat parties, helped make questions of integration a topic of policy debate. The late 1980s and early 1990s saw the creation of important new bodies, Her Majesty's Inspectorate of Pollution (HMIP), the National Rivers Authority (NRA) and the Waste Regulatory Authorities (WRAs), but still this did not quell the clamour for further reform. Within a month of the publication in 1990 of the government's White Paper on the environment, *This Common Inheritance*, the opposition parties had issued their own policy documents (*An Earthly Chance* and *What Price Our Planet?* by Labour and the Lib-Dems respectively), which, in contrast to the Conservatives, committed themselves to major institutional reforms.

Within a year the government fell into line, and in July 1991 John Major, in his first speech on the environment as Prime Minister, argued that 'it is right that the integrity and indivisibility of the environment should now be reflected in a unified agency' and announced the government's intention 'to create a new agency for environment protection and enhancement'.

The consultation paper *Improving Environmental Quality* (Department of the Environment, October 1991), which followed Major's speech revealed, however, not an environmental agency in the broadest sense (the nature conservation bodies were excluded) but a new pollution control body. Four options were set out:

1. a new agency to be responsible for emissions to air and land by taking over responsibility for most of the functions of HMIP together with those of waste regulation from local authorities; the NRA would take over HMIP's functions in the water environment;
2. an umbrella body to coordinate the work of HMIP and the NRA;
3. a single all-embracing agency combining waste regulation, HMIP and the NRA;

BOX 29.1   DEBATE

Key arguments for and against an integrated environment agency

For

- Company resource use and waste products need to be looked at as a whole, so that trade-offs can be made to find the 'best' receiving environment (i.e. air, land, water) for pollutants.

- Greater consistency in regulation.

- Larger companies only have to deal with one environmental regulator – the one-stop shop.

- Higher profile organisation that is better able to ensure its independence.

Against

- Organisations should be tailored to fit the resources they are to manage or the pollutants/processes to be regulated.

- Small, specialist bodies are more adaptable to changing circumstances.

- Cross-sectoral regulation is too complex.

- The focus should be on integrating the environment into sectoral policies.

4. as (3), but the NRA would retain its river, water and fisheries management functions.

The favoured response of most commentators, business and the environmental lobby was option 3. Progress, though, remained slow, and not until the Environment Act was passed in 1995 was the necessary legislation in place to create the Agency which came into being on 1 April 1996.

HMIP, the NRA and the WRAs together form the core of the Environment Agency in England and Wales. The Scottish Environment Protection Agency (the difference in name may be of some significance) has in addition to the three core groups the local authority environmental health officers who dealt with air pollution. In terms of the logic creating a unified and all-embracing, pollution regulation body, the inclusion of such staff makes sense. That it did not happen in England and Wales indicates the way in which organisational design in the public sector is invariably intertwined with political factors.

What does the Environment Agency mean for the work of its core groups and what effects might it have on those they regulate? The functions set out in Box 29.2 are derived from its constituent elements. Of these, HMIP was formed in 1987 as the result of interdepartmental disputes, embarrassment at pollution discharges at Sellafield nuclear power station, and pressures from the European Commission. It combined what had been distinct inspectorates in industrial air pollution, radiochemical, hazardous waste and water pollution. It was responsible for regulating discharges to air, land or water for some 2,000 industrial processes with the greatest polluting potential.

The NRA was a much larger and higher profile organisation than HMIP. It has gone on to form the largest part of the new agency and its former staff have secured a number of key positions within it. The NRA was created at the same time as the water authorities were privatised, under the Water Act 1989, and it took on the pollution control functions and some of the activities of these authorities. The latter were both guardians of the water environment and also major polluters as dischargers of sewage, that is, acting as both poacher and gamekeeper.

The formation of the NRA represented the separation of operational aspects (i.e. water supply) from its regulation. Whereas HMIP was involved in the regulation of industrial process, the NRA was

BOX 29.2

Principal functions of the Environment Agency

1. *Flood defence:* Protect people and the developed environment from flooding.

2. *Water resource management:* Conserve and secure the proper use of water.

3. *Pollution control:* Prevent or minimise gaseous, liquid or solid waste pollution to land, air or water.

4. *Fisheries:* Maintain and improve salmon, trout, freshwater and eel fisheries and issue angling licences.

5. *Navigation:* Over 800 km of inland waterways.

6. *Recreation:* Promote the recreational use of water and land.

7. *Conservation:* Of nature, landscape and archaeological heritage.

---

managing a resource, or, as it is more formally known, *river basin management*. As the quotation below implies, this involves the following:

1. flood defence (including land drainage) and coastal protection (involving about half of its staff of 7,800);
2. water resource management (including abstraction licences);
3. pollution control;
4. fisheries;
5. navigation on certain rivers; and
6. recreation and conservation.

The NRA and river basin management

> " The *concept* of integrated river basin management is quite straightforward. Rivers have water catchments, from which they are fed. There are inputs into rivers at all stages from their source to their eventual

discharge to the sea. There are also abstractions of water from rivers. Increasingly, rivers are subjected to recreational use, of which boating and angling are the most popular. Fish and other water-based life forms will thrive or die depending on the quality of river water. Since each of these factors is related to the others, and since all are at the mercy of an unmanageable factor: rainfall, it makes good sense to manage river basins in an integrated fashion.

HC 55, 1991–2, para. 94, p. xxxi **"**

Waste collection and disposal has been a traditional local government activity and in recent years has been subject to much reform in order to separate what were perceived to be conflicting responsibilities. Under the Environmental Protection Act 1990 three types of waste authority were created. **Waste Collection Authorities** (a local authority or contractor working for the authority) arrange for the collection of household and commercial waste. Its disposal is the responsibility of a **Waste Disposal Authority** (again this will be a part of local government or a Local Authority Waste Disposal Company). **Waste Regulation Authorities**, whose staff have been moved to the Environment Agency, are responsible for ensuring the safe treatment and disposal of so-called controlled waste (at present that is all wastes except that produced by households, mines and quarries and agriculture).

Clearly by bringing together in one organisation the control of water pollution, air pollution and the management of commercial waste there is the hope of providing a more integrated approach to environmental management as a way of contributing to more sustainable development. Whilst structures may be important in achieving this goal, the eventual success or otherwise of the new Agency will also depend upon the extent to which the various elements and professional groups from which it is formed can reconcile their different approaches and forge a common strategy, that it receives adequate funding, and can be seen to be independent of government and those it regulates. Much, then, rests upon the authority of the Agency and its willingness to exercise its power. In this regard HMIP had a patchy record whilst the NRA was perceived to be a more effective regulator. Much, though, will need to be done if it is to live up to its own claim of being one of the most powerful environmental regulators in the world. The

Agency is not helped in that it has received few additional powers, notably in preventing pollution, from those which its constituent bodies held. It is unlikely that most businesses will notice any difference in the way in which they are regulated.

Indeed, for some environmentalists the fear is that the Conservative government's approach to regulation may have quite adverse effects upon the Agency's activities. When developing new proposals for legislation or regulation the Agency is required to produce a compliance cost assessment, that is, to work out the costs complying with new rules will have on business. These are to be compared to any benefits which may accrue. The problem here, though, is that whilst the costs to business may be relatively easily ascertained, the benefits to the environment may not. To identify the financial benefits of, say, a cleaner river is no easy task. New regulations must show that benefits outweigh costs, and the outcome may be that reform becomes a more contested, incremental and lengthy process.

Local government and environmental policy

Traditionally, local councils have played a key and wide-ranging role in the UK's system of environmental regulation. Relations between central and local government, however, have often been fraught and have proved particularly challenging since 1979 with successive Conservative governments attempting to curb expenditure, curtail responsibilities and privatise services (see Chapter 22). Against this backdrop there have been developments in the role of local authorities in air pollution and waste regulation, the planning system, and local government's own environmental initiatives.

Pollution regulation by local authorities

While the Environment Agency is responsible for emissions from industrial processes scheduled under legislation, district councils are responsible for those from non-scheduled processes. These responsibilities stem principally from the Public Health Act 1936, the Clean Air Acts of 1956 and 1968 and the Environmental Protection Act 1990. Under the legislation, local authorities control emissions of smoke, dust, grit and odour, and, under the Control of Pollution Act 1974, noise.

As we have seen, however, local authorities play a more important role in *waste regulation*. Until quite recently local authorities collected, disposed and were responsible for regulation of the waste that was created in their areas. Under the Environmental Protection Act 1990, responsibility for the collection of household and some commercial and industrial waste is split between the different tiers of government, but the authorities, in this case largely county councils, are required to subject these services to private company bids in a process known as compulsory competitive tendering (see Chapter 22). The counties, however, remain responsible for waste regulation (Waste Regulation Authorities). (There is a more confused situation in some metropolitan areas where there can be joint responsibility for disposal and regulation.) Under the Environmental Protection Act, the Conservative government set a target for local authorities to recycle 25 per cent of household waste by the end of the century, which for some, it is already clear, is not attainable.

Local planning

The tensions of central–local relations have had a profound impact also on the operation of the planning system, one of the most sophisticated mechanisms for environmental regulation, more specifically for controlling and promoting *land use development*, in Britain. Although planning decisions are made under the broad supervision of the Department of the Environment (or the Scottish or Welsh Offices), councils are responsible for both drawing up plans and making decisions on proposed developments. Planning law grants wide discretion to councils to control and promote land use planning, including the content of plans, the granting of planning permission, the enforcement of breaches of control and the pursuit of positive planning. This discretion and decentralisation makes for both variability and vitality in local planning.

The reform of the planning system was a prime goal of the Conservative governments elected after 1979. The system was regarded as bureaucratic and an impediment to the working of the market. Government changes were therefore designed to reduce the scope of local authority involvement in the planning process and to remove some of the constraints faced by developers in securing planning approval. The reforms have profoundly affected the major urban and industrial areas where agencies of central government have replaced the local authorities. Enterprise zones, urban development corporations and simplified planning zones have awarded tax breaks to developers, taken over site development, and streamlined planning procedures.

Similar pressures for liberalisation have applied to rural areas but have not been reinforced by the centralising and interventionist measures deployed in urban areas, and so have not undermined local democratic control to the same extent. Thus development in rural areas has depended to a much greater extent on local discretion and the balance of local political forces, such as the strength of amenity interests or the involvement of local economic interests. Indeed, in areas of high environmental value such as national parks, areas of outstanding natural beauty (AONB), sites of special scientific interest (SSSI) and conservation areas, the government has introduced additional safeguards to protect them from development.

It is worthwhile speculating on why the Conservative government's deregulatory instincts were tempered in rural areas. Two factors would seem to be of critical importance. Firstly, the countryside remains the heartland of Toryism, a paternalistic and pragmatic brand of Conservatism, and this has shaped policy. Secondly, particularly in the more accessible countryside, Conservatism has been replenished by the successive immigration of middle-class groups. Attempts to liberalise rural planning, with the implication that this would hasten and broaden the rate of development, have produced a backlash from people concerned to protect their own environments and well able to articulate their interests in the political arena.

Local authority initiatives

Finally, despite, or perhaps more accurately because of, the criticism and restrictions to which local government has been subject, it has become increasingly involved in a series of measures by which it can promote the environment and at the same time promote itself not only as 'green' but as an active organ of government. The stimulus to which local government has responded has largely come from external bodies and events. Amongst the most significant was the launch by Friends of the Earth (1989) of its *Environmental Charter for Local Government*. Published at a time of considerable public and political interest in the environment, the Charter demanded a commitment from local authorities 'to promote the conservation and sustainable use of natural resources and to minimise environmental pollution in all its own activities, and through its influences over others' (Friends of the Earth, 1989, p. 4). The Charter provided guidelines on how councils might meet their commitment and nearly two hundred practical recommendations for action.

Other influences include the local authority associations, the European Commission and the UNCED Conference at Rio, where much of Agenda 21 (the global environmental agenda for the next century) was predicated upon local action. At the present time, however, because so many of the environmental initiatives in local government are of relatively recent origin, it is difficult to disentangle rhetoric from substance and so make a considered judgement. Many authorities have issued environmental statements. Some have undertaken thoroughgoing reviews of their activities and established environmental performance indicators, but others have been much more modest.

A test of central government's commitment to the environment will be to see whether it meets local government requests for more powers and resources to deal with Agenda 21. At a time of budgetary constraints, local government finds that it can do little more than carry out its statutory duties, and yet much that it does or wishes to do in the environmental field is of a non-statutory nature.

The conservation agencies

The part that *safeguarding and promoting the environment* may have played in the relatively recent restructuring of the statutory conservation agencies – the Countryside Commission, English Nature, Scottish Natural Heritage and the Countryside Council for Wales – out of their antecedents, the National Parks Commission and the Nature Conservancy Council, is a matter of some controversy. Certainly, the reforms are useful indicators of the way in which administrative structures

influence environmental policy-making and government thinking on the environment.

All the conservation bodies can trace their origins back to the 1949 National Parks and Access to the Countryside Act. Under the Act two sets of responsibilities were established. The first was for nature conservation. English Nature, for example (and its predecessor, the Nature Conservancy Council), is based on scientific and technical expertise and draws upon an elite tradition of interest in natural history and the preservation of flora and fauna. Despite the reorganisations and changing names, the major functions have remained largely unchanged:

1. the establishment and maintenance of national nature reserves and sites of special scientific interest (known as SSSIs);
2. the advising of government on nature conservation issues;
3. information and advice to interested parties, especially on how sites may be protected; and
4. supporting and commissioning research.

Meanwhile, the Countryside Commission, now operating in England alone, has as its main functions:

1. the extension of access and recreational opportunities in the countryside;
2. the conservation of the landscape beauty of the countryside; and
3. advising government on countryside matters, such as designating national parks and areas of outstanding natural beauty (AONBs), designating heritage coasts and establishing nature trails.

Thus was born a, perhaps, unique organisational division amongst public sector bodies in Europe of separating landscape and nature protection. The divide reflects some of the characteristics of British environmentalism. While English Nature might argue that the public should be excluded from nature reserves on scientific grounds, the Countryside Commission tends to favour access. But these are not the only differences between the agencies. English Nature has a much greater executive role through its management of national nature reserves (SSSIs are scheduled by English Nature but are often to be found on private land). Only recently has the Commission gained some modest executive functions through its management of the Countryside Stewardship Scheme, and the Countryside Premium Scheme, to protect valued landscapes, and the promotion of parish paths and hedgerows. Both organisations, however, are grant-in-aid bodies, i.e. they are funded from public funds.

In recent years the fortunes of the two bodies have diverged. English Nature has suffered budget cuts and an embargo placed on the creation of new nature reserves. Meanwhile, the Countryside Commission, benefiting from the rise of green issues, has seen its budget rise by £14 million, of which £10 million has been due to its new Countryside Premium Scheme. Judgements on the two organisations tend to be harsh but it is difficult to differ from that of Lowe and Goyder (1983, p. 67) that they 'have small budgets, little power and limited policy-making initiative, and they are politically marginal' (see quotation).

The political significance of conservation agencies

> The environmental agencies [also] act as negative filters to the environmental lobby. Demands from the lobby which are opposed by the agencies are unlikely to be taken seriously by government. However, the corollary – that demands supported by the agencies will command government attention – does not necessarily follow. Indeed, the environmental agencies tend to be regarded by government as pressure groups, whose views should be treated with scepticism and whose involvement in central policy making should be carefully circumscribed. The effect of such attitudes on the agencies is to induce them to behave 'responsibly' – to temper the demands made by environmental groups and to internalise the constraints which government regards as salient.
>
> *Lowe and Goyder, 1983, pp. 67–8*

The reorganisation of the conservation agencies has taken a different path from that of the pollution control bodies. Although there are signs of integration or unification of responsibilities amongst the bodies, it has taken different forms. For the conservation agencies the functional integration in 1989 in Wales and Scotland (in which landscape and nature were combined in the Countryside Council for Wales and Scottish Natural Heritage) has been allied to geographical fragmentation. In England, landscape protection and nature conservation remain the responsibility of separate bodies. It is not

a situation dictated by organisational logic or adherence to explicit environmental principles. What it represents is the current state of play in an organisational and policy framework that has developed in a largely *ad hoc* and pragmatic manner, and is a vivid testimony to the weakness of the statutory environmental bodies.

The political parties and the environment

These organisational reforms have revealed party political rivalry stronger than in any other aspect of environmental policy. Perhaps this is the area where the parties themselves feel they can respond most effectively without having to confront more fundamental challenges, such as curbing demand, or alienating traditional supporters. This suggests that although the environmental field has been party politicised, the parties remain unsure about how to confront the environmental problem.

The environment has emerged as a significant electoral issue. For a time in the late 1980s opinion pollsters recorded it in the top three. Although it has since subsequently declined, the way it has moved onto the agenda has both forced and encouraged the major parties to define their own positions and to compete for the votes of electors. As a new issue, it has forced the parties to compete across a broad front, although they have sought to define their positions in terms of traditional perspectives. Thus Labour is more committed to the benefits of public transport in its policies than the Conservatives are. Moreover, as an issue that does not always divide along neat left–right lines, it allows minor parties to play a more important part in defining the agenda as they would expect to be able to make gains by playing the environmental card. For the major parties, as competition has increased and they seek to maximise their appeal, their policies have converged.

The environment, however, is not quite like other policy areas. To begin with, the parties are generally defensive in their attitude, unsure of the environment's implications or its electoral potential. As a policy field, it has made its greatest impact *between* rather than during general elections. Nevertheless, the issues have steadily engulfed higher echelons within the parties, so that within little more than a decade the environment has moved from a minority concern to one which the party leaderships cannot ignore.

It would, however, be simplistic to regard the growing involvement of the political parties in environmental policy solely as a means to capture votes. They have also been responding to a changed policy context in which many of the certainties of the post-war years and the benefits of environmental reformism have been swept away. The adverse economic and political climate of the early 1980s led to new sets of relationships between environmental groups and government. One consequence has been that the political parties themselves have become an important vehicle for the promotion of environmental views as they responded to increasingly well-publicised and media-oriented issues commanding public attention. In contrast, therefore, to many other Western European countries, 'the party politicisation of the environment in Britain has not come about through the established parties having to respond to the threat posed by an ascendant green party. On the contrary, it was the increasing prominence of the environment in mainstream politics that helped the British Greens emerge from their obscurity in the late 1980s' (Flynn and Lowe, 1992, p. 12).

The Conservative Party

As the party of government between 1979 and 1997, the environmental debate in the Conservative Party has been of obvious consequence. Moreover, it has frequently been a vehicle for surrogate discussions of the ideological direction of the party and so assumed even more significant proportions. These arise from the inherent questions about the nature and extent of state action that are posed by environmental issues. Not surprisingly, the paternalistic and free market wings of the party have sought to outline their own agendas.

In the early 1980s, it was the paternalists who linked their brand of Conservatism and the environment (see quotation). Indeed, with neo-liberal ideas to the fore in the leadership, the environment, particularly where it had links to the countryside, became something of a refuge for those with a more paternalistic orientation. Such sentiments gained strength as the government's economic and deregulatory strategy gave rise to a number of unfortunate consequences, including increased house building in green belt areas in southern England and claims that weak pollution control made Britain 'the dirty man of Europe'.

Conservative paternalists and the environment

> "... green voters and conservative voters share an instinct for preserving what is good and fine around us and traditional around us. The nature conservationist is a natural conservative.
>
> *Paterson, 1984 p. 3*

Only in the late 1980s did the party leadership become actively involved and seek to leave its own imprint on the agenda. In the autumn of 1988, the then Prime Minister, Margaret Thatcher, launched a period of sustained competition between the parties on environmental policy when she made two major speeches on the subject, to the Royal Society and the Conservative Party conference. On the latter occasion she claimed: 'It is we Conservatives who are not merely friends of the earth. We are its guardians and trustees for generations to come.' The potency of these claims comes from the use of the name of a prominent environmental group and critic of the government, the links to paternalism, and the pitching of the environmental agenda above domestic concerns at the global level.

Having raised the environment to the top of the political agenda, however, the government found its own record and actions subject to greater scrutiny. It became increasingly obvious that clear principles needed to be enumerated to justify its position. What emerged, however, from the then Secretary of State for the Environment, Nicholas Ridley (1989), a noted free-marketeer, was largely conventional thinking supplemented by only two principles which could be regarded as neo-liberal. One was that production should be separated from regulation – a view supported by other parties – and the other was the polluter pays principle (interpreted as the polluters' customers must pay). Thus, the free-marketeers found it difficult to define a distinct environmental agenda.

The Labour Party

If the environment has been a difficult policy area for the Conservative Party, it has not been that much easier for Labour, despite the best efforts of committed groups (such as the Socialist Environmental and Resource Association) and prominent individuals. Indeed, until the late 1980s Labour's interest in the environment was sporadic and uncoordinated.

Labour's indifference towards the environment through much of the 1980s was partly determined by the issue's potential for internal disagreement. For some, it was an essentially middle-class issue dominated by amenity and rural preservation interests. It had little to do with the lives of the urban working class. Indeed, some environmental policies (for example, conservationist protection of villages from low-cost housing developments or preserving agricultural land from industrial uses) were and are still seen as antithetical to the interests of the working class. (For a classic statement of these views see Crosland, 1971.)

For others the environment was an unnecessary brake on economic development. Particularly in the early 1980s, when Labour reacted strongly to the recession which so badly hit its electoral strongholds, economic expansion to meet its employment and social policy commitments was a priority. This explains some strange alliances between organised labour and employers to defend existing practices from new environmental regulations on the grounds that it would lead to increased costs and consequently a loss of jobs.

Perhaps the clearest case of the unions seeking to defend their specific interests and influencing Labour Party thinking has been in the energy field. The National Union of Mineworkers (NUM) has been a critic of nuclear power, a competitor of coal-fired power stations, and keen to promote the latter as a more environmentally friendly form of electricity production. The NUM has, however, been dismissive of the effects those power stations have in acid rain production and on local conservation. Meanwhile those unions representing workers in the nuclear industry have sought to portray nuclear power as a clean and modern form of energy production and to play down the detrimental environmental impacts it may have. Nuclear power is, of course, one of the major concerns of many environmentalists, but Labour's front-bench spokesperson through much of the mid-1980s was Jack Cunningham, who represented the constituency in

which Sellafield nuclear power station is based. He has been a strong proponent of nuclear energy and in a handy position to influence party policy.

It was not until the mid-1980s that the environment become a matter for serious internal party debate. This arose from Labour's opposition to the Wildlife and Countryside Act 1981, which had brought it into close contact with conservation groups, and the explosion at the Chernobyl nuclear power station in 1986 which quickly threw into doubt the future of the nuclear industry. Moreover, following two successive general election defeats, there was an understandable desire to rethink some of the party's traditional ideas and extend its electoral base by capitalising, for example, on growing public concern for environmental issues. The Greens in West Germany had also enjoyed recent electoral success which had attracted much attention.

Labour's first comprehensive statement on the environment appeared in 1986. The party leadership, however, showed little inclination to build on the ideas until *An Earthly Chance*, published shortly after the government's White Paper in the autumn of 1990, attracted the support of environmentalists for its detailed promises of action, for example in the area of institutional reform and sulphur dioxide emissions. The document foresaw a more important role for the state in regulating environmental standards than the Conservatives had been prepared to concede, but did also recognise the role of market mechanisms in encouraging more environmentally benign behaviour from producers and consumers.

The policy differences between the two major parties have not been significant. Essentially they have reflected degrees of unwillingness to make commitments. If Labour has been marginally less inhibited, however, John Selwyn Gummer's very public warnings on global warming, made in the summer of 1996 as Secretary of State for the Environment, indicated an attempt to gain the moral high ground.

The Liberal Democrats

Unlike the two major parties, the Liberal Democrats and their predecessors have never been so closely linked to identifiable economic groups. This has allowed the party a much longer and closer involvement with the environment as a policy area. Indeed, the old Liberal Party debated environmental issues at its annual conference as long ago as 1971, and in 1974 the conference argued that economic growth should take place in the context of ecological constraints. Now the Liberal Democrats' constitution makes a commitment to safeguard the environment.

Throughout the 1980s and into the 1990s it is the Liberal Democrats and their predecessors who have provided the main challenge to the Conservative Party across much of southern England. Although rarely able to translate their support into seats, the party has been able to exploit environmental discontent and discomfort the Conservatives. This has often coincided with mid-term support for the Liberal Democrats and spectacular by-election successes.

The Liberal Democrats' statements on the environment are usually more detailed and wide-ranging than those of the other parties. *What Price Our Planet?*, produced at the same time as that of the Conservative and Labour parties' main policy pronouncements, was no exception. It leant heavily on environmental economics, particularly the work of David Pearce and his colleagues in a report that had been commissioned for the government. The Liberal Democrats have gone further than the Conservatives in seeking to link fiscal structures with environmental protection and have argued for a pollution added tax (PAT) and environmental grants and subsidies (EGS).

Despite their efforts, however, the Liberal Democrats have not been able to raise the environment to the national political stage in general elections or to differentiate their own position sufficiently from that of the other parties. Ground the Liberals originally trod has now become a well-travelled

Table 29.1 Environmental issue convergence in political parties

Issue	Conservative	Labour	Liberal Democrats
Agriculture and food		✓	
Conservation	✓		✓
Air pollution	✓	✓	
Water	✓	✓	✓
Energy	✓	✓	✓
Ozone layer	✓	✓	✓
Global warming		✓	✓
Rain forests		✓	✓
Waste	✓	✓	✓
Acid rain		✓	✓
Consumers	✓	✓	
Business		✓	
Economics	✓		
Land use	✓	✓	✓
Urban	✓		✓
Countryside	✓	✓	✓
Industry		✓	✓
Transport	✓		✓
Population			✓
Poverty			✓
Sea/coasts		✓	✓
Animals		✓	✓
Noise	✓	✓	
Heritage	✓	✓	

Source: Incidence of issues appearing in: Conservative Party, *This Common Inheritance*, 1990; Labour Party, *An Earthly Chance*, 1990; Liberal Democrats, *What Price Our Planet?*, 1990

path. Although the new party is more suffused with environmentalism and its latest proposals are more radical than those of the other two major parties, the overall thrust of policy does not differ dramatically from them, nor do the topics that the parties regard as legitimate elements of environmental policy (see Table 29.1).

What has happened is that as the environment has moved higher up the political agenda, so the competition between the parties has heightened. Therefore in their public pronouncements all three parties believe they can win (or at least not lose) what environmentalist votes there may be and they try to appeal to this group in broadly the same manner. Only if the parties believe they can secure a competitive advantage is policy differentiation likely to occur.

Plaid Cymru and the Scottish National Party

Whereas the Liberal Democrats have tried to cultivate an emergent environmental cleavage, based primarily in southern England, in Scotland and Wales green sentiments have been much weaker. There are at least two possible explanations for this. The first stems from the way material standards are important influences on people's attitudes towards the environment. Thus, in the northern and western parts of the country, where the effects of economic growth were much more patchy, incomes and wealth assets generally lower and unemployment a problem, the environmental message was not likely to be so well received. However, a different explanation is that any incipient environmental views in Scotland and Wales have been integrated within the nationalist parties.

For both nationalist parties, environmental policy is part and parcel of their overall political strategy. They believe that only as independent nations or in a highly decentralised Britain can the environmental issues that affect them be dealt with effectively. Their commitment to decentralisation means that it is often at the local level that their policies are strongest. Not surprisingly, the parties have formulated ambitious policies, set stiff targets for improving their environments and are committed to working with supranational bodies, thus bypassing the British state. Linking the protection of the environment with national identity is a potentially potent cocktail,

though there is no reason why nationalism should be an inherently environmental ideology.

The Green Party

No account of environmental policy would be complete without some reference to the Green Party, but, apart from one fleeting electoral success, it has been a marginal actor in British politics. Indeed, its significance from an analytical standpoint may not stem from its popular fortunes but from what it reveals about the structure of the environmental movement.

Britain's Green Party, founded in 1973 as 'People' and then relaunched two years later as the Ecology Party, was the first in Europe. Its formation was largely inspired by a series of articles in *The Ecologist* magazine in the early 1970s which warned of the need for immediate action if global collapse was to be avoided. To begin with, the party's focus was consequently rather narrow, being a set of ecological and quasi-sociological principles for action. Only in 1985 was the name Green Party adopted to emphasise its linkage with the more successful European green movement and to stop any other parties taking on the green mantle.

Despite the name changes, the party was remarkably unsuccessful in elections at least until 1989, when it secured 15 per cent of the vote in the European elections. This result was a major surprise and provoked much discussion on the future of green politics in Britain and further contributed to the flurry of party political activity. The vote, though, was largely dependent on the peculiar conditions of the time: an unpopular government, third party disarray with the botched merger of the Liberals and the Social Democrats, and people willing to express their protest views through the Green Party. Furthermore, at a European election voters may have been more willing to be more innovative in their voting behaviour, knowing that it would not lead to a change in government. Electors may even have been influenced by the relatively high-profile and successful Community environmental policy. By the next general election in 1992, however, the Greens' support had reverted to its traditional 1 per cent.

The party's electoral failure can be attributed to a number of internal and external factors. Almost throughout its existence the party has been bede-villed by conflicts as to what type of party it should be. Basically the division is between those who want the Greens to adopt a conventional form of party organisation and strategy and those who reject the idea of party politics and advocate a form of politics based around an alternative lifestyle. Following their achievements in the European elections, the disputes between the two sides became particularly fierce, and led to the resignation of one of its best-known members, Sara Parkin, one of those who wanted to reform the party's organisation to make it a viable electoral force.

Amongst the external factors limiting its electoral success has been the adeptness of the major parties to retain and recruit their own green supports by forming their own specialist groups (e.g. the Conservative Ecology Group, the Socialist Environmental and Resource Association). Moreover, in their formative years the Greens adopted a narrow perspective on the environment and were unable to cultivate the support of the environmental movement or more generally those on the left who may have been sympathetic to the party. That there should be a divorce within the environmental movement between political party and interest groups, when strong and mutually reinforcing links based around shared goals and values may well have been expected, is a feature of British environmental policy and owes much to the operation of the wider political process. It is to an analysis of environmental groups and their part in the political system that we now turn.

Environmental groups

Overall, the position of environmental groups stands in stark contrast to that of the Green Party. According to McCormick (1991, p. 34), 'Britain has the oldest, strongest, best-organized and most widely supported environmental lobby in the world'. By 1990 McCormick estimated the support for environmental groups to be around 4.5 million (about 8 per cent of the population).

The foundations of this lobby were laid in the late nineteenth century with subsequent bursts of growth in environmental groups in the late 1920s, the late 1950s, the early 1970s, as well as the late 1980s. The 1970s were distinguished from earlier periods by both the rapid growth of existing groups and the formation of new ones, such as Friends of the Earth (formed in the United States in 1969), Greenpeace (formed in Canada in 1972) and Transport 2000. The new groups made a significant impact upon the lobby by highlighting the international nature of many environmental problems, and providing radical analyses of environmental issues which linked them to contemporary social and economic conditions. New tactics also emerged with Friends of the Earth and Greenpeace adopting vigorous, high-profile campaigns to draw attention to a broad range of threats to the environment.

The success of the environmental lobby in increasing its membership has had an effect on its finances. One estimate is that by 1990 'the UK's 15 largest environmental groups, including the National Trust, had a combined annual budget of £163m' (Rawcliffe, 1992, p. 3), a not inconsiderable sum. As well as membership subscriptions, the other major sources of income for most groups are grants from government organisations, business sponsorship and other environmental groups, notably the World Wildlife Fund (WWF). As might be expected, groups differ quite considerably as regards whom they are prepared to do business with. On the one side there is Greenpeace, which makes a virtue of its financial independence, surviving entirely on its fund-raising, and on the other the WWF, which has been much more pragmatic. As business has become much more interested in promoting its environmental image, it has been much more willing to fund specific projects and sponsor groups. Friends of the Earth has responded to this situation by reversing its position of no links to business and appointed a corporate fund-raiser. In accepting sponsorship from those it regards as ethically sound, it seeks to promote environmental auditing and policy as a business concern. This may be a rather naive hope.

With greater income, groups have been able to employ more staff to monitor more accurately government activities, engage in more lobbying and prepare better critiques of official policy. Campaigns are much more sophisticated than they used to be, making still greater use of the media and, for the more radical groups, there has been a greater reliance on scientific and legal evidence to support their positions. The emphasis, therefore, has been on strengthening traditional styles of lobbying.

Although groups have, and seek, different relationships with government, most desire to work within the system, to be involved at the earliest stages in policy discussions, that is, before they reach the public arena. To do so, though, groups must be recognised by government as responsible in representing the views of their members. Responsibility implies discretion, trustworthiness, moderation and usually a formal political neutrality so that groups can work with governments of different political colour. Thus, even radical groups such as Friends of the Earth, who seek to maintain their relationships with government, will not wish to be seen to be to closely attached to a political party, even one as marginal as the Greens.

Greenpeace has confronted a more difficult situation. In some countries the nature of the political system is such that it can maintain its outsider position and still seek to influence debate. In Britain that is more difficult, and now that many of its concerns have become matters of public policy debate – Greenpeace's direct action tactics have been successful in helping to set the environmental agenda – it has to decide whether the same tactics are required for the next phase in the formulation and implementation of policy. As one commentator has written, 'Greenpeace faces a dilemma. If it does not insist on being very tough, it becomes little different from Friends of the Earth' (*The Independent*, 28 August 1992).

In many ways, therefore, environmental groups have performed remarkably well politically. They have been the main source of opposition to government policies and done much to raise the profile of the environment. Their links with government, although stronger than before, are not as deeply entrenched as those of producer interests. Some, though, would argue that such divisions are increasingly anachronistic and that an agenda shared by producers and consumers is beginning to emerge.

Issues en route to the green society

As we have seen, it has been the environmental groups rather than the political parties which have been successful in making the environment a matter of political debate. In the remainder of this chapter we will discuss three of the more important issues. The first, sustainable development, is of over-arching significance. The others, road-building programmes and ecological disasters, bring out some if its practical and sometimes more controversial implications.

Sustainable development

One of the classic confrontations of the late twentieth century has been between the environment and the economy. The two are regarded as incompatible: one either has ecological protection and no-growth or economic development and environmental degradation. The notion of sustainable development, and the belief of some that we are moving towards a greener society, integrates the economy and the environment and at one stroke sidesteps much of the traditional debate.

Much of the controversy now is over what is meant by sustainable development, for it has become something of a totem, a concept so powerful that no one should question it. But different interests seek to interpret it in various ways. As such sustainable development has become an object of contestation within the environmental debate. Originally developed within the ecological sciences, it was popularised in *Our Common Future* (more commonly known as the Brundtland Report) as that which 'meets the needs of the present without compromising the ability of future generations to meet their own needs'. At its minimum this would seem to involve little more than business as usual with a few added on commitments to environmental protection. This 'greening' of the business community and the consumer was especially popular in the late 1980s when environmental concern coincided with a period of economic growth. Books such as *The Green Consumer Guide* were bestsellers and a spate of products declared that they were 'natural' or 'environmentally friendly'. The belief was promoted that people could make a difference, that they could help protect the environment through their purchasing practices. A new breed of environmentally conscious consumer appeared to be emerging who was prepared to pay more for CFC- or phosphate-free products, for example.

Businesses in turn appeared to respond to consumer demands with retailers in particular leading the way. One of the business success stories of the late 1980s and early 1990s has been the Body Shop chain. It promotes itself on the basis of no animal testing of its products, recycling and refill facilities, and it promises environmentally friendly production methods. The very success of the Body Shop has inspired imitators and seemed to show that the environment made good business sense.

In order to show their commitment to environmental protection and exploit market opportunities businesses have engaged in such measures as environmental management systems and environmental auditing. Purchasing policies, production processes and waste disposal are all now much more carefully monitored. Eco-labelling schemes now exist in many European countries to show that products are produced to a certain standard and an EC-wide labelling scheme is likely to appear.

More recently, governments have shown a willingness to coordinate and act to address the issue of sustainable development. The Brundtland Report was endorsed by political leaders at the United Nations Conference on Environment and Development (the Earth Summit) in Rio de Janeiro in 1992. The summit produced the following:

1. the Rio declaration, which established a set of principles for action;
2. a programme of action for the next century, Agenda 21;
3. a Climate Change Convention to try to reduce the risks of global warming;
4. a Biodiversity Convention to protect species and habitats; and
5. a statement of principles for the conservation of the world's forests.

Each country was charged with taking forward these points.

The British Conservative government put some efforts into delivering its promises on implementing its action programme. After a year-long consultation period it published *Sustainable Development: The UK Strategy* (Cm 2426) in January 1994. The document was largely a restatement of existing policies and ideas but did contain some initiatives to promote new ideas. These included a Panel on Sustainable Development comprising five eminent experts who report directly to the Prime Minister; a Round Table on Sustainable Development made up of thirty representatives drawn from business, local government, environmental groups and other organisations; and a Going for Green programme to

carry the sustainable development message to local communities and individuals.

The government also published proposals on *Biodiversity: The UK Action Plan* (Cm 2428). Again, the policies were modest and often simply consolidated in one document existing actions but did at least represent a positive step forward. In contrast parts of local government have been much more innovative in developing sustainability indicators and action programmes though they remain hamstrung by lack of resources and powers.

In time the green consumer of the late 1980s may be seen to be a manufactured myth, an attempt to find an individual response to a collective problem, but one peculiarly suited to the politics and society of the time. However, many environmentalists are arguing that a more challenging version of sustainable development needs to be put into practice, one in which the state plays a much more positive role in ensuring the equitable distribution of resources through space and time. For them labelling or kite marking products is a diversion. Attention is switched away from total production to the methods of production of particular goods. It therefore fails to confront the major cause of the ecological crisis, the sheer amount of production and consumption. On this view, sustainable development does not mean no development but much more selective development.

Road-building programmes

One of the most bitterly contested areas of government policy has been that relating to road transport. The controversy it has excited has led to set-piece confrontations around proposed new developments, spawned a new wave of environmental activism and challenged the government's commitment to sustainable development. For the Conservative government the car was both a symbol and a provider of personal freedom, and traffic growth an indicator of economic development. Faced with a massive forecast for increases in traffic, the government committed itself to a large road-building programme in the suitably titled 1989 White Paper *Roads for Prosperity* (Cm 693). Environmentalists challenge each of these claims: the car, especially in urban areas, becomes a symbol of the right of individuals to pollute the air that others must breathe, projections of traffic growth pay insufficient attention to the environment and are therefore unsustainable, and more road-building does not ease congestion but creates new traffic.

Many local road improvement schemes will arouse little if any controversy. The road-building schemes that have aroused national attention, notably those at Twyford Down, Newbury and Honiton, are significant because of their scale and their impact on nationally important environments. They have thus become a focus, sometimes at a symbolic level, for the arguments for and against the road-building programme. The M3 protest at Twyford Down began in the mid-1980s and initially involved a classic local protest: concerned residents engaged in conventional campaigning tactics, such as lobbying and high-profile events (e.g. protest walks) in which they worked closely with national groups, notably Friends of the Earth.

As all legal avenues of protest disappeared a new form of protester appeared who was committed to non-violent direct action. The latter drew much of their inspiration from the American group Earth First! and disdained conventional politics as failing to protect the environment. The initially small group occupied part of the road-building site known as the Dongas, an area of deep hollows, and became known as the Dongas Tribe. Faced with overwhelming odds the Dongas Tribe could not hope to stop the building of the road. Nevertheless, their courage and commitment provoked enormous interest and inspired other protests such as that at Newbury. The Twyford Down campaign was also significant in another respect. As Barbara Bryant, a leading activist, has written:

almost for the first time …[the media] had witnessed middle-class Conservative voters, retired military men, elected politicians and a younger, less conventional group, coming together in an alliance against the Government's road building campaign.
(Bryant, 1996, p. 192)

Whilst it is important not to overemphasise the extent to which a coalition did exist (there were undoubted tensions between the different groups), it does mark a point at which diverse interests could come together to oppose a common policy.

There are many similarities between the Twyford Down protest and that at Newbury. Once again legal avenues of campaigning had been exhausted, leaving the protesters to try to disrupt and delay the

building programme sufficiently so that there might be a rethink of policy or a new government. The protests against the Newbury bypass began in earnest in late 1995 with the establishment of six protest camps. At the height of the campaign in the spring of 1996 this had mushroomed to twenty-nine. Some of the camps were based in trees, others in tunnels, and led to dramatic media coverage of the evictions of protesters as bailiffs brought in cranes and cherry-picking equipment to dislodge them. Once a site has been cleared for a new road it would be a dramatic event for a government to then halt operations.

Transport protests are now commonplace. Reclaim the Streets, an anti-car pressure group, has organised a number of events in London which have brought traffic to a standstill and a street party on a stretch of the M41 attended by some 7,000 people, at which parts of the road were dug up and trees planted. A central element to the protest movement now is the extent to which the organisers of different groups seek to link their activities and exchange ideas: a move from competing and exclusive organisations to supportive and overlapping disorganisations.

By helping to raise the profile of transport issues protesters have played a part in creating a climate in which a new agendum can develop. In the early 1990s the government was committed to an ambitious road-building programme, but by the mid-1990s a number of schemes had been dropped or shelved. The reasons for the change in heart are many but, perhaps, three were key. Firstly, the Treasury, desperate to retain a hold on the public finances, had been alarmed at the burgeoning expenditure on roads. Secondly, early in 1994 the government published its strategy on *Sustainable Development* in which in the cautious language of civil servants it acknowledged that unlimited traffic growth was incompatible with its environmental commitments. In other words demand would have to be managed, a key argument of the environmental lobby. Thirdly, later in 1994 saw the publication of two key reports on transport. One was by the influential Royal Commission on Environmental Pollution on Transport and the Environment in which it expressed its concern at the implications of current policy on health and the environment. It argued for a halving of the road-building programme and a doubling of the real price of petrol over the next decade. The other was by the Standing Advisory Committee on Trunk Road Assessment which concluded that new roads can generate or induce new traffic (i.e. that they may not ease congestion).

Thus, in the mid-1990s the party of the motor car, the Conservatives, finds itself having to rethink its traditional approach to road-building – just as it has relinquished its rail network to private industry.

Environmental disasters

The holing of the *Sea Empress*, a 150,000-tonne supertanker, and the release of over 70,000 tonnes of North Sea light crude oil into the sea off Pembrokeshire in West Wales in February 1996 raised in acute form the dilemma facing decision-makers of trying to manage development in environmentally sensitive locations.

Milford Haven, the port for which the *Sea Empress* was destined, is one of the busiest in the UK. It has grown markedly since the 1960s with the establishment of the oil industry in the area which sought to utilise its natural deep waters for the ever-increasing size of supertankers which transport oil and its products. In a relatively remote part of Britain the port, the oil refineries and their support sectors provide secure and well-paid employment. Other key occupations in the area are fishing, which is in long-term decline, and tourism, the major employer in the area, but one which is notoriously poorly paid and relies heavily on seasonal labour. Small oil spills were always likely to occur in the area but that of the *Sea Empress* was of a quite different magnitude and had major adverse effects on fishing and tourism which rely on the local marine environment.

The waters off south-west Wales support fish, such as bass and herring, and shellfish, such as cockles and oysters. The oil spill led to a temporary ban on all fishing in the area so that it would not get into the human food chain. Grey seals are also common to the area but fortunately seem to have missed the worse of the spill. Their health may suffer in the future, however, as they eat crabs and fish which have themselves been affected by the oil. The longer term effects on fish stocks and health are being monitored. Birds, though, were the species most visibly affected by the oil spill. The Royal Society for the Protection of Birds and the Royal Society for the Protection of Cruelty to Animals mounted a major rescue operation to clean up oiled birds. By the middle of April some 7,000 birds had been recovered dead or rescued. The worst affected species were the common scoter, with over 4,700 recovered, the guillemot, with over 1,100 recovered, and the cormorant, an entire colony of which, nesting in one of the small islands off of the Welsh coast, was believed to have been completely wiped out. Again, the longer terms effects of the spill on birdlife, such as the build up of toxicity in the food chain, are being monitored.

The full significance of the impacts of the oil spill on nature will only become apparent over time. What is not in doubt is the sensitivity of the environment of south-west Wales. Pembrokeshire is Britain's only coastal national park; the Island of Skomer is a national nature reserve and its shores and waters make up one of only three national marine nature reserves in the United Kingdom. Lundy Island is another. There are also numerous sites of special scientific interest along the south-west Wales coastline.

It is the beauty of the area's environment which provides the basis of its tourist industry. Not surprisingly widespread media coverage of the spill and pictures of oiled birds and beaches led to a marked drop of interest in the area by holidaymakers. The Welsh Tourist Board embarked on a rearguard action to minimise losses to the industry, but if the experience of the Shetlands after the *Braer* disaster is repeated, it may take at least three years for tourists to return in their former numbers.

In the subsequent inquiries into the spill much attention has centered on safety procedures and how this may avoid future accidents. Little comment has been made about what sort of activities are appropriate for such environmentally sensitive locations as the Pembrokeshire coast. The essence of sustainable development is that it brings together economic, social and environmental factors in decision-making and in this instance it has to be with the planning and development of an area of land. However, it requires considerable investment in decision-making procedures by government and a considerable act of faith in the value of strategic decision-making. One of the lessons to emerge from the incident is that pollution and environmental degradation are no respecters of traditional local government boundaries. Coordination is required to overcome administrative divisions and to bring together different economic interests (e.g. oil refining, fishing, tourism), environmental interests and local communities. Such a task is beyond the remit and competence of local bodies.

Conclusion

Issues related to sustainable development, including the communications infrastructure, pollution and conservation, as well as energy sources, are likely to figure strongly in the political agenda of the next decade. As yet, the main political parties have not risked being left behind but nor have they set out to make the policy area their own. Policies have tended, therefore, to reflect an interaction between the various institutions of environmental management (limited up to now but likely to be strengthened by EU interest and funds) and the various lobbyists.

Perhaps these factors make environmental policy different from more traditional areas such as economic management and social welfare. In time, of course, they may dissolve and the field will be characterised by the same sorts of institutional players, forces and rules as any other. For the time being, however, environmental politics remain unpredictably fascinating.

Chapter summary

This chapter began by asking what environmental policy might be and discovered a range of answers reflecting different interests in the policy field. Various key institutions were described, noting especially the new Environment Agency, which has been designed to integrate many of the functions of government. The activities of political parties and environmental groups were set out, revealing the way the groups had been much more successful in bringing issues onto the policy agenda. Finally, a trio of policy issues themselves were outlined to draw attention to the character of environmental policy in practice.

Discussion points

- Does environmental policy show similar or different characteristics from those of other more traditional fields?

- Why have political parties been less willing than interest groups to raise environmental issues on the political agenda?

- What are the factors which will determine the success or failure of the new Environment Agency?

- Are there any common issues involved in 'sustainable development', the road building programme and environmental disasters? What challenges do they pose for the British political system?

Further reading

A few general purpose books have begun to appear, including those by Gray (1995) (no relation!) and Young (1993). Of more specialised works, Wheale *et al.* (1991) contrasted pollution regulation in Britain and Germany and, although somewhat dated, Lowe and Goyder's (1983) study of environmental groups remains important and has been updated by an article by Grant (1995). One of the better books by activists on the policy issues is by Bryant (1996). But the best place of all to keep up to date, apart from regular reading of issues discussed in the mass media, is on the Internet. The Environment Agency is at http://www.envirnment-agency.gov.uk/. For an index of environmental topics go to http://www.lib.kth.se/~lg/index.htm. For an index of topics and organisations go to http://www.webdirectory.com. Friends of the Earth (England, Wales and Northern Ireland) is at http://www.foe.co.uk/ and Friends of the Earth (Scotland) is at http://www.foe-scotland.org.uk/, while Greenpeace is at http://www.greenpeace.org/greenpeace.htm.

References

Blowers, A. (1987) 'Transition or transformation? Environmental policy under Thatcher', *Public Administration*, Vol. 65, No. 3.

Bryant, (1996) *Twyford Down: Roads, Campaigning and Environmental law*, (E. and F.N. Spon).

Cm 693 (1989) *Roads for Prosperity* (HMSO).

Cm 1200 (1900) *This Common Inheritance* (HMSO).

Cm 2426 (1994) *Sustainable Development: The UK Strategy* (HMSO).

Cm 2428 (1994) *Biodiversity: The UK Action Plan* (HMSO).

Cmnd 4506 (1970) *The Reorganisation of Central Government* (HMSO).

Crosland, A. (1971) *A New Social Democratic Britain* (Fabian Tract).

Department of the Environment (1991) *Improving Environmental Quality.*

Flynn, A.C. and Lowe, P. (1992) 'The greening of the Tories: The Conservative Party and the environment', in W. Rudig (ed.), *Green Politics Two* (Edinburgh University Press).

Friends of the Earth (1989) *Environmental Charter for Local Government.*

Grant, W.P. (1995) 'Are environmental pressure groups effective?', *Politics Review*, September.

Gray, T. (ed.) (1995) *UK Environmental Policy in the 1990s* (Macmillan).

HC 55 (1991–2) *The Government's Proposals for an Environment Agency* (Environment Committee of the House of Commons) (HMSO).

Lowe, P. and Flynn, A.C. (1989) 'Environmental politics and policy in the 1980s', in J. Mohan (ed.), *The Political Geography of Contemporary Britain* (Macmillan).

Lowe, P. and Goyder, J. (1983) *Environmental Groups in Politics* (Allen and Unwin).

McCormick, J. (1991) *British Politics and the Environment* (Earthscan).

Paterson, T. (1984) *Conservation and the Conservatives* (Bow Group).

Rawcliffe, P. (1992) 'Swinging with the tide: environmental groups in the 1990s', *Ecos*, Vol. 13, No. 1.

Ridley, N. (1989) *Politics Against Pollution* (Centre for Policy Studies).

Rudig, W. (1990) 'Editorial', in W. Rudig (ed.), *Green Politics One* (Edinburgh University Press).

Wheale, A., O'Riordan, T. and Kramme, L. (1991) *Controlling Pollution in the Round* (Anglo-German Foundation).

Young, S. (1993) *The Politics of the Environment* (Baseline Books).

CHAPTER THIRTY

Northern Ireland

JONATHAN TONGE

LEARNING OBJECTIVES

- To explore the historical and political background to the problem of Northern Ireland.

- To outline differing explanations of the conflict.

- To discuss the respective roles of the political parties and paramilitary organisations.

- To examine the attempts to provide a political solution during recent years, culminating in the peace process of the 1990s.

INTRODUCTION

Politics in Northern Ireland is based upon a seemingly intractable problem. The province contains a divided population, split between two main groupings holding different loyalties. The majority within Northern Ireland, a minority within the entire island of Ireland, are adamant in their desire that Northern Ireland should remain part of Britain. A sizeable minority within Northern Ireland regard themselves as Irish and would prefer to see the island of Ireland united under a single, Irish authority.

This broad division between British Unionists and Irish nationalists or republicans is reinforced by a religious divide. Unionists are mainly Protestant, whilst nationalists are predominantly Catholic. In Scotland and Wales, debates over national identity are resolved through constitutional politics. In Northern Ireland, paramilitary and military solutions have also been attempted. Competing explanations of the nature of the Northern Ireland conflict exist. They reflect disputes over the historical origins of the problem and the extent to which the minority community in Northern Ireland has suffered social and economic deprivation.

The development of Northern Ireland

Historical quarrels

From the eleventh to the eighteenth century, Ireland existed under loose British colonial rule. The origins of modern problems lay with the conflict between Planter and Gael in the early seventeenth century. The latter were Irish natives, displaced by Scottish Presbyterians undertaking the plantation of Ulster, the nine-county province in the north-eastern quarter of the island.

Although the Act of Union in 1801 consolidated British sovereignty, Irish nationalism increased, assisted by the Great Famine. In response, the British government introduced a trio of Home Rule bills from 1886, designed to provide limited autonomy for Ireland.

Each bill was strenuously opposed by Protestants in Ulster, the descendants of the original planters.

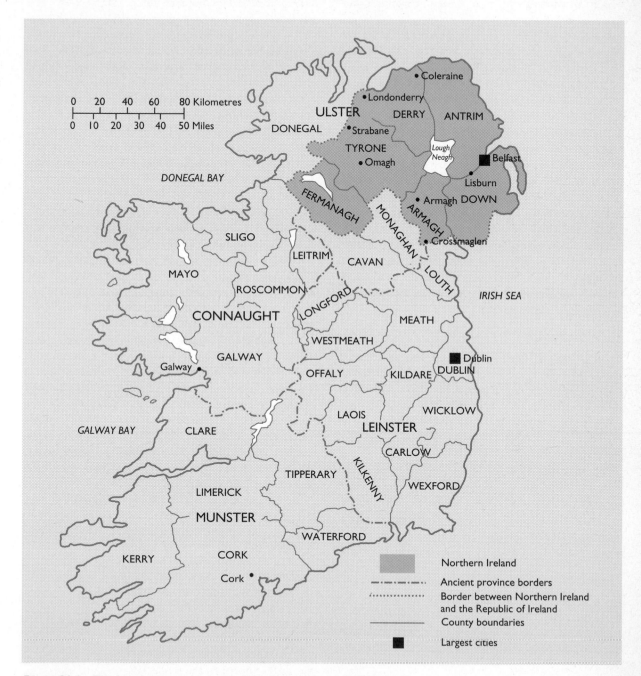

Figure 30.1 The four ancient provinces and thirty-two counties of Ireland: the nine counties of Ulster and the six counties of Northern Ireland

Source: McCullagh and O'Dowd, 1986

Unyielding in their determination to remain British, they argued that Home Rule would mean Rome Rule. With the overwhelming majority of the native population Catholic, Protestants feared absorption within an increasingly independent Ireland, dominated by the Roman Catholic church. In the south, nationalist sentiment for an independent Ireland increased after the British government executed the leaders of the 1916 Easter Rising.

Compromise provided a settlement, but not a solution. The Government of Ireland Act 1920 divided the country in an attempt to sate the desires of both identities. A twenty-six-county state was created in the south, later to become the Republic of Ireland. This was ruled by a parliament in Dublin which by 1949 was fully independent. In the north-eastern corner of the island, six of the nine counties of the ancient province of Ulster were incorporated within the new administrative unit of Northern Ireland. Exclusion of the remaining three counties, each with high Catholic populations, guaranteed Protestants a substantial majority in the new political unit (see Figure 30.1).

An 'Orange state', 1921–72?

From its outset, Northern Ireland was an insecure state, persistently under threat, real or imagined. Internal dissent was provided by a dissident Catholic–nationalist minority, amounting to one-third of the population. They resented the creation of what they saw as an artificial state, devoid of geographical, historical or political logic.

External threats came from the embryonic Irish state in the south. Under Eamon de Valera, Southern Ireland, later Eire, adopted a constitution in 1937 which laid claim to Northern Ireland, insisting that the national territory consisted of 'the whole island of Ireland, its islands and the territorial seas'.

Eternal vigilance characterised the Unionist response. As early as 1922, a Special Powers Act was enacted, providing the overwhelmingly Protestant security forces in Northern Ireland with vast, arbitrary powers. Although designed to reflect the population balance, the police force, the Royal Ulster Constabulary, averaged only 10 per cent Catholic membership. The auxiliary police force, the B Specials, was exclusively Protestant.

Discrimination against Catholics was common, although its extent is disputed (Whyte, 1990). Sir Basil Brooke, later Prime Minister of Northern Ireland, urged that wherever possible 'Protestant lads and lassies' should be hired. Many employers excluded Catholics from their workforce. High rates of Catholic unemployment deepened economic divisions between the two communities. The Protestant working class was also poor, but enjoyed marginal superiority over its Catholic counterpart. Other areas of discrimination included industrial location and housing.

Many Catholics felt alienated by the political system in Northern Ireland. The Unionist Party held power for fifty years. Each Prime Minister and most Cabinet members belonged to the exclusively Protestant Orange Order. In Stormont, the parliament of Northern Ireland, the only legislation successfully introduced by nationalists during this period was the Wild Birds Act in 1931.

Unionist domination was replicated locally, where Unionists controlled 85 per cent of councils. Dominance was increased through the process of gerrymandering. Large nationalist majorities were wasted in certain wards which yielded few councillors. Smaller Unionist wards produced large numbers of Unionist councillors. A notorious example was Londonderry City Council, where a Unionist council was returned even though Catholics amounted to almost two-thirds of the local voters (Arthur and Jeffery, 1988). Only ratepayers could vote in local elections, whilst many owners of businesses were entitled to extra votes. These measures particularly disadvantaged the poorer Catholic population.

In an attempt to challenge inequalities, the Northern Ireland Civil Rights Association (NICRA) was formed in 1967. Its demands were (Connolly, 1990):

1. one man one vote;
2. the ending of gerrymandering;
3. legislation against discrimination;
4. introduction of a points system in housing allocations;
5. repeal of the Special Powers Act;
6. disbandment of the B Specials.

Civil rights protests encountered a violent response from the police and loyalists. The moderate Prime

Minister of Northern Ireland, Terence O'Neill, was outflanked by hardline Protestant opposition and resigned.

Sectarian rioting in summer 1969 led the British government to send troops to restore order. For a brief 'honeymoon' period, the Army was welcomed by Catholics. As relations declined, nationalists once again began to use force in attempting to remove the British presence from Ireland.

Explanations of the problem

Part of the problem in solving the conflict in Northern Ireland is the lack of agreement over its cause. The main competing explanations are: ethnic or ethno-national; religious or ethno-religious; and economic.

Ethnic or ethno-national explanations

Two competing ethnic groups want their 'state to be ruled by their nation' (McGarry and O'Leary, 1995). Nationalists see themselves as Irish. They associate with the cultural traditions, history and religion of the population of the Irish Republic. Unionists wish to remain part of the United Kingdom. They assert their British identity and believe that they have far more in common with the people of the British mainland.

The ethnic conflict thesis has gained ground over the last two decades. Since 1972, when Stormont was abolished, Protestants in Northern Ireland have lacked institutional recognition of a distinctive Ulster identity. Nowadays, they are much more likely to see their primary identity as British (see Table 30.1).

Critics of ethnic conflict explanations argue that identities are not given, but instead are in a state of flux. Shared ethnic identity is not overwhelming. Only a small, decreasing majority of Catholics see themselves as Irish.

Religious or ethno-religious explanations

When sectarianism was rife during the early years of 'the Troubles', it was common to perceive the Northern Ireland problem in terms of two warring religious communities. Scenes of people fleeing from areas increasingly dominated by members of the

Table 30.1 Identity in Northern Ireland (per cent)

	1968		1989	
	Prot.	RC[a]	Prot.	RC
British	39	20	68	8
Ulster	32	5	10	2
Irish	20	76	3	60
N. Irish[b]	na	na	16	25

Note: [a] The total for RCs in 1968 amounts to 101 per cent
[b] The category Northern Irish did not appear in the 1968 survey
Source: Moxon-Browne, 1991

'other' religion fostered this idea of intercommunal conflict.

Bruce (1986, p. 249) argues:

The Northern Ireland conflict is a religious conflict. Economic and social differences are also crucial, but it was the fact that the competing populations in Ireland adhered and still adhere to competing religious traditions which has given the conflict its enduring and intractable quality.

Yet the killings in Northern Ireland have not occurred because of theological differences between Catholics and Protestants. The conflict is not a Holy War over matters such as the Virgin Birth. Religion none the less plays a crucial role in the following:

1. *Identification:* Almost nine in ten of the population identify themselves as Protestant or Catholic, as Table 30.2 indicates.
2. *Political influence:* To many, Protestantism and Unionism are inseparable, due to the variety of formal and informal links between Unionist political parties and organisations based upon the Protestant religion.

Table 30.2 Religious affiliation in Northern Ireland

Religion	%
Protestant	50.4
Roman Catholic	38.4
Not stated	7.3
None	3.7

Source: The Northern Ireland Census 1991 Religion Report

Economic explanations

Economic explanations of the conflict centre upon the impact of inequalities endured by the nationalist population in Northern Ireland. Despite political reforms and workforce monitoring, Catholics fare worse on certain economic indicators. Unemployment is twice the rate of that found amongst Protestants. During the 1980s, the percentage of Catholics in the lowest social strata in Northern Ireland was almost double that of Protestants (Moxon-Browne, 1983).

Nationalist antagonism is seen as a response to relative deprivation. Many of the IRA's recruits come from poor areas. Some Marxists see the disadvantaged position of the Catholic working class as a product of a divide and rule policy, designed to fragment the Protestant and Catholic working classes (Farrell, 1980). Irish republicans claim that Britain, acting as an imperial power, has exploited Ireland for gain, as part of a colonial strategy (Adams, 1986).

These arguments have all been subject to criticism. Firstly, variations in levels of unemployment have been attributed to skills differentials. Secondly, identity may be more important than wealth or status. Orangemen wish to remain as such, even though scant financial advantage accrues nowadays. Nationalists desire a united Ireland even though they might be worse off. Thirdly, allegations of British exploitation in Northern Ireland are countered by the cost of policing and subsidies. These costs, known as the subvention, amount to £4 billion annually, well over half of annual expenditure in Northern Ireland (Tomlinson, 1995).

The political parties

The largest political parties in Northern Ireland are divided into two main groupings, Unionist and nationalist. This divide is replicated by a polarisation of the base of support. Unionist parties attract almost exclusively Protestant support. Nationalist parties gain their support from Catholics. Recent election results are shown in Table 30.3.

The *Ulster Unionist Party* (UUP) is the main Unionist party. Its core beliefs are:

1. maintenance of the Union with Britain;

Table 30.3 Election results in Northern Ireland in the 1990s (% of votes cast)

Election	UUP	DUP	SDLP	SF	Others
1992 general	34.5	13.1	23.5	10.0	19.9
1993 local	29.4	17.3	22.0	12.4	18.9
1994 European	24.3	29.1	28.9	9.9	7.8
1996 Forum	24.2	19.0	21.0	15.5	20.3
1997 general	32.7	13.1	24.1	16.1	14.0

2. hostility to unity with the Irish Republic;
3. belief in the legitimacy of Northern Ireland as a distinct political, economic and cultural entity.

Debate within the party centres upon the most appropriate means of governing Northern Ireland. Integrationists tend to be the majority within the UUP. They believe that the Union is best preserved by treating the province in the same way as any other part of Britain. In many political aspects, Northern Ireland is treated in similar fashion to other parts of the United Kingdom. Budgetary matters are determined mainly in Westminster and aside from constitutional issues the region shares similar problems to other areas in Britain. Some Unionists argue that further integration would confirm the status of Northern Ireland and make its presence within the United Kingdom unconditional.

Formal party links with the Protestant Orange Order remain. The Order enjoys voting rights within the party. Although the link is in decline, many senior figures in the UUP are members of the Order. Some within the party believe that a more secular Unionism is needed (Aughey, 1989).

Regarded as advocates of a more hardline Unionism, the *Democratic Unionist Party* (DUP) shares the core beliefs of its bigger Unionist rival. Founded in 1971, the DUP has been led throughout its existence by the Reverend Ian Paisley. Many within the party fuse politics and religion. Over half of its activists are members of the fundamentalist Free Presbyterian Church, even though only 1 per cent of the population of Northern Ireland are members (Bruce, 1986). Support for the DUP is much more widely based.

The DUP sees the return of a devolved parliament as the best way forward. This would be based upon majority rule, but with some safeguards for the

BOX 30.1   DAVID TRIMBLE (1944–)   **BIOGRAPHY**

MP for Upper Bann, David Trimble was elected leader of the Ulster Unionist Party in 1995. Shortly after election he met the Irish Prime Minister for talks, the first such meeting for thirty years. In 1996, Trimble advocated a revision of the link between his party and the Orange Order and indicated a willingness to talk to Sinn Fein if the IRA began to decommission weapons. Many were critical of his role in both 'Sieges of Drumcree' (1995 and 1996) in which Trimble insisted upon the right of the Orange Order to march though a predominantly Catholic area.

By courtesy of Popperfoto/Reuter

minority. Arguing for a tough military policy to defeat the IRA, the DUP was critical of the peace process from the outset, describing it as a framework of 'shame and sham'.

The Social Democratic and Labour Party (SDLP) is the main nationalist party, attracting nearly two-thirds of the Catholic vote. Founded in 1970 following civil rights agitation, the party attempted to replace the old, abstentionist Nationalist Party with a more dynamic brand of left-wing politics.

Always in favour of a united Ireland, the SDLP advocates constitutional politics. It rejects the use of violence in pursuit of British withdrawal from Northern Ireland. Emphasising the need for an 'agreed Ireland', the SDLP accepts the need for the consent of Unionists for fundamental constitutional change.

The party also wishes to develop two other political relationships: north–south cooperation between representative bodies in Northern and Southern Ireland and east–west cooperation between the London (east) and Dublin (west) governments. Development of these links would forge structures to facilitate a united Ireland.

Sinn Fein (SF) is regarded as the political wing of the Provisional IRA. The party averages one-third of the Catholic vote. It has achieved this figure or better since the 1980s, when revived as a political organisation to provide a political outlet for the military campaign of the IRA. The link between the two organisations provided a strategy based upon a 'ballot paper in one hand and an armalite in the other', according to Sinn Fein's Director of Publicity, Danny Morrison, in 1981. Sympathy for IRA hunger strikers assisted Sinn Fein in the early 1980s.

Believing in the necessity of 'armed struggle' to enforce British withdrawal from Ireland, Sinn Fein

BOX 30.2   IAN PAISLEY (1926–)   BIOGRAPHY

By courtesy of Popperfoto/Reuter

Unchallenged leader of the DUP, the Reverend Ian Paisley has been MP for North Antrim since 1970 and a MEP since 1979. Paisley emerges as the most popular political figure in Northern Ireland's single-constituency European elections. Regarded as a demagogue by detractors, Paisley is seen by some supporters as a leader 'chosen by God to protect Ulster' (Connolly, 1990, p. 104). Unyielding in opposition to Irish republicanism, Paisley insists that his politics stem from his Free Presbyterian religion.

challenges the legitimacy of Northern Ireland. The party believes the partition of Ireland was unjust as it was never supported by a majority of Irish citizens. Sinn Fein won three-quarters of the seats in the last all-Ireland elections held in 1918. The refusal to recognise the state leads to Sinn Fein's demand that some of its institutions, such as the Royal Ulster Constabulary (RUC), be disbanded. Sinn Fein believes in self-determination for the Irish people as a single unit.

During the late 1980s and 1990s, policy documents hinted that seemingly fundamental demands might be the subject of compromise. *Scenario for Peace* (1987) and, to a much greater degree, *Towards a Lasting Peace* (1992) suggested that British *indications* of withdrawal might provide sufficient basis for negotiation. Sinn Fein declared that the consent of Unionists to a united Ireland was an

essential ingredient for lasting peace. It did not appear, however, that such consent was a *prerequisite* for the establishment of a unitary state. This issue lies at the heart of the Northern Ireland problem.

Other parties

The Alliance Party is one of the few parties in Northern Ireland which bridges the religious divide in its support. Although a Unionist party in respect of the constitution, it does attract some Catholic voters, mainly in middle-class areas. Gaining up to 10 per cent of the vote in elections, the Alliance advocates power-sharing as the best means of resolving problems.

Two parties with close links to the loyalist paramilitaries have attracted some support. *The*

BOX 30.3   JOHN HUME (1937–)   BIOGRAPHY

By courtesy of Popperfoto

John Hume is the leader of the SDLP. Elected to the post in 1979 after becoming a MEP in the same year, Hume is also MP for Foyle. A believer in Irish unity by consent, Hume has been criticised in some quarters for leading the SDLP in too 'green' (nationalist) a direction. He is widely credited with developing the peace process through his willingness to end the political isolation of Sinn Fein.

Progressive Unionist Party is close to the Ulster Volunteer Force. It argues for the constitutional status quo, but also for socialist politics within Northern Ireland. *The Ulster Democratic Party* is linked to the Ulster Defence Association, which has flirted with the idea of an independent Northern Ireland. It now argues for proportionality throughout government in the region to ensure fair representation.

British political parties

There is little division between the Conservative and Labour Parties on the question of Northern Ireland. *The Conservative Party* is seen as more pro-Union, although it has adopted a more neutral posture in recent years. Some on the right of the party are more stridently pro-Unionist.

Since 1981, *the Labour Party* has adopted a stance favouring Irish unity by consent. The party refuses to act as a persuader for Unionists to accept a united Ireland, although some, mainly but not exclusively on the left of the party, would prefer such an approach. Instead, a Labour government would act as a facilitator for a united Ireland should consent exist. In practice, this differs little from recent agreements supported by the Conservative government. Bipartisanship has characterised recent attempts to find a political solution. The Labour leader, Tony Blair, insisted that he did not wish to 'play politics' with the peace process of the 1990s.

The paramilitaries

The Irish Republican Army (IRA) was moribund and devoid of a military campaign between 1962 and 1969. It split in 1970, leading to the formation of the Provisional IRA. This comprised those who believed in the need for a military campaign to try to force the removal of Britain from Ireland.

BOX 30.4   GERRY ADAMS (1949–)   BIOGRAPHY

President of Sinn Fein since 1983, Gerry Adams was instrumental in changing Sinn Fein from an IRA support network to a developed political party. A former IRA member, Adams was MP for West Belfast from 1983 to 1992. As early as 1980, Adams acknowledged that the IRA could not win by military means alone. This perception meant that Adams sought the broader nationalist support which arrived in the peace process of the 1990s.

By courtesy of Popperfoto

Members of the new organisation rejected the Marxist social agitation which characterised the IRA of the 1960s. Instead, the Provisionals believed in the tradition of physical force common within republicanism. Following a permanent ceasefire of the old 'Official' IRA in 1972, the Provisionals were in effect *the* IRA.

Whilst the Provisional IRA claimed also to be a defender of nationalist areas, it soon launched an offensive. Curfews, the introduction of internment (detention without trial) and republican agitation soured relations between the British Army and the Catholic population. In February 1971, the first British soldier was killed by the IRA in its current campaign. After 30 January 1972, when the Army shot dead thirteen civilians in Derry ('Bloody Sunday'), the conflict escalated. The Army, RUC, Ulster Defence Regiment and businesses were targets

of the most prolonged and sustained campaign in the history of the IRA.

The 'long war' soon replaced the initial belief of the IRA that a military campaign would enforce an early British withdrawal. Brief negotiations with the British government in 1972 proved fruitless and the IRA declined in strength during the mid-1970s due to a combination of greater security, internal feuding and a ceasefire.

The processes of *Ulsterisation* and *criminalisation* were used to curb the IRA. Their aims were to reduce the military strength of the IRA whilst portraying its members as common criminals. Paramilitary prisoners were no longer treated as prisoners of war. This cessation of special category status led to the republican hunger strikes of 1980–1, in which ten prisoners died.

During the 1980s, the IRA was locked in stalemate with the British government. A military

Table 30.4 Deaths arising from 'the Troubles', 1969–96

British Army	445
Royal Ulster Constabulary	195
RUC Reserve	101
Ulster Defence Regiment	197
Royal Irish Regiment	7
Civilians	2,231
Total	3,172

Source: Northern Ireland Office

Table 30.5 Secretaries of State for Northern Ireland since direct rule in 1972

Secretary of State	Government	Duration
William Whitelaw	Conservative	1972–4
Francis Pym	Conservative	1973–4
Merlyn Rees	Labour	1974–6
Roy Mason	Labour	1976–9
Humphrey Atkins	Conservative	1979–81
James Prior	Conservative	1981–4
Douglas Hurd	Conservative	1984–5
Tom King	Conservative	1985–9
Peter Brooke	Conservative	1989–92
Patrick Mayhew	Conservative	1992–7
Mo Mowlam	Labour	1997–

campaign was insufficient to end British rule in Northern Ireland. It was also difficult to impose an outright military defeat upon the IRA. This was especially true after its reorganisation into a tighter cell structure and the procurement of armaments from Libya. As the campaign endured and the list of targets for killings broadened, twenty-five years of 'the Troubles' claimed over 3,000 victims, mainly civilians (see Table 30.4).

Almost 60 per cent of the above deaths are attributable to the IRA or a republican offshoot, *the Irish National Liberation Army* (Darby, 1994). Although purporting to defend the nationalist community, the IRA has killed more Catholics than the security forces. The loyalist paramilitary organisations of *the Ulster Volunteer Force, Ulster Freedom Fighters* and *Red Hand Commandos* have also carried out numerous killings, many amounting to random sectarian assassinations of Catholics. The security forces have also been responsible for a number of deaths.

Searching for political agreement

In 1972, Unionist rule in Northern Ireland was ended by the imposition of direct rule from Westminster, with the Secretary of State for Northern Ireland governing the province (see Table 30.5).

A number of attempts were made to find a political solution (Box 30.5). Most gave some prospect of the return of limited powers of government to Northern Ireland, whilst recognising that a purely internal settlement would be unacceptable to nationalists.

Although not all the above initiatives collapsed, none were jointly supported by the main Unionist and nationalist parties A central discord was apparent.

Unionists would not countenance any agreement which contained a substantial all-Ireland dimension. Nationalists would not support any set of arrangements in which the Irish government had little say.

Accordingly, the *Sunningdale Agreement* collapsed due to Unionist opposition to its proposed Council of Ireland. This was designed to create an equally weighted consultative forum of elected representatives from the north and south of Ireland and a council of ministers from both countries. Within Northern Ireland, the main political parties were to govern in a power-sharing executive.

Although the Agreement contained a declaration that there could be no change in the constitutional status of Northern Ireland without the consent of

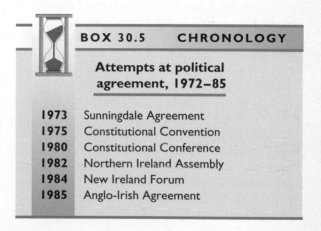

BOX 30.5   CHRONOLOGY

Attempts at political agreement, 1972–85

1973	Sunningdale Agreement
1975	Constitutional Convention
1980	Constitutional Conference
1982	Northern Ireland Assembly
1984	New Ireland Forum
1985	Anglo-Irish Agreement

the majority of its population, the Irish dimension was too strong for many Unionists. In the February 1974 general election, eleven of the twelve Unionists elected were opposed to the Sunningdale Agreement. Later that year, the power-sharing executive was defeated by a strike by Protestant workers which halted most activity in Northern Ireland.

A weak attempt to revive the concept of power-sharing was attempted through the **Northern Ireland Constitutional Convention** in 1975, but this foundered due to the absence of consensus over what powers should be shared and the extent of Irish involvement. For the following five years, no major proposals emerged. In 1980, the new Conservative government tentatively mooted the prospect of a return to some form of devolved administration.

Although profoundly Unionist by instinct, Margaret Thatcher saw the pragmatic advantages of a political accommodation acceptable to nationalists. A series of atrocities in 1979 helped shape this view. These included the assassination of her close friend and colleague Airey Neave; the murder of Lord Mountbatten; and the massacre of eighteen British soldiers at Warrenpoint.

Early political initiatives made little impact. Indeed the first lasted only three months. The **Constitutional Conference** called by the Secretary of State, Humphrey Atkins, failed to find common ground between the political parties. Atkins' successor, James Prior, launched the rolling devolution initiative in 1982. This attempted to coax the political groupings into cooperating with each other, in return for a steady return of power to a devolved administration.

A new **Northern Ireland Assembly** was to be the forum to which power returned. However, the lack of an all-Ireland dimension was deemed unsatisfactory by the nationalist SDLP, which refused to take seats. The Assembly acquired the status of a mere 'talking shop' for the Unionist parties and the Alliance Party (Bew and Patterson, 1985, p. 32).

Out! Out! Out!

Adamant that no purely internal settlement was possible, the SDLP attempted to forge a consensus amongst constitutional nationalists through the **New Ireland Forum**. Political parties in the Republic of Ireland deliberated on the best common approach to the future of the North. After a year's deliberation, the 1984 Forum Report proposed three alternative models:

1. a united Ireland;
2. a confederal Ireland;
3. joint London–Dublin authority over Northern Ireland.

The Thatcher rejection of each suggestion was characteristically brusque – 'that is out...that is out...that is out'.

Case study 1: the Anglo-Irish Agreement

An accord between the British and Irish governments was none the less reached the following year in the Anglo-Irish Agreement, signed at Hillsborough. The agreement was the culmination of Anglo-Irish cooperation promised by Margaret Thatcher and the Irish Taioseach (Prime Minister) Charles Haughey in 1980. They pledged to look at the 'totality of relationships between the two islands'.

Registered as an international treaty with the United Nations, the Agreement, signed by Thatcher and the new Irish Prime Minister Garret Fitzgerald:

1. guaranteed no change in the constitutional status of Northern Ireland without the consent of the majority;
2. accepted that no majority for change existed;
3. allowed the Republic of Ireland a consultative role in Northern Ireland.

A permanent intergovernmental conference was established which allowed the Irish government to assist in dealings on political, security, legal and cooperative measures in Northern Ireland. As with the Irish dimension of the Sunningdale Agreement a decade earlier, Unionists opposed the Anglo-Irish Agreement. Unlike Sunningdale, however, the new Agreement was difficult to boycott, as it effectively bypassed political parties. The agreement was *intergovernmental*.

Frustrated by its failure to achieve power-sharing, the British government was now prepared to allow the Irish government to 'put forward views and proposals' concerning matters that 'are not the responsibility of a devolved administration in Northern Ireland'. As no such devolved administration existed, some saw this as a wide remit.

'Ulster Says No' was the rallying cry of Unionist opposition. A protest rally at Belfast City Hall attracted 100,000 people. Although fifteen Unionist MPs resigned, the impact of this protest was muted when only fourteen were returned at subsequent by-elections. Resignations from public bodies were undertaken, but to little avail.

Most satisfied with the Agreement was the SDLP. It welcomed the all-Ireland dimension and the bolstering of constitutional nationalism. The SDLP was concerned with growing support for Sinn Fein, a process reversed after the Agreement. For constitutional nationalists, the Anglo-Irish Agreement provided parity of esteem for the nationalist minority and gave Dublin a representative role on behalf of the nationalist community.

Republicans opposed the accord. Gerry Adams of Sinn Fein insisted that it 'copper-fastened partition' by guaranteeing a Unionist veto over constitutional change. This view was endorsed by Charles Haughey, the leader of Fianna Fail, the main opposition party in the Republic.

Case study 2: the peace process

'Peace implies not merely the absence of war, but civilisation, a fully functional civil society. While para-militaries controlled districts or politicians radically disagreed on institutions, the outward signs of peace such as the demilitarisation of streets, the disappearance of searchers from shop doors and Belfast's consumer and restaurant boom all seemed slightly unreal.' Edna Longley, *The Independent on Sunday*, 11 February 1996'

As numerous political initiatives foundered, many wondered whether violence would ever end. Yet during the 1990s, there emerged the most sustained period of peace that Northern Ireland had enjoyed since 1969. For a brief period, it looked as if violence had ended, even if a political solution appeared a remote prospect. A carefully constructed process involved a series of initiatives (see Box 30.6). Proposals were designed to interest republicans whilst reassuring Unionists. Yet hopes were dashed.

Nationalist dialogue

The tortuous road to temporary peace began with a new nationalist dialogue. The intermittent talks between Gerry Adams and John Hume were an

---

> **BOX 30.6** **CHRONOLOGY**
>
> **The peace process**
>
> | | |
> |---|---|
> | **1988** | Hume–Adams talks begin |
> | **1990** | The Brooke initiative commences |
> | **1993** | Downing Street Declaration |
> | **1994** | Paramilitary ceasefires |
> | **1995** | Framework documents published |
> | **1996** | Mitchell Commission Report |
> | | Forum elections |
> | | End of IRA ceasefire |

attempt by the latter to persuade republicans that:

1. Britain was neutral on whether Northern Ireland should remain in the United Kingdom;
2. a united Ireland, or national self-determination, could only be achieved through the allegiance of both traditions;
3. violence was an impediment to such allegiance.

Hume was anxious to persuade Sinn Fein of the need to recognise that nationalists were not opposing a colonial aggressor. Rather, it was the opposition of one million Protestants within Northern Ireland to a united Ireland that was the problem.

In this respect, the dialogue was assisted by a declaration in 1990 by the Secretary of State for Northern Ireland, Peter Brooke, that Britain had no 'selfish, strategic or economic interest in Northern Ireland'. Brooke pursued public and private approaches towards peace. The former, based upon cross-party talks, achieved little. The latter involved a secret line of communication to the IRA, known as the Back Channel (Mallie and McKittrick, 1996).

Initiatives and ceasefires

Secret communication was followed by political initiatives. The British and Irish governments produced the Downing Street Declaration, or Joint Declaration for Peace, in December 1993. This attempted to:

1. satisfy Unionists by restating guarantees that there could be no change in the status of Northern Ireland without the consent of the majority;

2. use nationalist language supporting the right of the Irish people to self-determination, provided that consent was given, north and south;
3. confirm British neutrality.

Although the Declaration was never accepted by Sinn Fein, an IRA ceasefire was announced in 1994. The word 'permanent' was deliberately excluded from the declaration of a 'complete cessation' of military operations. A loyalist paramilitary ceasefire soon followed. The IRA believed it might advance its own cause via an unarmed strategy, due to the presence of a strong nationalist coalition. This embraced Sinn Fein, the SDLP, the Irish Prime Minister and leader of Fianna Fail, Albert Reynolds, and Irish America.

In 1995, the British and Irish governments produced the two 'Frameworks for the Future' documents. One outlined the principles of the Downing Street declaration of qualified self-determination, consent, non-violence and parity of esteem for the two traditions. The other provided the suggestions of the British government as to how Northern Ireland should be run. These included:

1. a new Northern Ireland Assembly;
2. a north–south cooperative body with compulsory membership for some members of the Northern Ireland Assembly;
3. a permanent Anglo-Irish intergovernmental conference.

Figure 30.2 Marching towards conflict? Orangemen assert their right to parade in 1996. Disputes over territory are highlighted in Northern Ireland's marching season; clashing cultural and religious identities deepen the problem.
Source: The *Independent*/Peter Macdiarmid

Problems of the process

Unionists were unhappy that their future governance of Northern Ireland would be conditional upon acceptance of dynamic cross-border cooperative institutions. As in the Anglo-Irish Agreement, they saw intergovernmentalism as a device to bypass political parties.

Meanwhile, the peace process was in jeopardy on the nationalist side. The resignation of the Irish Prime Minister Albert Reynolds weakened the nationalist coalition. Furthermore, the British government refused to enter into dialogue with Sinn Fein until the IRA began decommissioning its weapons. Appointed to break the deadlock, the American Senator George Mitchell suggested that decommissioning might take place during, rather than before, all-party peace talks.

The Mitchell Report of January 1996 produced six principles of non-violence. A less prominent suggestion of the Report was adopted, that of elections to a Forum to produce negotiating teams for all-party talks. During the following month, the IRA ceasefire ended with a huge bomb at Canary Wharf in London, killing two. Elections resulted in considerable success for Sinn Fein, but the party remained excluded from talks due to the failure of the IRA to resume its ceasefire.

By summer 1996, the peace process appeared close to collapse. The IRA campaign had resumed, concentrated initially outside Northern Ireland. Sectarian tension and serious rioting arose over the blocking and subsequent staging of an Orange Order march through an area in which Catholics resided (see Figure 30.2). Over 100 arson attacks on churches were recorded from 1995 to 1996. Meanwhile any political solution remained a most unlikely prospect.

Is a solution possible?

As hopes for peace faded, the question was again begged: is there a solution? A number of remedies have been advocated, each problematic.

1. *A United Ireland*:   Favoured by republicans, the absorption of Northern Ireland into a thirty-two county independent Irish Republic would almost certainly be met by armed resistance from loyalists. War might ensue throughout the entire island.

2. *Full integration into the United Kingdom*:   This is favoured by many Unionists on the grounds that it would end uncertainty over the future of the province. Supporters argue that this would assist in the reduction of violence. Detractors point out that the suggestion takes no account of the Irish identity of the minority population in Northern Ireland. The conflict may further polarise British versus Irish identities and increase violence.

3. *An independent Northern Ireland*:   Such an option has declined in its limited popularity. This proposal would end rule by the British government and rule out control from Dublin. It was attractive to some working-class loyalists sceptical of the value of the British link. Catholics, outnumbered in such a new state, would be fearful.

4. *Repartition*:   Any redrawing of the border would be beset by practical difficulties. It would be impossible to reshape without leaving a vulnerable minority Protestant community in the counties which were allocated to the Republic. Catholics in what remained of Northern Ireland might be equally unhappy.

5. *Joint authority*:   A sharing of power in Northern Ireland would require both traditions to accept that exclusive sovereignty cannot be exercised by a single government. Joint authority might be acceptable to many nationalists, but not to those republicans continuing to exercise romantic notions of a thirty-two-county independent Ireland. Unionists would reject joint authority, not least because it would be seen as an interim settlement towards a full abdication of British sovereignty.

6. *European authority*:   Some commentators have expressed interest in the possibilities raised by membership of the European Union (Boyle and Hadden, 1994). It has been hoped that membership of the European Union held by Britain and Ireland might produce one or more of the following:
   (a) the transfer of citizenship loyalties towards a new European identity;
   (b) the withering of the importance of the border as a range of cross-border institutions develop, promoted by European trade initiatives;
   (c) the emergence of a Europe of the Regions, replacing exclusive national loyalty with pooled sovereignty.

Thus far, none of these proposed developments has displaced traditional affiliations.

7. *Power-sharing*: In European countries formerly divided, such as Holland, consociational democracy was successfully introduced as a solution. Central to such arrangements was the notion of power-sharing, in which peoples of differing traditions came together in coalition. The success of such a system is conditional upon proportionality in elections (as opposed to majority rule) and guarantees of rights of autonomy. In Northern Ireland, the potential for this form of solution is impaired by the competing external loyalties (to Britain and Ireland) of both ethnic groups.

8. *Devolution*: The return of power to a Northern Ireland assembly is favoured by a substantial number of Unionists. Nationalists reject such an internal solution. They fear a return to the days of majoritarian rule under Stormont, with Unionists in perpetual control. Qualified majority voting, under which a large majority is required for certain decisions, might prevent this. However, this could lead to few important decisions ever being taken.

9. *Direct rule from Westminster*: Few see the continuation of the status quo as a solution. At best, direct rule produces reforms rather than resolution of the problem. Its persistence is symptomatic of the lack of consensus over the future of Northern Ireland.

10. *Demographic change*: Higher Catholic birth rates have led to speculation that Catholics might form a majority in Northern Ireland during the first half of the next century. This raises the possibility that the population might vote the state of Northern Ireland out of existence. Either possibility is unlikely. Firstly, large numbers of Catholics leave the province annually. Secondly, sufficient Catholics support the Union to ensure that a large Catholic majority would be required to end British control.

Chapter summary

Peace rallies staged after the end of the IRA ceasefire indicated that many in the population wished to avert a return to violence. However, clashing identities and traditions proved seemingly insurmountable barriers. Changes have occurred in Northern Ireland, including recognition of the Irishness of the minority and a steady growth in its confidence. Ethnic tensions are reinforced by economic and social divisions. The peace process indicated that continued violence is not *inevitable* in Northern Ireland. None the less, it remains the most probable scenario, as contests of sovereignty appear enduring.

Discussion points

■ To what extent is the Northern Ireland problem one of religious sectarianism?

■ Should the Irish Republic be given a substantial say in the affairs of Northern Ireland?

■ Same objectives, different methods? Is this an accurate assessment of the SDLP and Sinn Fein?

■ What factors enabled a peace process to develop?

■ Why has power-sharing been so difficult to achieve in Northern Ireland?

■ Has IRA violence achieved any of the goals held by the organisation?

■ Why do Unionists wish to remain British?

■ Which explanation of the Northern Ireland problem (pp. 523–4) is the most realistic?

■ Could nationalists be persuaded to accept the state of Northern Ireland?

■ Does discrimination explain continuing differences in economic status between the Protestant and Catholic communities?

Further reading

An outstanding recent scholarly work is provided by McGarry and O'Leary (1995). This goes further than the seminal study of Whyte (1990) in proposing solutions. Aughey and Morrow offer an excellent introduction to the politics and society of Northern Ireland (1996). Connolly (1990) provides a very sound basic text. Bruce (1986, 1994) gives illuminating studies of loyalism. Ryan (1995) provides an interesting account of republicanism.

Highly readable and informed accounts of the peace process are provided by Coogan (1995) and Mallie and McKittrick (1996).

References

Adams, G. (1986) *The Politics of Freedom* (Brandon).

Arthur, P. and Jeffrey, K. (1988) *Northern Ireland since 1968* (Blackwell).

Aughey, A. (1989) *Under Siege: Ulster Unionism and the Anglo-Irish Agreement* (Blackstaff).

Aughey, A. and Morrow, D. (eds) (1996) *Northern Ireland Politics* (Longman).

Bainer, A. (1996) 'Paramilitarism', in A. Aughey and D. Morrow (eds), *Northern Ireland Politics* (Longman).

Bew, P. and Patterson, H. (1985) *The British State and the Ulster Crisis* (Verso).

Boyle, K. and Hadden, T. (1994) *Northern Ireland: The Choice* (Penguin).

Bruce, S. (1986) *God Save Ulster: The Religion and Politics of Paisleyism* (Oxford University Press).

Bruce, S. (1994) *The Edge of the Union. The Ulster Loyalist Political Vision* (Oxford University Press).

Connolly, M. (1990) *Politics and Policy Making in Northern Ireland* (Philip Allan).

Coogan, T.P. (1995) *The Troubles. Ireland's Ordeal 1966–1995 and the Search for Peace* (Hutchinson).

Darby, J. (1994) 'Legitimate targets: a control on violence?' in A. Guelke (ed.), *New Perspectives on the Northern Ireland Conflict* (Avebury).

Farrell, M. (1980) *The Orange State* (Pluto).

McCullagh, M. and O'Dowd, L. (1986) 'Northern Ireland: the search for a solution', *Social Studies Review* March.

McGarry, J. and O'Leary, B. (1995) *Explaining Northern Ireland* (Blackwell).

Mallie, E. and McKittrick, D. (1996) *The Fight for Peace* (Heinemann).

Moxon-Browne, E. (1983) *Nation, Class and Creed in Northern Ireland* (Gower).

Moxon-Browne, E. (1991) 'National identity in Northern Ireland', in P. Singer and G. Robinson (eds), *Social Attitudes Survey 1991–92* (Blackstaff).

Ryan, M. (1995) *War and Peace in Ireland: Britain and the IRA in the New World Order* (Pluto).

Tomlinson, M. (1995) 'Can Britain leave Ireland? The political economy of war and peace', *Race and Class*, Vol. 37, No. 1.

Whyte, J. (1990) *Interpreting Northern Ireland* (Oxford University Press).

Britain and European integration

SIMON BULMER

LEARNING OBJECTIVES

- To explain the history of Britain's post-war relationship with the European integration process.

- To give an introduction to the institutions and policy process of the European Union.

- To explain the policy activities of the EU and give an idea of their impact upon Britain.

- To examine some of the current flashpoints of Britain's European policy.

INTRODUCTION

In 1973 the United Kingdom became a member of the three European Communities, the organisations which are now absorbed into the European Union (EU). In the subsequent period the UK's political system has become increasingly interlinked with, and affected by, the institutions and policies associated with the European integration process. In consequence, very few areas of British policy have escaped the impact of the EU. Similarly, almost all political forces and institutions have been affected by European integration. This chapter is designed to give an outline of this important dimension of British politics and policy.

Britain and European integration: the context

For Britain and the rest of Europe the period following the Second World War brought major change.

For Britain the global context changed significantly. Although emerging as one of the victorious allies, the UK effectively lost its status as a world power. The USA was to occupy the leadership role in the international economy and, politically, in the Western hemisphere. For Britain the new situation had two effects. Firstly, it had to manage the 'descent from power' in its foreign policy and adapt to being a medium-sized power. Secondly, it had to recognise that it no longer occupied the central role in the post-war economic order.

Of course, these patterns can look all too clear when viewed with the benefit of hindsight. Politicians had to contend with the day-to-day challenges of government as well as with electoral needs. In addition, there were other pressing issues, in particular popular pressures for the development of the welfare state and demands on the part of the colonies for independence. Hence successive governments did not confront the issue of reorienting British foreign policy to a new European-centred focus. For these and other reasons, governments led by both major parties were reluctant to participate in new forms of European integration that seemed to challenge national sovereignty. The nation-state was still an object of pride.

The post-war experience of continental Europe was rather different. By continental Europe, we mean first of all Western Europe but exclude Spain and Portugal (as rather isolated dictatorships until the mid-1970s) as well as the Scandinavian countries, which had different traditions as well as having escaped most of the worst excesses of fascism. The six member states which were to form the core of European integration until 1973 shared two particular experiences which encouraged them to develop a new form of cooperation. Firstly, they had all had their prestige undermined by virtue of national defeat: whether at the hands of Hitler's Germany or whether, as in the case of Germany and Italy, at the hands of the Allies. Secondly, in various ways they had all suffered from the excesses of state power, with the Nazi holocaust against the Jews the most extreme manifestation of this. These six states were France, Germany, Italy, Luxembourg, the Netherlands and Belgium.

For these countries – unlike Britain – the nation-state had been discredited, resulting in powerful political forces for new forms of interstate cooperation. These new forms of cooperation were needed for three reasons. Firstly, the six states all confronted the task of economic reconstruction but sought to solve particular economic policy issues in new ways. Secondly, most of the states bordered West Germany and sought an innovative way of constraining German power. Thirdly, the Cold War created a geopolitical division through the centre of Europe and a need to organise against a perceived external threat of communism that, together with worries in France and Italy about potential destabilisation by strong *domestic* communist parties, reinforced the need for cooperation. The consequence was that key continental political leaders, predominantly from the centre-right, developed supranational integration as a specific form of cooperation between states. Thus this supranational form of European integration and the first of the three European Communities were born.

Supranationalism involves not only a commitment on the part of member states to work together but, unlike other European or international organisations, also places formal constraints on national autonomy. Moreover, supranationalism expresses itself in a distinctive institutional structure: in a body of law that takes precedence over national law; in a dense network of institutions located chiefly in Brussels; and in a pattern of government which penetrates British politics and policies to a unique extent.

Before looking at the present-day interaction of Britain and the EU, however, we need a brief examination of the course of integration from the early 1950s in order to appreciate the current situation.

A range of European organisations were set up in the immediate post-war period, as well as the North Atlantic Treaty Organisation (NATO), a transatlantic organisation concerned with the defence of Western Europe. The first of the supranational organisations was the European Coal and Steel Community (ECSC). This was proposed in the Schuman Plan of 1950 and was a French attempt to place the German (and French) 'industries of war' under supranational control, thus facilitating the reconstruction of the two industries in a way that would not threaten peace, and indeed would form the basis for Franco-German reconciliation. This Franco-German plan was adopted by the Six, and the ECSC came into operation in 1952. The resultant Franco-German relationship has been a peaceful one but it followed some eighty years of recurrent hostilities. It has been the bedrock of supranational integration.

Despite some setbacks in the mid-1950s, the Six agreed in 1957 to extend the supranational approach. Two new communities were set up in the Treaties of Rome and came into operation in 1958. These were the European Atomic Energy Community and the European Economic Community (EEC). Of the three European Communities, it is the EEC which has been the most prominent. In 1967 the three communities merged their institutions, and from this time they were known collectively as the European Community/ies (EC). When the Maastricht Treaty came into effect in November 1993 the current term – 'the European Union' – was adopted.

Already by 1961 the strong economic performances of those states in the three communities prompted the UK government, under Prime Minister Harold Macmillan, to apply for membership (along with Denmark, Ireland and Norway). However, these applications coincided with a major internal challenge to supranational integration in the form of the new French President, Charles de Gaulle. He had come to power in 1958 with a view to restoring French pride. He was opposed to supranational forms of integration. Moreover, he saw an opportunity for French leadership of the Six as a way of restoring national pride. In consequence, both in 1963 and in 1967 he blocked British attempts to join, fearing the presence of a rival power.

No major new supranational initiatives were launched during the 1960s while de Gaulle was in office. However, progress was made on implementing parts of the EEC Treaty, including the creation of the Common Agricultural Policy (CAP) and the removal of tariffs on trade between the member states. Apart from blocking enlargement, de Gaulle also sought to undermine supranationalism through precipitating the 1965 'empty chair crisis'. The details of this episode cannot be recounted here (see Urwin, 1995, pp. 107–15), but de Gaulle withdrew France from ministerial meetings of the three communities. This episode only ended with the January 1966 Luxembourg Compromise. The significance of this was that he toned down some of the distinctive supranational features of integration by establishing an informal agreement that the principal decisions between governments would be taken on the basis of unanimity or consensus. This was a departure from the planned introduction of qualified majority voting. The effect was to dilute the supranational character of the EC for some twenty years until new momentum was provided by the Single European Act (see below).

For the UK this episode was also to be of importance at a later stage. When the first enlargement took place in 1973 (with the UK, Ireland and Denmark acceding), the British government presented the EC as an organisation which posed little major threat to sovereignty. In other words final and absolute authority would remain in the UK and not be challenged from outside. However, it is important to remember that this assumption about sovereignty was true only under the convention established in the Luxembourg Compromise and not under the formal rules set down in the treaties. When member states started to wish to return to the formal rules, and in particular to majority voting in the Council of Ministers (see below), the UK was less at ease because sovereignty was challenged.

A second point is also worth mentioning, arising out of this episode. Parallels have often been drawn between the perceptions of de Gaulle and Margaret Thatcher on the primacy of nation-states within the EC. There were indeed some similarities. But it is important to note that France occupied a much more powerful role in the Europe of the Six than the UK did in the enlarged EC. Thus British arguments with partners in the EC never had the impact of the 'empty chair crisis'. They may have slowed down the decision-making process in some respects. However, as the Maastricht Treaty of 1992 demonstrated, the UK's bargaining power has largely been limited to securing opt-out clauses from policies which it had been uncertain about, such as economic and monetary union (EMU), rather than influencing the direction of integration as a whole. This situation was again evident in May/June 1996 when John Major launched a policy of non-cooperation within the EU as a protest at the lack of a European solution to the BSE (or 'mad cow' disease) crisis. The policy of blocking EU decision-making was in no way comparable in its consequences to de Gaulle's 'empty chair' policy. Where de Gaulle's policy obstructed all significant decision-making within the EC for six months, the British government could only obstruct those decisions *where its agreement was needed*. The distinction in 1996 was that many EU decisions could be taken by a majority vote. Hence the impact of the British policy of non-cooperation was rather limited in nature because many decisions could be reached without British support. This episode merely served to underline the supranational character of the EU: decisions cannot be obstructed completely by the actions of one member state.

Despite these more recent developments of the 1980s and 1990s, the 'empty chair crisis' contributed to a stagnation of integration which lasted throughout the 1970s. There were some isolated advances, in particular the establishment of the European Monetary System (EMS) in 1979. However, it was in the

1980s that the integration process advanced in a striking way, through both widening and deepening. The EC was widened by virtue of two southern enlargements: in 1981 to encompass Greece, and in 1986 with the accession of Spain and Portugal. Deepening came about in the form of the Single European Act (SEA), which took effect in 1987.

The SEA was the first comprehensive set of revisions to the original treaties of the 1950s. Most prominently the SEA contained a commitment to accelerating economic integration. It was designed in part to put into practice an agreement reached in 1985 to create a single European market: the basis to reinvigorate the competitiveness of the European

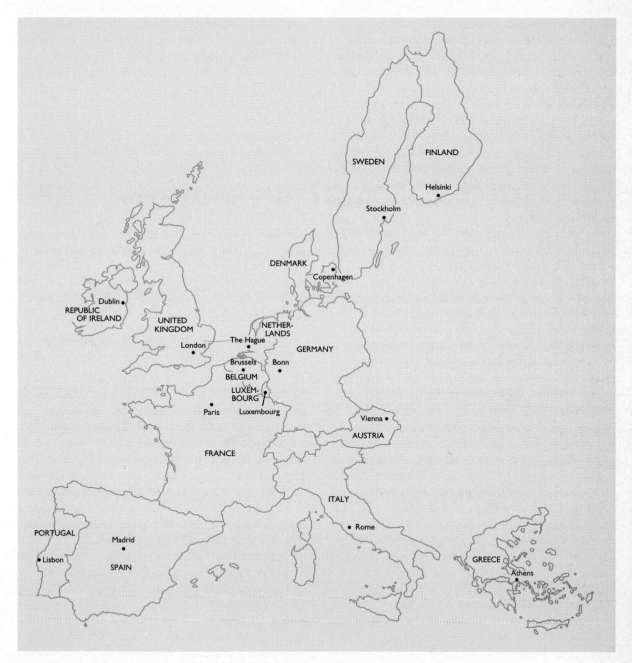

Figure 31.1 Map of European Union showing seats of government

economy. However, the SEA also strengthened the supranational institutions in order to speed up decision-making.

The renewed dynamism of the SEA brought with it a more widespread revival of momentum. The links between EC policies led to pressures for initiatives in other spheres, for instance the proposals for an EMU. These developments formed one of the sources of proposals that fed into a further exercise of treaty revision, in the Treaty on European Union (or, more popularly, the Maastricht Treaty), which was signed in February 1992. The other flow of developments arose from the dramatic changes in the map of European politics at the end of 1989. The end of the Cold War, as well as the reunification of Germany in October 1990, reopened some of the fundamental issues which the integration process had sought to address at the start of the 1950s. What should now be regarded as 'Europe'? Who was to be responsible for ensuring the economic prosperity and democratic stability of this 'new' Europe? How should Europe's international role be defined? What should be Germany's role in the 'new' Europe? Should the institutions of the EC be reformed in anticipation of much greater membership in the future? Hence, all these kinds of questions became intertwined with the existing questions, such as how to proceed to EMU.

The Maastricht Treaty represented an attempt at a structured blueprint for European integration. However, it was conceived against a background of considerable uncertainty about future developments in Europe. This uncertainty was compounded by related factors which became evident during the ratification process in 1992–3. In some member states German unification was viewed with considerable suspicion. Would Germany wish to return to an assertive central European role? Moreover, the popularity of some of the EC governments was very low, so that the Maastricht Treaty became a lightning conductor for domestic dissent. This explains why ratification of the treaty became so protracted. The Danish referendum of June 1992 rejected the treaty and threatened to derail the whole exercise until the decision was reversed in a further referendum in May 1993. The 1992 Danish referendum result in turn emboldened dissenters in the UK, resulting in protracted ratification in the House of Commons (see below).

One further development during the 1990s must be mentioned. The single market programme created particular concerns amongst Western European states not in the EC. How were they to have a voice in the new European economy? The picture became clearer with the end of the Cold War and the break-up of the Soviet Union. For Austria, Finland and Sweden, traditionally 'neutral' states, the solution now lay in applying to join the EC. These states successfully negotiated terms and joined in January 1995, thus bringing EU membership to fifteen (see Figure 31.1). Norway had also negotiated terms but its electorate rejected membership in a referendum. The passage of the Maastricht Treaty and enlargement to fifteen states had important consequences for the institutional structure of the EU, the subject of the next section.

The EU's institutions and decision-making

The European Union has five key institutions with which the student of British politics should be familiar. These are the European Commission, the Council of Ministers, the European Council, the European Parliament (EP) and, finally, the European Court of Justice (ECJ).

The European Commission

The Commission acts as the 'civil service' of the EU. However, it also has a fair amount of autonomy. This is what sets the Commission apart from the secretariats of other international organisations. This autonomy finds expression particularly in two of its functions. Firstly, it is the initiator of policy. This means that the Commission does not have to await instructions or guidelines from ministers but can propose legislation on its own initiative. Secondly, it is the 'conscience of the European Community'. This means that the Commission is supposed to develop ideas that transcend national interests, although the proposals have to be practical if they are to be sure of success. Amongst its other functions are helping construct agreement on policy by member governments, ensuring that they put such agreements into legal effect, and overseeing some of the detailed running of particular policies, notably the Common Agricultural Policy (CAP).

The Commission currently has a permanent staff establishment of some 14,000 but about 2,000 of these are assigned to translation and interpreting duties; the remainder have classical civil service functions. At the head of the Commission are twenty commissioners, each in charge of a policy area (Table 31.1). The Commission officials are organised overwhelmingly into directorates-general, which may be seen as the equivalent of ministries in Whitehall.

The commissioners are appointed by national governments (two each for the five larger member states) for terms which, from 1995, last five years and coincide with the electoral term of the European Parliament. One of the commissioners acts as president, from 1995 Jacques Santer. His predecessor was Jacques Delors, who served several terms lasting from 1985 to December 1994. Sir Leon Brittan, who has been a commissioner since 1989, and Neil Kinnock are the British commissioners appointed to cover the period 1995–99 (see also Table 31.1). Like Commission officials, the commissioners are supposed to reflect the European interest rather than that of their country of origin. With an eye on future eastward enlargement of the EU, the present figure of twenty commissioners is under review. As Table 31.1 shows, it is difficult finding enough portfolios for twenty commissioners: see the complicated sharing out of the external relations responsibilities. This situation would deteriorate further in an enlarged EU.

The Council of Ministers

The Council of Ministers is the main decision-making organ of the EU. Its official title was amended to 'Council of the European Union' when the Maastricht Treaty was implemented, but its former title, and the contraction, 'the Council', tend to be the terms in popular use. It comprises ministers from each of the fifteen member states. It meets almost a hundred times each year (1994 = 92) but does so in a number of different guises depending on the subject matter under discussion. Thus the Council of Agriculture Ministers brings together the fifteen ministers with responsibility for agriculture; the Council of Economic and Finance Ministers brings together the Chancellor of the Exchequer and his fourteen counterparts. Together with the General Council (of foreign ministers) these are the

Table 31.1 European Commissioners and their responsibilities, 1995–9

Jacques Santer (Luxembourg)	President of the Commission
Manuel Marin (Spain)	External relations with specific parts of the world
Martin Bangemann (Germany)	Industrial affairs, information technology, telecoms
Sir Leon Brittan (UK)	External relations with specific parts of the world; common commercial policy
Karel van Miert (Belgium)	Competition policy
Hans van den Broek (Netherlands)	External relations with specific parts of the world, including potential Central/Eastern European applicants, common foreign and security policy
João de Deus Pinheiro (Portugal)	External relations with specific parts of the world
Padraig Flynn (Ireland)	Employment and social affairs
Marcelino Oreja (Spain)	Relations with the EP, Intergovernmental Conference
Edith Cresson (France)	Science and Technology; training
Ritt Bjerregaard (Denmark)	Environment
Monika Wulf-Mathies (Germany)	Regional policies
Neil Kinnock (UK)	Transport
Mario Monti (Italy)	Internal Market, financial services
Emma Bonino (Italy)	Fisheries and consumer policy
Yves-Thibault de Silguy (France)	Financial and monetary affairs
Christos Papoutsis (Greece)	Energy, tourism, small- and medium-sized enterprise
Anita Gradin (Sweden)	Justice and home affairs, combating fraud
Franz Fischler (Austria)	Agriculture
Erkki Liikanen (Finland)	Budget, personnel

three principal formations in which the Council meets. It is indicative of the breadth of impact of the EU upon Whitehall that it met in 1994 in no fewer than twenty-one formations, including ministers responsible for energy, health, fisheries, culture and so on (see Corbett, 1995, p. 46). Of the principal policy-based departments of Whitehall – in other words, excluding the Scottish, Welsh and Northern Ireland Offices – only defence is absent from these formations. It is worth adding that the Maastricht Treaty formally brought ministerial meetings to discuss foreign policy as well as a range of Home Office and justice matters (in EU parlance, Justice and Home Affairs) under the umbrella of the Council.

The work of the Council is principally to take the many policy decisions of a political nature. This work requires considerable preparation. Three agencies are worth mentioning in this connection. The preparation of the work of the Council is largely undertaken by officials of national governments in conjunction with counterparts in the Commission. The main forum for preparation is the Committee of Permanent Representatives (COREPER). Like the Council, this meets in different guises according to what is on the agenda. COREPER meetings are attended either by national civil servants or diplomats who are based in the permanent representations, effectively member states' embassies in Brussels to the EU. It is in such meetings that the agenda is prepared for the forthcoming meetings of the Council of the EU. Given their heavy domestic schedules, meetings of the Council can thus be confined to either rubber stamping matters agreed in COREPER or to thrashing out the politically contentious issues.

The second agency is the presidency of the Council of Ministers. The presidency is held by each member state on a rota basis for a six-month term. The presidency is responsible for chairing Council and COREPER meetings. More generally it serves the function of trying to put together packages of agreements across a range of policy areas, and that have a sufficient balance to satisfy the interests of all member states. The UK held the presidency in the second half of 1992 and is next scheduled to do so in the first half of 1998. A six-month period is very short for the officials of a member state to master its brief. This is where the third agency comes in,

namely the permanent secretariat of the Council. This has some 2,000 staff, including a contingent of translators and interpreters. However, there are also key officials able to provide continuity.

What is distinctive about the EU, when compared to other international organisations, is the provision for the member governments to take decisions by weighted majority voting. Under majority voting each member state is assigned a weighting to its vote, based roughly according to the size of the country concerned. Thus the UK, France, Germany and Italy each have ten votes, while at the other extreme Luxembourg has two. Where qualified majority voting is used, it is necessary to secure a minimum of sixty-two of the available eighty-seven votes, in order to secure a majority. Such a system means that the British government may be overruled but it still has to give effect to the legislation agreed by the majority. Thus the importance of majority voting is that it is a clear way in which national sovereignty may be lost. In reality, and despite Treaty provision, little use was made of majority voting until the mid-1980s and the passage of the SEA. The Maastricht Treaty has extended provision still further. Even so, there are still important dynamics working towards a consensual approach. For example, it is a better guarantee of the implementation of policy.

The European Council

The European Council, established in 1974, has developed into an important institution covering all activities of the European Union created by the Maastricht Treaty (see below). It is broadly comparable to the Council of Ministers, except that it comprises the heads of government (or in France's case the President), the fifteen foreign ministers and two commissioners. It meets at least twice per year. It has initiated some of the key EC/EU developments, such as the European Monetary System, the SEA and the Maastricht Treaty itself (so called because it was agreed at the December 1991 meeting of the European Council in the Dutch city of that name). Given its composition, the European Council is best placed to provide leadership for strategic initiatives (such as the SEA or the EMS). However, its meetings equally may become media events resulting in little substantive progress.

The European Parliament

The EP comprises 626 members (or MEPs) in the EU of fifteen member states. Most of these MEPs sit in transnational parliamentary groups (see Figure 31.2 for the composition after the elections of 1994 and enlargement of 1995). Thus the main British political parties have had to come to terms with cooperating with their counterparts, often from different political traditions, in the other member states. This challenge has been the greatest for the Conservative Party, which has not been part of an international 'party-family', but its MEPs now sit with Christian Democrats in the Group of the European People's Party.

Directly elected for the first time in 1979, the Parliament has suffered from a number of weaknesses, although these are gradually being addressed. The principal weakness was its lack of powers. Until the mid-1980s its powers were largely limited to offering (non-binding) opinions on legislation; having the theoretical power to sack the Commission (never effected); and the right to scrutinise the work of the Commission and Council.

The first steps towards enhancing these powers came in the 1970s, when the EP gained important influence over the EC budget. Then, from 1987, the implementation of the SEA introduced a new legislative role for the EP in certain policy areas, known as the cooperation procedure. This procedure enhanced the EP's powers by giving it some bargaining chips with which it can seek to influence the Council during the legislative process. The EP's powers were further developed in the Maastricht Treaty by the introduction of a new co-decision power. In simplified terms this adds to the cooperation procedure by giving the EP the ultimate power to reject an item of legislation altogether. All in all, much European legislation now falls under either the cooperation or co-decision procedures. The EP has significant powers in respect of agreements between the EU and third countries as well as the

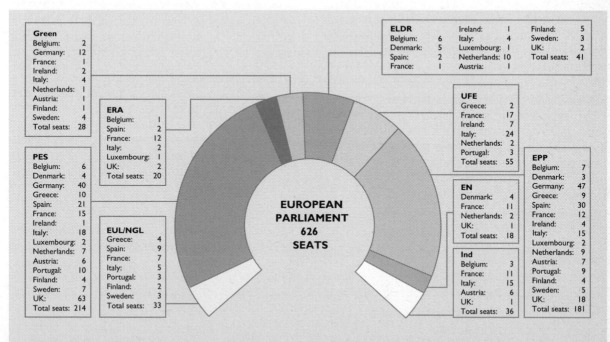

PES, Party of European Socialists – 214 seats; EUL/NGL, European United Left/Nordic Green Left – 33 seats; ERA, European Radical Alliance – 20 seats; GREEN, Rainbow Group – 28 seats; ELDR, European Liberal Democratic and Reformist Party – 41 seats; UFE, Union for Europe Group – 55 seats; EPP, European Peoples Party – 181 seats; EN, Europe of the Nations Group – 18 seats; Ind, Non-attached – 36 seats.

Figure 31.2 Seats in the European Parliament as of February 1997

power of veto over the accession of new member states.

Nevertheless, the EP's profile remains weak. The EP's work is not particularly suited to television, not least because a multilingual institution lacks the cut-and-thrust of the House of Commons. A further problem hampering the EP is the complex situation regarding its seat. Its plenary sessions are in Strasbourg; its committee meetings are in Brussels; its secretariat is in Luxembourg. This split-site operation scarcely helps the EP gain a clear profile. And the logistical arrangements seem to confirm the sceptical citizen's concern about the EU's remoteness and incomprehensibility. The EP's strong committee system is little known to those outside the EU policy-making 'network'. The EP remains the only directly elected parliament of any international organisation and potentially represents a competing focus for democratic legitimacy alongside national parliaments such as Westminster.

Indicative of the EP's problems with its profile is the turnout at European elections (see Table 31.2). When the fourth set of direct elections was held in 1994, EU-wide (then twelve states) turnout was only 56.5 per cent, a figure strikingly lower than for national elections. In the UK turnout has generally been the lowest of all member states: in 1994 it was 36.2 per cent. The UK elects eighty-seven MEPs: eighty-four from the British mainland by the traditional first-past-the-post system; and three from Northern Ireland using a single-constituency proportional representation method. The latter system is used to ensure the key shades of opinion in the province are represented in the EP.

The European Court of Justice and EC law

Consideration of the ECJ enables attention to be drawn to three important characteristics of the EU. Firstly, the significance of EC law and the treaties must not be underestimated. Within the UK, particularly in the absence of a formal, written constitution, it is difficult to appreciate continental traditions. A number of major developments in European integration have come about as a result of pathbreaking rulings by the ECJ in interpreting what the treaties 'meant'. Moreover, as the treaty basis of the EU widens, so a gradual constitutionalisation is taking place at the European level. It would not be too far-fetched to argue that the

Table 31.2   Turnout in European elections (per cent) and number of seats in the EP

Country	Year of election				No. of seats (1994)
	1979	1984	1989	1994	
Belgium	91.3	89.0	90.7	90.7	25
Denmark	47.1	52.3	46.1	52.5	16
Germany	65.7	56.8	62.4	58.0	99
Greece	na	77.2	79.9	71.1	25
Spain	na	na	54.8	59.6	64
France	60.7	57.0	48.7	53.3	87
Ireland	63.6	47.6	68.2	44.0	15
Italy	85.5	83.9	81.5	74.8	87
Luxembourg	88.9	87.0	87.4	90.0	6
Netherlands	57.8	50.5	47.2	35.6	31
Portugal	na	na	51.1	35.7	25
UK	31.6	32.6	36.2	36.2	87
EC average	62.5	59.4	58.5	56.5	–

Notes: na denotes not applicable, as the states had not yet joined the EC. Those states with turnout figures of 80 per cent or more have requirements (legal or otherwise) that citizens vote at elections. Election data for Germany prior to the 1994 election are for West Germany. Data for Austria (21 MEPs), Finland (16 MEPs) and Sweden (22 MEPs) are excluded, as their elections were held at a later stage.
Source: Agence Europe, 23 June 1994

constitutional law of the EC is bringing about a 'quiet revolution' in British constitutional practice.

A second important feature is to point out the existence of a body of EC law. What is distinctive about EC law, which remains the correct terminology, is that it has primacy over national law. Moreover, it may be directly applicable in not requiring the enactment of national legislation. It may also have direct effect meaning that EC law entails rights and obligations which may be tested before the national courts. These features of EC law are of fundamental importance to understanding the formal way in which EU membership challenges national sovereignty. In a 1990 ruling (the *Factortame* case) the ECJ effectively 'disapplied' British legislation because it did not comply with EC law (Steiner, 1992). This case clearly demonstrated the principle that Parliament is no longer sovereign.

The third feature is simply to draw attention to the ECJ itself. It comprises fifteen judges and is based in Luxembourg. It acts in a number of ways: interpreting the treaties, enforcing the law and so on. Nugent (1994, p. 234) summarises its role thus:

The Court of Justice has played an extremely important part in establishing the EU's legal order ... whether it is acting as an international court, a court of review, a court of appeal, or a court of referral ... the Court is also frequently a maker of law as well as an interpreter of law.

Other bodies and interest groups

There are a number of other EU institutions. These include the Court of Auditors, which scrutinises EU expenditure. The Economic and Social Committee is consulted on much legislation and acts as a kind of 'parliament of interests'. Its importance has been overshadowed somewhat in recent years by virtue of the increased power of the EP. Finally, the Maastricht Treaty provided for a Committee of the Regions. This new institution is designed to enhance the involvement of the regions particularly in those EU policy areas with spatial aspects, such as regional policy.

The final main category of participants in decision-making is the vast array of interest groups lobbying the EU institutions. There are over five hundred such groups, which bring together interest groups from the member states. One of the principal such organisations is the Committee of Professional Agricultural Organizations (COPA), which comprises most of the national-level farmer organisations, including the UK's National Farmers' Union. The extensive nature of European lobbying demonstrates another way in which the EU has penetrated UK politics, for it is now necessary for all British interest groups potentially affected by EU decisions to have some means of lobbying the relevant institutions, especially the Commission. Moreover, it is not normally feasible or effective for a UK interest group to lobby the Commission. The Commission has limited staffing resources and prefers only to consult groups representative of the EU as a whole. In this way it can consult one interest group rather than fifteen. However, what is also true is that UK interest groups lobby Whitehall about EU policies. Nevertheless, this strategy may not suffice, particularly given that the UK government may be overruled in the Council of Ministers through a majority vote.

A final further observation on lobbying at the EU level concerns local government. It has now become the rule for UK local authorities to have a European office of some kind within their organisation. In the case of those parts of the UK eligible to receive aid from the EU's funds, it is essential for local authorities to have effective contacts with the Commission. There is, in consequence, a significant impact on local authority activity in the UK. Of course, local authorities are not normally regarded as interest groups. However, in their relations with the EU authorities, this is the best kind of parallel to make for their activities.

EU decision-making

There are many different patterns for EU decision-making. However, it is important to give some kind of impression of the interaction of the agencies outlined above. Necessarily this requires some simplification. What follows sets out the decision-making process in the economic and social policy domains of the EU (the so called EC 'pillar' of the EU). Proposals normally originate from the Commission, which will usually have consulted with interested parties beforehand. The proposals are then sent to the Council of Ministers. There, deliberations take place initially at the specialist level amongst officials of the national governments, usually under the umbrella of COREPER. However, the proposal is simultaneously sent to the EP and the Economic and Social Committee. The latter submits an opinion on the proposal to the Council. The former, however, will make its views known through one of several procedures (consultation, cooperation or co-decision), depending on the legal base of the proposal. It is during this phase that a second stage of lobbying takes place through two channels: EU-level groups lobby the EP; national groups will lobby 'their' national governments. The final stage of the process is when the Council reaches its decision, taking into account the advice received, and in accordance with the prevailing voting method for the policy area under consideration. A schematic presentation of decision-making is set out in Figure 31.3.

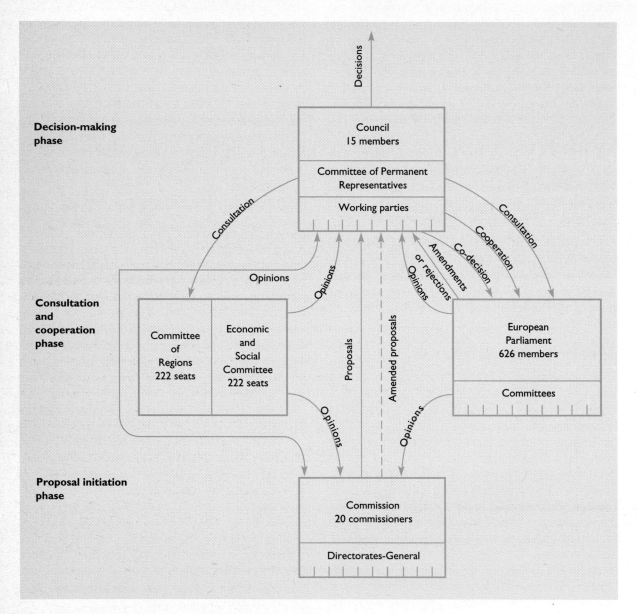

Figure 31.3 The Union's proposal and decision-making process
Source: Europe in Figures

Characteristics of EU decision-making

As has been seen, decision-making can follow several paths. Moreover, its characteristics are not especially familiar to the broader British public. Why is this so?

1. The procedure is remote by virtue of being centred on Brussels.
2. The constitutional-legal principles are different from those familiar in the UK.
3. The EU's policy responsibilities are wide. This means that it is easy to present the EU as 'interfering' with accepted British practice, even though this interference will probably have been sanctioned by a British minister.
4. The EU remains predominantly concerned with economic issues and its predominant mode of governing, in the absence of a large budget or of any equivalent to nationalised industries, is through acting as a regulator. Thus it sets the framework for economic activities (for instance, through competition policy); it regulates particular sections of the economy (for instance, agriculture or telecommunications); and it seeks to ensure that economic interests do not work against those of society at large (for instance, through environmental policy or equal opportunities policy). This regulatory mode of governing tends to be very much a matter for technical bargaining between governments, the EU institutions and interest groups. It is conducted away from the public eye.
5. Even for those specialising in the politics of the EU, the multiplicity of possible procedures makes decision-making difficult to penetrate.

All these characteristics have important ramifications for British politics because the UK and the EU are interlocked systems of government.

Two major concerns have arisen from this situation in the 1990s; and both came to a head during the ratification of the Maastricht Treaty. Firstly, European integration has been promoted by political elites rather than by the electorate as a whole. Right from the start of the ECSC this has been the case. But this method, pioneered and advocated by Jean Monnet, the author of the 1950 Schuman Plan, now appears to have reached its limits. Elite-led advances in European integration may not correspond to popular wishes, as the 1992 Danish referendum demonstrated when the Danes rejected the Maastricht Treaty. Secondly, the problem of remoteness has created concern, especially in Britain, that the Commission is a centralising agency undermining the authority of national government. It was this latter point that led to the exchanges between Margaret Thatcher and the then Commission President, Jacques Delors, in the autumn of 1988. Thatcher was very much concerned about the emergence of a 'European superstate' (see George, 1994) and regarded Delors as intent on centralising power in Brussels.

Two solutions have been developed to tackle these problems. The most discussed one of these is the EU's embracing of the subsidiarity principle. As expressed in Article 3(b) of the Maastricht Treaty, this states that:

the Community shall take action, in accordance with the subsidiarity principle, only if and in so far as the objectives of the proposed action cannot be sufficiently achieved by the Member States and can therefore, by reason of the scale or effects of the proposed action, be better achieved by the Community.

Despite the incorporation into the Maastricht Treaty of this check on centralisation, suspicions have remained because of different interpretations of subsidiarity. In centralised Britain it means keeping powers in Whitehall and Westminster, but in decentralised EU member states, such as Germany or Belgium, it means retention of powers at the regional level too, something which does not fit the practice of recent Conservative governments.

The second solution aims to make the functioning of the EU more transparent. At the Birmingham and Edinburgh European Council sessions in 1992 the member states agreed to disseminate information more widely and to allow television cameras into certain parts of meetings of the Council of Ministers. This must be regarded as only a small step towards solving this particular aspect of remoteness and something of a token gesture.

The European Union's 'architecture'

For many years the member states dealt with a handful of policy issues outside the the existing (EC) treaties. The best example of this was the foreign policy cooperation procedure, which was created in 1970. More recently, activities have extended to police cooperation, combating drug-smuggling, terrorism, cross-border crime and problems of immigration. These issues specifically were kept outside the EC treaties for a range of reasons. Governments have wanted to retain sovereignty over these matters (and thus keep the Commission and EP excluded) and they have found it convenient to conduct these activities away from the public eye. Under the Maastricht Treaty these activities have been given a clearer basis but continue to remain outside the supranational treaties. This kind of intergovernmental activity – conducted almost exclusively between the member governments – in fact exhibits even less openness than the supranational approach. It is one of the conundrums of the Conservative government's policy that it embraced the strengthening in the Maastricht Treaty of the intergovernmental activities even though they are at odds with its commitment to a more open form of EU government.

With the implementation of the Maastricht Treaty, the EU has taken on a somewhat peculiar 'architecture' resembling a temple (see Figure 31.4). All the collective activities of the fifteen member states are now under the 'roof' of the European Union. The existing economic treaties, as amended at Maastricht, form a supranational EC 'pillar' within the European Union. However, the EU is supported by two other pillars which comprise activities conducted in an intergovernmental manner. One of these pillars formalises foreign policy cooperation, now known as the Common Foreign and Security Policy (CFSP), in the EU. The other groups together Justice and Home Affairs (JHA) cooperation (police cooperation; combating drug-smuggling, illegal immigration and terrorism; and legal cooperation such as over extradition). The institutional structures of the CFSP and JHA pillars are dominated by governments, normally voting by unanimity and thus with no formal threat to sovereignty. It was largely to reflect these new areas under its auspices that the new name Council of the EU was adopted. Links with supranational institutions like the Commission and EP are quite limited in these areas of policy; there is no real accountability or legislative involvement. Similarly, decisions taken in these two pillars do not have the status of

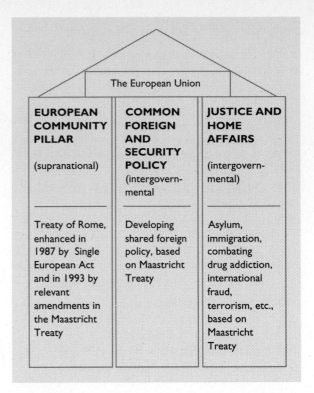

Figure 31.4 The architecture of the European Union

European law; that is why the term EC law is retained, since it only applies to the EC pillar of the EU. In the next section we look at the activities encompassed by the three pillars of the European Union but begin with those of the long-standing EC pillar.

The key policy areas

The integration process has involved an ever-widening portfolio of policies. The initial concern of integration was with the coal and steel industries, in the ECSC. In 1958 this was extended to cooperation on atomic energy, but this policy area never developed to the extent intended. By contrast, the EEC Treaty had a much wider policy impact. It comprised a large range of policies and, as they were put into operation, so the policy areas began to penetrate the activities of the member states, a phenomenon which we can call 'Europeanisation'.

The three main policies associated with the EEC Treaty have been the common market between the member states, the Common Agricultural Policy

(CAP), and a common commercial policy with the outside world.

The common market

The idea of creating a common market between the member states was to provide a stimulus to economic efficiency. A common market would allow consumers to choose between the most price-competitive producers from within the market. At the same time producers would be able to produce their goods and services for a market larger than their own state, thereby becoming able to generate economies of scale. This is the economic theory behind creating a common market but in political reality it entails some restructuring of the national economies. How, then, does it correspond to what has happened in the European context?

As set out in the EEC Treaty, the European common market provided essentially for three developments. These were: the removal of tariffs on trade between member states; the free movement of goods, persons, services and capital; and harmonising legislation that affects the operation of the common market. The first of these three was achieved without major difficulty in mid-1968, one year ahead of the Treaty schedule. However, other barriers to trade proved much more resistant to change. Member states used different technical requirements and a host of national measures to protect domestic producers. For example, German law defined very strictly what ingredients were permitted in beer. Beer including ingredients other than those could not be sold in Germany, so German law formed a barrier to trade. This kind of situation was pervasive.

As a result of such barriers, the EC's progress to achieving a true common market was, in reality, poor. However, this policy was revived by the single market programme, endorsed and accelerated by the SEA. As a result, most of the legislation needed to create a common (or internal) market had been agreed by the deadline of 31 December 1992. The UK government of Margaret Thatcher was one of

Table 31.3 The United Kingdom's changing trading patterns: exports to/imports from selected countries as a percentage of total trade in 1958 and 1992

	Exports from the UK		Imports into the UK	
Exports to/imports from	*1958*	*1992*	*1958*	*1992*
Belgium/Luxembourg	1.9	5.3	1.6	4.4
Denmark	2.4	1.3	3.1	1.9
Germany [a]	4.2	13.6	3.6	14.8
Greece	0.7	0.7	0.2	0.3
Spain	0.8	4.1	1.0	2.3
France	2.4	10.5	2.7	9.6
Ireland	3.5	5.3	2.9	4.0
Italy	2.1	5.6	2.1	5.3
Netherlands	3.2	7.9	4.2	7.3
Portugal	0.4	1.1	0.4	0.9
Total intra-EU trade	21.6	55.5	21.8	50.8
Developing countries	33.6	16.2	34.7	12.3
USA	8.8	11.5	9.4	11.7
Canada	5.8	1.5	8.2	1.6
Japan	0.6	2.1	0.9	5.7
Australia	7.2	1.3	5.4	0.8

Note: [a] 1958 figures are for West Germany; 1992 figures for reunified Germany.
Source: 'Annual Economic Report for 1995', *European Economy*, No. 59, 1995, pp. 237–8. Figures are rounded.

the main proponents of the single market programme, for it was consistent with the Conservatives' support for opening up markets and introducing more competitive economic conditions. This episode was one of quite a few where a British government succeeded in securing a strong correspondence between its national objectives and those of European integration. Linked to the common market is competition policy, which aims to ensure fair business practices prevail in trade between member states. The internal market and competition policy have very substantial effects on the day-to-day activities of businesses in the UK. This is reflected not least in the fact that the UK's fellow member states in the EU represent its most important trading partners (see Table 31.3).

The Common Agricultural Policy

The CAP was introduced in the 1960s. Although it now represents under 3 per cent of EU GNP and under 8 per cent of EU employment, agriculture was more important in 1958. Agriculture has also been of greater electoral importance on the continent than in the UK. Reflecting the interests of the then six member states, the CAP was created as a high cost, protectionist policy that in crude terms favoured the interests of farmers over those of consumers. Its high costs derived from the policy's price-setting policy, which aimed to cover the costs even of small, inefficient farmers. It was protectionist because it worked on the basis of 'Community preference'; lower cost producers from the world market were denied free access.

Prior to 1973 the UK had a different type of agricultural policy. It was expensive for the taxpayer but ensured cheap food supplies to consumers. Adaptation to the CAP proved controversial in the UK because food prices rose following accession. In addition, the lack of a large agricultural sector meant that Britain did not receive much revenue from the largest expenditure component of the modest EC budget. This in turn created a further imbalance, for the UK found itself becoming a major net contributor to the EC budget, alongside Germany. The costs of the CAP, along with the budgetary imbalance, led to Margaret Thatcher's demands, in the early 1980s, for the UK to have its 'own money back'. This dispute, which soured Britain's relations with the EC, also slowed progress on some other policies until the matter was resolved in 1984. From about that time a period of agricultural reforms began, aimed at reducing the policy's cost, and making it more in step with the liberalisation of world trade. Today Britain scarcely can be considered to have its own agricultural policy, for it is largely determined at EU level. This situation was displayed most graphically with the BSE crisis in 1996. National solutions to the eradication of 'mad cow disease' were an insufficient policy response; the other member states needed assurances that there were no risks to consumers, and a ban on the export of British beef was imposed. The search then had to begin for an EU policy solution to restore consumer confidence which had been damaged to a greater extent in some other member states than in Britain, the member state where concern about possible transmission of the disease to humans had first arisen.

The common commercial policy

The common commercial policy formed the external counterpart to creating a common internal European market. Hence, as internal tariffs were removed, so a common external tariff was created. This means that the EU is a powerful bloc in international trade negotiations. The UK government now has very limited powers in trade policy. The government's main involvement is in ensuring that the policy of the EU is consistent with British wishes. In the most recent international trade negotiations over the period 1986–93, the so-called Uruguay Round of the General Agreement on Tariffs and Trade (GATT), the bargaining with states such as Japan and the USA was conducted by representatives of the EC/EU rather than by the individual member states.

Other policies

Transport policy, despite considerable attention in the 1957 EEC Treaty, was of little significance due to the limited steps to implement the provisions. Only from the 1980s did the Common Transport Policy gain momentum, particularly with road haulage and air transport being integral to the single market programme. Subsequently, attention has turned to the creation of an integrated rail structure to augment the transport infrastructure of the single market. The building of the Channel Tunnel has contributed to this development of policy.

Social and regional policies came to be significant activities by the 1990s. Both these policies were of negligible significance in the original EEC Treaty. In the early 1970s a concern to give the EC more of a 'social' role led to policy proposals. The European Regional Development Fund was set up in 1975 to provide assistance to poorer areas in the EC. The European Social Fund has gradually been developed as a channel through which European funds are spent on such projects as employment training or retraining. The UK has been a substantial recipient of aid from these and associated funds. Both policies gained additional emphasis at the time of the SEA, for the EC developed an explicit interest in 'cohesion'. This term referred to a commitment to ensure that the poorer member states were neither socially nor regionally disadvantaged by completion of the internal market. With the commitment to EMU in the Maastricht Treaty a new Cohesion Fund was created to assist the economically weaker member states.

The regional policy in particular has been connected with the Commission's encouragement of the idea of a 'Europe of the Regions'. One example of this has been the Commission's encouragement of England's north-west to put together an integrated strategy document for regional development.

Social policy measures had been limited until the mid-1980s when a new direction was taken with the EC's attempts to ensure that the labour force did not suffer declining workplace conditions as a result of the more competitive single market. This policy was proposed in the Social Charter, accepted by eleven governments in 1989 (i.e. only the UK government of the then twelve states refused to sign up). Subsequently, steps were undertaken to develop a programme of implementing legislation and the British government argued that some of the measures adopted had gone beyond concerns about health and safety in the workplace and had 'interfered in' such matters as the length of the working week and maternity leave. The Conservative government took the view that such legislation ran against its own industrial relations reforms, which curtailed trade unions' power and liberalised

the labour market, and that it threatened to increase labour costs in the UK. This conflict then led on to the UK government's opt-out of the Maastricht Treaty's Social Chapter. The Social Chapter was designed to incorporate the Social Charter into the treaties, thus facilitating binding legislation in the policy area. The controversy about social policy continues.

Economic and monetary policy received considerable attention in the Maastricht Treaty, particularly with the commitment to EMU by 1999 at the latest. John Major negotiated an optout of this policy, meaning that the UK will not automatically accede to a single currency should the other member states press ahead. EMU, it should be noted, was already on the agenda in the early 1970s; indeed, it was due to have been completed by 1980! However, the 1973 oil crisis and upheaval in the international monetary system put a stop to that. In 1979 the more modest European Monetary System was introduced, but without UK membership of the all-important exchange rate mechanism (ERM). The British government was opposed to membership on the grounds that it would constrain domestic economic policy. However, in October 1990, John Major, the then Chancellor of the Exchequer, convinced Margaret Thatcher to join. Membership ended in September 1992 on Black Wednesday, when turmoil in the foreign exchanges forced the pound and the Italian lira to leave. This episode placed a major question mark against the already agreed Maastricht programme to create an EMU. More particularly, in Britain it strengthened the position of the opponents of EMU, who have been known to describe Britain's exit from the ERM as 'White Wednesday': something positive rather than negative.

All these economic and social policies are run with a very small EC budget. For 1995 it amounted to some £81 billion. This is only some 1.2 per cent of EU GNP, and is therefore a very small instrument for achieving any major policy impact. CAP spending, at its peak approaching three-quarters of the EC budget, is now down to approximately half of overall expenditure.

Other policies with major impacts on the UK include environmental policy and technology policy. In addition, there are the activities in the other two pillars of the European Union. In the

Justice and Home Affairs pillar there is extensive cooperation in combating international crime and increasing cooperation on immigration matters and asylum. Increasingly, the Home Office is undergoing the Europeanisation process which other Whitehall ministries experienced much earlier. In the area of foreign policy cooperation, the member states have extremely well-developed procedures. UK foreign policy can no longer be seen in isolation from the collective activities of the member states. However, it is certainly not possible to refer to a common European foreign policy as yet, for there are still occasions when member states break ranks. In the 1980s the UK government did this on several occasions, preferring to follow American foreign policy instead (George, 1994). The twelve member states revealed their collective foreign policy weakness during the 1990–1 Gulf crisis and in the face of the break up of Yugoslavia. The Maastricht Treaty has extended cooperation into the security domain, although the British government still regards defence policy to be the preserve of NATO. It fears that a new European military–security identity might lead to complete American disengagement from Europe, a situation that is considered too dangerous in light of the Europeans' inability to take decisive action in the Gulf War or over the crisis in Bosnia.

The impact upon the UK of the EC and the other policy pillars has been considerable (see Bulmer *et al.*, 1992). Central government, local authorities, political parties, interest groups, Parliament, the judicial system, capital and labour: all have to be aware of this impact to help them organise their interests. Of these, it has been the party political dimension which has been at the root of most of the continuing controversies within Britain about European integration. There is now an overwhelming consensus within the UK's political elite supporting membership, whereas in the early 1980s the Labour Party policy officially favoured withdrawal (see Chapter 6 on political parties in George, 1992). However, sharp divisions continue to exist over the desired kind of European Union. These divisions continue to be as much within the political parties as between them, with the divisions within the Conservative Party particularly strong in the period since ratification of the Maastricht Treaty. As will be seen in the next section, the issue

of sovereignty has played a pivotal role in the controversies concerning European integration.

The impact of EU policies on British government

EU policies now have a pervasive impact on British government, central and local. At the central level almost every ministry has had to establish institutional arrangements to deal with the European dimension of its policy activities. Overall responsibility for tactical policy coordination lies with the Cabinet Office, which has a European Secretariat to carry out these duties. The European Secretariat is also responsible for briefing the Prime Minister on policy, especially in the run up to meetings of the European Council. The four ministries most directly affected by the EU have been, with major policy responsibilities in parentheses: the Foreign and Commonwealth Office (external economic policy, foreign policy cooperation), the Treasury (the budget, the financial aspects of policies and EMU), the Department of Trade and Industry (most of the single market legislation) and the Ministry of Agriculture Fisheries and Food (the CAP). Some EU policy areas fall across several ministries, such as the EU's regional policy, which affects the Department of Trade and Industry as well as the territorial ministries (the Scottish, Welsh and Northern Ireland Offices). New EU policy areas, such as cooperation on Justice and Home Affairs, have impinged on additional ministries, notably the Home Office. Similarly, new Whitehall ministries, such as the Department of National Heritage, have had to take over EU responsibilities, such as the latter's efforts to regulate the media or the trade in fine arts. The EU's gradual extension into security policy may eventually intrude into the workings of the Ministry of Defence, but this remains the one ministry excluded from regular EU business.

A similar picture exists at the level of local government. Local government is responsible for implementing legislation which often owes its origins to EC law, for instance on weights and measures. Similarly, local authorities have had to remain alert to the possibilities of funding available from Brussels, such as to provide retraining for the local labour force, or to make infrastructural improvements to the local economy. Due to the scale of its economic difficulties, Merseyside has become a top priority area in EU terms for receiving financial assistance, thus creating particular challenges for its authorities. Most EU funding is contingent on partnerships, either with neighbouring authorities, with central government, with authorities in other member states, with the private sector, or with a combination of these. All this impacts significantly on many local authorities, adding to the effect on central government.

Continuing controversies: Britain and the EU in the 1990s

Supranational integration has provoked opposition in the UK since the 1950 Schuman Plan. It has been the cause of major political divisions within both parties. What have been the key instances of these divisions from the 1970s?

1. Already at the time of negotiating the terms of British membership and in the subsequent parliamentary ratification of the European Communities Act (1971–2), divisions emerged within both parties. Divisions within the Conservative Party meant that the Heath government's whips had to rely on pro-European Labour MPs refusing to vote against the accession legislation to secure the necessary votes to achieve membership. Within the opposition Labour Party divisions created serious problems for maintaining party unity: Harold Wilson's compromise position of advocating a referendum on membership resulted in the resignation of the deputy leader, Roy Jenkins, from the front bench.
2. The 1975 referendum, which was called by Harold Wilson's government with a view to resolving domestic disputes concerning EC membership, was a device aimed at preventing serious splits within the governing Labour Party (see above).
3. The defection in 1981 of four Labour MPs to found the Social Democratic Party (SDP) was in part the result of frustration at Labour's then policy of withdrawal from the EC.
4. Three senior Conservative ministers were casualties of divisions relating to supranational integration: Nigel Lawson on membership of the ERM (1989); the late Nicholas Ridley over German power in the EC (1990); and Sir Geoffrey Howe over the general direction of policy.
5. At the end of 1990 Margaret Thatcher was ousted as party leader as a result of matters brought to a head by a European disagreement concerning the development of proposals for EMU.
6. During 1992–3 the government of John Major found great difficulty maintaining the necessary party unity to secure the ratification of the Maastricht Treaty. The Labour Party was not opposed to the Treaty but opposed Britain's opt-out of the Social Chapter and made ratification very difficult for John Major's government. The Treaty was finally approved on 23 July 1993 only after the Conservative government had made the issue a vote of confidence, with the threat of a general election hanging over its rebels (see Baker *et al.*, 1994).
7. Subsequently, in December 1994, nine of the critics of the Maastricht Treaty from the Conservative back benches voted against the government over increasing contributions to the EU budget and had the party whip withdrawn, thus technically removing John Major's parliamentary majority.
8. In preparation for the 1997 general election the millionaire financier Sir James Goldsmith launched his Referendum Party in 1996. A referendum on continued EU membership was central to his electoral platform, to which he was thought to have committed up to £20 million, and he decided to run candidates in those constituencies where the sitting MP was opposed to such a referendum. This development caused great concern to a number of Conservative MPs, already fearful of their own re-election chances in view of the opinion poll ratings at the time.
9. Also in Spring 1996, and related to the perceived threat of the Referendum Party, John Major's Conservative government had to clarify its position on EMU because of divisions within the party. Its adopted position was one of keeping Britain's options open about whether to join a single currency. According to the Maastricht Treaty timetable, the key moves on

proceeding to an EMU only come in 1998, so the official government line was that it should wait until that point, and then calculate the costs and benefits of British participation. The 'clarification' was the Major government's declaration that, should it decide on joining the single currency, it would submit this decision to a referendum on the matter. This referendum device was designed to satisfy Conservative pro-Europeans, especially Chancellor of the Exchequer Kenneth Clarke, and anti-EMU Euro-sceptics alike. The government's delicate balancing act came under threat in July 1996 when a junior Treasury minister, David Heathcoat-Amory, resigned because he wanted the government to rule out EMU membership. It is worth pointing out that fifty Labour MPs were at the same time publishing a brochure arguing that Labour leader Tony Blair should rule out joining a single currency.

Thus, the divisions within the parties over integration in the run up to the 1997 general election were not so different from those at the time of the votes over accession. Although there is negligible parliamentary support for withdrawal from the EU, there remain hotly contested policy issues relating to integration. The parliamentary battle-lines on whether the UK should accede to the Social Chapter – with the Conservatives opposed and Labour in favour – are along orthodox government–opposition lines. It is this mixture of divisions between *and* within the two main parties that has characterised the European 'fault-line' in British party politics.

A continuing factor in these controversies has been the aversion to giving up sovereignty. This was a key factor explaining why the UK was a late participant in supranational integration. Since membership in 1973 it has remained a persistent issue. The sovereignty debate needs a little elaboration. First, it has to be pointed out that it is political sovereignty that is at the heart of controversy. Economic sovereignty, by contrast, has not been a feature of controversy in recent years. Successive Conservative governments have welcomed foreign investment or ownership, even though, cumulatively, this development increased foreign influence over the UK's destiny. Political sovereignty

has two dimensions. The first is *parliamentary sovereignty*. The House of Commons has been regarded as the formal centre of legislative power since the English Civil War in the mid-seventeenth century. This situation is challenged by the primacy of EC law and treaties. It is important to be rather sceptical when *governments* give voice to the threat of integration to parliamentary sovereignty. In reality, the executive has done more to undermine the power of parliament than integration has: hence the need for scepticism. However, the parliamentary sovereignty issue is a lightning conductor for worries about the impact of integration on Britain's constitutional order. A number of adverse rulings by the ECJ against the British government have fuelled concern about the impact of integration on Britain's constitution. In practice, governments are more concerned with a second form of sovereignty, namely *national sovereignty*, that is to say, the UK government's ability to pursue its own policies rather than be subject to the decisions taken externally.

Owing to the political sensitivity around these two notions of sovereignty, and to their symbolic importance in British politics, there is a serious danger of political conflict arising when European integration poses a challenge to sovereignty (Armstrong and Bulmer, 1996). Recent occasions of such dissent include:

1. the ratification of the Maastricht Treaty in 1992/3 in the House of Commons;
2. parliamentary reaction to the British exit from the ERM in September 1992;
3. British preparations for the 1996 EU Inter-Governmental Conference (IGC) on treaty revisions; and
4. the BSE (or mad cow disease) crisis.

Within the UK there are three principal camps concerning integration and the EU. The first camp consists of those Euro-sceptics who wish to halt the advance of supranational integration and, indeed, wish to reverse it in some respects, for instance by weakening the European Court or abolishing the CAP and the common fisheries policy. This camp is occupied chiefly by Conservative 'Euro-sceptics' but has a small number of Labour supporters that would doubtless grow under a Labour government. At the other extreme of the spectrum is the camp

BOX 31.1   **IDEAS AND PERSPECTIVES**

Key concepts in European integration

Supranationalism

Supranationalism refers to the characteristics that make the EU and its institutions unique amongst international organisations. These include the autonomy from national governments granted to specific institutions (the Commission, the EP, the Court of Justice); the primacy of EC law over national law; and the possibility of the Council of Ministers taking decisions by a majority vote. Supranationalism implies the placing of constraints upon national sovereignty. The EP, the Commission and the ECJ are often referred to as the supranational institutions of the EU.

Intergovernmentalism

Intergovernmentalism implies the primacy of the governments in decision-making. Although possessing the supranational attributes outlined above, the EU was frequently described as intergovernmental in character from the mid-1960s to the mid-1980s This was because the supranational institutions lost prestige following the 1965 'empty chair' crisis (see p. 538), and majority voting was not practised in the Council of Ministers. Since the strengthening of the supranational institutions in the SEA, it has become less fashionable to use the term 'intergovernmentalism' to characterise the EU. In reality, there are elements of both supranationalism and intergovernmentalism in the EU, and the balance between them has varied over time. UK governments have consistently favoured intergovernmentalism over supranationalism because it represents much less of a threat to sovereignty. The Council of Ministers and the European Council, which are composed of government ministers, are often referred to as the intergovernmental institutions of the EU. The two new 'pillars' of integration introduced by the Maastricht Treaty are intergovernmental in nature.

Sovereignty

Due to its long-established territorial integrity British (and especially English) politicians have been reluctant to see the limitations of the nation-state in assuring British welfare and security. Moreover, lengthy constitutional tradition has embedded the notion of parliamentary sovereignty in the thinking of the political elite. As a consequence of these two features, UK governments have been particularly unwilling to cede sovereignty (i.e. autonomy and power) to the EU. Many of the main disputes between Britain and its EU partners about the development of European integration have their origins in different notions of sovereignty.

Subsidiarity

This term has come into use from the late 1980s onwards. Essentially it means that the EU should only perform those tasks which the member states are unable to carry out themselves. In the UK subsidiarity is seen as a brake upon the centralisation of power in Brussels. In other member states subsidiarity is also seen as assuring the devolution of power to regional tiers of government.

Federalism

Federalism entails a clear constitutional ordering of relations between the EU and the member states, together with constitutional guarantees. The UK's lack of a formal written constitution, together with an aversion to giving up sovereignty, has resulted in federalism being used inaccurately to denote everything that is disliked about moves towards closer integration. This was symbolised during the Maastricht debates by British politicians' references to the 'F-word'.

consisting of those who advocate a federal Europe, in which an explicit constitutional reform takes place. A federal Europe would strengthen supranational institutions but would also aim to make them more accountable to the electorate. At present, the federalists are largely confined to the Liberal Party, although the Scottish National Party's policy on Europe bears some similarity. By far the largest camp is comprised of pragmatic Europeanists: those who are happy with European integration if it can deliver tangible economic and political benefits through policy results that are beyond the capability of a single national government, and with minimal impact on British constitutional practice.

Such divisions over the direction of integration are likely to remain for the foreseeable future because there is no sign that European integration is going to disappear from the political agenda over the coming years. The 1996 IGC, the Maastricht Treaty timetable for moving to EMU in 1999, and the eastward enlargement of the EU: these are important developments under way or scheduled for integration over the coming years and they are already having an impact on British politics. On the IGC the Conservative government sought to minimise the nature of the Treaty reforms. This position was as much the product of the internal politics of the Conservative Party as of an encompassing review of the British national interest. It is worth highlighting the basic principles of the Conservative government's European policy as set out in the March 1996 White Paper *A Partnership of Nations: The British Approach to the European Union Intergovernmental Conference 1996* (Cm 3181, 1996). There are five principles:

1. Integration should be built upon the cooperation of sovereign states (i.e. according to intergovernmental principles).
2. Integration should be pragmatic: 'we shall not accept harmonisation for its own sake, or further European integration which is driven by ideology rather than the prospect of practical benefit' (Cm 3181, 1996, p. 5).
3. The EU should encourage enterprise in the economy and be amenable to deregulation initiatives.
4. The EU should pursue an open (or liberal) trade policy.
5. Eastern enlargement of the EU is seen as an historical responsibility for European integration in the post-Cold War era.

The negotiating position of the Conservative government was viewed by its partners in the other states as very negative in that there were relatively few positive parts to its policy. Even the Major government's support for eastward enlargement to states such as Poland, Hungary and the Czech Republic was regarded with suspicion, since it seemed to entail an expectation that the EU would be diluted in the process and become less supranational. By late 1996 there were signs that some governments simply wished to drag out the IGC until after the 1997 general election in the expectation that an incoming Labour government would take a more constructive policy.

Following the resounding victory of Tony Blair's Labour Party in the election of 1 May 1997, the question was immediately raised: would the new government be significantly more positive about integration? Already during the election campaign, the Labour Party leadership had adopted a policy of it being very unlikely that the UK would join a single currency in the lifetime of the new parliament. This step, which was doubtless in part designed further to embarass the Conservative Party's internal divisions, suggested a cautious policy. However, following the formation of the Blair government, one of the first steps was for the new minister of state with European responsibilities in the Foreign Office, Doug Henderson, to attend a routine meeting preparing the IGC, where he announced that the new government wished to have a positive engagement with the integration process. The government moved to sign the Social Chapter and the new Foreign Secretary, Robin Cook, indicated support for increased majority voting in the Council and some strengthening of the European Parliament's powers. On some other policy areas, such as an extension of the EU into defence policy, its policy was not markedly different from that of the Major government. The announcement on 6 May that the Bank of England would be responsible for the independent management of interest-rate decisions brought the government into line with one of the prerequisites for the UK entering EMU.

Initial developments after the election, together with the new government's large majority, suggested that a more positive European policy could well be integrated into a wider strategy of modernising the British political system. Of course, nothing can be judged on the basis of the first days of a new government, for John Major enjoyed an initial honeymoon period on integration both with our European partners and with Cabinet colleagues. In that sense, therefore, it is important to conclude by underlining the theme of this chapter, namely that 'Europe' is a strongly established 'fault-line' in British politics.

Chapter summary

The UK's distinctive wartime experience, history of territorial integrity, distinctive form of parliamentary government, island mentality and former great power status are amongst the factors explaining late engagement with European integration. Joining at the third attempt, acceding to a community whose shape had been influenced by other states, and doing this in 1973 at the time of an international economic recession: these were not factors conducive to making EC/EU membership a painless matter. In fact, these circumstances merely added to the existing political divisions concerning membership. Even if EU membership is not seriously challenged almost twenty-five years later, there are highly controversial European policy issues causing divisions within the parties (e.g. EMU) and divisions between the parties (possible accession to the Social Chapter). With a review of the EU's treaties in progress 1996–7, and the need for any revisions agreed by the member states to be ratified in the House of Commons, European controversies look unlikely to subside during the remainder of the century.

Discussion points

- Why has the UK had such an uneasy relationship with European integration?

- What are the distinctive features of supranationalism and why have they created controversy in UK politics?

- Can British governments solve policy problems in isolation, or do they need to seek collective solutions through the EU?

Further reading

An important source of information on the EU is its own publications, many of which can be obtained free of charge from its offices. For an overview of the evolution of European integration, see Urwin (1995). The historical dimension is also covered in Nugent (1994), which additionally presents a most thorough outline of the EU's institutions. For general assessments of the policies and politics of the EU, see Nicoll and Salmon (1994), Lodge (1993) or Pinder (1995). Laffan (1992) presents an accessible but more conceptually organised approach to the subject matter. Nugent (1993) presents the first of an annual survey of developments in the EC, covering *inter alia* the problems encountered in 1992 in ratifying the Maastricht Treaty. The *Journal of Common Market Studies* is the principal academic journal covering integration. George (1994) provides a good, detailed account of the UK's European policy over the period up to 1993, while George (1991) presents a more general survey covering the post-war period. Young (1993) is an alternative source. George (1992) is a more interpretative study which not only covers UK policy but traces its origins to party politics, Parliament and other factors arising from domestic politics. Bulmer *et al.* (1992) present an overview of the impact of EC membership on UK policy and institutions. On specific issues, see Baker *et al.* (1994) on the parliamentary struggle to ratify the Maastricht Treaty; Armstrong and Bulmer (1996) for an analysis of European policy-making in the UK; and Cm 3181 (1996) for details of the Major government's European policy.

References

Armstrong, K. and Bulmer, S. (1996) 'The United Kingdom', in D. Rometsch and W. Wessels (eds), *The European Union and the Member States* (Manchester University Press).

Baker, D., Gamble, A. and Ludlam, S. (1994) 'The parliamentary siege of Maastricht 1993: Conservative divisions and British ratification', *Parliamentary Affairs*, Vol. 47, No. 1.

Bulmer, S., George, S. and Scott, A. (eds) (1992) *The United Kingdom and EC Membership Evaluated* (Pinter Publishers).

Cm 3181 (1996), *A Partnership of Nations: The British Approach to the European Union Intergovernmental Conference 1996*, (HMSO).

Corbett, R. (1995) 'Governance and institutional developments', in N. Nugent (ed.), *The European Union 1994: Annual Review of Activities* (Blackwell).

George, S. (1991) *Britain and European Integration since 1945* (Blackwell).

George, S. (ed.) (1992) *Britain and the European Community* (Clarendon Press).

George, S. (1994) *An Awkward Partner: Britain in the European Community*, 2nd edn (Oxford University Press).

Laffan, B. (1992) *Integration and Co-operation in Europe* (Routledge).

Lodge, J. (ed.) (1993) *The European Community and the Challenge of the Future*, 2nd edn (Pinter Publishers).

Nicoll, W. and Salmon, T. (1994) *Understanding the European Community*, 2nd edn (Harvester Wheatsheaf).

Nugent, N. (1993) *The European Community 1992: The Annual Review of Activities* (Blackwell).

Nugent, N. (1994) *The Government and Politics of the European Union*, 3rd edn (Macmillan).

Pinder, J. (1995) *European Community: The Building of a Union*, 2nd edn (Oxford University Press).

Steiner, J. (1992) 'Legal system', in S. Bulmer, S. George and A. Scott (eds), *The United Kingdom and EC Membership Evaluated* (Pinter).

Urwin, D. (1995) *The Community of Europe: A History of European Integration since 1945*, 2nd edn (Longman).

Young, J.W. (1993) *Britain and European Unity, 1945–1992* (Macmillan).

Index